ETHICS AND THE BETWEEN

SUNY series in Philosophy
George R. Lucas Jr., editor

ETHICS AND THE BETWEEN

William Desmond

State University of New York Press

Published by
State University of New York Press, Albany

© 2001 State University of New York

For information, address State University of New York Press,
90 State Street, Suite 700, Albany, NY 12207

Production by Michael Haggett
Marketing by Patrick Durocher

Library of Congress Cataloging-in-Publication Data

Desmond, William, 1951–
  Ethics and the between / William Desmond.
    p. cm. — (SUNY series in philosophy)
  Includes index.
  ISBN 0-7914-4847-9 (alk. paper) — ISBN 0-7914-4848-7 (pbk. : alk. paper)
  1. Ethics, Modern. I. Title. II. Series.

BJ301 .D47 2001
170—dc21
                                                                    00-032981

10 9 8 7 6 5 4 3 2 1

This book is dedicated to my father, Eugene Desmond, and the memory of my mother, Hannah Desmond (*née* Hannigan), who died while the book was in press. What I have known of goodness and generosity and gratitude, I first came to know from them, and through them. What I have received from my second family—Maria, William óg, Hugh, and Oisín—also is immeasurable. I dedicate the book with thanks.

And behold, a certain lawyer stood up, and tempted him, saying. Master, what shall I do to inherit eternal life? He said unto him. What is written in the law? How readest thou? And he answering said, Thou shalt love the Lord thy God, with all thy heart, and with all thy soul, and with all thy strength, and with all thy mind; and thy neighbor as thyself. And he said unto him. Thou hast answered right: this do and thou shalt live.

—Luke, 10, 25–28

CONTENTS

Part III: Ethical Selvings

INTRODUCTION

The *Incognito* of the Good

We live in an oddly equivocal time, alternatively blasé in its ethical relativism and intense in its moral earnestness. Being blasé and being earnest are perhaps not entirely unrelated. One sometimes wonders if both are faces turned away from what might be called the *incognito* of the good. Recent decades have seen a lush proliferation of writings on ethics, applied and theoretical, but with some exceptions philosophers seem hesitant to speak about the good. The blasé relativist is chirpy about our lack of names; the earnest moralist eagerly reminds us there must be names, else life is an anarchy of unjustified preferences; the good remains elusive. One of the reasons for this blasé attitude, this earnestness, and this incognito, I believe, is a very subtle ethos of valuelessness. I mean that we heirs of modernity inherit still a deep perplexity about the status of inherent value, indeed about the inherent value of being, of the "to be" as good. An unspoken ethical nihilism continues to be our nameless companion. Now we cheerfully live with this companion; now we earnestly struggle against it; now we find ourselves adrift, without a way of naming the good. Has the salt then lost its savor? Should we not separate wheat from chaff? Why then mix more chaff with the sparse wheat, making the whole pottage indigestible? Why then do we put ourselves on to a gluttony of husks?

A rethinking of the relation of being and being good is needed. This book develops the outlook articulated in *Being and the Between* by giving expression to the ethical understanding consistent with the metaphysics outlined there. Previously I sought a reconstruction of metaphysical thinking about what it means to be. My hope now is to effect some reconstructive thinking about the meaning of being good. *Being and the Between* outlined a metaphysics central to which was an understanding of being as *metaxu*, as between. By such a between, I intend an ontological milieu that is overdeterminate: both indeterminate and determinate, taking form in a plurivocal interplay between otherness and sameness, openness and definition, and yet excessive to final fixation. Our own being

1

also is intermediate. We come to be between an unacceptable relativism and an impossible absoluteness. We need not reject relativity: our being is to "be in relation." Nor need we deny absoluteness: we are marked by presentiments, in the midst of things, of what finally is most fundamental. In the between, our presentiments of the ultimate emerge in the deepest, richest forms of being in relation. The view I developed, a metaxological metaphysics, as I termed it, was inseparable from an affirmation of the fundamental relation between being and good. The first book addressed the question: "What does it mean to be?" The present work asks: "What does it mean to be good?" What is the meaning of "being good"?

As there are a number of fundamental senses of being, there is a plurality of senses of being good. I have proposed a response to the question "What does it mean to be?" in terms of a fourfold sense of being, namely, the univocal, the equivocal, the dialectical, and the metaxological. The univocal tends to stress fixed identity and determination. The equivocal emphasizes the indefinite and the unfixing of difference. The dialectical reminds us of the mediation of sameness and difference, but with the stress on self-mediating wholeness. The metaxological articulates the between as the overdetermined milieu of interplay of sameness and difference. It grants the indispensability of determination, the inescapability of ambiguity, the necessity of mediation, and some open wholeness. But it also acknowledges the crucial need to be unceasingly open to forms of otherness that are recalcitrant to dialectical mediation and univocal fixation, and that yet ask for more than lostness in equivocity. The metaxological interplay of self and other solicits a reformulation of the different meanings of identity, difference, and mediated wholeness. The recalcitrance of other-being is not merely a negative phenomenon, an opposing resistance to be overcome. Other-being, like self-being, is overdetermined, in excess of our final determination. We have to do with the rich inexhaustibility of being, not an indefinite indigence. What then does this fourfold sense do? It helps us unfold the recurrent forms of relation between same and other, identity and difference, self-being and other-being, oneness and manyness, singularity and community, and so forth. It helps us explore their becoming, mediations, interweavings, and intermediations. *Being and the Between* pursued this exploration relative to the ontological matrix of being. *Ethics and the Between* tries to do this relative to the unfoldings and interweavings of the manifold forms of being good in the ethos as ethical between.[1]

---

1. A third book to come, *God and the Between*, will pursue the exploration relative to the meaning of the divine and God, as gleaned from the between. All three works are contributions to one philosophical undertaking. I will henceforth refer to *Being and the Between* (Albany: SUNY Press, 1995) as *BB;* to my *Philosophy and its Others: Ways of Being and Mind* (Albany: SUNY Press, 1990) as *PO;* to *Beyond Hegel and Dialectic: Speculation, Cult and Comedy* (Albany: SUNY Press, 1992) as *BHD;* to *Perplexity and Ultimacy: Metaphys-*

Could one say that our current situation is marked, to a degree, by an oscillation between variants of univocal and equivocal ways? Consider: the univocal way feeds our desire for definiteness in a time of flux and for forms of moral sameness to mold an ethos that we are afraid is otherwise amorphous. By contrast, the equivocal way brings to mind the precariousness of many claims to moral fixity, and not necessarily with negating intent. We need constancy, we need improvisation. Yet at one extreme, univocity can fix on the one system of rules, commands, obligations, a monolithic foundationalism. Meanwhile, at the other extreme, equivocity can generate an antifoundationalism where sheer difference deconstructs all unities as false closures of life. Here, the stern order: This is commanded! There, the cheerful permission: All is allowed! But then the gyre goes around again. And then? Then there is no value; therefore, all is value; hence alas, all is valueless value. What then? The nihilist in us comes full circle, mounts his or her perch, and starts to preach.

A bare contrast of foundationalist unity and postmodern plurality proves too crude. Each needs the other to be itself, none turns out to be adequate, either on its own or in oscillation with the other. In fact, we are always somewhere in between. The task is to do justice to this ethical between. Some of the best work done now points in this direction, even if the systematic tools to do it justice are not always ready to hand. Why? In part because more systematic approaches are treated as suspect by postmodern pluralisms, and in part because dialectic is identified with a closed totality. How to move forward? I think we can reformulate the dialectical in a manner open beyond such closure and rethink the notion of system more metaxologically. Thus understood, the dialectical and metaxological are ways to do justice to that being between. They can offer modes of discerning mindfulness in the play of univocity and equivocity. The dialectical way can offer an approach to some mediated holism; the metaxological makes way for a community more hospitable to otherness as other. Both can point beyond an unsatisfactory dualism of foundationalism and postmodern pluralism, wherein much of our ethical thinking seems now becalmed.

That said, nevertheless our time seems to be very much one of equivocity. We appear to be certain about one thing, namely that, finally, uncertainty hovers over all, troubling our days and making our nights watchful. Perplexed equivocity seems to be a strong mark of our current ethos. You might demur and say: It is

ical Thoughts from the Middle (Albany: SUNY Press, 1992) as _PU._ Wherever convenient to do so, I will include any reference to these books within the present text itself. For their welcome help with proofreading and indexing, my thanks to Garth Green, John Hymers, Daniel Murphy, James McGuirk, and Miles Smit.

constitutive of our being to be in quest of what is good; and the meaning of that quest is itself in question—it always calls for interpretation. This is true. Nevertheless, given the extremities of equivocity pressed by postmodern perplexity, we need more than local rejoinders. We need a more fundamental rethinking of the ethos, the fundamental potencies of the ethical at work there, and determinate ethical configurations that come to be there. It is in this spirit that I have tried to articulate what an ethics of the metaxological might look like. As the reader will discover, the metaxological way asks for deep attunement to the equivocities of our being, and in that regard strikes out in a different direction to certain forms of dialectic that yield too much to the temptation to reinstate a mediated univocity.

Many of our perplexities stem from a retarded appreciation of the between as ethos, from questionable relations to the good emergent there, and from developments of forms of self, other, and community which, in giving undue superiority to self, produce an impoverished objectification of other-being, twist the possibilities of relation, twist also the relata, and thus deform the ethical promise of the ethos. The between as ethos is the promise of being good. The meaning of that promise must be approached through an articulate unfolding of some of its essential forms, deformations, possibilities, and perversions, and now and then, promises redeemed.

Four major factors went into the making of this book: first, the between as ethos; second, the fourfold sense of being good; third, the potencies of the ethical; fourth, the concretions of these potencies in selves and communities. Part I concerns the ethos, and especially the ethical implication of the devaluation of being in modernity. Part II concerns ethical ways. Here I deal with the plurivocal determination of the ethos in terms of the potencies of the ethical and the fourfold sense of being. Part III concerns what I call "ethical selving." I mean the concretion of being good in its immediate and self-mediating actualization: its given effectiveness and plurivocal becoming in human selving. This also includes an extended exploration of the different possibilities of being free. Part IV concerns the social intermediation of being good in certain fundamental forms of community. These range from the intimacy of family, through the network of use and serviceable disposability, to the communities of erotic sovereignty and agapeic service. But perhaps it will help to state briefly some preparatory points about metaxological ethics in light of these interconnected factors. I apologize for the fact that they will make more sense later, though they have to be ventured now, earlier, and so unavoidably, too early.

Ethos, Metaxological Ethics, and the Fourfold

First, *Primum vivere, deinde philosophari*—the old adage still applies. At first we do not understand explicitly what it means to be good "in the midst." This precedence of "being in the midst" applies to all human mindfulness, not just philosophical or ethical minding. Hence vigilant dwelling is needed, such that our best ethical thinking is a fidelity to the worth of what appears in the happening of the between. This makes us suspicious of a priori thinking, understood as the deduction of conclusive truths from categories already taken as fixed. Thinking so, we forget the process of emergence out of which such determinations have already emerged and treat them in abstraction from being in the between. We require primarily not thought thinking itself but thought open to the surprise of being as other, thought thinking the other to thought itself. If this is a kind of a posteriori way, recurrences and constancies do come to articulation. We discover later what was at work prior to the determination of our ethical mindfulness. Only in that sense can we make a qualified kind of a priori claim: there are relations and determinations shaping in advance what we are and are to become, though we only know these after having dwelled mindfully in the between. Instance: "Self, self, self"—says Dickens's Chuzzlewit. But oh what slipperiness there is in such a reiterated self! Ethically we come to know belatedly that others have been participant in our selving *all along*. We thought we were at home with ourselves, just through ourselves, but dwelling with this, we are surprised by the other—a second time. We remember others already enabling us to be so, and we see through this odd illusion of being through oneself alone. Odd, since it is one granted by the gift of the other, one that the generous other seems willing to let be. We become more mature as ourselves, and we realize that this being for self is an immaturity. There are debts deeper than ever one could say or pay. And then an *other giving* may be known and loved differently, an other giving that enables one's release to be oneself.

Second, the point is wider than self, self, self; or other, other, other. Suppose there is always some already given effectiveness of being good? Then though our task must focus on diverse ethical intermediations, it also must grant something elemental: rapport with the ethos of being as good. Can we say the between is good, because to be is good? Our answer cannot be direct, which does not mean we cannot answer, nor can our answer be dissonant with our more direct engagements with life. There is an existential as well as a systematic side to the task. Systematically, we might seem to ascend towards light; but like Plato's philosophers, existentially, we must descend again into the cave, down again into the chiaroscuro of the equivocal ethos. And if indeed the specter of nihilism still haunts us, this is even more urgent. Can we speak of the milieu of being as the elemental field of value? Is there given a primal sense of "It is good to be"? What is the "yes" that is here needed? Is there this field of the overdetermined good of the "to be" that cannot be identified with this good or that? Is there a primitive "It is good" in excess of all of our determinations of it? Do we already live the elemental field of value in this wise: our very being lives the ontological affirmation "to be is good"? We are in the middle, but does not this inchoate rapport with

the good of being define our own being? Is this rapport our inarticulate community with the good as overdetermined? A rapport that also is a love?

Third, the fourfold sense of being is helpful: it shapes different ways of being
ethical that dwell more and more intensively with what is at play in the ethos.
There is not just *one* approach that we canonize as *the* ethical: a teleological one,
or deontological one, or virtue approach, or ethics of will to power, or of alterity,
and so forth. The point for me is not finally to say: this is *the* ethical; let the other
ways go whistle. This is to distort the plurivocity of being ethical. This is not an
indifferent pluralism, since some ways show greater fidelity to the full promise of
being ethical. In my view, the metaxological way is truer to this promise than the
other ways alone. But all mindfulness is really metaxological: it gives a *logos* of the
metaxu, being true in greater or lesser degree to what is promised in the between.
To be human is to be metaxological: to be in the between, a between we do not
first create, within which we become ourselves, though we never become complete masters of ourselves or the between. To be ethical is to be in the milieu of
the good, between the conditioned goods we find and create in the web of relativities, and the unconditioned good that is shown or intimates itself in the happening, and to whose promise we respond in the lives we live. The metaxological
is not like a fourth layer that comes later on the scene, to be hoisted on top of the
other layers to form the penthouse level. It is effective from the start, but we lack
the thinking to do it justice. Its meaning only becomes more fully understood at
the end. The between is the milieu of the surplus good whose very overdetermination is just its hospitality to a plurality of ethical ways.

Fourth, metaxological ethics emerges *out* of equivocity, but it is not per se
inimical to more univocal signposts. The ethos is ambiguous, opaque, dense,
resistant, mysterious, but also luminous, transparent, supportive, shining with
light and warm. Both of these sides foster in us the feeling for its otherness.
Equivocity has its truth, for there are ambiguities that remain intractable to us.
But we also need to avoid postures of dualistic opposition that follow from a
fixation with unmediated differences. For instance, we are involved in an elemental play of trust and distrust, but unrelenting distrust sprouts its blooms of
destruction. We need to weed the garden and cultivate its compost for sweeter
fruits. The power of negation arises from a more affirmative power. The hostility to being, the feeling of the lack of value in being, are unintelligible apart
from some intimation of what is lacking, something not itself lacking, but the
good of which we feel cheated or robbed or disappointed. Aristotle said the
good is what all things seek. But this is not simply because now all things lack
the good; already we are with the good in a certain equivocal way. Not identical with it, not in dualistic opposition to it, we are with it and not with it, and
both of these at one and the same time. Only because we are with it equivocally, or it with us, can we seek it, and recognize it, or it be known, when we
find it, or it find us.

Fifth, such a seeming paradox suggests dialectical possibilities. In the ethos, the diverse interplays of self with other, and other with self, and both with themselves, have the character of transcending from one to the other, and both into the middle. One is not a univocal good without the other, or vice versa; each comes to be itself in a communicative being with the other. Dialectic can show us *something* of how the equivocity of the ethos is sifted by this process of communicative transcending. The good is in the coming to be of this togetherness, but this does not mean that the participants are nothing without the togetherness. The togetherness is not only an alleviation of the defects of the participants but also is shaped by their generosity from surplus, surplus already real and not solely realized in being spent for the other. It is already fulfilled before being spent, and fulfilled more in being spent, and not at all spent out in being spent, but augmented in its giving beyond itself.

What I have just said requires a thorough transformation of the dialectical way. This is very important for this work. The dialectical play is to be openly pluralistic: it cannot be closed in terms of any of its participants and the very nature of the togetherness being constituted. The forms of mediation are not exhausted by the self-mediation of its participants, not indeed of the milieu itself, taken as the embracing community of the whole. The *metaxu* is the ethos as the milieu wherein the plurivocal promise of the good comes to shape. Nor is an essential otherness and transcendence done away with, nor overcome or sublated, nor subject to our mastery or measure. Equivocity is not eradicated through a univocal concept or a dialectical one, though metaxological thought does seek to come to terms with it—even when there are no terms. We move into and through the equivocal, and come to appreciate a reserved sense of the good in the ambiguity. We read the ambiguity and comport ourselves differently in terms of what has been shown, or taken back. This means that there is no completely transparent rational ethics. Ethics is the reason of the ethos, but the reason of the ethos is itself attentiveness to the equivocity. Such attentiveness is a mindful finesse that must be renewed again and again, just as the equivocal milieu shifts into other shapes, even as we ourselves undergo equivocal shifts in our self-becomings and communications. There is no ethical stasis.

Sixth, all of this implies a certain relativization of the notion of *autonomy*. It is not that one denies the integrity of singularity—quite the opposite. There are reserves of otherness with both self and other, and marking the singularity of humans, as beings for themselves with infinite value. But this unfathomable integrity of singularity is communicative being. Self-transcending from the origin, singularity is defined in communicative relation to the other. Integrity is relatedness and, within the milieu of relativity, relatedness to others. This means that *auto nomos*, as the law of self, is a dissembling freedom, insofar as it does not show forth the communicative essence of the integral singularity, nor the essential relativity of singularity in community. We must formulate a conception of freedom in communication with the other, before and beyond autonomy.

The metaxological milieu offers the ethos of freedom, not the staging ground of autonomy. The meaning of freedom is not identical with or exhausted by autonomy. There is a freedom beyond autonomy: a release of self towards the other that is not determined by self-law, nor by a relation to the other which serves my self-law, and which is not legislated by me, if it is legislated at all, for it is a release beyond the law also. There is an ethics of the other in which being for the other becomes a free service for the good of the other, a service beyond the calculative self-interest of utilitarian prudence, beyond the self-determination of autonomous will, beyond a servile subordination to the will of the other. Agapeic service serves the good of the other out of a release of freedom towards the other, a release that is the overflow of a generosity without finite reckoning, and hence an image of excess relative to all finite measures. It is an image of the mad abandon of the good in our life. Autonomy, we might say, easily glories in being a rebel angel and it feels itself very righteous, but angels sing gloriously and otherwise when responsive to the divine hand. That hand relativizes all autonomy. It offers the manna of freedom, not the solitary stones of ourselves alone.

The freedom that gives good, gives good things just because this giving frees, and frees into the release of being as good in those who open themselves to the gift. It is the being of the good to give itself for no other reason but this. This reason may not look like a reason if we only look for a reason *for us*. This here is a reason for nothing, for nothing beyond the good of the giving itself. (Thus the return to nothing, hinted by "nihilism," can be the release of this good.) Being good thus is self-justifying, or rather it does not insist on justifying itself, for it is a generosity that even seems mindless of itself, so mindful is it of the good of the other, in its broadcast of the excess of generosity beyond itself. It does not think about itself, and hence seems not to think, or so we think; and so we think that it is idiotic. (Its right hand does not seem to know what its left hand is doing.) We have not been freed into that thinking which is beyond thinking for itself—mindfulness simply of the good at play in the ethos.

Seventh, such a freedom beyond autonomy also disturbs our idea of *will to power*. Much of human life is shaped by will to power that slyly, or shyly, dissembles itself in ethical ideals. It cloaks itself in the self-assertion of autonomy, expressing both our vulnerability in the ethos and our will to be ourselves in the mode of self-affirmation. Against the new ascetic preachers of otherness, I must say that self-affirmation is right and proper. But that said, we must still look anew on the community with otherness that upholds self-affirmation, despite any loud self-assertion that, in what really matters, it owes nothing to anybody, it is the absolute original. Suppose there is a willing beyond will to power? Suppose the ethos is the promise of freedom as this willing? Then we need an ethics of transcending in the genuine sense: the self is to be beyond itself, willing beyond itself, willing beyond willing itself. Freedom, as beyond autonomy, lives beyond the will that wills itself, in the ethical community of agapeic service. This is not easy, nor for us possible without passage through the fixations of moral univocity, the seductions and bewitchments of dissembling equivocity, the conflicts and false closures of dialectic. But the promise is there for us from the origin, more than a promise insofar as we are the issue of agapeic creation. In the openness of the between, we can strive to redeem the promise, even as we fail its full solicitation.

Eighth, does this not show us a crucial departure from the dialectical way? The metaxological way suggests a transcendence of any dialectical completion in terms of self-determining being, no matter that it be mediated through the other, and an engagement with the good as overdetermined. It points to the surplus of the good, its excess to dialectical self-determination. This point turns on a different understanding of the good as *arche*. Dialectical thinking tends to see the origin as an indefinite starting point, to be made more and more determinate, culminating in self-determination. The move from the indefinite to the determinate to the self-determining mirrors the supposed overcoming of the supposedly initial opaqueness of the good, through a more specific articulation of what it is, and in relation to what is other (for determination is impossible without reference to an other); dialectic moves towards a supposedly fuller articulation in which the other mediates the determination of the progress back to itself, thus possibilizing the self-determining autonomous good. So we see in Hegel the connection of the self-mediating good with a teleological orientation. Only in the end is the true good revealed, for only in the end is the process fulfilled. The end is self-realizing. It is the fulfillment of realized being for self, in Hegel's case, the good as the absolutely self-mediating whole.

The metaxological, by contrast, turns to the otherness of the origin, for the beginning intimates the overdetermination of the good—not indefinite, but too much. Determinate forms of good come to shape out of the initial excess. The overdetermined good is not a lack that seeks its self-realized form in the end. It is itself as already good; it is out of its being already good that it gives the good of the between and its different possibilities. This overdetermined good is an agapeic good: out of its surplus it communicates. Moreover, this overdetermined good shadows all of those other moves from indefinite to determinate to self-determination. An exclusively dialectical interpretation forgets this otherness of the good and tries to incorporate it into the movement from indefiniteness to self-determination. But the overdetermined good is above these, within these, accompanying these, supporting these, but as other to them, in that its surplus could never be measured on their measure, except insofar as it gives itself to them. This good is the agapeic origin. The metaxological way is attuned to the presence and absence of this good in the between, attentive to the signs of equivocity that give some hint of it, dialectically mediating in that we are called to answer for ourselves, but also vigilant to a further call to agapeic service for the other. Metaxological ethics asks the names of this initially incognito yet hyperbolic good.

The Potencies of the Ethical

I would I did not have to attempt these thoughts so early. If the jolt helps, well and good; if not, a slower caress may be better. But I still need to anticipate. To understand the promise of the ethos, do we need what Nietzsche sought—a transvaluation of all values? In the main, he offered us a flawed critique of "Christianity" and "Platonism," from the standpoint of a Dionysian will to power. I think what we need is less such a transvaluation as a renewal of discerning reflection on the basic sources of value, in terms of the plurivocal possibilities of the power of the "to be." The ontological promise of the power of the "to be" receives such plurivocal articulation in terms of what I will call the *potencies of the ethical*. These potencies—the idiotic, the aesthetic, the dianoetic, the transcendental, the eudaimonistic, the transcending, and the transcendent—will be more fully defined in due course, but they refer not to abstract possibilities but to the dynamical ethical endowment of the human. We are plurally endowed with the ethical promise of diverse potencies of the original power to be. These potencies assume different definitions, depending on the dominance of this or that sense of being, or of being good. To understand them is more fundamental than a critique of "Christianity," or "Platonism," or "Kantianism," or for that matter "Nietzscheanism." That understanding allows us to see these configurations of the ethos in new light and not simply play one off against the other. Since these potencies recur throughout this book, it will be helpful to note, again in a preliminary way, something of their metaxological meaning.

First, all potencies spring out of our immersion in the ethos as offering us an opaque intimation of the *surplus* of the good. There is nothing transparent about this; it is metaphysically enigmatic. Patience to this surplus otherness is especially significant for metaxological ethics. It awakens us to something inexhaustible about the good of being at all. But this is too much for us. It sustains us, but we fall into a familiarity that droops to its marvel. It is at work in giving us, astonishingly, the gift of being, the elemental good; at work when we develop ourselves and our determinate lives this way or that; at work when perplexity overtakes us and troubles us into anguish at the equivocal enigma of the good; at work when we determine to become ourselves, facing oppositions that rend us and stretch us on the rack; at work beyond our fullest stretch of self-determination, aiding fidelity to the "more" beyond every claim to final wholeness; at work in letting the giving others again come to us in a more mindful frame, and greeting us, as we greet them, as intimates become strange, and as strangers anew standing before us as givers of good beyond merit. This surplus good is always beyond measure, in all of the genuinely good things we do, though they seem anonymous and slight and merely routine.

Second, there is a sense of the *idiocy* of the good in the between. I refer to an elemental *intimacy* with the value of being: a predeterminate sense of the "rightness" of the "to be." This does not mean that we have made this "rightness" determinately clear to ourselves. Mostly it is in an unstated background that may come into sharper focus under the pressure of different stresses of being. This idiocy is beyond our determinate reason, but it is intimate and other at once. We are native to the world as good, but we are native with a mystery that demurs before our domestications. The idiocy of the good is especially important relative to the source of intimate worth in the human being. Humans wake up to this intimacy, and so begin to move beyond the living of this, to an express understanding and gratitude for it.

Third, there is the *aesthetic* potency. I mean that the otherness of the ethos involves a *showing* of the worth of being that is aesthetic—given to our senses and our bodies. The incarnate good of the world is in rapport with our response to goodness and our being as good. Most often we live this in our response to beauty; but we also create works of beauty; we bring to be, so to say, a courtesy of incarnation. The ethos of the body, as well as the "eco-system" as other to our will to master, are to be respected by metaxological ethics.

Fourth, there is the *dianoetic* potency. I mean that we seek some intelligible, law-like regularity to the ambiguities of the aesthetics of the good. This aesthetic showing is more full than we can manage, yet as we become discerning, we discover constancies and regularities. Metaxological ethics is attendant to the intelligible constancies emergent in the between. If this is a respect for sameness, it is not reductive. There are intelligible bonds that hold diversities together, and that command or ask for respect. Metaxological attendance must avoid the superimposition of orders on the inexhaustibility of being or its surplus worth. This does not mean that the constancies are always adequately formulated by us. We must guard against the false fixation and securing of ourselves through the spurious certainties we often mistake for dianoetic constancies.

Fifth, some constancies occupy a special position of being *transcendental* in this sense: without them, determinate ethical living would not be possible. The metaxological relation between self and other is transcendental in that regard: it is the condition of the possibility of more determinate forms of selving and "being together," of self-becoming and of being in community. Then there is the good as agapeic origin: the ultimate condition of the possibility of the between. This is not a "condition" at all, but if we call it a "condition of possibility," it is more in a "Platonic" than in a Kantian sense: the being of the good and the relativity of the metaxological as "original sources of possibilizing," presupposed by determinate approaches to the ethos and specific human formations of the ethical.

Sixth, there is the *eudaimonistic* potency of the ethical. In a way, the fullness of human flourishing resumes, with reference to the daimon, the idiotic and aesthetic potencies. There is a primordial "being pleased" with the fulfillment of powers: the determination of the indeterminate such that what was being sought and implicitly loved in the idiocy comes into its own and into its neighborhood with the good of other-being: comes into fullness, and in coming into fullness, rejoices even the more that being is the inexpressible good that it is. This is easier said than reached, but all the travail seeks it, though too much travail darkens the secret directedness on the daimon. We have to come to terms with this darkening in the chiaroscuro of the ethos.

Seventh, the *transcending* potency keeps in mind that the overdetermined comes to expression in human being as exceeding itself. We are determinate and more than determinate, and much of what we are, as determinate, is itself the crystallization of an indeterminate power of self-surpassing. This transcending potency cannot be fully understood in univocal, equivocal, or dialectical terms. The inward source of this transcending is a strange otherness in innerness itself, and it cannot mediate with itself entirely; for the presence of enigmatic otherness is always there before we come to ourselves in more determinate form. There is the surpassing mystery of self-surpassing itself, as we live it in the between— always something more than we can fix in our moving to something more. There is excess to that which we are seeking: the "end" is beyond us, even as we come into its neighborhood.

Eighth, metaxological ethics seeks the best way to keep our living in the ethos open to the call of *transcendence itself*—not just our self-transcendence but transcendence itself as the ultimate power that possibilizes all transcending, indeed all being, and possibilizes it because transcendence itself is good. The best word in ordinary language for transcendence itself is the extraordinary word, God. The extraordinary asks us to respect the ordinary usage. Metaxological ethics names the ethos as the space wherein the ultimate good intimates itself in the idiotic, aesthetic, dianoetic, transcendental, eudaimonistic, and transcending concretions of life in the finite between. This good is communicated into the between, opening its finite otherness, and through this, opening to the self-becomings of different beings, each becoming towards what is good for it. We are pointed to a community of the good beyond self-determination, a community already there from the start, enabling the powers of self to be determining of itself, giving it to be itself, giving also the ethos of possibility wherein that power can be more fully realized.

Relative to the ethical potencies, we need a fuller appreciation of the relation to otherness than dialectic offers, a more affirmative sense of the mystery than equivocity has, and a more open sense of determination than univocity fixes. And if all we say is a speaking from our human perspective, this need not be a mere projection of the human good, if from the outset the human is an undergoing: human being is a suffering of being, and a suffering of the good, before it is a doing of the good more proper to itself. Metaxological ethics is not a substitute for God's mind, but a human essay, always in the between, to read the opaque signs of being good. As a suffering, as well as a doing, as an opening to the other, as well as a self-forming, it must be alert, on edge, to what comes to it from beyond itself; otherwise it closes itself to traces of transcendence in the twilight of the middle or its dawn. The surplus of the good *asks for plurivocity:* not only because we are poor; not only because we are also rich in our poverty; but because the good of the between is beyond our measure; because we must do our best to stay true to what is given from it, and what is best in it. We need many ways. Nor is this antagonistic to the One, if this One is the agapeic giving of the plural between, and the broadcast of the good of being.

Concretions of Being Good

The fuller concretions of these potencies assume immediate, self-mediating, and intermediating form. This will especially occupy us in Parts III and IV. Immediate concretions have to do with the effective givenness of value, before we mindfully participate and contribute to its enrichment. We are guests at this feast, not overlords. And what is our freedom? It comes to us as guests who have been asked to make ourselves at home. This is an ethical task and has nothing to do with a rampage of will to power. The latter does not make a home, but more deeply makes us strangers to the gift of the good of the "to be." Still, our participation takes on a self-mediating form. In Part III, I will be particularly concerned with the self-becoming of the good in humans, through an unfolding of different forms of ethical selving: from rudimentary desire and its self-insistence to the release of freedom beyond autonomy, which comes to shape in community of agapeic service. Finally, in Part IV, we will explore the forms of social intermediation that most fully concretize the promise of the ethical potencies, as well as the richest possibilities of the fourfold sense of being. In different communities, from the family, through the network of use, to the communities of erotic sovereignty and agapeic service, the full ethical promise of the ethos becomes more richly concretized. It is only here in the consummate community of agapeic service that we find the meaning of the promise of ethical already incognito in the original indeterminacy of the ethos, the ontological milieu out of which we come to be together. This religious community points beyond the ethical.

How in all this should a philosopher appear? But philosophers want to disappear into their words—they want to speak no one's words—and everyone's. But thus to disappear is again to reappear, and one's words are still one's own. And yet still again, what is one's own is not just one's own. We are given to be, and to speak. How then appear? As oneself and as other selves, some of these oneself again, some showing the gift of goodness offered by true bestowing others: the little boy whose dash across the road was a brush with death; the good uncle whose kindness was an unwitting breach of trust; the mother who brought her children to devotions; the father who showed his son the secret sparrow's nest; the beloved woman the man would kiss, even in a note; and I too lapsing into my own Iago. But we do not want the fruit of the tree of knowledge to deprive us of the fruit of the tree of life. Alas, the first tree seems destined to rob us of the fruit of the second. Must this be so? Can we come to a knowing of the good that takes us back to life—to life itself as gift, and as "very good"?

PART I

ETHOS

CHAPTER ONE

THE ETHOS:
BEING AS WORTHY/BEING AS WORTHLESS

The Ethos in Question

Different ways of being good are not freestanding but come to formation in the ethos. By ethos, I mean the ontological context or overdetermined matrix of value in which our human ethos and ethics come to be articulated. This is prior to, and in excess of, every specific ethical determination that we define. For we reconfigure the elemental ethos, and so stay true or betray or disfigure its promise. What is at play in it cannot be stated univocally or made fully evident at the outset, since it is through the reconfigured *ethe* that we gain some sense of its potencies. This book tries to give some account of it, but now our first focus will be on certain stresses in modernity that mark our present predicaments. These stresses develop certain ambiguous possibilities, developments not altogether immune from their own deformations.

Many periods, or cultures, or communities, have been marked by relative stability, with ethical norms accepted and lived with significant constancy. These stabilities reveal livable resolutions to basic perplexities as well as offer sources for future decisiveness, reserves for resolve towards the good yet to be achieved. And now? Now we seem to lack a resolution that commands wide consensus. Being good is deeply in question. Indeed, part of its being in question appears in the dissent that rejects *even talk of being good*—we prefer to speak of preferences, or adaptations, or lifestyles, or options or whatever. Our current problematic is *not* the lack of a sense of what is right and wrong in particular situations, or more general orientations to what is more or less valuable. Despite dissensus, there is widespread agreement about the alleviation of poverty, care for the deprived, concern for the oppressed, basic tolerance, and so on. Decent people and communities struggle genuinely, even heroically, with the ethical challenges they face. There are cheap and tawdry things, but one might say the same of any era, yet they are distinctive difficulties.

17

It is not this or that distinctive difficulty that is the difficulty. The difficulty is less specific, more pervasive. It concerns a more indeterminate sense of "the whole." The difficulty is one of the ethos of ethics, and not this or that determinate problem within a specific system. In one regard, such an ethos has a *vagueness* to it, just because of its relative indetermination. In another regard, ethos has an *excess* character, making it resistant to clear objectification. Our difficulty, relative to the ethos, turns on what grounds our sense of the good. What is the ground of the good, and is there a good the ground of the determinate goods or values that direct and fulfill our lives? I suggest that our feeling for the ethos is tempted by the peculiar seductions of a kind of *valuelessness*.

At stake are basic metaphysical issues, not only practical difficulties in a more normal sense. This is why we need to ask: "What does it mean *to be* good?"; not only questions such as "Is this or that good or bad?" Here I side, if you will, with Plato rather than Aristotle. Did Aristotle fully appreciate the place of the Good within Plato's thinking, too quickly arguing to its questionable, perhaps redundant, role within ethics as he more practically conceived of it? At issue is more than a reflection on being good as we live this, say, in the polis. This too is at issue, of course, but we need to ask about the *to be of the good*. We are perplexed about the horizon, or context, or ground, relative to the determinate formations of ethical being in the between. Reference to the Good, such as Plato's, is not an optional metaphysical speculation one can bracket, while devoting oneself to the forms of ethical life in the midst of human community. I am not criticizing any detail of Aristotle's ethics, for which I have the highest respect. But the highly nuanced forms of determinate living are lived within the horizon of the ethos, understood in a more ontological way: a sense of "the whole," relative to what is worthy or worthwhile or precious, or loathsome, or ugly, or horrifying, or evil. This sense of "the whole" is not exhausted by the human good but invokes reference to a more ultimate sense of the good or evil of being: what being good is. Is there a sense of being good, or being as good, or perhaps of the being of the good that is not the good of this or that action or way of life? Plato, as I said, was more attuned to this perplexity than was Aristotle.

This invocation of ancient Plato brings us, perhaps surprisingly, to our current problematic. While many still claim to be Aristotelian, many seem to accept the redundancy of the Good. Some push well beyond redundancy. We do not benignly pension off the Good, as having done its good work in time, and now politely request it to shuffle off quietly into harmless superannuation. We retire it with indifference, or mockery, or even hostility. Our reply to Plato is less the argued sanity of Aristotle than the incredulous derision of Nietzsche. Some will be incredulous of inclusion among Nietzschean rhapsodists, those who think of themselves as more the kin of sane Aristotle. Alas, it is the *last men* who have become Nietzscheans. The last men are *now* a mongrel blend of the madness of

Nietzsche and the prudence of Aristotle (more accurately, Mill). We have invented happiness, they sing, and blink—and not in the way Nietzsche sang.

We have domesticated the disturbance that came from Nietzsche's hostility to Plato. Despite our metaphysical amnesia, perplexity in regard to the ethos does not go away. Willy-nilly we are influenced by unarticulated attitudes to being good, attitudes themselves the echo of philosophical, religious, and cultural formations shaping us behind our backs. We always live out of an ethos of the good that is not this or that good. Suppose our rejection of the Good takes the form of thinking the world or whole to be valueless. Do we escape the prior sense of ethos? Not at all. Our hostility to the Good itself functions as forming the ethos, playing a similar prior determining role as does the Good within the Platonic context. Whichever way we turn, we need to think about this prior determining of our sense of the good, a prior determining that is not itself a determinate good.

Why suggest that an ethos of valuelessness molds our values? First, in modernity, the issue of the ground of value as the good has been subordinated by the epistemological question of the ground(s) of knowing. Think of Descartes here: he seems happy enough with a provisional morality that is not always easy to distinguish from a set of Stoic platitudes, mixed with common sense cautions and Descartes's own curiously secretive nature. The assault takes place on knowing, and this in the context of a loss of faith in the deliverances of "immediate knowing" and perhaps the intelligibility of being. The deeper connections between being, the good, the true seem to have become lax, if not entirely invisible.

Not quite: Descartes remains equivocal on the provisional morality. What the *definitive* morality will be is secretively suggested.[1] This will have to do with the mastery and possession of nature, and the practical fruits for which we cultivate the tree of knowing. That there might be a ground of the good, more fundamental than all scientific knowing, and all our provisional accommodations, is not to the fore. In fact, some secret sense of the good is not obliterated. Its replacement is insinuated in the disjunction between mind and nature, subject and object. On the one side is the *res cogitans* that produces intelligibilities; on the other side is the *res extensa* that receives intelligibilities. Nowhere evident is any presentiment that the good is bound up with being as such. The dualism of inner and outer, subject and object, is already a loss of a more inherent sense of the good, a loss that defines how subsequently the specifics of a worldly ethics will take shape. The world will be there for our possible mastery. Made powerful by method, our minds will progressively assert their ascendancy over nature as other.

---

1. See Paul Bagley, "On the Moral Philosophy of René Descartes," in *Tijdschrift voor Filosofie* 58: 4 (1996): 673–696.

It is only a small step from our minds being the source of intelligibility to our affirmation of ourselves as the original of value.

Consider the claim in light of *God* as the good. Doubtless, religious belief was widespread, and perhaps even Descartes was a serious believer, though, like Pascal, I have my doubts. And doubtless, many currents of religious belief survived, even prospered, as they do now. Still, the issue is the peculiar way in which we face the world as there. Our secret presentiment of God, or lack of it, is extraordinarily important. Late medieval theology, with its dualistic outlook, slants God in a certain way: above and beyond perhaps, but in such wise that earthly creation shows fewer and fewer traces of divine presence; while down here, humans step into the newly cleared space of immanence, leveled for expropriation and appropriation. God's dualistic beyondness devalues the earth. Hidden in that dualism is the relentless erosion of belief that the ground of value is an ultimate other, irreducible to human power. And this, despite all Descartes's hullabaloo about God as absolute perfection, and so on. Again I agree with Pascal when he said: Descartes just needed God to give a fillip to creation, and then he no longer had need of God. And what is the fulfillment of the erosion? It is the hollow earth, our hollow earth, in whose hollowness Nietzsche's shout about the death of God echoes and reechoes, until it becomes mere white noise, humming in the background of our postmodern chatter.

The humming of white noise in cosmology, as we know, showed us traces of the way back to the first beginning. What of the white noise at the edges of our moral loquacity? Perhaps this may also offer traces of the good from the origin. We shall see. In any case, the question is absolutely crucial to ethics, as it is to metaphysics (and theology): What is the ground of the good? We live in light of the good and its difference from evil, but what is the ground and meaning of this difference? Is it not already given with our being, hence constitutive of what we are? Are we not given to be within this difference? We do not produce it, we are "produced" within it. If so, what constitutes this ethical opening that we are? And this opening, is it just the realization of a human power, so that we would say: it all comes to our autonomous being as the truth of the ethical opening, and indeed as the true ground of the good? Does not this question already start too late, in that the ground of the good has been lost or twisted? Do we not dangle in the twisting that then turns towards being as valueless? Meanwhile, stripped of its value, the thereness of other-being seems to turn us to *ourselves*, as powers necessarily bound to the difference of good and evil. What now? Of this necessity we now make a virtue, and reconfigure ourselves as grounds of value. I think, in fact, that this turning around ourselves is a deepening of the dark advent of valuelessness rather than its lightening. We prove not to be the measure of the good. Quite the opposite: when we make ourselves the measure, we end up inhabiting a deformed difference between good and evil. And the priority of the good to our being good comes back to haunt us in the eerie emptiness of value that follows our usurpation of the measure of value.

Ethos As Elemental—Preobjective/Presubjective Good

We shall come to this, but more must be said about the ethos. The ethos is not first revealed by thinking or by reflection; it is a *happening*, and happening *before* we make any firm difference between inner and outer, subject and object. Ethos is related to aesthetic value, though again this is already more determinate than what I mean. Perhaps we can try to name it by relating it to the idiocy of being (see *PU*, Chapter 3). By this I mean the intimate presence of being, in which there is an open, still not differentiated, rapport between self-being and other-being. In the idiocy of being the world is *undergone* as charged with preobjective and presubjective value. In the elemental ethos, the ground of our good cannot be made merely an *object* of detached reflection and analysis; for we are within what we think about; we cannot think *about* it, because it is about us; if we can think about it, it is from within it, as already all about. We do not and cannot stand outside of the ethos. We can only become awake to what we are in, and the ground on which we stand or fall.

There are peculiar problems here associated with a *nonobjective mindfulness*. This precedes all more specific reflection on this or that ethical problem. The ethos does not pose a problem as an object of specific curiosity; it occasions astonishment and perplexity in us (see *BB*, Chapter 1). The intimacy of the ethos calls for intimacy of mindfulness. Ethical mindfulness is an awakening to the intimacy of the good, not just as what we seek but as also enigmatically given. The point is hard to grasp, because when we grasp articulately, we are already beyond the original givenness of this idiocy of value. Nevertheless, the ethos always remains with us, no matter how we develop; every development is within it, including those developments that seem away from it, even hostile to it.

The matter is often more evident closer to the beginning of human life. A child lives in the aesthetic rapport of this idiocy more immediately and spontaneously. *Image*: a child sees a shadow on his or her bedroom wall and cries out in terror. We comfort the child and shush it saying: no, no, no, there is nothing there. And yes, there is nothing there, but in a deeper sense from which we adults have learned to hide our trepidation. Indeterminate terror and recoil are occasioned by the shadow: it is the shadow of *nothing* with which the child is in rapport. We say it is only infantile insecurity projected on an empty wall. This may be true, but there is more. The very insecurity points to the abyss of frailty that is our ontological condition. "Being as nothing": this is not in here or out there. The shadow is the occasion of a crystallization, out of which the recoil from nothing is startled into alarm. The happening is an undergoing and saturated with an indeterminate sense of the value/disvalue of the "whole." The happening is in excess of the determinations we will later lay on it, to make it more proportionate to the determinate being we can handle. And this predeterminate ethos of value is not just "back there" in an indefinite beginning but is with us always. It is more deeply constitutive of our being than this value or that. The ethos is the matrix of the *metaxu* as saturated with worth/worthlessness. Not just as a child, but at all stages of life, we live in this more or less unthematic envelopment by value.

Think of it this way. One awakes in the morning, but one tastes oneself with a certain savor, tastes the returning day as communicated through this savor. One wakes with weariness, as if the night of rest were really a restless tussle with shadows (vague monsters breaking the surface of a strange sea). Or one lies quietly in a dull amazement that one is at all, as if returning to life from burial in an unconscious grave. An undefined light of undefined mystery shines as one's eyes are opened once more. One is returned to being with a peculiar *indeterminate savor*, but this feel is charged with a sense of immediate value or disvalue. When we become busy with the things of day, we turn from this indeterminacy and occupy ourselves with this objective or that. But the feel of being at all, the rapport with its worth or worthlessness, is an unstated companion.

Of course, this elemental ethos can be both ontological and cultural, natural and humanized, a point to which I will return. If one dwells in an ugly ethos, such as an urban ghetto, one's soul will be affected (I do not say univocally determined) by that environment: the environment offers an idiotic and aesthetic milieu wherein the human soul is shaped, and in nameless as well as quite definite ways.[2] The rapport, the milieu, and the interplay cannot be made completely determinate; there is an openness for freedom and release in the interplay; there is a determining process that emerges from an indeterminacy that is in excess of every determination. The milieu, the ethos, the immediate between of value is tied to our deepest sense of being, and how we sense ourselves to be, and to be in the between.

I will come shortly to our rapport with the ethos in modernity: there is a peculiar darkening, as we insist on our own complete enlightenment. But more elementally, I want to suggest, our transcending in the between shows an indeterminate

---

2. Think of the way *weather* insinuates the idiocy of being. If the sun rarely shines, the world's shine also is tarnished. The rapport does not disappear, but it reforms as a grim enduring, or as a dreariness in the whole. One may chirp out a willed cheeriness, but a bass note of background drag is there. Our undergoing the world at this elemental level enters our feel for good and evil. Live in glorious light and our rapport may tend one way; dwell in darker forests and our rapport will mutate. This world is golden, that world more gray. Who does not recall sunlight after long nights and the marvel of its uplift? This interplay with the indeterminacy of the elemental must not be forgotten.

expectation that the other-being we meet will be good, that there will be community between ourselves and the other. Think of a child's reaching out to the mother, and not only the reflex reaching for the breast: the ingrained anticipation in reaching out, in transcending, is that there will be an other there that meets us, and meets our desire. We are centers of self-insistent being, for one could not be a center of the power to be if one did not affirm oneself self-insistently; but there is more, as the reaching out primitively shows. Think of the peculiarity of the smile: the child will respond to the smile, as if the gesture of welcome were preordained in its very flesh: a smiling face of the other arouses the joy of being in relation to the other, and a relation whose basic joy shows the prior dormancy of an *anticipation of hospitality*. The elemental aesthetics of being in the between suggests an already given community between self and other. Later the child will look for recognition to the mother, and to many others. The forms of communication, as well as self-insistence, will become more developed, often twisted from the elemental rapport. We will learn the equivocity of the smile. The face of the other is not always the smile of welcome; the smile is the trap to disarm the guileless one and woo it to its ruin. The false face betrays its own gesture of welcome by reserving in itself its own truth as the opposite of its appearance: for it is the lie that smiles. Hidden hostility works its hostility all the more effectively by cloaking itself in hospitality. The smile shows the incarnation of the *equivocity of value*. Hamlet: one may smile and smile and be a villain. From the hospitality of the other, we learn the hostility.

The elemental ethos namelessly offers us an overdetermined communication of the good. Our elemental transcending in the ethos is lived by the anticipation of hospitality, of the good as coming to meet us from the other. It is good to be, and we live towards the other as if it were good for the other to be, and to come to meet us, to welcome us in the between. Development brings some disappointment of this trust inherent in our thrust to the other. The other is not the *univocal* good that we anticipate. Our transcending in trust is turned back on itself in trepidation of betrayal by the equivocity of the other. And so the ethos, as the idiotic, and aesthetic appearance of the good, cannot be immunized from this equivocity of the trustworthy and untrustworthy. Indeed, perhaps the original sense of the good is just the genuinely trustworthy: what calls forth our complete and unconditional trust—the other whom we love, because we completely trust that we are loved. Perhaps by our parents. Or God. But even so, there is no avoiding the equivocity of the ethos.

Modernity and the Equivocity of the Ethos

The systematic aspect of this point is important, but it also throws a light on our current darkness. Modernity, as I understand it, takes form as a particular reaction to the equivocity of the ethos. I cannot outline all of the factors, yet it seems as if today we bring to the between less an expectation of hospitality, as a suspicion, indeed latent hostility. We know we are vulnerable and the trust-worthiness of being is not immediately univocal. So we suspect it of deceiving. The supporting, we fear, might turn out to be tottering, the venerable, worm eaten. Implicit hostility predominates over the implicit hospitality. One side of the equivocity overcomes the other. I believe the hospitable is ontologically more primordial than the hostile, but here there is reversal. We want to secure other-being as a place hospitable to us, hence a place whose face of otherness must be reformed in light of what we deem hospitable to our desire. Outcome: we do not desire the good as other; what is other is deemed good as far as it serves our desire. Then we do not set out in anticipation of the good of the other as hospitable to us; suspect of hostility, this other will be *made* hospitable by reformation in conformity with what our desires dictate. We do not love the good; what we love, we call the good. (Consult, if you will, Hobbes or Spinoza.)

This view entails that the good of the other *as other* is not essential to the truth of the ethos; the good of the other is what I deem good as good *for self*. There is no transcending to the good as other. If there is transcending to the other, it is only because of transcending towards self, as willing to realize and secure itself, through its disarming of the potentially hostile other. All of this seems quite understandable, *if* the equivocity is seen in light of the suspicion of hostile otherness. What if this suspicion risks defection from the truth of the equivocal ethos and turns from the elemental trust? Then it represents a poten-tially fatal loss of ontological faith in the trustworthiness of the ethos. The loss itself, in truth, cannot ever cut loose completely from the hospitality or anticipa-tion of the good ingrained in our being. It is the being of all beings that they seek the good. (Consult, if you will, Aristotle.)

This reaction cannot be separated from how the ground of the good comes to be understood. Perhaps I can make the point most clearly in terms of God, understood as the religious name for that ground. Early modernity exhibits a dualism of God and world that seems to preserve divine transcendence, but at the cost of making it redundant in this world. What does this dualistic opposition do? It opens an abyss between creation and the good as ground. But if this abyss can only be defined by dualistic opposition, no *immanent mediation* of the pres-ence of inherent good is communicated to creation. Result: first, an accentuation of God's transcendence to the point of its disappearance; then, a degradation of the good of creation; then further, our awakening on *this side* of the opposition to the degraded creation, a world so fallen it seems beyond redemption; then fur-ther again, either a *religious hatred* of fallen creation that would quit it quickly, or else the development of dualistic opposition along *another line*, namely, by oppo-sition towards the creation seen as degraded, seen as a hostile other, seen as an other whose fallen otherness has to be conquered and reformed under the pres-sure and power of human will. It is in this last line that the dualistic opposition of creation and God (as ground of good) is *reborn* in the human being, as itself in opposition to equivocal creation. Moreover, this opposition leads to *another rebirth* in the human being, namely, of *itself* as now having to claim for itself the power to be the ground of the good. Human beings, asserting their power to oppose the hostile other, redefine the vector of their own transcending as the original ground that defines what is good, what is good relative to their power to define, and this power as itself the measure of the good.

Simply put, if the dualistic transcendent God *is* the ground of good, as the opposing other it *cannot be* the ground of the good in creation. This sense of the ground actually drains creation of its good. If we wake up in this drained creation, we cannot find a ground, either beyond creation or immanent in it as other. And so we inevitably turn to ourselves as the only resort we seem to have to ground the good. So it is that a peculiar dualistic understanding of God leads us to ourselves as peculiar gods—dualistically opposed to the world, of which we must now assert our divine sovereignty. This is connected to the nominalistic God and voluntarism; to the breaking of mediating links of God and creation; and to the upsurgence of the human as the alleged center of unprecedented creativity. It is not sheer perversity that makes us will to be gods and the ground of the good. Nor is it sheer hubris, though this turn to ourselves, in fact, is swollen and debilitated by its own hubris. It is the outcome of a dualistic logic, as applied to God and the world.[3] Our will to be divine, though it will think of itself as releasing unprecedented human creativity, is the victim of bad theological logic. The badness of that logic is not purged by living it through to its conclusion and the final lunge for deicide. It is from the logic we must be released, not from God, for the logic builds itself a glittering palace that is only a gray prison.

On the Objectification and Subjectification of the Ethos

What is this palace, and how does it get built in the between? The process, we might say, is driven by a will to stand powerfully over against the given ethos, now viewed as riddled with equivocity. Think here of the characteristic beginning of modern thinkers with *doubt*. Doubt shows mind's infection with suspicion of being other than itself. Doubt springs from *diminished trust* in the good of the other. We doubt what we are estranged from, or suspect of being dissimulating or unfaithful. We do not doubt what we truly love. Doubt is a lack of love, turned from a more spontaneous expectation in the good of the other. Compare now the characteristic premodern beginning in *wonder*. Wonder and doubt seem similar, and in some ways they are: both can extend indeterminately to the whole; both

---

3. I have worked this out more fully in *God and the Between*, especially in Chapters 1–3.

can shake us out of taking things for granted. But wonder does this through an excess of marvel at the astonishing thereness of being, and so it arouses something of the deeper joy of unpremeditated rapport with the other. It cannot be understood outside of a latent love. Wonder wakes a latent love relative to the indeterminate appearing that the other is good. Doubt, by contrast, awakens out of a frustration, frustration that comes to anticipate a potential for dissimulation, if not actual duplicity, in the appearance of the other. It is not aroused to joy in the good of the other. It is on guard because it has been disappointed, and now it would rather hedge its bets and take the minimal position not to expect too much, or indeed the negative position to expect the worst, for then one will not be disappointed again.

This is unavoidable in certain respects. Our wonder gives way to perplexity at what exactly has made its appearance and the meaning of its good, especially as it grows on us that this is not univocally transparent. We *do* come to be perplexed by the other. Yet, as long as some astonishment remains alive, our rapport and communication also live on. Doubt is a development of perplexity in which trust in the other has been subordinated to distrust. If it seeks a new beginning, it is one that forgets the fuller meaning of the disappointment, namely, that there is a more primordial expectation of the goodness of the other. That will be all the more forgotten the more that doubt drives to overcome its own insecure starting point, and to make itself immune from disappointment, and the other. I see here a momentous shift in relation to the primal trust in the good of other-being.

This good is not unambiguous, but here doubt is a form of rational mistrust that wills *itself* to be the power that secures security for itself. In the insecurity itself lies the ambiguity. What ambiguity? Of an urge for power over the other. On guard against the other, the good will be what we secure in the face of the untrustworthy other; it will not be any *gift* from the other. Thus we secure the other as securing our desire. I believe that an implicit dialectical dynamic of an absolutely self-defining good is seeded here. This dynamic is built on an equivocal interplay of insecurity and power, distrust and seizure, self-assertion and subordination. I will have more to say on this autonomous good, but even in its embryonic form, it is a particular formation of the elemental ethos, a formation giving hegemony to a certain *dominant selving*, and already in defection from the fullness of the ethos. In our drive to univocalize the ambiguity of other-being, self-securing and self-certitude come to be our sense of what is its own good.

The premodern scheme looked to final causality: the good is what all seek as the aim, the purpose. But the premodern *archeology of the good* is as important as the teleology. If the origin is not in some deep way good, all subsequent movement to the good as final will be suspect of basic emptiness. This point is more Platonic than Aristotelian: the Good itself as origin, as original, not just as end. The mistrust of modern doubt is directed at this archeology, as well as the teleology. True, the latter mistrust seems more evident. The will to secure univocal intelligibility, to make the world as transparent to the new mathematicizing mind, dictates an extrusion of final causes. These are full of ambiguity, for who can say what is the end that this or that seeks, or that all seek. Thinkers may still bleat about God in a spirit of pious accommodation, but the shift in definition cannot hide the momentousness of what is happening. Why? Because the outlawing of teleology from any rational scheme of intelligibility has a boomerang effect on the archeology of the good.

I mean that the origin becomes itself defined as a source of effective power. And what we now claim to know of effective power is defined by the univocal mechanical energies that seem effective in nature, itself now stripped of any qualitative sense of value.[4] What has this to do with the Good? Elide the end, and what happens to the middle? It ceases to be a middle. What happens to the beginning? It ceases to be a genuine grounding origin. For if we call the beginning efficient causality, this too is just effective power. What do we have then? Nothing but *the play of homogenous effective power* in a middle that is no middle, for there is no real origin and end. There is just valueless power to effect the ceaseless passage from power to power, out of no good and towards no inherent good, from nothing and towards nothing. We have ongoingness ad infinitum that, as from nothing and to nothing, is ongoingness ad nauseam. We set out to univocalize the ethos, to conquer clearly the ambiguities that make us insecure and seem no good for us. Thus making it good for us, we end up with no good.

There is this further point: the denial of final causes is inseparable from our will to objectify the world as an other standing over against us, stripped of the ambiguity of qualitative value. Thus stripped, it is more effectively mathematicized and used. This is a homogenization of the world: ultimately, it is all the same. Thus the ethos is remade as a neutral medium of valueless happening. We see this in the classical doctrine of primary and secondary qualities. The truth of the other-being of nature has nothing to do with the qualitative values given in common sense: warm and cool, alluring or threatening, horrifying or charming. All of these spontaneous responses partake of the equivocity of value. They seem duplicitous—hot to me is cold to you, charming to me is repulsive to you. The aesthetic happening of the world is the show of dissimulation. But, of course, that

---

4. Many theologians will make God the absolute source of effective power, followed by intractable difficulties with predestination and theological determinism; this also will be reflected in notions of sovereignty, as we will see in Chapter 15. See L. Kolakowski, *God Owes Us Nothing: A Brief Remark on Pascal's Religion and on the Spirit of Jansenism* (Chicago: University of Chicago Press, 1995), and my review in *Modern Theology* 12: 4 (1996): 489–491.

happening is the showing of the ethos of value. The univocal *mathesis* of nature cannot accept this as the truth of the other. That truth must be objective; the other must be neutral to aesthetic happening; the truth must reflect the universal homogeneity of the primary qualities such as mass, velocity, and so on. And what are these? The "values" that a mathematical univocity can subject to its methodic ways of conceptualizing the world. These valueless "values" are said to be the truth of other-being. Their neutrality as "value" is what makes them univocally the same for all who methodically approach the middle with the mind of mathematical univocity. The truth of the other as object becomes a homogenous, valueless being-there: it becomes a *worthless thereness*.

Is this not the quantitative pulp of the indifferently neutral *res extensa*? This thereness is conceived of in terms of homogeneous effective power, and if it comes to be differentiated, this also is through the web of causality that is shaped by the effective power. Since this effective power is itself valueless, its web of causality can be subject to the neutral, valueless objectification of mathematical univocity. This means that the more mathematically intelligible we make the web of causes of the effective power, the more we make the same intelligibility and web worthless. Excess of mathematical univocity produces an enlightenment that is indistinguishable from darkness when it comes to the good. But what does this mean? It means that enlightenment itself is ultimately worthless. For centuries, enlightenment has been too busy, or distracted with itself, to notice the worthlessness, though the point is now seeping in. Pascal saw it more than three centuries ago, right at the start of the process.

Of course, there is more. For with this objectification of the world there proceeds, paradoxically, and with as much pace, the subjectification of value. We live in a world massively objectified, but we live in it as humans hugely subjectified. This has many consequences, but my present point is this: the objectification drains the world of values, considered as final causes; the world is purposeless, but we are purposeful, and cannot but be purposeful; the very neutralization of the world is itself no neutral project but the *product of a will to purpose*, the particular purpose of making being as univocal as possible. The draining of value reveals, ironically, a purpose saturated with value; and this very draining, as it were, redirects the flow back to the drainer. *We* become the source of purpose, *we* become the purpose in an otherwise purposeless world.[5] There is something disturbingly equivocal about this. The project of objective neutralization issues from a source that cannot be neutralized. Should we be

---

5. This is matched *cognitively* by the claimed dominance of the knower over other-being: the self as a grounding condition of knowing, and as a source of intelligibility, previously vested in other-being. It is matched *ontologically* by the extraordinary importance vested in human powers, verging on self-divinization.

surprised, then, if a subjectification with a vengeance follows this amnesia of the source? The extrusion of subjectification with radical objectification proves to be a tale of radical subjectification, albeit one that hides this full fact from itself.

Consider the example above: the secondary qualities are reduced in epistemic significance because ontologically they have no hard objective character but a kind of *double status* as mixing something in the thing with our subjective perspectives. This double status makes their value to be *dissimilating*. Value such as this hardly counts. It should not count really in the neutral objectification but, in fact, it comes to count for everything, for in the end nothing that we do can be done if it has no value. If the thing in itself has no value, we can have no concern with it, unless perchance we become the source that gives it value. To make the world have no value makes it necessary for us to make it of value, but this means making ourselves the real ground of all value. The seemingly secondary nature of the secondary qualities as related to the subject only masks the primacy of the subject, as *the source of relation* to other-being as valuable. Add to this the perception of the world in light of a network of effective powers. How to see the subject in this light? The subject too is effective power. Its great effective power seems to be its being the creator of values. So it cannot be (as in the official picture of secondary qualities) a mere passive subjectivity impressed by something in the thing. Quite the opposite, subjectivity as effective power *impresses itself* on other-being. The subjectification of effective power more than matches the objectification of the world as the network of effective power.

Here is the sting. The subject cannot live with this devaluation of otherness, and even less with the devaluing of its own valuing. It will not be passive to this. It will be active. The subjectification of value inevitably leads to the primacy of self-activity that impresses itself on the other. Objectification is itself a subjective production, and indeed is a kind of production of subjectivity itself. We witness the recoil of the subject on itself out of the hiding of neutrality it had schemed for itself. There is no escape from itself, but now when it awakens again to itself, it has been transformed into a more *radically self-assertive subjectivity*.

What do we see then? That the objectification as much produces the self as self-assertion, as that the objectification was itself secretly produced by self-assertion. This self-assertion forgets itself when it is univocalizing the world, and forgets itself because of its vulnerability to the equivocal other. It forgets itself by asserting itself, and in the process it diverts itself from this threat; its self-assertion as self-forgetful is self-protective, and what better protection than mathematics! For mathematics seems to offer the nobility of universality, the calm of objectivity, the quietness of mind with passion out of play, invulnerable to what comes from beyond its conceptual composure. Let it nobly forget itself when it was doing mathematics, nevertheless, the *ethos of its mathematicizing* was secretly self-assertive. Its knowing was a constructing,[6] and what it was constructing finally was itself, and the other as the image of itself.

Autonomy and Relation to the Other

It is important to paint the picture with sufficient nuance. There is a positive result in this, even if this too proves questionable. I mean that out of this maelstrom of equivocal being, the will to univocity issues in *the quest of radical autonomy*. This is a major landmark, if not the touchstone of almost all modern ethical thinking. Do we escape the equivocities of objectification/subjectification? I think not, for these reappear, as we will see. Nevertheless, a humanized ethos of autonomy emerges.[7] How so? The objectification of other-being drains objects of value, but the subjectification of value offers little consolation, if the stability of grounded values disappears into the vagaries of subjectivism. Moreover, there is the nemesis following the objectification, namely, that the subject is also made the object of a project of objectification—it too will be treated as a thing, drained of value. What does the ideal of autonomy do? It shores us against this last threat, as a defense action in which the value of subjectivity is preserved.

Again, there is more. For once this defense draws its breath, it proceeds to more constructive work. It announces the self as the privileged site of intrinsic value in a world otherwise devoid of value. The value drained from other-being, a draining that threatens even to deprive the human self of its value, coagulates in the self as the autonomous good. It seems that the process of objectification must lead to this. For one must ask about the source of the objectification, and of course it is the human being. The subject is not at all a passive object in relation to the objective; it is other than its other-being; it seems "autonomous" relative to it and the network of effective powers that defines the differential relativity of things in the world. It seems that there is only objectivity because humans are autonomous with respect to other-being. The self is for-itself, is its own law, for it is what finally gives the law to what is other-being.

Suppose we say that the law of self, or *nomos* of *to auto*, is first *freedom from*: it cannot be fit into the network of objectivities; it is over against them. As free-

---

6. See D. Lachterman on this and on the difference of a theorematic and problematic approach, *The Ethics of Geometry: A Genealogy of Modernity* (New York and London: Routledge, 1989).

7. See my "Autonomia Turannos: On Some Dialectical Equivocations of Self-Determination," in *Ethical Perspectives* 5:4 (December 1998): 233–252, especially 233–237.

dom from the other, is it not also a *freedom for?* Freedom for what? Not for the other, but for itself, and for itself as over against the other from which it is freed. A moment please. This is all very well, but the *inescapability of the other* is undeniable. Let us serenade our autonomy until we are hoarse, and the mocking laugh of others will still ring out at the end of the operatic performance. "Here we are!" How then are we autonomous? In turning to ourselves, even when we are in relation to the other, the other is not what defines our turn to self; this is self-initiated, we say. How then look at the remaining relation to the other? We can perhaps choose to decree it irrelevant, or as a source of inauthenticity, or even call it hell, as Sartre will do. Alas, this wins us a dubious autonomy—more reactive to what it would flee than affirmative of the law of its own being; more the reactive freedom of a slave than the grand self-assertion of a sovereign. How come to that sovereignty? *Turn the other in the same direction as the turn to the self.* I mean the self's relation to the other has to be turned into the other's relation to the self. Relating to the other must be turned into making the other relative to the self. *The other must be turned into a return to self.* I am autonomous because, even in relation to the other, that relation serves the primacy of self-relating freedom.

I am painting a move towards a more dialectical autonomy, but there are more dualistic versions. Kant is the hero of autonomy for many, but his autonomy is set in an ethos in which dualistic thinking dominates, indeed his understanding of heteronomy is dualistic through and through. His autonomy is a defense measure of human freedom in an ethos wherein the play of subjectivity and objectivity is defined by dualistic opposition, in which subjectivity, as empirical ego, is itself open to appropriation as an objective thing. Kant fits my suggestion of reactiveness to the interplay of objectification (à la Newton), and subjectification (à la Hume), and the rebound of objectification on the subject, as in the materialistic reductions of the human, and the eudaimonistic doctrines of the eighteenth century. In all of this Kant saw clearly the drain on all inherent value. Consequently, a place for true autonomy must be really other—other than objectivity, subjectivity, or subjectivity objectified. Yet the ethos of the latter still defines the reactive nature of the Kantian definition of autonomy, as not what these are.

The more dialectical view of idealistic philosophy carries this line further. It waters the seeds of self-activity in Kantian autonomy, and the growth that spurts from them overspreads the whole, and everything—subject, object, subjectified object, objectified subject—finds its niche under the lush, self-generating foliage of the absolute autonomous whole. Yet for all the surface of fertility, underneath, at the places of seeding, lies the sterile soil of devalued objectivity. Why sterile soil? Because if otherness is to have any value, it is to have its value from the self that actively gives it its worth, in the spread of self-determining being. This is a recipe for a wasteland, or a dust bowl, once the high wind of nihilism is whipped up.

The Valet of Reaction?

Sir, you are bitter! Do not speak for the valets of reaction! Your distemper retards you to the dawn of divine freedom newly breaking! Breaking, indeed. I agree. Self-generating autonomy does seem to assume divine characteristics, as God was defined in modernity, say by Descartes or Spinoza, so also the autonomous being seeks to be *causa sui*. Being for self is active, dynamic; it is a self-determining; it is not a being caused, it is a causing to be; and what it causes to be is worth and value, because it causes itself to be. Autonomy is truly a kind of god. Is this not the god we worship? We would be for ourselves; we would be self-realizing; we would be our own originals, and not the image or imitation of any other; we would not derive our being from any other. We would revolve round the circle of ourselves, as incense swings aloft and clanging symbols resound to that holy of holies, our sweet and sacred self.

You say: look how concerned we are, how caring, how humanitarian; behold our patient taming of base selfishness! Behold and glow! True. This is the mellow self-satisfaction of the sweet, sacred self. It is the idol in the Indian summer of its career. But bitter gusts of another and violent wind have already buffeted us. The revolving of the autonomous circle around itself need not be, I know, the precious narcissism of this self or that self. It may be the ethos of an epoch, within which decent folk protest rightly about forgotten righteousness. The idol may be mellow, but unwashed savages howl, and not outside the circle of the idol.

Again you protest: Look on the works autonomy has wrought! Have we not pushed back the boundary of suffering, buffered our flesh from frailty, made straight the roads joining city to city, if not heart to heart? Have we not steered the thunderbolt of Zeus? If this is an idol, its power has served us well. Very well, you want your power to be served. Consider how you want to be served. You want to be served, as more than any thing, more than anything you want to be served. You are not a mere objective thing. You are more, you are transcendent to mere things. I honor you with the name: you are transcendence. Is there mockery in the compliment? If so, the mockery is not mine alone. Once the name of transcendence was God; now you claim that name. You are self-transcending; you are free in going beyond, and going beyond yourself, overcoming not only the hazards of external things but navigating the rapids of the caverns of innerness. I honor this. You adventure in otherness. You are not a timid god, a tepid transcendence.

But how to connect your two names, autonomy, transcendence? You want to be called by both, and yet each does not name quite the same thing. As autonomous, you would be related to self, determining self, even in relation to the other. As transcending, you would be opening beyond self, perhaps to find self higher up, or deeper within, but still opening beyond, and hence ever risking relation to the other. But if autonomy is absolute, then opening to the other has to be subordinated to the circle of self-relation, hence transcendence has to be reined in, for then you are not quite the opening beyond you claim to be. If transcendence is absolute, the relativization of autonomy must be broached, whether in terms of what might be found higher up, such as the true God, or lower down, such as the dark labyrinths in the otherness of inwardness itself, or the seductive oblivion of materiality without mind.

Can one serve two masters as god? Is there not a certain *antinomy* of autonomy and transcendence? For both cannot be absolute together, in the terms proposed by the priority of autonomy. Absolutize the first, you relativize the second; absolutize the second, you relativize the first, and hence put a strain on the proposed priority of autonomy. Is this then the lesson: the antinomy points us further than autonomy?

For there is a price to be paid for the absolutization of autonomy relative to transcendence. If we take seriously the latter, as indeed beyond any objectification, we must ask if there is a freeing of self beyond the circle of itself, beyond autonomy. I think this move has *not* yet been properly made in modernity, or postmodernity. We still live in the idol of autonomy. For the further move shatters the circle that revolves around itself, and we still cling to that circle, for we fear the night outside, or the God; or we fight a rearguard action when a wave of the outside spills over the side of the circle, and we rebuild the breach in the stockade. Being free is extraordinarily elusive. It may also be more terrifying than the equivocity of other-being in reaction to which autonomy began to shape its circle or stockade. The terror is just in the relativity of all circles and in the impossibility of finally firm barriers against the other-being that drives us towards self-securing. We are fighting against ourselves all along: as autonomous we are fighting against our own transcendence, in the name of the transcendence that frees us beyond the objectification that drains being of value. The house that autonomy builds is divided against itself when freedom lets the voice of transcendence, its Siamese twin, speak.

Of course, such autonomous being is not lacking the intimation of its own inner dividedness. It would be free for itself, not be enclosed by the other. Yet it is racked by longing for the other against which it secures itself. And so transcendence again breaks out in it, as the indeterminate yearning to be connected to others. Within itself, it cannot constitute a seamless unity with itself. If it listens, it hears a quarrel of voices between autonomy and transcendence, a quarrel not resolvable within the circle of autonomy. Freedom must first give itself over to the nameless outside that transcending bespeaks. And perhaps the nameless outside may be more than outside, and encountered through the more intensive innerness of self-transcending. The giving over may also shatter the dualistic opposition of inner and outer, subject and object.

The Worthless Whole and Will to Power

Freedom beyond autonomy is a subtle matter, requiring a superlative trust willing to abandon itself to an outside, initially unnamed. It is idiotic, though, in a bad sense to the autonomous self. We will be occupied with such a freeing throughout this book, but there is more to be said about the consequences of the ethos of valuelessness. Satisfied with ourselves securing ourselves, we seem to lack the patience for this other freedom and transcending. We say, we have said: let us congratulate ourselves on our coming of age, on liberating ourselves from tutelage, self-incurred. Or if we are more modest, we will purr diffidently and exhort ourselves onward to this ideal. Suppose our modesty is a tissue of dissembling? Perhaps autonomy is not the unconditional good but is derived, and from sources in the ethos that give its absolutizing the lie? Will to power has many masks, but suppose autonomy is one of them, one that dissimulates the protean face behind it, the face that is finally faceless? If we think deeply enough on the modern ideal of autonomy, do we find it backed by anonymous power, the same anonymous effective power that supposedly rules the valueless whole?

To the true believers in autonomy its alliance with will to power will strike them as blasphemy. Should these worshipers complain if nonbelievers demur about their god? Idols generate their own faithless, as their own faithful. Idols irritate the faithless. Nietzsche was irritated by the idols of Kant, but suppose we have become, so to say, impious about Nietzsche's impiety towards Kantian piety. Suppose the piety of autonomy prepares the way for the impiety of will to power. Suppose also that the idol that shows its monstrousness in Nietzschean impiety was already recessive in Kantian piety. And suppose now it is no longer recessive, and now we can no more bow low.

Consider it this way. Autonomous humans believe that ethical right is within our power as self-legislating. We might even qualify this and speak of *rational* self-determining. Why do I smell the unmistakable whiff of power? To insist on being self-determining always risks placing what is other to oneself in a secondary or subordinate position. You say that we must take these others into account. Then either we do this to secure the fullest field for one's own self-determining, or one already breaches the circle of self-determining in invoking the necessary relation to the other.[8] Suppose we still insist on autonomy. But then our

---

8. Kant is caught between these: self-legislating and moral law; self-legislating and others as ends in the kingdom of ends. He never resolves this tension adequately, since the resolution requires a different form of *heteronomy* impossible on his terms. Kantian autonomy is a dissembling autonomy: equivocal about the ultimate ground of the good, about the status of the moral law itself, and about God in relation to the *summum bonum*. I say more about the complexity of this view in Chapter 4. My point now is that Kant prepares the way for Nietzsche, about whom I also will say more.

placing of the other indicates an *asymmetry*: it is the self who is the power so to place the other, and to do so, not for the other as other, but for its own self, and indeed for the securing of its own self-determining power, or its own power as self-determining.

I go further. Not only is subordinating power implicit, so is hostile power. Why secure oneself as self-determining power? Because just that power is insecure. What threatens it? What is other to itself.[9] How to deal with the threat? Subject the other to the self, and thus overcome the threat, overcome the other as threat. For instance, implicit in Stoic self-security is this latent hostility to what disturbs inner equanimity; it is also in Kantian autonomy, as secured for itself over against the heteronomous that is not within one's power. Autonomy as self-law hides from itself its own origin in will to power, for it cannot bear to think of itself as less than noble and ideal.

Further still, the hiding cannot be indefinitely sustained. This we see relative to the reconfigured *ethos of autonomy*. The ethos has seeds in it that do not blossom into the flowers of freedom, but into weeds that twine themselves around the flowers and sometimes choke their bloom. The ethos is equivocal, mixing trust and distrust relative to the ambiguity of good and evil. If a certain accentuation of distrust of other-being prepares for autonomy, that same distrust drains other-being of its inherent value, and just this drain places the spotlight on the autonomous self as the place where inherent value can be recuperated. Thus we have valueless other-being and the worthy autonomous self, the second seemingly uncontaminated by the first. Can we guard the autonomous self as this sanctuary of inherent value? No. Why? There is *another rebound effect*, that is, the draining of value in other-being returns to haunt the autonomous self, and it too cannot preserve itself uncontaminated from the ethos of valuelessness. It too is *exposed to valuelessness*, not only relative to the other, but *in the intimacy of its own self*.

How so? If we think of the good in terms of ends, and if in creation there are no ends, then creation as a whole is without good. It will not do to say that *we* are the end that rescues creation from its endless worthlessness. For we have made the *whole* of creation worthless; we also are creatures in creation; as part of the valueless whole, the human is also valueless, ultimately. You may want to delay this outcome by elevating humans above creation as noumenal beings (or overmen). And there may truly be more to us than other things in creation. But we are within creation, and when we would do the good, it is within the between we must do it. When we come to the concrete good, the noumenal self has to

---

9. Of course, what also threatens it is own inner ontological vulnerability, as beyond its power. And then there is, in the supposed self-mastery of autonomy, a subordination of *its own inner otherness*. So in mastering itself, it enslaves itself, it is the slave of itself. Its autonomy is bondage to itself.

reconnect with the other-being of creation from which this defense action severs it. And then even the severing is itself the fertile ground of hostile relations between the human and creation as other. The severing and elevation is itself an expression of the possibility of distrust, given within the ethos at the outset, and hence we do not escape this possibility, as we claim.

Or we might postpone the collapse thus: the whole of creation as other is devoid of inherent value, and this is just the reason why *we* must be the source of inherent value—namely, to give whatever value is necessary to this valueless whole. Autonomous self-determining of value is a *project* for the active self-generation of value. We bestow value, we bestow ourselves on other-being, we condescend to elevate it above its worthlessness. Notice the hostility in this bestowing: we are the worthy, the other is worthless; it is worthy because we make it worthy. Worthy of what? Worthy not for itself, but worthy for us. In other words, I am the good, the other is devoid of good; I am beauty, it is ugly. But how is it ugly? Does not my claim of beauty make it to be what it is? Am I not complicit in the uglification of the other? I am myself the worm in the apple that causes it to rot, even as I voice my outrage at its rottenness.

Strangely enough, in making myself the good I have only succeeded in showing how base I am, how evil. If I make the other worthless, what does that say about my claim? It shows not only its hypocrisy but its vileness. To claim that the self is the good is a claim made by a self that itself is vile. Honesty may finally bring out the hiddenness and confess the lie. The mask of this autonomous good reveals behind it a hateful self. What should we do when the mask begins to slip? We should turn to other-being and ask its forgiveness for visiting on it our ugly accusation. This is hard to do, of course, if we have become addicted to the sweetness of outraged righteousness.

If the whole of creation is devoid of inherent value, we cannot sustain the claim that humans alone can be the epitome of inherent value. The result has to be the opposite. Opposite, not only in the hypocrisy, indeed, the impotence of this will to power—impotency to acknowledge the good of other-being, of the good as other to us. But opposite also in this straightforward sense: if the whole is valueless, then every project of will (to power) to legislate value to the whole, or to whatever is within the whole, is doomed to failure. For every project of will (to power) is itself a manifestation of the truth of the valueless whole: will (to power) in creating values is itself ultimately valueless.

I say ultimately, because clearly we can endlessly carry on as if the name of the game were the creation of this value or that value, forgetting the sense of the whole that drives us to create this or that value, forgetting the ethos within which will (to power) takes it shape, as well as specific values, forgetting the ground and source of it all. We can become so insanely busy setting ends for ourselves that the ethos of our setting is ignored. But if the ethos is as will to power defines it, then these ends are, in the end, as in their source, all illusory. It may well be that, pragmatically speaking, we find it unbearable to live without such illusions. But the confession of this gives the game away, and we should give voice to the truth of our despair more nobly, not sing hymns to our secret self-deludings. The valueless whole, it may be confessed, is absurd. What now? Now we will sing hymns to human nobility in face of this absurdity. What is the ground of our singing? Is there some song of being not properly acknowledged in the picture of the whole as valueless? If so, there is more than the absurd, and if we are more than absurd, we are not so through ourselves alone; for if through ourselves alone, then we too collapse into the absurd. If we are more than absurd, it is because there is more in what we do than what we do, more in what we are than what we determine for ourselves, more indeed in the freedom of the ethical than the autonomous power of self-determining. The community with the other is already always there at work.

What this means remains to be seen, but I will make one last point here. The unmasking of will to power in the autonomous self opens us to otherness, even despite autonomy, and indeed will to power. I mean that once we see beyond the mask, the self is not self-legislating, and there is a power other than itself at work in it. In its efforts to secure itself as self-determining, it turns out that this is "determined" by something other, some other power than its own. In the ethos of equivocity, we may tend to call this other will to power, in which indeed the self-overcoming of its own otherness is part of the dynamic. I do not think will to power is the best word for this other to self-determining autonomy. Yet it can be an ambiguous opening to transcendence beyond self-determining autonomy.[10] If autonomy turns to itself, there comes a point when an otherness within the self comes to light—an *inward otherness*, if you like, but one in which the inescapability of the other, inner or outer reappears.

Just that inescapability can be given different interpretations. In the main, the ethos of modernity (and postmodernity) has continued its wonted line, interpreting it in terms of distrust vis à vis the equivocity of the given ethos, and in terms of a will to power that begins to pass out of the power of the will of autonomous selfhood. Let us say the hermeneutics of suspicion, far from properly passing into the opening, continues the draining of value, but now turns it towards the self. It bleeds the sovereign self, as doctors once bled patients, understanding their cuts as healthy care. The autonomous self is left weakened, further drained. And then it comes to know its nothingness as autonomous, comes to see a dark source dissembled in its idol of autonomy. But now it is left faithless and perhaps in despair before the monster in the idol. Alternatively, this suspicion

---

10. In a later discussion, I will touch more fully on will to power as self-affirming, relative to erotic transcendence and agapeic transcendence, as opening to the other, as genuine release and freeing.

will return the autonomous self to power as other, but other as non-self, power as indifferent to self, power as neutral and anonymous, power as the faceless face of nothing behind the cracked paint of noble autonomy.

The first alternative is the pathway into the darkness of subjectivity, more dark than autonomous subjectivity. The second is the way that returns subjectivity to the fate of effective power, believed to govern relentlessly the play of happening in the between. This effective power, though void of inherent value, cannot be called neutral power any more, for it has shown itself *finally hostile* to what has seemed the highest ethical construction of the human being, that is, its god, autonomy.

Desolate Ethos and the Waste of Power

Where does this leave us? Still in the equivocity of the ethos, but in sticky toils of our own making, perhaps sullen with the rage of disappointed idealism, perhaps frustrated by otherness within and without for mocking alike our power and autonomy. We seem to have no new way to turn. Secretly we worry if we have brought despair on ourselves, though if we could find something other to blame we would do so without a moment's hesitation. We have no right to shake our fists at the empty sky, yet we would like to shake our fists—at something, anything, parents, history, the color of our skin, teachers, the other sex, something, anything other, as long as it is other. We would really like to blame God if we could. But we cannot; though sometimes the passion brought to denouncing belief in God as "retrograde" seems shadowed by a rancor, the vehemence of whose bile is absurd, if atheism is, as it is claimed, the ultimate truth.

Should we learn the silence of Job? But there is no silence, and no patience, and no listening to the voice in the whirlwind. There is noise, louder and louder, drowning out the silence for subtlety. We have become impatient noise. We shake, not our fist, but simply shake ourselves, shake ourselves in all directions. We are the voice of the whirlwind, and the name the voice gives itself is will to power. We have become the whirlwind. We have become death. And this specter will sequester itself in the most relentless busyness. We must be busy, not only because we are the whirlwind, not only because we are transcendence as will to power, but because if we cease to be busy, we become as nothing. If we stop the circle of self-generating, we abort the cycle of *causa sui*, and the god becomes nothing. So we must continue to circle and circle, for ceasing is death. What does the circling and circling do to the between, to the rest of being as other? This must be relentlessly consumed into the circle, providing the energy when the internal motor seems to flag. The image might seem to be the perpetual motion or dynamism beloved of the Italian futurists. It might also be the vulture, since we have become death.

Everything other to self-circling autonomy will be a means for the circle to continue to circle around itself. This circling can be frenetic, not mostly when new sources of inspiration break out, but exactly the opposite, when the specter of death appears in the circle or casts a shadow on the circle. Then the frantic wheel is propelled one more time, and the whir of motion passes by the shadow so quickly there seems to be no shadow there, and death is no more. The world of other-being becomes a means by which the wheel is kept in such endless motion that the shadow of death is a mere blur, or a smudge that we are quickly past; and if the shadow has any power, then it may take the other; it is the other who dies, for the devil takes the hindmost. But move as quick as we will, it is flight and nothing but flight: flight not of transcendence, but flight from transcendence, and flight from death as the empty hole that opens into a nihilation where all of our will to power withers into its own risible pretentiousness. Let the sober catch their breath and not wince. One tries to name the fever of death that makes the face of will to power blush, as though it were flushed with the fullness of life, while, in truth, it is being consumed by its own waste, and its laying waste to other-being, as it voraciously consumes that otherness.

On the Totalizing of the Instrumental

Can the play of objectification and subjectification avoid an unbridled instrumentalization of all being? Ask again: What is the good of being? What does it mean to be good? And suppose you say: In itself what is, is no good: it is good as serving our desire or dominant will to power. "In itself it is no good"—this may be said without drawing attention to itself, but we pass over the violence in it. If one can only say, "In itself there is no good," one will come to say in the end, "In nothing is there any good." And this "nothing" will take over and seize the whole ethos. We configure the ethos as a milieu of seizure and nihilation. Let me elaborate relative to nature, man, and God.

Relative to *nature*: Nature as other is redefined in the image of will to power as the *network of effective power*. Entities are units of effective power, and our relation to them is to appropriate to our effective power these effective powers of nature as other. Everything is a means to this, nothing an end. The units of effective power are pulverized into a form we can turn to our effective power. This deprives things of their thingness, denies them any integrity as unities of being for themselves. Our self-insistent power reaches out, takes hold, overreaches their integrity, for it grants no integrity of their being as for themselves. They are homogenized into valueless thereness and sucked up into the voracious emptiness of our self-insistent will to be as self-serving *conatus*. This pulverization means a loss of the aesthetic value of the world, not merely a loss but a deformation. The garden of the earth becomes a fetid dump in the making. Nature's instrumentalization signals a decay of respect. Sly respect, yes, when we have to calculate our way around the otherness of things; but this is not respect in a true sense, since it is only a provisional standoff on our part till we find the way to further our power. This "respect" is calculative of its own "prospects," hence merely masked will to exploitation. In all genuine respect, there is a *reverence*. Nor is deficiency of reverence surprising, for the sources of the homogenization are not in wonder or astonishment but in a calculative curiosity that is not really curious about the other, except as the occasion in which unlocking its secret allows the penetrator to savor the feeling of his or her own superiority. Such calculative knowing is bereft of the reverence of wonder. And this deforms our being in the ethos. The charged value of aesthetic show counts for nothing, as does our anticipation of the hospitality of being to the good. The ethos is the stage on which we enact an unremitting struggle for ascendancy. The earth shrivels to nature neutered.[11]

Relative to *human being*: The instrumentalization is evident in different images of society. We say that we are ends in ourselves, but if this is defined in an ethos of oppositional dualism, at one level (the ideal) the other also may be said to be such an end, but at another level (the real) it will be treated as a means. The meaning of being as effective power makes this hard to sidestep. Nature reveals the effectiveness of units of power in opposition to each other, as each struggles to maintain itself and its niche in the indifferent or hostile ethos. Nature will be something like Hobbes's state of nature, inhabited by solitary, warring units of effective power. Movement beyond this to society will be continuous with the basic picture of being and its power. Society will be the most effective way to deal with the violence of effective powers, and this will itself partake of effective power, concentrated in the most overarching, overawing unit of effective power: the Leviathan. The power of the Leviathan will arouse terror in the units of power and cow them into cooperation, and this even when the language of rational self-interest is used.

Of course, "rational self-interest" is consistent with the absolutization of effective power, since it conceives of sociality in terms of a rational contract in

---

11. Suppose nature neutered is a counterfeit of creation and its glory. What then is "glory"? It is our *being above* nature neutered. If such an ethos of "neutralization" is an ontological contraction of the given milieu of being as saturated with value, why be surprised if such an ethos is implicated in "autonomy," as itself a contraction of freedom? Or that the ethos becomes a context of struggle for power ("survival of the fittest" or "nature red in tooth and claw" are only colorful examples of the view). Bacon sees the conquest of nature "for the relief of man's estate"; Hobbes sees that estate as "solitary, nasty, brutish, and short"; Locke thinks of nature as offering "the almost worthless material" for human progress. Do we remake the ethos as the excrement of our own despair, recycling ourselves in recycling the excrement? We assault without compunction. See my "On the Betrayals of Reverence," *Irish Theological Quarterly*, vol. 65:3 (2000): 211ff.

which the units of effective power become calculating units. Nevertheless, the whole calculation arises from and devolves around effective power. Reason is only another weapon of will to power. So while there may be dissimulating talk about the rationality of the Leviathan, the bottom line will be effective power, and the power to evoke terror that dampens, if not squashes, subordinated units of effective power, units tempted *simply to be themselves*, that is, tempted to give unrestrained expression to their will to power. Thus the social transformation of the understanding of self as a unit of effective power takes form in the ethos, understood as a milieu of threat and power. The escape into society does not escape the war, often the silent war, still secretly being waged in the peace of society itself.[12]

So we can restate the point concerning the grounding milieu of value: modernity's shaping of the ethos grows out of distrust of equivocity, expressed in the univocalizing mentality of dualistic opposition that produces a devaluing objectification of being on one side and a subjectification of value on the other side. Both sides deprive value of ontological ground, and this devaluation, in turn, forces the subject to step into the emptiness where it manifests itself in a reactive activism, itself expressing a will to power that wills to ground itself, or that claims to be self-generating, or indeed that in final exasperation dismisses all grounding and proudly stands there as groundless will to power that will brook no resistance from any other, that will make no apology for itself, but simply will insist that its way will be the way and the truth, and that it will get its way.

One of the great paradoxes of modernity becomes more intelligible. I mean this paradox: On the one hand, the widening recognition of the human as an end in itself, subject of inalienable human rights; on the other hand, the relentlessly growing instrumental reduction of humans to means, to useful units of effective power, and their depersonalization as anonymous concretions of faceless power. It is not enough to say that the first is caused by the process of subjectification, the second by the process of objectification. This is true to a point, but it forgets the interplay of objectification and subjectification; forgets in particular the rebound effect that each has on the other; forgets how underpinning both is the equivocity of the ethos that influences humans to react actively and to define

---

12. Hobbes is not determinative of the ethos, but he already revealed (to an extent, unwillingly, unwittingly) the fatality of an unfolding of will to power, if the basic presupposition about the character of being turns the ethos into a milieu of ontological war. Of course, on such an understanding of the ethos, different specific systems of morals can be erected. Hobbes clearly wanted to restrain the consequences of warring powers. Nietzsche was much more equivocal in glorifying the creative power of war. Likewise, pessimistic religious views will advocate, in the name of God, and the sinfulness of the fallen world, their own version of Leviathan, all with the sacred aim of curbing the darkness in fallen man, as unregenerate will to power. Versions of such ways of thinking can be found across the "ideological spectrum."

themselves as self-defining; forgets how the equivocity flowers into self-generating, self-determining will to power. But it is this that seeds the process of objectification and subjectification. And even if the latter, at a point, seeks a retrenchment of intrinsic value, the eruption of a particular formation of will to power in the ethos is hard to limit. It is hard to prevent the eruption from turning the subjectification into a more radical expression of itself as will to power, thus undermining the claim of the person to be an inviolable end in itself.[13]

Relative to *God:* Again Descartes's views are revealing. Many commentators think that Descartes was deeply concerned with God, occupying themselves with his proofs, his reformulation of the ontological argument, even locating him in the Augustinian tradition. I think Descartes has use for God, but his use for God eventually made God useless. The use he had for God was as a necessary means to further his new project. He needed God to guarantee the ontological import of his cognitive powers. He sought to ground the use of these powers in a new science of nature, which will not be useless, like the speculative philosophy of the ancients, but useful, so useful it may make us the "masters and possessors of nature." God is of use in furthering the power of knowing as itself effective power, not only to know nature but to have practical power over nature as other. God is of use in overcoming the equivocity of the ethos and in giving us confidence in our effective power to place univocal intelligibility in place of that equivocity. The equivocity of the ethos finds its expression not in wonder but in doubt, developed into the oppositional mentality of dualism and appeased by the use of God as serving to ground the confidence of our epistemic powers, hence as underwriting the project of power over nature itself.

Was Pascal then right when he said: I cannot forgive Descartes; all he wanted of God was to give a fillip to the world, and then he had no use of God?[14] Pascal should know: a mind obsessed with God, yet a mind capable of being a

---

13. I am not denying that the person is an end in self, but the equivocity of the ethos must be understood in different terms to prevent just this result. I will return later to the ferment of will to power in the ethos. For all of our talk of solidarity and interrelatedness, the social forms being globalized today, especially in terms of capital and the market, are grounded in an ethos of effective power, that itself is inseparable from a devalued nature, and an objectification of subjects into units of effective or productive power. The characteristic forms of interrelation are secretly issues of will to power and a rationalization that is the effective tool or weapon through which the absolutization of will to power effects itself. (See Chapter 14 on the dominion of serviceable disposability, relative to this "globalization.")

14. Blaise Pascal, *Pensées*, trans. A. J. Krailsheimer (Baltimore: Penguin, 1966), 355. Suppose that, despite what thinkers such as Kepler and Galileo might claim, finally it is not *geometry* that determines God's will? Suppose God is *finesse*? But if you will to absolutize the geometrical mind, you cannot quite see this.

greater Cartesian than the great Descartes, a superior mathematician in fact; and he is superior to Descartes because he knew you cannot use God thus. Descartes deigns to make the deity a partner in his project of the supreme rationalization of effective power. Of course, once he has "proved" God (if God is proved on the basis of the cogito, who then is the real basis, God or the cogito?—an old question), he then will go onto the real business at hand, namely, doing a myriad of experiments and projects, intervening in the ethos to overcome its resistance to our rationalizing, and so further the expansion of our effective power (see *Discourse on the Method*). Is this not an idolatrous use of God as useful: means to an end in a world devoid of value, underwriting the values of the Cartesian sovereign as rationalized will to power?

Compare this to Augustine's wonder: *Deum et animam scire cupio. Nihilne plus? Nihil omnino.* God and the soul I seek to know only. Nothing more? Nothing at all. Compare this to what I call Pascal's "invalid thinking"[15]—relative to God, our thinking is entirely other to will to power, entailing a certain impotence, in fact. God is defined as absolute perfection for Descartes, but what does this have to do with the good? Very little. Perfection pertains to a veracity that will guarantee our cognitive powers in the face of the evil genius. That God as the good might stand against the absolutization of effective will to power is entertained nowhere by Descartes, to my knowledge. Rather, one sees a mirroring relation: the idolatrous use of this God is mirrored in the project of power of the idolater. Does this God partake of the arbitrariness of effective power? The eternal truths are simply the fiat of the divine; God wills them, and that is that. Reason is the outcome of will. We look for a deeper sense that the "will" of God is already always, eternally good, not a groundless will that dictates. Moreover, though proved in the inner idea, this God, as a voluntaristic absolute, has only an extrinsic relation to the world. The extrinsic God decrees, and the world is as a machine that goes its own way, void of inherent value and of signs of God, and there seems no deeper community between the two. The voluntaristic God is a deistic transcendence that itself defines the ethos as either void of value or full of potentially hostile equivocity. As God is to creation, the Cartesian self will be to the equivocal ethos: a relation of will to effective power marks the second, as it is given unrestrained expression by the fiat of the first.

The milieu is not then the between of plurivocal community; connections are extrinsic between God and creation, between humans and the *res extensa* of externality, and the gap in either case is to be bridged by effective power. The uselessness of this God will become more pronounced, the more the human user

---

15. "Between Finitude and Infinity: Hegelian Reason and the Pascalian Heart," in *Hegel on the Modern World*, ed. A. Collins (Albany: State University of New York Press, 1995), 1–28.

develops his or her own effective power. God as useful becomes God as useless, once the circle of our self-generating power gets underway and works up enough steam. God as a means will be dispensed with for other means more useful. The self using God will now use itself, where before it used God. The useful God as useless is given his redundancy papers, with severance pay that will last for a few centuries. Now the gild of the golden handshake has worn off, and the lusterless iron shows through—God a discarded instrument, rusting in unremembered, out of the way, wastes.

More might be said, but let these last remarks suffice. Some forms of religion are covert instrumentalizations of the divine, hence conspire with atheism. But suppose God is the good that grounds the good of the ethos, even though the good of the ethos is undoubtedly equivocal? As this ground, God may have nothing to do with a univocalization of being, or the good that allows us to secure ourselves in self-satisfaction. The wonder expressing trust in the ethos, even in its equivocity, may already be a happening in which, perhaps caught off guard, we wonder if something of ultimate good is delicately communicated in the between. As beyond all instrumentalization, would not this God breach the self-circling of effective power? Has the circle not been constructed just as the exclusion of that idea of God? Another god is excogitated. We have constructed a variety of crystal palaces to be surrogates for the given ethos. We have recreated creation in the image of our understanding, or lack of it, or willful refusal.

What use is God? Useless and yet supremely "useful." Useful outside of any utilitarian frame: useful beyond utility, and so useless. This good is the one thing needful. The above instrumentalization reduces the overdetermined God to a determinate good, remade to take care of us, of our projects, as we dictate their value for us, a reduced God we place on our side and as for us in the peculiar terms we ourselves secrete: god as absolutely determining will, as mirrored in the human project of the willing of effective power. We turn around the God who would be for us into a God that we make to be for us, according to terms we dictate, terms not true to the fullness of the ethos. This instrumentalization means that God is not for us as an agapeic origin, but as a means by which we again secure ourselves in the world. This is an idolatrous use of God. Nor is God to be *used* to "secure" ethics.

Ethical Nihilism: Coming to Nothing, Beginning Again

Where do we now find ourselves? We have built our own *second* ethos in the first ethos of the metaxological milieu of value. This milieu is hospitable to human construction but is not a human construct, and it infiltrates our human shapings with the exigencies of different responsibilities to other-being. But the second ethos, as human construction, makes these exigencies hard to discern, and these responsibilities difficult to recognize or answer. Our situation, in fact, is one of out and out equivocity. We claim our power of construction, and we construct; but we construct in an ethos we do not construct. The ethos offers us the promise of constructive powers, but our living of the promise veers off into a constructing that wills to construct itself, to be as absolutely self-constructing as possible. What is given tries to reabsorb the ethos that gives the promise of constructing. *The constructed ethos tries to absorb the giving ethos.* Or the elemental ethos is assaulted by the constructing human who is after all a construction of the ethos. The flower tries to ingest the soil from whence it springs—it wants to be its own soil, seed, growth, and bloom. This is nonsense, of course, since the ground, even while giving growth, must always remain other; the flower is only relatively self-growing and never self-grounding. The self-grounding flower is folly. But we will ourselves to be thus blooming.

Self-willing will (to power) will dare the extreme and seems to raise the stakes one level higher. This raising shows us the folly of the tightrope act that tilts over the abyss. For this act, in the extreme, and in order to be self-creation, will ape creation from nothing. For what is the abyss? It is the emptiness below it, revealed to the high flying will, as it looks down from its exalted heights. There is nothing beneath it. And so, in a brief rush of exhilaration, it will breathe in the savor of absolute freedom, but in the blink of an eye it takes to taste that exhilaration, the sinking feeling will come that broke on Icarus as the first drips of melting were registered. The sinking feeling of emptiness, as false wings beat against nothing, and nothing holds Icarus aloft. Stalled in flight, shudder of terror, and then the long quick plunge that has its own delight, and another interim in which the whoosh of dynamism might again be reconfigured as exhilarating freedom. For after all, before the thud of hitting the ground, there is nothing standing in the way, and one is, as if one were unlimited, a god that will not anticipate its own future, as the broken body of a shattered idol.

This shattering should always have been anticipated, but it was not. Let us forgive those young to the exhilaration of freedom and those unwitting victims of an ethos of dualistic opposition and its latent hostility to otherness as other. What is not forgivable is persistence in that direction when the call of the other raises itself in a different voice, and when the ethos makes itself manifest as more than a context of dualistic opposition. That persistence is the real idolatry, the real sin, the real failure of humility, and hence the real failure of freedom. For that lack of humility—and humility always comes with reverence for the other—leads to the humiliation of the human being, just in its own self-elevation. This self-elevation, laboring on the steep slope of autonomy and touching the height of self-determination, plants its flag of victory there, but it knows a stab in its own heart from that same flag, as the surmise of the other, beyond self-determination, insinuates itself.

I mean that autonomy become will to power finds that will to power, and hence autonomy, are not sovereign faces, but useful masks of will to power itself, as impossible to exhaust in the mask of human identity. There is a darker origin, or a more original power, at work in our will to power, and that lives itself in us. We instrumentalize all being, and we end up feeling that we are instruments of a darker power, feeling that it is we who have been instrumentalized. We boldly proclaim our absolute freedom, and we end up suspecting that we are in the grip of a faceless fatality that mocks our freedom. This power has no face, because it has no name and no identity, for it is nothing. It is the power of nihilation that devours every definite face of being, including the human face. Nothing then can be univocally determined, as even self-determining power is undetermined and given over to this indeterminate nothing. Every definite sense of worth also is surrendered to this nothing. The will to power turns out to be more the nihilation of value than the creation of it. It does not create from nothing, it creates nothing as itself nothing. And why the somersault from self-affirming human autonomy to self-negating and negating power? Starved need of the other; malnourishment of spirit finally coming out, in a world imaging its own violent poverty.

We will to univocalize value in our own image, we end up equivocalizing all value, in here, out there, up there, down here. Will to power, as instrumentalizing of being, is really the nihilation of value as value in itself, whether in the other as for itself, or the self as in itself. In this situation, it seems that universal coming to be is indistinguishable from a universal coming to nothing. What then really matters in this malaise? Why this rather than that, if all comes to nothing? Why be patient and moderate if it all comes to nothing? Am I merely timid if all comes to nothing and I restrain my lusts? Why not grab, if it all comes to nothing? Why not cheat if it all comes to nothing, for otherwise one is cheated? Is one not cheated anyway? Why get out of bed in the morning, if it all comes to nothing? Why the blush of shame now that I have used another? Why can I not look the other in the eye? If it all comes to nothing and there is nothing more to say, why then the desolation?

Why to get out of bed? What a question! Yet the day will come when honesty will bitterly confess: I am as nothing, what do I matter? Why then rise? Habit? But habits can be broken, and life does break them with suffering. Easier to rise than not? But there will be a day when one is verging on paralysis, and one would sink into oblivious sleep. Rising again? Yet every day, we do it. And every day can be an act of faith and hope, a new beginning. But the why of beginning again, and again, this is enigmatic. I think it is the inescapability of the good, even when despair grips us. It is the sap from the ethos that still flows secretly in our flesh. Is this not rather minimal? Perhaps. But we are destitute and have almost nothing; we are as nothing, we are in the grip of nothing. We have returned to zero, our accounts are run down, and we must settle our account. How to begin again? Not autonomously, for we know the nothingness we are. Can trust spring up like a tiny mustard seed? Is not starting again always an act of trust—beyond ourselves? To be reborn, we have to consent to die, and shed false forms of selving. This is what coming to nothing can mean; this is what waking in the morning might offer. Arising can be a founding act of trust. It can enact a morning thanks.

Nihilism is this process of coming to nothing. Being brought to nothing, we are returned to the primal ethos. Are we not haunted by this: the resolution of the equivocity of the ethos into a moral desert, paradoxically produced by the will to overcome the primal ethos as a hostile other? The desert of nihilism is the doubling, redoubling of equivocity, in which the brambles of distrust tangle around distrust, making it hard for the tender shoots of basic trust to put out new growth. Returning to nothing is potentially the withering of the brambles. It can be suffered as an ethical ordeal in the constructed ethos. It can be the occasion of new mindfulness of the promise of the ethos, and the resolve to construct better.

That it can be so suffered, does not mean it will be so seen. For we are free, and we are sometimes lethally consistent, and we will continue on our way simply because we have taken it as *our way*, and we cannot say: I was wrong, and will return to the beginning. To begin again means to confess, and we heros of autonomy do not confess, we dictate and legislate. Very well, in this ordeal of coming to nothing, we can either be in hell and will to stay there; or we can hope it is purgatory. For if it is hell (and our time has had too many glimpses of hell), we are finished without confession.

PART II

ETHICAL WAYS

CHAPTER TWO

ETHOS AND UNIVOCAL ETHICS

The Play of Indetermination and Determination in the Ethos

The ethos is one of promise, and so open to different shapings in terms of the plurality of the potencies of the ethical. I now undertake (in this and subsequent chapters) a more intensive exploration of this promise and the shapings of such potencies. "Coming to nothing" returns us to the ethos at a level more fundamental than any Nietzschean transvaluation of values in terms of will to power. To understand the ethical potencies is more fundamental than a "critique" of "Christianity," or "Platonism," or "Kantianism," or "Nietzscheanism," though it will shed light on these ethical configurations and ask more of us than simply playing one off against the other. Univocity will help us see how sameness and identity mold the ethos by turning its overdetermination into a diversity of definite ethical forms. Equivocity will return us to the differences and ambiguities that give us pause concerning these determinations of univocal ethics. Dialectic will aid our dwelling in the equivocities, mediate in some measure the play of difference and sameness, and guide us towards an ethics of self-determining being. Finally, the metaxological way will further search the play of sameness and difference, but it will call for a recurrence to the overdetermined ethos, in renewed fidelity to the agapeic surplus of the good, its excess to self-determination, and its call to an ethical community of solidarity that is irreducible to any self-mediating totality.

The univocal way seeks to give determinate form to the overdetermination of the ethos. The ethos is not univocal, nevertheless we must find our way in it with some degree of definiteness and direction. There will be difficulties with this necessity. As not fully true to ethical promise, this necessary way leads to untrue ways—untrue ways that are just the truth of univocal ways. The ways of finding our way in the ethos can be many. For the ethos is defined by a plurivocal play between indeterminacy and determination. This indeterminacy is first felt in an intimation of an overdetermined good, communicated in an unarticulated way, when we are astonished by the givenness of being. Something strikes as rousing

in us a primal rapport with what is there. The rapport is an incognizant consent
to the worth of simply being: it is good to be. We do not *determinately know* this
in the beginning; and we may lose the feel for it. It is first *idiotic* and *aesthetic*.
Idiotic: with an intimacy hard to render more objectively, since it strikes into the
heart of selving, fermenting in our very flesh. Aesthetic: the worth of incarnate
being is intimated. The aesthetic show of being comes like a breath of beauty that
caresses with the aroma of released fragrance.[1]

The elemental givenness is in excess of our measure. It stuns us, so to say,
and the stunning can be both intoxicating and disorientating. We do not know
where we are, who we are, where we are going. But we begin to *come to ourselves*, in that, being struck by the otherness, we are rocked back on ourselves.
We might say: An incipience of self, as other to the otherness, is presented in
the very presenting of the otherness as other. That is, the rapport and primal
consent contain the seeds of developing differences. As we are given to ourselves, what is in us of our own singularity has to shape itself in face of, in relation to, this enigmatic showing of good in the ethos. Just the enigma of showing, and our own incipient selving, may make the showing perplexing:
perplexing in itself as to what it all signifies; perplexing to us and how we are
to find our way.

What of perplexity? Perplexity brings before us a face of uncertain smile.
Does this come from us? Does the showing arouse a hollow in us, and does
our vulnerability invest the showing with our trepidation? Yes, this is part of
it, but not all. Showing is itself equivocal: it is not simply we who project our
own equivocal being on it; we find in it the suggestion that there is more than
meets the eye, more than we can say, perhaps more than the inarticulate rapture of the primal consent. And this too: the very goodness of "to be" is shadowed by intimations of its own fragility: it is, but is as passing; and our being
full with the breath of its fullness wakens longing, but tinged with the sorrow
of transience. The hesitation at the edge of beauty is the harbinger that night
will come, not now, but come it will, and the sun will go under, and these
things too, this show of the given, and we too as given to be, will go under.
This hesitation at the edge also is given inarticulately, in our being given over
elementally to the ethos.

---

1. Think of being enveloped by a perfume of the good—the presence of an other so overcomes one that one is as if thrown into a swoon of longing. If one lacks such moments,
has one lived? The sun is shining, there is a gentle breeze, the light falls over things with
serene luminosity, and one wonders if one is just a step away from a secret paradise, and
the consenting "it is good." There is nothing strange about this, and yet it is exceedingly
strange: simply to be is good; the good given in the flesh of the world as aesthetic show of
being, in our own flesh as in idiotic rapport with creation, showing itself with allure
beyond words.

There is more, since now I name a gentle hint, but somehow we know *more* already in our flesh, know more of the nothing that does not show its face yet. We are tracked by horror. Not tracked, but ingrained in us is the inarticulate knowing that this flesh will fade; that now always it stands under threat, threat of the good of the "to be" being snatched from it, being given back. The glorious goodness given in the ethos, as it were, doubles the threat of fragility. For we so love what is given that hints of its *temporary being* place us in a posture of helplessness (as given, this gift is not something we master or can produce). Helplessness is the other face of the gift bestowed without our even asking. We are already given the gift, already in the gift, before we can ask for anything at all. The gift, once given, is so unbearably beautiful that it precipitates *horror* in us, at the thought that it is for our time, and then we must surrender again to the nothing. (This takes place in our flesh, not in rational self-consciousness.) This horror is not the opposite of the rapture but like a fragmentary palimpsest written into the overt text of consent. And there may be reversals: horror can become so prominent that consent becomes the palimpsest behind recoil and guardedness towards being.[2]

These themes will return again in different guises, but my present emphasis is on how the univocalization of the ethos arises from this doubleness: it seeks to have the measure of the ambiguity. Then the overdetermined astonishment will seem more like an undeveloped beginning to be conquered through a more transparent determination. We cannot live indefinitely with perplexity. We want to know *definitely* what is good in the between. We want to secure ourselves against vulnerability. We want to determine the good with the highest measure of definiteness. And this is what univocity signifies: to be is to be determinate; it is to be this thing, not that; and not anything more or less than this or that, but just this and not that. We want clear definitions and boundaries. We want intelligible markers and transparent signposts. We want well-defined maps of the murky terrain of the ethos and no vague tarrying with subtlety. One may grant: yes, here is confusion, for black mingles with white, unhealthy with healthy, corrupting ways of life with decent. But the task is to separate the opposites. We need stabilizing unities. Equivocation can be terrible, in some situations, fatal even. So we say: no more "ifs" and "buts." The play of indetermination and determination must be resolved in favor of determinable stabilities that exclude equivocation.

---

2. If some moderns fit the latter description, with a dominant emphasis on doubt and suspicion, and if some premoderns fit the former, with emphasis on wonder and harmony with the cosmos, in fact, consent and helplessness are not premodern or modern, or even postmodern; they are human. We seek to understand the consent and to consent, while knowing the struggle with horror and helplessness. It is the interplay of the two that is to be understood.

The One Good: Same and Supreme

This is very understandable. There are many kinds of good, and our desire is often riddled with conflict. We want this, then again its opposite; we seek this as if absolute, and quickly find sinking disappointment; we rush from one thing to the next, insatiably dissatisfied with satisfaction. The univocal way asks: Is there one good, the same and supreme above all else? But why seek at all to surpass the multiplicity? Among many reasons I will mention three.

First, *unity* or *oneness* seems to be intimately connected with good. A thing has a worth or value if it has a certain integrity of being. It is one with itself; its unity with itself suggests a certain perfection unto itself. This is related to the old ontological view that to be is to be one. Being and one are convertible, but so also are one and good. There is much to be said for this view; much depends on how richly we think the meaning of "the one" and the integrity of the *bonum honestum*. Second, the many goods are all deemed *as good*. What constitutes them all as good? It is not their difference simply, for they are good, or thought to be good, despite their differences. The suggestion is that there is a unifying good, underlying or standing above the surface of plurality. Third, diversity is not always the mellow tolerance, or lazy indifference, of "live and let live." Discordance seems an inescapable partner to pluralism. This is disharmonious with the harmonious integrity of good with itself. Discordance sets us in search of some unifying good. How to characterize the search? The univocal search is for the *same good* in all of the goods. The plurality of goods are goods not because of plurality but because of the sameness of the good. This, of course, is very formal and abstract, and indefinite in a manner that generally univocity eschews. Here the search is with the view to *determining* the good in all of the claimants to be good. Why are the many goods good? Because they are good. Their being good is the "same" that holds true, regardless of their being different. It is not their being manifold that makes them good, but the good that is the same throughout their being manifold.

I agree that this seems very indefinite, but in fact the *play* of sameness and difference runs through *all* forms of ethical reflection, including contemporary glorifications of diversity. This is not surprising, since that reflection cannot escape the meaning of the "to be" of good, insofar as this "to be" is defined by a play of sameness and difference. In the univocal reconfiguration of the interplay, pluralism seems merely indefinite, while the sameness points us towards determination. Here we favor placing sameness where plurality seems to reign. This, it is held, is to advance *determinately* towards the good, to *determine* it properly.

What of the contemporary glorification of difference? At one level, this is a reactive protest against the dominance of one/same. I believe it errs if it thinks it is an ethics of difference purely as difference. There is no such ethics. Why? First, the protest against sameness is defined by that against which it protests: there is no difference without sameness. Second, the ethical necessarily needs both sameness and difference. Hence any ethics of difference cannot avoid speaking about the sameness that runs throughout differences. This is most blatantly evident in the injunction: Respect difference! This is a command legislating the constancy of a respect that *is to be the same* throughout the manifold of differences. The command of respect for difference is promulgated under the legislating sign of the same. Does this mean that we cannot or should not talk about an ethics of difference? Not at all. But such talk should be seen properly as talk about the *play* of sameness and difference. The real issue is not difference or same but the play. Univocal ethics understands the play in terms of a certain dominance of the same; an ethics of difference enjoins the legislation of difference, but this cannot be except within the play of sameness and difference. As we shall see, the equivocal, dialectical, and metaxological ways are other approaches to deal further with this play.

Why then univocally determine the same good? First, because of the equivocity of the ethos. Second, because of our perplexity in process in the middle, *between* indetermination and determinacy. Third, because this process is expressed in our desire for the good, so that desire itself is a play of indetermination and determination. Fourth, because desire's indetermination is itself equivocal and not initially clear with respect to its own direction. Fifth, because the objective of that direction is also initially indefinite. Sixth, because human desire seems to unfold from the indeterminacy of a beginning towards an objective that determines desire and its express articulation. The univocalizing suggests one good, either immanent in all goods, or overarching them, standing above or under them, or the objective of all objectives that best directs all of the directions of human desire. The one good will be the good of goods and thus the supreme good, since all other goods take their worth relative to it. "To be is to be one" is thus supremely reflected in the belief that to be good is to be supremely one, or the supreme one.

I grant that those sympathetic to current critiques will charge that this is *reductive*. I grant that it can be so, as when nuances in the multiplicity of possibilities are shortchanged. But it need not be so. The supreme may subordinate others less supreme, but such subordination may be, more essentially, an *ordination*, an ordering of the many in relation to their good. There is no intrinsic necessity that this is a degrading of the many. The ordination may even *elevate* rather than reduce. The lower are, paradoxically, more valuable relative to the higher, because their true value is more authentically fulfilled in that ordination to the supreme. Of course, who can deny strange inversions here? Elevations can secretly serve the purpose of reduction. Think of the idealism of noble values that dissembles the reality of base connivances.

My stress now: univocal thinking influences the *entire* range of ethical possibilities. Ironically, being univocal about the good is not itself univocal. It is plural, depending on what aspect of the ethos or ethical potency is emphasized, and on what is deemed the one supreme good. Hence it makes no sense to imply an *overthrow* of the univocal. The univocal sense of the good is not something univocal that could be overthrown univocally. We must think into it and through it. To define its limitations is not to decree its dispensability. But whatever the one trustworthy good is, it must situate the deepest significance of other goods, not dismiss or distort them. Also, ironically *more than one* candidate has been proposed as the one good. Plurality pops up again in the effort to transcend plurality. Equivocity reappears in the best univocal efforts to conquer equivocity. This we shall now see with respect to diverse appreciations of the potencies of the ethical.

Aesthetic Univocity: Pleasure/Being Pleased

The most spontaneously striking good is what *seems* good for us and what is immediately determinate *for ourselves*. What pleases us seems to be good for us; what seems pleasing is pleasing. This "seeming" of the determinate good might be called its *aesthetic* univocity. The "aesthetic" signifies everything to do with the sensible and the sensitive. For we are aesthetic selves in an ethos that is itself aesthetic, as enveloping sensuous show. The good as seeming, so to say, caresses our fleshed being in the ethos. To be is to be aesthetic show, incarnate manifestation; and aesthetic show is nothing neutral but evidences the charge of attraction and repulsion, of drawing and recoil, a mingling of value and disvalue. We primitively sense good as what draws us to it, pleasing us, giving us pleasure.

Here the body is basic. How helpful are traditional forms of materialism? Generally, I think, they fail the body in not remotely capturing the charge of value carried by and to the body. Our very being as incarnate materializes good, just as the material manifestation of the world as other also is the sensuous show of value. The togetherness of these two in an inarticulate rapport is the ethos itself as aesthetic, and indeed as idiotic. For there is a *preobjective intimacy to this rapport*, lived in our own flesh. Materialistic ethics are usually abstractions from this aesthetic ethos that factor out the fullness of the charge of value. That is, materialistic ethics are not materialistic at all but function to determine "matter" as an abstract construct of univocal thought that objectifies the preobjective lived show of the ethos.

This preobjective aesthetics of the ethos asks us to acknowledge the flesh as alive with worth from the outset. We must acknowledge the play of the good in material manifestation itself. When we speak of pleasure, we are granting implicitly this "being pleased" with the aesthetic ethos and the rapport between us and the flesh of the world. Pleasure, we might suggest, has far deeper ethical, as well as ontological, import than standard materialisms can capture. I repeat, such materialisms are not material enough; they are, in fact, captive to univocalizing thought; they are dianoetic constructs that rightly insist on the material but in the process give us an abstract of its concreteness. They fail the living of the material good in the aesthetics of the ethos.

Since living itself is the appreciation of this aesthetics, not surprisingly pleasure often is taken to be the one good running throughout our being in the between. The argument is elemental: whatever we desire, we desire because it gives us some pleasure; even if we desire death, we do so because it is pleasing to us in some light; even the masochist seeks pain as strangely pleasing. Pleasure seems to be the one that ordains the manifold, that gives direction to all directions, that intimately relates to humans as in process of desire, and as seeking their own satisfaction in seeking objectives they value as worthy. Rightly, pleasure is central in many positions: Epicureanism, hedonisms ancient and modern, modern materialism, Hobbes, utilitarianism, Freud (pleasure principle), and so on. It is important in views that incorporate pleasure into a wider perspective, such as Aristotle's. My concern is not with distinctions such as those between psychological hedonism (we do always seek pleasure) or ethical (we must always seek pleasure). It is the significance of "being pleased" for the good of "to be."

If we are bodied beings in the aesthetics of the ethos, what is pleasure but the fleshed concretion of an elemental community between us and other-being, and between us and ourselves? Consider beauty. The harmony between the beholder and something beautiful shows an elemental, aesthetic togetherness. This may be true of a sunset, a child, a flower, or a woman, or it may extend beyond the immediately fleshed. Often it is an artist who offers us an image of the charge of the ethos as milieu of value. Reflective thought tends to distort it by moving away from the aesthetic as aesthetic. This also is why ethics has first to be aesthetic and not reflective. We need the image of value, or the story, or the living example. Only later will more reflective thought come into its own, but it too emerges from, and must be true to its emergence from, the aesthetic fullness of the ethos.

There is no mathematical univocity to this. There is the feeling of one thing pervasive. And yet, pleasure is strikingly determinate. For instance, we all know the enjoyment of food or drink and how our sense of well-being and the world's well-being are bound up with such elemental determinacies. Deprived of them, our feel for the good and the world can be radically changed, to the point of rage or despair. This aesthetic univocity of value is a prereflective univocity: lived in very definite ways, especially as defined by the common sense of communities; not made an object of determinate thinking unless there is a breakdown, an unforeseen change, or a deprivation.

The rapture of the aesthetic can only be univocal in a qualified sense. This is as one would expect: the aesthetic is overdetermined in its show of value. I see a beautiful face—univocal in that there is no doubt about *this* beautiful face—I am immediately captivated. But as I am drawn to it, I come to see subtler shades. The *seeming* of the aesthetic show contains more than what immediately seems. In time, too, we learn that the immediacy of being pleased does not sustain itself beyond a certain measure. The old sad song sings: love is pleasing, love is teasing, love is a pleasure, when first it's new; but as it grows older, then loves grows colder, and fades away like the morning dew. The truth of the pleasure is both the morning of rapture and the morning of fading: allure, passion, ecstasy; loss, pain, regret, something missed or betrayed. And all of this hidden there in the seeming of the aesthetics of the ethos, especially relative to desire's ambiguity, and the bliss that will be betrayed, just because it is bliss. We come to know this, the equivocity of the aesthetic univocity. We may learn to sing the loss, which in its own way is a celebration of the bliss that must be lost and betrayed. For we are grateful for the brevity of the glory, even though it must die.

Mostly we do not sing this equivocity of the univocal but seek strategies to continue the will to univocity. Think of how hedonism itself is riddled with this ambiguity. The popular image is wine, women, and song; or eat, drink, and be merry. Yet the classical hedonists are least of all libertines of the flesh. They are the *ascetics of the aesthetic*. The Epicureans' point is the equilibrium of the whole that balances the elements in a kind of material serenity. This cannot be achieved by simply saying "yes" to the body. Quite the opposite. We require a therapy for the equivocity of bodily desire. Desire indulged is desire stoking the fires of disturbance; and so desire indulged is equilibrium frustrated rather than *aesthesis* satiated. We must say "no" to desire's equivocity, say "no" to the seeming of pleasure that stings with pain.

The "seeming" of value shows the peril of taking things as immediately good. We have to learn the true from the seeming; and the true turns out to be a minimizing of desire. The best meal for Epicurus: bread and water. To desire almost nothing is almost to be as if all desire is satisfied. Minimal pleasure is maximum. Proper contraction is satiation. The good is to be attained by a univocity that goes beyond the equivocity of pleasure as seeming. We arrive at a kind of *ascetic univocity*, not in any overt violence but in a reduction of desire to a *homogeneity with itself*, for this keeps what is other and foreign to the minimum. In that respect, Stoicism shares much with Epicureanism: both look to security from disturbance. A *therapy of psychic univocity* must be fostered. To be beyond the aesthetics of value, desire must be disciplined to a more *inward univocity*.

Utilitarianism provides the modern example of the will to continue univocity beyond the ambiguity of the aesthetic. If pleasure is the univocal good, nevertheless the unavoidable equivocity must be obviated. We need a *calculative univocity*, regardless of whether pleasure is conceived of in terms of quantity, as with Bentham, or quality, as with Mill. Calculation moves beyond the equivocities of common sense and is reflective of the modern will to mathematical univocity. This quasimathematical univocity reformulates the one good in terms of the unit of calculation that provides, supposedly, a more rational measure of value than the wayward univocity of commonsense pleasure. It suggests what I call *dianoetic univocity* as needed to make more determinate the aesthetic ethos of value.

Dianoetic Univocity: Rational Rule, Law

Clearly there is no pure univocity in relation to the aesthetic, nor can there be. We find a play of equivocity and univocity in which one sides never really manages to dominate the other. To state the most obvious example: the pursuit of pleasure alone turns to pain, in satisfaction itself. We exceed a measure, and pleasure passes into its opposite. We laugh too much, our sides ache; we eat to excess, and we feel gorged. We are not pleased with our pleasures. Disappointment teaches distrust of the aesthetic seducer. We seek a different measure to moderate the flirtation of the aesthetic that leads us on to jilt us, just when we pout our lips for that final kiss of bliss.

One can call this measure dianoetic univocity, since dianoetic thinking is calculative and mathematical-like. It represents a more analytical approach to the ethos. To be determinate is to be a unit of more manageable character, made determinate by the precision of a kind of thinking that abstracts from the full ambiguity of the ethos and that accentuates certain aspects as being more essential than others. The ethos is a flux-like matrix on which the aesthetics of pleasure spread us abroad with a kind of indiscrimination. But we would pin down this flux, break it up into more analytically precise units, thus to get more univocal bearings. These dianoetic units are abstractions, the product of this will to a more precise determination. These units can take many forms.

They can take the calculative form indicated above: the hedonistic calculus in which reason serves the passions, though it is tempted to think itself sovereign. No, there are two sovereigns, pain and pleasure, as Bentham famously said. Dianoetic univocity serves their joint sovereignty. Dianoetic univocity is here clearly instrumental. Reason is and always will be the slave of the passions, Hume said. It serves to introduce a calculative foresight into the otherwise blind vehemence of passion. If the aesthetic in us were programmed according to a proper natural univocity (meaning here causal mechanism of effective power), instinct would automatically get us to our goal. For a variety of reasons (hard to explain mechanistically), this automatic aesthetic univocity does not work and is mingled with equivocity. Reason as instrument must take up the slack, must be the eyes of sightless urge. But these eyes lack the privileges of sovereignty, for they serve at the command of the blind king, pleasure.

This form of dianoetic univocity is understandable but limited in its understanding. Aesthetic being is too reductively understood in terms of the causal effective power of material mechanism. A freer mindfulness beyond utility, as

well as the release of aesthetic being in a fuller sweep of worthiness, is not properly appreciated. The fact is that no such univocal calculus can be really created.
Bentham's calculus is a joke; though if you are lost to this utilitarian mind-set, it
is no joke; indeed, for this mind-set, there are no jokes at all, one suspects. The
machine reason services the machine body and machine pleasure, all rather
earnest but also quite grim.

Look at the hedonistic calculus: it is a tissue of equivocity; all of the standards are vague and indefinite; they are shockingly absent of precise univocity;
they all allow a determination of more or less, and hence they are infected by just
the indefiniteness that univocal calculation was supposed to extrude. And there
is a darker side: the suggestion of a secret will to power that would impose its
measure on the waywardness of aesthetic being and on the subtleties of the ethos.
The units of dianoetic calculation are the instruments of this will. The danger
also is of a self-congratulating superiority that this will is, after all, rational, and
hence must be respected. If necessary, it will ruthlessly run roughshod over the
hints and hunches of a less precise aesthetics of value. The quality of compassion,
say, is not found in any calculus. For compassion suffers with the other, and so
calculates nothing. As compassion is beyond calculation, calculation risks closure
to the appeal of unaccommodated man.[3]

Some other forms of dianoetic univocity are more faithful to the emergence
of standards or norms, necessary to the discernment of the good in the equivocity of the ethos. Such standards, for instance, can take the form of rules, rules
that sometimes are calculative tools, but sometimes are more. There may be a
sense of the *law* arising in the immanence of the ethos, not reducible to an
epiphenomenon of aesthetic showing, but rather a more original source of ethical discrimination in whose light aesthetic being calls for transformation. The

---

3. The utilitarian idea of economic values produces a reduction to the one form of utility.
This is a contraction of the plurivocity of good and value to one and one form only. Recall
the mind-set of Gradgrind in Dickens's brilliant *Hard Times*. There is quantitative mea-
suring and the calculative reduction to averages of the value of humans being, as well as
other things. What does it matter if this individual suffers as long as the average works
out to a calculated measure of satisfaction? This is the principle of equation: put humans
in equations, and it does not matter as long as the equation is balanced in quantitative
terms, the social equation of utility and satisfaction. My great satisfaction cancels your
great misery; there are pluses and minuses always; if the equation works out, that is fine.
Strange that the people making the last judgment are usually on the plus side of the equation, buffered from the suffering of others on the minus side. They do not appear as singular humans in the equation; they are balancing ciphers, anonymous numbers in a faceless calculation. The economic thinking of capitalism, bewitched by this faceless power of
an abstract universality, can produce profoundly unethical outcomes with regard to the
"minus" men. (See Chapter 14 on the web of utility and serviceable disposability.)

fullness of what is at stake here has to be connected to dialectical self-mediation and metaxological intermediation. For the moment, we must stick with a less complex emergence.

There are rules that reflect regularities in a process and that show a constant pattern of determination recurring in the process. Dianoetic univocity can be attentive to these regular patterns and take its guidance from them. For instance, in the search for pleasure, certain patterns of recurrence can be discerned relative to eating and drinking, or in relation to sexual desire and conduct. Trespass against these regularities and the sought-for pleasure will be, at least in part, frustrated. A regime of order is necessary just to ensure the best in pleasure. We need disciplines of desire, disciplines at their best when discerning of regularities of order in aesthetic being. These disciplines will mark the accomplished libertine and gourmand, as much as the ascetical priest, or as much as the warrior, or the athlete who prepares for optimum performance. These disciplines first respect these regularities, then try to bend them perhaps to the increase of pleasure, or perhaps to the attainment of a more holistic equilibrium of self.

In that regard, at best, rules are promulgated on the basis of discerned regularities. Sometimes the rules genuinely serve a certain increase or equilibrium of pleasure. Sometimes, however, the rules can "lift off" (so to speak) the aesthetic level they are supposed to serve: a system of rules is produced, and its relation to the concrete life-forms out of which it emerged becomes tenuous. Then the dianoetic univocity takes on a life of its own, divorced from the aesthetic life it initially may have served to discriminate. As abstractions, the rules take on a life of their own, which ceases to serve the aesthetic life but rather imposes on it, and indeed sometimes to the distortion of the regularities at work there. When this happens, a system of rules can fail to serve the determination of the good. It becomes a self-enclosed system of abstract laws that does not release our discernment but dictates to human desire, as if from above. It dictates: it is legislative of the univocal standards that must be obeyed on pain of departure from the good. The system of laws becomes the ensemble of dianoetic units of ethical determination, dictated to the notorious ambiguity of aesthetic life and the murkiness of the ethos.

It is as if we rise above the ethos through the desire for more precise univocity, but the clarity we seem to gain is set in opposition to the originating matrix itself, including our own incarnate dwelling there. From above, the laws are imperial dianoetic units that charge the ethos and ourselves with conformity to them. If they stand *above* us and the ethos, we might think that we are in the company of the higher and perhaps supreme good. But, of course, we have forgotten that this "being above" has itself arisen in and from the ethos. For all of the precision of our clarity, we are unclear and imprecise about the precise character of these dianoetic units of ethical measure.

I will later suggest (in Chapter 5) that there is an inherent exigence for a sense of norms to arise immanently in some such fashion, arising from the most intimate heart of human being, and indeed communicating itself with the sense of the superior and the supreme. Forget that this is an arising in and from the ethos, and we end with a system of deracinated rules whose purpose to make univocally clear is not itself univocally clear. The legislating power of these rules is potentially even more dictatorial the more they lose sight of the nuances of the ethos they are to serve. Indeed, our sense of the *supreme* might even attribute the law to God, and armored with this divine authority, our own dictation may claim to be divine. Often it is not even benign. We become agents of the law, and in imposing it, we are imposing *ourselves*. The law serves our will to power, though we preach Law beyond will to power. Our legislation brings a kind of *wrath* to the ethos, and especially to aesthetic being. But the law was made for man, not man for the law. This is a good reminder that the ethos is to be served by law, and not to let law twist or truncate the ethos.[4]

Eudaimonistic Univocity: Happiness

As I implied, dianoetic norms *need not* be set in opposition to the ethos; their arising may stay more true to the exigencies of their immanent matrix. Moreover, the aesthetics of being pleased may assume a more comprehensive range when related to a more embracing unity. I mean not just the satisfaction of this or that desire but the *unity of a life as a whole*. The unity of a life requires a more generous definition of the univocity of the good. This is *the happiness of the whole* as the one, supreme good, directly and indirectly fostered by the multiplicity of this or that good. We can call this *eudaimonistic univocity* in deference to the Greek notion of happiness, emphasized, for example, by Aristotle. I make the following five points.

First, relative to the ethos: Eudaimonistic univocity is attractive in staying attuned to the immanent exigencies of the predeterminate context, already satu-

---

4. The natural law is differently understood in premodern and modern thought because of different concepts of nature and God. In the former, natural law is prior to positive law, but God is prior to natural law. The legalistic approach of the scholastics shows an emphasis on the univocal and the determinate that raises problems, and that certainly is not the best way to approach God. This univocity might even be suspected of creating the conditions for atheism. Modern natural law reflects the view of natural entities as units of effective power, hence it is tied to the will to self-preservation and self-perpetuation. The meaning of nature is contracted in terms of the univocal units of effective power. This is consonant with the unit selves of liberalism, capitalism, exploitative will to power, and so on. This view is not fully true to the ethos, both in terms of the ecological community of nature and the human community, as impossible to articulate fully in terms of self-interested aggregations or contractual arrangements of human units of effective power.

rated with values, whether implicit and explicit. One can become good only because this matrix offers us possibilities in excess of ourselves. It affords the social soil on which the flowers of excellences can flourish. Being good is always situated; there is no being good in the abstract. The modes of mindfulness and ways of life that are best are determinations arising from an ethos itself both determinate and indeterminate: determinate as the already given formation of value; indeterminate as open to further realization and harboring promise not initially budding in the open. We grant the ethos in the play of indeterminacy and determination as the context of further particular determinations.

Second, relative to the unity of the good: In our direction to different goods, we come to mindfulness of an immanent exigence to the best of goods, the good surpassing the rest, and for whose sake the others, finally, also are undertaken. There is a vector of transcending to the good in all seekings of this or that good. Not pleasure simply, not following the rules, but happiness, as the most flourishing functioning of the full human being, is sought. Everything seems to serve this maximum flourishing. The unity of the good is fulfilled in the fulfilling telos, named *eudaimonia*.

Third, relative to the aesthetics of value: Eudaimonistic oneness is more generous than aesthetic. Why? The latter can reduce pleasure to a measure less than the distinctive fullness of human being and desire. Happiness is a more inclusive measure of unity. For one might undergo immense pain and yet, in a way, be a happy person. Eudaimonistic univocity seems able to take into account not only the univocities of the aesthetic but also the *equivocities*. That said, it is not at all negating of the aesthetics of value: not dictating rules to its wayward equivocity, it actually seeks the good of the aesthetic, seeks to fulfill the promise of what is relatively ambiguous in the aesthetic. This is to seek a fulfillment of aesthetic being, beyond the play of univocity and equivocity, and hence to be implicitly dialectical, if not metaxological. To be happy means to be pleased with being—not in any simplistic sense, but with respect to the differentiated and discerning enjoyment of life proper to a human being. What measure of suffering can be included in eudaimonistic univocity? This is open to debate, since in some milieu the meaning of certain sufferings is not evident, so they can only be excluded from being good. I would say, the more inclusive the happiness, the greater its possible embrace of suffering, and the more inclusive its openness to the dark side of things, indeed, discernment with respect to the monstrousness in human existence itself.

Fourth, relative to the dianoetics of reason: There is less danger here that the univocal mind will rigidify laws and rules as weapons to subdue the ethos and ambiguous man. We must be discerning about the concretely reasonable thing to do in the situation. The situation is always this situation or that; there is no situation in general. Dianoetic univocity must be qualified by wariness of the danger of rules per se, the danger of abstract universals between which and this situation is a gap that cannot be univocally bridged by the abstract rules themselves. The subtleties of singular situations and the complex particulars of definite occasions must be respected. This is included in what it means to be ethically reasonable. Reason must discern the good of the whole; it does not impose it; it leads the whole to its own good. If it is not a slave of the passions, neither is it a tyrant over them. A relation of cooperation and solidarity is possible, even though there may be occasions when a more stern or forceful approach is necessary—again, depending on the concrete situation. We see a more inclusive univocity at work here: the will to be as determinate as possible, but as allowed by the situation, and not by forcing it into a form untrue to its proper possibility.

Fifth, relative to the whole: The whole of a human life has to be taken into account, if eudaimonia is to have its true meaning. We cannot fix on isolated acts, or become fixated with particular phases of a human development in abstraction from its further becoming. Happiness is what comes when the human is being made whole. There is no univocal fixation of passion as against reason, desire as against intelligence, pleasure as against the law. The human whole is inclusive of both and formed from a perspective that seeks the point of achieved unity beyond their current opposition. Such wholeness may include a variety of oppositions within itself, mitigating their stark antagonism.

This univocity is one of *integrity of life*, properly measured according to its full span. There can be no closure of this whole. Quite the opposite. Since we say, "Never call a man happy till he dies," there is clearly the willingness to suspend the judgment until the last. The race is not over till it is run; we must wait to hear the fat lady sing. Otherwise put, there is needed a kind of *patience* in the between, an openness in the interim that is life itself. For it is in the interim that the good is forged for us, or by us. The whole keeps its openness in the interim itself. This shows a profound respect for the otherness of the becoming of the process of life itself. We need a dianoetics that respects the otherness rather than legislating for it *ab extra*. Even when it does legislate for it, it is on the basis of this respect acquired over a span of living according to discerning mindfulness. It arises in, arises from, the ethos of life, and even when it seeks to rule the ambiguity of that ethos, it does so on the basis of this prior discerning respect.

Why not stick with this form of eudaimonistic univocity? Does it not have much to recommend it? Yes. But we can only see that properly from a position beyond univocity. Meanwhile, eudaimonia is often subjected to objections from the univocalizing approach for not being univocal enough. It might appear too complicit with ambiguities it does not cash into more flat, literal certainties, or more secure, rigid regulations. And the univocal mind frequently wants *more security of determinacy* than can be had here. Happiness is difficult to pin down and seems to have multiplicity built into it. This is a bad point for a more self-insistent univocity. Happiness varies too much with various people and places and communities. Its inclusion of pleasure and the aesthetic infects it with more variability. And the particularisms of the human ethos seem to deprive it of nonlocal universality: it seems Greek, too Greek, too dependent on the time and place and culture. All of this, of course, can be seen in a much more positive light;[5] but the univocal mind is not so inclined, given its will to have one universal standard that is the same, regardless of such variables.

Further, there seems to be a somewhat loose level of determinacy in its characteristic mindfulness. Its practical reason would seem not univocal enough. We may call it a discernment, or practical wisdom, and it cannot have any mathematical character (Aristotle: the mean between excess and defect cannot be a mathematical measure). Nor can we universally univocalize the particulars of different situations nor the singularities of different agents and peoples. Aristotle insists that this is what ethics is all about, hence it cannot have the scientific universality of other theoretical disciplines. The will to univocity is not satisfied with this entirely reasonable point of view. It would push the univocal to the limit; for only then can the good be made completely determinable, hence reasonable—as univocity understands reason. In truth, we have to live with ambiguity, but there is a will to univocity that cannot tolerate this and thinks the determination of the good is completely overthrown if we settle for this. A different demand on the integrity of the good will be made, which is supposed to free us from these vagaries.

What will the demand be? First, relative to the ethos, we must transcend its ambiguity. Second, relative to the unity of the good, this must be untied from particulars that rob it of its universality. Third, relative to the aesthetics of value, the good must be entirely freed from the equivocation of the aesthetic. Fourth, relative to the dianoetics of reason, a higher reason must be granted that has no complicity with the aesthetic and is beyond even the instrumental calculations of some forms of dianoetic reason. Fifth, relative to the whole, the integrity of the good cannot be defined by pleasure, calculative reason, or happiness; there is something more stern, a higher, more demanding univocity, so much higher that it should be called *transcendental univocity*. Dianoetic univocity must be purified of all of its complicities with ethos, aesthetics, calculating reason, and human happiness, and all in order to fulfill the radical univocity of the good.

Transcendental Univocity: Duty

Transcendental univocity, this purified form of the dianoetic, arises from the will to have a fortress of foundational certitude to ground all other ethical

5. Remember, the ethos of the between is not identifiable with this or that particular human ethos: it is the milieu of the good, which includes many particular humanized *ethe*. It is not just the humanized milieu, for beings other to humans, creation as other, God as other, also contribute to it.

considerations. I associate it primarily with Kant's claim to ground the ethical in the categorical universality of duty, which none of the prior forms of univocity can possibly attain. It reflects a noble motive, as it seeks to be true to the unconditional dimension of the ethical. It is akin to the emergence of the exigence of general norms with dianoetic univocity, but it pushes further, seeking an incontrovertible universality of duty rather that any generality, conditional or hypothetical, that may hold true, but only for the most part, or granting certain conditions.

Why align this approach with univocity? Because it seeks to be absolutely determinate about the unconditional ground and the norms arising on its basis. Like other forms of univocity, it looks to the one good that is always the same. It would have a universality without any of the "more or less," one that is absolutely binding and categorical. This cannot be rendered in terms of the diverse stabilities of common sense that help us "more or less" muddle through the middle. It does not claim a geometrization or mathematicization of the ethical (Kant uses the analogy with chemistry[6]), but it does seek a necessity and a rational universality that counterparts, in the ethical sphere, the same exceptionless bindingness we find in the former. The ethical is to be secured in a purely rational way that will be absolutely the same in its unconditional demands for all rational agents.

Later I will indicate that there are more than univocal features to this way. It does not escape equivocity; it has something in common with the dialectical way, with regard to self-determination; and it has a subterranean link to the metaxological, when it speaks of the community of moral agents as infinitely valuable for themselves, never to be made mere means. My concern now is its univocalizing of the ethical.

First, transcendental univocity turns away from the ethos, for this shows too much of indeterminate openness. This indeterminacy cannot provide the one ground said to be necessary. The ethos is a between and shows the interplay (for this view, risks the *contamination*) of the absolute and the relative, the unconditional and the complex conditions that define all beings in a network of relations to others. Such relativity to the other tells against its notion of the unconditional, which must be univocal as being for itself, unconditional for itself, and not in relation to anything other than itself. The peculiarly *transcendental* aspect of this univocalization is this: one unconditional good will be the ground making possible the moral quality of all other goods. This means that the ethos is subordinated to a putative moral absolute that remains itself in purity, regardless of the complexity of the ethos. Kant, for instance, names good will as the one unconditional good—not pleasure, not reason as dianoetically calculative, not eudai-

---

6. Chemical analysis is said to purify different elements involved in a complex substance (see *Critique of Practical Reason*); on the analogy of moral law and law in nature, see the second formulation of the categorical imperative in the *Groundwork*.

monistic reason or integrity. Good will reveals a moral sovereign above the ethos ("above," since it does not flower out of the "below"). The ethos, in turn, is never transcendental, always merely empirical. These two are defined by negation: the transcendental is what the empirical is not, and vice versa. This means continual difficulty in thinking the *interrelation* of the two in terms that are not dualistic. This it shares with a legislating dianoetic univocity, only it makes more majestic and sovereign claims for its legislation.

Second, there is a related turn against the aesthetic and its nuance. The aesthetics of value is reduced to the "merely" sensuous and impulsive. These have nothing to do with the properly moral. This approach perpetuates the dualistic attitude to the pleasing, the enjoyable, and so on. It is a kind of purifying univocity, a sort of puritan univocity. Earnest duty cleanses ethically.

Third, it raises to the height the claim made for reason. Dianoetic univocity is not reasonable enough, not relative to pure practical reason. It too must be purged of its relativities, especially its calculative and instrumental character. Reason is not, and never shall be, the slave of the passions. Pure practical reason is sovereign. Properly, it is the passions and calculative reason that must accept the dictation from on high. If the lower claims to be master, the whole course of the ethical is perverted, and we betray the integrity of moral duty.

Fourth, eudaimonistic univocity is not univocal enough, for it seeks discernment in the ethos, and with respect for the aesthetics of value, happy also if dianoetic thinking can collaborate. It is important to see that what Kant means by *eudaimonia* is not quite what Aristotle means. Kant's quarrel is with what he did not properly see as a debased version of eudaimonia, wherein not only has passion been instrumentalized but reason too, and both in line with the univocal *mathesis* of modernity. Kant reacts to a more empiricist, often materialistic, view, derived from post–Cartesian sources rather than from the richer discernment of the ethos we find in Greek ethics. I do not say that Kant would have agreed with Greek ethics had he understood them more deeply. He would charge the same lack of transcendental univocity to them as he would to post–Cartesian eudaimonia. There is a disjunction of virtue and happiness: to be good is more fundamental than to be happy, when faced with the choice between them. There is something transcendental about the demand of virtue, the voice of holy duty that would brook no resistance.

Why not be content with this? I will offer further discussion in subsequent chapters, but let these points suffice for now. This transcendental appreciation of the ethos is very thin. Why? Because it is the product of the modern play of objectification and subjectification. It sees that the empirical facts of the ethos, under the rule of objectification, become drained of value. Consequently, we need something entirely other than this valueless objectivism to ground value in a more fundamental sense—the transcendental ground. Coupled with that draining, this approach looks with equal trepidation at the dissolving of inherent value wrought by the accompanying process of the subjectification of value. It responds with a retrenchment of the ethical by pushing for a more radical univocity, beyond empirical objectivism, and above or beyond or transcendental to its unreliable ethos. Further, this approach drives beyond the subjectification process towards what it claims is a higher, more fundamental sense of self—the ethical subject as transcendental, hence not subjective in any more usual relativistic sense. Transcendental ethical subjectivity is the source of a moral objectivity higher and more fundamental than even scientific objectivism.

What if this view turns out to be *reactive* to an impoverishment of the ethos, as I think is the case? Then the fullness of the ethos is made redundant in *fundamental* ethical considerations. The aesthetics of the ethos are declared ethically irrelevant. Other-being tends to be an opposite over against the ethical subject who legislates its understanding of the truth of morals. Our own aesthetic incarnation is an other to the ethical. The body and its desires are to be subjected to the sovereign ethical subject, subjected with what looks like some ontological violence to our integral being. The perch of ethical height enjoyed by this majestic sovereign is supported on very thin stilts over the ethos, in otherness from other-being, in stressful tension with the incarnate human presence wherein we experience the concrete communication of value between the ethos and ourselves.

As defined by such dualistic opposition, transcendental univocity breeds a series of equivocities that subtly undermines its sovereign univocity. First, in being deracinated from the ethos, it deprives itself of the sap coming from the soil of the ground, hence the flower that blooms hovers over a void that will eventually drag it down again. Second, in relation to the aesthetic, it creates a house divided against itself, and it cannot guarantee the peace it tries to enforce by transcendental legislation; there must be more intimacy between the sovereign and the subject, between the ethical ruler and the body politic. In a way, there must be no difference at all; but if so, then there is no transcendental univocity as defined above, and we are back in the ethos, seeking and searching as fleshed humans.

Third, even transcendental reason itself begins to feel the cold of the void space in the high perch it has demanded for itself. It has the formal regalia of the sovereign, surveying from its high watchtower. But the banquet honoring the good is taking place in a hall downstairs, and it is locked out from the laughter and tears and wild abandon and sometimes intoxicatingly sweet music that drifts up from that hall of feast. Transcendental univocity feeds on the husks and chaff of the good blown up by the empty wind, not on the wheat and kernel that ripely fall to the ground and are eaten here below. It is laughing and weeping and fleshed humans who are called to the feast in the ethos. Transcendental univocity suspects something of this, for though it thinks itself good, it also knows it should be happy, though it is not. It painfully experiences this split within itself between its virtue and its longing for happiness. That painful split should not merely point it beyond to the next life; it should return it to the ethos with a chastened attitude concerning the univocity it can rightfully demand. It must descend from the high watchtower and partake of the feast of life, learn to laugh and weep, and even be willing to wander wayless in the ethos.

This is perhaps enough on this for now. The Kantian view, like the Aristotelian, deserves further thought at the proper place.

Transcending Univocity: Blessedness

If we come down from the high perch of transcendental univocity, can we still retain the commendable points of this and the other approaches? Here it helps to name what might be called a *transcending univocity* rather than a transcendental. The latter sets the height of the moral law above the ethos and denies itself the fullness of the between by seeming to take up abode at one extreme of it. In fact, it is not one extreme but an abstraction from the fullness of the between, an abstraction that focuses on the unconditional call of the good but misdescribes it in terms oppositional to the milieu. We need not deny this unconditional call but must place it with discernment relative to the ethos. The one thing needful makes a call on us in the between. We may be inclined to identify it with pleasure, or reason, or happiness, or duty, yet none of these is fully adequate.

How grant this one thing needful, namely, the exigence for the one unconditional good? Consider. There is a process of coming to mindfulness and fulfillment in the ethos; it may remain more or less in tune with the immanent exigencies of the between; yet the call of the unconditional, emergent in us, testifies to a power of transcending that *moves in and through* the milieu in search of the good. There is a dynamic power of transcending that holds us into integrities in the between, and that also provides a focal point of reference for the multiplicity of forays we make, seeking the good now here, now there. We ourselves provide a center of unity relative to the multiplicity of particular searchings. This center is not a static position. If we call it a unity, it is a unity in process; it is an integrity of being capable of a process of self-becoming, showing it more than any unity contracted into itself in abstraction from the milieu of the ethos, or from the other-being that is its partner, and whose solidarity it needs, to do the work of the good.

Why transcending rather than transcendental? Because though it is immanent in the ethos itself, not perched above it, it is in search for what is above it, as its ethical exemplar. I mean that its immanence is not any flat mirroring of a value-neutral factual situation. The situation is saturated with value, as is our transcending in the middle; but the call of the good as unconditional emerges in our transcending, and that call is the demand for discernment between more and less relative, more unconditional and less unconditional good. Within the humanized ethos, this transcending opens up the distinction of lower and higher, and this not as a dualistic opposition of two realms but as the distinction between less and more fulfilled responses to the call of the unconditional good. The search for the higher need not mean a hostile attitude to the lower. We may need to pass through one to get to the other. Sometimes, of course, we may need to instruct the lower, when it seizes for itself the claim of absolute good, instruct as we must exorcise usurping idols.

Transcending univocity refers to the implicit integrity of the whole that is gathered into some living unity in a life seeking and touching on its own proper fulfillment. Our transcending shows the becoming of an integrity of being. This integrity is open, for otherwise it would not transcend. We transcend not only to seek what we lack and need but also to express our community with what is other. Thus we live more expressly our community with the good in the ethos. We are in that community from the outset but not always living mindfully of it. As an integrity of transcending being, we also are in motion towards the telos of our own wholeness. We are open wholes in search of our own fulfilled wholeness. It is in the process of transcending that the fulfillment of wholeness can come.

There is more than the saying: pronounce no one happy till dead! Rather something of the fullness is *already at work* in the process of seeking the fullness. Something of the end as unifying comes to be in the process towards the end, because the beginning itself is not a mere lack but already evidences the effectiveness of an integrity of being. In other words, the good we seek in transcending is the good that is already at work from the beginning in the ecstasis of being that constitutes us as ethical creatures—creatures good in our being but in search of the good of being.

Notice we are already significantly beyond any simple univocity.[7] I am trying to describe the play of indeterminacy and determination, giving a more positive role to the former than is allowed by most forms of univocity. Because univocal thinking emphasizes determination and sameness, it has great difficulty dealing with any *being in process*, for such a process is more than a series of determinations, and more than any identical self-sameness. It is more than such a series, for there is a becoming *between* determinations that is not itself a determination. The process of becoming necessitates indeterminacy, hence an openness that requires thinking beyond univocity.

Moreover, the form of unity proper to such becoming cannot be identical self-sameness. For such a unity to become, it must indeed be itself, and yet not be fully coincident with itself; for it is itself in becoming itself; its very unity with

---

7. Transcending univocity refers to a one in the many; a one both a fullness and a search for fulfillment. This kind of one cannot be merely univocal, and clearly no numerical unit. See *BB*, Chapter 10, on the self as this kind of a one: one and all; all in one; or one in all; a whole in whom "the whole" is implicit; a whole participating in "the whole."

itself is in transcending itself, and hence in becoming other to anything that could be transparently captured in the language of identical self-sameness. There is as much determining as determination, as much fixing as fixation. And there is, so to say, unfixation, as each fixation reveals its finite nature and sets in motion once more the process of transcending.

In some ways, this transcending is closer to eudaimonistic univocity than are dianoetic or transcendental. It requires the willingness to be open to *improvisation* in the between. We have to move with the movement; we have to be open to revising our rules, perhaps even to jettison duty, if a greater good is in jeopardy. We have to cease being above the fray on the high stilts of transcendental univocity; it is sometimes quite wrong to superimpose rules from above. This transcending is an immanent arising in the ethos. As asking an opening mindfulness of the nuances of the between, it shares much with the aesthetic: there is a sweetness to transcending in the between; there is an ecstasy of the good we feel in our own surging enjoyment of the good of life itself. Alas, the word "happiness" has taken on too many of the restricted connotations of the contentment associated with the calculative mind of dianoetic univocity. This is especially true when happiness is matched with utilitarianism and its prudent apotheosis in the last man. But transcending need not be confined to the mediocre self-satisfaction of the last man. This is the caricature of transcending we find in the anemic soul, what elsewhere I dubbed *the neutral* (see *PO*, Chapter 1).

For transcending is connected with a kind of *blessedness*. This is happiness and *more*. There is a happiness before which we pause with a thankful silence, since it seems as much a gift of transcendence as our achievement. We also think certain people are already from the start blessed with goodness and by the good, and perhaps the good things of life. A different light shines upon them, shines out of them, from the start. We notice this in special cases, and we say the person is blessed with, say, a laughing temperament, or a good memory, or an amiable disposition: as much gift as achievement, a predisposition towards the good that already is a sharing in the good; a life seeking the good that already seems somehow blessed with the good; and this in terms of an enigmatic integrity or integral character that cannot be pinned down to this or that but rather plays around the life as a whole. The halo of the good shines around the person, because it is clear that something deeply good is at work in this person; and there is a sense of a fundamental unity at work, even in all of the multiplicity. This is a blessed condition.[8]

---

8. I mean more than what Spinoza in his *Ethics* seems to imply about blessedness. To make sense of it, some acknowledgment of the "personalism" of the divine is necessary. How can you be *blessed* by indifferent fate or necessity? I know those who revere Spinoza as a philosophical saint affect not to be bothered, but what do they think is implied by

Is this to exclude suffering and struggle? No. The suffering may be overt, but mostly it is quite hidden. It is as if the rough gem is being polished, but out of sight, and we onlookers see just the shine of light, we do not hear the hard striking that scrapes off encrustations of imperfection that pall the shining of the good. We see the results, we are deaf to the silence of the suffering—the idiocy of suffering so intimate that the one being shined on has only a dim intuition of what is going on.

I seem to say that this blessedness is only for a few, but I want to say that all have been blessed. The effective gift of the good is already at work in all transcending, for the good is not only in the end, and there would be no movement to the good were its perplexing gift not already at work in the process. True, we tend to notice those who seem specially blessed. Sometimes this is the success of the shine; sometimes it is a special gift to this person that defines the idiocy as its singularity. But we are all blessed, though we do not notice it. We are all already caught up in the ecstasy of transcending. We are all under the call of transcending—the integrity of being we are, the becoming of that integrity in search of fulfilled wholeness, or ethical integrity lived out to its maximum. We are blessed because we could not seek the good were not the good already at work in us. Being blessed entails the task of living up to the gift with which we have already been blessed. Even that task is not fully a task, since it has to be blessed along the way, in a manner that none of our achievements merit through themselves alone.

Blessedness come to wakefulness is dwelling in the ethos differently. How differently? Dwelling that sees the gift of aesthetic being as the good it is; dwelling, attuned to the call of the good emerging in human being; dwelling that seeks to live the life best appropriate to that call; dwelling that knows humans must answer the call in the most mindful way possible. Being good is a way of being mindful of the good. It is dwelling that knows there may be many suitable ways, depending on particulars that cannot be generalized. The dwelling has to

---

Spinoza's amazing claim (in *Ethics*, Part I, appendix)?: "Truth would be eternally hidden from the human race had not mathematics, which does not deal with ends but with the natures and properties of figures, shown to humankind another norm of truth." *Veritas humanum genus in aeternum lateret, nisi mathesis, quae non circa fines, sed tantum circa figurarum essentias et proprietates versatur, aliam veritatis normam hominibus ostendisset.* Mathematics seems a saving knowing, rescuing us from our otherwise eternal bondage to darkness—saving us from "ends," from purposes, which seems purely instrumental (as preceeding sentences indicate). Mathematical salvation: purposeless knowing in a purposeless universe? And this is an advance? Does this purposeless eternity of mathematical necessity console us with a counterfeit double of God? What monstrous blessedness that must wait for mathematics to lead us from the bondage of eternal ignorance. (For some further remarks, see below footnote 9, Chapter 8.)

be mindful of the singularity of the situation and person and tolerant of the many ways the call can be answered. The dwelling finds the same enigmatic call of the unconditional good emerging in itself on many occasions and in many different ways and forms, as if the speaking of the good had an unnumbered number of voices, and all of them loving in a different way. We are already blessed by being called to blessedness, even though the call makes reading the signs of the ethos both luminous and more mysterious.

It is impossible to avoid paradoxical language, and again we transgress univocity: uncertainty and sureness; fulfillment and yet expectation; being happy and full of longing; joy in the good and suffering; solidarity with others yet idiocy of intimacy; receptivity and decisive action; proper silence and speaking. The doubleness points to equivocity, and then to dialectic and metaxology.

Transcendent One: God

The final potency of the ethical is expressed relative to the transcendent one. I understand this in light of the foregoing forms, even as it causes us to look at these forms differently and to take our investigation to a different level. It cannot truly be called *univocal*, though a will to univocalize can seek to impose itself on it and our relation to it. In all of the foregoing, but becoming more explicit, there was some intimation of one unconditional good. None really shows itself to be that one good, though each has its claim. All risk reducing the one good to the good for us. Our relation to the good stands for so much that we risk fashioning it as the good for us.[9] This is not necessarily a mistake, for the good is for us, and is not really the good itself if it is not also for us, even as it is good for itself. The relativity of the good to us must be defended as much as its goodness for itself. At once unconditional and relative, the good works in us relative to the unfolding of immanent exigencies, and yet what works and comes to show itself is not something reducible to immanent exigencies, since an unconditional call emerges, and so in the very relativity an intimation of the absolute good comes to arise.

This we especially sensed in transcending; and this, even as nothing is absolutely static for us, and nothing is absolutely the same in any reductive sense of univocity. The one good that is the same remains the same in the flux of differences. While our transcending integrity is capable of a kind of constancy in flux (and so is a transcendent good, yet immanent in the relativities of ongoingness), developed ethical discernment (as can come with eudaimonistic univocity)

---

9. One might think of Kant as an exception, but I find Schopenhauer's critique of Kant (in *On the Basis of Morality*, trans. E. F. J. Payne [Indianapolis: Bobbs-Merrill, 1965]) hard to put out of mind.

begins to see that the one absolute good cannot be attributed to us. That the good is already at work before transcending points to a good transcendent to transcending, even while immanent in it. It is in the immanence of transcending that the call of the transcendent good makes itself felt, indicating that transcending itself would not be possible, were it not for the enigmatic work of this prior and superior transcendence of the good.

The transcendent sense of the one good shows itself as more than us, indeed as more than blessedness, and the other forms. It shows the good as other, and yet not as other in a dualistic opposition. It is other in community with the immanence of human transcending itself. The argument could be put like this: transcending desire seeks this good and that; it finds some fulfilment, perhaps some perfection in this and that good; it has an integrity as transcending that is not exhausted by this or that good; and so it is a good beyond this and that good; this *good beyond goods* is evident in the fact that the transcending is not exhausted, nor made completely whole, by its possession of this good or that; quite the opposite, there is something infinitely open about our ethical transcending, hence always beyond this determinate good and that; that infinite openness is also an infinite restlessness, and so its highest nobility as self-transcending also makes its living to be more perplexing and problematic, for there seems nothing finite that will slake its thirst or appease its hunger. What then can be the good that would allow this? It cannot be itself, for as itself transcending, it is in search of what it is not, and hence there is an other at issue from the beginning of the search.

You might say: this is just *our own otherness*—we will to be ourselves as other, other as completely whole or fulfilled. I think this cannot be the full story. For even the self-othering of our transcending finds that wholeness as blessedness is *not simply our own achievement*; it is as much gift as achievement. Were it absolute achievement, one might argue that it is all a matter of the self-fulfillment of human power; we make ourselves to be absolute wholes simply by following out the inherent exigencies of our transcending being. But we find that remaining true to the immanent exigencies of transcending does not make sense as solely a self-achievement. There is the advent of being blessed. Something other is at work, itself making possible our power to achieve ourselves.

What is that other? It cannot be a finite good, since we are dealing with the matter at the level of our infinite transcending restlessness and search. We are not univocally the object of this search. It is the good as other, the good that blesses us, that alone can be the proper object of that search. But this other is not an object at all; it cannot be objectified; it is a *nonobjective "objective,"* not only of finite desire but also of our infinite transcending. There would be no seeking, no transcending, whether finitely determinate or infinitely excessive, were not this nonobjective "objective" the most intimate participant in the arising of the good in the ethos and its unconditional call emergent in us.

The best name I know for this nonobjective "objective" is God.[10] God is the one supreme good. God is the good that always remains the same, with a constancy exceeding any loyalty humans know from humans. God is the most secret partner, the most anonymous helper, the most intimate prompter, the good that asks nothing for itself, for its nature as the good is simply to broadcast the good to the other, broadcast itself to the other as other, sustaining that otherness. This good is the absolute one. If this is "univocity," it is a perplexing transcendent "univocity." There is no quantitative or mathematical determination of it. There is no complete worldly or objective determination. There is no human determination, no definition in terms of law that will do justice to its being what it is. The ecstasis of transcending perhaps best gives us an understanding of a nonobjective integrity of being, hence an ecstatic univocity that is both absolutely at one with itself and yet absolutely in relation to what is other to itself: unconditional and yet involved in the immanences of relativity; one and yet partner with the plurality in the finite milieu of the between.

This is not a mere upward ascending move of our transcending, it is also, so to say, the descent of transcendence into the between (being blessed intimates this). There are repercussions for the following: First, we must look at the ethos anew, in terms of the signs of worth it shows. Ethos as a neutral context makes less and less sense. We do not come to the intimation of the divine by leaping outside of the ethos but by letting it speak itself and showing us an otherness not simply itself. It is not an ethos because we charge it with value either. This we undoubtedly do, but we now wonder at a more fundamental origin of its worth,

---

10. The question of God requires more extensive treatment, which I intend to offer in *God and the Between*. I have offered significant indications in *BB*, Chapters 6, 7, 13, and in *PU*, Chapters 4, 5, 6. See also my "God, Ethos, Ways," in *International Journal of the Philosophy of Religion* (1999) 45: 13–30. I mention some thinkers for whom the relation of good and the divine is at issue: while Parmenides's sense of the transcendent univocity of the ethos is connected with being as the whole, Plato suggests the transcendence of the Good to beings. Boethius in the *Consolation*: God is *summum bonum*. Augustine in the *Confessions*: Our hearts are restless till they rest in God—our transcending seeks the peace of transcendence itself. Aquinas: our natural desire to see God—beatitude is the *visio beatifica*: God is the absolute end. Bonaventure: *itinerarium* (transcending) to God. In modernity: Spinoza's different God: *amor intellectualis Dei*. The relation to God becomes mediated through autonomy in Kant. The *ethical* dimension of our relation to God I find equivocal in Hegel, despite talk of spirit. In others, our transcending tries to take the place of transcendence itself, whether social in Marx, species-defined in Feuerbach, or creative aristocratic in Nietzsche and many others—there is a reduction of transcendence itself to human self-transcending. I connect this to the antinomy of autonomy and transcendence (see Chapter 1), resolved in favor of different versions of "autonomy." This response is not enough, with respect to freedom (which is not identical to autonomy—see Part III), or self-transcending, or God. This will be more evident with dialectical and metaxological approaches.

an origin to us, and other to us, as sources of value. The value of the ethos is because it is valued, but not simply by us, but loved as good for itself. The integrity of the ethos is not our doing, being clearly much more than a homogenous empty stage on which we are allowed to strut. The enigmatic direction of the good is already in the play. Is the ethos saturated with value only because the good is somehow showing itself, and to us in an incognito way? We have a feeling that there is something there, but we are not at all sure what. We return to the ethos with a new astonishment and perplexity: less sure, yet strangely comforted that signs of good are enigmatically communicated. (Hopkins might sing: "The world is charged with the grandeur of God." You cannot univocally prove that.)

Second, the aesthetics of the ethos bring us to the border of and beyond any mathematical univocity. The aesthetics are the showings of value, self-showings that come to us, not simply our superimposition. We have to heed what is being shown—an exorbitant vigilance. There is the complication that we too are aesthetic showings—as incarnate beings, we are the aesthetics of value in our very flesh. This means: *we have to read ourselves as signs of the good.* We are enigmatic showings. Our fleshed being is an obscure sign. Respect for what the signs intimate must extend to basic corporeal respect for the good as coming to show in our sensuous mindful being. Pleasure and "being pleased" need new thought. Pleasure is being true to the joy of the showing, in ourselves, in other-being.

Third, relative to the law, the constancies of recurrence are other than dead mathematical eternities, other than permanences hovering over time, themselves devoid of dynamis. Suppose the constancies are quick with the energy of eternity; suppose they show themselves. Do we have the requisite discernment? The needed mindfulness cannot be any derivative of quasimathematical univocity. The ethical law cannot be that kind of constancy, if the divine lives in the law. Indeed, can law then be the ultimate? Not if the law is itself derived from the transcendent One. The One is not itself law or a law; it is more than law—even as transcending humans also are more than the law. The good as an *arche* is anarchic: it is outside of the law. The One that sources the law is not itself a law and in that sense is lawless. Why give the law? Not to coerce but to enable harmony with the fundamental constancies of life. If the law is the divine helpmate, this is not a marriage of equals; the divine is more ultimate than the law.

Fourth, concerning eudaimonia, happiness cannot be univocally identified with the good. Yet in our relation to the good, happiness is tied to the good as being for us. Can we say, God gives us the pleasure of being, gives us to be happy? This, I know, is hard to swallow in a world streaked with harrowing sorrow. The fact remains that the good is more than happiness; the good may give us happiness, but happiness is not the good, though it is surely a good that everyone wills to have. The good as *other* means that what we take as happiness is put under question mark. Consequence: happiness as the good for us has to be approached with less of a concern for ourselves. There is something quite contracted in how we define happiness as the good for us. The good as other may blast open that contraction. We experience the blast as suffering (see Chapter 12). The opening of the contraction may be because the good gives us to be happy, but not as we would be happy. The meaning of happiness becomes newly perplexing.

Fifth, with regard to duty and the "ought," there is a call made upon us in the ethos, drawing us out towards the infinite good. The call seems to be the presence of what appears to be far and away in the future, but it is not; it is here and very near; it is more intimate to me than I am to myself. Or the good is both an intimate call and a transcendent task, a present encouragement, a current challenge and a yet-to-come consummation. The "ought" itself is stressed by this tension between present promise and coming consummation. Both sides have to be maintained. Forget the first, and the second becomes a vain, idolatrous progressivism. Forget the second, and the first becomes a self-congratulating quietism. The "ought" makes us quiet and disquiets; consent to the good now, work for its coming, and yet refuse the current substitutes.

Sixth, in relation to blessedness, it becomes apparent that this cannot be a high-minded spiritual narcissism. Blessedness is to be blessed, hence the gift of the other is in the being blessed. Self-congratulation is out. There is a basic gratitude for the gift of the good. One is becoming good, because the good is coming to one. One is being invisibly lifted to see things, like a child at a game, and one's eyes slowly open to see the same things but now haloed with the shine of the good. I know one is not blessed with seeing this halo often. But one is, and then one feels the sink back into dulled familiarity, as the uplift lets one down again. Being struck now once stirs up a new sleeplessness of spirit. One is being blessed and wakes to each new morning with a tortured ache at the shabbiness of one's soul. One has been seized by the shine of the good, and after that one tastes oneself as a bowl of choking ashes. One has to eat the penitential bowl, for it is the price of waking to the good.

What does all of this mean? Does it mean that now we have the answer and that this is the end of the matter? That transcendent "univocity" brings us to rest, and that is all? Not at all. It means we have been cast back into the enigma of the between, back into the mystery of ourselves. The transcendent One is not amenable to any manipulable univocalization. The nonobjective "objective" also is most subjective, and in subjectivity itself also transsubjective, but transsubjective such as to resist the finality of any claim to definitive determination. Not only does our ethical transcending resist definitive determination; more so does its nonobjective, transsubjective, "objective." It is impossible to make God determinate and definite in terms of univocity, and we return to the equivocity of the ethos, to think it through more. We must seek to build another ladder of thought in its mud, and up it climb; or open a cave into the mud, a cavern into whose gloom we must climb down.

CHAPTER THREE

ETHOS AND EQUIVOCAL ETHICS

The Sowing of Confusion

Suppose God is the truth of transcendence; is not God also the *confusion* of our self-transcending? For we cannot determine the absolute good in an absolutely univocal way. Equivocity seems kneaded into all of our desire, even of God, especially of God. God is enigmatic, and the enigma confuses desire. So we love idols rather than God, thinking we love God. The desire of God is tempted to be the desire to be God. Does God then sow confusion, as at Babel? Is the ethos not also this: falling fragments, sharp shards, and our ruined tower to heaven? Behold, confusion! What then is this—some monstrous enchantment?

To many, equivocity will mean less an orientation to the ethical as a problem to be treated. This has its measure of truth; nevertheless, proper attunement to the equivocal is essential. The equivocal is not always a problem; on the contrary, it can coax us into deeper rapport with what is at play in the ethos. Ethics is not a definitive dissolving of the equivocal, but a way of dwelling in it, a dwelling that has its own equivocity. There is no evasion of the equivocal in the between. But first a number of preliminary contrasts will suggest what is at stake.

A first contrast is between *determinacy* and *indefiniteness*. One might propose that while univocity fosters a kind of "objectivism" in ethics, equivocity fosters a "subjectivism." This is too crude, of course. The equivocal is not the merely subjective; it has ontological import; and this, despite the fact that our situation as equivocal actually encourages the turn to "subjectivity" more so than does the univocal approach. Even here the contrast can be overdrawn. Univocity need not be merely objectivistic; for the search for absolute univocity to dissolve equivocity engenders its own equivocations. The will to absolute univocity proves self-subverting. What we always find, in the end, as in the beginning, is the interplay of the univocal and equivocal. This holds equally true for equivocity, for the will to absolute equivocity is also self-subverting. The *interplay* is the more fundamental thing. But we would not know the shape of this interplay, did we not try to think it, in terms of the univocal and equivocal.

A second contrast, again in broad strokes, is between *immediate unity* and *unmediated difference*. Equivocity puts the emphasis on the latter, stressing the inescapability of diversity. This will warm the cockles of many a contemporary heart. This emphasis also might claim an *incommensurability* between different ethical ways. The pluralism of "systems" will be celebrated as the truth of the moral; the seeming incommensurability of different systems will less raise a question as be taken as something final, beyond which we need not and ought not go. Not to accept this is to be in bondage to the principle of identity, nostalgic for a unity to dissolve differences. This is mesmeric music to many contemporary ears, but difference has its own bondages and its disguised yearnings.

A third contrast is between, so to say, *tradition* and *sophistry*. By sophistry I do not mean something merely negative (Plato's baptism). I mean more the critical examination of what passes as the pieties of the past, the unities of the good life, lived but not adjudicated before reason's bar. Tradition supposedly shows the sedimented univocities of valuation, passed on thoughtlessly from the past. To say that these univocities ("values") must be desedimented means, in part, that they must be uprooted from the *sedes*, their seat, their sediment, their soil. Tradition, as the social context of generally accepted univocities, must be called into question. And it is ethical difference that frequently gives the spur to this questioning. The Sophists often came from *outside* of Athens, bringing the point of view of the foreigner. They pluralized and diversified the ethos of the polis. Other peoples do not do it as we do, but perhaps with as much warrant as we. (Pascal, with a bow to Montaigne: on this side of the Pyrenees, good, on the far side, bad.) Ethical equivocity is produced by a kind of critical reason, itself the *further development* of the will to univocity in reason itself. So the Sophists contributed to the rational enlightenment of the Greeks. The heirs of modern Enlightenment share some of their impious pieties. Critical reason would glory in uprooting the univocities of traditional views. Sometimes this ends with the self-criticism of reason itself. Sometimes it yields to a more intractable equivocity that can neither return to tradition nor redeem itself otherwise.

Tradition finds expression in the "objectivism" of an inheritance, while sophistry involves the "subjectivism" of a more critical humanism that refuses any objective morality on the basis of traditional authority alone. To engage with the latter, some feeling for the equivocal is needed. I think it was Socrates's feel for sophistical equivocity that got him into trouble with the traditionalists. The contrast here verges on a conflict of sacred and profane. The tendency of the ethical univocalist towards a traditionalism easily becomes a fundamentalism or literalism. Sedimented in the ethos, ethical norms are invested with the highest authority of a sacred character: they come from the gods or God. The sacred tablets of the law are incontrovertible. Do not kick sand in our eyes with your critical reason! Before the sacred tablets fall silent, oh you profaner! What does equivocity do? It opens a blasphemous hemorrhage in the life blood of the ancient values.

Every question is a pin prick that drains one more drop of blood, until the tradition is bled dry by a thousand little needles.

One can understand those who executed Socrates. (Should postmodern philosophies of difference, if they are consistent, respect *their* difference?—I mean the executioners.) The executioners scented the equivocity of Socratic questioning as tainting the traditional univocity, as the benevolent poison bringing on the slow death of the inheritance. What seemed to be its fruits? Sons beat fathers; honesty counts for nothing; young men waste the substance their elders toiled to amass; they consume the inheritance with contempt for those who gave the luxury of the gift. Socrates was equivocal. He looked like the Sophist. He was a kind of Sophist. True, his condemners did not appreciate the equivocity of his equivocity. He went courting with the equivocal, but his courtship was ambiguous: he wooed but never wanted to wed the equivocal; he would win it to a different way, neither univocal nor equivocal. His affirmative way remained equivocal in his equivocal negation of what was taken without question. Do we inheritors of enlightened reason escape such equivocity, if in our onslaught on tradition we criticize what often makes possible our criticizing? Have we what Socrates seems to have: some self-knowledge beyond equivocity? Are our approaches to the equivocal duped by their own equivocations, or by sophistries of rhetoric that congratulate themselves on "free thinking"?

A final contrast, then, a more contemporary one: univocal "*foundationalism*" against equivocal "*relativism.*" One seeks a grounding unity; the other celebrates diversity without unity. Peculiarly, relativism often leads to a denial of relations. It separates different moral systems without judgment on any, except perhaps that each is as good as any other, which means that there is no one good to provide a common measure of judgment. In the first view, there is *the* correct ethics; in the second, only so many different interpretations of our situation. We cannot even speak of our situation, for there are many situations. There is no situation apart from interpretation; there is interpretation all the way up and down. What then counts as a good interpretation? This is hard to say, if "good" is already the *result* of interpretation: a good interpretation is good because it is an interpretation. But if one interpretation is as good as another, any interpretation is good enough, hence no interpretation is any good. The good of an interpretation is either no good, or it has to assert itself as good. If the latter, it is good because it says it is good; it has to assert itself, will itself. As we will see, this view is hard to separate from an ethics of will to power. The best interpretations are the most assertive forms of will to power. But this leads to nihilism.

There is an extreme living of the equivocal that will say there is no God. God sows confusion and returns us to the equivocal, but there is a glorying in the equivocal that wants to provoke our pieties by shouting out its own counterfeit majesty in the announcement that there is no God. It will enact the desideratum it yearned for all along: now I take down my pants, without guilt, for all is permitted. Salvation from guilt, it thinks it has, as it goes on to incur deeper guilts, all the while assuring itself that it is only interpretation or will to power. Lady Macbeth was that kind of ethical hermeneuticist: But screw your courage to the sticking point, and we'll not fail; our thoughts and not our deeds undo us. Think darker thoughts, go deeper into the evil, for there is no evil. At times Nietzsche tried to talk to himself as Lady Macbeth talked to Macbeth. The first two went mad. Macbeth showed some flawed superiority in that he knew he had done evil and did not interpret away his foulness. Interpretations will not wash out the damned spot. Evil is sticky, and destruction will come.[1]

Eschewing the traditionalist, the foundationalist, the fundamentalist, there is an equivocal approach that finds its relative food in a hyperskepticism. It may even rebaptize old practices with new names, themselves now aging fast, like "deconstruction." In the new excitement of debunking the same, the shadow of nihilism hangs over the different, and this shadow is the same shadow that has hung over the different for a long, long time. Nihilism is now a Western tradition that has turned on its own tradition—to be anti-establishment, the new establishment; to be critical, the new cliché; to be empowered, the new feebleness; on the margins, not the marginal, but crowds—crowds consoled by the comforting sameness of the rhetoric of difference. We might say we are bored with tradition, we might say, blasé, that it is passé, but this might be another exhausted way of shoring up our ruins, the ruins we ourselves are.

The Diaspora of Goods?

Can I put the matter more positively? The equivocal approach demurs about the one good that runs through all goods, or relative to which the others can be subordinated hierarchically. Diversity does not immediately call for reduction to unity; it is as much a value as unity; unity is one value among others. Is it clear there is any unity of unities? In this respect, the equivocal approach represents a return to the givenness of the middle where we live in and move through a variety of possibilities, without trouble about unity.

Such ease with diversity generally marks *sound common sense* in different cultures, despite cultural diversity itself. One is educated in different roles, in ways of acting and responding, some appropriate in this situation, others in others, and what is appropriate here may be ridiculous there, and part of the wisdom of common sense is to live with the difference, to have in one's bones a feel for differ-

---

1. See my "Sticky Evil: On *Macbeth* and the Karma of the Equivocal," in *Tender Poet of the World: Studies in God, Literative, and Process Thought*, D. Middleton, ed. (Albany: State University of New York Press, to appear).

ences. Without thinking things out, one is already more or less at ease in diversity—"more or less": there is no being absolutely at home. Diversity will see to that, for were we to become too much at home, we would begin to doze, and then the slip occurs, and we land on our backside. I deal differently with my children, my spouse, differently again with my neighbors, and then differently with bosses, and so on. I know how to relate appropriately by relating differently. I find my way in the ethos by light of that common sense whose mark is everyday alertness to differences.

An ethical attitude like this is perhaps at the basis of Wittgensteinian pluralism. This was developed in reaction to the will to univocity of scientism and positivism, and shaping the younger Wittgenstein.[2] The reaction is understandable. There is something already quite right about everyday responses that do not need reconstruction in terms of a more logically coherent univocity. What is quite right is just this ear for the nuances of differences, an ear not in need of the hearing aid of scientistic univocities or philosophical theories. Theories often are forms of dianoetic univocity that superimpose their own formal requirements on the everyday; they are then like hearing aids that clog the ear, or garble the calling of the good in the ethos. Return to the ordinary is the dismantling of the abstract constructions that a dianoetic univocity builds up out of the ordinary, only then to forget that it was out of the ordinary it had been building, as it reimposes on the ordinary, as if from above down, that abstract construction. Dianoetic univocity does not "improve" the ordinary; it makes a lofty nest of abstractions in which the rough work of the everyday ceases to be the fulfilling task it can be.

A person gives up robust food because it has a smell, and eats less and less, until an anorexia intervenes; but then it is too late, for the anorexic cannot but see too much, too much excess in healthy food. What the anorexic most needs is now disgusting to it. More, if the anorexic is a highly sophisticated intellectual, it feels the superiority of its reason, and hence is quite undeterred in dictating to the disgustingness of the robust. It dictates as the healthy diet its own empty plate of abstractions, succeeding in making others suspicious of their own healthy

---

2. This is the older Wittgenstein: walking in the Phoenix Park, autumn 1948, in conversation with Drury, who asks, "What about Hegel?" Wittgenstein replies, "No, I don't think I would get on with Hegel. Hegel seems to me to be always wanting to say that things that look different are really the same. Whereas my interest is in showing that things which look the same are really different. I was thinking of using as a motto for my book a quotation from *King Lear*, 'I'll teach you differences,' [then laughing] the remark, 'You'd be surprised' wouldn't be a bad motto either." In M. O'C.Drury, *The Danger of Words and Writings on Wittgenstein*, ed. and introduction by David Berman (Bristol: Thoemmes, 1996), 157. See pp. 115–116 on Wittgenstein's puzzlement with Socrates's search for the one exact definition, by contrast with his own interest in the many meanings of a word, and Drury's very intelligent response.

taste for the nuances of robust life. (Why do I think of Kafka's Hunger Artist?) Wittgenstein was a recovering anorexic in that sense. He may always have known that the diet of dianoetic abstractions amounted to little, as in his first work; but he also may have been recovering from the possible transcendent emptiness *above* the ladder, up which he climbed and kicked away. For there is a transcendent univocity that can produce its anorexia of spirit, a silence not full beyond the fullness of being in the between, but an empty silence reached by an askesis that negates, without being fed by the umbilical cord that ties it to the affirmative.

Wittgensteinian pluralism illustrates a possibility that took other forms in the past. Here I find the Platonic–Socratic approach very suggestive. This might seem extraordinary, for the ordinary view of this approach sees it as unrelentingly hostile to the ordinary. Is not the point to negate and transcend the everyday, wherein we are victims of *doxa*? Does anything but ethical grief follow from the equivocity of opinion? Let us have the univocity of *episteme*, and we will staunch this grief, conquer confusion. I will not deny a transcending movement in the Platonic–Socratic view; and there are places for aesthetic, dianoetic, eudaimonistic, and transcendent unity. But where does this occur? In the ethos of the ordinary, where the thought of much that is extraordinary emerges for reflection. Thus even when seeking a unifying, general definition, Socrates is tied to the ordinary particularities and must continue to respect what is presented to him in *doxa* itself. His guiding examples all spring from the world of common sense. Ethical knowing cannot be an escape from *doxa* but a new way of being in it, a new way born of a new thinking of what is truly manifest in *doxa*. This entails an ear for the ordinary, a mindfulness flowering in the equivocal itself, and so developed, it may suspect there something richer than the dianoetic theories proposed by philosophers.

Plato was unsettled by the suspicion that philosophizing might well be but a kind of game: something mocked it, not only the transcendent good, but something in the everyday itself. He is seen as the enemy of the poets, but I am always struck by his purported response to Dion when asked about what sort of people the Athenians were. In reply, he is said to have sent the works of Aristophanes. Aristophanes great comic artist, great debunker of Socrates as a head floating emptily in a basket of abstraction above the stage of life, Aristophanes who (in *Clouds*) has the Socratic *phrontisterion* burnt to the ground, who is full of a lewd laughter at the derisory abstractions of philosophy! Plato loved this comic poet! What impertinence! So much so that the story was told in antiquity that when Plato died, the works of Aristophanes were found under his bed pillow! (see *BHD*, Chapter 6)

I suggest: Plato was a philosopher of the equivocal, and philosophy's ethical practice must have respect for the equivocity of common sense. Its seeming confusion may harbor a richness unguessed by the abstractions of the intellectual. Mindfulness must move around in the equivocal and get its bearings from the differences manifest in *doxa*. Thus Socrates's turn to the *logoi*—what people say, ordinary opinions, already contain the sediment of vision of the truth; the sediment is not unambiguous, but this is not always a defect. There may be complexity that no simple univocity can adequately capture. We do not give up on univocity, but we need other ways of being mindful of the equivocal, such as dialectical and metaxological thinking.

What of Plato's "hostility" to the equivocities of common sense as they separate us from the dianoetic univocities of the Ideas and the supreme One which is the good itself? We must pass, I think, into and through the former to approach the latter. One is approached in and through the many. Think of Parmenides's question to the younger Socrates (*Parmenides*, 130c7ff.): Are there Ideas of things like hair, mud, and dung? I read the reply as a gentle rebuke to any philosopher who thinks that he can turn his back on such revolting realities. There is no transcending outside of relation to such things, even though transcending is not exhausted by relation to such things. Socrates is as much put to the question as he puts the question to others. And even when the highest, the Sun, is glimpsed, nothing is univocal; for excess of light produces blindness, and we must adapt to the loss of light that the light at first creates. More, the philosopher's *return* to the cave affirms justice for the cave itself. The cave cannot be negated, it must be transformed. The philosopher, again blinded on return, requires *adaptation to darkness*. In a word, we cannot but dwell in the equivocal. To dwell in it properly, this is the ethical task, not flight from or destruction of the cave. The dialogical emergence of philosophical mindfulness from close consideration of *doxa* evidences vigilance to the equivocity of the ordinary. We are to learn from the wisdom of the ordinary, even if also purging its corruptions. The result is not pure univocity but a more comprehending dwelling in the equivocal.

Much more could be said about the Socratic–Platonic approach, for it also is dialectical and metaxological.[3] I have said enough to indicate the play of the univocal and equivocal that suggests an opening to the good by way of the second as by the first. If all we had was an "either/or," the power of this approach,

---

3. In Socratic dialogue, our encountering of equivocal differences is evident in that you have to take *the other* into account when speaking. The full ambiguity of the other slowly unfolds in an interchange that tries to pin down some things, only to find that things are not quite so univocal as they might initially appear. Conversation is thus the unfolding of the equivocity of the self and the other, an unfolding also allowing an understanding of the equivocities and, to some degree, a transcending of equivocities that block rather than spur a deeper understanding. Conversation is one of the arts of the equivocal. It is nothing if there is not the living respect for the other as an equivocal presence that inflects the surrounding ethos in which both of us find ourselves. While this point emerges with equivocity, it comes out better in the metaxological, where the implicit *community* with the other is more explicit. (See *BB*, 374–375, 493ff., on the plurivocity of truth in dialogue.)

extending over millennia, to nourish and renew thinking on the good, would be incomprehensible. The approach is not immune from criticism. Plato embodied the practice, rather than making it a theme: he *shows* us dramatically the play of the univocal and equivocal; he shows us the show of the good in the play of the equivocal. This is one of the reasons the *imagistic* dimension of his philosophizing is absolutely essential, not a mere sop to inferior intellects. The dialogue enacts dramatically the truth of the equivocal and mediately comments within itself on this enactment. One has to be attuned to the equivocal to get a sense of the complex process enacted, without crudely calling attention to itself. As a philosopher of the equivocal, Plato is a masked thinker. Somewhere Nicholas of Cusa accuses Plato of a kind of cowardice in not coming straight out and stating directly his views. Cusa gets it wrong here: it is not cowardice; it is finesse and the reserve of truth.[4]

Of course, the point cannot be any unrestrained celebration of the equivocal, for it concerns the interplay of determinacy and openness, of sameness and difference. (This applies to Wittgensteinian ordinary pluralism as well as Platonic.) Ethical vigilance to the interplay is a living mindfulness of finesse, more like an art than a science, more a practice than a theory. It requires more than a theory, for it is the practice of a mindfulness. We have to be this mindfulness of finesse. Even if we are in the dark, we must be alert for every move, or sound, or shadow, or presentiment that may signal the slow ushering in of day—or a rough beast slouching in the gloom. We need *patience* for the play of determination and openness, sameness and difference. As the univocal mind can lose patience, so also can the equivocal. Manyness is all, we say, difference is king. But is this not self-defeating? When diversity is all, diversity becomes nothing much to write home about. Instead of having an ear for the different, we drown in trivialized difference. *If difference is so privileged, then no difference is privileged.* And we return, by a roundabout route, to a worthless univocity—a univocity of differences where, in the end, they all amount to the same thing. The homogenizing of the ethical follows from a false heterogenizing; just as a dissolving comes from a relativizing that seems to free us into the ethics of difference, but then all we hear is the cracked voice of the same ideological song, monotonously sung over and over.

To conclude: The ethos wherein we find ourselves is equivocal, and we must learn the art of dwelling with this. There are many ways of dwelling, but the art of every dwelling demands a truthfulness to what is given and shown in the

---

4. Whatever one thinks of the notion of the unwritten or secret teachings (and Plato teases us), the point is illustrated. Why should a univocalist have secret teaching? A true univocalist hates secret teachings, for they resist final fixation; they require initiation, catharsis, the right kind of soul, and none of these can be univocalized.

ethos. The equivocal is not simply our defect, nor are we to wallow in confusion. There is a truth of the equivocal, but it is more than the univocal, not less, and other approaches are necessary to reach it. We can only reach it if we pass into it, not only in its negative sides but also in its affirmative possibilities. All of the univocal formations of the ethical potencies (examined in the last chapter) are haunted by their equivocal counterpart, or a new shade of equivocity called up by their ceremonies of exorcism. We now look at these shades.

The Sorrow of Satisfaction: Aesthetic Equivocity

In informing our feel for the good, pleasure's indispensability is unequivocal; yet this indispensability is deeply equivocal. Not all pleasures, certainly not all bodily pleasures, are univocally bodied. "Being pleased" can seep out to the whole, in a way hard to encapsulate fully in more immediate bodily pleasure. There is something not immediately univocal about our embodiment. Our being embodied is our aesthetic presence to the world; it is the medium in which is expressed our rapport with the world itself as aesthetic show.

Out of this indeterminate rapport, determinate desires take form. We seek to satisfy this and that desire; these are differentiations more or less. Do we move from the indefinite to the definite? In one respect, yes; in another respect, not at all. We do not, cannot, satiate the indeterminate source. It seems that there is no serial way of satisfying a sequence of definite desires so that, having done so, the initial indeterminacy is completely conquered. Why? I seek and gain this satisfaction, or that; on doing so, I am satisfied, definitely satisfied; but the irony of definite satisfaction is its reopening of an indefinite dissatisfaction; perhaps not relative to this desire, perhaps relative to *nothing in particular*, yet there it is, this groundswell of unspecific unease.

Look: I have satisfied a whole set of determinate desires, and I know I have, and I am satisfied; but there is a different dissatisfying, not at all determinate. I come to say: I do not know why I am not satisfied! In a way, the reason is simple: the indeterminate opening cannot be answered by any one definite satisfaction or any sequence of them, because something more is playing in desire in excess of determination, both prior to the concretion of specific desires, and after such desires have been definitely satisfied. One is satisfied, one is still unsatisfied. Human desire is this equivocal wedding of opposites: dissatisfaction and satisfaction cannot live with each other, and cannot live without each other. Human desire: a marriage of excitation and disappointment, exhilaration and boredom, soaring tension and flaccid disgust, a marriage of heaven and hell.

What remains unsatisfied in such serial satisfaction of determinate desire? The answer is secreted somewhere in the promiscuous rapport first felt between self and other. This is the presubjective, preobjective stirring of ecstasy in us, as in the skin that is the excitation of being a medium in the between, a medium living the flux and reflux of life in the between (on the *skin*, see Chapter 6, §2). Determinate desire drives us into a differentiated world, full of more or less univocal identities. Desire drives to make this rapport more definite. The irony is that this definite satisfying also *distances us* from the initial rapport. The end of desire satisfied must be *both* consummation and the vague disappointment that something sought was missed, and worse, one does not know what was sought at all. The very mastery that lets us say I desire this, I desire that, I do this and do that, I am the measure of this desire and that, for see, I have done and enjoyed this and done and enjoyed that—all of this, well desired, well done, well enjoyed, all of this mastery is mocked by an indeterminate question: And so? So what? All magnificent ends, but to what end?

Vague longing, shapeless sorrow haunt us, like let down after coition. Is it just sorrow that ecstasy is now past? In part. Is it longing for more? Yes, that too. No matter what satisfaction, we are the longing for the more. We are excess longing, longing in excess of definite desire. Is the sorrow a sign of more again? I think so. The sorrow, less than the excess that wills for more, is an indeterminate grief, hence also an echo of distant indeterminate pleasure—"being pleased" when we were "pure" predeterminate desire. Many shadows crowd around our joys. We may immediately chase away such shadows. We may throw ourselves into new pleasures, or avoid pleasure to avoid pleasure's disappointment. Or we may become the hardheaded lovers of "fact," who tut-tut such longing as pointless. Alas, *the whole point is just the pointlessness.* There is a matter-of-factness that will wave its wand of "obviousness" and crowd out the pointlessness in a new, even frantic, busyness. This matter-of-fact wisdom, laudable in the efficacy of its daily prudence, diligently smothers what is at play in all human desire, and that daily has to be kept at bay. To deny it is to deny what one is, and to misunderstand, not only our bewilderment, but the greatness born out of a different accession to the indeterminacy at our heart.

This indeterminacy outlives the satisfaction of this, that, or the other. It sets in motion a search for something else besides pleasure, for instance, a quest of God, or a quest to be God. Or it may give rise to an aesthetic melancholy that only consumes itself in a deeper and vain hankering, for something that is nothing, for it knows not what it loves. We need mindfulness of the idiotic depth of the indeterminate "being pleased." The equivocal rapport with being goes into the deepest abysses of self, beyond self-consciousness. It is in the body itself.

At the end, desire reverses into a dissatisfaction to which there is also an excess, beyond all determinate pleasures and satisfaction. There is a trace of the infinite in bodily being: infinite restlessness comes to aesthetic concretion there. This sings in the morning with fresh and virgin rapport. But the morning is overtaken by noon and night. The fleshed place where the rapport is lived surges, ages, sickens, and declines.[5] In a way, this is always happening, in that from the point of view of a finite univocity, there is also something *sick* about human desire: it does not fit in definitely; it has its place, but it also has no place. It is inside and outside, in between, and yet on the extremes; a fullness of energy and a strange lack and nothingness; a definite fulfillment and a blind longing; most knowing of itself and its wants, most ignorant of what it is and wants.

The equivocity is captured in the word "want." "I want"—this means I know what I want, and I want that. "I want"—signal of imperial desire, dictating to being what it must give to me, yield to me. But then, "I want"—this means I am wanting. I want but do not know what I want; I am lacking, I am at a loss, I am strangely deficient. My desire does not dictate but suffers the loss of something it knows not what. I want and I want: will to power, and the powerlessness of will—both the opposites wrapped together, warped together.

Who are some who saw this equivocity? Many ancient thinkers were attuned to the disappointment of finite desire. I do not put this down merely to hatred of the body or ascetical revenge. It is a genuine feel for a peculiar kink in man, not at all like a healthy animal, even when we have devised sophisticated therapies to disarm desire's disappointment. The Epicureans saw it and developed their therapies of the soul. The ancient skeptics saw some of it. Despair over the nothingness of finitude is, as Hegel suggests, at the heart of ancient skepticism.[6] The Stoics realized the

---

5. Think here of our need of *sleep*. Tiredness wears down the effective energies of determinate desires—the day's return on living, a little satisfaction here, a minor frustration there, as the energy of desiring tires itself, tires itself in its body, and becomes, with tiredness, an indeterminate irritability, a state of negative arousal from which it must needs return to the rest of the predeterminate idiocy, like a grave out of which it will be resurrected again, on a renewed surge of definite desire. Dreams (as between the grave of sleep and the day's tiredness) reveal much that is predeterminate about self. The dreams of the twilight are different than the dreams of the dawn: the first, the shadows that crowd around the day of desire, just lived; the second, the mirages of anticipation of the day of desire, about to be lived. Tiredness and weariness show the equivocity of satisfied desire also: the unity of self is worn down in being fulfilled. It is augmented by satisfaction, but ground down in being augmented. The sweep of desire is implicitly infinite, but its satisfaction comes in the definiteness of finitude, and so blesses desire with the burden of something less than the depths of desire's love.

6. A critique of the senses' trustworthiness is the epistemic counterpart to ethical disappointment with, and distrust of, the aesthetic show of value. The issue here is, of course, relates to the dissolving power of thinking (such as we saw in the conflict of tradition and sophistry). Besides dianoetic dissolution, there is dialectical negation, as well as willful forms of it (a Nietzschean version in which will to power replaces *dianoia*?). Abstraction from the immediacy of life begins. In this case, skeptical dissolution leads to suspension, or ataraxia. The epistemic problem of equipollence also has its ethical counterpart: one

point, though again the emphasis falls on therapy to minimize the disappointment. Stoic therapy is quite elemental: do not expect too much, and you will not be too disappointed; expect too much, and you will be surely disappointed. The equivocal excess of desire is recognized, but the resulting guardedness does not allow desire to come into its full doubleness: desire's self-transcending, self-exceeding energy is kept on a leash. The Stoic draws a rational line around the potential for excess, for the most certain recipe for disappointment is faith in that excess. And yet what are we but faith in this excess? A faith perhaps more evident when we are young, when our heads have not been broken against walls; a faith companion to all life still receptive to life's goodness. Lose it, life grays. What then? We sidestep disappointment, and lo, the life we gain is just itself the incarnation of disappointment.

Stoic therapy against disappointment is already sickened by the disappointment for which it seems to offer the cure. The therapy itself shows the seepage of deep disappointment. What then? We may have to accept the living of the double, always with the shadow of disappointment. The price we pay for love of life is just disappointment. Without openness to the second, we do not love the first. Love of life is love in suffering. Stoic ethical therapy does not evade desire's equivocity but is itself permeated by this equivocity. Is it truly noble or high-minded escape? Is its inner tranquillity not corrupted by disgust? (Consult Marcus Aurelius.) Is it not built upon a more radical disappointment than "ordinary" disappointment that continues to muddle through the middle? Does it shape a secret despair into a show of nobility?

Religious responses are possible to the equivocity of desire.[7] The disappointment is that *no finite good* can ever satisfy the excess of infinite restlessness that can find peace finally only in an infinite good. Disappointment must shadow all finite desire, for the shadow is the longing of its own unsatisfied infinity, and this dissatisfied infinitude must be faced and made free. If this is the cousin of Stoic despair, it is without the same squinting at desire's infinitude. This is not just a

---

good is as good as the other. While this superficially seems a fine, tolerant pluralism, the attitude it breeds is one "good" is as worthless as the other. There is a dissolution of the difference of good and evil—these opposites are made to be the same, indifferently the same, since nothing ethical makes the difference. Equivocity here again returns us to nihilistic univocity.

7. Examples would be Augustine (*Confessions*), Aquinas (*Treatise on Happiness*), Pascal (*Pensées*), and Kierkegaard (*Sickness unto Death*), for instance. See my "St. Augustine's Confessions: On Desire, Conversion and Reflection," *Irish Theological Quarterly* 47: 1 (1980): 24–33; also "Between Finitude and Infinity: Hegelian Reason and the Pascalian Heart," in *Hegel on the Modern World*, Ardis Collins, ed. (Albany: State University of New York Press, 1995), 1–28. See also Harvie Ferguson's *Melancholy and the Critique of Modernity: Soren Kierkegaard's Religious Psychology* (London and New York: Routledge, 1995), and my review in *Tijdschrift voor Filosofie* 58: 4 (1996): 765–768.

sickness needing therapy. If it is a sickness, it is a homesickness, and this need not be a sickness. The sickness is rather infinite obsession with finite desire that does not let the excess come to its true freedom. There is a clinging to finitude that corrupts this free infinity. Of course, this infinity also can cause untold misery, since it gives us the opening of freedom, and so what makes us what we are. It is what transforms all finite desire. It is what ferments secretly in all seeking, from the infant's first mouth of the breast to the last gulping prayer of a dying human falling away. It is what drives all overcoming. It is what feeds the most megalomaniac egotism and the most selfless compassion for the wanting. It is need itself as infinitely open to the divine other and the needy human other. It is need that has the gift of the good in it, as far as it can give beyond itself. Does the equivocal excess finally mean nothing if the surplus of the human is not its homing on God or God on it?

The Virtues of the Promiscuous: Dianoetic Equivocity

Dianoetic univocity, we recall, claims to obviate the equivocity of the aesthetic by formulating rules that apply, or should be applied, in all instances. Dianoetic law regulates the grief of the aesthetic. Being ethical is not being pleased but following the law; if this brings pain, then be it so. The law is for the good, and this is not univocally what is pleasant. Thus dianoetic regulation claims to transcend the idiosyncrasy of the pleasurable and its particular occasion. It legislates a more than particular univocity, a general univocity. Rising above life's equivocity as aesthetically lived, it then turns back on that equivocity to regulate it with the clarity of general sameness. The lived aesthetics is promiscuous, the law is pure; it separates what is mixed; it purifies of particularity; it is puritan. At one level, this way seems to show something like a "selfless" universality. At a deeper level, its rising above life's aesthetic equivocity is itself mixed in with a skepticism generated by equivocity. It is less immune from despair than appearances lead one to believe.

Again, suppose I am serially disappointed. I might say: this disappointment is thus and so, but no matter, I move on, and will try again. Suppose I separate the disappointments, one from the other, and go on from one to the next, as if always rising again like a phoenix that no sooner burns than it comes to be again. I am no sooner disappointed than this disappears into a forgetfulness that allows life the faith to renew itself, again and again. Alas, the disappointment is not just lived but *known and minded*. In fact, disappointment makes us more and more thoughtful about what the good might be. It deepens mindfulness about desire's equivocity. It is not ours to live like a pointillistic phoenix; we make connections; we grow mindful that there is *recurrence in the series*; if nothing else, disappointment itself comes back again and again. Mindfulness is shown something *the same* about the very process of serially unfolding desire. Desire is serial but more than serial, for desire is made *mindful of itself* as wed forever to disappointment. This knowing in disappointment of a *continuity in* aesthetic life paradoxically fosters a *discontinuity with* aesthetic life. Mindfulness generates skepticism about desire, skepticism founded on desire's immanent disappointment but initiating a break with this immanence. We seek to be free from immersion in the seriality of disappointing desire. Thus is dianoetic univocity sought as discontinuous with aesthetic life.[8]

In this break, law seeks to provide the standard by which life's equivocity is to be judged and regulated. Judged: some forms of life are deemed not properly moral, some desires not licit; they are forbidden. Regulated: human waywardness is like a wild and too fertile flower and has to be domesticated, otherwise we transgress the ordered bounds of propriety. Without proper cultivation, we remain sunk in a savage state. Regulation is thus both a *defensive* response to desire's equivocity, and also an *offensive*, since the vitality of desire's excess has to be tackled, perhaps at its root, an offensive on what is outlaw, offspring less of twilight than of night. This double posture of defense and offense indicates law as both *rising above* the equivocity and *turning back* towards it. However—and this is the crucial point—the *equivocity of the law itself* appears in this double posture, especially in this turn back. The law is defined by a sameness that, as different to the aesthetic, is not reducible to life as lived. The sameness of the law turns its difference from life into an opposition and a negation, clearly evident in this double posture. You might say: well and good, as proper puritans we say "no" to life's promiscuity. Yet it is not enough to say "no": for even if one's regulation is to be negative, there must be a point of *contact* with what is negated. The purity, won in and out of opposition, at some point has to *descend* from its purity to influence the promiscuous equivocity it wills to regulate. But in this, it risks contamination by the very thing from which it seeks to be purified. The full meaning of its desire for purity cannot but risk impurity, if it is to *fulfill itself*.

I am pure, the other impure; I wish to purify the other; but in making the impure other pure, I risk making myself, as pure, impure. This risk of impurity is simply unavoidable, if the task of purification is to have any point. In a word: the purity of the law, to be pure, must run the risk of impurity. In the fullness of the

---

8. There can be more than the search for dianoetic univocity in that break, as, for example, in the complex skeptical response of suspense, the Stoic retreat in the sanctuary of inner virtue (there is a kind of dianoetic univocity here connected to natural law), or again in a number of religious responses. This dialectic of disappointment as recurring, as even tempting mindful desire with despair, is at stake in all skeptical approaches to ethics, where the very process of thinking about the good seems to dissolve faith in the already given sense of the good. We see this in Socrates, in the Sophists, in modern practitioners of critique, and in the hermeneutics of suspicion.

situation there can be no pure purity. There is only impure purity or purified impurity. Instead of the opposition of the two, we have the mutual interinvolvement of the opposites, and hence we return again to a promiscuity, itself riddled with equivocal possibilities. The mastery of the equivocal is itself overcome by equivocity one more time.

Let me put it differently. A puritan defines his or her purity by *negation relative* to the impurity of the promiscuous; the pure live by pure laws, yet the laws dictate that the impure shall be pure, or made pure; there is a *task in the law*, hence living by the law entails that the puritan set out to make the promiscuous more pure. But in the process of making the impure pure, the puritan is involved "with" the impure. Indeed, under the guidance of the good, the pure comes to see this "with" as a *community with the impure*, deeper than the negation and the opposition. Purity may dictate to impurity, but if that is all, then the imposition of purity is a dictatorial act that drags along its own characteristic impurity—and so there is again a community between them. Or purity may find that there is more to the other than impurity, and thus find its own form undergoing mutation under contact with the other—and so again there is community between them. Thus to live the law as *setting a task*, as dictating that one should do such and such, always entails *co-implication* with the other, and the *return* to the impure context above which the law seemed to stand. As enacting the task of the law, the human being cannot stand above but must return to the midst. To be in the midst is to be in the ethos wherein the law is to be enacted—and therein, avoidance of equivocity is impossible.

This is evident in the application of law: for application concerns the specific range of the law's task. This is what the *turn back* means: not to rise above, but to bring law to bear on what is muddled in the ethos. "Bringing it to bear" is *more fully* the meaning of law, for if law is to legislate, it must have *bearing on* the equivocity of the ethos. A law with no potential application is no law: it is an impotent generality, dictating nothing from a void into a void. The turn back is inherent in the vector of ethical transcending that generates law as dianoetic univocity.

Here a *first* equivocity of law itself is: It is not law that produces itself, but it emerges in this vector of transcending; hence law is not the pure primordiality of sameness it claims to be; something more primordial than law generates law, and this something more primordial is *beyond the law*. This is true even if we think of God as producing the moral law. There is something about God as good and origin not exhausted by moral law. The source that generates law is not a law. If this source is good, there is *good beyond the law*. If this source is not good, what good ultimately is the law then? In any case, even if the law does have dianoetic univocity, this cannot be the last word, for there would be no good to the law were there not good in a sense more primordial than law.

A *second* equivocity: Just as it is not law that produces itself, it is not law that applies itself. As it emerges in a vector of transcending, so it is applied in a *vector of descending* that *transcends downwards*, turns back to the ethos out of which transcending itself emerged. The law's application is an applying, and this is an activity that transcends from out of any dianoetic univocity towards the problematic situation or case that the law is to illuminate. The law does not judge; the judge judges in accordance with the law. But the judge is not a law, and her or his applying the law is more than the law. This is clearly more than the law as a general sameness, since the applying relates to this or that case. This also is more than the law, in perhaps a deeper sense, in that a discerning mindfulness is absolutely necessary to the proper application of the law.[9]

The application of univocal laws to cases is not itself univocal, for there is a gap between the law and the case, and the gap has to be mediated by the discerning judiciousness of the judge; this is not just a law but a mindfulness that *moves between* the law and the case. It is not one or the other but must be both, become both, while it remains neither one nor the other. From the standpoint of strict dianoetic univocity, this requirement seems entirely equivocal: "A something that is not one or the other, but must be both or become both, and yet remain neither one nor the other"—this has no meaning on purely univocal terms, where one is either one or the other, and one cannot be both, and become both, and so on.

The judge is more than the extremes of law and case as univocally fixed; to be in movement between them, the *indeterminate must have more power* than a mere regrettable indefinite; it must be the power of an open mindfulness, capable of attentiveness to the full nuances of a case, as well as the regulating principles that help us sort out ambiguities. The *task* of the law is such that no law has its full meaning in terms of dianoetic univocity, even though it is still essential that the law be formulated with as much univocity as possible. To do justice to the dianoetic univocity of law, we need mindfulness of more than univocity, not only vis-à-vis the equivocity of the ethos and human desire but also in relation to the character of self-transcending as ethical. This will be more evident later with dialectic and metaxology.

A *third* equivocity concerns law and *will to power*. Law can be used by will to power in its own game of self-mediation; within the law, the will to power camouflages itself. Marx and Nietzsche saw this. It is an important point. The law is dictatorial, because the will to power dictates through the law. Dianoetic univocity can be a mask of will to power. This also can happen with the law's exploitation by religious people. What better tool in the augmentation of my power than God's law.

---

9. The question of application also might be put in terms of the *correspondence* of the law and the case. But there are problems with the determination of the correspondence that is not itself simply either law or case. On analogous problems with the correspondence view of truth, see *BB*, Chapter 12.

A *fourth* equivocity might be stated in terms of *casuistry*. In casuistry we find the multiplication of cases in which all of the seeming exceptions are marshalled pro and con in terms of the law. Casuistry can become silly; it can become downright deceitful. You qualify the law to such an extent that there is really nothing left, but the exercise of infinitely subtle qualification camouflages this cancelling. So the casuistry is hypocritical: it wants to have its cake of law and eat its self-serving pleasures too. Why does casuistry easily become the hypocrisy of law? It wants to holds on to its own claim to univocity; to hold on to this, it must qualify itself again and again, all the while claiming to play the game of dianoetic univocity; but the reality is that this endless process of univocal qualification produces a jungle of cases, each with a tangle of intricacy grown up around it. Instead of the law's dianoetic univocity, we have this jungle of intricacy, itself created by the casuistical process of univocalization. Thus casuistically applied, eventually univocity produces an impossible equivocation: the seeming simplicity of the initial situation demands qualification, which itself demands qualification, and so on, until you have unmanageable complexity. Ungovernable complexity becomes the truth of the seeming simplicity. There comes a point when we say: let us sweep this aside and start again, for the law is now an ass, and it makes things worse rather than better.[10]

A problem here with univocal law is that it can fail, as it were, "*to let go*," to free: its rigid insistence on itself makes it such that it keeps painting itself into a corner to preserve its own consistency; but finally, all of the qualifications make one want to return more spontaneously to the ethos, as presenting itself *without* the accretions of these univocally generated qualifications. It then seems better to muddle through the promiscuity of the middle rather than, as it were, travel around it with one's book of casuistical cases, each time to be consulted as one hits a problem. How does the chicken cross the road? Just a minute—let me check how this is done in my book of rules! How do I deal with a weeping child? One minute, let me look up the book under feelings! Under the yearning moon, the lady seems to offer herself for kissing. One moment please, while I consult my manual! But in that twinkling of an eye, the moon is clouded, the yearning floats away, and the woman grows cold. And so the moment is lost, and the opportunity of life has passed. Life, we later learn, is what we missed while it was passing, as we willed to master it with our manuals.

---

10. The hypocrisy and self-serving nature of casuistical thinking might be illustrated by Pascal's polemic with the Jesuits. The point about will to power also applies: the Jesuits' use of casuistry seemed to ease the path of will to power, either making it more comfortable for the powerful and worldly to be Christians, or to give the Jesuits influence with powerful people, being the advisors and confessors who could be counted on to give the most "judicious" advice.

Something more than dianoetic thinking is needed to be open to and to receive the opportunity. One must go down again into the middle, and with faith; and not with less mindfulness but more, mindfulness that knows that univocal fixing cannot do the job, even the job it claims is its own speciality. This is one of the sins of dianoetic univocity: it tries to make a rational specialization of the ethical; it thinks it can be a specialist of the law and rule; and yes, one can have special knowledge of the law, but something essential, something more, is needed: a wisdom beyond univocity and equivocity. The wisdom of the judge cannot be either merely. A simply univocal judge would be a wooden fool, a merely equivocal judge a boneless wonder.

Judging means having an ear for the singular, not just by rising above the particular to the general but by descending into the nuances of the concrete situation. Knowledge of the general is not negligible, but even lacking it explicitly, one might yet be a good judge. Knowledge of the general, coupled with bad attunement to the particular, might make one a disastrous judge. One would be injudicious as if one tried to learn it all from a book. Good judgment demands a *justice of mind that must be won from life itself.* There is no ultimate specialization of the ethical. We need some indeterminate sense of the "whole" and the ethos and the nonunivocal mindfulness going with that. This is the mindfulness that law needs, to enact its own task as being applicable.[11]

The Stirring of the Subterranean: Transcendental Equivocity

The transcendental approach to ethics, as to all other issues in philosophy, is a continuation, purification, and radicalization of the dianoetic approach. Like the latter, it seeks to transcend the equivocity of lived aesthetics, but in a more thorough fashion relative to universality, necessity, and apodicticity. We cannot be content with the general over against the particular, but we need a universal necessity, free from the equivocities of even dianoetic generality. This latter too seems tied to the aesthetic, often here named the empirical. If dianoetic norms are tied to empirical generalizations, they are always open to the confutation of aesthetic happening, or experience, or "the given." The transcendental approach seeks the universal that not merely rises above and frees itself from the aesthetic

---

11. I return to the point below relative to *phronesis.* Plato saw the problem with the statesman; see S. Rosen, *Plato's Statesman* (New Haven, Conn.: Yale University Press, 1995). Aristotle saw the point relative to the *phronimos.* Kant saw the problem of judgment, especially in the *Critique of Judgment.* The issue is important in Gadamerian hermeneutics relative to the problem of application. See my "Phronesis and the Categorial Imperative," *Philosophical Studies* (Ireland) 27 (1980): 7–15.

but that *already is above*, always already free of the aesthetic, prior to the empirical. Such a universal, the claim is, makes the aesthetic possible, grounds it by giving it a foundation in intelligibility that it would not otherwise have, or could ever have, on its own terms. The foundation is the a priori that grounds the possibility of the ethical. It seems even more pure than the emergent purity of the dianoetic general, and more free of contamination from the promiscuous equivocities of experience.

The transcendental univocity that we find in the Kantian position is a form of ethical foundationalism: Kant was concerned with laying the ground (*Grundlegung*) of a metaphysics of morals. He does not deny a more "empirical" part of ethics, for he clearly offers us one, though he locates that in the doctrine of anthropology. Nor does he deny the need for something like casuistry, as we see in some of his discussions of particular duties, towards oneself and towards others. But there is a strict divide between the aesthetic/empirical and the transcendental. Relevantly, the ground laid for ethics does not pertain solely to human beings but to all and any rational being, I suppose spiritual beings not incarnated as we are, such as angels. This confirms the point that the necessity and universality sought is even more pure and exacting than the dianoetic. The latter yields a lazy or lax rationalism, also complicit with the cosy mentality of "more or less." All rational beings—no if and buts, no exceptions, and no qualification by extraneous factors.

A philosopher might perk up and cheer: our pride is in taking the issue to the root, and here surely we hear a prophetic call to bring ethics back from lostness in the merely empirical and general. These too end up in the labyrinth, but we seek the way. Transcendental reason must supply the thread. How? By transcending the aesthetic ambiguities of pleasure and desire and the logical ambiguities of generalizing reason that remains bound to aesthetic ambiguities and thus feeds the suspicion that reason is the slave of passion. Transcendental reason will be sovereign, the one sovereign commanding the final rout of ethical equivocity.

Has transcendental reason the freedom from equivocity claimed? One traditional criticism is this: the univocity of transcendental reason is formal, hence empty, when it comes to concrete material content for the ethical imperative. Many passages in Kant might seem to confirm this, though clearly he often intends more by transcendental reason than a formal logical operation. What kind of reason remains controversial. For instance, what does it mean to speak of *all* rational beings, since what we know of reason is of us, not of angels or of God's mind? How to give concrete content to reason, if in the end human reason is our guide? This is the whole question, in a way. For it has everything to do with *being good in the ethos of the between*.

You might claim that activities such as mathematics show us to be beings of pure reason. This claim is older than Kant, and its controversial nature outlives Kant, since again we remain humans even when we do mathematics. Moreover, is it at all reasonable to think in terms of any kind of "mathematical" paradigm when being mindful of the ethical? Mathematical reason may be the supreme example of the univocalizing mind, but that reason may be improper, that is, unreasonable, in dealing with the ethical. Kant knew that it was not mathematical reason, and he refers his ground laying to the analogy of a chemical rather than a geometrical analysis, but the will to absolute univocal determination is still crucial. It is not easy to isolate pure practical reason: the will to univocity is not easily fulfilled, and even the effort to fulfill it seems riddled with ambiguity, or the reentrance of what is not univocal.

What if the form of pure transcendental reason cannot find any content on its own? Content has to be secretly smuggled into it, coming from the ethical determinations already operative in the ambiguity of the ethos, determinations not themselves at all purified of equivocity. The duties found to be self-evidently universal seem, in some respects, to be relative to the social conditions prevailing with a certain people at a certain time with a certain tradition and culture. These seem less a priori than very specific ethical attitudes that have emerged to form in the ethos. The duties of transcendental reason seem to sound much like a rationalized reconfiguration of those of a German Protestant of pietistic bent around the end of the eighteenth century. The unconditional seems a complex echo of the conditioned times.

That there should be felt the need of *that kind of ground laying* is itself historically relative. Kant was driven to that extreme resort, just because the ethos was being drained of inherent ethical value by the basic metaphysical changes set in motion by the modern *mathesis* of nature. Kant's pure practical reason is unknowingly a defense measure against the ethical nihilism that must follow if that *mathesis* were the truth of the whole. Were it the truth of the whole, there would be no good to the whole, no point to the all, and no good or point to our awareness of being answerable for ourselves and to an unconditional good. Yet, and here's the rub, the defense measure is a *continuation* of the mentality shaped by the modern *mathesis* of nature, a kind of moral *mathesis*. But just as the first *mathesis* is a dianoetic abstraction from the fullness of aesthetic happening, the moral "*mathesis*," as a defense measure in the ethos, must fail. Why? Because it is already infected by the sickness it seeks to cure. The cure is itself a mutation bred by the deeper metaphysical malaise endemic in the univocalization of nature or the whole. It may be necessary to return to the equivocity of the ethos differently; perhaps even the fever (say, of "irrationalism") will have to rage before some peace is restored.[12]

---

12. If the ethical emptiness of the formal must be filled by X, itself not determined, then claims to a certain kind of necessity and universality may well be upheld, but at an ethical price not initially evident. For if X has to be surreptitiously presupposed to give concrete content, or if it has to be smuggled in, albeit not intentionally, transcendental form can be

Suppose the criticism of formalism is still controversial, not yet settled; we will leave the final judgment open. Yet this tolerant attitude of openness is revealing about the project's *failure—even if is a secret success*. Kantians may labor mightily to disarm the threat. How many tomes are excogitated, all trying to find some angle to show how the whole Kantian project hangs together? The fact that they have to labor shows that significant ambiguity attaches to the project. If you have to argue for a univocity not seen, something is not quite as univocal as it would seem. The fact that you have to argue for no equivocity shows the fact of some equivocity.

Or is it because, after all, we remain human and not transcendental reasons? But is this not itself full of the ambiguity in question, ambiguity not dispersed by waving the wand of transcendental reason, ambiguity calling transcendental reason into question? Is it not a very good thing that we remain human beings after all, and not pure reasons? So remaining means we do not and cannot forget the ethical as articulated in the ethos and its play of indetermination and determination. For the ethical is always in the midst, in the between. Pure transcendental reason is not in the midst thus—or if it is, it is so *ambiguously*, and we must spell out what it means to say it is in the between. And this shows, once again, its lack of univocal clarity.

Additional ambiguities concern a transcendental version of what I might call *dianoetic negativity* towards the "merely empirical." The "merely empirical," in fact, suggests a modern name (not a very good name) for everything given in the ethos, the matrix of value relative to which our sense of the unconditional is defined. Is there anything prior to this ethos? Is it not prior to our being ethical? Is it prior as a neutral context, or principle, or as already the milieu of value, not exhausted in value by our being ethical? Is a transcendental or dianoetic negativity necessary towards it? Perhaps, if the ethos has been neutered, thus seeming to necessitate what above I called the *defense measure* against ethical nihilism. But if the ethos is not drained of value, this defense measure does not make the same sense. Defense against what? Do we not need rather a further unfolding of what is already there? Not protection against the nihilism of the neutered ethos, but the fuller fruition of the promise of the ethical there? Our presentiment of the

---

complicit in a kind of bad faith. Its claim to be morally pure is belied by reliance on what is "impure," and this in order to be concretely ethical. The accusation of intentional hypocrisy is not needed; but there is the seed of an hypocrisy, if the pure ground cannot be a pure ground without actually depending on the "impure" it claims to be grounding, a dependency thereby denied, or masked, if not treated contemptuously. Such an hypocrisy hides the sin of an ingratitude: the independence claimed is dependent but despises dependence, hence despises what its "independence" *needs*. Were the gratitude granted, the pretension to purity would stand revealed as laughable. Transcendental ethics would be shown up as ridiculous, not the uncompromising nobility of pure duty it claims to be.

unconditional good comes to emergence for us there; we do not produce it; we find ourselves to be under its guidance and solicitation. Its priority is not quite Kant's transcendental priority, nor indeed is its excessive transcendence the difference of the transcendental as exceeding the empirical. It is in the midst and yet beyond, immanent and transcendent. To live ethically is to live in this doubleness.

The negative attitude to the "merely empirical" could be associated with a certain *ascetical* comportment. Transcendental askesis says "no" and generates its own transcending through a process of negation that turns the flesh of the aesthetic into an ethical inessential. Transcendental dutifulness is disciplined by this askesis towards everything to do with the body and vulnerability, to do with youth and aging, to do with fructifying and mortality, everything that makes us insecure humans. Everything that makes us *appealing* humans, who dare not call themselves pure practical reason, for the unasked largesse of youthful vitality, as well as the dull ache of age, all remind us that the process of life as good, and as evil, passes beyond what transcendental reason dictates to it.

Does transcendental reason then become another anorexia of life's fullness, presenting itself as the most healthful, because the most protected from life's vagaries—vagaries that offer us life's surprise and unasked opportunity? Is it an odd *partner* in an ethical nihilism when it cooperates in the draining of this fullness *off to one side*, where its *intrinsic* connection with the good is severed? The fullness of the good for us is in and through the vagaries of the ethos. These we must risk. Askesis is a strategy to reduce the risk while increasing the control.[13] But if the controller turns into a king of emptiness, what good then is this monarch of its own "no"?

Ascetics are proud of their "self-mastery." Do these sovereigns escape self-righteousness? When the "no" of the purest turns against the impure, is not its righteousness but wrath? Think here of the beautiful soul, an aesthetic exemplification of transcendental univocity.[14] It holds itself beautiful in itself, its own priority to all otherness; being itself beautiful in innerness, it makes everything outer contaminating, to be shunned if it is to remain beautiful. Thus its own beauty is the ugliness of the other. But if beautiful souls make others ugly, then it is itself ugly, as a source of ugliness in the other it shuns. And so the beautiful soul is the ugly soul. This dialectical reversal shows the ugliness there from the start.

---

13. A story is told of Kant being asked why he smoked only one pipe a day. His reply was to the effect, if I smoked more than one, you would not know where it all would end! This story suggests a lot, not least about the instability of the stabilizing "no" and the fragility of rigid limit.

14. The "beautiful soul" was a recognizable Romantic type, influenced by Kantian transcendental philosophy, though taken in a more aesthetic direction. Hegel is very critical.

Analogously, transcendental reason can be, in fact, a kind of *violence* towards humanity, even though it extolls the dignity of humanity in each of us. It is not able to love the whole, only the purity of humanity in us. The respect for ideal humanity is haunted by hatred of the "warts and all" of concrete persons. If so, ethical reason turns out to be a form of ethical evil. Couple this with the possible emptiness of the formal, and you have a potentially destructive combination. The vacuum of the form is easily filled by the "non-rational," and in reaction to the evil of reason. Moreover, these irrationalities filling the vacuum are marked reactively by *the self-righteousness they learned from reason*. They are further forms of reactive hostility and hatred. In seeking the hyperbolic purity of the transcendental univocity, we end up with far greater evil: from a priori purity there is a boomerang back to ethos still seen in its impure baseness, and now not ascetically negated but devoured with the gluttony of unreason. Do not bleat self-righteously: I told you so! Therefore, we need transcendental univocity all the more! No, it is the transcendental univocity that has hollowed out in the ethos the space of hunger, out of which the gluttony explodes.

I will mention one final, related equivocity in transcendental reason, namely, its vacillation between being a purely logical, formal reason and being a self-activating reason.[15] The latter was historically the more influential, because more consonant with the emphasis on self-legislating autonomy and self-creating humanity. Let this autonomous self-legislating humanity proceed to fill itself though its own proud self-activity. Why then am I startled by a miserable squeak? Is that not Dostoevski's underground man listening under the floor boards? Pure reason above stairs; below, the perverse self-will of the underground man looking up through the cracks in the ground—and with what a vile sneer!

What next? Sensing the anemic condition of pure reason above, now the subterranean self below starts to rebel with vital life. It struts out. And it struts out wearing the red cloak of self-activity, the cloak given in wan color by bloodless pure reason, but now flaunted with the tilt and swagger of a more idiosyncratic liberty. In the vacillation between form and self-activation, this active self of will to power was cloaked all along in transcendental reason. Behind it all, "self-activity" is god. Once more this god of transcendental askesis or subterranean revolt shows itself as wrath. The self-righteousness of self-

---

15. This is already contained in Kant's approach to the transcendental ego in the *Critique of Pure Reason*. See my *Desire, Dialectic and Otherness* (New Haven, Conn.: Yale University Press, 1987), Chapter 2; see also "Kant and the Terror of Genius: Between Enlightenment and Romanticism," *Kant's Aesthetics*, Herman Parret, ed. (Berlin and New York: De Gruyter, 1998), 594–614.

legislating reason mutates into the self-righteousness of dictatorial irrationalism. Instead of transcendental reason dictating to the aesthetic, the aesthetic
dictates to the transcendental. We behold two profiles of the same secret face:
equivocal will to power.

Nietzsche, we might say, is the posthumously born brother of Kant. We
ascetically negate aesthetic being, but the latter snarls at the wrath of transcendental reason, with a negation reverting, and with a roar of reversed wrath. Aesthetic being, before mastered, now seizes mastery. It rises from the grave of its
repression. Before it was subjected, now it claims to be sovereign subject. And if
sovereign reason is now subjected, we are back with reason as the slave of passion, though the passion is now more vehement and more clever than ever. Why
so clever? It exonerates its self-glorification with an aesthetic philosophy of will
to power.

Think of the logic in this reversal from Kant to Dostoevski. Kant was an
ethical foundationalist who also was a philosopher of freedom. The ground of the
ethical in its transcendental univocity makes possible a freedom that is self-legislating. At first this freedom is intent to do its duty, and it is contented; but it
comes to the discontent of finding such obligation confining and disappointing.
Now freedom rebels against rational necessity; it seeks to prove itself genuinely
free in its rebellion, not in its consent to duty. Thus Dostoevski's underground
man: he grants the truth of 2 + 2 = 4, but also spits at it: the wall is there for
breaking one's head but also for proving one's freedom.

When Kant came to the wall, he made it into two walls, the first wall only
phenomenal, the second noumenal. When we butt the head of freedom against
the phenomenal wall, it breaks down or parts and leaves a space for noumenal
freedom. Coming to *the second wall*, Kant fell in love with it, for he found necessity there, and the burden of freedom is lifted. By contrast, the underground man
finds one wall of necessity, and it does not move; yet there is this other necessity,
namely, that his freedom must insist on *itself*, and so perversely be self-legislating, not in consent to the wall but in vicious spite of it. Concerning the wall,
then, are the man of duty and the underground man so far apart? Yes, they differ on whether freedom means more a consent to the wall or an assault on it. But
consent is in secret complicity with assault, if consent itself is the withered child
of a univocal askesis of the ethos.

Transcendental foundationalism builds on ground undermined by its own
askesis: the man of duty *is* the underground man who has confined the perversity
of freedom to the cellar. The ground is the underground. Pure reason, with deep
equivocity, both cellars and lets loose its own impure other. The foundation is no
foundation, for it is all will. We slip from the good will of Kant to the willfulness
of Dostoevski's underground man to the will to power of Nietzsche's *Übermensch*
or *Untermensch* (his ranking of *über* and *unter* is finally impossible to uphold).

This principled foundationalism reverses into the subterranean groundlessness of anarchic freedom or will to power: not ethics in the ethos, not principles above it, but *alles ist erlaubt!*[16]

Wholeness and Death: Eudaimonistic Equivocity

Eudaimonistic univocity claims happiness to be the one good the same in all of our seeking. Desire multiplied is gathered to desire unified under the enfolding telos of happiness. All pleasures sought, all rules obeyed, all principles followed, are oriented to happiness as the one good.[17] This unity is not static but

16. Remember Rousseau as walking beside Kant: the sentimental and rational promenading together: this is the aesthetic companion of dianoetic or transcendental univocity. Is Kant not closer than he would find comfortable to the sentimental Rousseau (whom he so revered as to allow only his portrait in his study), the irrational Dostoevski, the rhapsodic Nietzsche? The underground man sees reason and thinking as a sickness, a disease, but he suffers from *hyper self-consciousness* and envies the sound common sense and general being-at-home with life of his former friends and colleagues. He exhibits an excess of reflection into self—but unanchored from ties, ungrounded. It is reflection turned against the other, turned against self, turning into a generalized indefinite negativity that even turns away from life with disgust. The sickness of reason is its despair. (Consider Sartre's nausea.) Thinking seems like a spreading infection that disturbs the health of customary and normal life—expels one from it, paralyzing one's powers, as Hamlet found. It seems innocuous but turns into a total way of undermining the vitality of life (aesthetic rapport). In its enfeeblement of the ties of human community, the excess of reflection makes the human being an impotent whining intellectual, devoid of spontaneity and solidarity, thoroughly alienated. Consider Hume's brush with despair before resorting to the *pharmakon* of claret and backgammon. One thinks of Rousseau's critique of the corrupting effect of the arts of civilization. One sees something analogous in Nietzsche's relation to Socrates: Socrates the sickness of rational thinking, corrupting the life of the Greeks, destroying the spontaneity of rich cultural and spiritual life (like the Sophists, corrupting the youth), destroying the confidence of the instincts. This is a dianoetic destruction of the vitality of aesthetic life and eudaimonistic flourishing. Socrates is an infection, a disease, a pestilence. These metaphors are used by Nietzsche in *Birth of Tragedy* (*Birth of Tragedy and the Case of Wagner*, W. Kaufmann, trans. [New York: Random House, 1967], 18, 96–97). There is a basic question here for the practice of philosophy itself.

17. Even Kant cannot, does not, avoid this. His sense of duty is set in potential opposition to happiness in *the short run. In the long run*, running into the afterlife, these two must be reduced to a unity, and the dutiful person must enjoy the happiness that his or her virtue merits. Kant's understanding of eudaimonia is restricted by the modern subjectification of desire, and the contraction of a desiring being into a unit of effective power, seeking its own self-satisfaction, directly or by wile.

embraces the fulfillment of the whole human being over a lifetime. Our fullest flourishing shows an active process of "becoming whole," and this must address the basic ambiguities of life. It happens and is enacted in the ethos, neither floating above it nor denying what lies below. Reaching for the highest good, it can come to include the subterranean—what is chaotic, dark, destructive, but now molded to the excellence of a human life that is whole.

This view offers us some of the best resources for dealing with the equivocities posed by aesthetic, dianoetic, and transcendental univocity. It suggests a discerning mindfulness attuned to the nuances of the ethos, including its subtler particularities, the singularity of different situations and unique persons. The ancients called this mindfulness practical wisdom, or *phronesis*. First, this discerning concerns the subtleties of pleasure, the qualitative differences so important in interpreting the rhythms of fleshed being. It is an openness to the equivocity of the aesthetic and yet not a collapse into it, or a being ambushed by its more perilous powers. Second, it is crucial for the application of law, an application not a law but requiring the ability to move back and forth between the general and particular. It is singular living mindfulness, impossible to objectify completely in fixed and abstract principles. For it is an exemplary person, one deeply judicious who is the actuality of this discerning mindfulness. This mindfulness cannot be made completely determinate, even though it is necessarily determinate as embodied in this person: a concrete determinacy of selfhood that cannot itself be made univocally determinate; an ability to unify or make connections in act and process; not a fixation on abstract differences erected into rigid and unrelated terms. This ability to *move between* allows it to deal with the equivocity of dianoetic univocity as law; it supplies what law needs but cannot itself offer; it lives *the task* of the law, not as a law but with a view to the enactment of the excellence of a whole life, or the wholeness of life lived in light of highest excellence.

Third, it addresses some of the equivocities of transcendental univocity, since it resists the bifurcation of singular and general and amends the claim that there is a further a priori universal. If there is something "prior," the purified universality of transcendental reason is not the best way to describe it. The good is prior, but not quite in terms of Kant's subject-turned transcendental; it is transcendental as disclosing the being of being as itself good.[18] Moving in the between, this mindfulness stands against any dualistic opposition of the rational and nonrational; a justified resistance to certain irrationalities may be needed; but there are

---

18. This is connected to the good of the "to be." See Aquinas on transcendental good. Here too the question arises about the Good being more than a highest principle, but as a living goodness that communicates goodness to the beings in the between. God is the living Good, not just a moral principle reached by a process of intellectual abstraction or erotic seeking.

others to reason not its enemy, but other in an intimacy that gives a vitality to reason itself and obviates its proclivity to desiccated formality. Moreover, if the point is the wholeness of a life, wholeness must include within itself the often discordant strains of human being. There is a wholeness more embracing of reason and the nonrational, not defined by setting these into enmity. Each as different has its place in the life of the whole, whose integrity in process this living mindfulness discerns and tries to enact in the middle of the ethos. The aesthetic and the "nonrational" are loved, with the consent proper to ethical living that is solicitous of the good of the whole; for being whole is good; and eudaimonia comes in this being whole.

If this approach helps us with the equivocities of the other approaches, what of *its own* equivocity? If the happiness of wholeness is not possible without practical wisdom, this integration of being is inseparable from a mindfulness that cannot be completely univocalized. This discerning power must move with the nuances of life and a life, hence must be an attunement to the equivocity of the ethos. Thus the truth of discerning *phronesis* that makes eudaimonia possible is not univocal. Eudaimonistic unity cannot be made completely univocal. And there is a more painful sting. I repeat the old saw, as Aristotle repeated it: "Count none happy till he is dead." This seems a platitude. It also shows a wise awareness of time's unpredictability, which can suddenly reverse good fortune, and in the wink of an eye land us in the pit of desolation. Think of the fate of Boethius: Boethius, well founded, fortunate beyond normal measure; then the wheel turns, and he is tipped to the bottom and doomed. And there is more here than the commonsense platitude and the respect for time's otherness. There is the *ever-present* shadow that is death, over all claims to fulfilled life. The task of being whole is under the curse of death. The platitude and the respect are more domestic acknowledgments of a potentially *violent equivocity* to the search for eudaimonistic fulfillment: wholeness is haunted, not only by brokenness, but by the terror of nothing. Not that life will come down to finally unconnected fragments, but that *it all may come to nothing*. We will come to nothing, and so any pretension to wholeness must, if honest, not turn its face from this mocking end. This end is not the end of wholeness but the mockery of all wholeness. Then it seems that death is the telos of life, not fulfillment. Or death is the fulfillment beyond the fulfillment of life that robs all joy of its savor. It seems we can only sustain the illusion of wholeness if we live in a kind of half forgetfulness of what our final end in truth is. We cannot face it full on, we cannot completely forget, and we half glance, half glance away, and mostly thrive on amnesia.

Why do we seek wholeness? Because we lack wholeness. We are wanting. Why are we wanting? Because we are want itself—a neediness, an indigence, a kind of nothing. *We are as if we were nothing.* The infinite restlessness we exhibit is the reactive activation of striving in response to being as if nothing: want to be, striving to be, because deeper in it all is the knowing of our being as if it were nothing. Our striving to be whole is befriended by its enemy, and an incognito companion of all striving is death. We seek to be fully what we are because we already are, from the outset, beings who are as nothing. The energy of life springs up in the stress of this middle between being and nothing, life and death, a middle itself their inextricable inseparability. Living the equivocity between wholeness and extinction, our odyssey towards fulfillment is the funeral procession to our own byre. The most joyous song has dirge in it, dirge drowned by life's energy early on, dirge drumming out as life later ebbs. The final refrain of time: your time has come.

This emergence of the nothing is something impossible to fix in univocal terms. It has to do with the *contingency* of the ethos: the between is good as given, but as given good just good, and it might not have been at all, and there is no absolute necessity to its given good. There is no absolute foundationalism possible that would put the good of given being on an absolutely unshakable ground; for the good of the given as given is contingent, and it might not have been given thus; and while it is good, there is no necessity that it be. The possibility of its not being so is ingrained in its happening to be thus and not otherwise.

The element of fortune in human affairs, in part, corresponds to this ontological contingency. The achievement of any wholeness has an unavoidable contingent side; it cannot be necessitated; all the more so, since there is an openness in free desire. Though we are free, we cannot be complete masters of our fates; our wholeness does not lie completely in our own hands. The fullest realization of our own best powers does not lie fully in the best of our powers. In the search for wholeness, we are and must always be lacking wholeness. We find ourselves in between the telos sought and the seeking, invaded by the nothingness emerging within, invaded also from beyond the present by the immanence of death, even when death is not imminent.[19]

Eudaimonistic wholeness also has to face evil, and not just this or that evil but the enigma of the good of the whole. What does it all come to? If it comes to nothing, how to sustain the good of the whole? Is the whole then simply destined to death? If we affirm the good of the whole, must there be more than the fact that it comes to nothing, something not merely perishing? Must the good of

---

19. The ethical twilight of the ethos is not just due to the doubleness of human beings projecting onto a neutral screen of thereness. Thereness is itself a twilight/dawn double, the full ontological meaning of which is to be referred to the contingency of creation: it is, but it might not be. Hence the nothing is ingredient as a possibility in its being so; its being is its possible not being. The sense of evil is inseparable from the nothing, at a primal level. For once in being, and tasting the sweetness of being, nothing is terrifying. Nothing is insinuated in the terror felt in the dissolving of being, as its sweet hold on being is taken away from it. These ontological dimensions to the current reflection on wholeness and death must not be forgotten.

life somehow outlive the life that is good? Then the good of life is not only in life itself but is itself *beyond life*. But does it all come to nothing? The question brings us to a wall that is no wall but a breach. There yawns a cessation or an opening, we know not which. Given this intimacy with death, and the "It comes to nothing," we might say that in the heart of wholeness is *the other to wholeness*, what we cannot make whole. Is there in wholeness something that either is the death of wholeness or that outlives wholeness? Death, I suggest, raises the issue of *the beyond of wholeness*. The good of the whole seems to point beyond this whole as good, if the final word is not to be "It comes to nothing."

How one further addresses this is still a question. But one can see that belief in another world, or in a life that outlives this life, is an understandable response to this perplexity. I stress, I am not talking about craven refusals to face death, though these can be. I am talking about perplexity raised by what arises in relation to the wholeness of life, as immanent within that wholeness itself. It is the wholeness of life that raises our perplexity about the beyondness of life to immanent wholeness. Many may deny this beyondness, but this perplexity arises from discerning mindfulness of the inner complications of wholeness. It arises from subtle finesse about the equivocity of the good, not a univocal will to escape the equivocities of life into the putative transparent certainties of another life. No doubt, the latter can occur. There is, however, a way of thinking the matter more profound than standard dismissals of the perplexity.[20]

I might put it otherwise: death is the great energizer, the spur to creation in us, even if also the destroyer, the reaper not always grim in driving us to seize the day. But to seize the day in search of wholeness means we risk the destruction of wholeness and the loss of eudaimonia. Another kind of hunger, and not just for

---

20. The issue invariably is tied to the ethical. I offer two different examples. First, Plato: the myth of Er (*Republic*): the issue of the other world has to do with the good of this life, the justice of this life. Immortality is not about securing one's own neck, but about the good of life beyond life that is intimate with the wholeness of life here. Our being in the between does not exhaust the thrust of transcending, nor the character of the good sought, relative to the unconditional, and relative to the evil here that is unredeemed. Perplexity about the good drives us to think of life beyond life, just to see the good of life and live it, not escape it. Second, Kant: the other world is necessary to deal with the affront to reason, namely, that the virtuous often are subjected to suffering and unhappiness. This is a question of justice, not revenge; a question about the proper fullness of fulfillment, fullness impossible here as shadowed by death, and the mocking of "It is nothing, it comes to nothing." The shadow of nothing is not mentioned by Kant, who would like to give a univocal argument for the postulate. But this argument is a self-restrained mask covering the secret terror. The secret is not at all hidden from those who think the matter itself. We know the restraint of mask—the need for disguise, for equivocation and hiddenness, serving the interests of truth as deeper than the surface, or beyond the limit of finite life.

happiness, springs up in us, when we remember our death. Of course, death can destroy even our modicum of more ordinary contentment, and we cannot eat our daily bread in peace. But the night of death also may make us ask about good beyond the night, and also beyond this day, our day. It can take the form of asking about life as other to life now in the ethos. It may take the form of a quest to produce creative works that outlive their maker, in art, or philosophy, or politics, or elsewhere. The desire for the immortal springs up in the happiness of eudaimonia, itself breaking open the contentment of any wholeness achieved.[21] The quest for a *good beyond wholeness* seizes the human spirit.

It is as if death sends a message about an other to wholeness that breaches fulfilled life, from an unknown bourn beyond fulfillment, making us unhappy with a strange and disproportionate discontent, for which there can never be any univocal alleviation in the between. Death shows the gift of eudaimonistic wholeness and yet drives that wholeness beyond itself into an unhappiness that is strangely happier in its disorientation and homelessness. Now and then intimations come on the wind that there is a rightness to this, rightness though mostly the winds are forbidding and icy, and we are desperately frail.

One final remark. Evidently, happiness can become a mediocre contentment. We settle into happiness, sink into self-satisfaction. Look at my works and no, do not tremble, but pat me on the back! This is especially tempting in the context of a well-accepted social sedimentation of the good. Our virtues and excellences are inseparable from habit; for habit allows us to realize our powers effortlessly; and what sweetness there is then in being thus without striving. Striving has vanished into forgetfulness in habitual excellence; the striving dies in the habit, the desire falls asleep, and devoid of questing, the happy man becomes deadly dull. What is the equivocity here? There is the *necessity* of habit as the concretion and sedimentation of ethical character. The peril of this necessity is the loss of ethical alertness in the habitation, as we pass from mind concretized into mindlessness void of discernment. What is necessary for excellence, habit, is such as then to let excellence fall into mere routine, with the inevitable withering of the excellence. Thus habit safeguards excellence; it is careless of excellence: it keeps in care, it wastes its achievement. Happiness has forgotten itself just because it is happy, and we have the wretched contentment such as Nietzsche mocked with the last men. We have forgotten the shadow of death and the hunger of good beyond life, the good that breaches the fulfillment of wholeness, as if from beyond life. We exhibit the loss of transcending towards human greatness or towards God. We are the anemic souls, the neuters, rather than the great souled (Aristotle), or the over-

---

21. Instances include Aristotle on immortalizing, Plato's account of eros, or Nietzsche (I love the one who creates beyond himself and so perishes).

men (Nietzsche), or the saints (such as Francis of Assisi). Mediocre contentment is a happiness that is wretched.

The wholeness that is breached from beyond, and energized by death into a
new stirring of seeking, is superior. It is the inchoate love of the superior, love of
what is above us, even more rich and good and whole than any rich life or goodness or wholeness we have, or could achieve solely through human power. Death
shows our powerlessness at the limit, but it also brings us again to the love in
transcending and the love of transcendence. It energizes the extremities of love
of the good, or curse.

Blessedness and Suffering: Transcending Equivocity

Human surpassing cannot be confined to opposites such as particularity and
universality but shows a doubleness of both within itself. Surpassing shows our
selving to be a unity incarnating opposition. The unity is self-opposition, being
able to be itself and to stand opposed to itself. Why stand opposed to itself? In
order to be itself, by being what it is not. Being itself by not being itself, not being
itself by simply being itself—such a unity incarnating self-opposition is a *self-
transcending one*. Such a unity cannot be univocally fixed to itself, and yet it is
itself and nothing but itself. It is equivocally indeterminate in that it can be other
to what it now is, and can move itself to be and become that other. That other it
becomes is again itself, and so is not simply other. Sameness of self and otherness
to itself are confused, fuse together (*fusio con*).

This description is already dialectical, but we must look at the equivocity of
transcending, following from what we said above. Our transcending seeks the
unity of itself, through the wholeness of perfected powers, sought for and won.
The unity sought is the immanence of this wholeness, and not only at the final
end, but somehow informing the self as it surpasses itself to a better expression
of its own already effective fullness. This is impossible to pin down to this or to
that; and yet, it is not unreal. We see it, for instance, in a certain integrity and
constancy of ethical character. Some persons have a reliability, a trustworthiness,
even in the dynamic process of self-surpassing and change. Becoming does not
contradict but concretizes this admirable constancy, testament to a certain wholeness or at homeness. Such persons serve as exemplars, "good examples," in modern jargon, "role models," in the older nomenclature, "heroes."

The blessedness of some such exemplars is *more* than eudaimonia, for there
is a fortune on the side of heroes that cannot be completely defined by their own
achievement of human promise. Much is achieved, yes, much is asked, yes, but
much more is made possible, given in the gift of outstanding promise. *The
promise is gift*, the realization of the promise the outcome of what the exemplar
does; but not only what is done but also the conniving of circumstances, or the

complicity of the course of things, or the beneficence of fortune, or the election of God. There is "more" to the exemplar, but there is also "more" than the human exemplar at work in the achievement. "Being blessed" carries this doubleness: already having the extraordinary power, and being its vehicle, such that one is the power; and yet there is a pathos, in that the blessing is given.

Blessedness transcends pleasure, law, principle, and happiness, and is not necessarily in conflict with them, though it may well conflict with them. The exemplar is not driven by pleasure, but may take great risks and endure depriva-tion and hardship. Further, there may be situations where being outlaw is unavoidable: the law shapes to definite forms, but the new possibility breaks through the already given or consolidated law with a new formlessness: the exemplar is on the edge of this formlessness, hence is ambiguously, sometimes dangerously, beyond the law.

Further again, the exemplar may be beyond principle by being himself or herself a source of newness: an original to be imitated, for what comes to serve as principle first has to emerge into definition out of the more primal formlessness; the hero is more intimate with this formlessness beyond univocal definiteness. Think of Jesus as blessed, but thought mad by his family: out of this original source, lives of Christian principle come to be formulated and imitated: it is the original life that serves as the more original source of the later definite principle; it is not the principle that the life merely instantiates; not that the life is unprin-cipled, but the principle is not an impersonal directive but more primally a living being as source, the source itself as a *being good*.

Finally, blessedness often will mean not so much shunning happiness as being bereft of it. The inbreaking of a demand creates disquiet, perpetually depriving the exemplar of the ease of being at home. Especially in relation to this last, do we find the equivocity of blessedness. Being blessed is an exalting gift; one is lifted up to the superior; but the exalting is often, perhaps always, matched by suffering. It is cursed by sorrow. The gift is too much, and to be up to it, we have to undergo breakdown, to let its breakthrough or inbreaking come. No breaking in, without breaking down.

We find this with religious exemplars:[22] the self has taken determinate form and risks freezing into the form. The congealed self is a confusion of good and

---

22. When we think of great religious examplars such as Buddha or Jesus, "hero" has the wrong connotation of "self-glorification." Blessedness is not self-glorification, though it is glory. Think of our tendency to denigrate blessedness (e.g., the holy/saints suffer from psy-chological defects). This tendency is self-consciously reductive; as if willing to drag things down, not even to our level, but *below* it; homogenizing, univocalizing, with a mass suspi-cion of superiority. It is what the neuter does. With blessedness, the point is *beyond* self-affirmation and self-glorification, hence more elusive, quiet, silent, hidden than self-affir-mation, which can be either glorified or dismissed as "arrogance." Either way, there is

evil, so the form must be unformed, deformed, in order to be reformed. There must be a return to zero, and to the original indetermination prior to the determination. The mixing has to be again put in motion, but put in motion to strain off the impurity. And the straining off is a strain on what one is, a purgation that is like a dying of what one now is. The glory of self-surpassing is that in order to be more, one has to become less than one's present stability. One has to return to being as nothing, in order to come to be again differently, out of the nothing.

To become again as nothing is to be nihilated, and so to suffer and to die. One is invited into the tent of the holy, but finds oneself wandering under the shadow of death. This is more than the disappointment of aesthetic being, or the incertitude motivating the search for law or principles, and more than the lack driving the quest for happiness. One is not terrified by death. One has to become as dead. The terror is the gift that is breaking into one, experienced as the breaking down of all held stable and constant. Going blind, going into a grave or tomb, wandering in the desert—these are some of the experiences, metaphorically described, perhaps, that bespeak this unforming and reforming. In the terror of the cave, or the grave, of subterranean emptiness, one is not sure of coming into the light again. It is black night that eats into the power of life.[23]

The surge of transcending is driven to extremes that rob it of normal happiness. There is no simple happiness. There is an extremity of deprivation, or of being under strain or pressure, or of being crushed. One has to suffer to see. Serenity dawns from excess of suffering. Seeing comes from being blinded. Of course, there is suffering that simply destroys. Even this blessed suffering destroys, but there are destructions out of which something purer comes, something more consenting, something purged of itself as willful self-insistence. Out of suffering the seed of agapeic mindfulness begins to grow. For this seed grows

---

nothing arrogant about blessedness. Does holiness have nothing to do with the ethical? It is expunged from ethics in modernity, not only because of the blindness of the above reductionism but because modern ethics tends to insist on some version of "autonomy," "self-determination." But blessedness and holiness are beyond this insistence. Yet if ethics deals with *being good*, it is senseless to expunge it. The blessed are good in eminent form—the great energizers of those of us who labor on the lower slopes, dreaming of the summit.

23. One is powerless and reaching down, or being dragged down, to rock bottom, and drowning down there, it seems, and struggling for air, then quiet, and quietly one is looking at the strange creatures of the deep, floating before one in a film of otherness, and then the turning around, and the reversal that turns back towards the light, not quite knowing what demons have been fought, what friends made, and what nameless interventions have aided one along the trackless way of the dimensionless abyss, for one has been in the nowhere, the "noplace."

in nothing, in one's own being as nothing; and yet one is, and is more than nothing, and hence the new serenity is just consent to the gift of this "more."

I stress the *gift* of serenity. Serenity is not the best word if it suggests a smug
complacency. Serenity is beyond happiness. What it does, it does for its goodness,
not for happiness as something of its own, something it would own. It is a state
of dispossession, or release from the entanglements of happiness that falsely tie
one to things as though they were ultimate, and one's possession of them
absolute. The release is an absolving from idolatrous attachment. One is in love
with the mortal, and this release is full of suffering, but one is not released to hate
the mortal but to love it differently, hence the detachment is a different attachment, an agapeic release of transcending towards its otherness as good for itself
and not for me simply. Nothing is for me simply; all beings are for themselves,
and for their participation in metaxological community.

This equivocity of transcending is powerfully evident in *tragic undergoing*. A
person is brought to an extremity of loss, just in the extremity of transcending.
Being at a loss brings one to a limit, brings a breakdown of self-transcending.
There turns out to be more to transcending than the self can ever master sovereignly. This "more" lifts the broken self beyond brokenness, for there is the breakthrough of release of transcending itself as always and ever beyond. This "more"
blesses. Its blessing is the gift of the good, not as simply moral but as holy. The
breakdown of wholeness is the possible breakthrough of the gift of the holy.

Something of the suffering of blessedness can be seen in the context of Greek
religion. There tragedy was inseparable from religious cult—tragedy was a ritual
drama enacted before the god Dionysus and his priests. "Count no man happy till
he dies"—but these are the last lines of the chorus of *Oedipus Turannos*. The eudaimonic must consent to the dark power of the daimon. Oedipus the cursed, at
Colonus becomes a blessing, for the land and the people, because the utmost of
his extreme suffering has blessed him beyond mortal measure. The blessed outlive
mortality and witness from a dimension beyond the moral measure. The blessed
know something of posthumous mind. The blessed are blinded like Gloucester (in
King Lear) or Oedipus, but they see differently in their affliction.[24]

Being blessed, as gift of the holy, can be found in entirely unexpected places:
not necessarily among the sovereigns but among those on the bottom, brought
bottom by providence or fortune, those broken and possessing nothing, those
who are as nothing. Hence the deepest words: blessed are the poor, blessed are
those who mourn. What are these beatitudes? Many Christians will pay lip service. Nietzscheans will heap haughty contempt on them—sly stratagems of feeble rabble who secretly insinuate their own perversion of superiority. Less

---

24. See "Being at a Loss," in *PU*, Chapter 2. Think also of the shaman who has to go into
the great solitude to come back gifted with other vision, second sight.

extremely, they have been dismissed as mere ideals that cannot have concretion in "real life." They can be put aside in a realistic, even cynical, gesture; or accepted in qualified ways as ideals that we must keep before and above us, perhaps even strive for, but which cannot be reached; or we reinterpret them in more and more figurative ways that serve to qualify their demanding nature, perhaps even qualifying them away. I suspect there is a harder realism, and a less vacillating idealism to which they speak. A harder realism: they reveal the reality of the good, the actual realization of what it is to be good; we are not good, hence, they seem as either wishful thinking or strenuous ideals. A less vacillating idealism: they are actualized in being good. Given the disjunction between our being and being good, the ideal is an impossible demand, yet it is the narrow gate of ethical possibility through which we must pass. They are *hyperbolic* demands, but they are not demands at all, since they force nobody, for they announce the hospitality of the good. The good solicits us in the beatitudes.

This hyperbolic demand, the risking of life and death, the setting before us of what is impossible for humans, show the disjunction of blessedness with enjoyment, law, principle, and happiness. None of the latter can do justice to what is contained in the beatitudes; only by going beyond them and into what is impossible for humans can blessedness be possible. Since it can be attained, or can be offered, and since not attained by us, this means that the impossible for us is not impossible, if we are aided by a higher power. Blessedness points beyond to transcendence itself, but not beyond in a manner that takes flight from inhabiting the between, but that lives a new ethical possibility there, transformed by the touch of the superior. Enjoyment is not enough, nor happiness, nor law, nor principle. The beatitudes point not to a command but to a solicitation that, consented to, may be releasing of human being. There is a release of self-transcending toward transcendence itself, because something of the possibilizing power of transcendence itself has been released to human self-transcendence, making possible what is impossible in human terms alone.

This is not a readily acceptable view, or even a comprehensible one, given the various currents of hedonism, utilitarianism, Kantian morality, ethics of autonomy, and so on that dominate the contemporary landscape. It demands a sacrifice of any claim to their being absolute. It relativizes in an extreme sense, in showing the powerlessness of the human to effect what it most needs to be itself, to be itself as fulfilled. Our modern and postmodern being is allergic to the risk of this sacrifice. It is too much to hazard, given the struggle of modernity to wrest something of autonomy from seemingly inhospitable circumstances. And there are postmoderns who would rather give their freedom over to something less than freedom and transcendence than to something above it or superior, a good more than our autonomy.

Blessedness is in another dimension, not fully reached by our transcending alone. The seizure of extreme transcending seems like an epilepsy of spirit (why do I think of Dostoevski?), and nothing is ever quite the same again. Of course, it does not have to come in this dramatic way. It may be working all along, like the waves of the ocean on a rock making slow inroads, and lo, after many tides and turns, a sparkling presence shines forth from the formless thereness. The extremity of self-transcending is ruptured by transcendence as other, and all sense of the good as determined in a common measure with our common measure of the good is washed away. The measureless good of transcendence itself, as other to human self-transcendence, kills the virus of conceited closure. The killing is the healing of the holy.[25]

God and the Dark Face of Evil: Transcendent Equivocity

The solicitation to transcendence itself in the equivocity of human transcending does not end equivocity but *intensifies it to a new extreme*. We are called to ultimate good, and yet as we labor up this steep incline, a monstrous weight seems perched on our shoulders. Drawn upwards by the good, we are dragged by a crushing heaviness, drawing us down into our greatest suffering. (To see God we must die.) There are breakdowns in life, there are the breakthroughs, there is the ultimate breakdown/breakthrough of death. Is this the moment of truth? Perhaps it is not the moment of complete truth, for we may have to be further purged. Purgatory is a name for this continuing need. Purgatory: ascent to good by descent into the mud of what is most mixed in oneself, the promiscuous confusion of good and evil in the idiocy of being. Every doing of the good is a dying of evil possibility, and in that, ascendency over death. But all of our victories are

---

25. Kant claimed that the supreme good (*summum bonum*) was not the same as happiness. He was right, if we connect the breakdown of happiness with the seizure of blessedness and the rupture of our contentment—the unconditional good is beyond all our measures, and the measureless measure is communicated to us. But Kant understood the "killing" of eudaimonia in moralistic terms, and not adequately in terms of the holy. And even though he speaks of the holy will, this too risks a moralizing. He did not understand the point I am trying to make; there is no moralization of the holy; the good of the holy is beyond our moralized good, and this is revealed in blessedness, beyond both eudaimonia and transcendental reason. Kant's collapse of the good of the holy into the moralized good is connected to his own equivocal attitude to transcendence as other (autonomy is highest, and he is unable to think of a freedom beyond autonomy). Religiously put, he has a disingenuous attitude to "grace." There is an extraordinary footnote in the *Critique of Practical Reason*, edited and trans. Lewis White Beck (Englewood Cliffs, NJ: Macmillan, 1993), 134, in which autonomy is blown open, I think. It is possible to retain a sense of the unconditional good that is to be admired about Kant, but to think it in terms quite different to Kant's moralization.

relative, as the weight of evil crushes with a relativity that devours us in the "It comes to nothing." None is good save God. If there is one alone good, and God alone is good, the face of this one is manifold; some of its faces may seem so other to us, so to exceed the measure of our good, that we wonder about their indifference, or cruelty, even evil; absolute good seems to present a face towards which we look and cannot look, disturbed by evil, beyond which we find it hard to move. We are not only shadowed by death, but by the darker shadow of evil that wills the triumph of death, in refusal of the agape of being.

Suppose we grant as imponderable any life to come, for that is a possibility shrouded in ambiguity. Yet if we must die, we must now die differently, and this different death means putting off the closure of transcending, or asking to be released from its closure on oneself, asking for the release that is transcending and not just for oneself or a detour back to oneself, as if the good were oneself, or for oneself alone. The asking for release, the willingness to die, is cognizant that our being turned around and back on ourselves like that is really death itself; it is being closed out from the feast of life, from the agape of the good. We must always die, always say "no" to the "no" that turns transcending back into a closed whole. This is a simulacrum of wholeness, in flight to itself only to find itself but as power to negate the other, negating power that will come to its own hollowness, destroying itself in the despair already consuming it. So we need rebirth to a new dwelling with the good, baptism into an openness to gift beyond human mastery. The good has been with one, unheeded, refused, abused, disdained. To die is to wake up to this: the elemental good of the "to be," always a gift. There is an ethics of gratitude: a living out of the heed of deepest gratitude for the good of being. Gratitude to whom? The blue of the sky, the master of the ocean deeps, the voice of quiet and silence, thanks to God.

The crushing weight of evil is carried, and we cannot carry it. Who carries it, if not God? The way of equivocity brings us to the question; but if we are the question, indeed questions to ourselves, we are not the answer. We cannot completely answer extreme evil; the answer is other to us. The answer is the goodness of the good, a power of living good that exceeds us. If God does not somehow bear evil, the whole thing comes to nothing. Do we perish at the thought? (Why do you squirm?) If only God can redeem evil, then God too must die. The good must embrace its own most extreme opposite and recreate its perverted power. This is the kenotic power of the good: as passing over, and passing away, it is a passing into finitude. God is passage of that good. If the good is passing, we grant the passing after it has passed (for we are granted by the passing). We always miss it, and in missing it we find it, since we come to realize that we have missed it passing. (The kenotic power of good means that agapeic transcending also must bear the most intensive equivocity of evil.) Death brings us to the passing of the good and the knowing of the good as passing always beyond us, and the chance of consent to its otherness in that passage. The pathos of the ultimate good is in this undergoing.

CHAPTER FOUR

ETHOS AND DIALECTICAL ETHICS

Why Dialectic?

Why turn now to a dialectical approach, since this is currently one of the most contested, even reviled, ways? On the one hand, various ethics of difference frequently define themselves over against dialectic as being too reductive of equivocity. On the other hand, approaches seeking univocal clarity often view dialectic as itself infected with too much equivocity. By contrast, I think we must both regather the energies of dialectic while reconnoitering its limits and extremities (a theme recurrent in many of my other works). Why? It helps us see what has been gained with equivocity in interplay with univocity. Moreover, it aids comprehension of what is at play in the ethos, particularly with respect to the importance of *self-becoming*. I might put the matter in terms of the determinate, the indefinite, the self-determining, and the overdeterminate good. First, the univocal way highlights the variety of guises in which the overdetermination of the ethos is subjected to *determination*. Second, the equivocal way opens up significant *indefiniteness* by attuning us to differences. Third, and this is now the issue, the dialectical way mediates, in some measure, the interplay of difference and sameness. Passing into the determinate, and thence into significant indefiniteness, the dialectical way approaches the overdetermined ethos in terms of *self-determination*. If to be is to be good, here to be good is to be self-determining. We are pointed towards an ethics of autonomy, but also beyond. At the extremity of the dialectical approach—and to this we will come—the metaxological way articulates ethical intermediation with the other beyond self-mediation, and in terms of the *overdetermined* good in its surplus to self-determination.

Generally, philosophers detect in the equivocal a failure to attain their desired telos, namely, univocal transparency. But while the latter is sometimes appropriate, it is not always, particularly in ethical matters. Ethics solicits an art of dealing with ambiguity, not a geometry generating deductive certainty. It requires the *esprit de finesse*, not the *esprit de géométrie*. This is especially needed with the human being, the equivocal animal par excellence: an animal not quite an animal; an animal more animalistic than any animal; a monster a little less

117

than a god; a summation of all other beings, and yet nothing in particular; continuity, contradiction, and unique creation, all knitted together tensely. The technician of univocity has little patience for this. The artist of equivocity is attuned to discern the fitting: the promise of the tension—and the danger.

When we see more deeply into the ethos, we see it is fitting that we move beyond simplistic certainties and see the shadow darkening all simplemindedness. It is fitting that we grow in perplexity about the good. It is fitting that we are perplexed about what is fitting. It is fitting to know that our "yes" cannot escape its "no." It is fitting that mindfulness be matured, even tortured by the mingling of "yes" and "no." It is fitting to be turned towards oneself in perplexity, bewildered by the ethos, perplexed by perplexity itself, for one has become a question answerable for itself. It is fitting to be shocked by the enigmatic reserves of violent darkness, the idiocy of the monstrous in the intimacy of the singular. It is as fitting to be drowned again in the overdetermined, as to learn to swim once more in the element of the good. It is fitting to see the fittingness of the unfitting.

And dialectic? Dialectic, I now suggest, is a way of attunement that mediates the process of selving in the labyrinth of the equivocal. It searches the play of affirmation and negation, self and other, striving to emerge above ground, out of the war of self with itself, of self with other. It is more than dianoetic or transcendental univocities that seek to cut themselves off from the war underground, under our nose, so to say. It is in the war, and it wants to rise above it by waging the war itself, and for the peace that may be immanent in it. Hegel profoundly called this peace: the rose in the cross of the present.

In the first part of this chapter, I will connect the dialectical way with themes significant so far, especially the ambiguous doubleness in the ethical potencies, the challenge of opposition to ethical self-becoming, and the hospitality of the ethos to inherent good, beyond subjectivism and objectivism. In the second part, I will explore the unstable ambiguity of the modern dialectic of self-determination. The equivocal relation to the other is pursued through a discussion of Kantian, Hegelian, Marxist, and Nietzschean approaches. This last brings us closer to our postmodern perplexities, but these are gestating in the equivocities of the former approaches. These views I situate relative to the interplay of the univocal and equivocal, their diverse contributions to an ethos of self-determination, and its denouement in Nietzsche's unmasked and unapologetic will to power. This outcome points us further, asking that we rethink the ethical relation to the other in metaxological terms.

Dialectic and Ethical Doubling

There is a dialectic answering to an *ambiguous doubling process* in each of the potencies of the ethical. I will first briefly make more overt the embryonic work of that dialectic, for it helps us take stock of how far we have come, bringing us again to ethical perplexity about human wholeness and its beyond.

What is the aesthetic dialectic? We saw the spontaneity of the happening of aesthetic value, in ourselves as fleshed. This is robustly determinate, yet also haunted with indefiniteness: the multiplying of definite satisfactions is indefinite, drawing forth its own disappointment. The dialectic here is the *dia-legein*, the speaking (*legein*) double (*dia*). We might say: desire is a double-speak: no determination without indetermination, no indetermination without determination. Indefinite desiring rises to definite desires, which give rise to new indefiniteness, and so on. Indeterminate longing or lack becomes specific seekings which do satisfy and yet never satisfy finally: episodes on the way, not ends of the way. But if we always find doubleness, this is more than equivocal, for there is a *rhythm of unfolding in the indefiniteness itself*. The interplay of the two, their final inseparability, is revealed by the dialectic of the two, as *the unity of the seemingly opposed*: satisfaction is dissatisfaction, dissatisfaction is satisfaction. Dialectic, attuned to the doubleness, acknowledges the tug of the two and their creative tension; that is, the *process* back and forth involves the unfolding of self-determination. The immediacy of the aesthetic also is self-mediation.

What is the dianoetic dialectic? Dianoetic law is a way to mediate the immediacy of the aesthetic; law gives a determinate form to the indeterminacies of the aesthetic. But as above the aesthetic, or beyond it, law is *non-showing*. As non-showing, and for all of its determinacy, it is also *indeterminate*: the law that makes determinate is supposedly determinate but, as not manifest, it also is seemingly indeterminate. So there is a doubleness in the law itself as both determinate and indeterminate. The doubleness is not only between law and the aesthetic; rather, law points to a unity of indeterminacy and determination, in law itself, and between law and its specific application. What is the dialectic? Simply coming to know that this is the truth of the law. The *task* of law as being applicable or applied shows implicitly this dialectic. Hence, dialectic demands attunement to the doubleness within the law and between the law and the aesthetic. It brings out these different sides as contributory to *a more inclusive process* marked by an internally complex development. Dialectic claims to hold true to the dynamism of the unfolding of the dianoetic universal, so that law and particular situations are phases in a more unitary process of ethical becoming.

What is the transcendental dialectic? It represents the continued search for the mediating universal, not just as a general law but as what is brought to the given situation. This is not necessarily a rigid or an abstract a priori. The transcendental approach, such as Kant's, vacillates between a formal condition of possibility and an active source of being, the synthesizing self. The formal condition is too tied to dianoetic generality, without proper vision of the source of law. At best, this approach can point to this source, not only as law, but as *law giving*, and as such a living reason, that is, a *self*, not just an abstract principle. We might say:

The being of pure practical reason is a transcendental *self as a mediating univer-sal*. What about the *negative* definition of the transcendental as *not* empirical? This does not seem adequate to the self as transcendentally *active*, for as such it seems to generate the law from itself; it seems an autonomous source of law—law giving, self-lawing, self-legislating. And yet the negative definition of the tran-scendental is implicitly dialectical in that what is negated in the definition is tied inseparably to what is defined, and vice versa. There is a hidden *co-implication* of empirical and transcendental, of determinate shape and indeterminate determin-ing source. To make the transcendental ego determinate is to connect it dialecti-cally with the empirical ego, and *this we must do in order to be and act ethically*. Both are the same, yet different: sameness and otherness must be connected, for each without the other makes no complete sense. To recognize this is the insight of dialectical thinking. Such thinking also helps more fully to articulate the char-acter of that necessary togetherness of the opposites. Dialectic is the mindful self-knowing of this togetherness, already at work in the aesthetic, dianoetic, and transcendental. This self-knowing mediates their limits, while acknowledging their necessity and comprehending their inseparability.

What is the eudaimonistic dialectic? This concerns the concrete embodiment of the above living doubleness. Aristotle presents us with a kind of concrete dialectical vision of *phronesis* in which the disparate strains of human beings and their situation are held together. There is a strong univocal tendency in Aristo-tle, but in ethics he shows attunement to the equivocal, hence also the *esprit de finesse*. Aristotle loves to say: *on the one hand* this, *on the other hand*, that. In some cases, the right hand contradicts the left hand, and it is hard to see them joining hands. In other cases, it is *absolutely essential* to say *both/and*, just in order to do justice to the many-sided nature of an issue or a situation. Also living, ethical selving, set apart by the transcendental way, is here placed in the ethos as a com-munal togetherness of human beings. The living human being of *phronesis* is cru-cial, not any abstract principle of self-mediation. Ethics entails a process of selv-ing in community and a process of communication between selves. Ethical self-mediation occurs within the intermediation of the ethos.[1]

What is the transcending dialectic? The answer turns on the fact that there is always a dynamism of becoming in the ethos. Beings participate in a self-sur-passing towards their own realization. This is a paradoxical movement: it is not just from A to B, from a starting point to a conclusion; especially in human becoming, there is no simple motion from A to B; rather, there is a motion that

---

1. I return to this below, relating it to Hegel's notion of *Sittlichkeit*. Ethical Hegelianism evidences a kind of dialectically concrete Aristotelianism. His word "spirit" adds some-thing new and rich, relative to the ontological grounding and the infinite value of the human self. This is mediated through the Jewish–Christian heritage.

returns on itself, as it *advances beyond itself.* We find a beginning that already has an end within it, even while, as a beginning, it sets out in search of an end. The end is with it from the beginning, and the becoming from beginning to end is both progressive and regressive at one and the same time. It is both exiting from itself and returning to itself. This complex conjunction of self-transcending and self-relating shows a self-realizing that is already self-realized; a beginning that is an end in itself, yet in search of an end beyond itself; a becoming that does not fully realize itself, yet is just itself in its fuller and fuller self-realizing. All human becoming as transcending has this double character, a character that is not any dualism of opposites but one that defines different phases of a process that integrates into itself the manifold of possibilities in strain with each other. We need dialectical thinking to make sense of this process of transcending.

Transcending is not simply something extraordinary. There is the "ordinary" transcending we live all the time; the everyday world is informed by countless acts of transcending, so common as to pass into not being noticed. The happening of transcending is indeed extraordinary, but the extraordinary has its more ordinary concretion and its transcendent incarnation. If for one we need Aristotelian common sense and *phronesis,* for the other we need a touch of Platonic madness. We need dialectic to find our way in *doxa*; we also need a dialectic to ascend above dialectic—towards the good. This latter dialectical ascent from lower to higher runs the limits of dialectic, for the absolute goal is not itself brought into being by our process of dialectical transcending.[2] This transcending towards transcendence as other to us is more metaxological than dialectical in Hegel's sense.[3]

Again, we have the play of determinacy and indeterminacy in self-surpassing. Dialectic emphasizes their togetherness, but primarily in the way an indefinite is turned into a determination, in a process that is on the way to being self-determining. This primacy of self-determining does not sit well with any *other* to self-determining being, or with transcendence as other to our self-transcending. The good in the end, as in the beginning, is not just our good, nor are we the good.

What is the transcendent dialectic? The transcendence of good must be in some way *immanent,* if it is to exert the call of the unconditional. A completely non-showing God would be analogous to a non-showing law—void for us. For

---

2. Aristotle shows some hesitation here as far as his sense of the ethical is tied to the more domesticated concretion of transcending. Even though his recognition of the contemplative life as the highest takes us beyond this, this "beyond" is more like the life of a god than of a human.

3. Hegelian dialectic has difficulties with any form of transcendence that is other to the dialectic of transcending. See my "Gothic Hegel," in *The Owl of Minerva* 30: 2 (1999): 237–252.

the unconditional to call on us, there must be showing in the between. The good, hence, must be *shown and not shown*. The transcendent dialectic claims a *self-showing* in the play of showing and not-showing. The issue is more complicated, however, since we can so stress self-show that we deny hiddenness. Or we can harness dialectic to convert all hiddenness into self-showing. This is what Hegel does, and with equivocal results relative to the realized eschatology of the good: the good is made immanent in history, in a manner that not only is contradicted by the idiocy of the monstrous, but by the transcendent hiddenness of the divine (see *BHD*, Chapters 1 and 4). I think we need to preserve the doubleness in the play of mystery and self-show. This means affirming the play of indeterminacy and determination and self-determination, so that the oversurplus of the indeterminate is not just converted into an indefinite to be conquered progressively by an increasingly inclusive process of dialectical self-mediation. This last point (a metaphysical as well as an ethical point) can only be handled by metaxology.

The Extremity of Opposition and the Ethical Exigence

In transcending towards transcendence, the suffering of darkness can be intensified to an extreme. Just as suffering and being blessed seem inseparable, approaching God's goodness seems less like dwelling in Eden than crossing a minefield strewn shockingly with evil. Dialectic possesses ethical import, for it brings us to face opposition, even alienation, driven to an extremity. Dialectic might be said to be an attunement to the equivocity of evil, in which something beyond evil is detected in evil. If we must forthrightly acknowledge alienation, we also must look for a goodness in the midst of what seems most opposed to goodness. This requires a more complex understanding of the ethos, a vigilance for any good immanently emerging in opposition itself, and a reconsideration of our quest for wholeness. Can the negative be overcome through the negative? Is the alien so alien as to make it impossible to enter into relation with the good? Is there a "being with" estrangement that immanently converts into a new "being at home" with the strange? What about the ethical dimension, since dialectic often is connected to logic, argument, and propositions? I suggest that in contrast to any complete logicization, the connection of desire and dialectic is crucial, and desire as leading to both free self-determination and ethical intermediation in community.[4]

---

4. Many significant points with dialectical import will be discussed in Part III in relation to desire, work, will, and so on. The ethical side of dialectic may have been neglected in the past, but it was always basic. This speaks against those who divorce ethics and first philosophy, but Levinas overstates his criticism of the tradition.

Suppose we say that either a way of being determines a way of thinking, or a way of thinking determines a way of being. In both cases, there will be a mutual mediation between being and thinking, which will express itself in a way of mindful being, or a way of being mindful. Suppose such latter ways are themselves grounds on which logic and argument and propositions are founded. The ontological significance is logical, but it is ethical as articulating what is valuable and worthless: it concerns sources of differentiation that discriminate between worthy and unworthy, true and false, and so on. It follows that dialectic need not be identical with a special method, such as Socratic dialectic or Hegelian. These methods are themselves grounded in a more fundamental movement of mindfulness and what this shows of human beings and our relation to being.[5]

More basically, dialectic concerns a certain process of articulation or development. This process is more clearly evident with human development, and so some have claimed dialectic to apply to human affairs, but not nature. I think the process cannot be univocally restricted to the human, not least because the process of becoming human is itself situated in the ethos, and the ethos is not just human. Yet there are dialectical features to the ethos that are relevant to human development, namely, its character as a process of becoming within which human self-becoming is defined or defines itself. It is not just we who generate the equivocity of the ethos. The ethos is itself equivocal. We see this in the universal impermanence. All things in the between become; become what they are not now, in becoming themselves, hence become what they are, in becoming what they are not. All things in the between are double, each a yesno, a lightdark, a fullempty. In relation to other things, they are in tension with them, and so they are selving, selfish, selfless. This is the twilight or the dawn of the ethos: the mixing of opposites, neither one nor the other, but both one and the other. I call it the chiaroscuro of the good.

In that chiaroscuro, contrariety and self-opposition are written into becoming, which at the same time is the opposite of contrariety and self-opposition, since becoming is also the fuller flowering of the being, the transcending of self-opposition in concord with the fuller self, towards some peace of consummated life that lifts contrariety beyond contrariety. With man this equivocity becomes explicit, becomes mindful of itself. All of the trouble starts then: not only the break with the determinism of the univocal, not only the freeing of human energies into their own indefiniteness, not only the mindfulness of that freeing, but the shaping of that freeing in accordance with mindfulness and with a lack of it.

---

5. See, for example, M. Westphal's *Hegel, Freedom and Modernity* (Albany: State University of New York Press, 1992), Chapter 1, where he proceeds from Hegel's philosophy of right to logic, not the other way around: the meaning of love and friendship go to determine the meaning of Hegel's *Begriff.*

And we *suffer* as well as *inaugurate* opposition in the ethos: opposition between us and nature, and within our nature, opposition with other humans, and between humans and the divine. The equivocity of good and evil extends to war between them, and we are in the middle. Rather, *we are a middle in which the opposites war*. We cannot stand above this fray, for standing above the fray we find *we are the fray* again. There is no escape, only different mitigations of its violence. While the point holds generally relative to the internal opposition of beings in process of becoming themselves, the opposition is most poignant, intense, and stressed with us. We live opposition, we are opposition.

How so? We seek the good, but find we do not know it, or worse, we know not ourselves, and our seeking is a flight from it. Or: We exist by relation to others, but lo, the other secretes in us dissembled revulsion or anxiety or will to dominate, and then our relation to the other has less to do with the other than with monstrous conceit. Contrariwise: We give ourselves to violence but hear behind our back a call welcoming us back to a more primordial peace. Or again: We will be lords, and turn out, not slaves, but beneficiaries of a good working incognito while we were rampant. Start with evil, we come to the good; start with the good, we come upon evil. Will the evil, we contribute to good; live for the good, we loose horrible consequences. We recognize in ourselves the knotted twining of the two.

Classically, dialectic claims to move into and beyond opposition. The opposition is not denied but redefined and transformed. How transformed? The energy of opposition shows the dynamism of a more affirmative becoming, and indeed it is directed to that becoming. In a previous image, twilight must become night before the light of day dawns. We pass from twilight into night to pass beyond them. What rises in the morning? Perhaps not the bewildered pilgrim, mourning the withdrawn good. Perhaps a sober sojourner, seasoned by adversity to the chiaroscuro of the good. But of course there are different seasonings. Kierkegaard offers a sojourner's dialectic not at home on earth but homesick for eternity. Plato is a dialectician who, in all maturity, was still a sojourner, and so not fully at home in immanence. Hegel was no sojourner, he was not going anywhere other, nor wanted to, though he had to work hard to convince himself of the consolations of immanence. Some dialecticians seek to turn the cave into home, some to surpass the cave and not towards another cave, even if it is rebaptized with an imposing name such as "world history."

Dialectic is a dwelling with doubleness.[6] How dwell? Willing to find in the double the lineaments of a more primordial togetherness. Take Socratic dialectic: there is an occasion of difference, perhaps violent opposition, such as between

---

6. See my "Thinking on the Double: The Equivocities of Dialectic," in *The Owl of Minerva* 25: 2 (Spring 1994): 221–234.

Socrates and Thrasymachus. The difference takes the forms of a *polemos* of *logoi*, a war of words. It is also a *polemos* of persons, and the *psyche* of each: different people incarnate different wisdoms or stupidities or corruptions. The dialectical claim is this: the difference has its *inherent exigence* for resolution. Disagreement is the occasion for the search for some agreement, even though "agreement" is sometimes effected by invalid argument or ad hominem abuse, or the subtle terrorizing of the other by sarcasm or irony. Even untrue resolutions can mimic the character of resolution in a deformed way, and thus the deformation pays its compliment to the immanent exigence of the initial opposition itself.

The antagonism of views and persons has its immanent dynamic that can turn itself, or be turned towards, an agreement not marked so extremely by antagonism. The agreement is not *univocally necessitated*, since the exigence is fragile and the telos difficult to fulfill. Even so, both exigence and telos are still evident in the distortions that constitute the failure to live up to agreement. (To force another to agree is to pay a complement to agreement, in its very absence or perversion.) Since it is persons who are tested, it is not only their propositions but their character, their integrity that is put under stress. The "wholeness" implied is not only the more inclusive coherence of different viewpoints and significant propositions, but the integral wholeness of persons, and their being bound together in a community that embraces the promise of discordance. The doubleness of discord is the showing of a more inherent exigence for the togetherness of more inclusive community. The discord of the ethos mediates its own overcoming. This involves a self-overcoming, since it is not extraneously imposed. The good is an integral one. Does this sound like a univocity? In a way, yes. But the one is now complexly mediated by a mindfulness of the equivocal, and an appreciation that discord can play its part in bringing about a more inclusive harmony. It is the discord of the ethos with itself that is being righted by that discord and ethos itself.

It might seem evident that we humans proceed to our good by a process that, at least in some measure, is self-correcting; but what of nonhuman dimensions of the ethos? I think the answer must include that there is an enigmatic rightness to the ethos, evident in the way things do come right, even despite the massive wrongness making ugly the beauty that is given. Things do come right. They come: this is nothing static, but they come as becoming. Right—not in denial of the wrong, but in and through the wrong. Things come right. But of course, a howl of derision will ascend to mock the empty thrones of heaven at this audacious, not to say distasteful, escapism. Look at the horror! Is it not what Beckett called "the mess"? Trust in a rightness—betrayal of the equivocal? More must be said.

Integrity appears with univocity: we are to be integral beings. We fall into the twilight of the equivocal. Losing ourselves for a while, some lose sight of the good, some lose and find themselves or are found, and some remain lost in the twilight or worse. But the exigence for integral good does not die. It may sleep, or atrophy, or grow weary, or come to hate itself, but it lives on in lostness. Dialectic finds life in this lostness, let us come as close as we can to staring death in the face. In this regard, it is figured by some of the undergoings we found in the suffering of blessedness, and the breakdown before breakthrough. It holds true to the integrity. This is right.

There is more. We can hold in check the promise of otherness as we hold on to the integral, and thus resist a different release beyond integrity. "Being integral" concerns transcendence towards some immanent wholeness, itself marked by a dynamic energy of self-articulation. But while such wholeness is essential, it is not enough, not "the whole." In the chiaroscuro, we are both in and beyond twilight, since in knowing our bewilderment, we show something more, not to be named as bewilderment. Wandering in the chiaroscuro of life, there is a light in the wandering; but while we are the wandering, we are not the light.

Coming to Self and the Immanent Standard

Can we state an affirmative outcome? Consider this: there is the recurrent promise of *a coming to self*, even though the ethos bewilders us with multiple possibilities, even though we ourselves are distended by multiplied desire. We can come round to ourselves. We come to selve in such a wise that we come to some resolve about self. What is one's resolve? It is one's will to deal with the equivocal this way, and not that way; one's will to be this kind of self dealing with the ethos, this way or not that.

This coming to self is happening *all of the time*, even if only as the promise of a less aimless life. To have a will is to have an aim, and some sense of the powers needed to pass from present desire to a completion of anticipation that allows one to say: I will do it, I do it, I have done it. Will mediates between desire and doing in this more decisive sense. Of course, we are always doing things, but there are degrees of decisiveness in the doing. A child may do things, but its will as self-directed desire may be relatively pliable. An older person properly does things, in that the directed becoming and energy of the self is concentrated into the will or willing itself. The will as immature is incompletely desired desire, and as desire open to diversion, distraction. It is not an owned will, owned desire. Such desire owes as much to pressure from irrelevance outside as to its own inner exigence. As the self comes round to itself, desire comes to itself as capable of directed self-becoming. Then it properly becomes will, or an agent of its own deeds. The I that comes around to itself also comes into its own *ownness*, and so it can take responsibility: it can stand up for its own doings and desires; it can own itself, own its own deeds. It can own up to deeds that are unworthy. Responsibility demands this owning of self that can own up when called to account, whether internally or externally.

A long development is needed before we can say that a human has a will in the above explicit sense (see Chapters 6 and 7). No doubt, will is there in the primitive self-insistence. Often what seems more mature is only the primitive self-insistence become more concealed and sly. Not always: there may come an owning of self that is less a matter of self-insistence than the recognition that there is no escape from self. One always will come round to self, hence one is answerable, for oneself before oneself, for oneself and others before a more ultimate bar. Why is decisiveness crucial here? Because decisiveness shows our ability to *live with* the equivocity of the ethos. If all were univocally determined, there would be no place for decisiveness; for no decisions would be necessary; a consequence would be determined by antecedents, and between them would be no play of openness between indeterminacy and determination. But since the ethos is equivocal, we face multiple possibilities, and which way we go depends on the choice of which we will. We are answerable for turning the equivocity of the ethos into this or that determinate formation. This turning is not its univocalization, though there may be decisions that would do that. It is participation in the promise of what is given in ambiguity.

The turning is *more* than a determination, since it involves a *self-determination*. One determines the ethos thus because one is determined to define it thus; but to be thus determined is to show oneself as determined by oneself, by one's own will. Coming round to self is happening all of the time, but the seizing of this coming round and becoming answerable for it decisively happens with will, properly speaking. Will is due to a self-determination that consents to *its own freedom as an inherent necessity*. It knows even that its own escaping from itself is the expression of the freedom that is this necessity. The coming round to self is *being resolved to be what one is*. This might seem a mere acquiescence, but this is not so, for the acquiescence knows that its consent is to a *task of self-becoming*, not to any static univocal fact. The task is inescapable, even when we divert ourselves into escape—for even the diversions fulfill the necessity evaded, for they determine us to be distracted selves. The task is not to be distracted, for distraction is freedom trying to free itself from its own inherent exigence. When the dialectic of desire becomes will, it leads to this mediated intertwining of freedom and necessity. It articulates the promise of freedom as a necessity of one's being, that is working always immanently as an initially unchosen exigence.

The coming round to self suggests the effectiveness of an *immanent standard* in all of our seeking of the good. This has decisive consequences for the aesthetic, dianoetic, transcendental, eudaimonistic, transcending, and transcendent potencies of the ethical and their defining of the good. (I return to this below.) If we are under the influence of univocity, we will want to fix the standard independently of the human being. If we are entirely under the sway of equivocity, we will dissolve such standards and find ourselves drifting or driven before the winds of relativities merely subjective. Dialectic finds a way beyond this dualism of literalism ("objectivism") and relativism ("subjectivism"). Or rather, there is some foundation, and there is some relativity; but the foundation must make reference to self; and the relativity is not necessarily an entanglement in subjective fantasy or projection, but the inseparability of self from its participation in a web of relations that shapes the good for it. There is no foundation we fix in abstraction from the dynamic energy of being as becoming; there is no relativity that does not find itself under obligations both to self and to others. The grounding is not static; the involvement in relations does not obviate the call of ethical responsibility.

Quite the opposite—to become discerning about the equivocal is to *move with it*, in some attunement to its bewitching power within us and without. This is not to be its prisoner but to see into and through it. And this is no escape from becoming to lifeless stasis; it is discernment of the living good that comes to show itself while remaining constant in itself, even as it comes out of itself into relation with the other. Selving can serve to show a form of being that can be both within itself and outside of itself, constant in its own integrity yet essentially involved with what is other, as it shows itself in such relations. Coming to concretion in such relations, its constancy over time need not be undermined by this. We manifest the immanence of the good, for we find ourselves as more than the passive receptors of an extraneous good superimposed from outside. From the origin, the call of an immanent standard sounds.

You object: we are born empty and as nothing; all we are within is just what has been stamped on us, what we have been conditioned to be; within self, we are nothing; take away those sources other to us and there is nothing left. I grant that we are shaped by the others to whom we relate. I add that these others coexist and are interiorized; they seep into us, we bring them into ourselves; their voices speak in us, as the father or mother comes to shape from within the child's soul, and not just by external diktat. But I deny that we are a merely empty nothing, if the web of relations is withdrawn (as if this were possible). We become what we are in debt to the other, but what we are to become is not so indigent as to be nothing for itself. Not at all: we are already concretions of the power of being as affirmative. This cannot be or be developed outside of relation and relativity. So much, so good. What is developed is what we are, both in present realized form and the promise of a more full realization. There is a richness to what we are as given to be, but we bring to relativity the promise of this richness. (This is not to deny a more significant sense of our nothingness.)

It is entirely abstract to separate self-relation from other-relation; nowhere are the two separated. In that doubleness, there is the call of an enigmatic standard. We must not immediately think that this call is simply the call of ourselves.[7] It

---

7. Heidegger seems to think this about "the call of conscience." One wonders to what extent it is an existentialized, "fundamental ontologized" variation on self-relation that wills to be resolved into its own auto-nomos: authentic *Dasein* calls *itself*; the inauthentic "they" (*Das Man*) seem to be under the sway of a "heteronomy" that "externally determines" them.

may well be that and *more*, depending on how we understand self. When we come round to self, it is not immediately clear what we come round to, and what is self, and whether truly coming round to self is to be catapulted beyond self within self to what is radically other to self. There may be an immanent standard in us, but we may not be that immanent standard, but participants in a good of which we are the beneficiaries along with all ethical beings, indeed all being. The light of the good may not be our light, though its shine be apparent in our intimate innermost.

Dialectic Beyond Objectivism and Subjectivism

The dialectical turn to immanence tells importantly against an "objectivizing" rendering of the good. This latter seems doomed to end up in antinomies that it cannot escape. For is it not the strangely *intimate* character of our relation to the good that is of the essence? We are called to live the best life possible. This may be our most important question: How am I to be? How am I to live? The question cannot be answered only objectively. "Nonobjective" need not imply any invidious subjectivism either. This is one of the powers of dialectic: to help us think beyond an oscillation between subjectivism and objectivism. Becoming sophisticated about the *aporiai* of objectivism does not mean that we give up acknowledging the otherness of the good; but *the otherness is intimate to us*; and as intimate to us, it is not identical to us, it is *not our own*, we do not own it. Becoming attuned to the equivocities of subjectivism does not mean drowning in a swamp of innerness. The character of one's selving is also at stake here: the kind of self we are, our being good, the ethical quality of the life lived. Intimacy and otherness are both demanded by the dialectic that turns us into the immanence of the good.

We see this need to go beyond an either/or, an oscillation of "objectivism" and "subjectivism" (recall our discussion of these and the ethos in Chapter 1), if we again look at the different potencies of the ethical.

Relative to the *aesthetic* potency: why should the aesthetic good be either "in here" or "out there"? It is both "in here" in the flesh and "out there" in the beauty of the good, its gift of goodness to us, as the food gives itself, and the drink and the air and everything we love in this still green earth. Why subjectivize the aesthetic or objectify it? Neither makes sense in opposition to the other; neither alone makes sense.

Relative to the *dianoetic*: why should the law be detached and hovering above the ethos? It is within the ethos as immanently emerging, and above the ethos as calling it to account. It requires the immanent power of judgment that comes to selving in the ethos. It is not subjectivized, though it comes to selving. It is not objectified, though it has its life that is beyond subjectivism. The law is within us and also above us. It brings us above ourselves, or lets us see that we have lived below ourselves.

Relative to the *transcendental*: why should the foundation be set in opposition to the ethos? Why should not the grounding good be emergent there, and emergent there relative to self? The transcendental approach sees the relation to self, since otherwise it is merely logical possibility. If the temptation of a kind of "objectivism" still haunts this approach, it is most important to see that "subject" need not be "subjective," and that "objective" need not be objectified, if we think of the objective as other in relation to selving.

Relative to the *eudaimonistic*: the point is evident in that one of the best accounts, namely the Aristotelian, is not formulated in terms of an opposition of subject and object. Something of the fullness of the ethos has been let be, such as to let humans be humans and nature be *phusis*, not a collocation of objectified, neutered effective powers. The standard is immanent in humans and shown in exemplars of certain realized powers and character. This is not antagonistic to the more than personal, since this human has the wide range of experience and rational discernment necessary to see what is the proper in the particular. There is a promise of the universal in the finesse that reaches beyond the particular, in reaching towards the particular.

Relative to the *transcending*: why render this in subjectivistic terms, even though a process of selving or self-becoming most helpfully points us to its truth? There is no objectification of transcending, though there is a determination to an objective that gives it direction and definition. And the lack of objectification does not mean subjectification but rather the dynamic becoming of self that is more than subjective, just in its realized power to surpass itself. Transcending is nonobjectifiable selving that is nevertheless self-surpassing, hence always in relation to the other. The other also is not seen as objectified but as entering into a living relation of community, the other as another self-transcending being.

Relative to *transcendence itself*: the concrete, living, and universal character of the good is crucial: concrete, as coming from showing and into showing; living, as coming from eudaimonistic and transcending insight into selving; and universal, as seen by dianoetic and transcendental thinking. But the showing is an immanentization that is not a diminution of transcendence; the selving is not intelligible apart from community with the other, communication that frees what is other into its own good; the universal is not intelligible apart from this community, hence is not a general abstraction nor a lifeless principle. This universal is the good that shines on the fair and the foul, and that in the shining lets be even unto evil, and lets be to allow for a metaxological community of free centers of existence, centers for whom the transcendent good is immanent in their being, and their being good, while being more than their being and their being good.

Hospitality to Inherent Good

The immanent standard beyond objectivism and subjectivism illuminates the question I posed (in Chapter 1) about being's hospitality to inherent good.

Dialectic, properly understood, can offer an extremely important approach to this. It can open to this hospitality by its probe of immanence.

Consider, for example, the Socratic–Platonic approach: were we to direct ourselves dialectically to what is now at work within us, and within the ethos, a sense of inherent value, and indeed the unconditional good, will not be wanting in showing itself. This is complex, in that the showing may be full of further qualification. But there is trust, articulated in *logos*, that dialectically we can approach the inherent good, and we can do so because it is already with us, though we do not determinately know it or know what it or its meaning determinately is. It is already with us before we chose to be directed to it. As *erotic* beings, we are from the start directedness to the good. As transcending, self-surpassing towards the good, the good is effective in our being from the origin, before we transcend. We have to seek the good, hence lack it, but that we have to seek means we have a presentiment of what we seek, hence do not completely lack what we lack. And since what we lack is the complete good, we then do not lack the complete good, or are not completely lacking of the good.

Dialectic must follow the unfolding of what is inherent in the inherent, even if enigmatic, presence of the good. It brings out from implicit inherence what is good for itself. This is not merely intellectual. It is the living of a kind of life. (Though this is identified with the life of philosophy by Socrates and Plato, there is more.) The mindful living of the good is the living dialectic. This way of life becomes itself good, because it is from the start an hospitality to good. And it is hospitable to the good because the good is and was and will be hospitable to it. This hospitality in no way downplays the equivocity of evil on one side, nor the transcendence of the unconditional good on the other. We are in the hospitality of the good somewhere *between* these two extremes. This will come back more with the metaxological.

What about that hospitality and that between, relative to more modern variations of the dialectical way, such as the Kantian, Hegelian, or Marxist? First I make a general point about modern dialectic, and then I turn to these in more detail.

Modern dialectic bears the legacy of the Cartesian dualism of objective and subjective, hence of a certain determination of the ethos in terms of objectivism and subjectivism. It shapes its own self-understanding in terms of such dualism, hence it is tainted with some of its deficiencies as a rendition of the ethos. In that rendition there is sedimented an antagonism between subject and object, itself harboring a reduction of the ethos to valueless neutrality: on the one side, a relentless objectivism that empties given being of value; on the other side, a rampant subjectivism trying to take complete possession of value, as itself allegedly the only ground of worth. This gets carried over into our understanding of self, of other, and of what their good is. The dualism tempts us to devalue the other, for this stands opposed to us; we take on the grounding of value, not only of ourselves but of the other, and of the other as there for us, as of value only as it is for us, as we have determined it to be.

Modern dialectic is still captive to an initial starting point opposing self and other. Its beginning is not the good already immanent in the between, as given by the origin or arche. It then sees how the self opposes the other opposing it. It begins to bring out some of the true character of genuine dialectic when it sees that harmony can come to be from the opposition to opposition, that in struggle a new wholeness or an integral value can be won. The accent falls on a *teleology* of the good, not on an *archeology*. If the self and the other are opposed, the self can mediate with the other, and in this can show itself as self-mediating; in determining itself in relation to the other, it is self-determining in and through the other. Relation to the other can serve the self-relation that is self-determining. Here's the rub: this now seems to be *the* inherent value, the value that is literally *for itself*. Notice, however, that this value for itself has altered or clouded over the full meaning of the hospitality of being to value. This hospitality has been dialectically displaced to the self as self-determining, has migrated under the pressure of dialectic to one being in the ethos. And so the ethos as well as the other still stand open to a dangerous devaluation.

Thus modern dialectic is hospitable to inherent value as the value that is for itself. This being for itself is the being for self of the self-relating, self-determining being. This not only risks shortchanging the ethos but makes the other a means for this inherent value, and then forgets inherent value of a different sort to any value that is *won* in a process of dialectical struggle. There is value already given before all battles for values, battles either lost or won. But if the valuable is always only won, never given, then *the gift of the good as gift is declined*. The given is made a pretext for struggle to win. If there is *a rebuff of the free giving of the good*, of what I call the agapeic transcendence of good, then also, I claim, the full ambiguity of the hospitality of the ethos is passed over rather than genuinely faced and surpassed. This passing over may have all the *appearance* of a self-surpassing, but it will have passed over what already is flattened by unwary self-surpassing.

I will now consider this central dialectical point in Kantian ethics, then turn to the Hegelian and Marxist variations. I will show how the ambiguity, passed over, resurfaces in the self-assertion of will to power that we find in Nietzschean ethics. This last, I think, is a possibility more or less latent in all of the others. This is especially the case insofar as we have not carded well enough the equivocal threads of the above form of self-determination.[8] I will be dealing with a *dialectical equivocity*—not a dialectic that overcomes an equivocity, but a dialectic enmeshed in equivocities it seems to mediate, but does not. Indeed, it cannot do so in the terms of a dialectic of self-determination. There is involved an other that is not a dialectical other.

---

8. This is the crucial point at stake here, not an exegesis of all of the dimensions of these thinkers. A volume could be devoted to the ethical views of each.

Anglo–American reflection on autonomy and self-determination tends to be a mixture of Kantianism and utilitarianism, but one also can detect a crucial line of unfolding from Kant through Nietzsche that has had immense significance (not least through Marxism, and now in the form of post–modern Nietzscheanism). These forms of self-determination (sometimes ambiguously or covertly) push its logic in ways that Enlightenment callowness, commonsense complacency, and Anglo–American pragmatism do not. We seem diffident about any ethics of "obedience" in which we are subject to command; our preference is for an ethics of will or choice, in which I exercise my own power of command— even when I find myself commanded. But this tension between obedience and willing my own choice keeps returning. We seem to have come to a form of self-governing ethics, but have we really left behind the old obedience and submission? Do we find *new obediences* to indeterminate powers we know to be and not to be our own? We seem to give up obedience, but what precisely are we obeying when we give up obedience?

Still, forms of being externally determined are all suspect of being obstacles to the free expression of my own being. We are to be ourselves through ourselves, not externally determined through another. If Kant seems the high point of self-determination, he reflects an ethos shared with other thinkers critical of him, even when they radicalize what is latent in him. This is true even of Nietzsche: the last man of German idealism and the sacred founder of an ethics of the post-modern non-self. His will to power does not simply come after the "deconstruction" of rational autonomy; it is already there at the roots in the ambiguity of autonomy's relation to what is other to self. "Below" both autonomy and will to power is the ethos as valueless and a devalued soil of otherness. Different constructions may be built upon this soil—Kantian, Hegelian, Marxist, Nietzschean, and now the further fruit of groundless will to power in some forms of post-modern thought. We move from the desire of the ideal to the project of the ideal to the dissolution of the ideal. Certain forms of "postmodern" thought seem to suggest more the *disillusion* of autonomy rather than its *dissolution*. We push away our autonomy yet equally hold on to it. This is the self-laceration of autonomy, not its abandonment.

Dialectic, Kant, Autonomy: Given the Law and Giving the Law

Kant articulates a viewpoint that is primarily an articulation of the *transcendental potency* of the ethical, and all that this entails relative to the other potencies, from the aesthetic to the transcendent. These potencies will be touched upon here, but given previous discussion, my main focus is on what one might call a virtual dialectic implicit in his view. What then of the dialectical equivocity? It resides in the tension between *being given the law* and *giving oneself the law*.

More generally, one can see Kant's moral philosophy as a defensive response to the valuelessness of being produced by the modern objectification of the ethos. He does not put it this way, does not even understand it as such. He is often extraordinarily innocent of the ethos and historical mutations in the understanding of the ontological situation, out of which his whole philosophical enterprise emerges. He simply accepts the Newtonian world-picture which, relative to nature's givenness, reduces being to a valueless thereness. This results, of course, in an entirely problematic place for morality, since mechanistic necessity undercuts the possibility of freedom: the determinism of the Newtonian machine has no place for self-determination in moral being. No freedom, no responsibility, no morality. Yet Kant was uncompromisingly aware of an unconditional demand or call that we normally name moral "obligation" or the "ought." How to do justice to that in the valueless machine?

Kant turns to the subject: not to the subjectification process as leading to subjectivism, but to the moral subject as immanently marked by an unconditional norm. Thus we see the lineaments of those themes we marked above along the dialectical way: response to a certain reduction brought about by dualism; the threat to any unconditional value by an unchecked objectivism or subjectivism; a coming around to, or turning to self; in that turn, a discovery of unconditional worth, beyond valueless objectivism and relativistic subjectivism. Hence Kant's ringing words: the goodwill is the only unconditional good, in this world, or out of it. The contrast is clear: nothing in the external has inherent value: the goodwill is the one unconditional good in this expanse of worthlessness.[9]

Kant does not reject the Newtonian world-picture—not at all. Rather, he interprets it such as to *reconfigure a view of the whole*, which allows space for

---

9. This is the significant opening of *Groundwork*. Why does he say out of this world? This opening, oddly, reminds me of Pascal—without his existential pathos: the I alone in the waste, the immensity without worth. We find the spirit of rational abstraction in Kant: see what he has to say about sympathy; there is a pathological and a practical version of it; see his praise of the Stoic in relation to his friend (stoic virtues, such as *apatheia*, alone are praised as sublime and noble in the *Critique of Judgment*, §29). Kant turns the transcendental potency of the ethical *away* from its aesthetic and eudaimonistic potencies, as he also claims to transcend the dianoetic. At times, one suspects a low view of human nature at the level of pathology: prudence as sly, cunning self-interest; happiness as the sum total of self-gratifications; we look for a sense of happiness as the joy that blesses a life of either erotic or agapeic self-transcending. There is a primacy of duties to oneself. See his view of sexuality and marriage—he has no feeling for the flesh as the aesthetic show of the good. Quite the contrary, his moral purity renders it impure. See the witness of one of his contemporaries, Charlotte von Schuller: Kant might have been one of the greatest phenomena of humankind if he had been capable of loving; but since this was not the case there was something defective in his nature (cited in E. Cassirer, *Kants Leben und Lehre* (Berlin, 1918), 441).

moral freedom. In my terms, ethos as the givenness of intermediate being counts for nothing morally; only the subject as moral can defend us against the ethical emptiness of the Newtonian machine world, emptiness if that machine is the truth of the whole. Kant's transcendental reconfiguration of Newtonian mechanism allows room for an other source of intelligibility, namely, the transcendental subject. This other source also gives room to freedom as itself a source of moral worth. The transcendental source of the intelligibility of the machine is not a machine, hence is free of external determinism. As a source, it is a free original of its own self-determination. It is noumenal, supersensible, and so on. The dualism of objectivism and subjectivism of the modern *mathesis* of nature is turned around so that, while the determinism of objectivism is maintained, a space is created for the subject's freedom. This latter possesses an unconditional status in the whole: without it, the whole would have no point: "What is the good of it all?" Without the unconditional good of the goodwill, there is no such good.

The above considerations define an implicitly dialectical context, but what about Kant's own usage of "dialectic," namely, as concerned with our tendency to be led astray into transcendental illusions? There is nothing positive about dialectic for Kant: it is another critical tool. Nevertheless, I think implicit in his practice is a more positive notion. Consonant with his own usage, he sees a "natural dialectic" (see *Groundwork*): not regarding the external dualism but the internal dualism, revealed in the strife in us between inclination and duty. Duty shows the unconditional; inclination draws us back to the determinisms of nonmoral nature. And when we yield to these determinations, as we are so inclined, we set in motion a corruption of the moral unconditional. Philosophy is helpful here in bringing us around to ourselves again, bringing before our reflection the moral norm already at work. The dualism internal to our being has to be fought and surmounted, but done so in terms of one side: duty must triumph over inclination. The Kantian subject is a site of strife, is the struggle of the two sides, and in that sense is both sides in one, already a unity of opposites, though Kant eschews such dialectical language.

The categorical imperative can be seen as Kant's way of defining the struggle: a way to lift the subject to the universal level, or to bring itself around to its union with the universal; for the subject is always tempted by subjectivism. Are we in the presence of the philosopher's old fear of the particular, and the old desire to lose self in the universal, to become selfless? And a new return to perhaps an old obedience? Kant expresses this in moral terms rather than metaphysical. The universal, fortunately, seems already at hand in the form of the moral law. As far as I can see, in Kant the moral law is given: we find ourselves under it; we do not create it; we bring ourselves into conformity with it, in doing our duty. This givenness of the moral is expressed in Kant's talk of "the fact of reason," the one "transcendental fact."[10] Thus *respect* also is the one moral feeling, itself a fact of reason. Respect has to do with granting the moral law in its dignity, given to us in that dignity which we grant as granted. The categorical imperative formalizes the process of coming into conformity with the universal. The moral universal under which we find ourselves is not a law such as is defined by Newtonian mechanism, though there is an analogy.[11]

We find ourselves under the moral law. Need we object to givenness, as do the idealists? No. Still we must ask about the *meaning of the givenness* in terms of its giving source. Kant avoided this question, purportedly as unanswerable. Why? I think because it would bring too uncomfortably to the fore the question of God as the ultimate ground of the good and the moral law. While Kant, at some decisive points,[12] lets God peep ambiguously through the thick curtain of the critical

---

10. Kant's idealistic successors ridiculed this—they wished to be rid of givenness as other to the self to whom the given is given; all the more to radicalize self-determining, self-giving, so to say. In its own way, Kant's equivocity here is superior to his critical successors.

11. It is interesting to see a new "objectivism" coming in: not the objectivism of externality but of the inner moral law: there is a compulsion and necessity there analogous to what we find in the mechanism of nature. The *quasi-machine* of freedom and morality? See *Groundwork* and the second formulation of the categorical imperative on this analogy of nature and morality; see *Critique of Practical Reason* on the "fact of reason."

12. See, for instance, the footnote in the *Critique of Practical Reason* (in "The Dialectic of Pure Practical Reason," when he discusses the postulate of God): there he seems to praise the Christian view for its hope that "what is not in our power will come to our aid from another source, whether we know in what way or not." If Kant is not being disingenuous here, the suggestion punctures the self-sufficiency of any claim to autonomy. His remarks on theological ethics in *Groundwork* concern, in the main, the morally corrupting potential of a divine heteronomy. In *Critique of Judgment*, his contempt is palpable in some remarks on abject begging and petitionary prayer. I cannot locate the source of this remark: the most shameful thing would be to be caught in the posture of prayer. In *Metaphysical Principles of Virtue*, English trans. by James W. Ellington in *Kant's Ethical Philosophy* (Indianapolis: Hackett, 1983), 99, in the section "Concerning Servility," he says: "Kneeling down or grovelling on the ground, even to express your reverence for heavenly things, is contrary to human dignity." In the *Critique of Practical Reason* (in the above Dialectic), he exempts Christianity from this heteronomy, identifying it with his own doctrine of moral autonomy: "The Christian principle of morality is not theological and thus heteronomous, being rather the autonomy of pure practical reason itself." Religion does not lead to morality; the moral law leads to religion. Here he speaks of religion as the recognition of duties as divine commands. He says the same in *Religion within the Limits of Reason Alone*. There Kant obviously talks about God quite a bit, but his response overall to any threat to autonomy's absoluteness seems to me to be a *study in evasion*, or perhaps, more accurately, a vacillating posture of *acknowledgment and evasion*, in which he seeks to defuse what he sees as a threat. I could write a book on that.

system, he does not always want to draw attention to the fact. Why? Because his view of theological ethics entails a heteronomy that for him is undignified for us: we risk submission to the commands of a tyrannical master and are turned into abject dependents. That does not accord with an ethics of autonomous self-determination. And yet who gives the law? Who is the lawgiver? Must God as other be represented by the ethical heteronomy of the domineering divinity? What kind of divine commander is this? Perhaps there is God beyond the law? In fact, if God is the source of law, God is beyond law, and this even if we agree that our ethical being is defined in the law. What if the source beyond law has a goodness transcendent to law: a living goodness from which law emerges but which is not and can never be a law or defined in terms of law? (This possibility has consequences for human goodness too.) The hiddenness of God is kept hidden by Kant.

If the law is given and we find ourselves under its obligating command, how does Kant square this with his emphasis on self-legislation? For to be autonomous and self-determining, we must be ourselves the givers of the law. How be a lawgiver if the law is already given? The first emphasizes self-determination; the second points to a submission. Kant's answer is that we give the law to ourselves: we are self-determining and submissive at once. This is not entirely off the mark: there is a freedom that comes with a fundamental consent or yes—I call it agapeic freedom. But Kant is more concerned with preserving autonomy, sometimes, it seems, at all costs. I mean, if there is a consent to something other as law, or source of law, autonomy is *relativized* in regard to this: autonomy cannot be the absolute Kant wants it to be. If autonomy is absolutized, this other must be relativized; if this other has a claim to be absolute, then autonomy must be relativized.

I think Kant did not fully appreciate this problem and its centrality. His view can be seen as coming to some expression of it; but he took the problem and (in some respects) simply baptized it as the solution. It is no solution. Autonomy functions only by relativizing this other source; and the more radically we insist on this autonomy, the more this relativizing must be completed. That is why the idealists saw Kant as halfhearted.[13] They wished to complete what he left unfinished, to entirely incorporate this other source into the self-determining of the (moral) subject. We will see something of this below with Hegel and others.

The antinomy: absolutize autonomy, and you relativize the good as other, or more than our self-determination; absolutize the good as other, and you must

---

13. They found their way to absolutely self-determining reason with Kant's help. In the latter, the law seems to be given *to* reason, and given *by* reason; it seems to be *reason itself*, as the form of the rational will. How can reason be recipient, giver, and given? It must be, or mimic, *causa sui*, or be "God." Some of Kant's descriptions of freedom make it a self-cause. How we differentiate a finite original from the absolute original here is crucial.

relativize autonomy. I think the givenness has to be acknowledged, relative to the ethos, and its milieu, and relative to the very gift of freedom with which we are endowed. I suggest this approach: the original givenness is not the kind of heteronomy of external determination that Kant rejects; it is not an internal determination; it is a freeing of finite being into its own freedom, prior to its being able to give itself to itself, or determine itself.[14] The origin frees agape-ically; it does not determine univocally, does not determine dialectically. We are given to be, and the giving is good; but given to be, we can participate in the giving of ourselves to be. We must move beyond an opposition of determination and self-determination, as beyond the empty indeterminacy of indefiniteness. The good is an overdetermined source that gives to be, but gives beings, given to be, the power to participate in their giving of themselves to be. Freedom is first a gift, and the primal gift lets us, allows us freely to be and to give ourselves. The primal givenness of this first good (and this is not the moral law) relativizes any proposal to absolutize autonomy.

Finally, I find Kant evasive. He retreats to equivocal showing and conceal-ing. Relative to his vacillation, I note the following seven continuing perplexities.

First, is there not something astonishing about human beings as ends in themselves? Kant would agree. One formulation of the categorical imperative enjoins us to treat humanity in ourselves and others as an end in itself. Humans have dignity, things have a price. This ascription is often repeated without much thought. We pay lip service to it, which does not mean that we live in accordance with it. Do we understand it? What grounds such an end in self? Such an end is a worth beyond quantification. We sometimes speak of the infinite value of the person. But what could ground such an immeasurable value, an infinite worth? It exceeds every calculation, and there could be no way to objectify it. Were we to have a bank check of infinite value, there is no way we could cash it; for there is no bank with the resources to deal out what is needed to be on a par with it. What is this strange value? And what source could be on a par with making sense of its given reality? For it is a given reality. We do not produce or create this end; it is what we are, constitutive of our being. It has no "cash value" (William James) that could be determined.

If we cannot ground it, can nature? But the same problem of objectivism arises in here: things in nature do have their price, but this has no price, so nature is not on a par with this end in self, this immeasurable value. (Kant saw this but expressed the point of the difference in misleading dualistic terms.) Not self, not nature? God then? Certainly some source that itself is on a par with the immea-surable: the unconditional that is constitutively in excess of any determinate or determinable calculation. Again, I find Kant evasive. Why? Because this possi-

---

14. See Part III for a fuller development of the different forms of freedom.

bility would bring him uncomfortably into the neighborhood of the divine once again. His strategy is equivocal, since what he proposes clearly points towards what he is intent on shrouding in silence.

Second, this points to another question, so obvious that Kant fudges it. Suppose there is, as Kant says, a realm (*Reich*) of ends? Who is sovereign ruler of this *Reich*? Kant does not speak of a king, but one could ask, who is the "king" of the realm of ends? We are not the king or kings; we are subjects in that kingdom, even if ends in ourselves.[15] Is God the king? The *Reich* is a community, but what kind of community? Why does Kant use the phrase *corpus mysticum* (in the *Critique of Pure Reason*, A808; B836)? Even if we permit Kant his reticence on the ultimate sovereign, we must ask what constitutes the *community* of moral subjects. If each is self-legislating, what of the other? Do I legislate for the other? Does the other legislate for me? Does not the *pluralizing* of self-legislation create serious difficulties to holding on to the notion of *self-legislation* as the primary model of moral freedom? Is the relation *between* a plurality of autonomous selves itself amenable to self-legislation? How could it possibly be, if the other and the between are what is at issue? Put otherwise, is the mediation *between* self-mediating beings just a more inclusive self-mediation? Or is it an intermediation which, as pluralized beyond finite calculation and univocal determination, exceeds all such self-legislation, even indeed a totalized self-mediation which putatively would include all finite beings within itself? Kant does not raise the question in that form, but the question is unavoidable once we begin to wonder about the truth of his ethics of autonomous self-legislation.

Third, how do the moral subjects *intermediate*? Through each other? Or through the universal? Or through the moral law? They relate, for Kant, through the categorical imperative, as lifting each to the universal level, hence beyond the singularity of their selves, where their self-legislation coincides with a universal legislation. Of course, we come back to the tension in self-legislation noted above, between the givenness of the moral law as the universal and the autonomy of my self-legislation as what I effect. But can this recourse to the universal as a mediating link between moral subjects deal entirely with the problem? For even granting some truth to it, how do we *come back down into the ethos*; come into the between as the ethical community? And we must come back down, for this is the between in which the entire drama ethically unfolds. For it is in the between that the universal and the particulars have to be mediated, not above it. And in that between, we come back to equivocity once again.

---

15. Kant explicitly says we are "subjects" not "sovereigns" in *Critique of Practical Reason*, though in *Groundwork*, we are both "sovereigns" and "members" of the kingdom of ends— as *Reich der Zwecke* has been translated, perhaps not entirely accurately.

Fourth, does not the between make us question any dualizing of the human being as an integrity of being? This integrity is made self-discordant by Kant in a manner that cannot be overcome in the terms his view proposes. Kant's solution to this self-discordance is to canonize a dualism, one side of which is claimed as the solution, namely, the moral side. But this solution is simply the problem once again, shifted to one of the poles of the opposition. And the *turn back to the other pole* cannot be prevented, since there is a dialectic in the situation that will effect this turnaround: the human being will *come to itself as the other pole*, hence as both poles, and just as soon will think of the *higher* pole as really the *subordinate* pole, as the other way around. And then, despite everything Kant says, and in some ways in reaction to the one-sidedness of what he does say, reason will *again* be made the slave of the passions.

Fifth, does the between also not make us raise again the issue of formalism as empty? If the universal is the form of reason, and if it mediates the will, the will itself will formally look like a universal will. But a universal will does not act in the between, as we act. Suppose it were true that the categorical imperative did raise the subjective will and its maxim to the universal will in that regard, the will of the singular subject would have to descend once again into the particularities of the situation, and what is required in that descending movement cannot be completely covered by the categorical imperative. For it goes in the reverse direction, and hence it requires the practical mindfulness that is ethical attention to the nuances of the particular. The question again is, what of the between? In the downward movement, we again meet ambiguity in the chiaroscuro of the good.[16] Since this equivocity keeps returning, as we are turned about in the between, the categorical imperative, while not inconsequential, is not, cannot be, enough.

Sixth, what of the ethos as community of intermediating others? Kant suggests that the *Reich* of ends is *an ideal*. When Kant uses the term *ideal* he tends to mean a regulative ideal. What kind of regulation? Surely this is an ideal that must *now* be working, even for it to be a regulative ideal. The kingdom cannot be merely a "pious" wish. While it sets a task or goal, it still must be effective here and now, and not only in some coming form. The ideal must be *constitutive* as well as regulative; indeed, it must be constitutive in order to be regulative. But if the kingdom is already given, like the moral law, what effect then on self-legislation? Perhaps we should talk about waking up to the *community already at work*, not only without, but within, and within which we too always already are. But

---

16. As I suggested with regard to the equivocal, Plato beautifully captures this in the image of the philosopher *returning* to the Cave: *blinded*, his sight must be adjusted to darkness, but his sight inside the Cave is not the same as looking at the Sun outside the Cave; adjustment to the twilight is of the essence for proper seeing, and for justice. Does this adjustment relativize the absolute? Yes and no.

wake up to such a community, and we quickly shed the language of autonomous self-determination. This last cannot be the deepest point, even though the community gives us to be as free beings who can consent freely to be what we are in community. If the ideal must be constitutive (and I do not mean in Hegel's sense), we must already be in this kingdom. The ethos as the between is community, the concrete place of emergence of the unconditional. It is in the immanence of the ethos, especially as ethical community, that the unconditional emerges, emerges for our relativity to the transcendent good, not in the "ideal" space of the dualized transcendence of Kant's unconditional.

Seventh, what of the *summum bonum* and Kant's view of this? There is a dialectic here, but not in relation to self-division and self-determination only. I will put it thus: we have to do with *a torment that the whole is not hospitable to value.* Kant saw what humans have always painfully seen: not only is there little justice, the suffering of the innocent tortures those who think. Why do the wicked prosper, the just suffer? I am virtuous, so why does my virtue not buffer me from woe? You are wicked, so why do you relish life, relish your very wickedness, and with impunity? There is something here intolerable to righteousness. Kant's views run the danger of self-righteousness, indeed, priggishness: the virtuous should be happy, the wicked should be wretched. I suspect Kant would find it hard to stomach the parable of Jesus about the workers in the vineyard and the agapeic generosity of the lord: those who have worked hard all day (dutifully) get the same wage as those who have lounged and loitered (following their inclinations; lolling in the sun, telling jokes, simply passing the time); and they come into work when the day's hard work is almost done, and the harsh sun is going down or moderating, and they get the same wages! This is wrong! Kant is like the older son in the parable of the prodigal son who resents the feast of welcome the dissipated son is given, resents the father's generous forgiving. The lost son deserves nothing, merits nothing, and is given everything! This is illogical, mad, evil, if reason dictates that happiness should be in exact measure to virtue. This is the univocal principle: one-to-one correspondence of virtue and merited happiness. The father gives everything, and not in terms of a measure of merit; nothing is merited on the measure of univocal reason. Is this not an abomination to Kantian morals?

The issue goes deeper. If the wicked prosper, there may be something *ontologically monstrous* here. There may be a vileness to the whole, if things do not come to right in the end. Kant speaks of virtue as the supreme good (*supremum*), but the unity of virtue and happiness is the *summum bonum* in the sense of the most complete (*consummatum*). Virtue is supreme but unconsummated without happiness. There is an injustice to the misery of the good. I think the question of the *good of the whole* comes in here, and in a deep, metaphysical sense. What is the good of it all? Is it consummated in the end, or does it all come to nothing? Kant does not outrightly ask the question in that form, but it is hidden behind his doctrine of the *summum bonum*.

Kant's answer is again a *virtual dialectic*: the dualism (of virtue and happiness) is tormenting, but it points beyond the limit, beyond the limit of this life, to a ground of unity beyond: God. But this is an asymptotic goal and a projected (postulated) unity. Equivocity remains: if the end is not now working, it cannot even function as an ideal: there must be a constitutive side to it. For if the final unity is only postulated or projected, why project *that*? Kant even speaks of the regulative ideal as a *focus imaginarius* (in the *Critique of Pure Reason*, A644, B672). God too as such a focus, as perhaps an imaginative projection? God as *but* an imaginary projection? And if God is just such a projection, why not *retract* the projection (as Feuerbach, Marx, Nietzsche, and others do; and as does Hegel, somewhat differently)? We are only projecting ourselves then. We project ourselves, we recover ourselves, by dissolving God back into ourselves, and thus we become truly self-legislating. We start as morally righteous Kantians and end as self-glorifying Nietzscheans beyond good and evil, ourselves the source of the moral law. Result: no givenness unless we give it to ourselves; and this includes our relation to the other; and a putatively higher, creative autonomy claims to free itself from all heteronomy and be itself the source of the true significance of the other. (This fatal ambiguity is already implicit in Hegel.)

Hegel, *Sittlichkeit*, Social Self-Determination: The Will That Wills Itself and Rational Obedience to the Whole

Reaction against the context of dualism, a transcending of Newtonian necessity, and acknowledgment of an immanent standard, these continue with Hegel. The Hegelian recuperation of intrinsic value against the devalued ethos is defined in terms of dialectical self-determination. This is not just the individual self-determination of Kantian *Moralität* but the self-determination of the whole. For Hegel, Kant does not go far enough. The "fact of reason" is ridiculed; all givenness and otherness, viewed through the lenses of dualistic opposition, is mediated into a dialectically self-mediating totality. Hegel is not opposed to self-determination but to Kant's limited version of it. He turns to the concrete social ethos of society. There we find a dialectic of *social self-determination*. Nevertheless, this is still self-determination. It is a kind of dialectical version of the *Reich* of ends—seen as constitutive and being constituted, not a Kantian ideal, which is only an "ought" that we dictate but that is not.

Beyond the Cartesian dualism of subject and object, Hegel appreciates a dialectic immanent in this dualism, pointing to a togetherness deeper than the opposition. Though he moves beyond the opposition, in his own way, he is still influenced by the privilege of self, and most especially in the wake of the so-called Copernican revolution of Kant's transcendental philosophy. The ever-present danger of devaluation of the other is not decisively overcome.

Hegel does think self must journey into otherness to be truly self, so he is much more complex than first appears. He certainly is ambiguous about nature as itself, relative to its contribution to the fullness of the ethos: it seems to be just there for humans to exert their right of self-hood, as property; owning it . . . and hence, owning themselves. He also is ambiguous with respect to forms of community. For *the logic of the whole* is the self-mediating whole; and while there is an essential place for the other, the other is placed within the self-mediating totality that mediates with itself in the other, as its own self in otherness; ultimately, there is no other as other. Though much could be said here, I must focus on the dialectical meaning of Hegel's view of social self-determination. Despite his very severe critique of Kant, he can be seen as Kant's heir, even more radical in his insistence on self-determining being. It is not that he denies a kind of "heteronomy," but it becomes sublated in a more inclusive social self-determination. And there also is a submission at the end of it all: dialectical obedience to the whole. What whole? Nature? No. The Idea? How so? God as the whole of wholes? The Weltgeist? Objective Geist as the historical totality of the immanences of time? Or does the mountain groan and give forth a mouse? Submission to the laws of one's own country or state.[17]

Thus freedom is, at its most primitive, understood as the *will that wills the free will itself* (*Philosophy of Right*, §27). But of course it cannot will itself in abstraction from its place in the ethos. Hence it must undergo an ethical education to make it concretely a will that wills itself. Otherwise, it is the mere abstraction of a power that remains in indigent indefiniteness. To be the will that wills itself, it must come to be with the others in such a way that, in willing in relation to them, it is simply willing itself. The different forms of freedom in the *Philosophy of Right* are more and more rich and complex forms of the will that wills itself in and through the other: the universal will is the will that wills itself in and through the other as its own other.

The point is to be found in abstract freedom, with property, contract, and so on; in morality with the inward absoluteness of the individual conscience. It is to be found in family life where the immediacy of the social will wills itself in the togetherness of parents and children. It is to be found in the civil society where the togetherness of calculative wills, each willing itself, comes to be a contributor and a participant in the more universal will that wills itself in and through these as others (these others mistakenly think of themselves as merely for themselves;

---

17. Did Bradley say it with less dialectical fuss and perhaps also less equivocation: My station and its duties? Indeed he cites Hegel on just this point, namely, his endorsement of the wisest men of antiquity when they recommend accordance with the laws of one's own country as the only true morality. See *Ethical Studies (Selected Essays)* (New York: Liberal Arts Press, 1951), 109.

finally they are not other to the more universal will that wills itself in and through their otherness). It is to be found in the state where the social will comes closest to being the earthly incarnation of the universal will that wills itself in and through the dialectical togetherness of all the participants. Even in this last inclusive community, the claim is that the individual self-determination of particular subjectivity also is included. For Hegel, one might say that Kant is reconciled with the Greeks and Christianity in a social *Sittlichkeit*, wherein the whole mediates with itself in mediating with its others, seen now not to be others at all.

The logic of the will that wills itself in and through its other follows this path. There is an initial *indeterminacy of freedom*; for Hegel, this is an indefinite retraction of subjectivity back into its own indefinite inwardness; this is its power to be free of all constricting otherness. But this "freedom from" is not true, concretized freedom; it is set over against the others and its ethos. To be concretely free, it must realize itself; it must give itself over to *determination*. This means it must come into the domain of the particular and the limited; its possibility must be limited thus and not otherwise. Only in determination and self-limitation is freedom concretized in the process of self-realization. Here we find Hegel's protests against one of the consequences of Kantian-style autonomy: an empty self-determination that keeps itself aloof from everything other; in that aloofness, it dissolves into an emptiness that is profoundly destructive (think of the Terror of the Revolution that comes from a form of abstract freedom). Here too we find Hegel's diatribes against the Romantic inwardness of the beautiful soul (though it, like moral conscience, is the immanence of the divine in the human, as he points out in the *Phenomenology*). Hegel opposes the cult of self-feeling that plumes itself on being superior freedom when, in fact, it risks being most in bondage to its own emptiness.

The determination essential to freedom is such that in giving ourselves over to the other, we begin to come round to ourselves, we come to ourselves in the other, and through the other. Why? Because we discover that the other is self, just as we are: it is the sameness of self and other that is truly discovered in determinate forms of being. Hence the relation to the other serves self-realization, coming back to self in determinate forms. What looks like the loss of autonomy in a heteronomous situation is not a loss but a discovery of the *heteros* as *auto*, and so a recovery of *auto*. Hence there arises a more inclusive *auto-determination* or *self-determination* in and through the other. This is the true freedom that wills itself in and through the other. This is freedom as concretely universal.[18] Again, this is

---

18. I have said something elsewhere about this inclusive self-determination and the other: "Being, Dialectic and Determination: On the Sources of Metaphysical Thinking," *The Review of Metaphysics* 48 (June 1995): 731–769; see also Chapter 4 of *BB*. Hegel's transformation of Kantian autonomy is in light of his sense of *the whole*. The resulting social

a social self-determination, not solitary autonomy; though in the whole, there is the majestic solitude of the One, and this despite the surfaces of manyness.[19]

It is worth noting how Hegel also uses the scheme of universal, particular, and individual. The first universal is an abstract universal; as indefinite, it needs the definiteness of determinate particularity. But this particularity comes to be seen by Hegel as the universal's own *self-particularization*. And so the universal *comes back to itself* in what Hegel calls the individual, which is the concrete universal. Is Hegel a defender of the individual? In a dialectically qualified sense, yes. His claims for individual subjectivity in modernity must be granted. Yet his individuality has a character that is dialectically self-mediating through and through. And the true individual as the true concrete universal means that there is really only one individual in the end. There is finally the concrete universality of the whole, which is the One that mediates with itself in and through its own otherness. Hegel will say Substance becomes Subject. He remains a Spinozist, a "transcendental" Spinozist. As Spinozistic freedom is rational consent to the necessity of whole, so the Hegelian freedom of the will that wills itself means consent to the rational necessity of the absolute self-determining whole. Hegelian freedom is holistic obedience.

Within that whole, that individual, there are finite individuals, yes, with a qualified separateness. These are not the absolute individual, not the truly concrete universal. In that regard, we must raise the question of the infinite value of the individual, understood now in the sense of the finite self. Properly speaking, for Hegel, only the absolute whole could have that value. How does it get reproduced in finite beings, like humans? It cannot be absolutely; the infinite value of humans can only be possible in a dialectically qualified sense. But this runs the risk of a *dialectical instrumentalizing* of the individual (again, in the more normal sense). This individual is a means wherein the whole mediates with itself, in that sense an instrument of the absolute whole: man, so to say, is the means by which God comes to self-detemination; man is the medium of God's self-knowing.

---

holism itself reflects his view of the ontological situation as the whole of wholes. It also echoes the nostalgia, rejected yet transformed, for the Greeks: the polis as aesthetic whole, as ethical whole. The modern principle of the subject allows this more immediate and substantial whole to be transformed into a whole mediated by *Geist* as itself the truth of the whole. Hegel has some feel for how we configure the ethos, with its aesthetic and religious dimensions as well as ethical and political. Overall, his dialectic contributes to the immanentization of the transcendent good, frog leaping the Christian incarnation and pentecostal community into the secular community of the absolute: the reconciled community of human and divine on earth—this is the modern state.

19. I mean, for instance, despite the usurped quotation of Schiller at the end of the *Phenomenology* regarding the life of the absolute, otherwise lifeless and alone.

And of course, there were some who claimed to be the privileged agents of that whole, and who had no compunction in instrumentalizing humans in the interests of the absolute good of the projected world-historical whole. Privileged agents, they felt justified in their invocation of the services of death to advance that whole. If the intrinsic good is only in this dialectically self-mediating whole, Hegel gives us a teleology of the good that honors the infinite worth of the human but at the same time sows the seeds of a temptation to dishonor it. Does he embrace it in the whole only to smother it, kiss it on the lips, but in the kiss, love it or betray it in finitude, like Judas?

Finally, I want to note another scheme of thinking used by Hegel. It runs like this: we must move from unity, through difference, to unity mediated through differences. First we have abstract unity; but this is not enough, for it does no justice to multiplicity and plurality. Then we have the necessity of differences; but such differences can extend to opposition and a being for the other that is over against a being for self. This difference is essential to unity, but it also is the undoing of unity; it is unity alienated into otherness. But if so, otherness also is unity, and the alienation itself must be surpassed. The otherness itself must be othered, and with this the unity returns to itself; it comes round to itself again. *Thus we come round the circle of the unity mediated with itself through difference.* This threefold scheme broadly corresponds to some possibilities in the threefold way of the univocal, the equivocal, and the dialectical.

Again we might see the different formations of freedom in *Philosophy of Right* following the above logic and moving towards the more and more inclusive self-determination that is social self-determination of the Idea or *Geist*. The point could be shown in detail, though this would take us too much afar. Where there are details that might suggest otherwise, these details must be situated in the whole, for that is the truth of the detail for Hegel.[20] God may be in the details, but

---

20. My point again is not to deny that in his social doctrine Hegel tries to think the relations of self and other, nor that he grants a certain otherness; the essential point concerns the logic of the whole that governs his thinking. I have simply mentioned different ways in which this logic shows itself to be that of the absolute whole that mediates with itself in and through its own other. Contemporary defenders of Hegel's social holism tend to downplay this *all-pervasive logic* of the dialectically self-mediating whole, for it confirms some traditional suspicions about Hegel as monistic that are found embarrassing in our pluralistic postmodern times. We end up with a *Hegel lite*. As an example of thinking genuinely in the spirit of Hegel but not hindered by such embarrassments, I think again of Bradley's ethics of the *moral organism*. This is less masked and equivocal, certainly, less tortured, perhaps, but it is still in the spirit of Hegel. On the moral organism and its logic of the whole, see *Ethical Studies (Selected Essays)*, 112ff. Dialectical ethics can equivocate regarding the immanent good: equivocate on the good as self, and as immanent in self but as other to self within self; on the tension of intersubjective plurality and self-mediating

for Hegel, the details are nothing without their dialectically mediated place within the One whole, which is more truly Hegel's God. This whole is the immanent standard and inherent exigence of the good. It is this, its immanence, in all of the parts, that works to drive the process forward to its teleological completion.[21]

This absolute completion is not accomplished for Hegel with the state. The state, he remarks, is not an ideal work of art: it exists in contingency and caprice.[22] World history is needed, yes, but even there, art, religion, and philosophy are more truly in community with the truth of the whole: the absolute accomplishes itself in its own self-comprehension, which happens in the Hegelian philosopher. Marx will nod to this in a qualified way but (in peculiarly Platonic fashion) will turn the Hegelian philosopher *back to the cave*—from contemplation, where thought thinks itself, to revolutionary praxis, where thought is enacted in the radical mutation of the given, indeed its transfiguration into paradise on earth through revolutionary work. For there, the true social self-determination of the essence occurs. The essence is not the divine essence realizing itself. It is essence as the species-being of humanity. A new god takes over

monism; equivocate on the good as arising in immanent self-transcendence, not exhausted thereby but rather articulating the call of good as absolute transcendence. In the coming round of self to itself, we find not just the good of self and the good for self, but the superior good beyond self, that opens up a new field of relations beyond all self-relating, even self-relating in and through the other. This is transcendence towards the other as other, because transcendence itself is the solicitation to agapeic being with self and other. This turns on the difference between dialectical self-mediation and metaxological intermediation: between the self-doubling of the one as inclusive whole, or the redoubling of the many in community as opening selving and othering.

21. In *Concluding Unscientific Postscript*, Kierkegaard denies that an ethics is possible for Hegel's system. Kierkegaard stands against the dialectical holism that forgets the singular. He tends to identify the ethical with the self-becoming of the *singular one*, in a somewhat Kantian vein—in protest against the "homogenization" of the system, and the "massification" of systematically organized modern life. Hegel claims that the modern state includes the principle of subjectivity. Kierkegaard denies the ultimacy of any such inclusion, since what is at issue ultimately with respect to the singular subject is beyond all finitude; it is God, not the earthly god (*Irdisch Göttliches*), which is the Hegelian state (see *Philosophy of Right*, §272, Zusatz). The massification of modernity follows the principle of the unit of quantity, multiplied indefinitely, indifferently. The self in mass is a function of this quantification. The idiocy of the singular is very important. It cannot be thus multiplied: a unity that ever escapes univocal quantification; this is the infinite value of the self as an end in itself.

22. This is against many aestheticizations of the ethical social, political world, for instance, that of Schiller, and by anticipation, many other descendants of the aesthetic state (see *Philosophy of Right*, §258, Zusatz).

the process of self-determination. This is now the social transfiguration in history's own absolute self-determination, through man, newly crowned the absolute subject of history, and its dialectical sovereign.

Dialectic, Marx, Historical Self-Determination: The Social Totality As Autonomy and Tyranny

The issue at stake here is evident relative to the "grand narratives" of history: namely, a historical teleology of the good, which follows a particular humanizing interpretation of the dialectical immanence of that good. If this immanence effects the whole, the process of history is not a mere becoming, but a self-becoming. This teleology also links up with progressive visions of history, reformulating religious hopes of a completion of time and the coming of the good in its unsurpassable fullness. This idea can take apocalyptic forms, such as in Joachim. Or we find secularized apocalypses in claims about the revolutionary fulfillment of time and the beginning of a higher history. The claim is that the self-becoming of the good is not that of the individual subject, à la Kant. It is social and historical. Likewise, the *summum bonum*, as the ground of unity of virtue and happiness, now comes to be claimed by the praxis of the dialectical revolutionaries. Nor need the subject of history be Hegelian *Geist*. This "mystical subject-object" is rejected by Marx in favor of the "real flesh-and-blood" human being.

Marx offers a variation on dialectical ethics. The process of history, he agrees, is recognized by Hegel as one of the real "self-creation" of man; but the self in "self-creation" is "mystified" into a supergeist, when it is really only humanity. Hegel was aware of the need to pitch the question at the level of the whole, but Marx rejects Hegel's whole, as he does anything other than the putatively true whole that will be created through human historical self-creation. Marx humanizes more crudely the teleology of the good: in the self-becoming of the immanent good, the god at work in history is always man, though his potential for apotheosis is initially hidden from him by his own "projection" of himself onto an illusory divine other.

This is all human projection, not divine projection. We might say that the potentially cautionary lesson of Kant's *als ob* is impatiently brushed aside—relative to the *focus imaginarius*, be this God or the counterfeit of God. But the fatal equivocation is already there with Kant. For all theories of "projection" imply an equivocal view of the other as the medium in which self-mediation is effected. Be it God's projection or humanity's projection, the other as other does not exist irreducibly; it is the mirror in which the projector comes to recognize self; the projector is *coming to itself* in the other, despite all detours through alien ways.[23] We are

---

23. Substitute "labor" for "projection," if you will—projection reminds us of Feuerbach's family transmission to Marx of the Hegelian gene: dialectical self-mediation in and through the other.

putatively freeing ourselves from the alienating other as a *focus imaginarius*, whose otherness is really *our investment*. We must redeem our investment in reality here, not in heaven beyond. When Marx rejects the Hegelian sense of the whole as he does, the value of the whole has to be reconfigured in relation to the projection of human power. Social will to power becomes the ultimate source of value; it makes valuable everything other than itself by imposing itself on that other.

There is a logic of tyranny implicit in this move. And we will repeat the old prison walk from the valueless whole to the nihilism of the humanism that has lost faith in the will to power that it previously disguised in its moralistic or socialistic ideals. We walk around ourselves as our own circles, or prisons, and we are back with raw power, and being as effective power, without worth. As caught in the logic of a certain self-determination, Hegelian, Marxist, and Nietzschean ethics lie on the same continuum.

With Marx, the historical immanence of the good is not immediate but must be mediated through historical opposition. We need to return to the discordance of social self-determination. Dualism comes back in the context of the class war that sets the human into antithetical groups and that must be overcome. Nor is the ethos devalued simply by doubt; it is made grim by the exploitative advances in industrial and productive power; this social situation reflects the fact that human powers have made human beings into merely effective power.[24] In the grim world of the early industrial proletariat, *the workers are nothings, they have become as nothing*; but this is the dialectical miracle—as nothing, they can become everything. Hence Marx's description of the proletariat: the universal class because they are nothing, the negative that will become everything. Very Hegelian.

In the meantime, the middle or interim time, their nothingness is turned into effective power by heteronomous powers—the exploiters. In the time to come, namely when the teleology of the good reaches its dialectical return to itself, this heteronomy will be destroyed. The nothings will become everything, because already as effective power, they are everything: the immanence of their radical self-determination is merely distorted by the heteronomous powers of the capitalist exploiters. As *nothing*, they are, in Hegel's phrase, the portentous power of the negative. And even though Hegel has suggested the freeing power of enforced work in the *Phenomenology*, Marx gives it economic and historical embodiment in the class war. True to the immanence of the good, the war itself

---

24. One might refer to the discussion of "utility," "value," and labor in *Capital*. I would say that here Marx shows himself heir to the devaluation of being in modernity and the loss of inherent value in other-being; value is defined in terms of human labor as the effective power. I do not see Marx as offering a defense measure of intrinsic value in Kant's manner, but as developing this devaluation in terms of, say, the industrial apotheosis of the powers of human labor which, as it turns out, conforms to a dialectical logic of social self-determination or species self-mediation, itself only lightly masking communist will to power.

will be the exacerbation of the opposition: heightening difference will bring about the collapse of difference in the class war.

There is finally to be *one mediation* beyond the antagonism of the class war: the whole will mediate with itself through its members. There is a principle of homogenization at work against the heterogeneity of discordant pluralism. There will be no irreducible others, for this is the sign of alienation, and this will be completely overcome. *The principle of totality embodies absolute autonomy*, for there is nothing other to it; it has immanently created itself through the productive power of the negative, the nothing that is the proletariat. The autonomous whole is, in that historical sense, *causa sui*, hence can be called an earthly God—Hegel's term for the state; or a mortal God—Hobbes's phrase for the Leviathan. Collective homogenizing, the pulverization of difference, both are driven by an ideal of absolute autonomy which here, in its logical consistency, mutates into *absolute tyranny*. And so this absolute autonomy shows its own truth as mastering will to power, that is, enslaving will to power.

This true "freedom" enforces obedience to the social totality. Does this our humanization become indistinguishable from the forced labor that dehumanizes? Such an autonomy would be a degrading heteronomy indeed. Why then should we be surprised if there is also the collapse of society and state and individual into one self-mediating whole? Is it because we too are bewitched by the ideal of absolute autonomy? We are now more willing to grant that this social holism has had the disastrous result of totalitarian politics. Have we awoken from the deeper bewitchment of absolute autonomy? The disastrous result can be traced to roots in a revolutionary interpretation of the dialectic of self-determination in which the negation of the other takes on a world-historical power that reaps the fruits of its own equivocity in the murder of millions. Magnified into world-historical visibility is the evil of a logic of *auto-nomos*: law of same, even as it rightly protests on behalf of the exploited other.

Of course, Marx was right to protest against the unjust exploitation of the worker; right to denounce the reduction of the human in alienated work; right to see the ideological superstructures as often masks of a will to power, the opposite of the ethical ideals the superstructures bespoke; right to see that masters do not yield their power easily, and may have to be fought. Yet his ethos of thinking is the very modern one of valueless being: for all his naturalism, ethos is one in which nature is for the human, a resource to be worked on by us, hence turned to our value. While a materialist, there is an idealism of the "for self" in his praxis. The lack of the agape of being is evident also in the privileged role of the master/slave dialectic and in the negativity of work as it imposes itself on the materiality of the other. In this dynamized instrumentalizing of being, there is the seed that will grow into a more overt will to power. But communist will to power is in exactly the same power play as capitalist will to power. The context of this dialectic of history is the very modern attitude to nature of mastery and possession.

In Marx, this finds expression in an ideology coarser than Hegel would countenance. We find an unstable mixture of dialectic and dualistic opposition here. Dialectic here more feeds the posture of crude opposition instead of leading to the discernment of the equivocal. The equivocal is flattened in one solution that will violently usher in the apocalypse—the revolution. The war is on God, on nature, on the class enemies, until finally the war turns on itself and the revolution cannibalizes its own children. It is the logic of negation that must negate itself in the end, a social self-determination that must become self-devouring. Why? Because it is unanchored from, because mutilating the agape of being, which is at the ground of value in the ethos.

Nietzsche's Higher Autonomy: Will to Power and Tyranny

Nietzsche would have it that the above scene socially dramatizes the revenge of the slaves, the nothings. In his unique way, Nietzsche is deeply attuned to the equivocal, here in the form of the dialectic of praxis relative to power. Yet for all of that, Nietzsche is a strange son of the ethics of self-determination. He revolted against the revolt of the many nothings, and in the name of the right to self-determination, of the few somethings. But in his hands, the all-pervasiveness of the thematics of will to power comes to the fore, not just relative to the so-called creative individual but to *the truth of the whole*. And this again brings us back to the fundamental question of the immanent good. The inherent exigence in self-becoming is connected to will to power. Thus so, as should be already clear, the ideal of autonomy can diversely mask will to power, especially when autonomy does not open beyond itself to relate to the other in another free way. This is a core equivocity in all of the above variations on dialectical ethics. If the equivocity is socially incarnate in Marxist ethics, it is individually incarnate in Nietzschean ethics. And if Marx is the equivocal doppelgänger of Hegel, Nietzsche is the equivocal doppelgänger of Kant—equivocal just because each had a lucidity that saw through some of the operative ambiguity in their forebears.

I understand Nietzsche in terms of the *transcending potency* of the ethical. This does not exclude, of course, the other potencies. He returns to the aesthetic potency insofar as the fleshed vitalities of life provide the matrix in which and out of which evaluations emerge: to be bodied is intrinsically to evaluate. This is so because the world as sensuous thereness, all being as aesthetic, is for him the show of will to power. Hence also Nietzsche's distemper with ascetical moralities that try to extirpate the will as at the root of life.[25] Likewise, the dianoetic potency

---

25. This Nietzschean aestheticization of the ethical, making oneself a work of art, is taken up by the later Foucault. Aesthetic self-creation is a poeticized form of auto-nomos, self-

of law has to be rooted in its originating source, as does any sense of transcendental self-determination. The source: proximately the creative lawgiver, mediately the will to power. And Nietzsche, at his best, is deeply aware of the living choreography between the eudaimonistic and transcending potencies—there is joy in self-surpassing itself, let the dreary last man in his dreamless self-satisfaction say what he will. What of the transcendent potency? Finally, there is no *transcendence as other* to human self-transcendence. God, as the hyperbolic good, is refused. Rather, the self-determining of the transcending potency *projects its own height*, its own transcendence, as the *Übermensch*. Transcendence as other is appropriated to immanent self-transcendence that glorifies itself in the *Übermensch* as *its own other*.

But why tie Nietzsche to dialectical ethics at all? First, because he is superbly attuned to the equivocal in relation to ethical value. Second, because he has a sense of the becoming of ethical value. Third, because he sees what is immanent in values not always concordant with the surface of what the values state. Thus he detects the secret self-discordance of ethical values. Fourth, because he is excellent in the way he instinctively has a feel for the transmutation of opposites into their opposites. Here he is not unlike Hegel, especially the Hegel of the *Phenomenology*.[26] This power of inversion became more pronounced as Nietzsche aged, and dialectical attunement to the equivocal becomes a masking of the *thinker himself* in the equivocal. This philosopher of the equivocal becomes more and more an equivocal philosopher. Here lies the difference with Hegel's dialectic: the latter sees the process of becoming as immanently exigent of an end. This end in Hegelian form goes in Nietzsche—there is no Hegelian *Aufhebung*. And yet there is an end, and it is a projected end, a postulated end, just like in Kant, but it is no longer the moral God. The immanent end is a higher human self-creation; it is ourselves as our own gods—or sacred cows.

Thus the self-legislation of Kantian morality is transformed into an autonomy that is *not under* any moral law, since it claims itself to be the source of the law. I am the law as the creative lawgiver; for in giving the law, I am both creator

---

legislation. If the aesthetic is important in metaxological ethics, and selving as aesthetic, and as a work of art, it is situated in a different sense of the ethos; hence the aesthetics of the ethical are not the same as Nietzsche's, which at best surpasses itself to erotic sovereignty, not agapeic selving. On this more fully, see my "Caesar with the Soul of Christ: Nietzsche's Highest Impossibility," *Tijdschrift voor Filosofie* 61 (1999): 27–61.

26. More might be said about master and slave morality in *On the Genealogy of Morals*. Nietzsche speaks of "the ripest fruit of the *sovereign individual*, liberated again from morality and custom, autonomous and supramoral (for "autonomous" and "moral" are mutually exclusive), in short, the man who has his own independent, protracted will, and *right to make promises*, . . . this master of a *free* will, this sovereign man" (*Genealogy*, second essay, section 2).

and created at once. Nietzsche knew the devaluation of being in modernity, though he took this valuelessness for the *truth of being*: no inherent value—value is what we stamp on the flux. Nietzsche recommends a more radical process of creative self-becoming. If there is an end, it is the human, as this also is the beginning and the middle. Postulating God becomes postulating self, and self becomes the *summum bonum*. Highest self-legislation: create *als ob* you were a god, create self *als ob* it were a god! [27]

The Nietzschean attunement to the equivocity of value detects the will to power at work in value, from low to high. This we must bring out and with hard honesty. There is no ground of the good other than ourselves as creators of the tablets of the law. As we create, so we can destroy; and destroy we must, in order to create ourselves again and anew. And we must create ourselves anew or we perish of despair and boredom. The law of life must include destruction, for without it there is no renewal of life. Hence Nietzsche's hymns to war: we need war to keep us awake to what we are. The dialectical posture of war was aesthetically appropriated by major lines of development in modern aesthetic culture: the creator, artist, poet, writer, or whatever must be set against what is, to stir up what has been repressed in the sedimentation of what is. The portentous power of the negative rides again, and not into the sunset but into the night, in the hope of a new dawn that—strangely—always seems aborted. Indeed, one wonders if it *must* be aborted. For were it to arrive, all hope of coming would perish, and the fulfilled future would reveal its hollowness.

In Nietzschean self-becoming, the good as other is turned back into self, and any transcendent good is reappropriated to human transcending (Zarathustra chants, man is a being who must be surpassed). Self-transcending becomes its own god, or good. The erotic sovereign is the highest in Hegel and Nietzsche, though we have a poetized sovereign with Nietzsche, with Hegel a more rational sovereign. Self-determining desire as will becomes will to power. *Transcendence is will to power.* If I am not mistaken, we are still in the horizon of Hegel's free will as the will that wills itself. It has now become the self-glorifying, self-affirming will to power.[28] I am aware of, I take pleasure in, Nietzsche's playful, pluralist, masking side, but there is *an earnest monist* in him too. This is most clear with the doctrine of will to power. He says, *Everything is will to power*, and nothing else besides; and we too are will to power and nothing else besides.[29] This is the

---

27. One of the first letters he wrote when he lost his sanity was to Burckhardt, in which he apologizes for being new to the business of being God: "I would much rather be a Basel professor than God," condemned to whiling away the next eternity by cracking bad jokes.

28. See again, "Caesar with the Soul of Christ."

29. On this more fully, see my "Rethinking the Origin: Hegel and Nietzsche," in *Hegel, History and Interpretation*, Shaun Gallagher, ed. (Albany: State University of New York Press, 1997), 92ff.

soul of the world, as well as its body. The incarnation of the truth is the aesthetic expression or show of will to power; goods also are the aesthetic bodies of will to power.

Nietzsche is the black sheep of the Kantian family, or the posthumously born bastard offspring of Kant. He carries the rogue gene of idealism that two generations later (having passed through idealism and the mutant Schopenhauer) throws up an offspring that would have horrified grandfather Kant. His genes also are from the family Idealism, where the constitutive subject determines the significance and intelligibility, even the being, of what is other. This subject is radicalized by Nietzsche in terms of creativity. It also is subverted, since the creative will to power that is now the thing in itself undermines the autonomous subject. Now you see sovereign subject; now there is no sovereign subject. Nietzsche is the dialectical union and rhapsodic peekaboo of these two extremes: self-glorification and *amor fati* in one: I am destiny, destiny is I. I am everything (all the names in history, Nietzsche says), I am nothing (perhaps a mere buffoon, he teases). Vates and clown.

Nietzsche is as much of a victim of the impoverished ethos of modernity as a fighter against that impoverishment. He is prescient about the nihilism that ensues on the absence of inherent good. But he is crude in connecting this too univocally to religion. And though he does see the relation to the equivocities of univocal scientistic objectification, he himself was not free of these equivocities. He wanted an ethics of rank, an aristocratic ethos restored, for such an ethos offers us the community that makes creative power genuinely possible. But his ethics of rank has its ethos drawn from an acceptance of the consequences of modern objectifying—I mean the lack of inherent meaning, the absence of inherent value. Values are projections of our will to power; there is nothing in the thing itself; there is no thing itself, only will to power, only interpretations. This is a voluntaristic idealism of the "for-self." But if *all* value is projection of will to power, how to establish *rank*? For if all is will to power and there is no inherent value, the whole is valueless and the truth of rank in value is actually *homogeneity*, since high and low each is a projection of will to power.

If we want to say that the higher is a more valuable projection of will to power, then something inherent in will to power is expressed more truly, more affirmatively, in such rank; and then we are back to some form of inherent value. The will to power must have some inherent exigence for good, if there are values that are inherently higher, that is, if like Nietzsche, we want an ethics that can *discriminate and discern differences*. This is what rank means. If an ethics of rank is to be retained, we must reformulate will to power to make it inherently hospitable to the discrimination of higher and lower values. If we reject that inherent hospitality, every assertion of will to power is merely the reassertion of nihilism.

Nietzsche so wanted to avoid inherent value that he was trapped in the latter nihilism, despite his excess of rhetoric about overcoming nihilism. And he wanted to avoid inherent value, because he wanted to avoid God, just as Kant wanted to put God in epoche to cling to the sacred cow of his own autonomy. Nietzsche may present himself as the all-too-knowing insider of the skeptical and ironical posture, but there are fundamental evasions that perhaps he suspected in his more lucid moments. Let us say: jealousy of Jesus and his superiority; the lie of godlessness that absolute autonomy perpetuates; the lie of autonomy that autonomy (become squintingly honest) wants to hide dishonestly in a subversion of autonomy, so that in its intoxication with subversion, it is actually a hiding of the truth from itself—even while it declaims ever louder about its own hard honesty.[30]

The ethics of will to power owes too much to the modern project of mastery, even if it aestheticizes, poeticizes the project, instead of mathematicizing it. We may diagnose nihilism, and do so brilliantly, but the diagnosis is no response to nihilism, if the question of inherent value is fudged, and fudged because of horror before God. Nietzsche was a good diagnostician but a miserable doctor or healer. His laughter briefly uplifts us, but there comes an emptiness to its forced buffoonery. The claim to be beyond good and evil reflects a kind of dialectical transcending of the ordinary opposition of good and evil. But there is an emptiness about this beyond, if it is the putative place from which a revaluation of all values is to be launched. Here there is no ground that can make that revaluation persuasive. We are asked to give ourselves over to Nietzsche's bewitchment. But this is poetic sorcery, even black magic. The enchantment does not last, even if it entrances many arrested in the adolescent posture of desire desiring itself, or the will willing itself, or eros in love with eros.

Far from being beyond opposition, Nietzsche is twisted in an antinomy for which he can provide no resolution. Let us say: Pagan mysticism of the primordial One versus the modern individualistic self-apotheosis. Or: self-affirming will to power as my will to power versus love of fate as the necessity of the will to power of the whole. (This is another variation of *the antinomy of autonomy and transcendence*.[31]) Nietzsche is both and neither. He lived the antinomy,

---

30. In Chapter 3, I mentioned the possible equivocity in relation to law and will to power: law can be used by the will to power as a means in its own game of self-mediation; within the law, the will to power camouflages itself. Marx and Nietzsche saw this. It is an important point. The law can be dictatorial, because the will to power dictates through the law; dianoetic univocity can be a mask of will to power. This can happen with the use of the law by religious people also: God's law becomes a good tool in the augmentation of my own will to power, and so on. Nietzsche is hypersensitive to some of these twisted equivocities.

31. Recall that if we absolutize autonomy, we relativize transcendence. If we absolutize transcendence, we must relativize autonomy. Subsuming both into human immanent self-transcendence will not do; we take the second path and less give up autonomy as we see its conversion into a different freedom.

was sometimes tortured by it, sometimes released by it into a beyond. But philosophically he could give no satisfactory account of it or the happening of release. He knew not himself nor of what he spoke, nor what he did, nor what was happening to him. He would say: it is good, would sing it is good—all that is, is to be affirmed. But how and why, if there is no inherent good or exigence to thus affirm, sing thus? Will to power could just as justifiably be disgusted with what is (Nietzsche's admitted temptation about man); or curse being, and say, "better not to be" (as Nietzsche, echoing the Silenus, did also say). Did Nietzsche ever surpass this? Is this not why we need lies, "noble lies"—at bottom being is horror? Once one knows this, how can one take any *focus imaginarius* seriously? To pretend these "noble lies" redeem life—is this to collude in bad faith with mere lies?

The upshot: there is no justification one way or the other; injustice is as justified or not, as justice; that is, there is no justice, which means there is no injustice. And Nietzsche does not demand Kant's *summum bonum* in response. He simply affirms the sheer fatality of all as the *"summum bonum"* (a *"summum bonum"* that, properly speaking, is no good at all). We have no right to or claim on anything, even as—astonishingly—we toy with the supreme claim to be as gods.

You might say: This is where nay-saying and yea-saying coincide in Nietzsche: the higher autonomy is obedience. Revolt is submission. But submission to what? What is the difference between the tyranny of will to power and fate? Why consent to *that*? Is this not another *servitude*? One can imagine old Kant turning in his grave and plaintively querying: What kind of an improvement is *that* on my dear *"summum bonum"*?

Nietzsche, however, was tortured by the face of meaningless evil, all of his braggadocio notwithstanding. He was one of the most tortured on this score, he could not stand it, and more often than not, he tried to hide it, from others, from himself. The solitude of Nietzsche was as much despair as dithyramb. He remained a sufferer from nihilism. His aestheticization of the good and the world is such that there can be no good, no rank, will it otherwise though he may. There is no transcendence to a meaningful end, since all ends are homogenized as projections of valueless will to power groundlessly willing values. They all come to nothing. You speak of destiny or fate, but if fate and the good cannot be brought together, it is all wishful thinking. All of the affirmation is vanity and a puff of wind. Too human, perhaps all too human; but it all comes to nothing.

Dialectic, Plato, Justice

This denouement of self-determination in will to power cannot mask the fact that the absence of inherent good is covered up by excessive noise about our purported creation of value. We distract ourselves from the death of the ethos with encomiums to our self-proclaimed creativity. Are the possibilities of dialectic all spent? No. Dialectic still has the power to bring us back to ourselves, hence also from this high-flying distraction that wings on enthrallment to self. Where there is only self, there is no self; where only self-affirming, no affirmation of self. Icarus needs a hidden hand to keep him aloft. What is that hidden hand?

Dialectic can return us to ourselves from the instability of the spurious self-satisfaction that touts its own creativity. Yet since this matter concerns the openness of freedom, no one can be forced out of this labyrinth of equivocal will to power. I know that hymns to the sacred cow of our creativity are sung widely and loud, but the noise of the singing is the index of its incredibility. If in the extremity of will to power we are strangely returned to nothing, this "nothing" might just be our interface with creation, hence the promise of always beginning again. Who knows? When we wake up to the baseless fabric of this self-hypnosis, perhaps a century hence, we will rub our eyes and say, what silly hymns we have sung—or shouted; let us again find a God worthy of song!

One aspect of the issue might be put this way: the archaic Platonic question asks some rehabilitation. This too is the question of tyranny. Is justice more fundamental than power? Is will to power more basic than good? Dialectic brings us back to ourselves, yes, but also to the immanent exigence we are and to the immanent sense of the good. The question is, is this immanent exigence will to power, or is it eros, itself marked by an immanent exigence for the absolute good? Absolute good already at work in eros, else we would not seek what we lack? Or is it more than eros, the "more" eros lacks and seeks—the plenitude of the agapeic power of being, immanent in the already given good of the "to be"? *Eros turranos* is matched by its heavenly double, *eros uranos*. Is there a superior other to free us from bondage to *autonomia turranos*?

Dialectic is self-mediating, but it is clear that the self it mediates can be diversely interpreted. The emphasis on autonomous self-determination as absolute leaves us with a fatal ambiguity about the transcendent good and this is liable to decline into a will to power in which there is finally not even self. Is the exigence for ultimate good just an exigence for absolute self-determining self-mediation, or is there an immanence of absolute transcendence in the self-transcendence of human desire? Does Nietzsche's default bring us back to Plato's promise? If efforts to absolutize an ethics of autonomous self-determination seem to break down finally into will to power, or the closure of self on itself, hence into bondage not freedom, what then? Being brought back to ourselves, are we turned back to consider ultimate good as other to our self-determination, even in our self-determination. Having been brought back to ourselves as exigence for absolute goodness, we are turned back to consider the good as absolute, as other to our self-mediation, even in our self-mediation. In the claim to autonomy, a true self-knowing comes to open to the good beyond autonomy. This also is a freeing of the ethical self—beyond the bondage of autonomous freedom. This leads to the metaxological way.

The question is not transcendence versus immanence; not heteronomy versus autonomy; not Hegel's unhappy consciousness versus the satisfactions of autonomous immanence; not "Plato versus Homer," as Nietzsche would have it. These forms of "versus" are the residues of dualism in the inheritance of dialectical self-determining. The question concerns the transcendence of the good to self-transcendence. The breach in autonomous self-mediation, and the opening of freedom beyond autonomy, mediate anew the option: the good versus the valueless whole. Clearly Plato does not put the question in such post–Hegelian, post–Nietzschean terms. Yet these terms are not unfaithful to the reserve of promise in Platonic dialectic as showing the insinuation or pull or solicitation of transcendence itself in our erotic self-transcendence. Platonic dialectic rivets us back on ourselves by the hiddenness of transcendence shown in our own words—our *logoi* turn us back to ourselves, where we are turned beyond and above ourselves.

What is the Cave? It is the equivocal as the dissimulation of *logoi*, our words as screens or shadows or silhouettes of truth. What is the release? Seeing the truth in the equivocal, seeing in the *logoi*, seeing who and what we are, but also seeing beyond. For the *logoi* make desire of the good mindful: words give mind to desire. *Logos* gives *nous* to *eros*. What mindfulness discovers is our transcendence towards the good. Dialectic is the self-return of words that raise words above equivocal immanence, and releases the *logoi* into the truth of the good.

As much as Nietzsche, Plato was a philosopher of the equivocal. As attuned to the equivocity of value as Nietzsche, his dialectic is a way of discerning the genuine in the equivocal itself. What Plato discovered is finally more complex and more subtle than either Hegel or Nietzsche, since the stunning realization of the good beyond all of our mediation appears in all of our efforts to mediate. The extremity of mediation is approached, and something beyond the medium, the middle, comes to be understood. This Plato calls the good *epikeina tes ousias*. This is the ultimate horizon in which the hospitality of being to good is approached. It is not a determinate good, but goodness itself as the overdeterminate source without which nothing would be and nothing would be as good. The naming of the good thus shows Plato to be deeply attuned to the ultimate question concerning the good of it all, the question of nihilism, as we might now formulate it.

Here we also meet the question of the good beyond good and evil, as proportioned to our moralities in the middle. This is the question of *the beyond of the good* and of the limits of self-determination. We are pushed back and beyond modern autonomy, hence beyond its form of dialectic towards a renewal of the *metaxu*. This has nothing to do with a tyrannous heteronomy. The transcendence of the good is, as later we will see more fully, an agapeic *heteros* that releases a different freedom beyond autonomy. The transcendence of the good is yet in deep community with our self-transcending. It is beyond will to power, beyond justice too, as measured on an exact one-to-one univocal correspondence. This good as other is the agapeic origin that releases.

Socratic–Platonic dialectic is enacted in dialogue and in relation to others. But I and the others stand under the good, whose exigence appears in our *eros*, *nous*, and *logos*. This dialectic is an interplay of many, in the ethos of the good, each an incarnation of the good working in their *eros, nous, logos*, and working so that the interplay itself brings the good at play into mindfulness and life, pointing to the transformation of soul, of life, of communities.[32] Plato, it will be said, has been "refuted." True, he is not to the taste of many today. Taste is as fickle as the weather. The night falls, the day comes. The many who mass, with the courage of crowds, under the banner of Nietzsche, will mass under another flag, when the weather shifts.

Equivocal Dialectic, Erotic Sovereignty, Agapeic Relation

You might ask: Can we avoid obedience? The answer seems to be no. But then who or what do we obey? God? Nature? Ourselves? Society? Nothing? Total autonomy might seem to be to obey nothing but oneself; but then we must submit to ourselves; and so as masters of ourselves, we end up as slaves of ourselves. Or if we obey nothing, we are nihilists; but even here we end up as puppets of the nothing; for all of our gestures of originality come to nothing; our being bound by nothing gives us up to the fate of being as nothing. No doubt, we might dismiss this again. But in the name of what? If we are as nothing, then if it is in the name of ourselves, it is again in the name of nothing. You might say: these possibilities are all exaggerations and extremes. Perhaps. But that is precisely the point: once we worship the god "autonomy," it is not evident that we can place boundaries so easily, since to place a boundary is to determine, and hence to *relativize* autonomy, in the crucial sense of bringing it into relation to something other to itself. And is this not to court again some form of "obedience"? There is a lethal consistency in these exaggerations or extremes that plots remorselessly the destiny of autonomy unbound. You might say: forsake the extremes for the moderate middle. But what if the modern middle has been relentlessly eaten away by the presence there of these extremes that here and there take off the mask of extremism and show the truth of what is secretly at work? Though we might shrink from this, if we look thoughtfully at many trends of our world, this is no exaggeration. We say we are autonomous not obedient humans, but in our autonomy we know not what we obey. We know not what god we serve, if now it can be called a god at all.

But perhaps the issue is not quite unbound autonomy versus obedience; or unbounded autonomy that falls into the bondage of equivocal submissions.

---

32. See *BB*, Chapter 9, on intelligibilities with respect to Socratic–Platonic dialogue.

Suppose unbound autonomy is already a bind, a contraction of the promise of freedom? Suppose autonomy is freedom contracted onto "self"? The promise of freedom is a being free, but before that, it is being freed. Being freed, we are free. But being free(d) is not originally the product of freedom but the gift of freedom. The giving of freedom is not first either obedience or autonomy; it is not a being subject to the law as other or to self-law. It comes from a giving beyond the law. This giving is not our own. This giving gives us to be ourselves. But freed to be ourselves, we turn around ourselves, turn back to ourselves, and reck not this giving source as other, as not our own. Becoming heedless of, or refusing, or revolting against, the giving origin, our destiny is to be bound to ourselves as, so to say, the false double of God. We usurp the freedom to create ourselves, and our autonomy produces itself, but it gives birth to itself as the counterfeit of God. Many thinkers in modernity have come to see God as the false double of man. It seems truer, in fact, to say the opposite. Modernity too often was, and is, a project for the production of man as the false double of God. If all of our values are shaped within the ethos of this project, they all are tinged with the counterfeits of God. This is true even for the very same values that are genuine and true within an ethos where God is the original. Good men, without God, become themselves false doubles of God.

The difficulty extends to the doubling of the ethos that we have created around ourselves. We *redouble ourselves* in the ethos that we have reconfigured: nature neutered rather than the ambiguous milieu of being, saturated with the equivocal showings of value; and in whatever direction we turn, the spellbinding power of the human being seems to redouble itself indefinitely. This reconfiguration may well secrete a derived ethos that is made for the self-doubling of autonomy, but it offers stony soil for a freedom beyond autonomy, beyond self-doubling. In the chiaroscuro of the ethos, the false doubles of freedom cast their spell. They are mimicries of release and they cannot be discerned for what they are unless we have the finesse to interpret the counterfeits of God. The false doubles of freedom enthrall us with the bewitching power of a god. What power exorcises us and releases us from the thrall of the false doubles? Do we not need a reborn finesse to understand agapeic release—originally as giving us to be, but as calling us to be ourselves as free; and then to be free as released into being agapeic and into the fling of joyful generosity, beyond our endlessly dissimulating circulation of ourselves around ourselves? Who or what can give us this reborn finesse?

At best, modern dialectic tends to make freedom into what I call erotic sovereignty, that is, the coming of self to itself, out of its initial lack, but in interplay with the other, realizing its own power to be, in such a way as to attain some self-fulfillment. This fullness is never absolute wholeness, nevertheless some finite wholeness is not impossible. Transcending can come to some finite measure of self-fulfillment: the lack driving beyond comes into itself so that it is no longer driven beyond by lack merely; it is in some deep and enigmatic way at home with itself. This does not mean transcending ceases, but where it continues, it shows some fullness realized, rather than lack to be realized. This realized selving is not self-constituted, for it does not come to be outside of mediation with the others. In fact, the other is needed not only to fulfill the lack but also to give us back to ourselves. I am given to be myself because the other gives me to myself; without the other, the circuit of self-mediation would be short-circuited.

That said, erotic sovereignty is tempted to come to rest in itself and to stress the self attained rather than the giving of the other needed for self-attaining.[33] Highest dialectical freedom is then not a simple autonomy but a release to self that remembers the others that give that freedom to itself. *We are relatively self-determining, because we are qualified in our release by the giving of the other which allows us to be as other.* Dialectical freedom as erotic sovereignty is already in seed beyond autonomy, because its community with the allowing other is already immanent in its self-determining. The giving of the others is immanent in the giving of the self to itself. Thus the immanent exigence is not just the voice of the self calling to itself (as it seems to be in Heideggerian conscience). The voices of others are sounding in one, and not just the human others in fellowship with one (sometimes dominating one). Against an ethics of autonomy that equivocates on the relation to the other, the point is not a heteronomy that stifles freedom but a different heteronomy, an other otherness that is releasing rather than constraining.[34] The point is the agapeic relation.

This concerns our being in the between insofar as our self-surpassing goes beyond itself from more than lack, and beyond erotic self-determination. There is a release towards the other for the sake of the other. This also is implied from the side of the other as giving me to be myself, hence opening the space between us as one of pluralized freedom beyond self-determination. We are returned to the ethos in terms of its being *criss-crossed by the agapeic relation*, by its being from the origin the promise of the agapeic community which, given the internal complexity of its participants, is quickly stressed this way, that way, and indeed stressed into a distress where the agapeic relation becomes incredible. We need metaxological ethics to make sense of the service of the other in the agapeic relation.

We also return to the hospitality of the ethos to the good. If there is agapeic selving, it does not come to be out of the emptiness of the good but out of its

---

33. See my "Dream Monologues of Autonomy," in *Ethical Perspectives* 5:4 (1998): 305–321, in which I retell the story of the prodigal son from the standpoints of Kant, Hegel, Marx, and Nietzsche, and the old man.

34. Kant is not at all clear about this other heteronomy. He just sees heteronomy as the source of all false moralities, though the kingdom of ends is unintelligible without this other other, which is not the external determination of Newtonian causality.

effective being at work before I come to myself, without which I would never be given the power to come to self. Similarly, with community, the agapeic relation suggests a promise already at work in order for community, in a more overt, determinate sense, to be constituted. The ethos is the promise of the agape of being. In bringing us back to ourselves, dialectic also sends us beyond ourselves in a new restless transcending in which the immanent exigence comes into its own in mindfulness that the ethos is the promise of this agape. We are the charge to realize freely this promise. This is the charge to be agapeic in free community beyond self-determination. There is a dialogue of transcendence in the immanence of self-determining; but our self-determining is participant in a dialogue that is not immanence at home with itself, but the converse of transcendence and immanence within the immanence of self and community. The metaxological way is to articulate the agapeic relation as the fuller truth of dialectical ethics.

CHAPTER FIVE

ETHOS AND METAXOLOGICAL ETHICS

The Archeology of the Good

Where are we? Still in the play of indetermination and determination of the ethos. What there is the difference between the dialectical and metaxological ways? Both mediate the play of univocity and equivocity, the first with respect to self-determining being, the second with a fuller intermediation with otherness. The latter calls for a different *archeology* of the good, not just its teleology. For dialectic, the beginning is an indefinite, to be made more and more determinate, to the end of self-determination. In the end is the true good. This is faithful to the Aristotelian line or the Hegelian erotic teleology: the end is self-realizing, or realized being for self. By contrast, the metaxological is recalled to the *otherness of the origin*. The beginning intimates the overdetermination of the good—not indefinite, but too much: out of this surplus, determinate forms of good come to shape. This is the origin as agapeic good. This overdetermined good companions all moves from indefinite to determinate to self-determination. An exclusively dialectical view is not fully mindful of this companionship.

The origin as agapeic suggests an elemental worth to the "to be" (see *BB*, Chapters 6 and 13). To be is to be given to be by the origin; but given being is other to the origin, and for itself, and good as for itself. This "being good" is not antithetical to being in communication with other-being. To give being is to communicate the good of being. Finite beings also communicate the good: in some cases, simply by what they are, fulfilling their natures according to allotted destinies; in other cases, greater openness goes with a more extensive range of self-transcending, as well as more intensive selving and depth of original power. In the latter cases, by responding to the call of being good, the creature answers for what it is. This call and answering are themselves communications calling for communities. Being good is a doing of the good in community. And if in our open transcending we find the *promise of allowance*, there can be no one simple way to fulfill that promise. The goodness of being is surplus, and we are guests of a feast that surpasses us.

Singulars within creation also are good—concretions of the "to be" as good. Singulars are harmonies of integral being. Their coming to be is inseparable from such integrity; were they not "one" in a fundamental sense, they would not be at all. But this is no block creation. There is a pluralism to creation, reflected in the pluralism of original powers marking different beings. The good of beings is shown in the ontological integrity, out of which a being's powers emerge into expression, and shown in the harmony of wholeness it seeks to attain in fulfilling these its powers. Given to be, beings are open to the promise of realizing themselves, as for themselves. The good of beings is thus inseparable from the original power of transcending (the very *doing* of its being) that the gift of the finite "to be" concretizes.

The openness of creation means that it is not the self-determination of the divine, not the necessary block of nature that is the body of Spinoza's God, or the necessitated finiteness that is the self-externalization of Hegel's God. The agapeic origin gives a world for itself, and as in promise to be itself through itself. The promise seeks out fulfillment, and in that regard the good is in the end; but this is possible because the good as original releases the finite into its own being for itself. This is not to be forgotten, even as we transcend towards an end. Ends sought in the between may be genuinely good, but they are not the absolute good. Nothing finite is a final measure of what this is.

If promising beings seek the redemption of their promise, do we have the dominance of being for-self? This is not so, since the range of powers of being remains metaxological rather than exclusively self-mediating. This range involves other-relating as well as self-relating powers. We find a tense doubleness here. In fact, this is the basis for the intense equivocity of good/evil, as well as the labyrinth of the heart. This is the juncture of plural possibilities at the heart of the potencies of the ethical: the coming together of self-transcending and transcendence as other, or their splitting or wounding. This doubleness defines the communicative promise in the original power of all beings.

The range of goods cannot be separated from the range of metaxological power to dwell in the fullness of the between, open to the other as transcendent in the very unfolding of self-transcending. Communication with the other goes hand in hand with intensive self-relation, which is exhibited variously at different levels of ontological richness. The range of transcendence towards the other is expressive of depth of ontological intensity. Thus communicative power as metaxological, the ability to be self beyond self with the other, cannot be separated from the richness of the concretion of singular power, reflected in the intensive innerness of selving. This is why the human being (as far as we know) is the most communicative in creation and the most intensively singular: most selfless, most selfish; most open and out in the open, and most idiotic, reserved and secret.

The doubleness directs us to these two sides. First, there is the good of "wholeness" that expresses the integrity of being as seeking to fulfill its power most completely. Second, the relation to the other brings us back to the surplus of the good. The good as more than our good becomes more of moment. Our transcending to wholeness gives way in itself to an infinite restlessness that seeks what as good in itself is no finite good. There is no rest in a self-determining autonomy but a breach beyond finite wholeness, which offers the breakthrough of a freedom beyond autonomy. This freedom releases the energy of the good in giving towards the other. Beyond autonomy it brings us to goodness as agapeic giving, as well as sends us in search of a different telos beyond self-determining: to be ourselves agapeic and in community with the origin as agapeic.

This doubleness is reflected in the difference between erotic sovereignty and agapeic service. These are the flowers of our self-transcending as coming to itself and its justified autonomy, and as exceeding itself and its autonomy in the release of a more ultimate freedom that communicates in a being for the other that is a giving of good. What is intimated in the arche here becomes community in humanity, itself now called to be a concretion of agapeic community and witness to the ultimate agapeic source. This end is participation in community with the arche and hence itself is a finite form of the community of agapeic service. This is the good we must seek to be, failing again and again, and beginning again and again, as we must. I now explore the metaxological meaning of the potencies of the ethical, but first a word about the surplus of the good.

The Surplus Generosity of the Good

Sometimes the "too muchness" of thereness is oppressive; other times it falls into the invisibility of everydayness; and still other times it is alive with a shimmer of inexpressible worth. To be in the between is to suffer the thereness. This is first an undergoing; we do not choose it but find ourselves in it, now buoyed up, now flat, now weighted down. In every instance, thereness is saturated with some communication of value. Even insipid life is not flat of value, and this is clearly so with being weighted down, or elevated. There is an otherness to *being at all* that now seems void of meaning, now assumes the urgency of a message, communicating a good that teases, or torments, or turns tender on our terrible exposure. Univocity and dialectic seek too much to determine the surplus; metaxological mindfulness, like equivocal attunement, comes into the knowing of surplus beyond our mediation. The equivocal attunement does not always see that, beyond our mediation, this surplus sends its own shoots of communication and thus mediates with us: to feel the oppressive weight of being there, or to be lifted by a release, both are beyond mediation as self-mediation. They are opaque communications, intermediations from beyond us. We alone do not intermediate the good.

Suppose we have the presentiment even in the oppressiveness: it is good. What communicates this? Are we ourselves communicating with ourselves?

Something other? Would there be any between did not that other come? The very being of the between is constituted by communication. Creation is a communication, and in the middle we have a presentiment of its mysterious goodness, as we live the feeling of "it is good to be," and are called to live up to the "it is good" of being. The communication is extremely enigmatic to us, and first we have no ken what it is we touch or what touches us. We are like tiny insects, laboring to climb a spiky stalk, and we put out feelers into the wide and empty air; and when we know a warmth on our surfaces, it is beautiful, but we do not know it is the sun that shines, and that the vast expanse of open air is the inexhaustibility of the between. Our feelers twitch, and our small minds are given the spasm of a glimpse that all this is the great mystery of the good. We baptize as "world" our twitch and feel. Some twitches, say, some dialectical and univocal ones, even feel their "world-historical significance," or feel assured of their "scientific-technological progress." Yet something about the touch of air and warmth has passed into us, and life is more difficult yet more true. The metaxological way is chastened by knowing the meagerness of its knowing, knows it does not know. More affirmatively than the equivocal way, it lives on this border of mystery. This too we may come to know more wakefully as the chiaroscuro of the good.

Our argument comes later, but if it is not grounded on the givenness of the ethos, then it is the insect flying through empty air and thinking that the freedom of the air is its only ground. The argument comes from what we cannot know at the beginning, for knowing of a more determinate sort comes later. The later argument tries to construct determinate accounts of the surplus given in the beginning. We come to be out of an origin that initially we cannot know determinately, for there is an indeterminacy prior to such cognitive determination. Being given to be is not best described as a thrownness into absurdity, or a condemnation to a hostile environment. It is being offered the gift of life as itself the elemental good we live. No doubt this gift is not Paradise, and there are too many occasions when the gift of life itself is communicated in circumstances hostile to its receipt; or that conspire against its joy; or that evoke hatred in those who are being gifted; or that sometimes come with a baffling deformation that tempts us to see evil there, not good.

Image: A deformed child is born. We recoil. Why? The child lacks the full promise of the good we anticipated. We need not recoil, we can have faith that there is good in this, though this faith is hard, maybe divine. But *that we recoil* is a secret compliment to the good that seems to be not given; we have expected the properly formed, perhaps taken it for granted; we may have forgotten that all of life, formed or deformed, or what we take as such, is given, is gift. This is not something we can demand, or over which we have command, or can count on, absolutely. We are dependent on the giving source. And when we see the (to us) deformed, we may be tempted to see the source as other than good; as no source, or perhaps as impotent, or perhaps as malicious.

But why *recoil* at all? What is it in us that recoils? Can it be pinned down, made completely determinate? Does it not suggest an anticipation of good inscribed in our being, an expectation that is our being? The ontological inscription of that indeterminate anticipation suggests that the recoil is an *indirect mediation of our relativity* to the source as good. The recoil testifies to an elemental expectation that the givenness of being is good, more elemental than the determinate deformations and disappointments that will later come on the scene and trouble us and make us suffer, and maybe rebel or revolt. The indeterminate intimation of the good of the giving source is mirrored in the indeterminate expectation of the good of being that we are and live. Our dwelling in the ethos, our being in the between, testifies to an original indeterminate togetherness of these two overdetermined sources.

You say: all this seems quite "metaphysical." Very well: this is because "being good" has to be understood all the way down, as well as all the way up. Can we otherwise avoid being pulled into the orbit of ethical nihilism? For this nihilism is not first the failure of humans to be ethical, to live up to genuine ideals. More elementally, is it not a loss of a full feeling for the fullness of the ethos? Loss signaled by the loss of presentiment of the giving source as good, and the trust that there is a good in the giving, not of our doing or making but in which we enigmatically participate? The loss of the ethos takes the form of the so-called death of God. And this is correct in that this is the loss of the elemental good of being in the between. It is not primarily a matter of finding the arguments for God unconvincing, or finding oneself living fine without God, or indeed even of turning against God. It is a loss of the mindful attunement between the indeterminate openness of elemental expectation in us and the goodness of the source.

This loss can take place behind our backs, occasioned by the formation of ways of life that cumulatively turn the ethos more into a mirror of the human being than the source of otherness which gifts all being with the goodness of its being at all. We live the ethos with an emphasis on our own powers of self-mediation, but in the process we crowd out, slowly, inexorably, with a gentle stifling, the subtle communication of the source as good. We are responsible for the loss and not responsible; responsible though we do not know it, and we think we are being the most responsible, since we answer primarily to our own powers of self-mediation, and not to anything other. But this answering just to ourselves is the rub. The ethos communicates the source as other, and this the metaxological way must recall, but this recall means breaking the circuit of self-mediation that has crowded out, or subordinated, or refused the more elemental character of this primal relatedness to the other. The fundamental enabling power of being is forgotten, in our being enabled to be ourselves, as we claim to define the good for ourselves and through ourselves. Metaxological mindfulness returns us to a new rapport with the between as good, as ethos in communication with the origin.

Is not late modernity anomalous in this regard? We have set ourselves up over against the surplus of otherness; stripping it of the charge of the good, we also have stripped it of the signs that point towards the ground of the good. As we saw, being there becomes worthless. In tandem, we set ourselves up as ground of value who impose on this valueless thereness values of our construction. This construction is really based upon a destruction and itself is an aggression that congratulates itself on its own superiority to other-being as other. All of this is the result of certain developments of being in the between, especially the absolutization of our being as self-determining. Previous epochs, we may say, were less powerful, in being determined by what was other; and yet this "impotence" was not without its glory, in that beyond the wretchedness, humans were sometimes visited with glory, in the breakthrough of the gift of the origin, the vision that the between is truly beyond our power, and that this is a good thing, that it is just the good of the between that its good is not our production. Its gift is the good, albeit ambiguous to us, sometimes threatening, sometimes destructive of us. Just this appreciation of gift can nurture a gratitude to the ground of good. We are not in our own hands. We receive the gift. We can be thankful; we can rage, or whine, or find sly ways to get our own way, to the end of finding that it is not ours, and will be taken from us, as we go as naked into death, as when we first came into birth. Naked, we spend our lives covering ourselves, but in the end, as at the beginning, there is nakedness: exposure and vulnerability beyond all human power, beyond the power of nature itself as a totality; vulnerability and exposure beyond the whole.

The nakedness can be lived with hard-won consent, or perhaps with a gift of "yes" that comes out of nothing, or with anxiety and trembling, or with wrath. And yet for all of this, an *ethics of gratitude* can be called forth. This ethics is not supinely impotent because the ground is beyond our power; it generates a response in us, a corresponding *ethics of generosity*. We are grateful for the generosity of the ground, and we respond to this with thanks, and with thanks lived as a form of existence. For it is not only the generosity of the giver that is important but the generosity of the receiver. We are the receivers, and strangely, it is the generosity of the other that possibilizes our comportment of generosity towards the other. Generosity entails no servile reception or abjection before the other. In fact, the other's generosity does more than occasion our gratitude; it charges us with the living of generosity. Only a generous person can properly receive a gift. The *receiver* must have generosity to receive the generosity of the giver, otherwise the gift is perverted in thankless grabbing. Think of a person who cannot receive a compliment. Think of those who are unable to be gracious—their inability turns the gift into something else, turning it aside. The gift needs the graciousness of the receiver to be itself fulfilled as gift. Thus the gift is the promise of a fulfilled community. The promise can be lost in more than one place. The gift is an occasion that occasions giving, as much by the receiver as by the giver. There is a reception that is a giving, for it is an opening of the self to the other, and this opening is the greatest gift—not the thing given, but the mode of being of the giver and receiver, as with the widow who gave her last mite.

So also generosity is not only relative to the giver. Those who cannot receive a gift lack the spirit of generosity. We must be generous to allow the generous other to offer its gift. It is the spirit of generosity that is more than us and makes us more than ourselves, and that comes over us in the gift of the ground. If we are obsessed with doing all for ourselves, of proving that we are in charge or in control, even if we seem utterly noble in insisting on giving to others, we may, in fact, have perverted the occasion of generosity. Our "generosity" may be the pride that insists on itself and hence may not be generous at all.[1] The depth of generosity is sustained by humility in relation to the ultimate.

This means the willingness to put oneself in the relative position, not the unconditional. Strangely, the relative position is the absolute position, insofar as it is the position of relativity in which being there for the other becomes an ethical reality. Being relative in the spirit of generosity is the unconditional relation, not the unconditional self-relation that would only relate to the other out of its prior securing of itself. Relative to the surplus, this prior securing is a perversion of what the prior is, for what is prior is the gift of being as good. Securing ourselves as mastering powers cuts us off from the fullness of the gift, even though it is the gift itself that allows this cutting off of the gift. If the project of modernity is this securing of itself, it must risk the loss of the metaxological between and hence of the ethos as ambiguous cipher of the grounding good. Before that, and still for many in their heart of hearts, the good is God and nothing but God. The singularity of this good is alone what makes more than aloneness possible. This good communicates the being of the good as being in relation to the other, and of enabling self-being in the web of relations that constitutes the between. That there are communities of being in the between is already a sign of the communication of the good. We have taken up domesticated residence in these communities and have forgotten how astonishing it all is. There is an ethical need for the rebirth of agapeic astonishment, for this is the opening in which the ethics of gratitude and generosity is born for us.

You sigh with faint exasperation: But are we not all now postmodern—not modern, not premodern? I sigh too. The equivocal again dons its seductive mask. There is a "postmodernity" that, in all humility, seems to be coming around to a new insight into the patience of the human before God, and the active patience that is the ethics of generosity, and the life of service going with it. There also is a "postmodernity," and this seems the more frequent, which is an accentuation of

---

1. Aristotle's *megalopsuchia?* Descartes's *generosité?* Nietzsche's *gift-giving virtue?* Finally they bathe in their own self-worth, or self-esteem.

the modern, an aggravation of the powers of self-determining, but now grown skeptical and bitter about themselves: wanting still to be absolute, insisting on themselves always, secretly now, overtly now; and yet knowing that these cannot be absolute, for a presentiment of the other has made its way into the heart of humanity, puffing itself up as a project; but the project is wounded by a shadow or a compassion or a terror or an abyss or . . . some indeterminate nothing.

Then the self-determining human lacerates itself, as it still clings to itself; preaches about the other, while still shouting about its right to be in control; vacillates between knowing in its heart of hearts that the tale is told and the impotence to let go of its own power. The laceration brings us to no self, no God; and we are in the between with a bewilderment we hysterically call creative freedom, all the while without wise counsel about our bewilderment and our hysteria. "Having your cake and eating it" is an old phrase for this; but the cake that is had is just as deficient in nourishment as the cake that is eaten. The simple answer is to rethink the good of the human as more ultimate than the human; to have the humility to say that numberless generations of humans were there before us, closer to the divine traces of the ethos than we are, and for all the sound and fury and mire of man, quietly aware that the ultimate "yes" is the "yes" of the divine and our "yes" to it.

The Idiocy of Being Good in the Between

As there is an idiocy of being, so there is an idiocy of being good. "Idiocy" names the initially unarticulated intimacy with the good. This is not a sameness to be caught in a definition of generality or that univocal mind can formulate in stable identities. I mean a singular happening that as intimate is not straightforwardly public, not fully available for mastery in terms of neutral objectifiable standards. Nor is this happening any monadism that closes into a knot of solitude or circle of being for itself, without relation or community. A kind of solitude may mark singularity, but no solitude is absolutely cut off from community. The intimacy of the idiocy is both a self-intimacy and also an unthematic mindfulness that self is with others always and from the start. The ontological definition of the intimate "*solo*" is always to be with the other, even when not knowing this, and indeed when not knowing itself.[2]

"Idiocy" also names an indeterminate preobjective and presubjective "awareness" that is not any definite awareness, and that floats with a predeterminate sense of "self" that is no definite self, that yet precedes any definite formation of

2. See my "The Solitudes of Philosophy," in *Loneliness*, Lee Rouner, ed. (Notre Dame, Indiana: Notre Dame University Press, 1998), 63–78.

self, and out of which crystalize different formations of selving. The innerness to self initially is not itself determinate, and, as alone, not for itself alone. A dualism of "being alone" and "being with others" is a later crystallization of determinate formations of self and other out of the indeterminacy. If dualism is not always helpful here, neither is dialectic, since it thinks in terms of determining the inde-terminate, even if in terms of self-determination. The opening or beginning is idiotic in a bad sense for it: merely indefinite. Metaxological thinking better sees the overdetermination of this intimacy, the surplus not only of being and the ethos but of the human self that comes to itself more determinately out of this surplus. It acknowledges the place of determination and self-determination but sees beyond the negative equivocal, sees more than ambiguous confusion to be put in its categorial place.

This idiocy is an awakening. The community of being as good comes to indeterminate mindfulness in the *innerness of selving* that is the mysterious com-ing to self in primal self-awakening to the "to be"—a coming that is of the essence to singular selfhood and yet irreducibly communal, at once a relation to itself and a relation to what is other. It includes a relation to self given to itself, not by itself, but by the agape of the origin; and given to itself, not solely for itself, but in relation to all that is other. The idiocy awakens to the agapeic relation. This is the relation of community in which self-relation and other-relatedness are always in togetherness, yet irreducible to each. The idiocy of being good shows the agapeic relation coming to mindfulness of itself in the irreducible singularity of human innerness as itself, always from the origin, in intimacy with what is other to itself.

I connect this to the elemental, nondeterminate mindfulness of *simply being*. This indeterminate awareness/nonawareness of simply being is saturated with the value of being, but we cannot uninterruptedly endure this value. Our being shuns it in the tiredness of our bodies and minds.[3] Interestingly, children do not willingly shun it, since there seems to be nothing more they fight than having to go to sleep. The surge is young, and it lives in the good of being, and would play in it sleeplessly, did not the frailty or weakness of its incarnation return it to mindlessness. The play of the child is "mindless" in another sense, in that it sim-ply lives the elemental good of the "to be." Insomnia is for those who have been rent by time; for memory and anticipation, and the frustration of time born of them, or the excitement, all these make one sleepless. This is not the child's lived,

---

3. For instance, experiences such as insomnia (see *PU*, Chapter 3) bring us back to this idiocy: sleepless we would escape the "that it is" into the rest of sleep, but we cannot. This weariness of being is the necessity that we finite entities have to return to the other side of the wakening up to the good of being; we can only endure that awakening intermit-tently; it is too much for us, and we must sleep.

affirming sleeplessness. Insomnia is the sleeplessness that would be rid of itself, and turn off from reality, and return to non-knowing, back through the idiocy and out of the equivocity of good and evil.[4]

The elemental good of "to be" is idiotic. Simply to be is good: not just good for a purpose or a use, though this is true too. Just good: elemental simpliciter; good without a determinate why or wherefore or wherefrom. And this more-than-determinate good is strangely always singular, not vague good in general, just as the elemental being of the "to be" also is not vague being in general. This person, that flower, that horse, but as pervaded by a suggestion of the good of simply being: zoned on the singular, but in the good of the singular a sense of the good of simply being, a good that is not the possession of any singular; the goodness of the gift of being incarnated in the being of this, this, this, as each an irreducible good. How to prove this? There is no "proof." We must wake up to it. Some ways of seeming to wake up are only fallings into a deeper slumber. Since we cannot fully wake up, uncertainty and indeterminacy always go with this presentiment. Communicating it is difficult. Images help. Here are some.

Image: A baby is born. We have waited for many months with expectancy. The waiting now is not disappointed and there we hear the scream of the new arrival: eyes crunched up against the strain of passage and perhaps in possum protection against the otherness that waits it; wet body, blood, fluid, disheveled arrival, mysterious newness, unformed and indeterminate, yet completely formed and intricately singular; startled, sleepy eyes look out on this strange world for the first time, and it knows not who or where it is. It is in the idiocy of being, and already the indeterminacy of that idiocy begins to be shaped in terms of the relentless unfolding of time and its own self-becoming.

What is it like to look at the world, fresh to the between, as a baby? We have done it, and we do not know, we cannot know. And yet, close perhaps to the newborn baby is the Tao, said to be an unborn baby, and the way of heaven. It is the way of the good of being. Are we shocked into an intimation of this by this arrival of the intimate stranger? Often yes; though we may be too far from rapport with the idiocy in ourselves to let ourselves be startled by the new coming; so busy, so consumed with ambition to manage the determinacies of life, fooled by feeling that one is in charge of the middle. How are we to look on the child? With wakefulness to the fact that it is good that it is; that it is at all, is its good; one is to love it for itself. The freshness of this intimate stranger may be peculiarly burdensome. We see the virgin snow and flare with the shame that we are stained.

---

4. There are other experiences: sexual orgasm is idiotic; like the face of grief, the contorted outcry of pleasure sometimes sounds like pain; paroxysm of the flesh not knowing the difference between pain and pleasure, violence and tenderness; a mixture of intensification of life and the loss of life.

The idiocy has been shaped in us, and the freshness of its first beginning has been formed but deformed. We feel full of sin. This is a rebound effect from the originality of its elemental good. We are stirred into being ashamed of ourselves. Its newness also is the promise of the good of life. Time has proved for us to be the windy plain of broken promises. And yet this shame is salutary, not morbid. The beginning of life anew in this other makes us eager to renew life in ourselves: the new idiocy rebounds back on us and makes us idiotically want to begin again, and to be good, afresh.

The child arrives, but now it is malformed. The shock of disappointment can be crushing. The energies that would celebrate retract into a formless void and sit stunned by a face of idiocy that takes the life from one, even as this new strange life has come. This retraction also is into the idiocy of being. And that we are stunned or aghast shows the saturation of the idiocy with value, disvalue, shunned and hard to bear. Sitting in the inarticulate silence, the idiot self is struggling with its yes or no; coming to terms takes place mostly out of sight, out of hearing, in an abyss of interior silence. But is not the disappointment here a secret homage to the idiocy as good? For it is the lack of this that we shun. And were it there, we would not give it a second thought, we would take it for granted. Not being there, we strain to come to terms with our deprivation of the good we anticipated. We have to see the good of what is there before us; hence this idiotic struggle is all the harder and heroic than the more normal, often unthinking assent to what is there. That "normal" assent happens and forgets itself in happening, and then the happening of the good also is forgotten. This is not possible now. Something elemental disappoints and crushes us. At the deepest level, we strain to find good in the absence of the good anticipated. Completely to lose the elemental good of the "to be" would be to despair. We are made to struggle for some consent or hope or perhaps a different dawning, albeit in terms different than anticipated.[5]

You leave your home for a foreign land; away, you grow aware of something away—the good that was there, but in unstated intimacy. In separation there is a

5. When something goes wrong at this level, or almost goes wrong, we meet an instinctive regress to idiotic rapport with the good. A two-year-old child is posting a letter with his mother and rushes across a busy street in eagerness. By a mere two seconds, the child is not hit by the car approaching over the hill. How does one feel? One breaks out in sweat at the hair's breath that separated eager life from catastrophe, at the contingency that saved or did not save the life, itself completely singular. Contemplate the death of the child, and the idiotic singularity brings on the sweat of an ontological terror. This sweat is inseparable from the elemental good of life itself, as mysteriously beyond us always. One might awaken to the nighttime terror of the moment in which life and death are poised as on a edge, and be grateful the child was spared. It might have been otherwise, and terror would become mourning and perhaps despair.

rupture of intimacy and yet its heightening, just because it is no longer there. You awaken to the delicacy of presence, previously surrounding one, but not now. One remembers, say, children, as now they are not here, or one is not there. A singularity haunts one as it appears, then to fade. Or it appears what it delicately is in its fading. For it is the fading that stirs up the delicate savor of presence; presence that when present was too much for us, and so was not properly minded. Of course, leave taking or rupture is not necessary, but intimate familiarity mostly dulls us to what is intimate. And presences can come to one like overwhelming invisibilities—nuances of "being there" that break through the crust of domestication. One is, as if one were, *simply skin*—vulnerable medium of caress and communication. The overwhelming may be such that one is, as it were, *flayed*—deprived of even the last elemental protection. As if stripped to the skin, one is stripped again of the skin. Yet such an undergoing of presences comes to one as still saturated with value. The wave of the overwhelming swamps but also retreats and leaves us knowing that presence is always fading, even as it is always too much there. And both the thereness and the fading are too much for us.

Distance does not lend enchantment to the view, for distance is grief at what was there and is not now. This grief is not a wan holding onto what a stout soul would let go, singing its brave new world without "nostalgia" and other "regressions," now denounced so cheaply. The grief is a weeping love. The grief is indirectly a confession that we lived as sleepwalkers of the good of being that was there all around us, and we blithely passed it by, as we passed on. It is because we participate in the idiotic good of elemental being that we are beings who weep. No other animal weeps. Why? Because we are woken up to mindfulness of the intimacy of being and its good. Our pain before the loss of the good takes on this new mindfulness, for weeping is intimate mindfulness, idiotic mindfulness. Weeping is in the flesh itself, weeping is elemental. There is something deeply metaphysical about weeping. And this astonishingly is called a beatitude: Blessed are those who weep.[6]

Does suffering intimate the intimacy of what is good? Does it advance appreciation of the idiocy of the good of "to be"? A person dies whom one loved; one mourns the loss. All negative, you say. What is mourning? A love of the lost

---

6. Compensatory anticipation that we weepers will get ours in the next life? Surely there is something deeper? There is a weeping that intuits something of the heart of things: not into the evil of things, but into the good, but the good that is withdrawn from present enjoyment. Weeping is in the flesh, but it shows an extraordinary openness and vulnerability: the mindfulness of undergoing, only possible to a creature hiddenly in rapport with the divine, in rapport in the intimacy of being itself. A physiology of weeping that tells us the mechanism involved is very interesting. But this is not the deeper level. The elemental nature of weeping makes it of metaphysical import: revealing something about our being, and about being, and about being good.

that memorializes the good of the one gone. It can be a clinging, a will to hold on, and many other things; but in all, it is a love; for clinging, and bereaving, and sorrow are all loves, lost love or love of the lost. The death of a person, in the rupture of passing on or over, or going under, or vanishing, can bring us into mindfulness of the strangely astonishing "that it is at all" of the being now gone, and of the incalculable singular value of that one who is no more: once and now no more, but now appreciated as having passed beyond all human power. The "it is good" of the "that it is," incarnated in this singular, has now gone, and the rupture resurrects the strangeness of that good: the gift of life itself as there always as the unstated elemental good that it is. I am not talking about a calculative clinging to life as my own and my possession. I am talking about coming into a mindfulness, or about being dropped painfully, even violently, into a dawning that the incomprehensible goodness of life is there all along and we do not and cannot see it, and we have lived the gift and lost the awareness of the gift. It is not a calculative holding on at all, but a mourning coming out of a chastening of the soul, a quietening that makes the self pensive, in the most intimate recesses of its hiddenness, and in a manner eluding complete public conceptualization. Death is an event that brings a hiddenness out of its hiddenness, but as it does so it thrusts us into an idiotic hiddenness in which we are enveloped by the mystery of being at all.

A final image of the idiocy (I multiply images too much? Perhaps; but that is the point here—the pervasive intimacy, hardly noticed; images are needed *reminders*): the friend now shockingly dead I saw last week, met him on the street. Life was surging, he said, flying, very good for him. We promised to communicate. A few days later he went to sleep and never woke up. He was, so it seems, *taken*. There is no reason we know why this good man, eager for the best of life, seeking to live to the best, should be taken. What comes? An impotence that can rage but does not, an impotence whose face crumbles into the idiocy of grief, deforming the composed face, yet comes out of depths none has plumbed; and terror that life is so fragile, a thin wafer of "now" and "once" coming between one and "gone" and "never"; the terror of a tightrope walker who is assaulted by the dizziness of frail balance over a depthless chasm; dizziness that knows it too will fall, it too is falling, but there seem no depths to fall into, the depths are so deep; the depths are the openness of the future, and all forward motion into the future is falling into this abyss.

Singularity of the self, singularity of the life, singularity of the unexpected occurrence of rupture, singularity of not-being any more—and this last singularity producing the recoil effect on us and on itself, and we are startled into troubled awareness that we were less than alert, less than watchful, less than mindful, even when we struggle towards our best mindfulness. We were lost in the elemental good of being, as if we were sleepwalkers, and sleepwalkers who could pride themselves on sophisticated self-consciousness. As if we sleepwalkers could write these ambitious books, and discourse on this and that, and give forth thoughtful opinions and judgments, and plan and manage and put forth immense energy in doing everything needful for human life to survive and prosper, and yet the elemental truth is, we were sleepwalkers, and are sleepwalking.

The singular falls so deep into the chasm that there is an imperceptible point of vanishing, and the singular is not there any more. Or it flies up: as if I see a balloon being lifted higher and higher, and I can keep my eye on it, and my eye does not stray from it, and to the attentive eye, inexplicably, there is a split moment when the balloon, now visible, now vanishes. It is there, it is gone, and all scanning of the sky reveals nothing of it or its whereabouts. At death, we look at the flying balloon and then are shocked by the transition that seems nothing and yet after it, it is nothing that reigns: no longer, not there. But what is this? It is the shadow side of the mystery of the good of being about which, as the balloon flies higher, we were mindless. Or say the death of an oppressive parent suddenly makes a child feel as if a burden was lifted; this also makes the point: the new release of fresh energy, fresh being in the world, as if one's previous bond with the other was a bondage, and death not only releases one, it releases the idiocy of the goodness of being. Look at that middle-aged bachelor whose domineering mother died these past six months; he is a like a young buck of eighteen again. What is it like to become young again? It is to have the idiocy of being and its goodness given back to one. A new bounce to the step; a smile, a carefree manner not seen for years; a laughing that startles friends who did not know him when first he was young. They will say, he should act his age, be middle-aged solemn, and there, will you look at him, guffawing with gusto.

This might be called the event of being brought *back from the dead*. The man has been brought back to life.[7] One can rise in the morning and the world seems restored to its miracle. Or one can rise and feel oppressed by its burden and yet say yes to it, and know that one's eyes have become cataracted, one's ears waxed up, one's flesh cold and stony. What I am is the barrier between me and life; and that barrier must die; I am dead, and I must die so the flow of life can move again. The experience of dying is a shock that may let that flow flow again. There is a

---

7. There can be more violent cases. Dostoevski: condemned to death, and on the morning the sentence was to be executed, reprieved at the last moment; as if he were already half over into death, being his own nothingness, and the terror and the struggle to consent; then reprieve and a kind of resurrection: he noticed the air, bird's song, the morning freshness; simple elemental things, tasted as inexpressibly good; simple things some dying people tell us strike them as miraculously there. Is this an agapeic savoring of the good of life: knowing something of its gift, that gratitude is really the enjoying of the gift, just in the goodness of its being there? But another of the reprieved prisoners went mad.

gratitude for simply being that matches a sense of the elemental good of being at all. One is rescued, saved, offered again the chance to live in the elemental good. (In some religious traditions, becoming a child again is symbolic of such regeneration.) This is never to define the good as *for us*, for all of the above are on the *other side* of self-mediating power. They reveal an otherness preceding or haunting or breaking through self-mediating power. This is the good of being as elemental. There is a gratitude that goes with it that is the basis of an ethics of generosity, and gratitude. This primal level must be remembered: it is enlivening and chastening, releasing and humbling.

I am talking about what elsewhere I approach in terms of a *posthumous mindfulness*. Does this posthumous character contradict what seems to be the *priority* of the idiotic? Not necessarily. It means we do not determinately know the idiotic at the start; posthumous mind is the later knowing of what was and is prior; it is knowing the elemental from a distance that undergoes the otherness of life, yet in the intimacy also knows no distance. We come later to this knowing, we almost always come too late. But this is the nature of the idiocy of the good; we are given it, and we do not know it, and it is gone before we know it and have taken the trouble to thank it. It is a hidden good, one that does not insist on itself or shout to call attention to itself. Its quietness is the invitation of our generosity and gratitude. This is an agapeic good: giving, receding; coming, standing aside; always making a way, ever making way. Do we come to the time of prayer, where the only kind of prayer is thanksgiving—the yes to life, the yes to death? Prayer is a return of love to the idiocy of being in whose indeterminacy the divine can come, though what comes seems as nothing. To die is to be born as prayer.

The Aesthetics of Being Good in the Between

The worth of being is shown aesthetically in the ethos—given to our senses and to our bodies. This is rapport with the incarnate good of the world, lived in our responses to beauty and ugliness. The aesthetic worth of being is the sensuous showing of the agape of the good. Respect for the incarnate world is inseparable from an environmental ethics in which the aesthetic horizons of our lives are the occasions of our becoming good, occasions both shaping us, as well as allowing us to shape our own dignified dwelling in the midst of things. The milieu as aesthetic ethos, open to our influence, opens us to respect of givenness. And there are *doings* responsive to this: how mundanely we care for the incarnate; cultivate the land; tend to bodily things, including feeding the hungry and clothing the naked; the respect shown to ourselves and others in not exploiting the flesh as property simply for us, to own and use as we please. The gift of the body, understood as such, induces reverence for the embodied other as the incarnation of singular but infinite worth.[8] The response can occasion the creation of works of beauty, not only in art but in how we shape our bodies and thus our whole being. The aesthetic and the ethical are not opposites, despite the aestheticism empty in its formal preciousness, despite the moral rigorism that in its righteousness cuts off, and cuts us off from, the sensuous showing of the agape of the good.

First consideration: The aesthetics of the good relates to the incarnation of the idiot/intimate. Any dualism of same and other is strained; the other is same, and same is other; or, rather, the intimate is other, and yet not other but familiar. The feel of the goodness of being is incarnated in the flesh. We speak about *feeling good*; but feeling good has much to do with the being of the body, feeling *being itself* to be good, being as finding singular incarnation in this bodied person. "Feeling good" entails a kind of *self-savoring*. This *can* be selfish in excluding the other or in being hostile. But at the bottom of self-being there is always self-savoring as this taste of self—exultant, or weary, or crushed, or thrilled, and so on. It can be vague, but "vague" is not the best word; it is affirmatively indeterminate, and so easily overlooked, since we normally live in determinate objectifications of selving, forgetting the feel of self tasted prior to this. The rationalist dismisses this as mere subjectivity; the sentimentalist puts it in emotional apartheid; yet the whole being of self is felt in the body in this taste of self. The idealistic reduction to merely indefinite immediacy also diminishes it. The immediate is full with more significance, even when the experience is one of feeling entirely empty. Take away this elemental feel of self, and you also take away the savor of being at all. Life would be insipid, perhaps even unbearable. There would be a kind of living death. The intimate is strange, the strange is intimate. If it is hard to fix it categorially, yet it is elementally real.

How is the metaxological way relevant? Attuned to the between, our bodies, our senses are through and through metaxological. There is both an *undergoing* to our bodies and an energy of *transcending*, playing in and around them. The aesthetic values to which they open are shown as both intimate and beyond, in deep rapport with our being and yet remaining other. The sensuous being there of our selves and of beings, neither are closed in themselves, because both are mediated into the between, wherein each is mediated to itself, intermediated with the other, but never so as to mediate entirely the otherness, either in the self or in the other. The feel of the good in our good feeling is the sensuous rapport with the good as shown—shown in the between as world, shown to us as dwellers

---

8. An ethics of the body must question its exploitation, for instance, in certain sexual behaviors, or in the corruption of pornography. It respects the show of intimacy manifest in the human body. It responds to the vulnerability, as well as the power of the body, training healthy physical powers as well as nursing sickness. Those who care for the bodies of children, of the sick, the aged, the hungry, live the hospitality of being.

in the between. Against the dialectical self-mediation that would interpret this feel of the good in terms of a return to inclusive selfhood, the metaxological attunement lets be the sensuous showing as other, as surplus. The beyond of its good is there, and yet not there.

Second consideration: The more standard contrast of aesthetics and ethics cannot be finally upheld. We think of beauty as an aesthetic category, but it also is ethical. Beauty is the singular formation of harmonious integrity of being within the ambience of value pervading the ethos. As there is a singularization of value in embodiment, there is an attunement to value in our response to beauty, as embodied in singularly striking beings and events in the world. To be is to be a harmony, and the world is full of integrities in just that sense; and not only vis-à-vis singular things, but vis-à-vis the halo that radiates from singularity and that does much to propagate the charge of the ethos. It is not that the value of the beautiful is directly moral in a human sense. It is not that those who are connoisseurs of great beauty are necessarily persons of upright moral integrity (a point Adorno reminds us about some perpetrators of the Holocaust). Rather, if the shaping of the ethos is bound to beauty, the promise of human doing is all the more rich, which does not mean that the promise will be acted on properly. Ethical goodness and beauty are sisters, both children of the same elemental mother energy of being as good.

Harmony and wholeness are proportioned, to a degree, to our measure. In the shaping of excess, a measure of vital equilibrium of powers is reached. Our attraction to beauty has a certain immediacy, most evident in response to human beauty, especially of the face. The proportion is a kind of intimate community of rapport. There is a *call from* the beautiful (*to kalos* has been connected to "calling"), and there is an answer in our being *called out* of ourselves: a transcendence of the beautiful as other to us and a self-transcendence on our part, and the two meet in the middle; their coming together is a lived appreciation for the value of the beautiful, as well as a savoring of the feel of something good. This coming into the middle also is metaxological as far as the call of beauty's otherness is not simply mediated by self. Beauty may be proportioned to us, but we are not the measure of that proportion. There is a receiving never to be accounted for in terms of our self-activity, even though the receiving energizes quiet, yet exhilarating, activity. First there is the opening, only later our activity. While dialectic tends to a holism, hence being quite well made for beauty, there is something about the wholeness here beyond closure: it is an open wholeness and opens us beyond any achieved wholeness we think we have attained. There is the presence of something more in both the beautiful object and in our being called beyond ourselves—presence of transcendence that is not yet present as fixed determination.

Even in this wholeness and harmony, beauty is intimate and mysterious in ways similar to the idiocy of being. There is something astonishing about beauty: not only that *this* or *that* should be so beautiful but that *it is beautiful at all*. The character of the beauty of being is not a property or quality and certainly not a mere subjective fancy; it is transobjective and transsubjective, yet embodied in singular objects and calling forth in the subject its power of transcending. *That there is beauty at all is astonishing.* This is really another voice heard in the plurivocal happening of agapeic astonishment: that being is at all, in being rather than nothing, and good.

Is this a nice and pretty aestheticism? No. It is a defense of beauty, and as met in out-of-the-way places and persons, beyond more standardly recognized forms. Suppose we live in an ugly world. The ugly will infiltrate our souls and lives and relations. We may then perceive being as ugly, even hateful; we may ourselves become shaped in the image of ugliness. There is nothing necessary about this, though given our rapport with the beautiful, the dissonance of this rapport is likely to create discord in our lives and hence to make us self-discordant. It is a great ethical task to shape the milieu of life in a manner that diminishes the prevalence of squalor, material and spiritual. Squalor of environment often can go with squalid human life, but there is no univocal determination between them. These humans live in sumptuous, tasteful surrounds, but their souls are sordid though their hair is coiffed, their delicate hands manicured. These others live in a mud hut, but the nobility about them is of the stars. The equivocal openness of interplay remains open.

Yet too often a squalid milieu can be too much to overcome. The squalor passes unnoticed as the habitual surrounds of our lives, shapes us behind our backs, and then it may be too late. The aesthetics of environment points us towards an important ethical *task*. We are not simply prisoners of environment, though there are environments that are prisons; but even in these, the possibility of transcending is never entirely cut off. The aesthetics of the good asks for mindfulness of the environment, not only of nature but of the human setting we create to enable us to continue and prosper. There is something beyond functionality in function itself. The value of both beauty and ugliness is beyond function, even in functional settings.

The idiocy of good comes back here in an unexpected guise. Think of an ugly human being; add uselessness to ugliness. (Freaks were *used* in past times as shows in circuses, such as the elephant man.) What is the showing of the value of this ugly self? Is it not the idiocy of good as beyond determinate measure, and beyond the value of functional usefulness? For function can be measured, calibrated in terms of more univocal standards of value: value for this, for that. Thus an ugly person may feel worthless, since he or she is valued for nothing, found to be of no use. But suppose there is a different value in the useless, beyond the function. The being of the ugly shows this other value as simply being.

Look again. We recoil at the malformed man because of the natural rapport with the beautiful. In the ethics of the metaxological, there is room for a *double recoil*—a recoil from our recoil, back to looking at what is there, in light of another light that is never functional. Here returns the agape of astonishment. It is not easy or painless: to gaze on the malformed can have its torment. Yet the ugly man can be the presence of the divine (see *PU*, 162–163 on the ugly man of Clonakilty). God is shown in the face of the monstrous. Beauty still shines in the squalor. We need to become different persons to be able to greet this shining. We have to be completely transformed. The basis of the beauty of the ugly remains the trace of infinity that is there in the intimacy of idiocy, the overdetermined good that is prior to all determinations, even the aesthetic determination that marks this singular beauty. Being is good, even when it is good for nothing. There is a goodness that is good for nothing, since it is simply good to be.[9]

Third consideration: The recalcitrance of the aesthetic to *being for us* is manifest in our suffering of *sublimity*. This undergoing is not *for us* simply, since it is a showing of nature's power in its otherness to our mastery. The "too muchness" of this other power comes to manifestness in the middle, and in such wise that we feel as if reduced to nothing. There seems nothing we can do except flee, but to flee is not to allow the revelation of the undergoing. Nature's power as other overwhelms us, and when it does not destroy us, in the distance of relative safety, we can come to acknowledgment of what is being manifest. The sublime communicates the complex excess of the showing. There is a play between harmony and discordance, between rapport and rupture. The first is more evident in the beautiful, the second in the sublime. The "too muchness" of other-power in the sublime makes it more forthrightly metaxological than is the beautiful. The threat of destruction causes both diminishment and uplifting. There is a *double* movement: first, the breaking down of the pretense of self-mediation; then, the releasing of a different energy of being in us beyond self-mediation. This second is a form of transcending that cannot be simply for the self, for it is the other that has struck us out of ourselves, and while we are shocked by the striking, we are also freed into something unexpected. The breakdown prepares a breakthrough, and though there is a self-transcending, it is for the transcendent and not for the self. The self is for the other in this movement of breaking through and breaking beyond itself.

---

9. It is clearly not enough to locate the question of environmental ethics with reference to more sophisticated ways of ensuring the functioning of the environment as the context of our projects; for then all value is still relative to us, or for us. We need a different thinking of its goodness for itself. This means going beyond the return to self in dialectical self-mediation and accepting the ecstasies of metaxological outgoing, which itself is an elemental realism that is beyond itself and for the other as other, or beyond itself in a letting of the other be in its otherness, a letting be that is a respect, bordering on the transcendence of religious reverence. There is no adequate environmental ethics without reverence beyond all functionality; simply joy in the being other of the world, joy that enacts a lived praise of its worth.

While true to many aspects of the sublime, Kant errs, I think, in his *moralization* of it. Here is how he describes it. The sublime reduces us in the face of nature's superior might, but in this reduction we find the elevation of our superior identity, superior to nature as moral beings—the phenomenal otherness of aesthetic showing is transcended in the noumenal ideal of morality. I do not deny a connection with the "moral" but think that this is beyond Kantian moralizing. It relates to the sublime as revealing the ethos, ethos in its non-human value, and non-human value such as to release in humans values that are not susceptible to Kantian moralizing. The point is not at all the elevation of our self-mediating morality, self-determining freedom; it is precisely to rupture its pretension to superiority, not by destroying the human but by releasing the possibility of a freedom in excess of autonomous self-determination.

The release is the breakthrough in response to the communication of a different sense of the being there of nature as other, revealed in the sublime. The sublime is the aesthetics of excess shown in the between, through nature as other; it is not the mediation of moral destiny understood in Kantian terms. There is, it is true, a sublimity peculiar to humans, insofar as our nature also is *other* to rational moral self-determination; this is its religious destiny to come into the company of the divine. The given being of nature as other comes to shine with a strange, unmastered power in the undergoing of the sublime. This does something to us: it humbles and chastens us, makes us quiet and silences us; it also makes us celebrate and sing; something other sings in us in our singing in the overwhelming sublimity of nature.

The affirmation of value is not my value, or my moral value; it is the value of being as other that I now am released to sing. There is a self-transcending towards the transcendence of nature as other, a transcending not for self but for this other as other. At last I find myself at home, there where I had always been tending towards, namely, to be beyond myself in the between, there with the gifts of creation, though I know I am frail, and a small swat will snuff out my singularity. And yet there is the "yes." This is an agapeic "yes," not an erotic "yes"; and not the rational "yes" to the moral destiny of self, understood in Kantian terms.[10]

---

10. Kant makes reference to Ideas, which are unpresentable, beyond our immanent determination. We might see the Ideas as invoking the transcendent as other, and yet as somehow manifest. The moral Idea is the most important for Kant, and in that regard, the sublime is related to the ethical, and perhaps to the ethos as aesthetic. But relative to the metaxological and more affirmative relativity to the otherness of the transcendent, this moralization of the sublime tends to domesticate a more radical breaking into, and breaking through, and breaking out of the confines of self-sufficient autonomy. The sublime, in promise, is related to a freedom beyond autonomy, just in bringing us to our interface with an otherness that cannot be included within the self-sufficient circle of self-mediating autonomy. There are more helpful hints in Kant here than perhaps in Hegel, for whom

The sublime is the finite manifestation of the infinite, beyond the measure of our moral evaluations of good and evil. In rocking us back on our powerlessness, a new power of consent to the otherness of being may be released. The voice in the whirlwind, heard by Job, is heard in other seasons and places. The sublime is an aesthetic manifestation of the good beyond good and evil. As such, of course, it remains ambiguous. Some will take this as offering them license to deride the more human measure of good. They will think themselves

---

the dialectic of self-determination is more complete, and the willingness to let the transcendent be transcendent less full. Kant's view is expressed in a dualistic framework, my view in a metaxological context, where the pluralism of the double is not the same as dualistic opposition, hence not amenable to the appropriating move of *Aufhebung* by Hegel's dialectic. The other as manifest while still being other is apparent in the sublime. The sublime also is connected to refreshing our feeling for the "it is good" in the face of the power of being there that could in the flick of a finger wipe us out. The sublime harbors an interplay between being and nothing, and the confrontation with nothing throws us back to the refreshed affirmation of the goodness of the elemental "to be." This is related to posthumous mind. The sublime is like a death and a resurrection, and what is resurrected is not the self of moral autonomy simply but a self released into a different freedom. Note also that the famous passage, at the end of the *Critique of Practical Reason*, about the moral law within and the starry skies above, all but exactly anticipates what Kant says in the *Critique of Judgment* about the sublime. The same movement by which, in the end, moral self-mediation is privileged is present there. This is more consistent with the dialectic of self-mediation, and it is not metaxological, as I mean this. Kant may be in the between, but finally he pulls back from the power and enigma of the other and seeks the consolation of the moral self. My point is not the squashing of the human self; I agree, our destiny is to do the good; but the release of affirmation of the good of being there, even though it may destroy me, leads to a different appreciation of good. The ground of the good is indeed insinuated more by the power of the sublime than Kant thinks. But this ground is not measured by our moral self-determination. It is a good beyond the measure of our moral difference of good and evil. The good beyond good and evil (see *BB*, Chapter 13) has to be faced, as showing through the sublime, to let us come to the freedom beyond autonomy; a freedom that also brings home to us that we are native to the world, at home in creation while also strangers on the earth. And what of Hegel? His account continues the Kantian line. Perhaps better than Kant, he sees the transcendence revealed, but he criticizes just this transcendence for being an other that is not fully mediated within the circle of self-determining being, at home with itself and for itself. The transcendence is an as yet unassimilated other, not a final barrier to a more complete self-mediation. I say there is a different being-at-home in the homelessness induced by the sublime: not a self-mediating being-at-home; but a being-at-home from out of the gift of an enigmatic, unmastered other; a gift of serenity coming from the severest suffering; a gift of affirmative immanence coming from the transcendent, one still caught "between two worlds," insofar as the being-at-home also is a not being-at-home. See my "Gothic Hegel"; also "Art and the Impossible Burden of Transcendence," in *Hegel-Jahrbuch*, 2000.

sublime in loosing the monster in themselves. This is a monstrous deformation. This is evil beyond good and evil.

The good beyond good and evil does not execrate the human measure but more completely stretches its promise in a new freedom beyond our measure. All of the demands of moral integrity remain in place but are transformed by this new freedom. Indeed, what previously was a burden can seem now as natural as to breathe fresh air. In sensing good in the overwhelming power of being, we are released to more full life with others and with ourselves. What is shown in the sublime passes into the heart, but the heart returns from its sanctuary and goes forth towards others, natural and human, with a new love that the measure of moral good and evil could never release in it.

This showing of excess may bring us to a conversion, but it also is dangerous, because discordant with our more sedative domestications of life. Its equivocal show may tempt us to think of *ourselves* as beyond the measure of good and evil, like wicked gods, or like naughty Nietzsche. The new freedom opens onto the equivocal snare of a baser monstrousness. The closer we come to the highest, the more the danger of debasement. There can be a kind of *perverse infinite depth* in the doing of evil, as there can be a miraculous generosity in some humans lifted up by the release. The latter we call holy, or sanctified; the former we call cursed, though they be the terrible kings of the feeble day.

Fourth consideration: What of the peril of the monstrous? It is important to keep faith with the elemental sources of the good. The recoil effect from the sublime reawakens our deadened feelings for the good of the elemental. Simply to be in the flesh is not just to be there but to live incarnation as aesthetic good. It is lived all of the time, though we pay no notice to it. The incarnate value of being fleshed is not of my own being but plays around my being, like a caressing breeze. The flesh itself is the feeling of the goodness of the "to be." Think again of recoil from malformation, or life in a squalid milieu. This recoil is not the result of decision or deliberation. Prior to that, it will happen spontaneously, as when a child sees a midget passing by and cannot help but point and stare with eyes as big as saucers. The child has not yet learned to control the spontaneous bodily response to the other. It is not rude, though the child will be told not to stare, for it is rude. The spontaneous body will learn to embody respect for the other, or a least a certain disguise of its own fascinated recoil. The recoil is in being surprised by the wonder or freakishness of what is there. In principle it is not only the flesh of the freak that may cause this; it is all flesh, the flesh of the world—crabs, cats, spiders, leaves of grass, odd-smelling uncles.

We come to the world in agapeic astonishment, and the flesh is the incarnation of this. This is an antidote to the monstrous, in that the *benignity of the strange* is intimated here, indeed, the benignity of the innocent response that really knows no harm and means no harm. The monstrous is what is shown (*monstrare* is to show). This can be the spectacle of the freakish and the outlandish, but also the shining of the most divine (consider the way the Eucharist was shown at benediction or devotions in the Monstrance). Again, it is the "too muchness" that is there as shown, but shown with a possible doubleness: it prepares the ground for a more explicit freedom but itself does not know the calculation of options between alternatives. We are spontaneously in the play of same and other in the flesh itself, in the play of the incarnate good and threatening evil.

The human body is a *sublimity in miniature*, even when it exhibits the highest harmony in its beauty. Thus the recoiling attraction to its excessive sides—its hairiness, or its rank smell, the salty fishiness of something primeval, as if the sea washes in the secret fluids, or the ugliness of the genitals as peculiarly fascinating, or the obsession with the excremental we find in children, and not only there. There is a violence to beauty about the body, as well as a desire for the body in its beauty. This is more manifest when the excess of self-transcending energy becomes more restlessly wakeful, after puberty when eros in sexual form shapes the body into a double vitality: desirous of its own fulfillment, desirous of the other, without which it is all but a lonely nothing. The bodies of innocent children are beautiful, and only sublime in an evil, monstrous way to those who would defile them, those who defile the name of *philia* by being called pedophiles.

Fifth consideration: The aesthetics of the body takes on a more *active form*— we are *adorning animals*. The aesthetic value of flesh is a given but also is a task and a courtesy. That we adorn is deep testament to the waking up of transcending in us; to adorn is already to be beyond what is given sensuously; it is to originate an other form of self-being in which an envisaged other also is implicit. I mean: to be adorning is only possible on the basis of imagination that sees what is not, that envisages what is other to the present sameness, and that has the effective power to work on what is given and give it new form. Adorning is a form of self-mediating of the flesh; it is made possible by the imaginative envisagement of otherness; and to the extent that imagination is metaxological, it shows us as transcending bodies communicated in the between. For though we adorn self, we adorn self because another will see us. The other is *in* the process of envisaging how the self might be itself other. What I become as other is not possible without the other that is not me. That other serves to spur the imagination of myself as other, myself as the other sees or might see me. That other allows me to imagine myself as seen as other, thus brings me outside of myself. Imagination is a form of metaxological self-transcendence and a freeing from the flesh in the flesh. It is the flesh waking up to the possibility of envisaging itself as possibility to be other.

There are many sides to this, and much of human life is concerned with the images here created, how they free us, how bewitch (see Chapter 8). In advertisements, in clothing, in cosmetics, in "image" generally, the other is always present, even as the self envisages itself as other. We could not mediate with ourselves did not the other come to us in the image. The image is always double: an articulation of intermediation that allows self-mediation. There is no self-image without the other. It is misleading to speak of self-image as if the image were generated from a self alone with itself. It could not do this at all, were it so alone. Imagination is a happening of communication in us, a communication that as from the other comes to the self as possibly other to itself. *Hence the imagined other incites self-communication beyond the idiotic self-relation.* Of course, there is still always something idiotic to this, since the image cannot be completely analyzed into neutrally public, discursive concepts. The idiocy is not just back at the inarticulate beginning; it is there with every development, and it has much more power than we think. We forget it as we become lost in the preoccupation with determinate formations of self and community. Nevertheless, the creative indeterminacy is there incognito, always.

Adornment has much to do with the fact that we make ourselves into kinds of *works of art.* The great work of art is not always the painting, play, or poem but the *human being* who has managed to become itself. How so? By originating the form of itself that answers to the reserve of promise that wells up in the indeterminate and idiotic depths. This self-work is the more or less public concretion of what is there as presentiment in the idiocy of being. As the latter is presentiment of overdetermination, the former may be the concretion of overfullness. It may be an integrity of being that has both a suggestion of inexhaustibility and an elusive reserve about it. The human being as integrity intimates wholeness, with an intimacy that is singular and personal, yet cannot be entirely objectified in fixed determinations; and this, even though there is absolutely no doubt that this person is there determinately as this peculiar presence, marked by its own singular signature of being—itself, and nothing but itself, and yet more than anything that can be objectively fixed, and as more always in play with what is other to itself, the powers of nature, the people whose lives it shares, the God it loves in secret, or curses.

Sixth consideration: This open wholeness again means that we are at the limits of any dialectic of self-mediation and its autonomous self-determining. The human whole is open in the beginning, because it is a singularity of self-transcending power; it is open in the middle, as always more than what it concretizes as itself; it is open at the end, as always more than its attainment. There is more to transcending than transcending. The open whole is an overwhole. The "more" is a halo of gift, in the child's beginning; a halo of promise in the growing human; a halo of achievement in the mature adult. But there also is a halo of the "more" that is something more than any halo of self: an other power plays around the whole self, always remaining in an intimate togetherness with the self, even when not known or acknowledged or refused or vilified.

The open overwhole has to do with the *surplus of integrity.* "Integrity" does not fully capture the infinity of the human being, its infinite value, nor the kind of community between such beings. Integrity has too much self-sufficiency about it, while it is not so much lack that we here acknowledge as surplus to self-sufficiency. There is something more than integrity, more than autonomy. This is not the betrayal of the integrity but a flowing of the fuller energy of transcending beyond its borders. The good person flows out from self, and it is always out beyond, knowingly or not. This "being out beyond" is what it always is to be in communication. The surplus of community is always flowing and it does not come into play only once self-integrity has been attained. On the contrary, the integrity itself is grounded on the surplus that gives it to itself, and now gives it more mindfully to be more than itself.

The work of art that is the human being cannot be closed. The consolation of other works of art is that they seem more closed, more contained, and in some ways they are. They seem wholes in the muddy flow of promiscuous life. But they too have their halo of the "more." They intimate the "more," are presentiments of what is not and cannot be presented within the artifice of the artistic frame. The work of art of a human life is a far more enigmatic drama, and we cannot be its spectators. We have episodic presentiments about its inherent rightness or wrongness.

Seventh consideration: If I question more usual separations of the ethical and aesthetic, I also suggest that their togetherness points us further again to the *religious*. Their community comes from their concern with worth: elemental, in process, and achieved, and with our perplexity about the worth of being at all: not just human being, though often this more than what is other, but also the worth of being simply, the struggle for consent to the goodness of being, often in the face of the meaningless and the malign. There is something metaphysical about the matter, since the question comes down to the ultimate "yes," and how this comes to expression in sensuous concretions of our participation in creative power. I sing the praises of Kierkegaard, but perhaps the aesthetic is more ethical than he suggests, just as the ethical has its necessary aesthetics. Kierkegaard owes much to Kant's conception of the moral, but even Kant has teasing hints about the aesthetic and ethical in which his intention to separate them is nibbled away. The between as ethos reemerges at this point of undermining their separation. The undermining is less important than the fruitful matrix, out of which the separated aesthetic and ethical often are defined. Both get defined in the ethos. I think "being ethical" in a more fundamental, rich sense includes them both as articulating what is at play in the ethos. This is one reason why great works of art, such as a Greek or Shakespearean tragedy, are *works of ethics*, ethics not only in a humanistic sense but in probing our perplexity about the metaphysical consent to the ultimate goodness of being.[11]

---

11. I am not endorsing the aestheticization of the ethical in the Nietzschean sense, nor any such aestheticization of the religious; there is an aestheticization that amounts to a trivialization in the end. I want the aesthetic invested with the power of its ethical and religious affiliation. I want a more archaic sense of the aesthetic rather than a post–Kantian aestheticism.

The fact that there is something "more" shown in and through such works manifests the effectiveness of transcending desire in the aesthetics of the flesh. There is an indeterminacy to this transcending power, yet it is made concretely determinate in works, indeed, in the best of works it shows itself as determining itself to be itself more fully in the work. I will note two sides of this.

First, the work is a showing of self-determining power. The making of the work is a self-making, so the human is both artist and work, artist of itself, work of itself. The "more" relates to the indeterminacy of freedom, and while it means more than self-determination, it does mean that too. For the making of oneself as a determinate being, more or less realized in some harmonious whole, is inseparable from a feeling for the worth of the human being. The aesthetics of the ethical is bound up with the *dignity* of man: a being of special and unique worth. This worth is not just tied to our beauty. It is irreducible, even in our ugliness. That we adorn ourselves is not only a matter of changing and disguising who we are, of putting on a mask to deceive, but of showing that we are worthy to be valued. We would show ourselves as worthy to be recognized by the other. What is to be recognized is the worth of the singular.[12] There is nothing solitary about this dignity at all, since the showing is always in relation to an other.

Second, this aesthetics of selving goes beyond self-mastery. If there is a dignity beyond beauty, there also is our infinite restlessness that figures forth the open surplus of free self-transcending. There is a *sublimity to self beyond wholeness*. Thus, the *ugly Socrates* could be a sublime soul, just because there was something more to his being, shown in not being shown aesthetically. Beyond the ugliness is intimated a sublimer beauty more than can be aesthetically manifest. How do we measure this worth? It seems that there is *no finite measure*, since each is a singular infinite, and there is no common whole that would place each in its status relative to the others. The measure of the infinite must itself be infinite. The measure of the infinite value of the self must itself be infinite, more than the infinite restlessness but actually infinite. This is not a human measure.

This showing of infinite desire that is also a non-showing, again shows the *impossibility of closing the circle of self-mediation*. Since there is always the "more" to our most comprehensive wholeness, the integral self is a witness to what is beyond. Ugly Socrates was perfectly correct in using the language of divine mission to describe who he was: a servant of the god, aided by the daimon as a negative guide. Is this a quaint, figurative language that thankfully we can now translate into secular psychological language, so that we have at last the real,

---

12. And this, even when the singular is hidden in the crowd in those societies that adorn to show the bonds that bind a many together; the worth of the singular is in its being dressed as the others, or in a being along with them in various guises, through clothes, paintings, markings, lacerations, and so on.

comfortable truth? I doubt it. This latter strikes one as flattening the "more" of the former. The former is the truer. Otherwise we lose the entire point—that there is more to the human than can be captured in human showing. That we have diminished capacity to live in the mindfulness of the "more" does not tell of the need to translate the latter. It tells of our need for words more than our accommodating humanisms. The current words being thin, we have to learn old languages anew.

The religious continues to call. I mean that the "more" enfolds us back deeper into ourselves, where elemental community with the divine is effective from the origin. The indeterminacy of the idiot self wells up in the determinacies of aesthetic showing. We need to become again as idiots, as children to learn the language of the divine. We must come down from our stony castles of humanistic parlance, play again on the sunny grass, caught dazzlingly in the shine of God. And perhaps we will never be those children again, except in death. In the between we have the sublime within, what is presented as unpresentable, what is revealed as hidden, what is given as withheld, in the restlessness of transcending desire that desires not desire but the divine. Within us, this is more than us, and the "more" we are longs for what is *above* us, and in its travail comes into the company of what is beyond. How many voices and whispers and wastes awaken in this restlessness and travail and suffering!

Eighth consideration: Though there is a center of dignity coming into show in the aesthetics of incarnation, the restlessness of desire also means that the self coming to show is a creature of *multiplicity*. The "too muchness," the "more" within, realizes itself in a process of self-multiplication, *self-diversification*. I paint my face, and lo, I make myself other to what I now am. I make a different self. This other self is not me, yet it is me. It may be *more me* than the former self! Indeed in acting, or in adornment, or in wearing a mask, or certain clothes, some people find themselves more genuinely freed into being who they really are. They had a presentiment that they were other, and the act of aesthetic incarnation shows who they are to themselves, as to the other. They find themselves by painting themselves or singing themselves: a stutterer is suddenly released into communication by *singing the words* instead of struggling to say them. We *perform ourselves* in a bodily show: a shy child at table suddenly becomes different when he or she sees that he or she can act, . . . and act up; a show is put on for the others, but the child is finding itself in the show, and also, as we say, "showing off," . . . showing who he or she is, in perhaps an exaggeration of his or her histrionic gifts.

This aesthetic pluralization of the self is within the between, for the other is always taken into account, though not known. There is the self-othering of self; there is the other that enters into the between from the other side, that other also aesthetically incarnate, and othering itself into the between. The between becomes the ethos of *the seemingly unlimited multiplication of different selvings*.

There is a difficulty in putting any determinate limit on this process of plural-ization; and this not as a plurality of constituents, but as the self-pluralization of the participants in the between. This self-pluralization contributes to the com-municative mediation of each one in the plurality, but it is not itself masterable by any form of mediation. It is an intermediation, but an intermediation that cannot be given a determinate or self-determining form. There is a formlessness to it that is the happening of freedom, freedom happening in a plurality, and the self-pluralization of participants as themselves free. This is also why the excess is never completely mediated in intermediation, since the "inter" is always open. It comes to be what it is from sources of mediation that are not either completely self-mediating, or in mediation with other. The sources of mediation are idiotic.

Ninth consideration: The infinitely restless desire attests to the "too much-ness" at the idiotic source. This powers the open-ended pluralization of selving in aesthetic incarnation. Inherent in every process of incarnation, it exceeds every determinate incarnation. Its expression is not simply a move from indefi-niteness to determinateness to self-determination. For it is no mere indefinite-ness in the beginning; while determinate, and in a qualified way self-determin-ing, it is as a concretion of the surplus of the source that it is so; and this surplus is just the origin that grounds its infinite restlessness, and also indirectly the infinite value of self as end in self. Here we see the affirmative side. The human self is an aesthetic incarnation of infinite value. As such, it is a value beyond dialectical self-mediation. Indeed, it is beyond the intermediation that consti-tutes a community of human others. If all humans are of such infinite worth, neither they, nor the community of humans, create this worth. Without relation to a source of infinite worth other than the human, the infinite worth of the human hardly makes sense.

All of this is shrouded in ambiguity and not easy to grasp. The ambiguity is evident in the idea of *person*. The word has its history, as we well know. The *per-sona* is bound up with dramatic performance, hence with the acting aesthetically shown in art. The person comes on stage as masked (perhaps as the mask, *proso-pon* of Dionysus). The acting self, the one on stage, *is* the mask: there is no dual-ism of mask and character—the mask shows the character and shows it in such wise as to be the character. The mask is aesthetic appearance or incarnation as *doubling*—showing the self, being the self, and yet incarnation in the mask is here now on the stage. When the idiotic source and the ethos shift, the mask is no longer a mask, no longer a show, and the source that is shown has its life withdrawn from the mask. In a word, showing is always both showing and keep-ing in reserve. It is incarnating a mystery, or the finite presentation of an infi-nite that otherwise is unpresentable, not present in being present, or present in not being present.

The mystery as incarnate is the infinite value that is shown in the person as mask. If being a person is tied to the dignity of being an end in self and of infinite value, this always points beyond itself to a deeper mystery that is not our being or value. The one that creates the art releases the mask into its own freedom on the stage. But the one that creates withdraws from univocally determining what is done in the play. The work is open, because the artist is agapeic. The mask or person is an incarnation of the gift of openness. Without this openness, there is no self-pluralization and no complex community between plurals. The mask, as defined in this self-pluralization, is the incarnate aesthetics of the good. The person as masked is a showing of idiocy, and hence also a showing of singularity in community.

And so we come again to the *unavoidable equivocity of good and evil.* The mask of person is bound up with *the masquerade* of community. How so? Community involves the plural showing of many beings in process of aesthetic selving. This communicative showing is caught in a double play of candor and deceit, truthfulness and dissimulation. The doubleness of person/mask (as revealing and hidden) occurs in an opening wherein evasions and treasons also are carried out. Moreover, our equivocal self-multiplication can lead to a loss of singularity in distraction. In the masquerade of community, one can revel in being other as *not being true.* One plays a role that corrupts, though not always with explicit awareness. This equivocity of the aesthetics of the good calls out for *constancies.*

Dianoetic Constancies of Being Good

If the aesthetics of the ethical middle multiplies ambiguity, it also calls forth our search for reliable intelligibility. Freedom opens up the delight of surprise and the shock of inconstancy. Nature is astonishingly diverse, yet there are recurrent determinacies in the harmonies of happening, in the lawfulness of processes. Why should we be completely other to this? Our being is not an anarchy of unbridled possibility. In the polyvalent showing of the between, metaxological ethics is vigilant to what might be called *ethical constancies.*

What are these? Not rigid rules imposed on the ethos, not dualistic opposites dominating its ambiguity, but reliable directions *emergent* in its plurivocity. Metaxological vigilance requires respect for emergent "sameness," but in no reductive sense. As diversities are held together by intelligible bonds, constancies bear upon ways of "being together" (see *BB* on intelligibilities, Chapter 9, and communities, Chapter 11). Why do ethical constancies often take the form of commands or directives? *Because our openness asks direction*: we not only live these bonds but contribute actively to their constitution. Ethical directives emerge from natural and human constancies, but the latter exhibit greater creative freedom and a wider range of self-transcendence. Our openness indicates why the constancies both reflect what is and direct us to what should be. The value of what should be emerges from the value of constancies already operative. These two are joined as different phases in the unfolding of ways of "being together," or in community. Intelligibilities are modes of "being together," but these will differ depending on the powers of transcending shown by the beings that are together. With us the freedom of transcending power shows "being together" to be as much enterprise to be achieved, as given fact.

And so ethical constancies both point towards intrinsic value and command moral respect. Ethical mindfulness is intensive attunement to the play of sameness and difference in the ethos, where insistent, subtle constancies emerge in the flux of impermanence. The point is not first our dictation of orders. It is letting appear such orders as come to show themselves in unfoldings of self-becoming and communicative being with others. Some orders direct us to a task, thus are formulated as commands and obligations—not you "may" do this, not you "will" do this, but you "must" do this. "May" and "will" discern within themselves directions that "must" be answered on pain of betraying exigencies inherent in human possibility and willingness. Willingness comes to see that its own character must be metaxological in the double sense of remaining faithful, both to the integral exigencies inherent in self-becoming, and to the opening of transcending desire towards the other as an other of infinite worth. The constancies reflect dynamic patterns of integrity and commonality in the changing flux of the ethos. They are forms of "being together" that, already at work, make a call on humans to realize more fully their given promise.

There is an *ananke* within the heart of freedom itself, expressed by this double exigence: truth to self, truth to the other; love of self, love of the other. Freedom is a freeing, a releasing. What is releasing? Release of self into the fullness of its own being; release of the other into its own fullness; release of both into their community which, it turns out, actually grounds their self-release and release beyond themselves. The character of release is metaxological, but this takes shape within orders of relation between self and other, or constancies of community. This does not mean that we formulate the constancies with absolute adequacy, as we try to articulate what they ask of us. The overdetermination, the play, the plurality of the between, the flux of its becoming, all call into question our fixation of the constancies into unquestionable certainties by which we dubiously secure ourselves, rather than let the more ultimate good impel us beyond the narrows of ourselves.

We must think beyond any dualism of nature and the human. The modern objectivizing of the human and opposite subjectivizing of being express an exaggerated assertion of human freedom from nature. Nature is first a matter of coming to be: *natura* is a "being born," to be seen in light of *coming to be*. If we become this or that, what we become is not indefinite. If there is an overdeterminacy, nevertheless its promise takes determinate shape. We all have natures in this sense: we are concretions of definite patterns of coming to be that have a relative reliability in the passage of the universal impermanence.[13]

Consider again the idea of natural law. Did its pre-modern form tend towards a certain "objectivism"? This was not its deepest intention, I think. The primal exigence "Do good and avoid evil" reveals an absolute constancy of human existence, reflecting an ontological condition already real and communicating a task to be faithfully accomplished.[14] In the necessity of the first there emerges the openness of the second, since in the ambiguity of the between we must read the signs that tell us what exactly the concrete good is here in this particular situation. Quandaries emerge when we approach the specifics of a singular situation. This is not an objection, since every thinking ethically has something of this difficulty. It is inherent in our being ethical: to find one's way in the midst. The pre-modern grounding of natural law on a more ultimate divine origin reflected and affected the way human beings understood themselves—participants in a more encompassing adventure of the good. To move from the mystery of the divine, through the universal constancy of the natural law, to the impermanent variabilities of the particular, was to be thrust more and more into the equivocity of good and evil—but with a basic faith that there was a fundamental ground in the good that was the ultimate constancy. It is not fair to speak of "objectivism" here, since it really concerns more a sense of the grounding good as other to the human, not as a dualistic opposite but as the giver of the good within which we participate, and of which we are never masters.

In modernity we find changes in the meaning of natural law, in line with a changed conception of nature and "objectivity." The natural is univocalized as effective power, crystallized in units of being that assert themselves, seek to expand their power, and protect themselves from the intrusion of other units. Natural law blends with a view of the ethos as the context of effective power relations.[15] Modes of togetherness take on an indelible tinge of threat: the other, whether external nature or human, is a possible infringement on my being as per

---

13. Admittedly, the openness of our naturing, our coming to birth, tempts us to speak of "self-birthing" in a qualified sense. This cannot mean some absolute "self-creation." It is our free self-defining of what we are to be that qualifies the powers already given us in the singularity of our "to be."

14. See Aquinas, *Summa Contra Gentiles*, on reason and law as connected, God and the eternal law, and the natural law as participant in Godself as eternal law; and the precept "Do good and avoid evil" as the first precept of the natural law.

15. And this, despite the surface of "life, liberty, and the pursuit of happiness." Life: my life; liberty: as unhindered as possible an expression of my power; happiness: my self-satisfaction as the unit of desire. See how Hobbes and Locke define "natural right."

se and its self-assertion. Being "for self" dominates the modes of "being with," so being for the other is not seen in its full promise as the supporting context of community that actually allows the assertion of the self for itself. This is reversed, and communities have to be reconstructed by a plurality of "for selves," out of their self-assertive power, now moderated through threat and the intimate knowing of their vulnerability in a hostile universe. I think this is to start too late (rather than re-start), with one particular crystallization of the plurivocal possibility of the metaxological ethos. Equally the beings that assert themselves thus in the ethos have been already made possible by the metaxological ethos, as an always effective "being together."

Thus now natural law and right show diminished redolence of the metaxological community, because saturated within the estranging effects of a dualizing univocalization of being. Modern objectivism is a kind of "subjective/objectivism," since the two opposites define each other (see Chapter 1) as we oscillate between mindless objectivity and objectless subjectivity. The community suggested by natural law cannot be rendered adequately in these terms. Such a rendition must inevitably undermine its own "objectivism," since its sense of effective power will come, in the end, to war with others, a war always impending, if not always declared. This objectivism degenerates into willful subjectivism, while subjectivism descends into objective powers at war with the other powers. Natural law is then the rule of the stronger. If so, we lack the basis for integral value, and our talk about inalienable right becomes dubious.

Let me reformulate the point positively. What is called natural law, I suggest, reflects the truth of the ontological gift: to be is good, and it is good to be. This is very elemental and also indeterminate, since it does not specify the way in which this or that is good. There is an indeterminate sense of the good of being underlying and permeating and outliving all definite and qualified goods. This way of reformulating the matter covers the pre-modern conception: the directive "Do good, avoid evil" is seen as the exigence of being, and of definite beings, to the extent that they are creatures of becoming, hence implicated in the seeking of their proper good in the universal impermanence. It also covers the modern concept, to the extent that this focuses on the way the good of the "to be" is particularized in beings, especially human beings, as the urge to preserve, perpetuate, and fulfill their own being and its power.

This modern particularization is more than it seems on the surface, however. Embedded in a context of a *mathesis* of nature, it lacks resources deep enough to rethink the particularization in terms of the good of the "to be." The pre-moderns were in a better position here, due in the main to the Platonic and Judeo-Christian heritages. The modern view might accuse these of anthropomorphism, but the point here is precisely not anthropomorphism: the good of the "to be" is not a human good; it is not primarily defined as good for us; and what is good for us is defined in train of this first "to be is good." This is precisely to point beyond human specificity to a more universal constant, albeit indeterminate, and requiring further determination. It is in the very constant nature of the "to be" to be "good." The modern view might be said to be far more anthropomorphic, since it models the good of the otherness of being in terms of human metaphors such as the machine (now the computer), or in terms of a human ideal such as "objectivity." It is not any the less anthropomorphic for saying that it is not so; it sees the good of the world in terms of its characteristic evaluation in favor of devalued objectivity (itself a value). The value of pre-modern metaphors is precisely that humans cannot be the measure of this universal constancy—to be is to be good. Rather, this serves as an indeterminate measure of the particular values to which humans resort to evaluate specific goods.

This is more in accordance with the receptive attunement to the other of metaxological mindfulness. For the indeterminacy of this constant is not merely indefinite; it is more than determinate, overdetermined. The incontrovertible unsurpassable good is the inexpressible sweetness of the "to be"—so sweet in its uncomprehended absoluteness that paradoxically we might kill another who tries to deprive us of it. The affirmation of being in one's own being need not be seen as some miserable clinging to the self, or violent rage against the other. Such clinging or rage, paradoxically, are specific formations of the first sweetness and love. It is with reference to love of this surplus of the gift that all reverence, gratitude, respect, dignity, obligation, and consideration are alive. Reverence: it is worthy in itself. Gratitude: we return goodness in the "yes" to its goodness. Respect: we must not violate it, we must allow or let be its goodness. Dignity: it calls for a sense of inherent integrity in us, in others. Obligation: it asks of us something like its own incontrovertible goodness. Consideration: it solicits care for the delicacy of nuance first elementally communicated in the inexpressible sweetness.

Beyond the elemental affirmation of the surplus good of being, further constancies are determined, relative to different forms of communicative interplay in the metaxological ethos. There is no denial of the universal impermanence, nevertheless, within it relative constancies are stabilized. The ethos is a community of relativity defined differently by the good as origin, by nature as non-human other, by humans as selves for themselves, as well as for others, both human and non-human. The constancies are stabilized relative to the communicative interplay between origin, humans and nature. The constancies will refer to the origin as good, and then to self and other, and each of these in light of self-becoming and relatedness to other. The origin is the ultimate giver of the gift of the good of being in the between. Self and others are recipients of the gift in the between, and both in community by their being and called to realize the promise of community. Thus the good of God must be reverenced first; then the good of the being of self and other, and everything pertaining to the flourishing of this in the between. This will be in the face of the opposition and violence revealed by the equivocal and the dialectical. There is no escape from strife, since the tension between self-relation and other-relation can open up a Pandora's box of woes.

In face of these equivocities, it is understandable why the constancies often are formulated in categorical terms: Thou shalt not kill, thou shalt not lie, and so on. But there can be no complete univocalization of the constancies because of the metaxological nature of the ethos. Much equivocity will have to be traversed in the quest to discover the constancies, and even when discovered, there will be ambiguity that we forget on pain of actually distorting what they call for. We find a dialectic of insecurity and constancy. If we return to self out of the equivocity, attaining mindfulness despite distraction, we may open to the constancy of what is given from the other. The exigency of the other is inseparable from the inner exigencies emergent in self. Attainment of metaxological mindfulness is then a homecoming to the constancy, given relative to the other, given from the outset. Metaxological mindfulness frees us from the definition of constancy through the power of our self-mediation—this last is a subtle way for us to univocalize the constant in our own image. The constant stands with us, by us. What do we find is the constant? We approach very close to the elementals: worship and thanks, reverence and honor, love, birth, marriage, death, covetousness and liberality, possession and hospitality. The elemental constancies bring us to the elemental powers guarding our moment in the sun, and the recurrences governing the twisting course of our moment. The sun: the giving of the absolute other and its offer of the gift of agapeic being. Our moment: integrity of being, and fidelity of community with human and non-human others in the between.

I think the Ten Commandments[16] offer a succinct codification of the constancies as passing from God's absolute constancy, and the gift of the "to be," through the other more qualified constancies related to self and other: mortal life, family, marriage, birth, death, one's place in the sun, what one may possess and what one should not usurp, the elementals above named.[17] The point is not mindless submission to dead law. The constancies formulate deep and elemental exigencies of human being, formulate them often as tasks, but tasks based on what we are, for what we are is an openness to become what we are and to answer the exigencies immanent in our being. These immanences are not merely immanent—the exigencies are those of transcending and of transcendence as other, so

---

16. 1. I am the Lord your God, you shall have no other God but me. 2. Do not take the name of the Lord in vain. 3. Remember to keep holy the Sabbath. 4. Honor your father and your mother. 5. You shall not kill. 6. You shall not commit adultery. 7. You shall not steal. 8. You shall not bear false witness against your neighbor. 9. You shall not covet your neighbor's wife. 10. You shall not covet your neighbor's goods.

17. These elementals also are of great moment in the community of agapeic service (see Chapter 16).

that this other is already, from the origin, in community with our transcending. Community with the good is not a subsequent construction; there is a primal community with the good that emerges into diverse articulation and more explicit formation of ethical community in the between.

Hence the first commandment: I am the Lord: the origin. God demands nothing and demands everything. Finite being is given for itself and given as good; it is given for nothing; but as being, it is the promise of agapeic self-becoming and self-transcendence, hence being in metaxological community. This promise reflects what we are and what we are to become. Relative to what we are to become, we come to understand *promise as command relative to inner exigence.* It is command that we can ignore or refuse. The law, in a sense, is a falsification of freedom if it is understood as a merely extrinsic imposition. There is nothing imposed on freedom; rather, the nature of freedom as a freeing is only released when it is faithful to the truth of being good, hence to the truth of itself. Freeing is agapeic release in community. Commands of the law have much to do with the need to give some qualified univocity to the flux of the equivocal, in ourselves and in relation to the other. But the truth of law is freedom, freeing beings into the good. The first truth of finite freedom is the gift of being as agapeic. God is at the origin of this.

The first command is thus a statement of ultimate truth and the formulation of the truth of transcending: God alone is good; no false gods; no bewitchments by false gods, including ourselves as false gods, for all idols seem to come to this, namely, self-divinization. To be under the law is to recognize oneself as finite creature, not in any respect that squashes one's being, though command often is understood that way. I also connect the first command with the elemental good of the "to be": from the origin, being is good, and our own being free is fundamentally a matter of being released into the joy of the good of the "to be." There need be nothing negating about this. The negating view has been attributed to law, but this is due to a view of freedom as at bottom inseparable from self-affirmation as self-assertion. Once again there is a self-affirmation that is idolatry and is not affirming in the releasing regard of agapeic self-transcending.

The source of the law is as enigmatic and mysterious as God is. The source of law is not law but exceeds its determinations, even as our freedom is in excess of it. The source will never be subjected fully to any form of dialectical self-mediation. Its nature is more than that; and our efforts to render the whole in terms of dialectical self-mediation remake the otherness of the source in terms of our immanences, that is, in terms of idols. The metaxological sense of otherness reminds us of the mystery of the origin, even as the exigence to do the good in light of agapeic being is communicated to us, sometimes categorically, sometimes more subtly, sometimes even playfully. (The beatitudes are more tied to transcending than to law, hence they show the reference of the constancies beyond univocal stabilization.)

If the first command names the origin as absolute good, the other commands follow relative to more finitely bounded contexts. They reflect more of the qualification of the between, its potentially equivocal plurivocity in recurrent relations of human selves and others, commencing with the elemental community of being born into and of a family. Hence constancies have to be qualified by mindfulness of context and all of the nuance of the ethos. Consider this general point in relation to the fifth, "Thou shalt not kill." This has a categorical ring to it, creating the impression that it is an absolutely unqualified constancy. Yet there also is something indeterminate about it. There is hence an openness that makes the categoricality more complex than any univocal imperative. Killing is killing, but there is killing and killing. The sentence is seemingly nonsensical, yet there is a move from the seeming univocity of the first part to the potential equivocity of the second. Both are true: killing is killing; but there is killing and killing. The first articulates the imperative that embodies absolute reverence for the good of life, of the "to be." The second qualifies this relative to the ethos. It invokes the need of dialectical and metaxological mindfulness for discerning deeds in the plurivocal ethos.

The command is determinate, but also indeterminate, so we must couple constancy with context. Is there not a justified killing, for instance, in self-defense? For it is the worth of the "to be" that is defended here too, but in limiting circumstances wherein the absoluteness of the good is qualified by finite promise and possibility. This is a very elemental example. It shows that we cannot avoid discernment relative to the qualification of the ethos.[18] In the between as concrete context we need mindfulness both of principles and particulars. Such mindfulness can take a transcendental and a eudaimonistic form, the former relative to the community of self and other, the latter relative to a practical wisdom in the between.

Transcendental Constancies of Being Good

Does change then dominate constancy, diversity sameness, perishing permanence? This would be too simple. Thus the constancy of origin cannot be univo-

---

18. The necessity of qualification also will extend to attitudes to spouse, family, and goods. What was enframed in the command has some openness to further determination, which must take into account the truth of the ethos. Towards spouse: we come to recognize the crippling effects of treating a woman as a chattel, and the task of the command shifts. The prohibition against adultery: this is a violation to the community of marriage and family— breaking its vow or promise (in more senses than one: the promise to the spouse, also of the marriage as a whole, which infidelity can wreck). Attitudes to goods: nature is not just to be possessed; we reformulate the meaning of property—not as what we own absolutely but as what we have provisionally been gifted with. Covetousness then: the will to usurpation.

cally defined either as being or becoming, same or other, since it is beyond these as dualistic opposites. Often our demand for an "either/or" between, say, permanence and change, is the product of univocalizing mind. But after all, we are in the between, and while sometimes we do face a radical "either/or, such occasions are not always univocally clear, and we need discernment. More frequently we remain between, hence involved in an interplay or in a community that intermediates the opposites into a more fulfilled togetherness, or failing that falls apart into indifference or war. The greatest enigma is the interplay between the origin as good and the good of the between as gift, and between the origin and humans, bewildered often or lost or without a way. Here again being ethical shades into being religious. But do we find constancies so insistent as to be called transcendental in the general sense that without them determinate ethical living would not be possible? I think the agapeic relation between origin and the ethos is transcendental in that sense, as well as the metaxological relation between self and other within the ethos. Both relations condition the possibility of more determinate possibilities of selving and being together. These relations are a "being in community," where "being" as much as "community" must be emphasized.

What I mean by transcendental here is not any logical or epistemological possibility; it is ontological as pertaining to the constitution of what it means to be, and what it means to be good. It also is metaphysical in that if we name the origin of the *meta*, the *meta* refers both to "being in the midst" and "being beyond."[19] We brood on the double meaning of "*meta*": being in the midst is a being beyond; being beyond also is a being in the midst. Why this doubleness? Because what is in play is communicative being: being in community as a togetherness in the middle, but of beings that are beyond themselves as self-transcending. Community cannot be understood apart from the communicative energy of self-transcending being. There is a transcendental/ontological meaning of metaxological community that is the ground that makes possible determinate formations of ethical community, such as we find in definite forms

---

19. The two *metas*, being beyond (*meta*) and being in the midst (also *meta*) correspond to the good as beyond beings and in the community of the between. These two *metas* are themselves joined and separated metaxologically. Were we talking about a mere beyond, it would have little to do with the between. Were we talking about a separated between, it would have little to do with the ultimate and original good. The beyond is transcendence as other, but it is communicated; so while absolute as other, it also is shown, hence it is communicated to the between and has to do with it; transcendence as other communicates the good and its charge. The between as given being is itself a community that is open to its own giver: for the beings in the between are self-transcending, hence they relate beyond their finiteness towards the unconditioned. Self-communicating transcendence as other; the between as community of creation groaning for the good: it is not right to emphasize the extremes, if we fail to see the modes of intermediation between them.

of ethical selving and communal intermediation. These will occupy us more fully in Parts III and IV.

What then are the transcendental/ontological grounds? There is the agapeic origin as the ultimate grounding good. This grounding good releases the finite between into its freedom, and in that way it is the ethical/ontological condition of the possibility of the metaxological between. This "condition" is unconditioned, not in a Kantian but in a more Platonic sense—the being of the good beyond beings. This unconditioned conditions the being of the relativity of the metaxological. The latter is a transcendental condition in a derivative sense, though more seemingly proximate to our finite being in the ethos. It offers the conditions presupposed by determinate approaches to the ethos and specific human formations of the ethical, including both the promise of human self-becoming and of being together in community with others.

There is a given community of self and other that grounds the doing of the good in the ethos. We do not first create metaxological community. It is given. What we are given in its given betweenness is the freedom to realize more fully the promise of agapeic transcending, in self-integrity and forms of community that concretize its truth in the world. One might find some echoes of this when Kant speaks of the person as end in self, and of the kingdom of ends. The human being as an end is already emergent in its infinite value with respect to the aesthetics of the metaxological (as we saw). Once we understand this, it is difficult to deny it as a transcendental constancy. While the concrete working out of its implications may vary, and people will argue what exactly person is, that we are ends in self stands as incontrovertible. But I situate this matter in a different context to Kant. Indeed, Kant's way wants to be decontextualized, since this is his approach to transcendental constancy: with him, context is little more than variable empirical reality. Contextualized in the between, a metaxological view of humans as ends in self does not require the dualizing of the noumenal and phenomenal into oppositional domains. The noumenal apppears; the depth of infinity in the intimacy of idiocy shows itself in aesthetic incarnation, and in the constancies of life. True, the showing is not univocal, but then no showing is univocal; as taking us into the between it is equivocal, and dialectical and metaxological. The idiot self concretizes the infinite value in the ontological roots of human being as given to itself by the origin. In the idiocy is metaxological community; the showing is its more determinate communication and formation in the between.[20]

---

20. The implication here might be put in a more theological way: the notion of the end in self cannot be made fully intelligible if we exclude reference to God, and to God as the agapeic "valuer" who values infinitely; outside of this, all talk of "infinite" value seems ultimately meaningless. Infinite value only makes sense in relation to the infinite. Kant wants to hide reference to the infinite for fear of returning to some dreaded heteronomy. We need not dread heteronomy, though in relation to the *heteros* as divine, there is, of course, a holy dread.

The infinite value of person is on the other side of the couplet autonomy/ heteronomy. It is not defined by autonomy, for this is a freedom that affirms its own self-determining powers over against any intrusion of the other. There is a metaxological freedom on the other side of this couplet as normally used: it is a kind of heteronomy, since the other is constitutively implicated with self from the primal origin. And there is a kind of *autonomy*, in that identity to self is primally given—but this given is not completely self-determining; it is self-determining only because it is already given to itself as free. In the metaxological ethos, relativity to the origin as the ultimate other grounds the infinite value of self, but beyond the inadequacy of more usual dualistic categories. Original good is being agapeic, as giving the self its infinite value, out of which it becomes itself, with a freedom first given to the person, before directed and appropriated by that person.

This also contextualizes the kingdom of ends differently. Kant's transcendental strategy decontextualizes the kingdom of ends and lacks a full appreciation of the ethos—that kingdom *is* from the start, and is not only an ideal, as Kant claims. It is a given *arche*; not the absolute *arche*, but a created *arche* within which we already live our ethical being. The kingdom of ends is not in the end, but is in the end that is given in the beginning. The ends we are in community are not lacking beings from the beginning; we are the concretion of the surplus of the good from the origin, and ourselves surplus to finite determination. Should we think of the kingdom of heaven? Among us and within us, even if also always coming? Is there incompatibility between its being already here and its being a promise of what is to come? Suppose it cannot be exhausted by any univocal temporal determination? Suppose again it is *meta* in the double sense—beyond time and in the midst of time; communicated into the between, and yet beyond the between? Then it would cut into and across time: the incognito community of solidarity that is also always promise, even if only in rarer revelations is its name more expressly spoken.

Can the kingdom of ends be made properly intelligible without God? Of course, it can be acknowledged, or we can live in accordance with it. But how do we make it intelligible? Nothing in nature, and the human being as a creature in nature, has the requisite unconditionality. And to say that above nature or beyond nature, we have this unconditionality, as Kant does, is still only to postpone the issue. For we are not the explanation; it makes us ends unto ourselves; it does not explain itself through itself, for its very nature is marked by reference to transcendence as other. Is this the God whom Kant was intent on keeping out of the picture, as much as possible, for fear of "heteronomy"?

The transcendental question asks, what makes being good possible? The answer must include a denial of any merely solitary ethics. Even the idiocy of self-being is inseparable from the metaxological community with the other prior to autonomy. This is prior to self-mediation, haunting it in the middle, before it as a solicitation to fuller realization in service beyond autonomy. The priority here is not just the relation to the other, not a simple heteronomy prior to autonomy. The prior is a *mixed double*, so to say—the twinning of other-relation and self-relation: there is no self-relation without the other, and yet with the other, self-relation is irreducible as singular and idiotic. Responsibility to the other is prior to autonomy, yet not prior to a different sense of freedom. Being responsible is being answerable. To whom? To the other before self; to self before other; to self before self. Yet we come before ourselves as first given to be ourselves. Given by whom? Not by ourselves. We come before ourselves because there is a giver of self before ourselves. We can come before ourselves because before this we are given to ourselves.

This rules out any project of complete self-determination from the outset. It also rules out a merely determining or dominating heteronomy.[21] The origin that gives freedom is *releasing* of self and other and their community. Freedom is not identical with autonomy; there is a different freedom in releasing. The agapeic relation is solicitude for the release, not of the other over against me, but of all selves, including the other as singular idiot.[22] "Autonomy" that takes responsibility for self presupposes responsibility to the other: answerability to self and answering to the other, answering for self, for the other.[23] There is in responsibility itself a different freedom. This is approached by the metaxological way as the condition of the possibility of responsibility in a more usual sense, as well as autonomy. The primal giving of the beginning, as creation, is the giving of freedom as the release of the finite being into its own being. Its own being is its being given to itself, and hence is gift. It is a gift that is all but forgotten as gift, almost as soon as it is given, just because the giving gives it for itself. The giving hides itself in giving. We humans are coarse receivers who take wing on the delight of the gift and neglect

21. I mean, for instance, the tendency at times for Levinas to reverse autonomy into a dominating heteronomy, with a traumatizing, mastering other rather than an agapeic source.

22. Think here of parental love for the child. This relation, when agapeic, is for the *freeing* of the child. It is not indebtedness prior to autonomy (nor overpowering source), hence there is something wrong with parents who later will insist on reminding their children that they owe them everything. Rather, this freeing can be a generosity in relation to the child as other and as self for itself, primally concerned with releasing the child's freedom, its own being released. This is a kind of "saving" that begins or originates, and also completes or fulfills. It is a release that creates and that redeems, that allows freedom, and that also fulfills freedom.

23. One may agree with Levinas, and more recently with Derrida, that there is a responsibility prior to autonomy. I would add, however, that freedom is not exhausted by autonomy, and that there is a freedom as a "being freed," which makes possible "being free": this "being freed" into "being free," in a sense, is prior to responsibility.

its giving source (as the parent's love will be enjoyed and taken for granted by the child). Enjoyment of the good of the gift leads to forgetting the source. Let that forgetting continue, and there is no gift, and no good, and I claim enjoyment as my right, but then there is no enjoyment any more, only seizure.

The Eudaimonics of Being Good:
The Daimon and Homage to the Gift

The need to acknowledge context finds expression in modes of mindfulness attentive to the nuances of being in the between, modes informed by a "feel" for the "whole." Savoring mindfulness leads to more particular discernments in the plurivocity that find out ways through the chiaroscuro of the ethos. We come to the eudaimonics of being good.

The needful discernment is neither a fixation on rigid principles nor a lax yielding to every passing impulse. It is principled and yet ever vigilant to the nuance of situation. It is a *living constancy* in the midst of the passing. It is an intermediation with the passing that is mindful of the constant and how it gives direction in the midst. This does not mean that we can automatically apply univocal principles to this particular situation. This would be too abstract, though it does happen in delimited circumstances. More often the savoring mindfulness has passed into the second nature of habit and is enacted seemingly without thought. It is intermediating vigilance become as like immediate instinct.

The person of practical wisdom is simply the embodied discernment of what, right now, is the appropriate response or course of action. Being this embodiment telescopes a long history of intermediation with others, familial, fraternal, societal, and so on. This does not obviate an *improvisatory wisdom*—the ability to face the new, and with new eyes to discern the proper that yet has no precedent. To be intermediating in the between is to meet the surprise of the unexpected, as well as the confirmation of the well tried. Since this middle mindfulness is only as concretely incarnated in this person, it is a living mindfulness that has its being simply as responsiveness to what is called for in the situation. It has an *original side* that probes the unknown, as well as a *conserving side* that confirms and guards what is worthy in what has already been. Such practical wisdom is what it means to be between ethically in the ambiguity of the ethos, both in its general encompassing character and in the specificity of this particular situation (see *PO*, 176–178).

This middle mindfulness is not merely a domesticated prudence, calculating its own best advantage and otherwise secure in a life of contented mediocrity. The tie to eudaimonia is crucially revealing. We must take this with a seriousness lacking, say, in the eighteenth-century version of eudaimonism, as rejected by

Kant. Eudaimonia may be in the middle, but there are *extremes in its middleness*: it is a being at home that has been visited by the communication of a more ultimate otherness. Thus, eudaimonia carries this in its reference to the daimon. Contrary to the calculative prudence that revolves in the narrow circle of its own advantage, human beings are guarded: they may be aided by or seek the aid of their daimon. What is the daimon? It is an in-between power, midway between mortals and gods, creatures and the divine. It is the guarding power between our finitude and transcendence as other, towards which we in our finite transcendence tend. Metaxological well-being comes in the company of the daimonic which shatters, with a visiting otherness from beyond, the finite self-satisfaction of calculative prudence.

The daimon is ambiguous. When it is beneficent, it is not so with univocal clarity. Being blessed with the daimon echoes or mirrors something we found in the idiotic and aesthetic: a primordial being pleased with the fulfillment of powers. What this might mean we can now see more lucidly. There is an articulation of the overdetermined good that brings to mindfulness the secret love of the human, and what was given as presentiment in the idiocy and the aesthetic. We sought and did not know what we sought. What stirred in the idiocy, what sought to show itself in the aesthetic, what struggled to steady or stabilize itself in the dianoetic and transcendental constancies, comes out into finite concreteness. The human being both comes into its own and into its neighborhood with the good of other being. A fullness is touched, redoubling the original stirring of affirming life, rejoicing in the inexpressible good that "to be" is. This is what it is to flourish: in one's very existence, as it were, to sing the good of the "to be." This is not something we can *just will* (as if we were autonomously in control). It approaches the release for which we all travail: peace that intensifies the fructifying powers of life. We cannot come to this without the daimon.

What actualizes being good is not only a transcendental condition of possibility: it is the *real enabling power* of goodness. *The realization of our power comes in the realization that no realization of our power is ours alone.* Thus, metaxological ethics demands more than an ethics of self-realization simply in the classical sense. Though there is a realization of self, in that realization we realize that it is made actual by the original gift of the good. As we realize self, realize we are in debt to others, and to the ultimate other,[24] we find realization as a release from self, self as cabbined, cribbed, confined by itself. The release releases one to be oneself, but being oneself is lifted by a power that is not one's own. Is this some-

---

24. "Debt" is not the right word if it implies that there is something to be paid back; there is nothing to be paid back in that the good gives itself and extorts nothing from us; it does have a paradoxical coercive power, but this is releasing rather than constraining.

thing like a grace? In some ways, for we do not effect it ourselves, though we effect it. It involves a being effected, and we are participants in the effecting, not overseers or directors. Concretion of self is due to self, but not due to self alone, and not due only to all the other human powers in whose debt we are. A mysterious providence is intimated in the singularities of unfolding. Think of how an artist may speak of a muse or inspiration. Or the way we speak of "genius" as an informing spirit. Thus, the genius of a place—you cannot make it determinate, nor completely mediate it, yet there it is, haunting the place, though it floats from grasp as we try to stay its elusiveness.

This is why we keep the word "eudaimonia." The daimon is ethos, Heraclitus said; but ethos is character, and more; it suggests also the spirit of the good haunting the between as the milieu of good. The daimon is not a quaint exoticism we find among unenlightened primitives. It may be the true word to describe the tutelary powers that aid us to become and be ourselves. (Think of the similar idea of the guardian angel.) We are in the care of something other and greater. Transcending is not in our power, but our powers are in the power of transcending. The daimon must be with us, or we with the daimon, for our power of being to come into its flourishing. Eudaimonia is thus both singularly intimate and yet a relation to a more ultimate other.[25]

The daimon is connected to *death*. There is a demonic side to the daimon, relative to the terror of the nihilating powers that rear up in us as creatures, that shadow all transcending, and that gather their counterposing power the more transcending itself is carried beyond itself to the ultimate other. Since the gift of the "to be" is for a time, kneaded into it is the seed of its return to the nothing from which it was created. Is this all? No: we cling to the sweetness of this timed "to be," which means we also revolt against its transience and its being given back, revolt against its being beyond us, even as we soar on its power. The seed that is there grows into its own countering flower, for we have eaten of the fruit of death, and we eat of it the more we cling to being as if it were simply ours. Thus the demonic is connected to the fall into evil and the fruition of the energy of nihilation that usurps the original power of the "to be." Hence the deep ambiguity of the eudaimonistic good: the tension between our will to wholeness and the strain of other powers that shatter that will, sometimes irremediably, sometimes as the purgatory prior to the breakthrough of a new willing beyond will to wholeness.

---

25. Socrates's daimon is not to be interpreted in merely psychologized terms. The daimon names a sacred enigma. That many today can make no sense of this may reflect how far we are from the meaning of happiness as eudaimonia. The daimon calls attention to fulfilling life as *gift*—or curse. Is the daimon confined only to singular singulars, such as Socrates's?

This issue spans both the ancients and moderns.[26] The human being can work to bring itself to a perfection of body, soul, and spirit. The human being is a work of art, first of divine art, then of the free art of living well. Inner being is to be developed into harmony with outward manifestation, so the person becomes itself and stands there like a god—blessed and serene, in equilibrium with the world, a world of equilibrium in itself. Like a Greek god: an inner principle worked into complete accord with its own concrete corporeality, and in complete consonance with its own inner possession of itself, as well as the world that is its sacred ethos. It graces the world in its graceful body. If there is something like this in Aristotle's ideal, it also is in Nietzsche. *It is the eudaimonia of the erotic sovereign*: justified in self, with a proper pride, with physical "perfection" and strength of decisive will, intelligent in a more than ordinary sense. The artist of eudaimonia is the erotic sovereign coming to perfection of self, as if it were the beauty of an art work.

But there is more. There is the ugly, there is suffering, there is evil. These too are to be affirmed! A more expansive affirmation is needed: a higher sublimity that paradoxically is willing to descend into consent to the ugly. There is more to the idiocy of self than can be captured in sensuous beauty; more to the good as overdetermined; more to the human being than its attainment of erotic sovereignty. If eudaimonia implies reference to the gifted nature of man as special (be we gifted by fate or fortune or gods or God), we can never be absolutely sovereign, nor simply erotic either. There is another grace before the gift, the knowing that the attained perfection is really not one's property. One has truly done one's best, but the gift solicited this best, and the achievement was really, most deeply, a *homage to the gift*. Erotic sovereignty hides gratitude for the generosity of the gift. And the hiding can be double, either a denial or a pushing aside, or something that, more shyly, will not coarsely claim as owned the gift of great powers. Homage to the gift is gratitude to the daimon.

This gratitude makes one look upon the ugly differently. Beyond contempt, homage to the gift makes one affirm the good in the ugly. If erotic sovereignty just affirms its own beauty, it fails in the higher nobility that affirms what is other to itself as good, and good even as ugly. If the aesthetics of eudaimonia are geared to beauty, that *beauty must be found in the other to the beautiful*: the beauty of the ugly, the good of the despised, the deprived, even the depraved. Here eudaimo-

---

26. Think not only of Aristotle but of Schiller: the fragmentation of the modern soul to be healed in a new wholeness of nature, art, morality. He develops a view beyond Kant's dualism of sense and moral freedom through a new aesthetic education (something hinted at in Kant's *Critique of Judgment*). This is a modern resurgence of something like Greek *kalokagathia*: a wholeness, natural, ethical, aesthetic. Schiller, of course, influenced thinkers as diverse as Hölderlin, Hegel, and Nietzsche.

nia turns into agapeic opening to the other. This is a daimon that is more than eros, but still as daimon it is between the human and the divine. But the divine, like the human, is not the good as self-sufficient perfection but as generosity that exceeds itself, and that, in overflowing the boundaries of wholeness, flows towards those beings that are refused. There is an image of the god here too, but it is more than the god of the Greeks as above suffering. It is the God who enters into the midst of suffering and who comes to suffer with the despised others; who communicates the truth of the agapeic relation in the willingness to suffer with and for the other. In some ways, this ruptures the wholeness of eudaimonia, but it is still a being blessed, graced by a daimon, an intermediary between us and God. There also is an aesthetics to it, though it does not shrink from the showing of our suffering flesh.

All honor to the noble athlete, to the beautiful and vigorous powers of youthful life that find extraordinary expression in this body, a person graced with powerful selving and noble embodiment. We are in the presence of something divine that is entirely human and yet more than human. But homage also to the blind man who dimly taps his way along an unseen way, whose blank eyes shock us, more than the blank eyes of the Greek statue, into a startled thought of the God of all. Homage to those whose legs cannot walk, let alone run, the cripple, the lame, and the maimed: a God looks on them with joy, though they and we know it not; we too must bring that joy.

We cannot do it. The ugly causes us to recoil. In that repulsion, we are thrown back upon ourselves, and there another war with consent struggles to form. Recoiled back and recalled to self, the offer is opened of "yes" or "no" to the ugly. The ugly breaks down the serenity of harmonious wholeness; in recoil, we can simply negate the ugly; but this negation is, in fact, also a negation of the range of self-transcendence.[27] For what is a wholeness that is only sustained by a retreat into itself, that cannot live with the other's ugliness that disturbs its equilibrium? It is a wholeness of escape, not a wholeness that opens beyond itself out of the strength of affirmation. Thus the recoil from the ugly is analogous to the experience of a kind of death wherein the self-affirming life of erotic sovereignty is challenged to an *affirmation of life beyond self-affirmation*, and life that is a death to its own serenity with itself.

---

27. That the beautiful soul becomes the ugly soul is recognized by the dialectical way, nevertheless, the issue here is more than dialectical, since what is at stake is the laying of the self open to the other, so that its very being may be attacked, or destroyed, or shattered, just in the hoping of its vulnerability. This asks for a naked consent in the between in which all of the guards of self-mediation are in abeyance. It is a different, idiotic beauty to that of any beautiful soul. One thinks of Francis stripping in the snow, like a newborn babe, and without shame. God weeps over the forlorn beauty of the naked dead. We do not weep, and we stifle the comfort of the angel. The matter is one of transfiguration.

Recoiled back on itself, erotic sovereignty faces a new form of the double: either affirm the being of what is other and ugly, as good in its own way, good as for itself; or affirm the good of one's sovereign being that excludes the ugly from itself, as much as possible. In the first affirmation, a new self-transcending towards the other comes to be that is more than the first erotic self-transcendence that has come into its own self-affirmation. It is the more radical and open consent to the good of being as other, and is agapeic as released towards this good. When it occurs, it is both a consent and yet more than our consent, for there is released in us a joy that is a gift and not an achievement. St. Francis kissed the leper and was given this joy. I consent to reconciliation with my enemy, and I am released into this gift that is in this world, but also not of it.

I speak of the ugly, but I also must speak of the *enemy.*[28] Asked to love our enemies, what is the point? The enemy is the one who negates me; I cannot affirm my erotic sovereignty, not so much because I am negated, but because the more ultimate affirmation of good must face into the enemy's negation, and offer the "yes" that places one in the between, where the enemy's negation might yet be turned to consent. Facing the enemy is more perilous than recoil from the ugly. That recoil would negate the ugly presence, but *the enemy is active in negating me.* I do not just recoil from the enemy; the enemy actively seeks to negate me, and from that active threat to my own being I recoil. Hence the struggle for consent is both the struggle to convert one's own negation into affirmation and the hope that the enemy's negation will also be converted. This conversion to "yes" will not be effected by negation. Rather the openness of the between must be shaped to make a way for those at war to come together to ask forgiveness and to forgive.

Being in the between in a community of forgiveness is metaxological rather than dialectical. Those in enmity are doubled in themselves and doubled in a

---

28. The following suggests something more transcendental than dianoetic, and more phronetic than transcendental, relative to story and image. It also invokes transcending, beyond the recoil from the ugly: it is beyond the hatred of the enemy that self-love lives. I mean the answer of Jesus to the young lawyer trying to trick him, which affirms what is written in the Law (Luke, 10: 25–37; Matthew, 22:37, 39): Love the Lord, your God with your whole heart and soul and strength, and your neighbor as yourself for the love of God. The young man presses further, and Jesus tells the story of the Good Samaritan: who is my neighbor? The young lawyer, trying to trick Jesus, plays a game of univocity and equivocity. He makes use of clarity in order to obscure. Lawyers are managers of rules and believe themselves masters of dianoetic precision. Jesus tells a story instead of giving a rule; or rather, he shows the concreteness of the law by telling a human story. The law must be known with the imaginative sympathy and rapport (here sacrificial compassion) that a story captures and evokes. The story is not univocal, but it is clearer than a set of univocal rules, for it shows the good as incarnate, and in the most unexpected of persons and places.

redoubled way, in relation and out of relation to each other, so that the redoubled doubles cannot be two sides of a more encompassing one that includes them both in its own self-mediation. Dialectical *self*-mediation in the other is just what has to be renounced here, both in trying to consent to the ugly and the enemy, and in trying to be open to forgiveness in the between.[29]

Metaxological Transcending: Ethical Desire in Extremis

What is noteworthy about a metaxological understanding of *trancending*? Mindfulness of what is overdetermined, in ourselves and in other-being. Though determinate beings, we exceed complete determination, for our determinate being is the concretion of an open power of self-surpassing that exceeds univocal, equivocal, or dialectical terms. The metaxological points to the inward source of this transcending—strange otherness in innerness itself, not susceptible to complete self-mediation. The enigmatic other is with us prior to our coming to ourselves in determinate character. Our self-surpassing is a surpassing enigma, as is the "end" we seek: an end that is endless, always beyond us, and yet intimately involved, doubly related to us as enigmatic and yet still there, for were it not there already, there would be no moving towards it as not yet there.

Metaxological transcending shows ethical desire *in extremis*. Think of it this way. Desire's distention is a voracious seeking of this and that as good. In that distention, our coming to some completion is lost in the very energy of going towards all of these goods. I love this and that, and soon it is less the love that counts, but that I am caught in a spiral of rush, in which I no sooner have this than then I want that. I seek, I own, I crow, I sink back into indifference, inquietude stirs afresh, I seek again, but now this other and that other, and always I am seeking and gaining, gaining everything but gaining nothing. The energy of self-surpassing towards things takes over as a flight from self that is most a flight when it is most in search of itself as the empty voraciousness that must be satiated. Satiation of self secretes now boredom, now disgust with self, and hates itself in the very puffery of its supreme self-seeking.

Seeking self, I find nothing but myself, but in this I drink the cup of gall I really am. I want everything, and I may have everything, but I have nothing, for what I am is not what I have, and what I am is nothing, for I am nothing except what I have. What I have I know is not what will fulfill me, and I know this in the bitterness of satisfied desire. Everything I have is still not enough, and in

---

29. I suspect that Hegel's account in the *Phenomenology* gives us a dialectical simulation of forgiveness; perhaps he has something of the right *intuition*, but he does not, and cannot, give an adequate *account*; see *BHD*, 192ff.

getting everything I have, I have not myself, indeed what I have may have twisted what I am and might be into an image of my own possessions. I will to possess, but I end up possessed by what I possess.

This is something terrifying. One spends a life in seeking, and is successful, but the success comes to nothing the morning one sees the emptiness of the face in the mirror. A child at play reminds one of the energy of self-surpassing, played in joy, and played without will to possess, played in the elemental joy of being itself. One has lost what one is at the elemental level. The mask of success covers the face, and to remove it would be now like scaling off one's skin: being flayed of one's success. It is not myself I have become; or I have only too much become myself; but I hate what I behold, for it is the image of the things I took as good. I have sought to bring the "more" to an end, but reducing it to a level below its sweep, I find myself lacerated between an irritable restlessness that persists with all that has been gained, and a deeper restlessness that still is haunted by the presentiment of "more." The irritability of the first mimics the misery of the second; for the first is a deformation of the second that has become in bondage to finite things, which it both loves and hates at once, which shows it both to be self-seeking and in flight from itself.

This doubleness betrays our condition as one of inward laceration or being torn. Desire's doubleness is twisted into a knot of self-closure, clasping to itself what things outside it has possessed. The doubleness is not the problem but how it has been twisted in the process of self-surpassing: surpassing as released towards the other is twined around itself. The doubleness is the spring of transcending which, when true to itself, is released towards the other. But in this inward laceration, self-seeking is flight from self, being in love with things is hating things, being master of all is being slave of everything. *I am the contradiction*: dissonance of self with self in self-surpassing that is not self-surpassing, since in being in bondage to what I possess, I am in bondage to myself. I twist and turn in this prison that is myself, and my twisting and turning is simply my closed self-surpassing knotted around itself.

The loss of self in satiation with self is not altogether negative. It can occasion a reawakening in us. The infinite restlessness discovers itself not in the pleasures but in the frustrations and the futility. We seek this, gain it, enjoy it, move on, move on because we are not satisfied in being satisfied. Our successful sallies renew disquietude, more looking not final serenity. We can career on this path for a long time. It is amazing the amount of unhappiness, even self-torture, we will put up with. And put up with, not because it is forced on us, but because we consent to be bewitched by our favored misery. We come to love, indeed to need our misery. We love what we hate and hate what we love.[30] This miserable discord will

---

30. For example, a person starting to smoke has to overcome the natural revulsion of the body; one has to force oneself beyond the body's natural disgust; then one becomes

hide from itself in crowing about its inalienable choice and such guff. The stark truth is we foul our own nest. We are misery incarnate. Desire's unfolding comes to this: a wretchedness of suffering without precedent in nature. The very depth of our nature is matched by the incalculable quality of our wretchedness.

Look again at the sweep of human desire, sweeping all before it as if it were majestic master of this and that finite possession. The range of its possessions exceeds all animals in nature. It should be the subject of the greatest happiness of the greatest being. Instead, it is wretched. Its wretchedness is its boredom with the finitude it has mastered. What is boredom? It is the simulacrum of peace— peace without peace, satisfaction unsatisfied, desire that desires but with dry and withered longing. One should not be fooled by appearances. A person seems full of lust for life. But there is desire and desire. Dry desire is lust for life that wills itself forwards but inwardly there is nothing but dust in the well. Wet desire is love of life that flows from a source even deeper than the well of desire, so deep it overflows even the majestic sweep that impels forward the most grandiose greed for it all. It is not a greed for it all; it is a different being towards the other in which inarticulate love wells forth, unknowing to itself and perhaps of itself, for there is water in the well.

Wretchedness is a grand master, a tough teacher. It teaches us to take stock. The truth of wretchedness is the beginning of self-knowledge. A favorite son, still young, asks, demands his patrimony from the generous parent. The parent gives, since there is no forcing impetuous natures greedy for all that life offers. The son goes afar and spends the patrimony in unrestraint and riot. He comes to have nothing. But he comes to himself only when *he has come to nothing*. He finds himself feeding among swine. He has had his day in the sun, and now he makes friends with the muck of things. It is only when he comes into the knowing that he has come to nothing that he wakes up to himself differently, and to the generous other that gave him his freedom and resource. And then? He turns around and sets off for home. He is not greeted with admonition but in joy and celebration: generosity in welcoming back, generosity in allowing the youth to go forth and be for self.[31]

---

addicted and finds it hard to break the habit; but suppose one does, yet is tempted to smoke again. One has to once more force the body to overcome its natural revulsion; one inhales, and the result may be a kind of relief, but it also is nausea and dizziness and the secret groaning of the healthy body. We have to force ourselves into our addictions at one level, while we also love just that addiction. We seek what we flee, and we flee what we seek.

31. Of course, this is the parable of the prodigal son. It is an extraordinary tale. Why are philosophers liable to be embarrassed? After all, are we not free thinkers? Are we free enough to see the profundity in the elemental—sometimes more profoundly captured in a story than in fifty tomes or treatises? The older son is very dutiful, but his righteousness

A restlessness emerges that testifies to an infinite dimension to human desire. We cannot force all desire into the mold of finite appetite. To live in terms of that forcing is to deform ourselves. The infinite restlessness must be given allowance to be itself. Allowing it so, however, risks futility on one side, our coming into something more transcendent, on the other. Both sides have to be taken together. The futility is frequently inseparable from awakening to the transcendent. Happy the one whose eyes are opened to the second without having to endure the agonies of the first. Most of us must go through the racking of desire, stretched to the breaking point, and beyond, to begin to come into the second. The breaking point is the emerging of the infinite dimension, in a form true to the infinite. Memory of this is often stirred only when we are in the mire.[32]

The infinite restlessness privileges the human with a taste for *infinite loss*. No other being has this taste. It is beyond the calculable measures of objective science; it has no determinate measure. It is born in us in a different dimension; or we are reborn as a different desire in this other dimension. The pain we pay for being reborn is awakening to the possibility of infinite loss. What is this loss? For

---

is no shield against resentment. He does not appreciate love beyond duty, generosity beyond righteousness, good beyond regulative obligation. Why do I think of Kant again, as I did with the story of the vineyard? Motiveless love is not so easy to place in the system of categorical imperatives. The philosophy of duty hides in high-minded morality unconquered traces of the resentment of righteousness. The prodigal son has no right to anything, except perhaps respect for humanity in his person. But the celebrating father is not respecting humanity in the person of his son. Certainly he is an end in himself, but that is not the point either as a universal moral truth about the human being. The point is the "thisness" of the this: this singular human, loved beyond moral measure, and loved in an ethics beyond dutiful morality, and in a sense beyond every right to be loved, not to mention even being respected. Indeed the prodigal son has besmirched the figure of humanity in himself in debauching himself. From the standpoint of accepting love, this does not matter finally. This love is an idiot wisdom. No accounting is demanded; instead, immediate song and dance, that is, a return at a height of generosity to the elemental and the aesthetic, and to the idiot too, since it is the singular this that is loved and appreciated, being pleased with, joyed in. For different retellings of the parable, see my "Dream Monologues of Autonomy."

32. There are a number of senses of *losing self*. There is losing self in the distention on things; there is the loss of self that is transcending towards the other, which is beyond self, and in a way lost to self; there is the breaking point at which the self seems to be lost, coming to nothing, though actually being brought to the border of what is transcendent, on the verge of a different finding on the other side of a breaking through, of itself and of what is other. The second loss is often conditioned by the first. Some lucky humans find themselves beyond, from the outset; they do not lose touch with themselves in always losing themselves; they live transcendence in which they are finding themselves in the other, even in losing themselves, and indeed in not at all thinking about themselves in all of this.

what do we mourn, for what do we weep? Have we any science of this suffering? Does this suffering decree a different vision of the good of life, beyond all objective rationalization? Surely this is not a lack of knowing, a mere irrationality? Is there a knowing aroused from suffering, a reorientation?

Often art and religion articulate the infinite loss. Tragic being at a loss is such that no finite good can compensate or help us towards a recovery. Beyond any definite recuperation, tragic loss has *no finite atonement*. It brings us to the verge of infinitude as other to any finite mastery, not even human mastery marked by its own infinite restlessness. The restlessness *cannot bring itself to rest*, cannot give itself the peace it needs. It seems that infinite loss can only be matched by an infinite finding. No finite good, no aggregate of finite goods, not even an indefinite sequences of such goods will meet the loss. The infinity here is not quantitative or successive but of another dimension. This transcending of desire is lived vertically to quantitative succession.

Ethical desire *in extremis* is brought to the verge of the religious, beyond all finite objectification. Here showing is as important as mystery, manifestation as hiddenness. What is manifest is not finitely objectifiable, and the one to whom manifestation is given is not also thus objectifiable. We have to be infinitely disturbed and energized by the restlessness to have a glimmer of what might be manifesting itself. Since we live in an age of objectification, we frequently falter here. Our enlightenment casts a light that blinds us. The result is a secret mourning that we are unable to name, or afraid. It is as if we were suffering a spiritual hemorrhage, and weakening, even as we compensate for loss by hyperactivity. The fever of busyness is a mask of self-importance hiding from itself its own hollowness. The mask of bustle and glee keeps out of sight the soul that weeps.

Loss and finding take on a different meaning in this other dimension beyond finite objectification. In transcending desire, we suffer not just the opening of any lack but the upsurge of infinite lack. The notion of infinite lack makes little sense in terms of finitely determinable entities. A lack is always the lack of something, and something is always determinate: I lack food, clothing, housing, and so on. What then could an infinite lack be? It is beyond univocal determination. It seems *hyperbolic*. It refers to the impotence of the finite to quell our extraordinary transcending. Defined in an interplay between our desire and the goods it seeks, infinite lack opens up in the disjunction between seeking and sought, though no determinate name can be given to what is being sought.

We do not really know what we seek. If we did, we would be on a par with it, and there would be no undergoing of this lack, except perhaps the boredom that comes from conquering. But boredom itself is a revelation of the infinite lack. Only a being capable of boredom, and this alone is the human being, testifies to the thrust to the "more"—again a thrust that cannot univocally name its goal. The infinite lack is a lacking, a dynamic happening that also is a patient undergoing. For in the dynamic interplay of desire and finite goods, we discover that unchosen, unwilled, the insufficiency of finite goods tells their tale; unwilled, we are thrust by a transcendence towards something more.

An abyss breaks open within, bringing terror as well as excitement. What is this abyss? An infinite neediness gapes in our desire. One must resist conceiving of this neediness in terms of the compensating achievement of this or that item of wealth. Clearly we often live this misconception, when we believe that the acquisition of more and more things will assuage the neediness. The abyss is beyond finite determination; the neediness is beyond finite alleviation. *It is not an infinite lacking that stands only in need of itself.* For what would its neediness do to itself except close a circle of insufficiency, even though it presents the face of absolute self-sufficiency to the world? It stands in need of what is other, the good that is other: not this good or that good, but the good as other. The infinite need of the good as other seeks another good that, to meet the lack, must itself be infinite. Short of this, our desire is a futile passion. Transcending would be our absurd overreaching into the void. Without an infinite good that comes into relation with our transcending, desire is an emptiness that must end in emptiness, a void that calls and must call to void.

Since we come to the verge of profound transformation here, the void we face can send us back into recoil towards reimmersion in finitude. We stare bleakly at nothing, and we conclude with a shudder that there is nothing there, and haste to retreat to the familiar comfort of finite goods: I have my car, my house, my friends, and so on, and these are my goods. These are my consolation against despair. They shore up a secret ruin. The signs of ruin are not easy to read. Those touched by the angel of death wander as if in deserted villages, peopled by unquiet ghosts, shadows passing the empty streets in twilight, horror deep in their eyes, or beseechment. The visible marks of flourishing can dissemble the opposite. The settlement of the living dead may be a thriving city.

If we have eyes doubled by death, eyes prescient with the double vision that is the angel's gift, one sees what is finitely there, and what is beyond and not there, or there with a truth the finite carapace serves to falsify. In the carapace is the shell of a life, and we remember the absolute vulnerability of the idiot self, which also is the source of its openness; remember that we are that vulnerable openness, and always will be; and realize there is horror in the protectiveness and self-assurance we have secreted around ourselves. The shell will be cracked, the golden bowl be buried in silt, the house will gape with glassless windows, the walls will tumble in on themselves, and in the rubble there will be only the idiot self, crying out in appeal, or hissing in execration.

The infinite lack is despair, without the enigmatic orientation of transcending desire towards the good as itself infinite. What kind of good could this be? It is not a good of this world, insofar as that is dominated by determinable objectivities. It is other. It is beyond self-mediation too insofar as the energy of desire cannot be the source of value that defines it as good. It is good absolutely for itself, and as other. Our relation to it beyond self-mediation is an undergoing and a receiving. It is in suffering this good that we are saved from despair. There is an open dialectic here between us as finite, even though infinitely restless, and the other good as infinite in a dimension to which we aspire but which we neither define nor can conquer.

Our doubleness comes back: finite and infinite; but infinite restlessness emerging in and beyond our finitude, thrusting for something more; and infinite restlessness teaches us our finitude in a deeper sense, since we come to despair if we get no further than finite goods. The infinite restlessness throws us back upon finitude in a way that opens up the possibility of another sense of the infinite, an infinite not at all defined by the mediation of finitude and infinity in our self-mediation: an appearance of the infinite into the middle and in a relation of superiority relative to our infinite restlessness. The doubleness, properly interiorized, pushes us towards the double vision that blindly sees beyond death, by itself being touched by death. The other of which it is blindly prescient is above it. It comes from the height of transcendence as other.

The anomalous being of the human is revealed in this freedom of infinite desire. Infinite desire emerges in finite being—excess of being rises up in the human being as selving: transcending as more, and towards the more. This "more" means enigmatic otherness in inwardness itself: the very interiority of being is the coming to show of infinity, the transcending power of the being, the transcendence towards infinity of the human being. As I said, this excess is both our misery and majesty, source of our futility and our drive towards nobility. Neither of these can be defined through our powers of self-mediation. Infinite desire is for the ultimate good, but this enigmatically intimates itself in the doubleness of transcending desire, as beyond the self-mediation of desire itself. There is a release of unique transcending power in us—a release beyond the self towards the ultimate other. Yet the release is in and into the maelstrom of the equivocal, hence it risks the perilous outcome of merely dissolving endlessness. Our transcending desire has to pass into its own precarious *equivocality*, pass through to its *erotic* possibility, and beyond this again to *agapeic freedom*. The move from the first two, especially beyond the second, occurs in the confrontation with the infinite lack. The infinite lack discovers the original power in transcending itself but is seized with temptations either to intoxication with its own energy or to absolutize itself in erotic sovereignty. Or it may be opened to the release into agapeic service.

With *equivocal transcending*, lostness induces a flight into the vehemence of unchecked desire. There is first the lostness of equivocal desiring: from mania to boredom, shouting to implosion, ending up stretched on the extremes, shattering any genuine being in the *between*. There can follow this our loss of the constancies, lack of phronesis and eudaimonia, for transcending is corrupted at the idiot level, as shown in violence in and towards the aesthetic, the beauty of being, bodily in us, and the world of nature despoiled. We become incapable of properly marking difference, then swallowed by differences into a promiscuous univocity, wherein all is lost. For self and other must be set apart and held together in communicative togetherness, for the self to be in proper self-relation, for the relation to the other to be as it should be.

With *erotic transcending*, there is struggle with the equivocal within: the chaos, the anger, the monster; there is confronting the lack and the undergoing of life as lost; there is struggle with the opening within and seeking to overcome the lack in self-transcending. Transcendence is *self*-transcending; the self is coming to itself in its going beyond itself, coming back to itself, and through the other, since this is complexly mediated: the other gives me back my self, and I come to myself. There is this immense struggle to come back to self in relation to the other, and this means coming into some overcoming of the monster within. (Some end up as monsters, conquered by what they think they conquer.) This form of transcending is in the between, but with a predominance of a kind of dialectical self-mediation, in which I come back to myself through my relation to the other, thereby attaining a kind of self-determining power.

This relates to erotic sovereignty, where there is a will to life, a will to affirm life, even despite the abyss of lack. The will to affirm is expressed as self-affirmation: I am I; I still am I, in the face of the abyss of emptiness. Often in erotic sovereignty there is a defiance of the negative, a revolt against the emptiness or lack or loss, a revolt that affirms itself in its refusal of the lack. And there is a rightness to this. We must not turn against the good of the "to be." This defiance of the emptiness is a rightful affirmation that despite the worst there is still life to be lived, no matter how squalid or in travail. But the peril of the revolt is that the I becomes a self in revolt against the conditions of life and less an affirmer, *despite the lack and the loss*, of the good of the "to be." The revolting I then can become an incarnation of evil will to life, even as its revolt is carried by the affirmation of the good of the "to be," manifested in its own particular being. Affirming life, it has an evil eye for life; for the life it affirms first and foremost, and also last and most of all, is the particularization of the good "to be" that is *itself.* Then ensues the self-deification of the erotic sovereign. This self-affirmation turns to evil, and paradoxically an evil produced by the ambiguity of its "no" to the evil it sees outside of itself.[33] It has not learned its solidarity with those evils; it has not learned forgiveness and compassion; these would put it in a different relation to what is other.

33. How relate the daimon and this self-deification? I think the daimon is here turned into *my* daimon and its otherness to possession blurred in the false belief that I am the daimon; the daimon is usurped in this form of the daimonic. Is this what was called "possession" in the good old days—diabolic possession? The ambiguous power of the daimon is perverted by being appropriated—that is, by being misappropriated. I usurp the daimon and find myself usurped.

I am not claiming that erotic sovereignty is necessitated to become this monstrous god. If, as Plato suggests, eros is a daimon, midway between mortals and gods, its reference is to the latter in the between. There are concretions of great nobility that have faced the monster and faced it down and that maintain a wholeness and integrity in the face of it. If these nobles do not make the next step and learn the wisdom of forgiveness, and if they have learned something of the humbling effect that follows struggle with the monster, the sadness of infinite lack will come upon them again and again, and purely in terms of their nobility, their erotic sovereignty, they will not be able to shake off the distress. They must become open to a further struggle with transcendence, and with the pride in their great achievements that, first bringing them back to affirm the good of life, now may cut them off from that good.

In *agapeic transcending*, there is the great struggle that is no struggle, for nothing we can do as just willed by us will bring us the release of this form of self-transcending. How struggle to let go; and to see and live in the light of the inexpressible good of the gift of being? The relation is to the other, not to the exclusion of the good of I. We affirm the good of the "to be" as beyond the good of self but not hostile to it. We affirm the good as the source of this good: God. Affirming is consent to *gift*. Generosity is born of a primal gratitude. Ethics springs from gratitude. This is lived in ethical and religious service beyond autonomy. What is this service? It is a willingness beyond will, beyond will to power, beyond my will to power. (The religious say: It is serving the will of God, insofar as this is possible for human beings.) The great venture that moves from erotic to agapeic self-transcending has to do with the realization in soul and body, in the life of the person, that there is a transcendence other than self-transcendence.[34] If erotic sovereignty is tempted to close the circle of desire and make self both desiring and desired, by contrast agapeic service cannot close any circle, for the desired is not the same as the desiring—when I desire I desire the good as other to my desire: the communal reference to the good as other is in the dynamism of our self-transcending. Desire itself is a primal openness to the other and the beyond. Desire of the good is desire of God.

Transcendence and the Metaxological: The Agape of the Good

Is it possible for humans to sustain an ethics of agapeic service? Extremely hard. We are always drawn back into the being of selving as for-itself. The doubleness of

---

34. Transcending always refers the ethical constancies beyond their own univocal stabilization and in the constancy of the law itself. Thus the beatitudes reveal the truth of transcending, in the surprise, rupture, and breakthrough of its agapeic form, and beyond fixation in law.

our transcending, as seeking its own fulfillment and going beyond itself to the other, resists definition by one or either side. Yet no absolute closure on ourselves is possible; we always stand in relation to others; though there can be a retraction of self back on itself, as if, in its necessary relation to the other, it would that it were only in relation to itself and nothing but itself. But in this "would," it is always fighting against the exigence of transcending to be for the other.

Equally, on the other side, we cannot absolutely leave ourselves behind, in our being for the other; there is no transcending for us so absolutely selfless as to be nothing but a service for the other; for our self-transcending, even when maximum, is still the self as other, in its being beyond itself, and so it always brings itself with its self-surpassing, hence there is always a "for-itself," even in the purest form of its being for the other. This means concretely that just as self-love cannot be defined absolutely to exclude the other, neither can love of the other exclude self-love. Moreover, there is a proper self-love; this is the love of the good of the "to be" as singularized in the I; this I is to be loved as good, as much as the good of the other. Concretely, this proper self-love is mixed with more retracted selfishness so that agapeic service also is mingled with other considerations: the need to get something back, to get something out of the relation, to get a return, whether thanks, recognition, a smile, or a mere nod. The agape of being is entirely forgiving and will laugh at these mischiefs of selfishness. The human is to be loved still.

Acting on the call of agapeic service is not sustainable by our will alone. It is not enacted by autonomous will deliberately setting out to be beyond itself in service for the other. Transcending desire discovers that, in being fully itself, it is more than itself and called forth by transcendence as more than itself, transcendence as superior to it. The call is a sustaining that is prior to the hearing of the call. The hearing is sustained by the call that, in being sounded, opens up the middle of communication, even before the middle serves as the medium of its transmission and reception.

That is why I speak of a willingness before and beyond will, or any will to power. For this willingness is the laying of selving open to this calling. And it is in the strength that comes to one in laying oneself open that the support is offered for living something of the life of agapeic service. Strength comes from laying oneself open, or being opened. The power of being good grows with knowing that one is not the good; the power of doing good comes from knowing that good is being done to one; the power of willing the good comes from beyond the powerlessness of will to power.

Needless to say, the call of the transcendent good is enigmatic in our self-transcending. Hence our laying of ourselves as open seems like a constant striving, or like a pathway through a wilderness that often vanishes, making us think we had been fooling ourselves, only then to reappear suddenly further along and hearten us that our faith in the good, faith without certitude, is not without unexpected fruit. The life of agapeic service is impossible if we are alone and without the sustaining power of the good as other. As I suggested before, the familiar word (and I think best word) for transcendence itself is God. The fullest community with the good is reflected in the openness of the metaxological way towards God as the ultimate other. The metaxological is a way of trying to give articulation to the ethos as the finite between wherein God is intimated and reserved in the idiotic, aesthetic, dianoetic, transcendental, eudaimonistic, and transcending potencies of the ethical.

There is a reversal here: being open finds itself being opened. The ultimate power is turned towards us: transcendence itself possibilizes all transcending, indeed all being, and possibilizes it because transcendence itself is good. It is not only good but the good. The good communicates itself into the between, communicating the space that sustains the community of finite being and the variety of self-becomings of different beings, as each strives towards what is good for it, or what is good. There is a community of the good beyond self-determination, given from the origin, giving the ethos and the power of "to be" as good, giving the self the power to be determining of itself, giving it itself to be itself, giving all beings their distinctive promise of agapeic community with other beings.

The ethos as good is not any projection of the human good. The gift means an undergoing of the good from the origin. The supreme suffering of self-transcending reveals ultimate receptivity, not mastering power. We do not understand the mystery of God. Metaxological mindfulness mulls over the signs of God in the between, alert to what comes to it from beyond itself. Traces of transcendence are communicated in many ways to the twilight or dawn of the middle. The many ways and the one good are not antagonistic, for the one good as agapeic gives the plural between, communicates to it its being as good, whence comes the good of the "to be." The many ways are possible ways to serve the communication of the good in the community of agapeic service. This is true even of our finite vulnerability, which strangely heightens the good rather than simply being the occasion of despair. It is because we love the good that we despair, when we are not with what our being secretly tells us we should be with. Despair is love of God frustrated, frustrated by overwhelming perplexity about the equivocal face of evil, or perhaps by our frustrating or corrupting the exigence of transcending in ourselves.

The relation to the good as other is more complex than dialectic comprehends; the mystery is more affirmative than equivocity knows; determination is more open than univocity allows. The intimation of transcendence as other is not within our univocal or dialectical grasp, though the equivocal brings us to its threshold. Those who have the finesse of the equivocal often are closer to the divine, though their finesse seems like a laughing mockery of the certitudes of univocity or the premature inclusions of dialectic. Nor is the intimation separable from the glory of creation, its show of aesthetic value in the ontological splendor of the incarnate "to be." Love of creation is secret love of God, for the time of creation is our time to sing.

There is no univocal proof of what is suggested in the intimation. There is probing with respect to the ultimate perplexities, especially, "What is the good of it all?" This perplexity we have shunned in our obsession with this or that finite good. Yet if there is no response to it, our busy obsession is much ado about nothing, and we had better face this honestly, for the emptiness will stalk abroad as hatred of life and leave us finally in the lurch. The probe is dependent on discipline that purifies itself in the direction of spiritual discernment. This archaic truth is neither old nor new, it is elemental and perennial, always promised, always betrayed, but in strange ways, also redeemed. The agape of being is first given to us, but we are called to an agapeic being that is the doing of living, in an ethics of gratitude to the origin, and of generosity to self and other. The agape of being intimates a fullness, but it is not being full of oneself. One does nothing to merit it, and no payment is exacted, for it offers itself simply as the life of the good, a life we are to live. It has no reason, beyond itself, which is to be beyond itself, in being itself.

PART III

ETHICAL SELVINGS

CHAPTER SIX

FIRST ETHICAL SELVING:
THE IDIOCY OF ROOT WILL

Ethical Selvings

Our task now is to explore the ethos of the between, less relative to the more "metaethical" ways of the previous part, than relative to *being ethical as a becoming good*. To speak about this is difficult, since it involves more than a linear unfolding; it is more a process of forward movement and backward tracking, in which the unfolding recurs deeper and deeper to the sources of being ethical, all the while also articulating fuller expressions of transcending. In Part III, I consider the self-mediations of the good from rudimentary desire to agapeic freedom beyond autonomy. In Part IV, I explore different communal shapings, from the family to agapeic service, that make up the intermediations of the good.

Beyond the immediate equivocity of the good, its more overt self-mediation occurs with humans. Other things selve, but our selving is more extensive and intensive. Nothing is so closed into itself as to lack some energy of self-transcendence, but with us this energy becomes more startlingly evident, and the more so as it wakes to itself as mindfulness. With the deepening of the intensiveness of self-transcending is the widening of its extensiveness. We are the selving of being good. Of course, we cannot separate the self-mediation of being good from the intermediation with the other. But for purposes of clarification, self-mediation can be correlated with a more dialectical slant, intermediation with a more metaxological. In truth, ethical selving is intermediated through and through, and is hence metaxological. The intermediate sustains the self-mediation.

These selvings of being good might be said to follow broadly the lines of a human genesis: infancy, childhood, adolescence, adulthood, age. This and subsequent chapters in Part III will follow, more or less, this unfolding. *First selving*: the idiocy of root will surges up as spontaneous desire/need—elemental self-insistence. *Second selving*: the age of "reason"—mindfulness comes and willing, and the doubling of will; "conscience" comes in this doubling between self and other, and the intimacy of the other within self. *Third selving*: desire's new adolescent upsurge. Puberty: the unruliness of eros ferments in the opening of the

223

interior space of selving. It shatters and remakes with a new aesthetic, and idiotic upsurge, and this in virgin flesh itself. Self-identity undergoes crisis and difference though the equivocity of eros (adolescent infatuation with the other is self-infatuation). *Fourth selving*: beyond an equivocal liberty ethical selving works for an adult autonomy, not least by dialectically seeking to appropriate its own powers of negation. *Fifth selving*: adult eros seeks its sovereignty (there is "autonomy" and mature autonomy). *Sixth selving*: eros begins to be a giving over to agapeic willing (philia: friends as *others* count). *Seventh selving*: being freed beyond autonomy and erotic sovereignty, sifted by suffering into agapeic service and the passion of being. These selvings articulate the transformation of root will into agapeic willingness. Is there any wisdom of age? A time that serves as herald of eternity? Is there a Sabbath of willing—a kind of idiocy that is holy?

Desire's Bodied Flush: Skin and Seepage

There is an immediacy of the good of "to be" prior to its express self-mediation and intermediation. This immediacy is intimated in the happening of sensuous givenness, in our bodies, in desire as surging up spontaneously. Such an immediate aesthetics of value is double: a showing, it also is a concealing; a manifesting, it is the reticence of something retained in hiddenness. We come to know this of our given place in nature: human life flourishes more or less, sometimes less than more; then we know not only nature's generosity but also the harshness, the scarcity, the bitterness of eking toil. We know the extremes: nature so indifferent our soft flesh hardens itself, as if in a landscape of penance; nature itself soft, as on a golden day, fragrant with secrets scented but not entered, brimming us with satiety. Now hostile, disquieting; now caressing, almost loving. And we ourselves also are double: coming to ourselves or stunted; confident that life's conditions are good, or dismayed they are so grim. The doubleness is not clear-cut, for sometimes it is good we have to fight, otherwise we would still sleep; so much so, we wonder if nature's opposition is secretly a support. What is good in it and bad, what is good for us and bad, concerning these we are left unsure. This reflects the immediate equivocity of the ethos.

At first we lack determinate cognition of this; we have a presentiment of it. We find ourselves living thus, being lived thus in the *flesh*, where rudimentary mindfulness is sparked with stray flashes of intimation. Our embodiment: a joy in the good of the "to be"; and yet, almost on the instant, this enjoyment of "to be" retracts into a protectiveness, when the ambiguous other precipitates the presentiment of our exposure. The joy of being turns to the guarding of joy of being in my "to be." It is turned thus by trepidation for itself. What am I then? Insecurity rather than trust. The other? Threat rather than the welcoming face. This is our immediately doubled condition. *Within ourselves*: confidence and inconstancy. *Without ourselves*: the glorious draw of the world, but danger round that bend, filling us with dread. Our presentiment within of the danger without deepens the insecurity within. And when danger does materialize without, it redirects that inner insecurity outwards, in the defensive posture of aggression. What does this do? It materializes all the more the danger without, while aggravating the more our defensiveness into aggression. This knotted result flows from the love of being as good that we know in the love of our own given being.

Our bodies live this equivocal conjunction of trust and distrust. This conjunction is doubled over into itself, twisted into a tension-filled torque. The thereness of other-being, the ethos itself, as an overdetermined milieu of value, ferments in its tense singularity. The human body is a tangled site of sameness and otherness, at-homeness and alienness, rooted in itself and exposed to being ungrounded. Thus its extraordinary *responsiveness*: not a response to a stimulus but an overdetermined world unto itself, containing multiplicities in its own immanences, recklessly generous and insanely selfish. The flick of an eyebrow can send this world into gyres of mutation that may come to the top as smiles of appreciation or roars of ire. The body concretizes our rapport with the world as aesthetic show. The body is the fleshed matrix of our pleasure in the between as milieu of the good of "to be." The body is not here and the outer world over there, nor vice versa, even though both are different. It is hard to fix the body into a univocal unity set in strict opposition to what is other to itself as world. There is an interplay, indeed a *seepage*, from one to the other. The world seeps into us, even as our bodies primitively are already seepages beyond themselves.

Think of our skin. It is a porous, two-way passage between different sides of the aesthetic show of being. We are an aesthetic skin, not just a set of fixed, determinate organs of sensation. The organs of sensation are themselves specifications and specializations of this more pervasive porosity. What is skin? A membrane that separates, but that also can be breached, or that breathes and opens and sweats; that may be wounded and healed or suppurate. It is an indeterminate medium of rapport between; a vulnerable middle in which pain and pleasure find their register. This indeterminacy in our being as elementally embodied suggests an aesthetic equivocity *prior to* univocal fixation into this feeling organ or that, this or that specific pleasure. It gives us a feel for how we are in the world, and how the world is for us and towards us: it gives us a sense of how we are in the midst of things.

Think of the infant at the breast: all mouth, all skin, gurgling on the mother's skin. There is an indeterminate "being pleased" in which skin is the porous between aroused with aesthetic community in which one and the other meet. This is why some of the most intense pleasures are a kind of return to this indeterminacy; not just pleasure in this or that but an indeterminate pleasure that suffuses the being as a whole. Erotic arousal means intense pleasure, because it is the skin that is most aroused, most in rapport, most desiring the caress and also disturbed, as it seeks to be as close as possible to the other; so close it would want to be on the other side of the skin, but of course it cannot be. This skin: intimate yet granting intimacy; a surface that wants not to be a surface, that wants to vanish and yet all it wants is to be more there, there more intensely than ever, there as urgent excess of indeterminate arousal and rapport. One can be bewitched by this pleasure, as if a "narcissistic" return to the mother skin were sought. Of course, the presentiment of difference also can make the skin cold and a mask. The face is especially the skin of personal presence, but this is equivocal, not ethically univocal, as Levinas seems to suggest. This is one reason we *adorn* the skin. We put on another face, we put our best face forward, lest we lose face or lest the other sees the gargoyle self.[1]

The flush of indeterminate desire comes to suffuse skin. Think of these porosities: I am hungry—and so withdrawn into self and yet outside of myself foraging. I have a hearty meal, I am sated. What is the effect? I am full, yes, but then seepage comes: the world of other-being is touched with a glow—no longer prey but in rapport again. The lion hungry: rapport with the deer, but it is predatory. The lion full: rapport again, but now it is a fleshed peace. Since humans are marked by an *excess of hunger*, predation is always suspended in the rapport. The flesh of peace is subtended by an insatiable hunger whose irritable flame rarely sleeps. The intensive depth and extensive range of our desire mean a ceaseless reformulation of the entire field of desire, hence the possibilities of the rapport. Our doubleness is perilous: our skins caress and are caressed; they also are surfaces of slapping and betrayal.[2]

This, then, is the point: out of the indeterminate porosity of the embodied skin, we are in rapport with other-being and self, and we make no separation between one and the other; there is a lived ecstasy not first known, but lived, though it enters into some awareness of itself, in an indefinite way, for otherwise it could not be the "being pleased" that it is. It is preobjective and presubjective but also transsubjective and transobjective, because both subjective and objective, though these terms are not adequate to express what it is (they are the product of univocalization and determination). There is the happening of an idiotic pleasure with being—felt rather than cognized, lived rather than reflected on, surging rather than directed, pervasive rather than fixed, overall instead of specific.

This happening, nevertheless, is articulated into different, determinate desires. Spontaneous desire takes more specific form, and the rapport is mapped, so to say. The skin becomes zoned into definite organs and places, each with

---

1. Some feel exposed in the skin, as if without a skin; being seen may feel like a flaying; inordinately shy people live the skin as the porosity that exposes them.

2. Other examples of the porosity: getting drunk—intoxication as the dissolving of hostile difference, though in some cases the violence within comes then to the surface, comes to the skin; being in love, especially with adolescent infatuation—how everything glows differently in the seepage; and prayer, a kind of return to a *primal porosity*, and one is as if not there, and is nothing but the passage of divine energy. This is related to the idiot self.

more specific needs and powers. The initial rapport and arousal is made more and more determinate. This is the point where we more normally speak about pleasure: the pleasure of the senses, not of indeterminate sensing: of the eye, the ear, the mouth, the genitals and so on. There is a spontaneous movement to a more univocalized desire: hunger to food, drink to liquid, ear to song, hand to hand, and so on. There are cases where this specification takes longer to develop, as with the genital pleasure—the vagueness and indeterminacy of pre-puberty becoming more determinate with puberty and beyond. Again, here the determinate is relative, not absolute, since there is tremendous indeterminacy about the arousal occasioned onward from puberty, and bewildering flux in the movement of desires, desires that happen with a new vehemence, not chosen desires, desires that live us rather than we directing them.

The Idiocy of Root Will

There are degrees of intensiveness to desire as well as different amplitudes to its extensiveness. The indeterminacy means our desire is potentially an unlimited openness to what is other, even as it drives us to seek to be whole. No finite limit can be imposed on it a priori, either with respect to its intensive depth or extensive range. It manifests an infinite restlessness. Mindfulness is the waking up of this self-transcending power. The power to be is the original of desire and mindfulness; they are different crystalizations of its initial idiotic indeterminacy. This original power to be exceeds what mindfulness can determinately grasp or desire exhaust. This excess does not undercut its powerful thrust. Quite the opposite—the thrust continues its surge, though it does not clearly know where it heads or definitely comprehend what it desires. Often it is out in front of what mindfulness expressly understands or desire defines. This excess energy finds its expression in willing.

Will means different things, but first will is more elemental than this or that determinate choice. Elementally, will names the root self-insistence of selving. A child expresses itself, plays effortlessly an energy of being that seems tireless. In its indeterminate reaching out, there is this quite determinate insistence of self: this singular concretion of energy of "to be," just in its expression, is self-insistence. This is the singular stress of "to be" that a definite human is, relative to the particularization of its own energy of being for itself. This elemental will, while completely determinate, cannot be completely determinated. (Consider the obdurate will of a stubborn child—absolutely determinate, yet when we try to determine it in terms of our order, or command, it completely escapes that determination.)

This elemental will shows the root energy of the idiot self. Out of it is unfolded the singularization of the maturing self. Maturing will point forward, as we will see, to a willingness beyond determinate wills. Mostly human life is shaped in the *middle range* between the elemental will of root self-insistence, and this other willingness. All strivings of will are determinations of the original energy of the "to be," but most are in the middle range between these extremes.[3] In this middle range, will itself, willing the good, works to be a mediation of the equivocity of the ethos, often in terms of projects that reflect our will to power. This equivocity excites us, bewilders us, bewitches us. Sometimes we just drift along, content to let things happen to us. In time, however, we have to *will the good* in the equivocity of the ethos. We have to choose ourselves and our form of life. Of course, we may be deprived of the opportunity of certain choices; nevertheless, we have to relate ourselves to ourselves and our situation, if only to revolt against it. Negation too is a form of willing, in which the self insists that the current situation cannot stand.

The elemental root of will has to be more than self-insistence. Ethical selving, in this middle range of willing, has to undergo the education of the between. It must be free: self-determining rather than simply self-insistent. Sometimes the difference here is hard to see. A person insists on self, and it looks like mere pigheadedness. It may be that, but it also may spring from the will to be oneself, defined through one's feel for what is appropriate. The equivocal faces of selving require a nuanced understanding. The root will is in the idiot self—sheer idiosyncrasy in one sense, but in another sense, it is the intimacy of being, hence the happening of deep presence both to self and to others. The truth of community, of communicative being with a uniquely personal intonation, is already there in the root will. The unfolding, the communication of that root into the between, is fraught with ambiguity, for the closure of the root will back into itself has to be weaned from a self-insistence careless of community. By its very nature, it is self-defining, though not such as to exclude the other, but it must be educated towards a truthfulness to its own being as communicative personhood.

The root will is always at work, even when self-determination mediates it. There is goodness to this root will: the self-insistence is the very energy in which the unique self-being of this being gives expression to itself. Every being is thus, simply as a being of dynamic energy; this is the spontaneous affirmation of its own being, of this being as good, and of the good of this being. The real challenge is

---

3. Most ethical discussion does not focus on this willingness beyond will, beyond willpower, but on will in the middle range. But we distort this middle range if we forget the extremes. The extremes relate also to the indeterminacy of the original energy of the "to be," not particularized into a self-insistent singularity of being for self, but released beyond self in a way that cannot be definitely determined in advance. This willing beyond definite will is not just at the end; it is the promise of a universal openness there from the start, lived in mindfulness as thinking what is other to thought, loved secretly and unknowingly in the restless sweep of infinite desire, imagined now and then in breathtaking moments of inspiring vision, remembered with elegiac tenderness when finitude makes its flare subside. Overall, Part III outlines the transformation of root will, beyond willfulness into self-determining willing, to the willingness beyond self-determination that echoes in articulated life what is inarticulate in the indeterminate original energy of the idiotic self.

one of being genuinely truthful to this exigence of being. For this exigence includes more than the root will in its unique stress of self. It includes community with the other. There can be no truthfulness to self that excludes faithfulness to the truth of the other. The challenge includes this twist: the root will sometimes masks its refusal to acknowledge the truth of the other by spouting the language of freedom as self-determination. It will run roughshod over the other, preaching the virtues of its own self-determination, concealing thus the truncation of self-transcendence that refuses to pass beyond itself. The masks of equivocity also include the ruses of self-relation: I mask myself in forms of self-*manifestation* that, while manifesting myself, disguise and deceive. How many times do we see it? I perch in a high pulpit, and I preach my right of self-determination, and what I really mean is my right to do what the hell I want. Ideal freedom, base selfishness. A deeper discernment of the communicative exigence of the idiot self, and freedom beyond autonomy, detects the self-serving hollowness of this rhetoric.

Ethical selving is inseparable from crucial transformations of the idiot root. The mindful selving of the good is tied up with desire, memory, and imagination. *Desire*: as orienting us towards what we seek. *Imagination*: as allowing us to envisage being as other than it now is, hence as shaping desire's orientation. *Memory*: as stabilizing desire in the lessons it has learned from its forays towards its goal, beyond the immediacy of its first upsurge into unchosen self-surpassing. All three form the process of self-surpassing, shape the unfolding of our distinctive transcending as metaxologically mindful.

Desire is basic: it is the very energy of the original power to be as self-surpassing, which takes form from an immanent exigence at first not chosen but lived—immediately undergone, though able to assume a more self-defining shape. Imagination begins the freeing of desire from its own immediacy in a double differentiation: undergoing desire, we also come to ourselves, and we come into the envisaging of what is other. Immersed in immediacy, imagination frees from immersion. Thus the image's power to effect us: it takes us out of ourselves spontaneously; it may rivet us or stir passions we had not dreamed existed. If it takes us out of ourselves, it also brings us to ourselves, for we come to display the power by which we can enter into the life of the other as other. The image touches deeply the idiotic, and aesthetic self, and thus is immersed in "subjectivity." But by letting us envisage beyond immediate presentness, it places us in a life beyond "subjectivity." It is an immediate concretion of the vector of transcendence as it surpasses the inwardly idiotic and aesthetically incarnate. Only humans seem to be marked by this capacity for free images.[4] Human desire is energized by the image itself. It

---

4. Such are images freed from more univocally determined patterns of stimulus and response. A hiatus is interjected between the stimulus and the response; we can pause in not immediately responding, and in that pause is the power to respond otherwise or differently. That space of being other is impossible without imagination, for imagination imagines that the other might be other, that we might be other. (See *PO*, Chapter 2.)

is not that there is a basic desire upon which the image superimposes another layer. Imagination permeates the freeing of the energy of human desire. An image releases desire or, in some cases, it suppresses desire. A latent world of "subjectivity" is carried by the image, as is a presentiment of the other as possibility. This intimation tantalizes desire with the dream of its secret bliss.[5]

It is not simply that desire frees imagination, or imagination desire: rather, both are modes of the freeing of the original power of transcending being in us. Imagination is free in us, because desire is the freeing of itself from the univocal immediacy of stimulus and response, response that is really no response but a determined reaction, for a response means the responding of the I to the other. Genuine response presupposes first that pause of consideration in which the other is considered for itself as other. Imagination shapes the freeing of self and the sense of other as it is for itself and for the responding self.

What about memory? Without orientation to the possible, freeing is not itself possible: desire and imagination live towards the possible; but the possible is not enough. For freeing concerns an actualizing beyond the currently concretized actuality. But there is no possibilizing without the original power of being as actualizing the power of possibilizing. Memory is turned towards the inescapability of the actualizing and actual. Memory often is seen as bound to necessities that already have taken place and hence are beyond freedom. This is true in the sense that what has been has passed into already determined actuality; but as having passed, it is not absolutely past, since it provides the actuality on whose ground actualizing and hence possibilizing continue. Memory in us is the release of mindfulness towards this grounding. There is no orientation of desire towards future possibility, no imaginative envisagement of being-other, without this ground which itself provides the opening by which the surpassing is a surpassing of self. Without memory, there is nothing that surpasses itself. Memory frees freedom from its own danger of defining itself as merely the negation of what now is.[6] For what was and is are not rigid, univocal determinations whose iron chains freedom must break. What was and is include the hospitality of the gift of being to the release of free being. Freedom defined as merely negative relation to the past is freedom undercutting its own promise of fulfillment. It has cut itself off from the more basic hospitality, given in the ethos, to its own self-actualization. Memory is more like the plow that must continually turn up the soil to make it fertile for freedom. Nothing grows on soil that has become hardened on the surface. Nor

---

5. Advertisers know this well: the image seduces unformed desire (see Chapter 14). Of course, the image also may be an exemplary life that unlocks ethical hope. It may release a reserve of longing that carries us towards the unconditional good, a reserve we thought dead or nonexistent.

6. We misunderstand freedom if we only emphasize the relation to possibility and futurity; we can fixate on negation (as in Sartre, or thinkers who privilege future orientation).

does anything take root when there is a mere whirlwind of change on the surface of the earth. This erodes the fertile topsoil and the coming of winds of devastation stirs up the dust. Memory entails the necessary reverence for being as other to our complete determination, without which our own self-determination withers at the roots. This is one reason memory was called the mother of the muses.

Here there are different forms of memory (see *BB*, 389ff.). First is the *elemental recurrence to self* that happens always in human self-transcendence. Second is the *derived memory* that a human being builds up over a lifetime trajectory, which includes what has been done as well as undergone. Third is the *integral memory* that strives to bring derived and elemental memory into some existential harmony. This third form seeks an integration of what one elementally is and might be, with what one is, as having become that character. This last entails achievement but also a kind of confession of failure (thus guilt and evil doing must be faced). It also harbors the promise of forgiveness, for not being what one is, or not responding to the ethical solicitation of the other. This third memory is not at all closed to the *fourth recollection*, so to say, where self-transcending is renewed, while the release of freedom is converted to a new going out of itself towards the other. The very hiatus of the first and second, confessed in the third, does not mean a return to self-satisfaction or self-security, but calls for a further release of freedom beyond one's own integral being.

Transformations in Root Will (1): Selving and the Ideal

Desire is not a mere emptiness that needs to be filled. Its very demand to be filled reveals the emptiness to be self-insistent. What a strange thing—a self-insistent emptiness! A self-insistent lack, just by being self-insistent, is not a mere lack. It is an original center of energy whose being is to give expression to itself, in its obdurate presence as there, in its incontrovertible demand that it be noted and satisfied, in the recalcitrant singularity that is itself and not anything other. We need a plurality of paradoxical descriptions to get at what is elemental here at the root: an idiot self that is indeterminate, and in no merely indefinite sense, since it is uniquely singular; and yet also, though indeterminate, this self determinately insists upon itself, and shows the obdurate concreteness that seeks to make other-being form a circle of relevance around its need.

There is intelligibility in this plurality. First, this singular concretion also is plural; it is metaxologically double—self-related and other-implicated, singular and communicative being in one. Second, this concretion is not a determinate univocal but an overdetermined source of origination—this is its originality as a center of "to be." Third, that overdetermined source exceeds determinate boundaries, hence it is self-expressive and communicative, an origin of self-transcendence and communication. Fourth, in the original self-exceeding, the doubleness shows itself as a complex interplay of its own energy of being and its relation to other-being. In this interplay, it is both affirmative energy and also lack.

This is where we situate the lack: emergent in an equivocal situation where the affirmative original energy shows itself in need of the other to be itself fully: its fullness with itself is emptiness if not also constituted by relation to the other. Need of the other is not then a deficiency but a self-manifestation of what it is as a communicative being, enabled to be for itself only through its implication with what is other. Need would be a defect only if the truth of full being were a kind of inert univocity of sameness. But any such inert univocity must exclude the energy of self-manifestation and self-communication. Need is something positive for a being whose being for itself is inseparable from other-being. This reflects the nature of metaxological being as doubly mediated.

Of course, there is tension between being for self and relation to the other. Since the source of self-transcending is concretized in this singular self, there is a tension, within self, between the self and the transcending. Selving shows the exigence to affirm one's singularity as an integrity to be maintained; transcending shows the exigence to be beyond self, risking the adventure of the other; the stress of what is beyond the integrity may shatter its integrity. Inevitably, the self-insistence of the center will protect itself against possible shattering, even while its being cannot but be in process of exceeding itself. Both are necessities of its being, but they show a dialectic of singularity and self-surpassing, self-expression and communication. The singularity of our being in the between always modulates the specific tonality with which we live the double mediation. Our quandary: How is the energy of transcendence released without loss of either the fullness of singularity or of communicative being? Response: The process need not destroy the singularity, and yet a "destruction" may be needed. I mean that the idiotic center must concretize itself in definite ways of being, thus come to constitute a definite character. But just that determinate concretion may be not fully true to the elemental truth of the metaxological. It may be necessary to destroy the false sedimentation of determinate selfhood to release again the primal energy of transcendence. I will come back to this, having run through some of the stages of determination.

For the idiot self has an intimacy with the good of the "to be," which is predeterminate, yet it tends to close in around its own self-insistence, hence it comes out as *the insistence on my being*: I am, and my being as such is good, and will be preserved and perpetuated. This is the elemental "narrowness" involved in the idiot which, however, is not at all determinate. In a way, I am the good; except this good of the "I am" is not possible without the gift of the other, nor its expression possible without the continuing gift. Yet *here* this gift is turned around into being as for me; its good is good, but it is primarily for me, when the good of my self-being is elementally stressed—as indeed it must be. How then understand the transformation of rudimentary desire into a more determinate form? I suggest that we understand it in terms of the potencies of the ethical.

First, it is *aesthetic* when the root will seeks its pleasure: in being pleased with being other, and in being pleased with itself. Pleasure is the flower of being pleased. Thus the basic amen to the elemental "to be" finds its incarnate expansion in a multiplication of pleasure: the "please" that asks what is needed of the other, the being pleased that is fruit of the answer given; the displeasure in finding the giving or refusal of the other not as good for one. Aesthetic good is not simply selfish, for it is always defined in a reaching beyond, and the body itself is this reaching beyond, an incarnation of transcending. The value of the pleasing is an extension of the elemental good of the "to be." It too has its ontological ground in the inarticulate metaxological community of the ethos. There is no escaping it, nor should there be, as ascetics will recommend. What then is the problem? It is the *short-circuiting of "being pleased"* simply to the elemental self-affirmation. When this occurs, we suspect the "narcissistic" personality: the idiot self-pleasure fails to go beyond its own affirmation of itself and retracts even the gift of community into its own closeted intimacy. This is the opposite of transcending in the fullness of being pleased: being pleased is a being pleased *with*, and the full meaning of "with" cannot be confined to "with self."

Second, the labyrinth of the intimate nevertheless calls for more *dianoetic* constancies. But these too are related to self-transcending desire. They are not reached by extirpating root will but by desire becoming *mindful*: mindfulness emerges in the body and is in the body, even as it reaches beyond the surface of exteriority. Mindful interiority suggests something both shown and yet beyond showing. Thus the dianoetic constancies come to expression as *ideals* that a mindful self finds making demands on the course of its self-transcending. Desire itself undergoes transformation in light of ideals; it becomes itself ideal. The ideals may be ends it seeks as worthy, or commands it must follow to be itself the integral good it seeks to be. Thus ideals transform the root will into something more than either languid drift of pleasure or root self-insistence. Something more inherent emerges that makes a demand on its own self-transformation. What we more normally call *will* emerges here. This will is mediated in desire by dianoetic mindfulness—it demands and enacts decisiveness.

It is at this point that we may more properly speak of selving as the *becoming of an agency*. The becoming of agency faces new equivocity: it has to act not on whim but according to an ethical order that makes its demand on it through the ideal. The self chooses itself as an ethical agent in coming into the neighborhood of this demand of the ideal. But what is this order? Alas, the condition of Babel repeats itself here. There are many efforts to state the ideal or ideals thought to constitute the ethical order. Some formulations are more lax, others more rigorous. All testify to the inescapability of the demand of the ideal. The answer we have already given is relative to the metaxological community: a double ideal—truth to self that is inseparable from truth to the other.

Third, the *transcendental* order of the ideal is connected to this double demand of relativity: integrity of self-being and communicative being with the other human, and each as an infinite value.[7] For the *infinite depth* of the self, evident in restless desire and in the overdeterimination of the intimate, means that the value inherent in both self and other is more than finite. This infinite value cuts across the divide of self and other, and serves to give more concrete flesh to the ideal. Of course, further interpretations of the ideal will be controversial. For a more objectivistic, univocal one, ideals are just there, as quasi things; for a more subjectivistic, equivocal one, they are projections of secret desire. If there is some truth to both, they must be situated in a dialectic of innerness and otherness, hence redefined relative to the between wherein desire is *both unfolding and being converted*. The ideal will be the integral wholeness of humanity such as is possible for a singular self; it also will be more than self and will issue the demand of the community of ethical persons. This metaxological side of communicative openness to the other gives rise to the ideal, such as we find in the community of agapeic service.

Fourth, relative to the *eudaimonistic* potency, there is the call on the willing agent to concretize in a life this plurivocal ideal. The integrity of self must be enacted: the ideal and the real, the ethical and the aesthetic, and so on have to be brought to some harmony. This does not exclude struggle nor occasions of sacrifice when one side has to be secondary, as the ethical judgment sees fit. One might wish a seamless "being pleased with," but the metaxological ideal strains us between multiple calls. We are stretched on the plurivocity of the ethos, trying to do the best we can. Choice, mediated by mindfulness, must mediate further the elemental immediacy of desire. All of this can be the education of the elemental self-insistence to full membership in the metaxological.

We also must face the shadow side: insistence on obligation and choice can smother the vital energies of life; there is a righteousness that kills.[8] Nevertheless,

---

7. This is not the end of the transcendental, since the issue of the ground of this value has to be answered. Transcendence is the reply to this. This comes to ethical mindfulness but also transforms willingness, as offering the ground, not only of the elemental good of the "to be" but of the infinite value of the person and ideals such as Kant's kingdom of ends. These have their roots in the ontological constitution of the self as within the metaxological community: this is transcendental as ontological, and not just in terms of Kant's more "subject-related" transcendentalism. We avoid the dualism plaguing Kant's way: the ideal is defined in the between, not on one side of the divide of inner and outer, or higher and lower.

8. The killjoy who hates the child who is simply enjoying himself; the person of rancor that severs the ideal from pleasure in being, and hence betrays both the elemental good of the "to be," as well as the infinite value of the person—all in the name of an ideal masking its refusal of life by preaching from its lofty superiority. The political revolutionary can do this, or one convinced that the good is on his or her side; condescension and pride all hide refusal of the equivocal plurivocity of the human in between. This righteousness can be a hatred of the good.

the eudaimonistic transformation of desire turns the willing agent into a person of some practical savvy: knowing what is proper on the proper occasion, the proper time, how to respond appropriately, and so on. This is the will mediated by mindfulness that is intermediate between impulse and principle, the aesthetic and transcendental: it knows the human heart as well as the chiaroscuro of the objective occasion. It is properly decisive, when that is proper; properly tentative, when that is right; properly angry, when the mediocrity exceeds patience; gentle when frailty requires; merciful when a turnabout can be coaxed; walking in trepidation when the perils of perdition assail; laughing when the absurdities catch us off guard; capable of praise at achievement, not stingy with encouragement; grateful and generous, since the promise of the between is not an economy of scarcity.[9]

Fifth, desire's *transcending* transformation of root will is a recurrence of the infinite dimension of exceeding. Are the nobilities and squalors of the finite between all there is? Is the depth of the idiot hidden in the divine ground? Are we longing for what is more than well achieved intermediacy? Is this hope of deeper community with good? What grounds the elemental good of the "to be" and the glory of the world? What grounds the infinite value of person that gives us measureless joy, especially in those we love? Does this measureless joy not seem to seek a value beyond finitude? Deathless destiny for that beloved? Consent to the elemental good of the "to be," thanks rinsed of rancor, even given one's death-destined being? If we say yes, we are taken to the verge of the religious. Desire is converted, since its ideal is hard to call simply an ideal, for it concerns what is beyond the doubleness of the ideal above: not love of self and neighbor but love of the divine, and this as the first and the last. Will and agency reach their limit here, though we may well wonder about the giving of transcendence in a willingness beyond our will to power.

In all of these determinations we must fix ourselves to this and to that. But we may be straying. We may be making ourselves prison houses rather than vessels of the energy of transcendence. We may have to die to come back to the idiot and be recreated into what we are and were: made newly to be what simply we were to be, before we refused the expansion and release of the root will; refused, at each turn of desire towards what always was its heart's desire, and this was never its own heart, for its heart was its root exigence of transcending to transcendence.

Transformations in Root Will (2): Intention and Directed Selving

Back to the middle range of ethical selving! To direct desire is to intend. What is intention? This is a major question, with many subtleties. In one way, all human

---

9. Consider Aristotle's middle as charting something like the above, but with somewhat different virtues.

desire might seem intentional, insofar as it is directed towards some objective or goal that it seeks or wills to be. But intention also refers to the mindfulness of the self involved in desire's transcending. It entails not only impelled desire or driven desire, but directed desire. It is the self of desire that directs desire and directs itself in directing desire. Directed desire is desire that mediates with itself in terms of its anticipation of its own future, a future also full with others. Hence intention is inseparable from time and the becoming of a being of self-mediating mindfulness. Intention specifies an anticipation of the future that is willed to be. But the future willed to be includes an anticipated concretion of self. I intend includes: I intend myself to be such and such. What of my intention was that *you* should benefit? Then I give myself over to a future anticipated for the other. Thus the plurivocity: "I intend" testifies to the will of desire to be self-directing, but in anticipating the future form of my self-mediation, intention exceeds the self towards the other in transcending. In its involvement with the other, intention is given over to what exceeds its own self-direction.

Thus the vector of intending passes beyond the intention of its own self-mediating power. Something more intervenes in the carrying out of the intention, even when the intention is, in fact, successfully carried out. The distribution of the full truth of the intention is communicated abroad in the between, where it effects not only what the self wills but what the other receives or places before the intention through resistance or cooperation.

This is especially evident with respect to *consequences*. The consequences of an intention carried out are not coincident with the consequences intended, even when all of the consequences intended are, in fact, realized. By being broadcast in the between, consequences take on a life other than the self-directing desire of the source of the intention. Some people can be paralyzed for acting when they realize that the consequences intended are exceeded by consequences other than those intended. They fear to make a move, for they sense that to move at all is to be deprived of the power of self-mediation that directs the intentional desire. Yet move they must in order to be self-directing. To be self-directing, the move towards what is other must be taken, but once taken, the intention of complete self-direction will always be resisted and called into question by what exceeds intention.

This is a *loss of self* necessary to be self-directing. To come to ourselves, we have to forget ourselves; to find ourselves, we must forget that we must lose ourselves. The intention itself has to have in it something of a kind of acceptance or grace that is other than its power of intending: a gaiety and faith that intending the best as it may, there will be something other to bend the course of becoming to consequences not foreseen or chosen, and this bending beyond intention contributes to the good of the course of becoming.[10]

---

10. See the self of innerness like the beautiful soul who is paralyzed by this *irony of intending*. The self of innerness who lacks the faith to live with the uncontrolled becomes a victim of this irony—fails, in fact, to be self-directing and self-mediating, and hence loses the power of intending anything.

Persons seek exculpation from the unintended consequences of their deeds. They claim only to be responsible for and guilty of what was intended by them. Yet we all know that evil consequences can follow from good intentions: the way to Hell is paved with them. This means that there is a possible guilt and responsibility more extensive than what can be made answerable to self-mediating desire. The excess to intention (mentioned above), in being "carried out," gives intending over to a larger otherness, and necessarily so. We are not personally responsible for all unintended consequences, yet we are called to a responsibility that seeks the most extensive mindfulness of the context of consequences. This asks for mindfulness of the fullness of the between, insofar as it includes the community of others, and not some solitary absolute preaching the duties of its own self-determining will. The between indicates that there is a guilt and responsibility in excess of personal guilt and responsibility, in a more normal sense. No one's hands are absolutely clean.

To live is to be mixed. This is no excuse for the further self-exculpation. I mean the one that says all are tinged with guilt beyond the personal, so why should I worry; I shrug it off, or go to evil with more relish, since whatever I intend will come out mixed in any case. So we dodge the meaning of the excess of guilt, which is humility and farsightedness, dove and serpent: humility in granting our inevitable lack of pure goodness, farsightedness in reconnoitering the occasion and full context of carrying out the intention. To know what is happening is needed to know what is needed to happen. The character of one's knowing is steeped in, seeps into, one's character.

Transformations in Root Will (3): The Enigmatic Excess of Purpose

Selving purposes or is purposive. We tend to think of purposes in purely human terms, since the ethos of modernity involves the superannuation of natural ends. Purposes "are" only where self-conscious agents can project "themselves" onto the valueless thereness. This is a stark contrast, but it is fairly characteristic of the arc of development in modernity. Intelligibility is determined in terms of efficient causes, with modifications of formal and material in light of a methodical *mathesis* of nature, but final causes in the Aristotelian sense were excluded. "All things desire the good." Now things desire nothing but materially live out the mechanisms of their efficient causes, and these at best can be formulated in mathematical ("purposeless") terms. The full consequences of this only dawned with the diagnosis of nihilism by Nietzsche, though some—Pascal, Leibniz, Hegel, Kierkegaard—sensed it earlier. Earlier I recalled this tale of the ethos.

But suppose Aristotle was right, in a way: all things desire the good? I do not mean that we think of non-human things as if they were human. I mean that every being affirms its original energy of being, and this self-affirmation is its being what it is. Suppose this expression of original being is "desire" in the sense that it expresses the nisus of the being to affirm and maintain the integrity of being it is. Since the integrity is not static, it must be affirmed and reaffirmed to be maintained. All things "desire," in that they concretize the energy of self-maintaining and self-surpassing being. Since the self-maintaining affirmation cannot be sustained without self-surpassing, each being "desires" in the sense of being defined in a dynamic relativity that forms it in relation to all others. Beings as self-affirming are ecstatic: they exceed themselves as themselves; their imma-nent identity is defined in itself and by itself, but also outside of itself and beyond itself in relation to what is other and transcendent. All things "desire" in a self-becoming in the universal impermanence of creation. Ecstasies of transcending define the relativities of beings in the between.

To see our desiring the good as the ecstasy of transcending become mindful of itself need not entail that we see other things as dead therenesses. The ability to see things as other is deeply related to being able to acknowledge the elemen-tal good of the "to be." Strangely enough, this latter way is dependent on *humans* being able to open up to the good of the other as other, as non-human: the good of "to be" is not confined to us. Strangely again, the so-called nonanthropomor-phic scientific view is far more anthropocentric, since it creates difficulties for value beyond human value. It lacks metaphysical imagination for the deeper pos-sibilities in the view: all things seek the good. Its basic orientation to being reveals an anthropocentric contraction of the good.

I connect purpose to the ecstasy of transcending in the self-becoming of beings. There is a process of self-mediating involved in this self-becoming. This is not to confine purposes to self-mediation; for the process of transcending exceeds the self into the between; hence the self-affirming of any being impli-cates its relativity to the other, so the promise of affirming the good extends beyond the self maintaining and affirming itself. Purpose is never just my pur-pose. Purpose is a mediation of the between, wherein harmonies of togetherness are formed. Some of these formations are already operative in the web of relativ-ity that is the between; some are being effected in the human world behind the back of this individual or that; some have an otherness resistant to the determi-nation of human mediation—a mysterious boon is being effected in the course of things. As tied to the ecstasies of transcending, there is an excess to purpose.

To purpose is not only to intend but to intend in light of a goal. I have a pur-pose means I have a future goal towards which I will to work. Purpose confers on the space between then and now a directional meaning or intelligibility. Of course, not all purposes as goals are articulated with the same amount of deter-minacy. I purpose to do such and such, but since the "such and such" is still in the future, there is about it a necessary indeterminacy. It will only become more fully determinate when the purpose is realized. Now I can be more or less determinate about what I purpose, but as unrealized there is still an openness in play. The goal is thus the union of a proposed definite future and an openness of indeterminacy that just is future. Desire is thrown forward, or throws itself forward towards an anticipated goal; the very transcending is one that makes a possibility or range of possibilities more and more definite; but the purpose retains both the lure of indeterminacy and its elusiveness until it is made determinate in the now.

The purpose as goal is not a merely indefinite possibility. Were it such, it would be powerless to exert an influence on the present. Quite the contrary, to have a purpose is to be energized; it is to discover the power of the possible from the future, as entering into the originative disturbance of the present and its shadow of past inertia. The purpose looks to the future; the goal may be future, but it is present as purposed, and as such it is an active telos that ferments the process by means of which its indeterminacy will be made more determinate. Clearly this kind of process would not be possible if the purpose were something entirely different to the very becoming of a self. The goal, in being purposed, becomes appropriate to the unfolding of a selving. And it is not always cooly and rationally appropriated. Often, it is just the opposite. The selving finds itself gripped by an enthusiasm for a desired goal. It is not the self that chooses the purpose but the purpose that chooses the self.

Image: an indolent young man, drifting, lying-a-bed, bored, truculent; a purpose appears, for whatever reason, a purpose appropriate, somehow "fit" for him; and suddenly there is a transformation from indolence to vitality, from boredom to tireless application. Finding the fit purpose, the purpose fits the self, and the purpose finds the self who finds the purpose. Result: excitation of an ecstasis of self-becoming. We marvel and say: You would hardly recognize that person anymore, so complete is the change!

All of this means that purpose is more enigmatic than might appear. We think that all we need is a little rational calculation, a dose of planning, the setting out of goals, and that's the end of the matter. The purpose thus conceived is too extrinsic. Perhaps this fits instrumental purposes: ends that are mere means, means for further ends, and so on. But purpose has a more immanent power, and it is not at all so univocally calculable; it has reserves of motivating power on the other side of calculative self-interest. Purpose as proper is fitting: it shows a fit between the goal and the intimacy of a person caught up in the process of living the purpose. Purpose is thus resonant with the reserves of self that are prior to univocal determination, and that exceed it. Intrinsic purpose is sought, not instrumental. Intrinsic purpose appeals to what is most fit and intimate to the human heart: to desire as itself drawing from the fount of its energy deep in the idiocy of being.

We may say that the purpose is intrinsic because, in one sense, it is the self that is the purpose. I purpose, but the telos I propose, while other, is yet deeply intimate; and it has that power not just to be out there because of its power to appeal to what is deeply immanent in self; its appeal is the appeal of self to itself in the form of its foreseen goal or anticipated perfection. Its power to ferment is the power of the self-becoming to ferment itself from within, ferment by the very power to be outside of itself and beyond itself. If we connect this with self-mediation, this cannot be any simple self-transparency. It is quite enigmatic, as enigmatic as the meaning of that purpose that gripped the young man and transformed his life.

The self-mediation of purpose is not any simple self-control. We are not simply in control of it. Obviously, there can be an increase in control: the indefinite future is before us, but we take steps in the time between now and then, and we test our powers in taking these steps. Initially tentative, these steps may become increasingly sure. Or one may find the purpose beyond one's power and falter in one's steps. I may fall and get up again; I may fall and stay down. The openness of the middle time is incontrovertible. But let us persevere and, all things being equal and the purpose being proper to the person, the initial indefiniteness will be turned into a definite outcome. The very commonness of definite outcomes makes us think of the process of self-mediation as one of progressive mastery of self, turning the idiot indeterminacy into a definite autonomous self-determination. I deny that this is the full story of purpose, even purpose related to self-mediation. Why? This picture forgets eros—the unpredictable power whose roots go deep beyond calculation and whose reaching out stretches beyond the rational. This is an important point, in giving us pause, say in relation to the Kantian image of pure, rational self-legislation, or the utilitarian image of the calculative control of self-interest. There is something beyond both, relative to something more sublime than the first, and relative to something deeper, and ontologically more intimate than the second. We have seen something of this above in the bodied flush of desire.

So our calculative control often is subverted by the upsurge of eros that turns awry our cunning, well-laid plans. I plan to marry a rich woman because I calculate wisely: worldly prudence dictates I tailor my purpose to my self-interest. But I discover I cannot calculate for eros. The poorer woman is the more beautiful; unpredictably, she who has nothing seems to have everything. I am overcome by unplanned desire; eros has shredded my calculations. Something more deeply intimate wells up and receives some answer from the other. For this other has nothing except the power to appear as "fitting" to my unchosen desire. I seem chosen, I do not choose.

Some of the best novels concern the strife between rational self-interest and these incalculables of eros. The deeper stirrings of the heart stir desire itself, stir the very energy of willing in a more moving and urgent way. The univocity of the calculated purpose is subverted by the equivocity of the unpredictable heart. The heart is vitalized by an unbidden impulse that turns into a purpose that overtakes and overturns it. Perhaps the equivocity can then be willed and the dialectic of the two sides be integrated into a life that comes to a fuller resolution of its own fuller purposiveness. But even in this dialectical self-mediation, the shadow of the excess remains. Were it to be forgotten, the withered eros would die into little more than dry desire and calculative coupling.

An analogous point applies to the Kantian image of rational self-legislation. Kant opposes both calculative self-interest and "pathological" desire, here the upsurge of eros.[11] He thinks of purposes as calculated consequences, ends that desire calculates in terms of its own self-interest.[12] I want to say that the erotic character of desire shows it to exceed its own calculative self-interest, not only from the origin but also relative to the end. This is why a proper purpose can energize not this or that act or deed but can transform a *life as a whole*. Example: Francis of Assisi—he awoke from dreams of knightly glory, his life was transformed, when he came to see the fitting purpose as the service of God. The rebound effect of this purpose was to shatter the old self and overturn all aspects of life. The process of this transformation exceeded the purposes of rational self-legislation. The eros is for the sublime or the height, or transcendence. The height itself becomes the transforming end that redirects a life. The point is not confined to religious exemplars. Nietzsche: this is his point when he says man is something to be overcome: the purpose is beyond rational self-legislation, since all purposes are rooted in the depths of eros, which exceeds every partial determination of itself.

The issue, of course, has its own dark ambiguity. There is what might be called the *fanaticism of purpose*. The purpose takes hold of one, and one is transfixed. One's life has its direction now, and this is lived with a vehement zeal that is uncompromising. I not only hate the old self, now mediocre and unworthy, I hate all those others still at ease in this mediocrity. Everything now is plain to me; why do they still not see the light? They are mired in desire's middle range; overtaken by purpose, I am carried in a swirl of driven certainty. My driven love creates, alas, what love should drive out—hatred. Love creates hatred, because love hates what now mocks it with emptiness, namely, purposelessness. And this, it seems, is the state of those who cannot see.

What is this fanaticism of purpose? To be overtaken by the drive of a love not yet purged of its own self-love: a breakthrough of the purpose without a breakdown of the self-love. The purpose that makes me new now becomes me,

---

11. "Pathological" because it concerns what we undergo, suffer; for Kant, our lower natures. Yes, it overtakes us, but is it lower? Or deeper and more intimate in an ontological sense that grants the good of the "to be" in its fleshed concretion?

12. Kant seems to think predominantly of purposes in terms of "one's own purposes" and hence links "prudence" to happiness considered as the maximum fulfillment of "one's own" desire (see, e.g., *Grounding for the Metaphysics of Morals*, trans. James W. Ellington (Indianapolis: Hackett, 1993, 26). I am taking issue with this view of purposes as just "one's own".

as the purpose that must make all things new. This is the strange inversion in the very dialectic of conversion: a turn of the recurrence of self-mediation that recurs to self, but without the purgation that allows the intimate depths to appear with their diabolic possibilities moderated. The discipline of this moderation is not here evident, for the person is still green to the vehemence of overpowering purpose. Given time, a person may learn the moderation, without negating the power of the purpose. Often it happens that the fanaticism of *good* purpose produces profoundly destructive results. This can be evident in different areas of life. Witness the zeal of the religious fanatic—the shadow of the divine ardor of the saint. The religious zealot has the purpose, and his whole self is consumed in living for the purpose. He would bring all others to the power of the purpose, but they are sightless or they resist. They must be made to see, their resistance resisted. Instead of release, the fanaticism of purpose builds a new prison and forces freedom to room in its confines. Making no distinction between itself and the purpose, it does not distinguish the purpose from its own will to power. We see something analogous with the political revolutionary or terrorist.[13]

Purpose is inseparable from the self-mediation of the good, but there are depths to the self and the mediation not taken into account when we confine ourselves to self-mediation and more univocally determinable aims. And what we have said hardly scratches the surface of how the other enters purpose as a process of intermediation. For in the between (as we saw with intentions and consequences), we are communicated abroad into a network of relativity that exceeds self-mediation. So too with purposes. In being successfully completed, they are always failures; for there is more purposed in our purposes than we can purpose. Our purposes are not our purposes, even as they are our purposes. Another purposiveness than self-mediating purpose has its purposes in the realization of our own purposes.

Transformations in Root Will (4): Ardor of the Heart

Because root will ascends in the *heart*, the transformation must descend into the heart. Self-conscious purpose puts its roots into the idiocy of the heart, just as the heart's longing exceeds determinate purpose, just as also the enactment of its purposes involves it in purposiveness beyond its own purposes. The human heart

---

13. The fanaticism of purpose in relation to the terrorist: an *eros uranos* for the good "cause" becomes an *eros turannos* corrupting the ardor of the heart; consult Dostoevski's *The Devils (The Possessed)*. Adolf Hitler: What was the outbreak of World War I for him? The occasion of his being overtaken by the fanaticism of purpose. *Now* he felt he had a meaning, a life.

is equivocal: seat of ardor, it also is often wounded; and these two go together. Ardor: the stirring, the warming of selving that melts it for the good of life: it is a secret love; an eagerness for life's sweetness, a reaching beyond to meet others who confirm the sweetness. Wounded: not always confirmed, the heart is thrown back into itself and thrown around, bewildered. We do not know what comes out of us. First is a kind of outburst. We are surprised by ourselves; the ardor overtakes us, and more so when we are young. With age, disconfirmation makes cold the heart; it is not its nature to be cold, yet it cannot but become cold when the determinate forms of life disappoint; disappointment makes its ardor a suffering.

The elemental vulnerability of the ardent heart can make it aggressive. Its self-affirmation can only endure so much, and there is a limit to the ingression of disrupting otherness. It must protect itself in the deeper delicacy of its desire. Many strategies of defense will be developed: sullenness and retraction; laughter (one protects the heart by making others laugh); diligence (the hard worker, the conscientious one—a way of not calling attention to oneself); pleasing others (my anxiety that others are happy is my shield against my unhappy vulnerability); aggression as defense; yieldingness as decoy; acting with supreme consideration for others as protection *from* their violences.[14] So the heart becomes tangled around itself, and its ardor loses its purity of longing for the good, just in its self-affirmation, exposure, self-protectiveness, and self-aggrandizement. It becomes a monstrous labyrinth.[15] A discipline of gentleness, consideration, diligence is

---

14. Despite so much fancy talk about the other, the other can be the *school bully* who makes one's life miserable, for no reason but his own malignant glee in terrorizing those who cannot fight back. The bully is also self-protecting but his heart has swollen with the unexpected ease with which he finds others fear him. Tormenting others often springs from self-loathing.

15. Think of the *jealous heart*. *Othello*: There is an outburst of rage at the *thought* of betrayal by the other, yet behind the rage, what infinite vulnerability! How touchy the heart, how infinitely responsive to being touched at a certain depth to being radically hurt; how insecure the heart, though, outside, one is all power; as if one were walking on ice, or suspended over an abyss, and the slightest touch sends one tumbling; but it is in hurtling into the abyss that the greatest power of the rage receives expression. The murderous outburst of raging power is really the heart's manifestation of maximum powerlessness, helplessness. There is the infinite will of the heart to hold to itself the beloved one, and when that cannot be, the infinite rage in helplessness against helplessness. And this, even though the rage shows all the absolute power of life and death, when it murders the beloved, for not loving it as it sees love. Think of Augustine's image of the child who is jealous of its sibling suckling at the breast—murderous rage of jealousy that would kill the other, the brother that deprives one of the beloved, yet cannot do so because it is helpless. We are very lucky that looks cannot always kill; otherwise we would all be murderers. If looks could kill, Sartre's look would make us mass murderers. Should we primly preach in rationalistic fashion about jealousy, as if it were some dirty, atavistic thing, like the jealous god?

needed. To remain true to itself, it must know love, love of the other. The heart can become more fiery as it ages, more intensive by being banked by the strictures of finite life. Great passion can smolder in the ashes of aging. The greener passions of life are easier, but they flower and fall autumnally. Subtler passions sleep under the heap; they may awake to love of life's inexpressible sweetness, reminded by the purer face of a child. There also is the great passion that cries out to God: Show us your face that we may die and live.

Not always is the ardor an internal purity, while it is the coldness of the outer or other that is hurting. The ardent heart often is too much in love with itself: in love with life, yes, but in the form of its love of itself; its heat composes a sweet hymn to its own beauty, hence dulls it to the stirring of ardor as truly a call to the good of all, the other as well as itself. The sweet air of itself circulates around itself, inhaling the perfume of its own preciousness, monstrously remiss about the heart of others. This self-love of the heart, drowsing in its own perfume, proves itself beautifully, brutally loveless. This lovelessness is itself an inner wounding of the ardor: it transfixes itself and feels itself in piercing itself and swoons in the blood of itself, but its ardor is hemorrhaging into itself and it pines in the wanness of its own self-consumption. This might be the "beautiful flower" of ardor and wound, but there are spikier plants and more cannibalistic blooms. These are flowers that devour others as their prey, prey seduced just by the beauty of the flower, or perhaps by the strange allure of monstrousness itself. It is as if the one seduced were also pining within, and welcomed being devoured by the monstrous other, rather than hemorrhaging away its loveless days.

But its idiocy reaches into the ontological roots of desire, where self-insistence mingles with an intimate love of the other, so intimate that it is perverted into power and impotence to let the other be as other. Calculative reason is not the proper judge, though in a court of law the heart cannot hold sway. The truth of the jealous heart must be punished for its "crime of passion," the crime of a hate that comes from love perverted.

CHAPTER SEVEN

SECOND ETHICAL SELVING:
THE REDOUBLING OF WILL

The Willing Self and Its Doubling

The heart is a reserve, but what comes out of the reserve is related to what a person wills. The self must will itself, will itself to be itself. Will is a directing of desire out of the reserve of the heart. The basic self-affirmation of a being is the root will, but the root is shaped as it wills itself in the interplay of ardor and wounding. Willing is a decisive transformation of desire: not just lived by the original energy of being, but living it, as both what one is, and what impels one to be beyond oneself. Hence desire is not just for this and that but also for *its own* fulfillment. This appears with will: not just the will to this or that but the will to be such and such a person. Not only do I will to have, or do, or be, such and such; *I will myself* to be such and such, in having or doing or being such and such. This is a more decisive self-mediation than any immediate happening of desire.

Thus will is always implicitly an answerability for self. To will is to be answerable: to be open to acknowledge that what has been willed has been willed by *this* self, as the original of *this* willing. This answerability means that the root will that merely insists on itself here decisively steps in the direction of ethical responsibility. The will that is answerable for itself is more than the will that insists on itself. Answerability lays itself open to judgment, while self-insistence calls for attention to itself, announcing its being there as a claim on the other. Answerability may be the willingness to judge oneself, as well as to be laid open to the other's judgment. The two cannot be separated.

We find here a kind of immanent *doubling of selving*: the self opening itself to judgment in willing, and the self judging itself as not quite what it would will to be. This immanent doubling is not the same as the doubling *between* self and other. Still, it is essential to the immanent drama of ethical selving. The root will of self-insistence is not so explicitly doubled, though it is implicitly. Thus the heart caught between ardor and wound gives witness to a breach within selving, hence to the doubling. In the breach someone is being born, or reborn. With willing, the doubling explicitly stands forth: in willing, the self is itself but is also willing to be itself, and as willing itself, willing to answer for itself; and yet as answering for itself, it must be able to judge itself, as if other; it must be able to stand above itself, so to say, and not merely surge up from inarticulate reserves welling up from secret sources. The doubling of will explicitly introduces the notion of the higher, the above; the higher that is itself again, since it is both as answerable and judge that the willing self finds itself. The doubling we find in willing is tied to the rebirth of self as a mediation in and through and by ideals, and thus intimately tied to ideal selfhood.

With this doubling of willing, the transformations of desire are turned over themselves, even as they are ejected outside of and beyond themselves. A decisive complexification of ethical selving comes to be. We are near the origin of *shame* and *esteem*—both are forms of answerability. Shame is an immediate sense of exposure to answerability; esteem is the satisfaction that one is up to the call of answerability. *A blush* is the immediate incarnation of exposure; it is a kind of silent, yet loudly eloquent expression of answerability in the flesh itself. And it clearly brings out how the doubling of the self in willing puts its roots down into the inarticulate reserves of the idiot self. This idiocy flashes into the flesh, as the face of the one blushing is flushed with blood. There also is an immediate posture of esteem that we see in the spontaneous grace with which a person carries himself or herself. Answerability is evident in the human flesh itself, even though it extends beyond what can be adequately manifested in the flesh.

The question here is this extensibility to self. What is selving here? Matching the infinite character of desire's restlessness, there is a potentially unlimited extensiveness to selving. Hence there is *no determinate limit to answerability to self*: one is infinitely answerable for self. This is why, even when one gains the esteem of completing a definite task in a satisfactory way, one is still not satisfied, for there is a further answerability whose silent call yet awaits its timely word, always and ever a further call. Unavoidably, there enters into self-satisfaction the necessary complement of failure. Though it be no necessity that we will succeed, it is an *unavoidable necessity that we must always fail—even when we most succeed.* There is an asymmetry between success and failure. There is unavoidable necessity to the latter that exceeds the likelihood of the former. Why? Because our satisfactions always answer to this willing or that willing, but none satisfies the infinite answerability. There is the exceeding of the determinate satisfaction in willing as doubling, as always redoubling itself, and this is infinitely open. Answerability is to something infinitely open. There cannot be a determinate closure or satisfaction to this.

Thus the sense of failure *must* emerge. Our answerability to ourselves is infinite, and we cannot fully answer this answerability. We exceed the measure of ourselves, even when we ourselves are our own measures. Even being our own measure, we do not own our own measure, and hence as our own measure, we are always in excess of ourselves. We are called to live up to ourselves, yet we cannot live up to ourselves, for the measure of answerability at work in us exceeds all of the finite measures that are within our command. The doubling of the will means a deepening of the enigma of human being. From the point of view of univocal logic, we are contradictory, self-contradictory, and yet our very glory is just in this—to be an answerable self is to be able to contradict oneself, to go against the finite satisfactions that tempt us with spiritual smugness. There is a paradoxical glory in this incessant self-subversion. The entry into failure is itself a kind of paradoxical success of another sort, since it shows the continued vitality of an energy of transcendence that is called by and oriented to the infinite. To be that energy of transcendence is always to stare failure in the face, for one is not the infinite.

The doubling of the will is doubled over *again* here, for there is a willing that will refuse this failure and claim itself to be the infinite. The doubling of the will introduces the exhilaration of purpose, the energization of self-becoming that is directionally thrust forward towards a goal, but it also introduces the shadow of failure, hence the possibility of shame and guilt. These two are in tension; the selving is just this tension, this between. There is an infinite restlessness to the first energizing of purpose; there is a stop or an arrest to that energizing with the second. The second finitizes the first and hence qualifies the infinite restlessness as not actually infinite. It also dampens the tendency to overreaching that self-surpassing carries in its very nature. For this latter is a surge that is full of the joy of its own self-affirmation; and now there is the damper from the realization that there is another necessary failure, if the infinite restlessness takes itself as actually infinite. The failure is an education of finitude, but also an education of the infinite restlessness. By the nature of the exhilarating self-affirmation, this education is not soon learned, not learned willingly, since it cuts into the temptation to self-absolutizing. It is hard to be weaned from that.

The lesson will be rejected often, for the lesson seems to turn against self-transcendence, and the immediate surge of this self-transcendence will take the arrest as something still to be overcome, so that this overcoming enhances the absolutizing of self-affirmation. In other words, the very doubleness will not at all be taken as the education of finitude but as the occasion of a self-infinitizing. The truth of the failure will be seen as something to be brushed aside, a mere barrier to self-overcoming before which only the fainthearted quail. For the intrepid, glory is the challenge to self-infinitizing. There *will* be no failure, even if there is now some failure. The doubling of the will now comes to be seen as a self-doubling that ought to issue in the redoubling of the will affirming itself, not the truth that an *other limit* reveals itself in failure that doubles the self-affirmation back on itself, where it learns the humility of the created being that consents to this truth—I am not the infinite.

I am not absolute, and my sense of failure, and shame, and guilt is the ingression of implicit mindfulness that I am under the infinite, under the absolute good, and that hence the infinite restlessness has to be radically transformed rather than puffed up further into the illusory feeling of its own absoluteness. So the intrepid self-doubling, the redoubling of the will, risks being the refusal whereby the self falls into evil, even as it elevates itself in the reiteration of its own self-infinitizing. Will willing to be itself absolute, to be itself the absolute: this is, in one sense, a natural development of the root will; in another sense, it is the result of a perversion of the doubleness that necessarily emerges in the self-unfolding of the root will.

Will Willing Itself: Self-Doubling, Ethical Answerability

Here we come to a clear, yet enigmatic, revelation of being in the between with respect to our relativity to the good. That relativity is not just a seeking of what we lack, though it is a seeking of what we lack. We are somehow already in relation to the good, else we would not seek it, or have the hope of being otherwise with it, were we to find it. We both lack and have the good, hence our doubleness. This is not reducible either to a univocal or dialectical identity. Nor is it only equivocal, nor a dualistic opposition. The ambiguity of our integrity is its necessary relativity both to itself and to what is other. The doubleness allows of intermediation but not of absolute self-mediation. Willing shows itself to involve a metaxological doubling.[1]

Desire shows us to be finite: we desire because we lack; we seek to make up the lack and so fulfill ourselves. Desire shows us to be dynamic, reaching out to what is beyond, the other to requite the lack. Desire seeks what is good for itself, or what appears so. It is sometimes mistaken. Desire values as good what serves its lack and fulfillment. Its distentions occur under the lure of good as deemed desirable for me. This fact makes some say: the good is the desirable; it is what is desired; desire defines the good, not the good desire. This is a widespread modern view, from Hobbes onward. The ancients took the other side of the ambiguity: the good is the desirable, it is desired as desirable, but it is desirable because it is good; the good is desired because it is good, not good because it is desired. I take the second view to be the truer, but the first has its partial truth. We must locate the matter relative to the doubleness of desire: both seeking what is desired as good for it and seeking beyond itself for the good that is good. The double corresponds to good for self, good for itself, even as other to self.

---

1. We must keep before us this "*with*" the good: seeking the good, hence not with it absolutely; strange tension of human beings that drives us forward in search of what always is there with us from the start. The human being: one who goes elsewhere and nowhere; great adventurer in the foreign and not yet, even in the never never; and yet the home lover who always comes back to where he or she always was and is.

Let me put it this way. Desire is indeterminate as simply desire but determinate as oriented to this particular outcome. It is always both: indetermi-
nate/determinate, and yet again more than any determinate desire. There is a
univocity to the process: I desire this, this, this—and the "this" can often be
determined with strong univocity—food, drink, shelter. Yet this univocity leads
to this good, this good and so on, ad infinitum. It is this *multiplication* that introduces the "*more*" in *equivocal form*. The excess of desire meets the excess of things,
always more than desire, and at the same time desire is more than they. They are
more than it can possess; it wills to possess more than they can give. There is a
double "more" on both sides. The ad infinitum of desire suggests *futility*: ad nauseam. It is the same damn thing again and again, in every different object. And
as the same, it is now not anymore the more that desire seeks. An orgy of satisfaction comes to sing the dirges of dissatisfaction.

What of the *will willing to be itself absolute*? This is a self-doubling that
expresses the root energy of our being as self-transcending. But this is a self-transcending that does *not* transcend self. The self-doubling is no doubling at all; it
is the insistent reiteration of the I as alone to be affirmed, and as I alone. This is
a will to self-reiteration: self-insistent solitude in the absolute of will willing
itself. You might say that the I voluntaristically mimics the God of Aristotle—
not thought thinking itself but will willing itself. Both descriptions of God, theoretical and voluntaristic, leave out the other, hence they do not do justice to
transcendence as self-exceeding towards what is not self—self-exceeding as a different thinking than thought thinking itself, and a different willing than the will
willing itself.

This will willing to be itself can succumb to the temptation to be a false dissimulating self-doubling, since in redoubling itself it never gets beyond or away
from itself. In essence, it reveals itself not to be a willing but to be a *refusal*. This
is evil. It is a kind of infinitely subtle shift, an infinitesimal dislocation of the *love*
of itself that is *proper* to all being. For it is not even *love* of itself that is here in
will willing itself. In willing itself, it hates itself, for it has refused the I as other
that shames it, that shows it its own failure. It has refused the witness of the other
that casts down its pretense of being ab-solo, absolute. The infinitesimal shift
occurs *invisibly* in the intimacy of the idiot self. Nevertheless, the infinitesimal
shift in the root will occasions bitter fruit, as the original refusal, masked as affirmation, expresses and consolidates itself in action, deed, word, character, way of
life, community. The seed has undergone a secret mutation from love of being to
refusal. Much of living is the growing of the seed, a growing in which we collude.
Sometimes the monster flowers, and we are shocked to discover what can come
out of the mutant seed. Or we glory in giving the monster all the encouragement
it craves to feed its delight on darkness.

There is no *determinate explanation* for the mutation. It occurs in the darkness of indeterminacy—in the root will before it has determined itself, so to say,

above ground. The mutation is in the heart. It is a secret refusal of being as good, hence an affirmation of death, that occurs because our own death is prefigured in the presentiment of our failure and shame. If it has no determinate explanation, yet it is very understandable as a mutating of life affirming *itself*. It is a violence of life on itself, even as it seems to affirm itself. In rejecting its failure, its death, it has refused the truth of its own life, which is to be a finite creature. Its primal refusal is the will to be god; and this will is *grown* in the horror of freedom itself when it dawns on it that it is not God.

Will willing itself to be absolute has been the implicit definition of the absolute since Hegel. Thought thinking itself (Hegel) was dethroned, but its voluntaristic *twin*, seemingly other but not so, now mounts the throne. The thought that thinks the other may seem to be answered for here, but in truth the mutation of will willing itself is not at all a release to the true other. It is the darker twin of thought thinking itself, even though it prides itself on the energy of seeming otherness in the vehemence of willing rather than the quietness of thinking. Think of *Streben* (and not only in Fichte), or Schelling exalting will to absolute being, or Schopenhauer—but he sees the darkness, the "evil." Then think of Nietzsche, who most *vehemently* shows will willing itself, making its evil now be the good, and this quite self-consciously. It is the voluntaristic idolatry of the dark twin of thought thinking itself. It is the apotheosis of the idol lurking in self-mediating being. It is the evil autonomy—the false double of freedom.

How does the will become evil? In the doubling that is its nature, its love of itself is hatred of the revelation that it is not absolute, a revelation coming to it from the presentiment in self-doubling itself that it is always *below* the infinite. It hates the revelation that its being is gift. The consent to the gift mutates into hatred of the giver, because it has become intoxicated with the image of infinity that it feels in its own self-transcending. Deceived by its own intoxication, the double promises to undeceive it—undeceive it not always overtly but as intimating the living of a lie involved in its being taken up into the unbound intoxication of its own self-affirmation. The will, here become a doubled will, is actually in opposition to itself, by being in opposition to the source of the gift. The strange paradox is the feeling of intoxication that appears in this self-opposition. Why paradox? Because it is really beginning to tear itself apart, to lacerate itself. It experiences this laceration as the fascinated freedom of negation. We see it in the child: freedom announcing its stubborn presence in its incessant repetition of the word "no." This is not the "self-propelling wheel" called "yes" of Zarathustra's child.

This paradox helps us make sense of two opposite evaluations of the doubling. Call one, the *Augustinian*: the evil will is a will that cannot will what it really wills. The evil will is itself in bondage to itself—its self-willfulness is not finally a free willing, since it has made itself into its own punishment. This only comes to be felt when the will wants to convert or be converted—to become other in the image of the good. It finds it cannot do it, cannot will what it wants to will, has become enslaved to itself. Far from being at home with itself, it is in essential self-discord, in disarray. The willfulness is a will-lessness—since its freedom has been lost by being used, and yet not completely, since it wills to be other. It is at least the possibility of repentance. How is the circle of this self-enclosing will willing itself, and so unable to will itself, broken open? Not simply in the will itself. By the gift of some power beyond will willing itself: by the renewed giving of freedom of an other that wills my will as it would be, were it its proper desire and directionality to the good. This renewed giving takes us beyond the ethical self-mediation of the good.

Call the other evaluation, the *Nietzschean*: the doubling of will that wills itself throws itself with rhapsody or frenzy into the intoxication of will willing itself. This Nietzschean adventure in evil shamelessly borrows the language of affirmation to cover its unashamed self-affirmation. Self-opposition is not denied—it is turned to this end—and so the refrain, man is the being who must be overcome. Intensification of self-surpassing is said simply to be the truth of what we are. Desire desiring itself seems to desire what looks other to itself—but the seeming affirmation of the other is merely the occasion in which the self affirms itself once more. If an empty stage (hail my solitude!) could allow the self-affirmation, well and good. More often, the stage needs others as props, but props to the only drama, my self-dramatization, my song of self singing itself to itself. (Why though does it peep sideways at others, as hopefully the mirrors or echoes by which the song to itself is reflected back to the singer?) Nietzsche is all alone, as sealed in self-affirmation, as Aristotle's god is sealed in self-thinking. This is an intoxication of evil, of a rhapsodic auto-nomos. This self-conceit is mired in self-deceit, with potential for great violence, not only on the other but on itself. Its "great yes" is the defensive hyperbole or bombast that hides or drowns out the cry of desperation that gives it its fake energy. It is the energy of the fevered patient when the fever is at its most intense. Not health of will but sickness of the will energizes this "great yes."

Why must this fail? Because answerability to self becomes inane without answerability to the other. This second double makes it radically impossible that the first self-doubling can be indefinitely self-sustained, much less be infinitely self-sustaining. The latter must collapse, for inner *emptiness* is just its meaning. The ministering of intoxicated energy serves to fill this emptiness that it perfidiously thinks it serves to heal.

Self-Doubling and Answerability to the Other

Answerability to the other also has a double aspect. The doubling within self is inseparable from relation to the other. It reflects as much a doubleness *between* I and other as well as a breach between I and itself. Indeed, it is the otherness of the other that firms up the sense of immanent doubling, since it is concretely impossible to separate the envisagement of the *self as other* from the presentiment of the *other as an other self* who witnesses to my deed. I cannot stand as witness for my own deed in separation from the knowing of the other as witness to my deed, hence as my witness. Witnessing is responsibility to self; it also is answerability before and to the other.[2] The other as witness gives me back to myself or does not give me back to myself. The truth of my self-return is not a pure auto-effecting, but hetero-influenced; my coming to myself is always with the aid of the witness of the other. Of course, coming to myself I can forget the other who aided me on my way. Self-recall ceases to recall that the call of the other aided the call and recall to self.

This is an *intermediation* in the very intimate heart of self-mediation. The double aspect of answerability to the other is not only the necessary participation of the other in my own self-mediation but the sense of difference between my self-relation and the witness of the other. There cannot be a complete coincidence between how I see myself, even as envisaged other, and how the other witnesses me, sees me from an outside otherness. And even though I interiorize the envisagement of the other, this disjunction, this sense, remains of there always being something more that is not within the power of my self-mediation. This something more is ineradicable.

On the one hand, one can consent to these limits of self-mediation. This can be the beginning of responsibility, as genuinely seeking to participate in community beyond self, in which self also is affirmed and indeed given to itself. As given to itself, it may acknowledge its gratitude to the other—generous in consent, as the other was generous in giving. Here the sense of failure, or guilt, mutates from shame into a form of humility, perhaps a joyous modesty—an entirely energizing affirmation of the sweet gift of being given to self. The indeterminate restlessness is released differently into its own infinite dimension; this consent to finitude leavens our propensity to hubris—excess in the evil sense. Answerability to the other energizes the restlessness in a new ethical direction, which is not just in search of itself and its own completion, for it is already mindful of always having been given to itself. Its gratitude for the gift shifts restlessness into the self-surpassing of an ethical generosity.

On the other hand, the smart of disjunction can secrete rancor in the restlessness and nurse its brood of impotence. Consent does not leave the restlessness. I am given to myself by the other; I am stung by the disjunction beyond my power; vulnerable now to the witness of the other, I hate to be seen, for this makes my touchy core even more exposed. I hate the other's witness, for I fear that the ignobility of my rancor may be betrayed. The call of the other must be

---

2. Witness: one who sees with their *own eyes*; standing for what one claims to see; honest owner of one's judgment.

stifled, for it is the witness of my fault. The stifling is committed by something that *looks just like* the above consent but is exactly the opposite—desire's restlessness is energized, but through its own self-insistence on its infinite restlessness.

In both cases, the energy of "to be" is set in motion. In one, consent to the other's witness releases a new energy of overcoming or going out. In the other, refusal of the other as witness looses a release of energy, but it is the self-willing of the restlessness forward *despite*, not in consort with, the witness of the other, and to spite that witness, to do away with its presence. The second energizing turns its own answerability to the other into the other's answerability to it. The other is made to stand naked before one. (The torturer strips the other while remaining dressed himself; the tyrant sits or stands above his prey.) There is induced an asymmetry in self-communication; the one willing to reveal nothing except its power over the other, not to be witness to itself or the other; the other forced into display, despite its gift as witness. The exposure of the other is both its vulnerability and petrification—subjectified, objectified. I will not be judged; I will judge—ab-solo. But there is no absolution in this absolute judging. For where the witness is denied, I cannot be my own witness. So I cannot confess. And when I cannot confess, I cannot be absolved. Thus refusal of witness is the refusal of forgiveness. Its issue is the stillborn child who would be named generous.

Answerability to and before the other turns out to be radically equivocal. There is a fork in the road: one way leads to community of generous consent; the other way to perdition. The second way mimics or counterfeits the first. To some, it will seem the truer release of self-transcending. But it has not purified this self-transcending of the ambiguity of self-insistence. It has turned from its patience to the other. It wants to be the only witness, hence wants no witnesses. It must murder to effect this, and the final murder attempted must be the murder of God in the heart—or perhaps this is the first.

The other may love one and may bring us to love. The other may love one and bring out in us our hatred of being patient to any other. Love precipitates the great mystery of absolute hatred—a hatred without a why, beyond the hatred that it is at all in relation to an other beyond its own power. Its hatred of the other cannot be divorced from the hatred of its own helplessness, a helplessness that displays itself as offensive will for power. A paradox again—consent to powerlessness over the other releases power in deep community with the other; refusal of one's powerlessness before the other ends in helplessness before oneself.

Consent to the witness of the other is consent to powerlessness—an expectant helplessness willing to wait on the other. This helplessness releases an empowering of self-transcending. By contrast, refusal of the witness reveals a core of helplessness that refuses its own helplessness. Paradoxically, this helplessness betrays itself in the power of will to absolute power, the release of which brings one to the impotence of being condemned to oneself, as one's own infernal stronghold—or bolthole.

Willing Doubled into Acting: The Deed

Willing acts its own doubling in enacting itself. It redoubles itself in deeds. Prior to the act, the will can play with possibilities. Once the act is done, the will has enacted itself, wills itself to be and become thus. It passes from the play of indefinite possibility, through decisive determination, into the public world of determinate deeds. The decisive determination is a self-enactment, hence a self-determination that finds its immediate concretion in the deed. The deed is not an optional extra added onto an inner drama, essentially complete in itself. The deed is the immediate end of the drama of the idiot: it is the beginning of passage from the intimate to the public, mediated through the aesthetic concretion of will that is the enacted deed.

The deed is an acting of mindfulness in the practical ecstasis of self. There is a dialectical interplay[3] in the deed between will as intending and the integral self as realizing the intention, both in light of the purposed outcome. This is not always explicit, though it is at work. The dialectic is one of indeterminacy and determination. The indeterminacy of innerness is made determinate by intention and purpose. But the latter are indeterminate relative to being in the world, while still being determinate, more or less relative to the innerness of the idiot self. The deed makes the second indeterminacy determinate and so completes the orientation of self-transcending into a definite term that both concludes and begins something new—concludes the passage into otherness, and begins the adventure in otherness and all its chances.

The dialectical interplay conditions not only implicit self-determination but begins to confirm and consolidate explicit autonomy. The deed comes to show the self "objectively" to itself. It knows itself in the deed—and so in going out of itself, it is carried back to itself. The deed shows the power of the doer—shows it to the doer. The deed is the self-enactment of the doer, the selving as practically "objectified." Without it, the consolidation of the doer as self-mediating would not occur. This is to put into question the idea of a merely inner sanctum of subjectivity. As Hegel saw, one cannot sustain this view, say in the aestheticized version of the Kantian subject, such as the beautiful soul. Our tendency towards narcissistic self-relation contradicts our being as communicative of itself in the deed. So too Stoicism must be questioned in this respect: no complete retreat is possible into an inner sanctum cut off from public enactment, divorced from the deed

---

3. Kant will underplay the ethical essence of purposes, as he will say that it is not action but the inner principle of will that is moral. As Hegel saw, his view is not dialectical enough: you cannot separate the inner and outer—the principle, the action, the purpose that inwardly mediates between them, the consequence that outwardly enters the judgment of rightness of both.

that shows the doer as communicative being. Equally questionable is a dualism of private and public as an opposition of "subject" and "object" (where privacy is sometimes a reactive retreat into innerness from devalued objectivity). The truth of the deed is both intimate and public—intimate as a showing of the integral self, and public as communicative of itself to the world and to the other. The deed is an enactment of selving within a community of otherness, which gives the self back to itself.

The risk of adventure *towards the other*, mediated by the deed, is crucial. The deed *exposes* one to the other. It is much more than a display of power in which power expresses itself. It puts one on show as potentially answerable. It puts one before the other, opened up to the other's judgment, or violation. If I want to be confirmed by the other, I intimately apprehend that I cannot count absolutely on this confirmation. For already I know the rift of failure that is insinuated out of the doubling. So I cannot count on what I expect of the deed. In this further rift, a deeper chink of uncertainty and wariness appears. Exposure in the deed is open to the possibility of threat from the other. My immediate faith in my own being as affirming itself might be snatched from me, unceremoniously.

There is no way to avoid this exposure; nor to obviate the possibility that one will be betrayed by the other, in betraying oneself in the deed. The deed is not only a doubling of inner into outer, but since the inner knows itself in the outer, the outer is retrieved back with a mindfulness of "mineness." This retrieval and mineness is both manifest in, and put under threat by, the deed as exposure to the other. It is self-discordant in just retrieving its own mineness in the deed. At once the deed is absolutely and essentially *mine*, and yet necessarily and in essence snatched from me, and not mine at all but in the power of the other. Power of self expressed in the deed is exposed to powerlessness of self, just in power exposed to the other. This is the *travail* of the deed.

This also is the public emergence of *distrust*, of the wavering of a faith whose issue can be violence. In exposure to the violation of the other, the thrust of the now distrusting self turns violent against the other, in turning towards it. This is dialectical through and through, and more than dialectical, but here I focus on a dialectic of trust and distrust. The deed exposes both our power and our vulnerable enactment of selving before the other. The latter exposes our insecurity, the former our resource to deal with it. Distrust of the other generates a trust in self in the form of self-expression of power over against the unsecured other. But note: here this trust in self is grounded in distrust, this power willed over the other in powerlessness. Trust is inseparable from distrust, power from impotence, not only between self and other, but within each self as in process of selving.

On the one hand, it is possible to continue the thrust of self-affirmation as self-centered: the root will perpetuates its elemental self-insistence into the deed, so its exposure is not an exposure of the self to the other but the pretext for close security of the self, always preemptively striking against the other. This strike may be the hand extended to shake, or the broadest smile. But the handshake and smile are weapons. War may rarely be declared; but undeclared, it is even more rarely subject to a cease-fire. Thrasymachus, Hobbes, Nietzsche, Sartre, and such, make hay.

On the other hand, the deed may be lived in differently—depending on the heart and its hardness. When the deed shows the heart that is not stone, the exposure of self is there as its own witness. My deed witnesses to what I am; I witness to myself in the deed. I am in my deed, and I stand by my deed. I own myself, I own up to myself. My deed declares: I am responsible. Of course, the other as witness may be equivocal. This is just my singular travail. I must stand fast in a faith that has no absolute guarantee to do justice to the *double witness*. Holding fast is holding on faithfully in the dialectic of trust and distrust. This is the faith of will in the good, the witness of the good. In the insecurity of exposure, I must resist the temptation to strike out. There is a self-affirmation that extends beyond self-affirmation; it lives in unsecured trust in the promise of the good of the other. This is to be the witness of the good as exceeding the self-contracted will of unbound self-affirmation. Witnessing allows the other to behold my deed, communicates to my being beholden to the deed, but it also reveals each of us as beholden to the good in a sense that exceeds us both.

I hold fast, I hold good, because somehow I live from a deeper reserve of trust, even in the abyss of insecurity opened by the deed. In that trust I find the way to exposing myself to the witness of the other, with faith that good will come to be between us, in the between. And still, of course, the witness of the other remains fraught with ambiguity. I do not always know when I can trust, hence my way of doing will accommodate itself to the other. While open, I may still be guarded, and at the wink of an eye I will retract into security, like a hermit crab into its shell. The great difficulty is to know the unknowable insecurity of what is before one, and still to remain open to the good as it may come. Witness to the good in the deed exposes me to violence but also is necessary to create the hospitality in the between wherein the good of the other is welcomed, the good of the other as its witness.

Witness to the good in the deed clearly moves beyond self-mediation but paradoxically only by deepening the mediation of self. For the *character* of self is both expressed and forged in the deeds that enact our willing.

The Doer Redoubled As Character

There are a number of dimensions to this. The deed not only brings us before the other but *intensifies* the demands of ethical selving: intensiveness of self is deepened as the extensiveness of its self-surpassing expands in relation to the other. A deeper *interiority* is conditioned by the deed as mediating a confirmation of selving. This intensiveness and the inward abyss drive us back unto the intimacy of the idiot self, as we have been driven out of ourselves in deeds, or willed ourselves to be enacted outside in the body and beyond. The doer of deeds is the actor who is the character in play with what is other. But the character shows a *prior* and a *posterior* form: prior "essence" (our being in promise) and posterior "manifestation" (our being as performance). Going outside to the manifestation turns us back to the "essence" that we discover within. We discover, so to say, *our interior selves outside of ourselves* in exteriority and action.[4]

Character is *unique*: it is the thisness of the self, known in the singular, idiosyncratic savor of its deeds. Deeds may seem general and average, but they are always done with unique modulation: the will as mine is in the deed and makes it my own. My deeds are exactly the same as yours, but they are never exactly the same as yours, for your deeds are yours, and mine are mine. Such uniqueness has everything to do with character as my own—never a general character, always a "this." The idiot reveals the destiny of singularity. Character is the destiny of singularity (character is destiny).[5] I would put it this way: Each singular is given to be just itself from and by the origin.[6] Character is not just something, it is gift. The gift is good: gift of life as good, this life, irreplaceable, once; and not condemned

---

4. The going outside of ourselves in the deed thus mediates the most intensive self-knowledge that exceeds even itself: we do not *know this* at the beginning; we live it, are lived by it. Self-transcendence in deed is necessary to bring us back to what we are most deeply.

5. Consider undertaking a *pledge*: standing surety for the deed, or friend. See Schopenhauer, *On the Basis of Morality*, trans. E. F. J. Payne (Indianapolis: Bobbs-Merrill, 1965), 106, his remark concerning the Delphic Oracle: pledges and "trouble" go together. Standing for *oneself* in one's deeds is the basis of *honor* also. My word is my pledge, that is enough: my word alone is the deed that stands surety for my trustworthiness—my honor. Pledge of honor: you can trust me, rely on me. Do not look for extrinsic confirmations or substitutes for honor, for me—not money, etc. No other security is needed: my word is my essential security. See *Rob Roy*: giving my word is giving my complete self. My *character* is honorable. I will honor my pledge, my promise. The intimacy of intrinsic character eschews extrinsic accidental securities. Honor may become very angry if my word is not enough. This rejection of my word is an insult to honor and takes the extrinsic to be more of a surety than the intrinsic. Yet there persists the *dishonorable* ("trouble" above). Honor is a war with the dishonorable, which besmirches the inner integrity of the actor. Schopenhauer has interesting things to say (*Basis*, 110) about character and Kant's unalterable thing in itself. In this regard, Kant's greatest achievement was to understand the *coexistence* of freedom and necessity, noumenon and phenomenon—character as *destiny*. (See the Spanish proverb Schopenhauer quotes, 111.)

6. Consider the religious view: each of us is given a unique soul: this is coherent with previous explorations trying to account for the "infinite value" we ascribe to the self—the infinite end originates in the gift of the origin.

to exist; not cursed with character; not thrown; given the gift of its own "to be"; and beyond root self-insistence, we must come to love it properly. This means being diffident about the view that all is "nurture." Character as posterior is subject to the formation of "nurture." Character as prior is "nature," idiotic as overdetermined this, but open to later determination, including the determinations influenced by nurture. The child: already a singular presence from the moment of birth. Parents know intimately this feel of self, this savor of singularity—they have intimation of character as gift.

I call on an old distinction—nature as nature *naturing* and as nature *natured*. Character is, relative to the gift of the origin's naturing, a nature natured; relative to itself as given, it is this singular nature naturing (prior); and this singular will become this character in time as this nature natured (posterior). I mean that original character as gift does not give itself to itself; it is given to itself, but as having been given to itself, original character is original in a derived self; it can begin a finite process of giving itself to itself (and of giving itself to others), so that its character as *second nature* takes form, forming itself in a temporal self-becoming. The elemental giving of *original character* suggests the origin as *more* than self-mediation in giving us ourselves as self-mediating. Character as posterior follows the originative promise of original character. The gift is originally unchosen, but it includes the free power to choose. Through this choosing, a new "destiny" is elected. The first necessity is unchosen; the second necessity comes to firm concretion through the choices we elect.[7]

Through the latter, we now come to character in a sense more usually recognized: *result* of self-formation, issue into time of original character. Such a second character in some ways answers to Aristotle's description. First character as the unchosen gift of singularity is what I am and will remain, despite all changes. Second character (in the derived sense) has to do with the kind of selves we make ourselves through the habitual pattern of our willing, enacting the original character of self in deeds proper to it. This is not the elemental character that is a gift from the origin but the character that is the second nature built up over a lifetime of choice of this or that. First character is not fixedly formed from the beginning. It becomes formed as we give expression to our desires, choose and will certain acts and ways of life, find ourselves recurrently choosing, willing, and enacting ourselves in a definite way. Our desires issue in choices, issue in willings, issue in deeds that are the repeated enactment of the self, as a singular concretion of being whose originally hidden promise is the idiot self. Second character is one that is firmed over a lifetime; not this or that enactment of self but the habitual enactment of a definite character.

---

7. Is it something similar to this that Plato was communicating in his Myth of Er and the prenatal choice of lots?

We come to have, so to say, our own distinctive voice. It is like a signature on all we do, a second signature that is the fuller signing of the first signature signed by the agapeic origin in the singular as this singular. To enact one's being with this second signature, some intimate knowing of the first signature is important: us being signed, not we signing ourselves, and signing for ourselves. Without intimate knowing of the first signature, us being signed, we mistakenly think of ourselves as unconstrained signs—signing and consigning beings.[8] Singularity is first a sign, a being signed, a consignment. Our own signing for ourselves, our own being as sign of self, is first on the basis of being signed, as bearing a signature that is character in the prior sense. We sign ourselves out of the gift of the first sign.

This view is not widely accepted today, due perhaps mainly to a questionable theory of autonomy, and of what it means to be as original. Any original as other is seen to curb my own being as original. Originality must be self-origination, as signs must be self-signifying, as art works self-referring. Freedom is my freedom, extending to the character I can choose to be. In different forms, this is the attitude: we have no original character (all character is derived; from what?); in the derived character, we can be anything we will to be. Drive this view in a certain direction and it will turn out that we hardly yet exist as originals. Oddly, this conclusion is not seen as humbling—on the contrary, it renews a relentless, always unfulfilled exhortation: *become* original!

But there is something singular given from the origin, and this is not within our will. What is given is free, since the original self is an indeterminate power to be. Indeterminate does not mean that it is absolutely indefinite. It is overdetermined, in that it is a very determinate singularity of different and definite powers; yet it is more than determinate, since there is a freedom to the manner in which it can realize its singular being, singularize itself in second character. It is this determinate singularity of original power to be; as determinate, it is defined by definite powers but also by the power to be that, as originative, is potentially in excess of determinate characterization.[9] The givenness of the singularity, with its

---

8. On that view, are we not then signing beings that consign all other-being in accordance with the dictation of our signature alone? As if that signature were unconstrained power over the consignee? How does this relate to the post–structuralist view that there are no signified, only signifiers, and endless chains of signifiers? On the contrary: we sign ourselves, but we are first signs or signed; as a sign, or signature, we signify more than ourselves, and this is already signed, signified in the first sign of character.

9. Thus the power to maintain itself, to grow, to feel, to remember, to desire, to think, and so on—these are definite powers, but in their definiteness they have the potential to be in excess of determinacy; freedom ferments in them, since this openness of the overdetermined is given from the beginning.

determinate powers, determines the range of possibility to which the overdetermined power to be gives expression. It is not unconditioned freedom but singularized freedom, hence dependent on conditions not of its own choice.[10]

It is fatal to second character if it thinks it is what it is through itself alone. Tempted to think it can be anything at all, it ends by being nothing at all. If it can be any character at all, why be this character rather than that? Better perhaps to try all, to taste and see. But in being them all, it is really nothing intrinsic in itself. Instead of the promised fullness of character, we become a nothing in particular: a jack of all trades, master of none; capable of playing many roles but never being itself in any role; never being oneself, nothing but one's roles, acts, nothing. And so we behold the empty actor who is briefly excited and struts in his or her paints and powders before an inciting crowd, a jostle of onlookers, themselves supposed to be similar nothings. The hot breath of their interest lifts this balloon of self and it floats, as if a something, for its brief performance. It retires to the back room. It is nothing again, not even with the masks stripped, the costumes divested. It is a tired nothing staring into a mirror casting back no reflection of realness, only the shine of desolation. The freedom of this nothing is a fatal freedom. If we can be any character, we have no character. Our great creative autonomy is the sign of nothing. I can never be myself, never, for what I am is nothing. Being everything means being nothing, and coming to nothing.

Character Redoubled in Community

Just as we should not forget the first signature on character, we should not think that derived character is *only* self-derived. Family, friends, and multiple communities enter its singular formation. The self-mediation in second character passes into one through these others. One also is derivatively given to oneself by virtue of relation to others. One's character becomes one's own in the second sense, only because self-mediation itself is supported by numberless, nameless others who offer us the gift of allowing us to see ourselves as others see us, hence aiding us in realizing the promise of a self-transcendence that as an exodus from self is a coming to oneself.

---

10. Differently stated, character as "destiny" always shadows character as "chosen." The second nature that we build up over a lifetime of choice is "chaperoned" as it were by character that is unchosen. Part of the wisdom of time is to come to live with the chaperon! This "chaperon" is the truth of the old view that each of us, in being signed by the absolute original and consigned to be ourselves individually, is assigned our own genius or daimon or guardian angel.

This *socially* mirrors the deed. As I have said, we must go outside self to discover what we are within: the external deed mediates interiority. Here relation to others, or more, the others' relation to one, gives us to ourselves: the relation outside possibilizes more intensive self-relation. For one goes within in the measure that intensive life is revealed to one, but one does not produce that revelation through oneself, but it comes in the company of others. The view of the other on us, as we come to see from the view of the other, releases us into a fuller discernment of what we are. Too close to ourselves to see ourselves intimately, we need the outsider to turn us back to ourselves. Even more, we need the intimate other to free our mindfulness of hidden recesses of intimacy in our idiot being.

There is no necessary opposition of self-mediation and social intermediation, as might be claimed by those who take an excessively "atomistic" view or an exclusively "relational" view. The "atomistic" view is tempted to set "character" over against the others, to be affirmed by opposition to what others think of one. The "relational" view is tempted to overlook an integrity of self that is not derived from relations to the other; character is a social construction, and we underplay both the givenness of original character and the self-mediation of derived character. When we see the cooperative community of self-mediation and intermediation, we see this opposition as enforcing a dubious choice. The "atom" of self contains all the depths of the intimate idiot, even with the presence of community in the deepest intimacy of integral self-being. The "relational" self is multiply modulated in that the self-being is not constituted by human social relations; this would reduce the self, whether original or derived, into an empty nothing. (This possible reductionism in the "relational" view mirrors a complementary reductionism in the "atomistic" view.)

Nevertheless, if the self-mediation of character is shaped through the mediation of the other, *conflict* is possible as well as support. The pervasive forms of life in other-being may be at odds with subtleties of original character. Example: a child is by nature shy, but surrounding social forms are brash and pushy; inevitably, she feels pressured into a loudness not concordant with her nature; she may have to submerge the flow of original character, to feel definable at all; her derived character does not embody who she genuinely is; she has to shout a song, so to say, not harmonious with the quieter music of her soul.[11] We all have to play such roles, and none is entirely consonant with the subtler stirrings. It may take a lifetime of seeking for honesty with self, a kind of fearlessness, to come into the peace of accord with these subtleties of soul. Some never come into this accord. They are distorted or mutilated by what they have become. They accept what was given from the other, but that gift proved a poisoned cup.

---

11. Boys: some are intelligent and sensitive and like to read books, but they are *bullied* into being jocks; they learn to *hide* themselves.

The ambiguity of character relative to self (between original and derived) is matched by a similar ambiguity relative to community. What is given from the community may as much oppress as liberate. Think of character as a determinate role within a dramatic play. The drama has many characters, some major or dominant, some minor or recessive. The character is a singular presence who lives itself in dramatic interplay with other characters. Singularity of character and its dramatic enactment cannot be absolutely separated; yet the drama is more than the character, even as the character is more than the drama. The role played by major characters is important: they dominate the drama and shape more the others than the others shape them. There will always be dominant characters shaping the self-mediation of the many. These may be actual persons—a soldier, a saint, or statesman, a kind of hero of character who has made a singular contribution to the community. They also may be pervasive types of character who significantly influence the models of achievement the society values and inculcates. The latter types veer from the singularity of heroes. They are general distillations of characters crystallized in the ethos of a society.[12]

This generalized other can give us back an image of impoverished humanity in the indigence of human possibility realized and communicated in the type. We still yearn for rich singularity: not flat, typical character, but character of integrity and width of soul, and depth of wisdom and compassion. If the social intermediation of character has come under flattening influence, we become deficient in the taste for such nobility. We have been fed on husks, and we continue to clamor for more husks, and cannot participate in the banquet of superior excellence. We may be secretly shamed by excellence, shame not shown in repentance and renewed striving upwards but in rancorous aggression on the excellence for insulting our mediocrity with its superiority. We will draw it down to our level instead of consenting to being drawn upwards.

This averaging type of character enacts the fata morgana of human possibility. The type then functions as a kind of *social bewitchment*. We find ourselves mesmerized by the fata morgana. If we suspect their emptiness, we try to flee, but we find our legs heavy as lead, and we cannot move them to our will. We are paralyzed by these bewitchments, overwhelmed by a nameless fate. Not character is destiny but is a fate as fata morgana. Character then is the enactment in self of bewitchment, and those who struggle to awake from the dream know something is horribly wrong, though quite what is hard to say. Their struggle for concordance is experienced as an exacerbation of discordance. They

---

12. Among the influential general types in our time, as MacIntyre reminds us (*After Virtue*), are the efficient manager, the aesthete, the therapist. There are others—the braggart sportsman; the celebrity businessman; the pseudo-wise talk show host; the flat-souled rock singer . . .

experience the appeal for release as a further suffering and travail. It seems easier to slip back into dreamless sleep than to struggle for wakefulness beyond the dreaming bewitchment.

That is why the singularity of character as encountered in the family is absolutely important. Father and mother are not first general types but living singular presences. Good parents can give us to ourselves out of their reality of fleshed character, can give us impressive reality before the fata morgana of social bewitchments wafts seductive illusions towards impressionable green desire. Family can give the bedrock of real character before the corruption of social character goes to work. Nor do I mean to say that social being is simply corrupting something that is otherwise pristine. There can be corrupting families too.

Character Redoubled As Singular Person

Willing redoubled in deeds makes us acting characters in community, wherein the ethical selvings of many enmesh and communicate. Again, there is no self-mediation of the good without communal intermediation. This inseparability of singularity and community shows itself in the idea of the *person*. Person is *recognized* in community. Recognition: something is acknowledged that already is what it is, even when not fully self-unfolded. Person highlights character as of intrinsic value. We see the matter from the viewpoint of both origin and end: origin relative to the gift of the beginning, end relative to the fulfillment of the promise of the gift given in the beginning. The promise of character is revealed in the ethical person.

Personhood recalls us to the singularity of the idiot self and the givenness of first character. One is not a person in virtue of what one does but in terms of what one is. One first acts thus and thus in terms of what one is. Then acting thus and thus comes to constitute what one is in virtue of a process of self-becoming, in terms of second character. A proper understanding of personhood acknowledges first character.[13] The process of the transformation of the will does not *produce* personhood in the most fundamental sense; it *realizes the person* as from the start the promise of a certain singular character. Community serves the recognition of personhood in the first sense, while serving its formation in the second sense.

The first gift of personhood is not a static thereness but an ethical gift to time, of time: the promise of a future in which the good is to be lived and enjoyed. The promise of time is the gift of freedom—freedom to become fully a

---

13. See the remarks in Chapter 8 relative to the *person as mask*, as showing. The mask shows a proper character, even though equivocally; the mask hides and betrays the signature of singularity; it shows and conceals character.

self in community with others. The gift of personhood is from the outset self-mediated in intermediation with others. The express realization of self-mediation means participation in community that influences the formation of the person. The ethical formation needs to remain true to the being of self as person, being not first formed but given in virtue of the infinite value the human being is.

Why not say that the idiocy of self is grounded in apersonal, neutral powers? Because the idiocy is known to itself in the patience of intimacy, hence some personal note of singularity always genuinely marks our idiocy of being, our idiosyncrasy. This springs forth in the idiosyncratic uniqueness of the person. If person as self-mediated points us back to the idiotic gift of first character, then "value" is not a later production simply, an addition to a basic substratum stripped of value. Rather, personhood reveals the saturation of the idiotic with "value." So it is dubious to think of person as something that supposedly comes to be at a certain point in human development, say when a child is such and such an age. There is no such point, for the value of the gift of the person is given from the idiotic beginning. (This has consequences for the issue of abortion.)

How could the "value" of person be produced later on the basis of what prior to this is supposedly without such value—magic supervenience of infinite, sacred value? It is less this magic we need than acknowledgment of the mystery of singular personal life to which no human is on a par. Nor is that mystery dissolved by our more and more intricate knowledge of the various mechanisms involved in the growth of the embryo human. That is not the level at which the mystery is: this is not the neutral fact that it is as such and such, but the value saturated fact of its being at all: that it is, and is as a good. We have a glimpse of this mystery when a child first comes into the world, though it be bloody and wrapped in debris from the womb. There she is, he is, this astonishing singularity that now is, once is, and never was before, and in time will never thus be here in the middle world again (see *BB*, also *PU* on the "once" and the "never").

The person comes to recognize its value as self and for itself when it is recognized. On both the side of itself and the other, it is *recognition* that occurs, pointing to a "cognition" that was with the process from the start: the self's intimate sense of its own idiocy, the other's granting that there is a return to the self *of itself*, in the knowing of it that the others allow. I mean: First, that there is self before there is recognition that self is person; and this first self is not produced by process but participates in it, and is not produced either by itself (what could "itself" here mean if self is produced by itself?) nor by the other, for in either case there is recognition. And second, that the other's recognition contains the release of the self back to itself as other to the other's knowing of it. Recognition is not an idealistic constitution of the object recognized, but a respectful letting be of the other as other, a letting that is filled with the presence of "value."

The person acts in community, and the community is saturated with value, as is the inner sense of selving as living the transformation of its own root will into a singular presence, capable of giving itself to the world and receiving what comes to it. Deeds are not just the self-expression of indifferent power. It is the moral power of character that transforms the self-affirming power, the sense of unity marking its will to integrity, as well as the mode of "being with" concretized in community. The responsibility we have seen, the upsurge of the heart with root will, the slow weaning of self-insistence from itself as just insisting of itself, all testify to a process that places the delicate singularity there as personal presence, presence not only unintelligible but concretely impossible without the presence of the communal others, themselves singular presences.

Singular Person Redoubled As Ethical Discernment in the Middle

Singular presence can unfold and redouble itself into the ripeness of achieved character: heir of a life of judicious choice and tempered desire; heir of the wisdom of ancestors who have smoothed the way for the newest generations; singulars of an integrity that commands authority, without pressing this by extraneous means; commanding presence that invites confidence beyond all self-insistence, though the one commanding respect is a quite singular presence. So we come to the person of singular discernment, one who enacts practical wisdom.[14]

This is appropriate here for the following reasons. We have seen the transformation of self-insistence, without extirpation of the ethical exigence that comes from fuller selving; seen the concrete discipline of desire, and its result in character; seen the incarnation of mindfulness that is discerning of the appropriate; seen the doubleness of character, enacting self-mediation in the community of intermediation, and thrusting the acting person into the between, beyond any solipsism. But practical wisdom has to deliberate, make its judgment, and enact its decision, all in that between. So it emerges from the transformation of root will into forms of self-transcendence that transcend self-insistence while not stifling the vitality that carries us as beings of desire into the between. For practical wisdom is a kind of wisdom of the between. It is a discernment of singularity in community and respect for the subtlety of community as it finds its communicative forms in different singularities. Properly, it is metaxological, but as relative to its singular concretion in the character of this or that person. It shows one of the acmes of ethical selving (the saint is higher).

What is this discernment? *First*, it is the discernment of a person of integral character, one who has extensive contact with many aspects of life, and intensive understanding of the nuances of the overt and unstated in the ethos. *Second*, this

---

14. See *Nichomachean Ethics*, end bk. 6, where phronesis is compared to *aisthesis*. This a propos of discernment.

integral character is the fruit of a lifetime of enacting discernment, result of habitual willing that has constancy, has tolerance, has willingness to revise in light of the new, has sobriety when the situation is somber, laughter when lightness is right, intoxication when the divine powers draw near, trepidation when the monster growls and sets out on prowl.[15]

Third, the discernment draws on deep self-knowledge, but its knowing is beyond self, since it has finesse for the nuance of the between. It is a form of mindful self-transcendence, especially attuned to the appropriate appraisal and action in the shifting scene of the ethos. *Fourth*, it is not capable of univocalization in mathematical terms: it is beyond the geometrical mind as a mind of finesse that dwells as much in the indeterminate as the determinate.

Fifth, it is improvisatory, since it has to move with the dynamic happening of the indeterminate. It is not at all a self-satisfied smugness that knows the right things just because things have always been done that way. The ethos shifts, and we must discern the right in the shift, and this is no easy or mechanical application of rules inherited from embalmed ancestors. The living truth of the elders must be resurrected, brought back from the dead to the dynamic ethos of life itself. There is no *mathesis* of this resurrection, nor indeed is the life of this discernment just this resurrection, since it now must dwell in the present, hence forge its own life. It must extemporize when time itself demands a new approach or shows us possibilities of the good coming to us from hitherto unanticipated angles. Beyond univocity, it is not lost in equivocity but rather is carried by the fruits of dialectical self-mediation and metaxological intermediation into the between where the ambiguity must be mediated anew.

Sixth, though this discernment cannot be univocally mathematicized, it is embodied in this person or that. It is never an abstract wisdom. It cannot be abstracted from its concretion in personhood. It is incarnate in the ethical selving of the singular. And while general descriptions can be offered of it, none can exhaust or fully do justice to it. Such a person may contribute much to life, but when he or she dies, something is lost, something that cannot be recuperated in abstract general terms, even though the spirit of this exemplar may live on. Something was there in this singular that was nowhere else: once

---

15. The elders can *generally* be wiser, and a society that values age will have more respect for this discernment. A society that flatters youth tends to be deficient in it. And, of course, there are individuals whose character is marked with its promise from a young age: they exhibit the gift of exceptional powers. A wise society will nurture such gifts, for its own good depends on their fuller realization. Mindful discernment is not biased between youth and age, but in the nature of the case age generally brings what youth cannot have, most especially suffering and its wisdom, and not just suffering of the body, though that too, but suffering that comes from a more intensive knowing of the human heart and its travail.

there, and contributing its gift of gratitude for the powers of the good, through mindfulness that wills to foster the good anew.

Seventh, when we wish to know the appropriate, we cannot learn it in the abstract, as if from a manual. We have to look to its incarnation in the praxis of the singular. We must imitate this incarnation to come ourselves to know discernment. Hence to know discernment is first to be a follower or a disciple. There we have an ethical selving enabled by an other, and so a decisive breach with self-mediation entirely defined by autonomy. There is a mimesis of the good person.

Eighth, it is perhaps easiest to find such person in societies where a long and stable order has fostered the slow fructifying of human powers. Discernment and mindfulness do not grow quickly. They must be steeped in the fullness of life, which means also steeped in suffering. The long and stable order allows the slow judgment that has weight to it, for it has weighed many possibilities before it comes decisively to the judgment of the appropriate. There is no hurry in such an ethos, not because the issues are not pressing, indeed sometimes ultimate, but just because these ethical issues are so pressing and ultimate. In a way, this needs a kind of priesthood of the wise, who are freed into an honesty for which they will not be punished, when they utter any considered truth.

Finally, the singular who is practically discerning is not confined to the idiotic, aesthetic, dianoetic, transcendental, and eudaimonistic potencies of the ethical. She or he is in tune with the transcending powers of the human, and in the highest instances in rapport with the transcendent. He or she knows the idiotic in knowing the heart and its intimacy. She or he knows the aesthetic in appreciating beauty, the glory of creation, and the vitalities of the body—no world negation here. He or she knows the dianoetic and transcendental, for constancies recur, even in the uniqueness of singular ethical selving. She or he knows the eudaimonistic, for humans crave happiness, not just superficial contentment but happiness that has the peace of depth, as well as its disturbance.

But she or he also knows that the intimacy of the heart cries out beyond itself; that the glory of the world is evanescent; that the constancies cannot be made rigid and the exceptional and the new confound the best wisdom; that peace often comes after war, and the scar of indelible suffering has scripted its sign on joy; that there is a suffering beyond happiness in the shock of evils that makes of us a terrible sleepless something.

It is in transcending that we know both of these sides, from the intimate to the tragic. There is no mediocre middleness about this. There is no self-satisfaction. One is cast into the middle space between domestic perfections and extreme conditions that stretch the human heart to its limits and test it to the marrow. One is then in the middle, yes, but the reassuring earth has now lost its comfort, for one is placed between heaven and hell, not placed there, racked there. In extreme transcending, these things come to be discerned, but at this extreme there is no human help that will do. It is the transcendent we need to aid and save. This too is known.

CHAPTER EIGHT

THIRD ETHICAL SELVING:
THE BECOMING OF FREEDOM

Freedoms and Self-Transcending

Ethical selving issues in the enactment of freedom in life. This is implicit in what we have so far explored: at one extreme, in the singularity of the root self-insistence, that in asserting itself, is not univocally determined; at the other extreme, in the singular discernment of practical wisdom that must improvise as much a new path as steer a course by well-established marks. This discernment is not the end of ethical selving. We must pass through further intermediate steps in the shaping of freedom. Remember, we are not dealing with a simple, linear unfolding but a process of forward movement and backtracking, in which the further unfolding recurs deeper and deeper to the sources of being ethical, while also articulating fuller expressions of transcending. We follow a recurrence now, as in our further explorations in the rest of Part III we move more from the middle range towards the extremes of the ethical between.

If the freedom that ferments in ethical selving is not univocal but plurivocal, it follows that there are different freedoms, corresponding to different formations of self-transcending. What freedom means for a child is not the same as what it is for a grown person, nor for youth what it is for age. As it is inappropriate for the young to be old before their time, it is unfitting for the old to act as though still adolescent. Sometimes the freedom of youth is refusal, that of age consent; sometimes age rages and lacks liberty, while youth is sweetly in the right and carelessly free. Freedom undergoes a becoming: the will ages, as the I ages. Freedom itself ages; it is not eternal, though perhaps it brings us to a border between time and eternity.[1] Ethical selving is in the between time, the interim of the aging of freedom.

Freedom, of course, seems the catch cry of modernity. Is there anything so affirmed without demur? When even tyrant and torturer appeal to freedom, we

---

1. As Kant implies about the noumenal self, *Critique of Practical Reason*, 121. Aquinas speaks of the human soul as being on the border of time and eternity.

wonder if we must quickly genuflect, as if in the presence of a god. And what many idolatrous forms of itself mimic this god! Freedom is our bewitching word. But does it free us from the spell of other bewitchings? Or send us into another bewitchment, more spellbinding because we are smug about being released, and all the while we pad our comfortable cells? What mendacity the seduction of freedom serves! The main name given to freedom in Western modernity is "autonomy." Are there further freedoms? Is there a bewitchment of autonomy so widespread that, to have a glimmer of a further freedom, we must be startled out of the slumber that dreams its own self-sufficiency? The question is not only relative to negative freedom, "freedom from" the hindrance of external impediments; it is relative to origin, that is, "freedom whence." Is that "whence" more than a negative source? Is it releasing, perhaps in an agapeic way? Has freedom to do with original power coming to us? Nor is the question just relative to positive freedom, "freedom to": the freedom of original self-becoming, the freedom to realize self as power to be. Further than this "freedom to," there is a "freedom towards": being free as transcending, released towards. . . . Towards what? Itself and our own self-realization? To that and something other? Or something other and then to that? Towards human others? Towards transcendent good as other?

These questions turn on whether the self-mediation of freedom is itself the good as end; or whether the human as end suggested by free self-mediation points to a good beyond it, more ultimate than self-mediating freedom. The latter view is more true to the intermediation of the metaxological. Freedom is relative to a source other than itself that, as preceding it, exceeds it always. The origin and end of freedom, even when freedom in the middle is both original and an end in itself, point to a freedom beyond self-mediating freedom, beyond autonomy. Beyond any univocal determination, freedom opens up in the unfolding of original power in the indeterminate. It unfolds as the expression of overdetermined power in integrities of being that exceed complete univocal determinism. Overall, we will need to distinguish these formations: call them equivocal liberty, dialectical autonomy, erotic sovereignty, and agapeic release. These are increasingly richer concretions of the creative power of the overdeterminacy of being. In meeting the ambiguous challenge of the indefinite, they also reflect the different emphases in "freedom from," "freedom whence," "freedom to," and "freedom towards." In this chapter, we are concerned with equivocal liberty, while in subsequent chapters we will treat of the other forms.

"Freedom From" and Equivocal Liberty: Ontological Difference and Being for Self

First freedom is given to us as the release into being for ourselves. Can this be understood in human terms or in terms of nature? Is there something in excess about freedom as given? Some reduce the human to the natural and both to a univocally determined mechanism. Others grant the excess relative to nature but ascribe this exclusively to the human. Is there an excess more than such naturalistic and humanistic terms? In both the natural and the human, an open indeterminacy is given in which the release of freedom is given into its own promise. Of course, we ascribe the promise of freedom in a stronger sense to the human, but were there no convenience of freedom with nature, it is hard to see how freedom would just pop up unintelligibly. Suppose freedom were prepared in the earth itself; but the openness of earth as creation is itself not self-grounding; the origin creates beyond itself and frees finite creation into its own being for itself; meanwhile that intermediate being is most essentially the promise of community, both in its own terms and in terms of its ultimate relativity to the origin itself. (This makes more sense in light of the discussion of origin and creation, in *Being and the Between*, Chapters 6 and 7.)

The givenness of creation as other manifests the complex happening of community in which a plurality of things is together. Things are not thereby univocally determined in an absolute way. They exhibit their being for themselves, which may variously take shape in interplay with others in the environment of creation. Their self-becoming exhibits a conjunction of determination and indeterminacy. With the human, the freedom of the indeterminate becomes awake to itself, as does the integrity of this being centered on itself. This comes to expression in the root will, the self-will, in which the human affirms the "to be" in affirming its own being. This affirmation is not subject to completely univocal determinism in which antecedents and consequents are rigidly bound to each other in a one-to-one relation. The one (the human as an integrity) is open to a plurality of different determinations, some of which are impossible to determine in advance in terms of such a one-to-one univocal relation. We show the given possibility of variability, difference, indeed, self-pluralization, in ways that are original—original relative to our integrity, original relative to the novel and surprising. First freedom is not our self-determining: it is "determined" to be as it is by an other source than itself; not "determined" but "offered itself" as full with promise.

This first freedom opens equivocity: equivocity between our dependence on the other origin, our relativity to other things and persons in creation, and our own integrity of being for self. I have said that my being is an affirmation of the "to be" in the self-affirming of my being for self. This affirmation is a freeing of the original power of the "to be." It is a primordial *ontological* freedom. It is an ontological release more embracing than any integral thing or singular person, but it is concretized just in the particularity of these things and persons. Hence the equivocality between the necessity of an overdetermined release of ontological freedom and the necessity that this be concretized in particular things or singular persons. Neither side is avoidable, but just this tense doubleness tempts the singular to think of *its own* self-affirmation, its own self-affirming "to be," as first freedom. This temptation seems most intimate to the singular self just as idiotic. In fact, *the other affirmation is more deeply intimate*, more intimate than the intimacy of the self for itself, since it is a more elemental idiocy that gives the possibility of just that intimacy of the self for itself.

When a being wakes up mindfully to itself, it enjoys the sweet affirming of being that is its own life and is intoxicated with *itself* (though that intoxication is only possible through the sweet nectar that comes from the other affirming release). We wake up to the idiocy of freedom, its sweet intimacy, and we fall in love with ourselves at first kiss, at first sight. We do not then notice the more intimate and more patient suitor that waits there with us, and who, unlike ourselves, is not self-insistent, who takes pleasure in the sweet pleasure we take in ourselves as the gift of good life in love with itself.

Here begins a kind of slippage in freedom: we see it as related to a first love, of the self for itself. In fact, this first love is second, as is the freedom. We may have to live a long life to find again that the first is not first, and the last not last. This "first" love that falls in love with itself goes on to a long career. We call this career a life. From the outset, it is tempted to fly on one wing—its own. It flies, but it also is in flight, and in flight from the more intimate realization that its wings are gifts, and that there is more than one.

This flight or fugue suggests why first freedom is often viewed in terms of "freedom from"—understood as the absence of impediments to one's own sweet will. To be free, then, is to have all obstacles removed that obstruct the sweet satisfaction one takes in oneself. Defenders of such a view are quite clear that, realistically speaking, there is much more than I; there are others, and limiting conditions of nature, culture, and so on. But these are just the obstacles that one would were overcome, and a path beaten smooth to the sweeter self-satisfaction, to the will that obtains what it wills when it wills.

What happens? We make a primacy of the self-affirmation of the root self-insistence and fall into an equivocity from which we spend a life seeking extrication. It is not that we choose this fall. At this primary level, we have no choice in a clear, explicit sense. We live in the elemental mixing of freedom as being released into the gift of life, and freedom as the self-affirmation given to be itself by this release from the origin. We do not know clearly the difference between these two, for what we are as given to be is simply release into difference, release experienced intimately in the affirming of root self-insistence. We fall into the equivocal primacy of the latter; or we find ourselves already coming to ourselves more wakefully, subsequent to a more elemental clinging to self that we do not choose. Or rather, we are chosen, and in a sleeping way we have "chosen" ourselves, before we find ourselves in a position to choose ourselves more wakefully. In another respect, the gift of being centered in self is immediately the possibility of seizure, and before we know it, the gift has been both usurped and turned into a usurpation. It almost seems as if this fall into ourselves is so unavoidable that the fall into evil cannot be obviated. Or, the fall into the possibility of evil is not first "chosen" but itself becomes the necessary fall that precedes the second fall in which evil is more explicitly chosen.

Think again of the child, in some ways the epitome of self-insistence, hence not only given to itself but given over to the immediacy of elemental self-affirmation. This is *not* the fall into evil, though it is the "fall" into the possibility of evil. The child is indeed an immeasurable "to be," given over to be as an integrity marked by self-affirming original power. This is not evil, since it is the gift of the good "to be," as singularized in this self. But this is what allows and also tempts the fall into evil. In the floating mingling of the first release by the origin and the release of self-affirming insistence, the latter as given to itself so insists on itself that the givenness is swamped by the surge of self-affirming insistence. This is where the usurpation begins, and *it is entirely the work of what is good*, namely, the self-affirming of the good of the "to be" as singularized in this self.

The fall into evil is the result of an expansion of this self-affirming good to be *the* good, an expansion that is really a radical contraction; for the floating community of primal release and self-affirming release has now been focused on the self-affirming, in such wise that it is no longer released to what is other as other. It has turned back into itself by turning itself outward to all others in the posture of affirming itself as *the* good: the strange self-contradiction of self-transcendence that is self-contraction. Henceforth, freedom in us will be lived in the inheritance of this contradiction. Strangely also, we as free can only move forward to freedom by moving backward to first freedom. Hence we advance by return, or we become self-transcending by a forgetting of self that remembers itself as primally given to be.

The sweet taste of the self-affirming root insistence, insisting on itself and affirming itself, contains a grain of poison that may sicken the promise of freedom. This is not known at first in tasting the sweetness. One may say that there is poison in the resistance that the will of others inevitably places before one. Yes, there is recalcitrance soon known and resisted in turn, even hated. But this is not the real poison; it is the congruence of wills that in congruence only clash, for *all fall* into their own singularity that usurps the release of freedom. Each is in a cell of solitude as it tastes the sweetness of itself, hence resents the disturbance of the other to that tasting, for the disturbance threatens to usurp its usurpation. And yet in the sweetness, it soon grows bored with itself and feels a disgust with itself that is inexplicable, if it is the good. In truth, this disgusted boredom is one of the first offspring of the contraction into self that narrows self-transcendence while seeming to expand it.

Dwell quietly with oneself in a quiet room and how soon restive boredom and disgust come over one and the itch to be distracted from oneself. The self-insistence is a deep distraction from oneself; the contraction is a diversion. Why? Because it is the heritage of an emptying and a secret negation. And the emptying is not only the negation of the primal freedom but of itself also. The self-affirming self-insistence that insists on itself turns out to be negating itself in negating what relates to it and gives it its givenness. In this wise, its self-insistence is indistinguishable from a hollowing out of itself. It usurps the gift of freedom, but rather than being free for itself more fully, it is taking away from itself its own freedom, even as it wills to give itself more and more freedom. Its willing of itself as free is hence indistinguishable from its bondage to itself. And this is not a bondage that simply closes down everything and preserves it in the state it is in. No, the willing to be free as this bondage is an extensive detraction from the promise of freedom, even as it ostensibly seems to extend freedom. The usurping self-insistence hollows itself out more and more radically, as it more and more extensively wants to will itself as absolute freedom.

What seems to appear from the above? The mutation of self as affirming into self as negating, even as it is affirming itself. There is the emergence of the "no" in the self-affirming self-insistence, whose willing of its own will becomes its negation of what is other, and indeed, unknown to itself, the undoing of its own willing: a willing that in willing itself is not willing itself, not willing to be itself; an affirmation of self that in affirming itself is undermining itself. The seed of the "no" brings us into guilt, not only before ourselves, but before the origin. It also drives us as self-affirming away from ourselves into a life of deeds as distractions from guilt, or as ways of coming to terms with, or to resolution of, the guilt. There is cunning in this "no." For the "no" prompts self-affirming willing into transcending, in which it is indirectly offered itself back to itself—always offered this, in that the origin does not abandon the will that has willed against it, but remains faithful to the agape of being. This only appears later. The prodigal son, so to say, has to squander his legacy, and descend to the squalor of his own destitution, before he knows patient love that forgives unconditionally.

This freedom I am now exploring is indeed like the equivocal independence of the prodigal son. This phrase is full with an ambiguity. To be a son is to be given to be, and to be gifted. To be prodigal is to be generous, even to the point of recklessness and unstinting generosity; it is also to risk loss. First freedom oscillates between these extremes. We are given to be as free by the generosity of the origin, and the gift we are given is a rich inheritance. We go and live in riot, and we spend the gift on what is beneath it, and beneath us. In willing our freedom, thus, we become what we will, namely, something beneath us, devouring husks with swine. We come into the fair-weather friendship of a crowd the mere grouping of calculative wills. These friends know which side their bread is buttered on, as long as there is bread and butter, and you or someone else can pay. When the bread is eaten, there is no friendship.

This elevation of the will by its own willing into *the* good must lead to the subordination of others. *I am number one*, the others always number two. If my freedom also is freedom from constraint, these others, while unavoidable, are nevertheless defined in the image of my negation: they become the negative other potentially curbing my freedom, hence I cannot but approach them with double tongue, forked. I need them, I would I did not need them. I would be free, but they are there; I would they were not there curbing me, and then I would be free. The negative relation to the other emerges from the "no" sown in the will that wills itself, the affirming that affirms itself. This negative relation constitutes the dynamic character of the will willing its own freedom. In this form, my willing must necessarily relate to the other as finally hostile to my project to be free. Even my need of the other, which I cannot escape, may disguise itself in the outwards of love, but in its inners it is tinged with hate. This willing as willing itself must be infected by hatred for the other, for the very existence of the other is a source of its shame, a living witness of deluded grandeur. The mirror in which I see my shame becomes a spring to elevate me once more, for the shaming other is hated all the more for reminding me of what I am. My grandeur is my betrayal. The usurpation refuses to turn back from its willing of itself, for to turn back would be to repent, and this will that wills itself cannot stomach repentance. In the needed humility all it sees is a hateful humiliation.

And so there is forgetfulness of first freedom, and in place of the call of metaxological community, hostility assumes primacy. The war of the will against itself is redoubled in its own willing of itself. It will not pay heed to any reminder that it is as gift in the agape of being, or to offers from others that would break the seizure of its own self-willing. This war is not within one, it is within us all, and hence outside us all, and it shapes the concord of discord of human togetherness.

If this exhausted freedom, we would be given over to the necessary instrumentalizing of all others. You might want to say the person is an end in self. But this claim loses its proper meaning here, for the inner self-relation of the person is infected with a constitutive suspicion of the other. Having turned from the agape and its possibilizing of basic trust, a basic distrust of the other must take over. Nor is the distruster immune from his or her own posture to the other. *He or she is distrust*, and so must become himself or herself the inward distrust of self. This will that wills itself ends up lacking trust, not only in others but in itself too. It cannot be the will that wills itself, for its distrust contaminates its willingness to affirm its own willing. It has the foreboding that at the bottom of it all is a cry of horror in a handful of dust.[2]

---

2. One version of "freedom from" is a dominant liberal understanding of freedom; the social milieu is supposedly a more or less neutral matrix, while individual self-interested units optimize their satisfaction. The neutrality is humbug. The truth of the neutral is a formation of the ethos in which distrust and secret struggle are ushered towards an inordinate role, a role one would not guess were one to take the rhetoric of neutrality at face value; but faces here are double, triple, multiple; there is no face value. The ultimate truth

Who is really free in this equivocal liberty of self-affirming? Not the other, whose will presents a limit that must be sidestepped, thwarted, or subdued. Not the self willing itself, for it is not at all free from itself as set in a posture of oppugnancy. This will is riveted to itself in its willing of itself; it forfeits its freedom of self-transcending, as it insists without limit on its own freedom. Freedom's assertion is freedom's treason, for the will makes a regal palace for itself out of itself, but its palace is a hovel that holds it fast. In enslaving, it becomes enslaved; in seeking to enslave at all, it is already the slave of itself and has begun the forfeiture of glorious self-transcending. The twist here is that we prisoners are still self-transcending, and thus our bondage is a *prison in process*. The self is its own mobile dungeon, even though as moving, the dungeon seems the embodiment of free access to the world around it. At the heart of it, at the depth of the intimate, the self mediating with itself is not at all released to be itself, as released beyond itself into the community of the between.

The Chiaroscuro of the Ethos

But all of this is even more equivocal. For where does this happen? We recur to the chiaroscuro of the ethos. This is either a twilight or a dawn. Twilight: there is light, but it is fading and we cannot catch it, as we cannot grasp the thicker darkness coming on surely and seditiously; we strain to see what the gloaming shrouds; we see, but we are not sure if what we see is so as we see it; we have squinted to see, and in the falling dark, we peer and weary, without sureness. Dawn: light is promised, but it has not come clear; we awake in presentiment to amorphous outline dim; regions drowned deep in black, spectral shadows, streaks of light streaked of night; and even in the daylight, the shadow between brightness and creation. For the ethos also is a nocturnal between. I do not say the ethos is night, but there is night to the ethos. We look for high noon, thinking we will surely fix the sun; instead, shadows lengthen, reason wearies of day and seeks its rest in sleep. What dawns in dreams is no univocal sun but night terrors—the shadows of the inward sun.

We are the cave made flesh. What is the cave? It is the between as shadowed by darkness we cannot dispel; the inward sun always casts its own shadows. We find ourselves there and find ourselves all but lost. We know where we are, and we know not where we are. The cave is the underground. It also is *our own* subterranean being. Our opening into the ground goes into our own underground.

---

of freelance desire optimizing itself is unsurpation or despair. The truth of this "freedom from" is too often bondage to the dominant bewitchments whose spells are cast by the social means of communication.

If we are the cave, the deeper darkness is simply our being; the cave is like our grave. We grow used to the cave and call it home. This—our familiarity—we name the world. We call the half shadows, the light; our tracings of the dusk, the truth; the dim purposes we project, the good. We purr and find it reasonable to be at home. The cave *now* is not a cave. We have squinted so long we no longer squint. We are at home in the half light, half dark. We have grown to be ourselves in this half-and-half world, and we are half-and-half humans, but we do not know this, for we have sunk our sedentary souls into this split double. Legion are the names for home. Every generation builds its own. Every people furnishes it with the trophies of its self-satisfactions. Every epoch sanctifies its squintings as gospel. This is the familiar between, the world made ordinary.

I know this seems solemn and gray; I also know the chiaroscuro is what makes us young and gay. The cave is the carnival. What is the carnival? It is the feast of the equivocal.[3] It is the time of masks and the wearing of masks. Some

---

3. Think of Halloween as being between two worlds: the mingling of death and life, grave and womb, the other world in this world, this world in the other world. The cave is not separable from death and the other world: the cave reserves the presentiment of nothing. Halloween is a good image, for this is the time of death but also the time of the most powerful magic. It is the time of bewitchment, of temptation; it is also the time of dissimulating identity—we mask ourselves; we play the masquerade of the evil ones who are in the cave or the other world. The dead come back to life; or we assume the mask of the dead, or the mask of savage powers, or the face of the monstrous, or the mask of the witch. These evil powers are related to us in a strange, ambivalent way, since we are those powers and yet not them, intimate with them, and yet they are other to us. Profane daylight is univocity; Halloween is equivocity. This is a holy time, even though sinister powers stir abroad. This time too is the conjunction of opposites: time of curse and also of blessing— All Soul's Day; All Saints Day: the dead in purgatory, the blessed in heaven; and the threat of the hellish powers. We pray for the dead; we cross Styx to help rescue them from death. Must ethics also go into death for the blessing of life? Allow the visitation of hell and enter the purgatory of the in-between state and its vastation? The modern West has lost much of this as a result of a pervasive univocalization of the ethos. We indulge the remnant in children. We often do not understand what we indulge. We indulge a different cave as created by the modern media, with perhaps less potential for salutary spiritual benefit than the older mythologies. Must ethics remember the witching hour, the bewitched time, the time of curse and blessing? The dead, the attendance of the underworld and otherworld awaken our being to its finitude. These mythologically image the emergence into life of the powers of negation and their ambiguous mix with renewal and affirmative power: death and life as twins. The metaphorical is not a mere addition to some univocal and neutral bedrock. Quite the opposite, it often is closer to what is elemental than the univocalization of the ethos. More primordial than the latter, we have to return creatively to its more primal power to get a better sense of the origins of value in the ethos. We need imagination to dip into the darker wells. The awakening of death in us goes with the awaken-

wear the mask and know there are other faces behind the mask. Others are their masks, for they live in the equivocality of the show with univocal minds, hence do not know that the show is show. They are asleep to the fact that the show hides even as its shows. Others who are attuned to the equivocal are able to divine the unshown in the shown, or at the least are delicately alert to it. The shown may be very other to what it appears to be. Its identity may be just in concealing its identity, if the identity shown is its false face. False face: leading us on to betray us, seducing us to give ourselves over to sedition.

The cave thus can become a masquerade. Children play the game of "pretend" and do so in relative innocence. Adults play "pretend" but rarely innocently. Our play acting has designs, some with dubious detours to monstrous aims. What is the masquerade? It is the play of "pretend" in the feast of life when the sun goes down, and night licenses temptation the day would blush to think. The masquerade allows the masking of the good in the other of the good. The good seems not the same as itself; it seems other to itself, while presenting itself to itself. It masks itself in the enticements of pleasure, be they of the table, the bed, the bottle, or the company of others. Masks are not put on; all is under mask, always. The play of pretense is the insinuation of corruption that will not present itself directly. Indeed, it must needs be insinuation in order to seduce with the half-light of the good. It must keep the ambiguity in play, for the allure of possibility is held out as the lure towards unwitting woe. Evil contrives to play with the good, not for the good, but for itself. It needs the complicity of others to enact the play, for this makes the treason towards the good all the sweeter.

The masquerade is not just for hard-hearted seducers. It also is the daily play of deceit and betrayal that wears the mask of reliable decency. There are indecent things in the inner heart of decency that decency cannot confess to itself. It has worn the mask so long that the memory of its other face has grown vague. To remove the mask would be like having its face flayed. I want to say the masquerade is *constitutive* of our ethical situation. The grief of being ethical arises out of the hiddenness of good and evil, in their very showing of themselves. If the showing is double, it is as much secrecy as it is manifestation. Such equivocal showing conditions the possibility of deceit, and lies and distortion and cunning and conspiracy and other treacheries. It also conditions the possibility of man's innerness, which as innerness never completely shows itself, even as it shows itself. Hid-

---

ing of mindfulness: knowing is a gift of death. A metaphorical mindfulness is not a deficiency but is essential: to read the equivocal images, to be attuned to the power of doubleness, to shatter the illusory fixation of univocal literalness. The equivocal is the matrix of the univocal. Metaphor is more primordial than literal language, poetry more than prose, religion and myth more than philosophy and science, image more primal than analysis and concept. We who live in the derived world often lack finesse for the more primal: the derived has become our home and prison: its clarity bewitches us, its light blinds.

denness belongs essentially to the otherness of the ethical situation. The doubleness of show and secrecy also is inseparable from the openness of freedom. The equivocity of the masquerade cuts both ways. We trust the face of that person who faces us with a show of the good, but buried in the smile is the snarl of malice. Meanwhile, that tax collector we hate turns his face towards God in the secrecy of the night.

Underneath the stabilities of univocal determinacy are arational sources. Value is shown in the mire and the blood. Mire: the underground dips into the excremental. Blood: fires of passion pass through the very flesh, brooding brutally and with inarticulate love. Why does the dream of univocal reason sweat monsters? Because in the brood of the body are the seeds of savage gods. Flesh floats on a sea of equivocity in which confusion reigns—confusion in the fusing together of things that univocal reason refuses. Our body dreams in the theater of underground desire. These dreams themselves are the masquerade of the equivocal innerness of human desire. A son sleeps with his mother, a father rapes his daughter, a person flies, or cuts off the head of a dog and himself becomes a wolf, only to mutate into a butterfly in flight and then instantly to become the sky itself floating serenely in blue nothingness. Plato knew the shameful shamelessness of dreams. Underground is the theater of our monsters: the masquerade that materializes from dark sources, clothing itself in gaudy dress, taken from animal or fish or fowl or the very earth itself. After all, we humans are shapings of the *humus*. We are a breathing compost, intermittently and fitfully mindful. This is the darkness of the equivocal: the ferment of a compost heap. The heap gives forth gassy heat and dreams of violent dominion. The compost heap dreams itself to be the cock that crows on the dung hill that is itself.

If this seems too excremental, let us not forget that excrement is fertile. (One of the elemental words for "evil" is *kakos, cach*, excrement.) We are dust, but this dust is not sterile ash; it is alive with strange and exotic life, maggots, slugs, all crawl there, and this array of incestuous slime is the matrix out of which desiring energy emerges. The slime is the fertile soil, and only in fertile soil do flowers grow, do souls flower. Look to singing Orpheus who must charm Hades and release beauty out of death. This singing is not *outside* of the equivocal. The equivocal must be outwitted by the show of the equivocal itself. There is no passing the savage that does not undergo the savage, come right up to its repugnant face and seek deeper resources in the underground to sing a sweeter song. One thinks of the Titans—the savagery coming out of the fertile earth; Gaia's power as mixing, as confusing, destruction and creation, death and fertility; of Anteus— the giant who must keep his feet on the ground to retain his strength, and who is enfeebled the moment his legs lift off. Univocity without its feet in the mud of equivocity breeds enfeebled humanity. Should we be so horrified when our dreams walk abroad in daylight? They are the waking monsters we suckled in sleep. Least of all should we whine righteously if it is our superior univocity, our stupid superiority, that incubates the monstrous. There is a complicit ignorance that thinks it knows, but it ignores our being as danger and in danger.

Adolescent Freedom

Equivocal liberty as "freedom from" is released in this chiaroscuro and initially correlates to desire as enthralled with its own ungathered play of differences. I mean something like this. In its upsurge, desire discovers freedom, both in its power to possess this thing and that, and in its dissatisfaction in excess of all of these possessions. Its knowing of this "more" about itself means it is "free from" these things: it is beyond them, even though it needs them. Its dissatisfaction paradoxically is inseparable from its *superiority*: it tastes the unlimited range of its self-transcending and sees this lack of limit as revealing its power. Its unhappiness shows its power, even though as it ages it will know more from this the meaning of its impotence. Now here the virgin freshness of desire, new to its own restlessness, is intoxicating. Desire is desire affirming itself as desire. Its drunkenness consists of its own self-intoxication, even as "freedom from" takes form out of the will willing itself, or self-affirming affirming itself.

This equivocal liberty also might be correlated to *adolescence*: desire's upsurge is beyond control immediately, but there is something longingly indeterminate in it, experienced as a sweet, self-indulgent melancholy, strangely pleased with itself. Its dissatisfaction with itself is strangely satisfied with itself; its discontent is indulged paradoxically to savor the happiness with self the unhappiness brings. Eros also is equivocal, for it is precipitated unpredictably with the appearance of new others. And there is an instability to it, so much so that the ever-new beloved is never the beloved at all but the occasion in which the infatuated lover loves itself. It needs the other, but its pleasure is in its own being in love, not in the beloved. There is no real beloved. Rather, there is the bewitchment of the other that casts its spell on uncertain eros, that, in fact, is quite certain that it itself is the desire to be requited. The beloved is bewitching, but I cast this bewitchment on myself, not self-consciously, of course, but idiotically. The bewitchment is the self-communication of the intimacy of the idiot self, the self-transcendence that finds itself in the other and is enthralled by the seeming transcendent other, when it is really the sweet exhilaration of its own self-transcending with which it is falling in love. It swoons, but it swoons into itself, as if it swooned into an other.[4]

---

4. The beautiful soul thinks the other ugly, because the other is a limit on "freedom from"; but the beautiful soul makes the other ugly, so its own beauty is itself ugliness. It lacks graciousness, lacks the agape of "freedom towards," hence the release that is receptive to the

There is unbearable pleasure and agony as the other as other now serves the bewitchment, now resists it: as if the bewitching other now was the glorious acme, and then in the twinkling of an eye was just an acned girl or boy. The wavering of the bewitchment is the wavering in self-intoxicated transcending as it comes upon the other, as at a certain point limiting the power of the spell. We wake up from the bewitchment, not because we have rationally seen the truth, but because the otherness of the other breaks the spell of self-intoxicated transcending. We wake as if from a drunken reverie, and how different the same things then look. "Freedom from" may be intoxicated with itself, but it cannot completely evade the limiting otherness of the other, hence its drunkenness must at some point hit against a wall and come to a tumble.

Of course, this is too simple, for there will be many walls, many tumbles, hence also many beloveds before the waking of this self-intoxication effects a more released self-transcending. Self-transcending falls into itself and makes of itself its own coop; for the transcending is for the self, hence as transcending it is not transcending but bewitches itself with the feeling of release that is the pleasure of transcending; it is not released at all, it transcends itself to itself, and it does not transcend itself at all; or where it does, the other is in the blink of an eye embraced in self-transcending that transcends to itself again, and hence does not transcend itself.[5]

Some persons hit walls and learn more quickly from the tumbling. Many remain in adolescent eros for a long, long time. The tantrum-prone self-insistence may be submerged; it may seem to be conquered; but it has become more sly, since it senses its own heart as being more complex than the vehement I that asserts itself; it senses its own need as subtly in need of the other, but in need as for itself; and hence games of the masquerade must be perfected and played. The

---

beauty of the ugly. The look (pace Sartre) it casts is the dart of the evil eye: the evil eye casts a spell, but it is an evil bewitchment, not enchantment, and in this case it is the spellbinder that is in the thrall of its own spell.

5. One would be vile not to grant the beauty of young love too: the idealism, the purity of motive, the delicacy of modesty, the innocence of shyness, the tenderness of affection, the uncalculated grief over separation, the laughter of the morning, and the rush of easter energies. There are persons in whom the idiot has remained more chaste, and in whom gentleness of consideration has been inculcated from a young age; they show a courtesy and chivalry that shames the skepticism of the aged, who sneer out of their grunting disappointments. These young live naively the agape; we sour elders are the treasonous ones, not the wise. There is horror in that treasonous ones often too dominate the communication of images of the soul, and eros. Grown wise in calculative ways, they exploit eros as a powerful instrumentality and project the shadow of their ugliness. The young are unguarded, as is the nature of the young, and easily defiled. Justice fashions a millstone, and with it time will garland the necks of those treasonous.

mask must go on, and so go on that the faces behind the mask forget even themselves, as they slyly set out to get their way. The masks can be extraordinarily
diverse, including even noble masks of selflessly living for the other as other. The
forgotten face behind the altruism is the root self-insistence, now superbly
groomed in the intricacies of sincere deviousness.

Temptation: Presentiment of Evil

The presentiment of evil arises with the intimated show of the good. We
deal with a difference that is an undifferentiated difference, a confused and confusing difference, not at all a univocal difference. It is a baffling difference. Often
we treat the difference of good and evil as a fairly fixed opposition between more
or less irreducible others. We think we have the free ability to set options before
us, to assess their relative merits, and to judge, choose, and act on the most worthy. We do come to have this power, but it is because already a prior, more confused situation has been intermediated. There is a more primitive sense of confusing difference, in the chiaroscuro of the good, the evil. Our baffled feeling for
the difference takes form in relation to its relative absence of form.

The difficulty here is an indefinite sense of the good, of the evil, and we cannot say it is this or that. An indefinite difference is surely a strange type of difference, where it is hard to make clear the difference or set forth what constitutes
the difference. In this chiaroscuro, we cannot easily set apart what is good from
what is not, even though we are entirely energized with respect to this difference:
at once aroused by a sense of the good, but in an undifferentiated, confusing way
that cannot make definite what or why or towards what it is aroused. There is an
indefinite longing for what draws us to itself. What draws us carries a halo of
good or a vague air of corruption: either what we would love to have, or what we
would have, because it has a slight stain whose curdle of gone-offness is just its
pleasure: like a cheese smell or a shell fish or briny mucous . . . attracting us in
sweetly repelling us, thrilling us by secretly disgusting us, as sometimes happens
with the grossness of the body.

And so the univocities of biological straightforwardness are gone by. We eat,
drink, and so on, but these appetites reveal themselves tangled in equivocity,
because entangled around themselves. The simplest determinate desire can be
invested with this indeterminacy, but this is not just a mere formlessness that we
abhor. Quite the opposite: we take all the sweeter pleasure in the formlessness.
The sweet formlessness answers to something amorphous in ourselves. Void calls
to void, and is sweetly glad to meet void, for we thrill to come into our own excess
to definite actualities, right from the start. The confused presentiment of equivocal difference in which evil passes into good and good into evil is correlative to
the immanent indeterminacy of our desire. In that regard, it more truly matches

our transcendence than any arrayal of a sequence of definite goods that, serially enjoyed, might be said to constitute desire's satisfaction. This is not to our satisfaction. More to our satisfaction is the very openness of indeterminacy that generates and crystallizes into determinate form but that accompanies all definite forms as a kind of undefined heat of desire that is not of this or of that. Pure, indeterminate heat of openness and indefinite expectation for anything at all, for nothing in particular—this is the formless feel of adventure that tempts the embryo of equivocal freedom.

Ad-venture: a venturing towards. Towards what? This is not clear or definite. It remains open, hence *adventure is excited by itself as venturing* and by any needed object around which it congeals into temporary form. The temporary is temptation: the good tempts us here, the evil tempts us here. Temptation beckons in the equivocal. Temptation refers us to an openness to possibility that enjoys its hovering in indefiniteness, enjoys the confusion of possibilities, the confusion of opposites where the evil is tinctured with the good, the good with the evil.

What is temptation? To be aroused by the lure of the attractive. It is to be initially aroused, for one can be indefinitely tempted but not definitely decided. In this gap between indefinition and definiteness, a sweet playing with possibility is savored. Tempted by a beautiful woman, I do not decide to sleep with her. I am tempted by her, her beauty, by the luring possibility over which I linger. But I have not given myself over. Or, rather, I am given over to her but given over as not yet given over. I have my foot on the bank of the Rubicon, but I do not feel the rush of water swirl round it yet. I *imagine* I have made the step, but I have not. Temptation is an imagination of the equivocal good. If I am tempted, I still play back and forth between the evil and the good. In that play, I may be given to think that I ought not to give in to temptation; and I may revise the imagined act with a new rationalization. I want to do it; I do not want to do it. I tell myself, or am told by promptings, to do it; I tell myself, or am told by contrary promptings, not to do it. I am in the in-between of indefinite possibility that in being tempted also is in the process of yet becoming more and more definite, leading towards perhaps a fateful decision one way or the other. The decision may ask for something more univocal, but until that point, I swirl in the fog of possibility.

This in-between of confused possibility is reflected in the fact that I am *toying* with an act. Or am I being toyed with? I think *I* am being tempted, but I am *being tempted*, and the initiative is where I least suspect it to be. I am the victim of temptation as much as the master. I am both at once. I could not be tempted did I not acquiesce, yet to be tempted is not quite to acquiesce, yet. I could not be tempted if I were my own complete master, and yet were I just simply the victim of an external impulse, I could not be tempted either—I would simply be put upon. I am "responsible" for being tempted, and yet I do not simply choose to be tempted, hence I am not "responsible." Temptation *happens* to me, but temptation is something I *entertain*, thus it does not happen, for I am complicit. I am

complicit and not complicit in one act that itself is not an act but an active indefinition that entertains the possibility of a definite act. Hence the strange indeterminate in-between character of temptation. Only if the ethos is equivocal, as
is our freedom, can we make sense of it.

More, temptation is not only toying with a guilty act or deed; it is a toying
that experiences itself already as an indefinite guilty feeling. I did not go out of
my way to be tempted, but I come across the occasion, and I feel a vague guilt
that seems disproportionate to my indefinite responsibility, responsibility that is
profoundly mitigated since what happens to me is just what happens to me. Why
then the indefinite guilt? It does not seem to be merely due to something outside
of me. For there is nothing definite to correspond to it as its source or cause. It
seems to spring up in me, as if the soil, at a preobjective and predeterminate level,
were already prepared for a free possibility that properly brings us into the guilti-
ness of freedom. Embryo freedom is already guilty about itself, because it is the
upsurge of open difference that, as it were, violates the stability and unity with
self of a more total univocity of being. The hints of guilt stir up with the transcendence of the innocence of univocity. It is as if the entertainment of possibility itself contaminated one. To be tempted is already to be complicit or in the evil,
though one has *done nothing* that brings one into the evil.

Why is this? Once again, we have to say that there is an abyss of innerness
here, an uneasy idiocy of the most intimate ontological level, which is dormant
only to be awakened, as if from a most deep sleep, and we spring up on being
awakened with almost a cry or a shout. As if in the sleep one cannot recall one
was wrestling with monsters and angels, only to wake and unknowingly know
that one has been closer to a source of happiness or horror in sleep. I cry out on
coming to waking mindfulness. I cry out because I have come to the shore of
articulation, and what was compacted into the inarticulateness of innerness now
breaks forth with anxiety and a kind of helplessness. The ferment in the compost
heap releases a pocket of openness; but what forms itself in the gap of the pocket
is a cry of both the incipient anguish and the ecstasy of free difference.

Consider our bent for the *forbidden*. The forbidden emerges from equivocity, imposing a difference on the good and the evil. The forbidden seems the evil,
the allowed the good. The prohibited serves to fix the difference. But is this so?
Why does the forbidden have such a double effect on us—bringing us to a halt
and yet releasing us into a different longing? The forbidden fixes something yet
unfixes something else, makes definite and yet releases the seduction of the
indefinite. We have equivocity again, and again we are found toying with the
imagined, with what is other as imagined. What is, is released into an imagined
otherness, hence what is, as it is, may in truth be other than what it appears to
be. *The appearance is doubled over as a showing* by the release in it of imagined possibilities that peep out in being imagined but which yet keep themselves in
reserve, since they remain possibilities. This is the raising of aesthetic showing to

a new level of showing in which the imagined otherness is immanent in the very appearance itself, but immanent indefinitely, hence in a way not immanent but transcendent, even in its being thus immanent. This may sound very confusing. It is confusing, because *it is confusion*. The expectation of univocity, again in an ironic way, only adds to the confusion. The willingness to live with equivocity ironically mitigates the confusion somewhat, while it does not dispel it.

The happening of temptation points to an important aspect of the twilight of the in-between zone that constitutes the ethos more primally than any univocal fixation and that outlives all univocal fixations. The indefinite also has the more affirmative side of the overderminacy of original freedom, divine freedom to do and be the good. Freedom ferments in the equivocal, but the truth of the indefinite is really a secret love of the unconditional good, love that is given a presentiment of its consummation in equivocal form in the seduction of the chiaroscuro, given also a taste of itself as infinite transcending that transcends itself towards the true infinite that, like the equivocal ethos, cannot be univocally determined or fixed. The truth of the temptation is not the temptation itself but the release of freedom beyond freedom in the form of temptation. There is a freedom beyond entanglement in the ambiguity of the forbidden. The promise of this is in temptation itself.[6]

Bewitchment

The intimacy of this equivocity of good/evil is other but resists objectification. It is preobjective but not first determinately subjective—it is indefinitely subjective. This is why it is intimate, idiotic. And yet it is an ontological condition. It first happens to us, we do not produce it. It is spontaneously secreted, secreted in us most intimately. The equivocity *turns back* the difference of good and evil, back into predeterminate selfhood. We later have more determinate experiences of this: we seek a standard outside of ourselves but upon experiencing the lack of univocal fixity about these objective standards, we are turned back to ourselves by our own bafflement—we seek within what we cannot find without. The univocity of objectivism produces the equivocity of a kind of subjectivism. This is not a self-conscious happening now. This is why I call it a secretion rather than a production. The serpent slithers in inwardness itself. As its own tempter and temptation, innerness is an indeterminate in-between, toying with openness beyond univocal fixation, felt as a wound or lack one moment and at another as an exhilarating presentiment of fuller enjoyment, or self-enjoyment of

---

6. That this in-between zone is unavoidable all the way up, as well as down, is suggested by the fact that even Christ was tempted. On these temptations, see footnote 11, Chapter 10.

enjoyment of self as opening beyond its own inertia of identity. The monstrous is sensed as a serpentine stirring in the humus of the idiocy of being, in the most intimate innerness of incarnation itself, being fleshed beyond determinate objectification, even though the flesh is there solidly with all of the massiveness of incontrovertible determinacy. This stirring is at the origin of original freedom.

The monstrous is the serpent taking form in the idiocy of being, in the most intimate innerness, beyond determinate objectification. The monstrous and the divine are both together in a confusing promiscuity close to the idiotic origin: angels and devils mingle, for devils are fallen angels, hence the fall and the source of divine freedom are promiscuously entwined each around the other, here in the depth of intimate being. The idiocy of the divine also is the idiocy of the monstrous. The divine and the monstrous mingle in a confusing promiscuity at the origin of a different ethical freedom for us. Angels and devils are one and the same, for devils are rebel angels; the fall and the spring of divine freedom twine themselves around each other in an embrace blasphemous and holy. Blessing and curse are the equivocal partners in the depth of intimate being. The idiocy of the monstrous is a shadow cast by light from the idiocy of the divine.

The stirring of an indeterminate opening has the peculiar effect of freeing freedom, but also of ensnaring it. For the indeterminacy, while free of determinacy, cannot escape being ensnared to determinacy. But this is not any kind of determinacy, not a neutral determinate thing, void of value, whether alluring or repulsive. Quite the opposite, the embrace of intertwining between the divine and monstrous enchants the determinacy with the inchoate halo of the indeterminate opening. Put differently, the stirring of our infinite desire is in excess of finite objects but cannot escape finite objects; and its being ensnared by the finite is really its own self-ensnarement; hence the finite is never a neutral entity; it is embraced by the halo of equivocal freedom that wells up with the welling up of the indeterminate opening. The finite object is invested with the enchanting freedom of open desire which, in being freed to openness, enchains itself to the object, because it is chaining itself to itself in the object it can neither escape nor completely surpass. It is ensnared with itself in ensnaring itself in this or that determinate object.

The result is bewitchment. Bewitchment is a happening governed by the freedom and snare of the equivocal. Bewitchment is enthrallment to an idol. The idol is not known as an idol: it is loved as a god. The idol can take numerous forms. It is protean, or hydralike, many headed, or its name is legion. There are bewitchments of the body, of property and power, of mind and spirit In all is shown the equivocal confusion of finite and infinite, relative and absolute: the finite infinitized, the relative absolutized, the infinite finitized, the absolute relativized. Bewitchment is the spell equivocal desire casts on itself through the false doubles of god, that is, itself. Desire as equivocal freedom is the duplicitious power: I finitize the infinite, infinitize the finite. But bewitchment is not merely subjective. The thing as good is equivocal: its finite goodness lends itself to being a dissembling of the good: it stands there because of the good, but it also can stand there in the way of the good. In that sense, nothing is absolutely innocent. And when we are freed towards the value of things, the possibilities of duplicity are doubled, redoubled again and again—infinitized. As within this redoubling process, we are bewitched. If we have not been freed beyond this redoubling process towards another infinite, we may think we are beyond bewitchment, but this thought is itself bewitched.

Freedom Seducing and Seduced

This equivocal liberty reminds one of Don Juan (so fascinating to Kierkegaard and others): the great seducer, great lover, who really loves no one, since each conquest, once possessed, is the mixing bowl of weariness and the spur to new search. The *metanoia* of will involved in commitment to *this* one is short-circuited, and the desire that desires itself turns the circle back around to itself. Not the quarry, but the excitement of the chase; and the investment of device and deviousness in the seduction; these serve the excitation of energy, without which loathing might descend. It is that self-excitation that is sought, it seems so much like the ecstasis of self-transcending. It is not finally an ecstasis at all, just because "freedom towards," and the "ex-" of being beyond self have been retracted. It is the simulacrum of ecstasis, the false ecstasy of simulating love.

There is no power of seduction without the power of bewitchment. What is seduction? There are many seductions, some cold-blooded, some warm enough to deceive even the seducer who feels he or she loves what he or she exploits. Seduction entails the half-truth, the half-lie. It is an erotic exploitation of the equivocity of desire; it exploits the chiaroscuro in desire itself that does not know what it desires, and yet has an indeterminate presentiment of what it desires. It caresses the doubleness of desire: caught between its own self-satisfaction and its openness to what is other; between its self-affirming insistence on itself and its necessary relation to the other; between its self-love and its freedom in loving others. This doubleness fosters the strong power of the half-truth; for the half-truth speaks to the secret intimacy of the idiot self, speaks to the equivocity between narcissistic self-regard, and ardor for another in whom I find myself beyond myself. The seducer knows how to place himself or herself, his or her strategy, his or her probe and thrust, just in between these two sides; and thus between, he or she can move now one way, now the other, indeed can let ring a suggestion that echoes on both sides, silently appealing to the depth of inarticulate narcissism and to the highest idealism of our ardent seeking.

The seducer must be a magician to cast these kinds of spells in this tender middle place where the will to trust, to believe in another, is most receptive, and where the pleasure in self-affirming also is most liable to excitation. The spell rouses both sides in a promiscuous amalgam, wherein the seduced does not know, does not want to know, which is which, and what is going on. To be a seducer, one has to be extremely discerning; but the discernment is turned towards the excitation of the equivocity of the heart, with the purpose of pleasure in the spectacle of power over the submitting other. Seduction is deceit that works through truth, half-truth; is consideration that works through rousal of the vulnerable point in the other; is discernment of both the weakness of the heart in the other, and the mysterious place where an ambiguous ardor takes fire.

This description applies to an *asymmetrical* seduction, where one is seducer, the other seduced. When you have two or more willing to be the seducer, these tender subtleties tend to harden more quickly into masks, behind which take place calculated gambits in a cold game of will to power; even though the point will be to probe into, thrust into, the tender spot of intimacy and vulnerability, that then becomes the wound through which the weakened, swooning other can be overcome. This discernment of the tender is discernment of the idiot self, the intimate singularity. This is what the person of practical wisdom has also, though the heart of the seducer has not at all been transformed by love. The "freedom from," hidden in the seducer's motivation, comes to cold will to power; cold because it is a refusal of the vulnerability of the flesh; will to power because it hates not only being limited by another but having to receive from another, hence being in debt. Behind all this: the inability to thank; gracelessness and the deficit of the ethics of gratitude; impotence to receive and accept a gift.

That this desire desiring itself may end up in despair, or fighting off despair, is imaged in the story of Don Juan, the great libertine, ending up in a monastery: the life of simulated desire of desire seeks its final "freedom from" when it wills to be "free from" *itself*. It cannot bear its own emptiness; it would be free from itself in a self-negation that would negate all. This too contains another simulacrum of "freedom from." For to be "free from" self can mean to be "freed towards" the other, can mean the beginning of agapeic "freedom towards." Here, however, there is no "freedom towards" beyond the courtship of the void: this self-negation is born of despair of self, not love of the other, a despair that is just despair, not a despair of false forms of self, and a longing for truer forms.

The will that wills itself is a double will, and it seems affirmative in redoubling itself, but it doubles itself against itself when it just affirms itself. It has refused or forgotten or trampled on the first "freedom from," freedom as gift, and has refashioned its own willing of itself into the essence of "freedom from." This "freedom from" defines enmity with the other, and rebounds on itself as the enmity of itself, not redoubling itself in an ecstasis of self-transcending but doubling itself against itself in a self-undermining self-apotheosis, a self-hating self-love. It is the double as war against itself, just because it has betrayed the double as community with the other, betrayed its own transcending self-doubling, as placing itself before the other in answerable availability.

Despite appearances, this self-circling excitation of desire desiring itself is not fulfilled desire. Desire fills itself with itself. One is "full of oneself," we say. Is this fulfillment "being full of oneself"? Is it the plenitude of agapeic generosity that would give beyond itself? Is it the power to bestow itself on the other? No. It is the self-consummation that consumes itself and only itself, and in its own self-consumption it finds the bitter taste of its own nothingness. In thus "being full of oneself," there is no fulfillment. Freedom is ordained towards its fulfillment in the metaxological community of self and other, which affirms self and other as being together in agapeic freedom. The fulfilling relation to the other has been usurped by the self-relation that, full of itself, retracts into itself. In being pleased with itself, it deprives itself of pleasure, the inexpressibly sweet communication with the other that gives, and to whom we might give. The "freedom from" that is full of itself leads to the doubleness that betrays the brokenness of self-insistent will. Despair here is an empty self full of itself, circling on empty in its own lacking fullness with self.

Freedom in Flight From the Determinate

Deeper equivocities eventually overtake this "freedom from." Consider the relation to purpose. Without some purpose, desire dissipates itself. But to have some purpose is to be more than "free from"; it is to be "free towards . . ." If we have made our settled abode in "freedom from," we are in trouble. Why? Because purpose *constrains* desire. If I have a purpose, I am not "free from" anymore, and I have to direct, to discipline, desire towards that objective. This means placing restraint on desire. If "freedom from" is *the* meaning of freedom, then this constraint betrays freedom. What results? A disrespect for definite purpose and the discipline of desire that goes with this respect; a desire to retain an indefiniteness of desire, outside of or beyond all definite purposes.

There is an important truth to this, insofar as desire is infinitely self-transcending. Nevertheless, here this takes the form of a *flight from the determinate* into an indefiniteness in which desire can *feel itself as free*, in its refusal of the restraint of definite purpose. To have a purpose then seems to be hemmed in; rather be purposeless. What value can this purposelessness have? Freedom become indistinguishable from aimlessness, from a kind of cunning capriciousness, or an arbitrariness calculated just in its purposed rejection of purpose. It is a purposelessness with a purpose, and so it is already in self-contradiction.

Who lingers in this freedom? Those who, bored with adolescent infatuation, will not advance to a different maturity but want to reawaken the intoxication of infatuation. How to do it? Random, purposeless acts, sometimes perverse acts, seem to reawaken the feeling of freedom's intoxication with itself. A settled person runs away from her or his family. Another cocks a Dadaistic snout at the domesticities. Another walks on his head because there is no excitement in walking on one's feet; everyone else does that. Another decamps for the exotic foreign, dull to the marvel now here around us. Here, there is a loss of the agape of being; there, tricks, or pranks, or desperate measures, recover some feel for it. Another may descend into abuse to feel something, anything, in face of the soul's anesthesia; or into mutilation, or evil and death, as the last excitements in a world become fatal futility. And there will be the hatred of discipline, or training, or the slow education of skills to serve a purpose that demands one's life. One will have immediate gratification, and that becomes one's purpose without purpose. To wait longer demands a more patient faith. Equivocal liberty must continually stir desire up, just to feel itself alive. We find a cult of the immediate in this inebriation with instant glory. Because it wills no purpose, and hates definite content, it is hunted by anxiety about its own aimlessness. Its alarm siren continuously warns it to those holding to definite purposes with an enduring faith and a constancy.

Its alarm at the definite purpose cannot avoid the necessity of purpose, twist and turn as it will. Remember, it is the absolutization of a certain "freedom from" that shuns definite purposes. But how escape and still desire? By turning desire into its own end. Purposes may serve to arouse desire initially; but since freedom is "freedom from," purposes must now serve to deflect the energy of desire back to desire itself. The particular purpose arouses desire, desire energizes itself towards it, but the "freedom towards" is again overtaken by "freedom from." The dynamism of desire must be deflected back in a rebound upon itself, and thus, just at the last moment, it escapes with relief the restraint of the definite purpose, and alone with itself, it is thankful for its still unlost "freedom from."

It is like a young man, aroused by a beautiful girl, impelled towards her, impelled even to commitment, but then on the approach of the other suddenly overtaken by trembling at the loss of "freedom from" in this commitment, and breaking out in cold sweat at the *metanoia* this commitment may ask, and then just in the nick of time, withdrawing back to safe aloneness. Of course, the withdrawal may not be as straightforward as this, for the game of commitment may well be played; and the young man will swear undying love to the beloved, and insinuate himself into her affections and perform the role of dedication, but the other will be used all along, for the full transformation of "freedom from" into "freedom towards" will not have been given consent, and the man remains secured in his "freedom from." The other is my means for I myself to be for myself, but not now bored with self but purring in my prowess as seducer or conquistador. The superiority is all pretense, for I am still the prisoner of myself as pretender.

True, I need the other to overcome the lassitude that the sameness of self induces. A little spice of otherness serves nicely the desire desiring itself. It is indeed its own goal, almost like a self-pleasuring god, an aesthetic/erotic cousin of the old god, thought thinking itself. Thought is boring or bored, so let us have desire, for desire carries us, inebriates us, and feels its own reality in feeling itself inspired from sources within itself. Desire desiring itself marvels at the divine secrets harbored within itself, secrets that the little shock of the other or the jolt of the perverse or unexpected lets loose from it, sparks shaken out of a smoldering ember that suddenly revives with the pleasure in its own light, generated surprisingly from itself. Why I contain multitudes! I sing a song of myself. I say: Ecce homo! And then oh so wickedly whisper, or shout: I am not a man, I am dynamite! What folk are impressed. We love that naughty liberty, that Dionysian mischievousness, and pick for the incarnate god the sweetest grapes on our street stall.

Stuff and stuff. This is perverse parody of divine, self-generating light: forgivable in a child, comic in a mature person, absurd in a philosopher.

Dissimulating, Inordinate Desire

What bewitchment shows is what cannot be objectively shown, namely, the excess of desire that shows itself as freely letting itself be seduced by spells it casts unfreely from itself onto things. The spellbinding things are as nothing if not already enchanted by a desire enchanted with itself. This is something that differentiates human from animal desire. The latter is in a more univocal correlation between seeking and sought: the hunger setting the cow to seek food is correlated to the grass she chews to cud. The grass does not enchant. While there is openness in the relation of seeking and sought, the openness is a determinate, not an indeterminate, one. By contrast, an indeterminate openness sustains the peculiar freedom of human desire in its excess to determinacy. There is no univocal correlation of seeking and sought. The openness allows, so to say, the musk of the seeking to envelop the sought with its own aroma; hence it is seeking itself, breathing in as much itself as what is other to itself, seeking itself as much as something other also sought. You might say it is self-seeking, but this is deeply ambiguous, for the first secretions of self-seeking are in thrall to what is other, though, in fact, in thrall to themselves, unbeknownst to themselves.

The excess of our desire is prized off the determinacy of univocal appetite. Thus we lose the definiteness of instinct. The slackness ensuing can make us envy the surety of touch that the beast brings to being at home in its world. Our indeterminate opening breeds bewilderment—a rupture with the animal peace of sure instinct. It also is the secret knowing of death—the rupture floats us above the immediate and univocal now, articulates a temporal sense of the seeking and the sought: the not yet, the not yet any longer, and the puzzle of the present. The opening of freedom and its enchanted self-seeking is paid for with the presentiment of death. It is the latter that silently mediates the sense of what is evil. We drown the presentiment in the glut of satiation. The tide of glut will ebb, and the jagged rock of future death will jut its sharp edge above the submersion. Much of desire's self-seeking will expend its energy to keep the sharp jut below the tide level of glut.

Of course, this equivocity of desire is the despair of many ethical thinkers. Kant was in the grip of that despair. Others sought therapies to mitigate its destructive excesses. Others sought not therapy but calculative coordination, not empty of the fear of death, and of the power of terror to enforce coordination. Others again glory in that equivocity, as the self-exciting enthrallment of desire desiring itself. Others demur: endless excitement, yes, but endless ad nauseam—exhilaration collapses into self-disgust.

I say the equivocity is itself equivocal. For it also seems close to the origins of our originality and offers access to the matrix of our creativity. I say matrix, not the self-realization, of that creativity. After all, there is no clear sense of self or of originality here: the exhilaration of first freedom threatens to swamp all excitement in a formlessness, as much destructive of creativity as fostering of it. The upsurge is doubly ambiguous. Those who glory in desire's equivocity are right to a point, but wrong if the equivocity is not further mediated. Desire is dissimulating—it shows itself and what it wants; it hides itself and retreats into itself, frequently not knowing itself. It expresses itself, it represses itself. Its expression of itself is drawn out; it also is censored against its communicating exigence. It grows now uprightly, now waywardly. It is a straight flower shooting to the sun, it is a bush bent by a badgering wind. It is a flower that stunts itself because that is what freedom will do, namely, be perverse when the sun shines, and call down bitter rain and blight.

Man is the equivocal animal par excellence—the superior animal who dishonors the innocence of animality, the emptiness that is full of itself. This animal wants to slake its thirst, but refuses to drink, for some black block, hidden within and hidden from it, casts a spell from its own unknowing darkness, and it cannot drink from the beaker of life. It wants to eat, and it chokes on its own hunger, for some secret malnourishment makes it recoil at the bread of life it so hates just because it is made to desire it. It will say it wants solitude, while eagerly hoping for a warm hand. It will be proud of its self-sufficiency, but behind the bluster long for support. It dissimulates what it seeks and seeks what it says it seeks not. It reveals and hides itself—reveals itself in hiding itself, hides itself in revealing itself. It is in the masquerade, for it is always masked.

Why? Because the appearance of the indeterminate openness creates the gap between inner and outer, available and reserved, on show and secret, visible and invisible. The gap is not a space between univocal correlatives but a dynamic between which turns dynamically around, and in turning around twists into many shapes of possibility, some of which twist showing into secrecy, inner into outer, visible into invisible, and vice versa. The between becomes the knowing of confusion, or the serpent that in being twined around itself makes it hard for us to see where the head is and where the tail, for the height and the depth, the beginning and the end, and the thinking part and the excremental part are twinned and entwined.

The excess of desire is coiled around itself in this twisting. This excess shows freedom being given; it makes monsters of us. It reaches beyond univocal determination, energizes itself in the bewilderment of slack instinct, and sets itself out as the good in the ambiguous all. We are excess to animality, so much so that we can behave just like the animals, but we do it from *above down*, which is why it is a shaming with us, and so unlike the animals. I insist that this is not a shaming of the animal: we cannot behave like the beasts, because they have a limit and lack the excess, hence they are innocent in a way we cannot be. We behave like the beasts when freedom forms itself into being below its own promise; it seeks itself in what is less than itself, resulting in an even sterner bondage than bewitchment. Only because we are not beasts can we behave like the beasts. The possibilizing ground of this is the excess of freedom that can be other to itself in being itself, or in forming itself deform itself.

The excess of freedom means the absence of animal innocence. But is there not innocence, especially with the child? Psychoanalysis alerts us to the ambiguity of childhood innocence, but it is real. Desire's excess has not exerted itself with the vehemence of self-insistence that is more than merely desiring itself, but insisting itself, willing itself and nothing but itself. There is a selfishness to innocence, hence innocence is not ethically neutral. Already seeds have begun to sprout in this way and that, but the fruits are still in growth; these wild or bitter fruits, the glorious blossom, these await their season. Beyond the selfishness of innocence is a different willful selfishness beyond innocence. The two are not entirely disjoined, since the excess begins to appear right from the origin. There was never a time when we were not human in desire. We were never beasts in that sense, even if the best-bred human beings relive a bestial ancestry. Human desire is excess transcendence from the origin. It is an inordinate possibility beyond any neutral objectivism. It is monstrous. No univocity can explain this inordinateness. Humanity and hubris are conceived together. The kiss of transcendence was there at this maculate conception.

Hubris and Ananke

Excess of desire expresses freedom; freedom grounds reaching beyond self; reaching beyond breeds overreaching; excess of freedom feeds hubris. This is the dark equivocity of freedom. Freedom makes us more than any determinate thing, goes beyond the univocity of predetermined limitations, unloosens the "no" that turns against those limitations, a "no" also a possible "yes" to a fuller existence. Our transcending cannot be halted at any determinate limit, for the source dynamizing desire is beyond determination, as is the goal tantalizing transcending. A "yes" and a "no" are at work together in the original power of free transcending. But the "yes" and the "no" are again promiscuously confused.

How so? This way. If freedom is exhilarating, exhilaration also is the temptation to exult in the "no" that enacts the irreducibility of freedom to determination. The energy of "yes" flows together with the excitement of "no," so that it is unclear if "yes" is "no" or "no" is "yes." The opposites are not opposites but pass into one another seemingly. Seemingly: because this yeast of freedom that ferments the vintage of human surpassing also stews a witches' brew of darker portents: fair is foul and foul is fair. And what hovers in the fog and filthy air? The apparition of freedom—apparition, as if out of its own nothingness.

The intoxicating power in being able to say "no" crystalizes the apparition that can be confused with what is affirmative about the power of transcending. Being able to say "no" is taken as freedom's essence, or rather there lurks a "no" in the "yes." Say: I do this deed, and congratulate myself on a deed well done, but the goodness is seeming: the "no" dissembles itself in the show of the good, masks itself from itself, for it is taken in by its own mask, so incontrovertible seems the good "yes." The "no" is parasitical on the "yes," but it does not conspire *deliberately* to dissemble. The truth of what is happening is hidden from the happening. Thus it is with freedom's equivocity—we do not know what is negative, what is affirmative, for original freedom mixes the two, and we have not yet learned to sift the mixture. We need to be tumbled in the mixture before we can see the difference differently.

There is another equivocity of freedom. If free desire is more than determinate specification, if not exhausted by this or that possibility or option or decision, so it is undefined, and in that regard, unreal. It is all very well to proclaim one's freedom indeterminately, but merely indefinite freedom seems indistinguishable from its opposite. Though desire can be more than determinate, it cannot escape being necessitated to determination. It is a necessitation to determination if it is to be a realized freedom, otherwise it remains a freedom of mere possibility which, as indefinite, is not free at all. The indeterminacy and determinacy cannot be disjoined. The doubleness reappears.

Relative to hubris, this necessitation to determination is the rub. There is an intoxication of self-enjoyment in the excess that is *undefined*; but there is something irritating to this self-enjoyment, when circumstances, or its own nature, demand determination. This necessity is not *first chosen* but is given. It is desire's own exigence in fact, but it is felt as an imposition placed on it, placed on it in such a way that it partially closes down the indefinite opening of the original freeing. Hence there is an *intimate irritation of desire with limitation* at the very ontological core of self-being.

This introduces stress into the heart of freedom itself. To know its own exigence as necessitated to determination means that it is not entirely self-master. This does not result from its choice; its choices result from it. That it is no result of choice shows original freedom to be promiscuously mixed with necessitation to determination. It may think itself imposed upon, but it is not imposed upon, for it is what it is by virtue of just this exigence, in tension with its given nature as an indeterminate transcending. Hence its unlimited opening is not definable through itself as such. Rather, its power to be self-defining presupposes a more primal happening in which the indeterminate opening is given as a happening, which is not produced as the result of a choice or decision. In this, the indeterminate opening, even as it transcends determinacy, knows its ordination to determination, necessitated by an inner *ananke* that exercises on it a pull not of its own self-production. There is this intense and tense coexistence of limit and unlimitedness, closing and opening. The equivocity of primal freedom is just its being subject to such a necessity that is not of its own making, that cannot be of its own making, if it is the freedom that it is.

The knot is more twisted if we take into account that its freedom also is the power to say "no," even in saying "yes." The surge of excess, dreaming of possibility unlimited, is tempted to flood over the banks of determination. The surge of freedom in its "yes" flows over, and in its "no" it is tempted to refuse limits. The intoxication with itself is a drunkenness that is not aware that it is drunk on itself; and as intoxicated with itself, it either is oblivious to boundaries or irritated when a wall hits against it, as it reels in its formless energies. In this drunken dance, the vim of hubris foams.

The hubris is not first a cold, self-conscious election to overreach the necessities of freedom. It is the half-awake, half-asleep, will-less will to self-seeking or self-enjoying that brews itself in us. It is the twilight/dawn "yes" to ourselves, half-awake/half-asleep to itself and the other, a "yes" that leaps out of its drowsiness with a will that suddenly roars, announcing its own claim to dominion of the day. It is a kind of leap, but a leap that is not first done by a leaper who knows what he or she is doing. That is why the leap leads also to a fall. Hubris *flares* up in us; we do not choose it; rather, it lives us before we know what is happening; it is more like an anger than a willing; a subjectless, objectless wrath. It is a kind of will-less willing, and yet it is a fiery insistence of self, an urgency of self here that has all the directed power of willing.

Two brothers: one is praised, the other not; the brother not praised suddenly flares with an unknowing hatred, not only of the other brother but of the one who praises, and indeed the flare passes beyond these determinate objects of hatred; the flare has a halo of hatred to it; it has an indeterminacy of reaction, but it is not a reaction merely, for it also is a refusal—thus a will-less will, a passive action, an active passion, a free necessitation, a necessary freeing. For the flare is like the release of a power long pent up darkly in one, yet like a destiny that befalls one. The flare interests me. It is the flaring of self but also of something other to self in self.[7] The blood boils, we say; not as a *thumos* midway between appetite and reason (as in Plato) but as a kind of *thumos* prior to determinate appetite, and not totally conceptualizable in purely rational categories.

Again, the opposites are promiscuously mixed, and suddenly we become aware that a fearful power of negation and refusal, with self-affirmation and self-insistence, has flared in us, been released in us. What releases it, what makes it befall us? We do not do it, and yet we do it. It happens to us, and yet is it just ourselves that is happening in this flare that happens to us? We are not passive, not active, but prior to that usual more determinate distinction. And at each stage of determinate distinction, this more prior freeing, this necessitation, can make itself felt and in terms not completely defined by the specific, determinate situation in which one is.[8]

We fall in a darkness that also befalls us. We do not first stand in an open meadow and weigh the options and then decide on evil as opposed to good. One is swirled around in a witches' brew, and one comes out of the brew already contaminated. Perhaps we should not call this a fall. Nevertheless, the taint is not self-consciously chosen; it is finding oneself already in a kind of complicity with evil, before one finds oneself actually choosing to be in league with it. One is not sure if one has chosen evil or has been chosen by evil. The dark swirl of the brew throws one this way and that, and even while tempted and still resisting, one is still stained with a sorrow beyond innocence; or one is a glee, eager to go further into the exhilaration of the fall that feels itself as a free fall into openness, though the openness, in truth, is emptiness.

This means that to speak of evil as originating in an act of free will cannot be entirely right. To be able to act thus freely happens later. There is a different freedom prior to this kind of deliberate free choice; evil ferments first there. For there to be a free choice of evil, one must already "know" evil, hence not be completely outside of it in some unknowing innocence but already intimate with it. This is only possible given the prior fermentation in the equivocity, here now torturing us. The first fall takes place in a fevered twilight; the second fall may be willed later in an infected night or dawn.

---

7. I am thinking less of Cain and Abel here as of the quality of absoluteness that may flare in the jealousy of one brother for the good of the other; not jealously of the other, but the strange sense of being deprived or robbed of the praise that one feels one ought to enjoy— jealously as secretly an expression of the self as the absolute whose majesty has been slighted when the other is given a preference. One does not hate the other; one hates the other other who has not preferred me; and then one hates the brother who is preferred.

8. Consider *blushing* again. This also is a flaring of the sense of shame or modesty. What has coursed through the body in that upsurge of the blush? There is a sense of good/evil felt in the very flesh itself, but it is not just of the flesh. It is a happening, predeterminate and yet amazingly anchored, suffused in this trembling red face.

Usurpation

The basic usurpation is the urge to be God. This is evident in the elemental self-seeking, self-enjoyment of desire: transcending urges itself to be transcendence itself. The circle of self-enjoyment would be the self-sufficient plenitude attributed to the gods. They need nothing but are for themselves alone. The usurping self wills to be its own ground: to be original in a radical sense, hence its own source and process and goal, absolutely for itself. This is to find it hard to consent to any derivation from another. Desire would be self-generating; self would generate self. Any releasing of desire into freedom as itself given to it will be redefined in terms of the circle of the self-generating, self-seeking, self-enjoying self. There is no gift. The self is the gift it gives to the universe. I bestow myself on things. I stand ready to receive the gratitude of the universe.

The *ananke* in this equivocity calls forth nemesis. Self-grounding finds itself as a groundless freedom. There is something to this. Freedom, in one sense, has no ground except in itself. The question is, is it its own ground, or is the ground of itself in it, but not entirely to be identified with it? Freedom's ground is within freedom, but freedom is not its own ground, for it is first given as a promise of being, not itself the product of the being so free or freed. Its source in immanence is given from another, not from the free being itself. The happening of freedom is an opening that is not first produced by the human self but given to it. Only on the basis of the gift of this happening that opens one is it possible to give oneself to oneself.

What is the temptation here? This: the doubleness within self is reduced to the single self being its own saviour: not first freed to be itself, and given its freedom, free in itself to be itself; rather allegedly giving itself its own freedom from the origin, its freedom nothing but its freedom to be itself. So there must be no ground of its freedom except its own enactment of freedom. It is either like Munchausen or like a finite mimicry of the divine fiat that just decrees the act and the actuality is enacted.

The giving at the origin not being granted, the relation to the other remains in thrall to ambiguity, in the derived use of freedom, in the between, and in the objective this use sets for itself. The other is drawn into our power to negate, placed within the definition of the self-seeking, self-enjoying circle. The other curbs the untrammeled expression of my self-affirming "yes." I must say "no" to the other to say "yes" to myself. This "yes" is the absolute act, and the other compromises that act, it must be put in its place, that is, disarmed, that is, robbed of its otherness as other. Self-grounding freedom issues, equivocally, in a strangely *dictatorial univocity*: I am the one who absolutely matters; I dictate the terms on which the other is to come into my company. It might be best if I were king of a country without need continually thus to subordinate the other and disarm the threat. Self-generating freedom dictates the kingdom of the same in which I am monarch of myself, the sovereign that is the only subject.

Here's the rub: In making claim to absolute mastery, I consign myself to a *subjection* that is the nemesis of equivocal freedom. I am Lord and must be Lord over myself. The dictatorial desire I am becomes the dictation of desire to the I that seems to be free, but in fact now turns out to be the slave of its own majestic whim. I am absolute master; I am absolute slave; I am both, and the one has generated the other so that the absolute freedom I claim becomes the generating source of a prison house that is nothing but myself and my subjection to myself.

Freedom becomes an *unanchored freedom* when it keeps itself alive in the equivocity of a potentially subjecting relation to the other. Unanchored from, ungrounded in an other, it seems to float free of encumbrances. It floats above it all in its pure superiority. It floats so freely, it makes little of the too much it has usurped. What is that to such as I, I who am, I big with big desire? A trifle. A feather as light as my own free-floating freedom.

Alas, the monsters in the excess have not been tamed, not transformed. The height on which I float is not above the savagery, for the monster is as light as I am and flies as high. On that cloud of unanchored freedom, I am not uplifted above the mire. I am besmirching the heavens, for in the heights I am the besmirchment. The monsters growl in the empyrean. If they do not quite bring me down to earth, they will slouch out of hiding in time and show the truth of the free-floating freedom: it is a fall into bondage, because the self is its own prison, is its own bondage. And it carries this with itself everywhere; it is this bondage pervasively in its being anywhere. It cannot escape its own shadow, even in soaring into itself as a sun; for this shadow is itself, and there is no difference between itself, its sun, and its shadow.

Unanchored self-affirmation may pursue this sun or shadow with a vengeance. Nevertheless, the other necessarily stands there before one, appealing against the temptation of this self-affirmation. There is no time when this affirmation is pure. It must puff itself always by negation. And it is not that there is first a snip of negation and then the self floats free of its moorings into the heights; no first snip is enough, nor any further snip of connection; there is no snipping that will free itself from the appeal of the other. It must continue to be that process of disconnection just to be the self it desires itself to be. Then it becomes a self that is only itself in negating the other. And where then is the affirmation? The nemesis of its free floating is that its affirmation is swamped by its negation of the other, hence it turns out to be more in bondage to the other than it could ever have been, did it not set out to free itself from the other. Its will to be free makes its subject to the other, subject to the other it would make subject to itself. The line it snips and snips again turns around against it, and it finds itself entwined and enslaved.

This freedom fashions its own new prison house in making for itself alone its own house of liberty. It may never be as clear as this to it, never as univocal. Most often what we find are more and more subtle forms of bewitchment. Freedom casts its spell before itself, casts the spells of itself before itself, but when it meets itself, it meets this spell and so finds itself again enthralled by itself. This self-enthrallment is its own being in thrall to itself. It binds itself to its own bewitchment; for it is spell-maker, spell and spellbinder in one.

You might say: well and good, there is nothing as admirable as a human being so at home with itself that it breathes the air of self-contentment, self-absorption to the point of being self-sufficient—with the charisma of a surging, self-affirming presence, radiance of itself as a kind of unbrookable stream of forceful singularity. Were this true, it might be something, but remember the monster. Monstrous self-closure has its charisma. But it is like an infinite bladder that must be filled with air and more air, blown up and up, and cajoled into further self-inflating puffery. The air is infected: fair is foul and foul is fair, and the air in which we hover is filthy. The monster stabs the bladder, not to deflate it but to increase its puffery, to ferment the infectious brew, to make it noxious. How then does desire show itself bewitched? As in thrall to *craving*.

Craving

What is craving? A hunger that gnaws at itself as an emptiness that is never replete, that must be infinitely fed, even as it ceaselessly devours everything. Craving: desire that is mine and that is not mine anymore, for I am not free in my craving. Craving: my desire freed, but so freed that it is the prisoner of necessitation, hence not free at all. Craving: free desire, but having freed itself it is the subject of its own dictation; but what dictates is the monster, hence it is the monster that is free, and the free monster is not freedom but rampage and desecration; freedom is necessitation but now in the vile form of bondage to the evil one has become.[9]

---

9. Spinoza speaks about human bondage, and rightly so. I think the bondage is deeper than Spinoza knew. Spinoza thinks that there is a necessity in the course of human emotions, of which we are ignorant; the necessity lives us, and we are in bondage to our own passions. Once we properly understand them, we are released from the bondage; a knowledge of necessity somehow (but how?) frees us from the bondage. First, his sense of necessity is tied to the univocity of the universal determinism marking the *mathesis* of nature in modernity. This is not a deep enough understanding of necessity relative to the ethical. Necessity here is deeply equivocal—a peculiar thing to say, I know, given standard views of necessity that invariably tie it to a more or less univocal view of intelligibility, correlation, causation, and connectedness. The necessity of bondage is produced out of the equivocity of human desire—an equivocity not dispelled by being subject to a univocal *mathesis*. There is a constitutive equivocity that is not a mere confusion that univocal ethics will get rid of, returning us to a univocal continuity with the characteristic modes of determination in the rest

What is craving? It is impulse become compulsion. To be under impulse is to be impelled, as if a strange hand were pushing my back, or an unseen hand drawing me forward. But there seems to be nothing there at all, except me. Why then this grip of obsession? Being obsessed is not being able to let go, not being let go. It is not being able to free oneself. And paradoxically, one is not *tempted anymore*, just inexorably drawn down a path one would not now go, though there is nothing more insistently one desires than to walk down that path. I am now the living embodiment of equivocity of compulsion and choice, necessity and freedom, feverish and frozen into a habitual posture like a straitjacket in whose grip I am helpless. I am riveted to the obsession: riven in two between opposites tearing me apart; paralyzed in the rift between, frozen in the middle where the opposites coincide with my own internally contradictory being. I have become war: war in myself, war against myself, war devouring itself in my self; the war that is the self devouring the self that is war. I have become desolation.

What is craving? Free desire, unanchored from God, seeking to be God—in its own emptiness. How so? Free desire is excessive just because it desires God. The craving for God is an insatiable hunger, but it does not feed the monster or free it. The craving that is bondage breaks the bond to the other that keeps it in ontological equipoise. It sees itself as the lord of the equivocal, but it is servile to

---

of nature. There is a necessity of freedom as a happening; but this happening, once it happens, is itself equivocal between a further freedom and necessity. How one lives that equivocity shapes, though it does not absolutely determine, the kind of bondage in which one will come to live. We do not just deliberately choose our bondage, but we live half-awake and find ourselves in a self-created bondage. This is not to deny that we can also choose a way wherein lies bondage to evil, and choose not in being half-awake but in being fully awake, knowing the good but willing and choosing the evil. The bondage we find ourselves in is both more equivocally shaped and on some occasions the result of knowing evil, not the result of not knowing. And it is not just knowing that will free us from the bondage. The cravings of which I speak are not just misunderstood passions. They are *exigencies of transcending of which we have no control*; and which cannot be brought back to harmony simply by being known. A new self has to be shaped in which the waywardness is slowly converted to the way of freedom as a different necessity of love of the other, and indeed of God as giver of freedom. Is there too much of the rationalism of the Stoic in Spinoza's view of bondage and blessedness? Not enough of the recalcitrant equivocity of evil and good; not enough of the shattering and remaking, the breakdown and breakthrough necessary to bring freedom back to its own true necessities and its own being freed, freeing into what I call agapeic transcending? The cave, the masquerade, bewitchments, and bondage hold us in their vice far more fastly than Spinoza does justice to. Spinoza's therapeutic attitude to equivocity and his desire to bring it back to geometric univocity fail to see the complexities of equivocity that cannot be brought back to univocity, since they point beyond to more dialectical and metaxological ways and to other necessities and freedoms that cannot be defined in terms of the interplay of univocity and equivocity.

its own equivocity. Its craving shows it must feed its own openness, for this becomes more insatiably hollow the more its affirming transcending is swamped by the negating of the other that fuels its free flight. Negating becomes its destiny, not out there but in the heart it has made for itself, the heart that has not just grown cold but grown violent in its will to be free for itself alone. As it is more for itself, it also is more void. Craving is the life of transcending still surviving in this void. The craving, though violent, is still a hope of life, be it the craving of malnourishment that would devour scraps and shreds to palliate the hollow it has made itself to be. In its radical emptiness, it might again become ready for good. Sunken into the prison of its own made soul, that soul may have to be shattered to be made a new opening. It cannot break the spell of itself it has cast on itself. There must be the in-breaking of a releasing other. Fair is foul and foul is fair. But the hurly burly's never done; and the battle's always to be lost and won.

CHAPTER NINE

FOURTH ETHICAL SELVING: DIALECTICAL AUTONOMY

Prodigal Freedom

Suppose we take stock in terms of the parable of *the prodigal son*. The younger son has adventure in his blood, and we might cheer his pluck to risk the foreign. The dutiful son, by contrast, stays at home and seems to play it safe. The youthful prodigal chooses his liberty as "freedom from." What is his "freedom towards"? Initially this is not known: he will risk the peril of "freedom towards." The son is not unconsidering; he wants his patrimony; he wants his share; he asks for what we thinks is his by right. It is given. Is the giving of the father a generosity or a foolhardiness? Surely he has some presentiment of a dubious end? Is he reluctant to let him go? Why does he release him? How could he? And the son goes off, spends what he is given. He is prodigal: giving out what he was given. As he gives it out, expends it, he is "freedom from." While the resource of the patrimony lasts, all seems well. Friends appear, the fair-weather friends who know a good thing and extend the fond hand that would wash the hand—as long as its own palm is crossed with silver. The prodigal perhaps is so caught up, he does not calculate; coming into his own, he hardly notes their sham service; he is bewitched—under the spell of his power to command comrades, while he commands a purse. Company will keep at bay the hour of irritated weariness and the burden of oneself; for this is the end of the "freedom from"—oneself as an intolerable burden. The purse buys the company of "living tools"; and when it runs out, one can do nothing but become a burden on their purses. The meaning of their acceptance shows itself as rejection, their friendship as hostility. They snarl, or take their leave, without courtesy. The upward exhilaration of spending and spending reverses into a downward spiral from request to pleading to begging to squalor and the last company of innocent swine. The spell begins to break.

It is not at the apex of "freedom from" that the prodigal knows himself; it is in the nadir of his despair. When he is lost, he then tastes the ashes of prodigality as distended to profligacy and forgetfulness of the first giving. In the sty of squalor, light is born: born of necessity and need, born of despair, and born of last hope in the father. It is in going down to the bottom and discovering the nothingness of his equivocal liberty that he reconsiders who he is: not who he wants to be, but who he is—a son. The nothingness of his "freedom from" stems from his turn from the other "freedom from," a "freeing towards" that released him into his own self-becoming. He could give himself to himself because he was first given to himself. He must grant an other origin as first the giver of freedom's promise. One might say that the squalor of his own descent into nothingness brings him back to point zero. This zero is the point of maximum contraction of the bewitchment, and so also, because of this, it reveals the renewed offer of the granting source. The zero is what we are without the gift, and what we become without granting the gift as granted. Acknowledging that we are as nothing opens the offer of being free in a new way. We turn towards the giver in hope of being accepted. The story says we are, unconditionally. We are astonished to find ourselves feasted.

Is the restored son free at last? Certainly there is much of self-interest in his return. He considers his situation. He sees how even as the lowest in his father's house he would be higher than his low squalor now. He is willing to be a low servant in that house, and there is a strong element of self-consideration in this. If he has lost the pride of being full of himself, he calculates also in response to his loss. Is this willingness to be a servant simply a reverse of the forms of enslavement his purse allowed him so recently? Would he still be the will willing itself did he still have the purse for it? Would he be so willing to be a servant did he have the purse to make others his servants? There are turnings around that are no more than reversals in the mutual definition of masters and slaves. Their opposed views of "freedom to" may each be still enslaved to this form of "freedom from."

It is necessary for a different turn to take hold. The coming to nothing may strain the heart of its hubris, chasten its willing of itself, purify it, may purify it. And, of course, the monstrous hubris also may just lie in waiting, lying low while the tide of things seems to go against it, only to spring out again with its old, wily willfulness, once the tide turns in its direction again. The difference cannot be decided easily. The difference is in the heart, and this is in the intimacy of the idiotic, and this always retains a hiddenness and reserve. A purification by descent into nothing is necessary, for the descent to zero is being brought back to the origin in which this doubleness of first freedom can be faced again: freedom as first gift releasing us to be ourselves, and freedom as the "freedom from" that allows us to affirm ourselves, once given to be ourselves. Being brought to zero is being brought back to this intimate double condition.

Brought back to zero, the prodigal still has a life to resurrect. Perhaps the festive acceptance will so stun him that the form of his squalor will strike home even more, not destroying him again but shaking him into a love baffled by reconciliation. This return to community also is a different intermediation of the good in gratitude—not gratitude resenting its debt to the other but gratitude astonished that it has been delivered from its own nothingness and given back its life. The son has come to his own death and has undergone one death; he may have to undergo more deaths ("My son was dead and now he is alive again! . . . your brother was dead and has come back to life," Luke, 15: 24, 31–32). Has he begun to be a posthumous gratitude: not resentful of the goodness of the other but released from itself because it has learned the release given by the love of the other? But the story can be retold differently, as we shall see. *New bewitchments* can be cast by free desire as it is resurrected from zero. What of *the dutiful son*? He finds his place in a different freedom (tempted by the resentments of righteousness, something of an embryo Kantian, stressing duty, autonomy, submission to the moral law). What of *the father*? What freedom here? Generosity beyond the measure of righteousness? Forgiving that is reckless; that exceeds the measure of duty; that exceeds all autonomous self-determination; pure release towards the loved other, like the agapeic origin? We will come to this too.[1]

Coming to Self: "Freedom To" and the "No"

What are the words when the prodigal hits bottom in a far and foreign country? "And he came to himself. . . ." This is my clue in thinking further about "freedom to . . ." I shall put it this way: not every wandering son comes to himself in the same way; some hit bottom and come to themselves, but *they will to*

---

1. Why should a philosopher invoke such parables? A scripture scholar: " You trespass without competence! You need to read the New Testament in the original language, and you need to know the different theories of composition, and so on and on." An academic philosopher: "Where is your intellectual self-respect? We expect from you a set of non-sectarian arguments. I hate to admit it, but the theologians are right: religion is one thing, philosophy another. At least that gets it right. You are muddying the waters." All honor to academic competence! Is this the point, though? Do these parables have an elemental power that exceeds the most complex theories any scriptural scholar or academic philosopher could concoct? Is it not this elemental power that draws us back, especially the heart grown in mindfulness and suffering and love. Think of Rembrandt's drawings of the prodigal's return. He was no scriptural scholar, no academic philosopher. Should he have been refused a license to create those drawings? Yet they show he has drawn near to the truth of the parables. The power of the elemental shines out in the drawings. Monsieurs, the professional philosophers—how cutting your condescension! It practices an etiquette with a long pedigree—the old protocol that parables are for children, while intellectuals walk in the mature ways of conceptual sophistication. But would one exchange tomes of ethical analysis for one of these parables? Suppose their power exceeds the professorial measure, outliving the pomp of our academic respectabilities? One should play by the rules of the guild, I suppose, but some things, alas, are without the shelter of the guild house.

come to themselves in a different way; others, as in the parable, see that they must *come back* to the father's house, having come to themselves. This first possibility is now my concern.

Both ways are possible. The first can yet turn to the second, but the one who travels away may still be in the intoxication of "freedom from." To return home suggests my mistake, and I bridle at that. My pride cannot endure it, and I have no ken of compassion that does not want to shame. Astray, I cannot see this. Since I still think of my being as "freedom from," return to the first giver seems only a submission or a loss of face. What then? I will come to myself differently, come to be differently than I am now, here hitting bottom and coming to myself as a nothing. I will *convert my nothingness* into something of note, convert it through a new willing. I come to myself as nothing; I come to myself as despair over myself; I will climb up from the bottom of the pit. How? *Through a determination that insists on itself as the will to self-determination.* I will not forfeit my own self-willing, but I am not the adolescent in love with its own being in love, or desire seduced with its own equivocity. I am someone. I am a human being at work: I will cease the play of equivocal liberty. I will mediate a maturer freedom that is self-determining. This may sound straightforward, but it is not. It demands the conversion of our power to say "no" in a certain direction. The power to say "no," indeed to be "no," is worked closely into the texture of being free. It is sleeping there from the beginning, and it takes on different configurations in different forms of freedom. The "no" is not a human creation, nor does it appear out of nothing with the human and our power to say "no." Rather, the "no" is there in an ontological way, constitutive of the being of finitude, hence kneaded into the ethos, sleeping in the givenness of the good of being. For the good of being that is given is other to the origin, and as originated, it is defined by having come to be out of nothing, and the nothing is not something left behind but it constitutively marks finite being, both as being and as possibly not being: the possibility of not being is an actuality in the finite being of given being. This is the ontological character of the finite in its contingency. This also means that the good or perfection of the finite is always host to its own possible nothingness—the "no" that is other to being, the nothingness that is overcome in the coming to be of finite being is an other intimate to the contingency of finite being.

This intimacy of the nothing comes to awakening with us. We are beings that can be mindful of being; so also we can be mindful of the nothing that is the intimate other of finite being. Hence we can refuse or consent, over and above the consent of simply being alive. And we also have the *knowing* of good and evil, not just the being of good and evil, so we have the *knowing presentiment of death* in all that we do, in all of our lives. The knowing of the nothing introduces a mindfulness of possible rupture in being that has repercussions throughout our entire human being. An earthquake deep underground shakes the surface many miles away: the surface returns to calm, but we wonder what shifts have taken place. Sometimes the shifts disclose themselves as huge and gaping rifts on the surface. These wounds break out in human being; but it is the abyss underground that we must acknowledge as much as the more evident breaches on the surface. These breaches are the showings of rupture, but the abyss out of which the showings come is often a reservoir in secret of trembling, precarious being.

Our desiring being shows the equivocal excess that mixes "yes" and "no." I come to myself as nothing, but as coming to myself, I say "no" to this "being nothing." I will be something. In affirming myself, I can stand, I can come to a stand in myself, against what is other. This self-affirmation then contains the dangerous ambiguity that, just as affirmation, it is also negation of the other. The "yes" to being in self is ambiguously a "no" to the being of the other. Yet this "no" is not an absolute necessity. The indeterminacy of our possibility opens the *temptation* that "yes" to self—altogether natural, necessary and unavoidable—may be "no" to the other. In necessarily affirming itself, my freedom is tempted to negate freedom in the other. The "yes" of my freedom is also the possibility of the "no" that subjects what is other.

This is an outcome that, while free, seems fated, though not in an absolutely univocal sense. Temptations are turned into necessities, but not univocal necessities that are externally determined, since the turning itself is just a free self-determining. Self-affirming is an expression of free being; it also is a necessity of free being. The power to say "no" also is an expression of free being, and a necessity as far as the self-affirming is to be what it is. Thus a *necessary temptation* of free being is negation, exclusion, refusal, and subordination of the other to the self, just in ordination to itself. This ordination to self makes it will to be its own end. It lacks itself; it seeks itself; it affirms itself; it enjoys itself; it is its own end because, beginning with itself, it wills to mediate with itself.

Strangely, this will for the mastery of self-mediation also is at the origin of *the slave*. For this will willing itself, as free from the other, is tempted to turn the other, through negative relation, into the means of its own willing of itself. The will of the other as willing itself is to count for nothing, except to confirm or serve my primary will. The other is thus deprived of will as for itself, and turned into will for me, the first, number one. For the slave is the one denied his will as for itself. His will is not so much destroyed as bent from its own self-affirming towards serving my more dominant willing. Sometimes this bending means breaking his root self-insistence; the other, like a horse, has to be broken, to be broken in. Sometimes the submission is less violent, for the root self-insistence may not be as vehement as the dominating will, hence is more easily overpowered. The will of the other is made to serve the self-mediation of the more dominant will.

Thus a certain *logic of self-mediation* in and through the other defines the emergence of the slave (and not quite the emergence beyond the slave, as Hegel seems to think). The slave emerges when there is a struggle for the dominance of a *number one*. The self-affirming will looks out for number one. It thinks it is nothing if it is not number one. The others who oppose it also want to be number one. Since there can be only one one, plurality must mean war—if we think in terms of a logic of self-mediation and negative relation. What is more than one, what exceeds one, is always violation. The "more" is not an affirmative excess, just because the one who would be number one asserts its singularity exclusively.[2] This means negating the other pretenders, and the successful pretender is not successful due to the truth of its pretense, but because it activates in itself greater strength to affirm itself and negate the other. All is pretense, in fact, but it is pretense in power or power in pretense. If so, might is right, but might also is as much pretense as right.[3]

In a word, master and slave come to form out of the will that wills itself and the self-mediating logic of being number one.[4] It is first freedom that first creates slavery. Slavery is not the univocal deprivation of this "freedom from," as if a slave becomes a slave because he or she is deprived of freedom to be released from the dominating one. This is true in a subordinate sense. The first equivocal liberty is itself the seedbed of a certain slavery and mastery. The unfolding of a certain dialectical self-mediation brings to fruit these seeds.

---

2. If the slave is denied a will of his or her own, this inevitably is a violence, whether overt or not. What is violated? It is the gift proper to freedom that includes its being given for itself. If a certain self-assertion of "freedom from" leads to this violence on freedom, clearly there must be *more* to freedom—that is, if it is not to destroy itself in self-evisceration. Without this "more," the self-insistence would never be the proper self-love that loves itself in affirming itself.

3. It seems inadequate to describe slavery as either an internal or an external happening; it is clearly both; but it has its roots in the idiotic, as this is enacted in deeds in the community, even as the communal deed shapes the indeterminacy of the idiotic. Nor is liberation only a matter of taking off the external chains, or of reforming violated inwardness. These could be done and done well, and one might still lack real release. Enslavement sends its roots deep into the idiotic, as it shoots its baleful legacy abroad in community. There are further freedoms beyond the enslavement that *freedom still finds itself in*, even though we are released from these first constraints. The intimacy of the condition of slavery to the idiocy of freedom makes one think that there is some shocking truth to the Aristotelian and Nietzschean views that some are "by nature" more slavish, at least in this sense: their *first character* presents less spontaneous resistance to the conditions of slavery that freedom itself secretes.

4. My treatment here tilts slightly more towards slaves, since it is more apposite to treat masters below in terms of a further freedom, relative to erotic sovereignty.

Making Freedom Work

What are these fruits? These concern "freedom to," where the directionality of the "to" is towards the self who mediates with itself. The root self-insistence is to be further transformed in a willing of the self that *seeks to appropriate the multiple ambiguities of its own internal equivocity and the recalcitrances of resisting others*. Such "freedom to" looks towards a kind of dialectical autonomy in which the objective is the constitution of self-determining life. Autonomy as *nomos* of the *auto*: law of the same that comes to determination and self-determination in this further self-mediation of the root will.

Autonomous self-determination is indeed self-insistent, but now the naivete of my own self-affirmation has been tempered: I have tasted the despair in an undirected intoxication of desire; I have known the dubious fidelity of others who stand more against me than with me; coming to myself, I must calculate for myself and not be prodigal; I must work and not spend and work for myself; and work for myself as *one works to make oneself be something*. I must climb out of the sty of the hired hand and be my own master, owning not only my own property but my own life. I see that my further freedom is closely connected to negation and work, beckoning me to autonomy as a dialectical freedom, and perhaps the further selving of erotic sovereignty. But I must again return to the nothing and face it further. Why so?

Consider. The will's self-mediation, when childish and adolescent, hardly knows death. It has a presentiment of it, and it may often be overcome with nameless horrors, just because the presentiment is of nothing, and the nothing strikes terror into the elemental love of the "to be" rising up in our self-insistence. The nameless presentiment of death also makes the young susceptible to bewitchments, even as they also are more subject to fascination, ardor, and idealistic zeal. Nevertheless, the seed of our own nothingness is in the seed of our own self-becoming. The seed may barely stir for a long time; its mere stirring can send shudders of dread through the will, and send it into a fever of distraction, though the distraction looks like creative energy. (The adult counterpart—work as a narcotic.) The young will is susceptible to agents of ecstasy in which it forgets itself: the *immediacy* of the good of the "to be" coexists with the threat of nothingness to that good. Because the original "to be" is given, it is not in the will's own power completely, and time will take it away. Just its *contingency* means that the seed of its self-becoming grows in the same soil as the twin seed of its own nothingness. This will later flower, often just when the bloom of life seems to sing out its song of completer self-possession.

The twin seeds, the intertwining of the elemental good of the "to be" and its own mortal fate, mean that freedom always has the presentiment of its own *temporariness*. Mindfulness awakens it to the unmastered nature of the universal impermanence, the flux of time on which it is broadcast. Presentiment of nothingness becomes mindfulness of time relative to its own "to be," mindfulness of its own time as temporary. The selving of freedom comes to itself in the mindfulness that it now is and is *once*, but that there will come a time when its "once" will be spent, and it will not be, and *never* be thus again, as it now is, tasting the sweet air of simply being at all.

To enter fully the mindfulness of the twinning of this sweetness of being and its temporariness is not easy, and not chosen by us. Most of our lives we flee it, because minding it means entering into our own death, and we cannot savor the sweetness when that doom hangs over us. We remain suffering animals. "Freedom from" and "freedom to" may will to be master of fate, but death is their fate, and if fate is their master, that master is death. Freedom initially recoils from this master, as its own self-negation. It will later learn that it must make its peace, even when it comes into some qualified self-mastery. It must take the measure of its suffering, and when it is defeated, it must learn that it cannot take the measure of its own death, even as it must try to take the measure of death.

The presentiment of nameless death takes form in peculiarly creative and original shape. *Carpe diem*—seize the day. For the darkness will come, when the hand of man will wither, and no work will be done. Work must be done now, if it is to be done at all. There is a discipline of freedom in this work that takes it beyond its own younger self-insistent form of "freedom from." The work of the nothing is in the exigence that drives us to work. Mindfulness of our nothingness turns us into workers, but work itself is possible only because, in our share of the original free power of the "to be," there is twinned the power to negate, to say "no."

Suppose again that the prodigal comes to himself, and will not go home, out of shame or refusal; he will stay and work, and work himself out of the sty; his coming to himself is inseparable from his power to say "no" to his present condition. We know we are hemmed in by limits; we know our "freedom from" hits against walls, some obdurately evident, some invisible. If we would be "free from" them, we must exert that freedom by saying "no" to such limits. By saying "no" to such limits, "freedom from" can be turned towards a "freedom to." Negation is inseparable from the power of freedom, but also inseparable from the realization of limits, of constraint on will, of our finitude, and most deeply, of our mortality. The negation that death will be comes alive in us as the negation of that negative. *The nothingness we are comes alive in us as the power to negate.* The fever of our freedom, willing to be more than "freedom from," passes into its own powers of negation, and by those very powers we *pass beyond* our nothingness, at least we essay to do so.

Original power to be free is mixed with nothingness in us, but that mix wills against its own nothingness. In one way, it is nothingness fighting nothingness. It is freedom asserting itself against the suffering of being, though freedom itself is born in the most primal suffering of the gift. The terror of its temporariness temporally blinds it to the gift as good, even as the nothingness seeks to transform its own nameless indeterminacy into a definite power that transmutes the suffering nothingness into a good, into a new being good. This is more than the rebellious refusal of the adolescent will; it is the liberation of itself from its present constraining form, through a new willing. This is a new willing of itself, new because it is *subsequent* to the self-knowledge of coming to itself, subsequent to the knowing that it must take responsibility for itself or be doomed to remain as it is. There is a self-willing in this will to be responsible.[5]

Suppose this form of "freedom to" means we have to retell the story this way:[6] the hired hand sees his destitution and sees that the master eats and enjoys, while he is deprived of his own will. Will he rebel, seek to usurp the master, and take over his inheritance? Perhaps his violence will make him master. Has he already stepped down the road to tyranny? Is this a more violent form of the will willing itself, willing itself to such a pitch that it will murder the other that stands over it? Can a tyrannous rejoinder to tyranny be avoided here? That is the question.

Suppose we say that this hired hand comes to himself as knowing he is responsible for himself, that no one else is to blame. He may then say, I will put my shoulder to the grindstone and work to overcome my predicament; my very work will be my negation, but a negation that does not destroy but builds something that is not here now; this work may build me into a different freedom. (Perhaps he remembers vaguely something of the father who is good even to his servants and allows them freedom in their work and even respect. He may aspire to be that kind of master, but through the power of his own responsible work.) His work will be the token of his freedom, as it transforms itself from "freedom from" into "freedom to." Even the slave whose will is not his own and who is deprived of "freedom from" might embody a kind of "freedom to," insofar as his work releases the original power of being into the construction of new life, in the refusal of present limits. For this refusal is beyond mere refusal; it is refusal of the now that builds, hence affirms, something of the future.[7]

---

5. This prefigures in a more self-willed form, the fuller ethics of generosity in its transmutation of the suffering in being good into gratitude for the gift. It prefigures, but it also disfigures, just because of the self-insistence, hence it does not fully transfigure.

6. A number of such retellings are possible. I try to do this in Kantian, Hegelian, Marxist, and Nietzschean ways in "Dream Monologues of Autonomy," in *Ethical Perspectives* 5: 4 (1998): 305–321.

7. The servant expends himself, earns his master's respect by the quality of his work, and makes himself indispensable to the master, who now finds it impossible to do without him; and then indeed the servant begins to see his own worth in the prizing of another. Being pleased with self in being pleasing to another may further release "freedom to"; though it may also enslave one to "being pleasing." Hegel's dialectic of master and slave is relevant here, though his emphasis, significantly, is on struggle, not on "being pleasing" or "being pleased."

In all work, there is the seed of a "freedom to," even though the bloom of that seed may be snatched from the one who is it. Work is a kind of constructive violence of freedom. Other animals do not work in our sense, for none has our intimate presentiment of death. We work to secure ourselves, but this means to secure our own time: we work not for today, not even for tomorrow, but for the day after tomorrow, which we now hope to defer, for the day after tomorrow is the day we would were the day of our death. Work is death haunted, and death bound. It also is incited to create, in the short day before the sudden fall of the winter night.

There is no escaping work, once we have fallen out of paradise, and the immediacy of mindless enjoyment.[8] Our freedom falls into necessities not first chosen. We must work, but this necessity is the way freedom wins its way with necessity. Work shows "freedom from": subjected to matter, we will to make matter subject to us. Our subjection becomes a making subject and a liberation of the human subject from its subjection. Work also shows "freedom to" in the further sense: we make ourselves subjects in making the necessities of life subject to us. Work allows the freed self to come into itself as realizing itself as the power to determine the necessities of life as other to it. It determines itself in determining these others. It can free from external determination, allowing freedom to be self-determining. It can mediate a more autonomous freedom: a mediation with other-being that is a self-determining.

Work entails dynamic forms of relating, transforming forms of relatedness. For the terms in relation are dynamic, and *the relatings themselves change the terms that are in relation*, insofar as the dynamic powers of the terms come to expression and concrete formation in the work. Let us say that I work on this matter. I form and indeed transform the matter; but I also am formed by the matter on which I work, and in that way the matter works on me. Even as active to its passivity, I must be passive to its otherness, otherwise the work as a relation will not be possible. The matter influences the kind of work that can be applied to it, just because it has an integral otherness that is not absolutely plastic to my power, though it does indeed show a plasticity and a cooperative side. The matter works on me and transforms me.

More: I do not only transform matter; I find myself knowing my power in its self-expression, hence I become different in making the matter different. I am

---

8. The Adamic story has it that work is a result of our fall into evil: punishment for sin, sin connected to self-insistence; to be expelled from paradise is to be punished with hope for a future, since one has been deprived of a past; for us, any hope for the future is twinned with the terror of death, which nestles close to every consummation. Thus we see the double view of work, discussed briefly in *PO*, 178–184: penitential/upbuilding; punishment for freedom's misuse/the saving hope of freedom; a curse of impotence/the way power overcomes curse; a necessity to be avoided/a freedom that allows us to overcome necessity.

making myself, in working on what is other to me; for I am invested in the deed and its incarnation in the material work. The worked thing seems to rob me of myself, insofar as it is the public presence of my self-transcending power. The work is the body of my freedom, its incorporation in the world beyond. Yet I am as much *given back* to myself as robbed of myself by the worked thing. I come again to myself in being incarnated outside of myself, and indeed come to myself in a way I could not, were I to remain just with myself, without risking the venture of working on or with the other. In this further coming to self as "freedom to do," a more affirmative liberty than "freedom from" comes to embodiment. The discipline of the work and the otherness of the material serve to bring me to myself, so I am in debt to this discipline and this otherness for my more affirmative freedom. I am only "free to" as far as I can renounce an empty "freedom from." Hence such a "freedom to" is inseparable from a *consent to necessity* and a new respect for the otherness of incarnate restraint that previously seemed nothing but a barrier to freedom.

The subtle question concerns that consent and respect. The solidarity of necessity with freedom and the influence of the constraining otherness infiltrate "freedom to." In what guise? We are tempted to think that the point of the working is just the self-mediation that is self-determining freedom. This is true, but in an importantly qualified sense, in that this freedom must itself be qualified: it must not be absolutized, since then just that consent and respect are turned over or refused.

In fact, we risk once again a new bewitchment with self-determining as nothing but *self-confirming power*. This bewitchment must be broken too, though the breaking will be more like a Golgotha of the will, rather than a benign waving of a wand that dispels the enchantment. The communication from beyond is already there in even the most elemental form of working on or with the other as in, say, carving a piece of wood. There is a communication from the integral otherness of the other, and this is not our own self-communication. It often is so subtle that we need the finesse of mindfulness to hear it at all. The greatest workers hear it, as the great artist hears it, such as Michelangelo heard the call of the figures in the rock, calling out to him to be released by his work. What is the highest work of art but a work of freeing?

Of course, there are many different kinds of work, from forced labor, at one extreme, to works of love, at the other extreme. Something of self-determining freedom can be found in all, though on the verge of extinction as we move closer to the former extreme and to transcendence of itself at the other. Hegel's dialectic of master and slave implies the freeing and reversal involved even in forced labor. The danger with all dialectical accounts is that the dominance of the doublet "active/passive" shapes one's thinking, and we cannot see the subtler releases that transcend this doublet. This is more and more the case, more and more important, as we come closer to the other extreme, as in works of love. This also is true of works of art. All ethical work is a work of love, and this work of love can work in any kind of work, even in forced labor. The work of love transforms all work, frees it into a different dimension.

What of work as implied by the saying, *laborare est orare*? This is work as a creative contribution to the agape of being; work as vocation; work that wills to do the divine will. This work is acutely attentive to the thereness of things and others as gifts of the origin. It seeks to mitigate the negation on being involved in much work. It works out of an ethics of generosity, freeing human energies toward the goodness of things and others. This work is a communication that renders thanks. It takes time with the perfection of the work. There is time, because it is given, and there is not more time because one rushes and finishes the task shoddily. To be grateful for the time given is a consent, not a negation.

Compare this to the rush of forms of work that distract one from what one is. One works and works and works, throws oneself into this task and that task. As if in a mystical ecstasy, one vanishes into the work, and not I work, no the work lives, and I live in the work. This is indeed a self-forgetting, and the work a losing of oneself. It is an impressive expenditure of the energies of original self-transcendence, but in flight from itself. There is something other we will not face. We cannot endure the emptiness apparent when we pause in our headlong rush. When the excitement palls, there is disquietude and suppressed terror. Work is a narcotic, an anesthetic, yet it makes one feel good about oneself—one is successful or contributing something useful, and so on. All of this may be true, but the worker does not come to self, does not come to the verge of his or her own nothingness, to the death he or she works to hide. The worker's "workaholism" is a pragmatic bewitchment, a spell cast upon his or her own selving by the expenditure of organized energy. One is in bondage to being busy.

Let there be a time of rest, and then the monsters rear their sleepy heads: I cannot sit still, I must be doing something. I cannot gaze into the open world and marvel. I am supposed to be enjoying myself, and I am miserable! I have nothing to do, so I take flight again, say, into drinking, and lo I am quarreling with my wife! Instead of peace after effort, there is the irritable inability to enjoy the elemental good of the "to be." Holidays are not holidays, but often times of violence and the surfacing of suppressed despair. The particular bewitchment with work, cast by work itself, is most extreme in societies where the utilitarian spirit is most pronounced. If instrumental work is king, there is no king, only servants, but then again no servants, for nothing is being served. Everything becomes a means to an end, and there is no intrinsic meaning to the work, or indeed to the elemental good of the "to be," and joy in that good, for there is no profit in doing nothing. Or rather, even here there will be a profit to make: voila the leisure industry—an impossible conjunction of opposites that produces an abomination of industry—not forced labor, but forced leisure! What peace is there in that?

It goes without saying that work can be demeaning, debasing, when there is no recognition of our dignity. Work can be "dehumanizing" as well as humanizing. Yet all work, even dehumanizing work, where men are beasts of burden, is human and nothing but human. Only human beings work. Busy beavers do not work, in the sense intended here, namely, as willed externalization of original power with a purpose in view. We speak of the dignity of work and imply its moral dimension. Does a busy beaver have dignity? What is dignity? What is an indignity? A kind of insult or an affront to the inherent worth of person. What is indignation? The outcry of affronted dignity. Dignity is bound up with the sacredness of person. Hence even demeaning work can be done with dignity. The worker refuses to turn himself into a slave, or a tyrant, even as he works his way out of his lower position in the sty. He must continually remember himself, and hence never cease to come to himself: remember dignity as inherent worth, that is given and goes down into the intimacy of idiotic selfhood. This ("being with self," even as self is demeaned) is very hard, since the deprivation of "freedom from" by subjection to a master often makes equal difficulties with "freedom to" and its confirmation. There must be a struggle to sustain the process of "coming to oneself." Much of the time, this is more ideal than historical reality, which more often than not is the war between masters and slaves, owners and possessed, war that calls forth the violent reaction in which the murder of the mastering other is contemplated, and now and then enacted.[9]

As a self-mediation of freedom, work always involves relation to the other. It is defined in the relations of power *between* humans. In truth, it is always an *intermediation* beyond self-mediation.[10] We labor in the between. Laboring names the burden of finitude; we labor under this burden, we labor to lift it. Labor is a travail of freedom. Hence there is no understanding of work without granting suffering—our being passive to certain conditions, our being active relative to these conditions to mitigate the burden of their necessity. The labor of one can help the other: if work is a form of "freedom to," it also is "work for." For whom or what? For ourselves, yes, but also for others. But this "for others" can be double: free labor on behalf of the other—or working for others enforced by the circumstances of life. This second "working for" can take the form of being indentured to that other. The communicative transcending of self involved in work places it always in a communal network of

---

9. Marx and Hegel are quite right to highlight this struggle, but there are freedoms before, and freedoms after, and if we think that this struggle is the whole, then full freedom is in trouble. The freedom beyond antagonism and *agon* will be more evident with agapeic selving.

10. These social intermediations of the good will be addressed in Part IV, but see especially Chapter 14 on the network of utility and serviceable disposability.

power relations. In that network, the work of the worker can be turned from the "for self" of the worker and made to serve the "for self" of a constraining other, such as a work master. We must work for the other in working for ourselves, but in both cases the "freedom to" of the will finds itself in harness to bitter limitation. Work schools *the adulthood of the will* in which freedom creates the conditions for self-determination.[11]

In sum: No work without the transformation of desire into will; no work without will transcending itself to form and transform what is other to self; no transcending without the original power of being as free to be released beyond itself in its own self-becoming; no work without the possibility of the freely transcending will coming to itself again, in being outside itself in the work; no work without that "freedom to" be itself, which is the mark of the particular autonomy of which humans are capable; no work without autonomy as an implicit telos; and no work without intermediation with the other.

Dialectical Freedom and Autonomy

Autonomy is a self-fulfilled actualization of the release of the power of the "to be" in "freedom to." Self-fulfilled, in that it is freedom willing to be itself, but willing to work for itself through the expenditure of its being that is answerable for its own self-expenditure. If I come to myself as answering for myself, *I show my coming and answerability in the work* I perform. My selving is a working: it is a doing of itself, a commitment of itself in deeds, and into deeds. It comes to itself as standing for itself in deeds, and standing by its deeds as its own, willed as its own and hence decisively owned. In the work of autonomy, the self wills to uplift its own willing from its idiotic uniqueness into a *measure of willing*, indeed the measure of all willing. Thus, *auto-nomos* suggests self-law. I am self-legislating, but the roots of this are in the will that imposes itself on the recalcitrant other in work. A working will is a will that legislates to the recalcitrant that it come under the measure of the self-willing.

---

11. That is why we object to *child labor*. The child's will is not yet sufficiently mature so that it can work. Instead of work, this is a forced expenditure of energy, driven by another's will; the will of the doer is not properly in the work. The young will is not yet mature in directedness and decisiveness, not a will that wills itself forwards in the face of obstacles and against them. This is a relative matter, of course, and one cannot quantify exactly when the will shows working power. Forced labor can indeed force a development of will that otherwise would emerge later. Thus the constraints of limiting conditions or of an other can call forth earlier the working will that faces the recalcitrance and nevertheless wills itself to continue. *Willing itself to continue* entails that will has *come to itself*, at least in some rudimentary form. The child's will has not quite come to itself thus.

There is much to be said about this kind of freedom, and I have already touched on it in the chapter on dialectic. Here I confine myself to these further points. First I note a *tendency* in modernity to identify autonomy with freedom: the negative form of "freedom from" is transposed into the positive form of "freedom to." Indeed, the language of autonomy is so pervasive that its identification with freedom seems incontrovertible. That a kind of autonomy might seem a wretched thing, say to some of the ancients, does not worry us: the autonomous was one cast out of his community, an exile, a law to himself certainly, but there was nothing in this but the loss of one's essential humanity. "Autonomy" then was not to come to self but to be cast out from self, for what one was was in community, and there no law of absolute autonomy could reign. The one who willed to make himself his own law was closer to the tyrant than to, say, the creative genius who often is believed to give expression to the modern version of autonomy.

Let this identification be as widespread as you like, this does not mean affirmative freedom is exhausted by autonomy. Autonomy risks always the return of its own "freedom from" in the shape of the self as a unit of power, indeed as negative power turned to predatory power, that is, as implicitly tyrannical in the idiocy of the heart, there where the monstrous slumbers. Autonomy is self-legislating, but which "self" legislates? Rousseau's sentimental self, Kant's rational self, or the Dionysian self of Nietzsche? Or the tyrannical self of ordinary impatience with philosophical subtlety, that self whose heart's desire is the glorification of its own will to power? Or the underground man whose rancor legislates spite out of impotence? Or the revolutionary self whose vehement ardor legislates terror in the name of the cause? And do not say: but is it not the universal self? For the universal self often universalizes, that is, elevates into the ideal, just our secret will to power, still unpurged in the idiotic sources of selving that is turned from the first freedom as gift. Thus do children of darkness hide themselves in the light.

Second, there is a justified *truth* to the idea of autonomy, insofar as humans are answerable for their willing, hence for the fullness of what they are, as expressed through the work of their willing. We live life, we are not just lived by it: we are recipients of the gift, nevertheless, the *promise* of the gift is to be expressed in a way of life, itself to be expressed in characteristic ways of being and doing, characteristic in that again the agent is responsible for itself in what it does. There is a justified autonomy in which the human does for itself what is proper for the human to do for itself: lord of itself, master of its passion, captain of its bark. Within the limits of the allowable, this is to give direction to one's life as seeking the fullest flourishing of its powers, powers that are the flowering of what is given in seed. This is a rightful self-mediation of ethical selving that mediates its own goodness by setting its course by the good to which it commits itself. I am answerable for myself, no one else is. But to be answerable is not simply to be self-legislating; it may mean to submit to the law, as Kant claimed, or to bow before a good that comes before one, coming before one from another source of goodness. The truth of autonomy is the freedom of a self-becoming that chooses itself, but with an answerability that does not shirk saying, should it be called upon: I am not the law.

Third, there is some *equivocity* to its truth, since it implies a self-mediation that places the other in an ambiguous position. If its own self-determination is the meaning of freedom, the other cannot be completely fitted into the seamless circle of its own self-mediation. Something here is inherited from the ambiguity of "freedom from." For the latter, to be free for self is to be free from the other as a restraining curb, hence the latency of hostile relations: the "from" is shaped by the negation that springs up with the "no" to the other standing in the way of my freedom. But since there is no escaping the other, the other must be "put in its place." Autonomy continues "freedom from" into "freedom to," and in terms of the will willing itself. It is this continuity of the will willing itself that inevitably places the other in an equivocal position.

Since we can never be away from the other, there is no "pure" self-determination, hence no pure autonomy: the *heteros* is always there, whether it is rejected, subjected, or merely scorned. If *self*-legislation is king, to which self-legislation must the *other* submit? If my own, I place the other self in an ambiguous position. If the other's, I am placed in an ambiguous position. In the instability between these two, every claim of autonomy harbors the temptations of caprice. What is caprice? It is the idiot self expressed as the willful idiosyncrasy of the I. It was the terror of this that forced Kant to create the strategy of the categorical imperative: to seem to impute or create a seamless continuity between my self-legislation and the self-legislation of all the others. Since we are all self-legislating, the universality of autonomy seems to be safely preserved. But this will not work, as will become evident.

Fourth, the absolutization of autonomy is impossible, for it requires a *necessary qualification*, indeed, a *relativization*. The absolutization aims at the transcendental univocity of freedom completely at home with itself, the will absolutely at home with itself. This transcendental univocity is really transcendental equivocity, in that the doubling of the predicament (which the necessary presence of the absent other creates) *divides the one*; hence this freedom cannot be thus absolutely at home with itself, as long as there is more than one center of freedom. Freedom cannot just be the autonomous freedom to be oneself as long as there are others who will themselves in difference from me, and whose willing of their own willing even seeks to include my willing within itself. More likely it is a kind of *universal ethical cannibalism* in which the eater also is eaten, and the eaten in turn begins to devour the host that seemed to have gained the upper hand. There is a perpetual instability regarding who has the upper hand, who is the master who determines the more inclusive agent of self-legislating. Again, one asks: Who is the "self" that legislates? With Kant, again, you may say the rational self. But given the roots of freedom in the elemental self-insistence, and the flowering of the good of the "to be" into the will willing itself, this answer will evoke little patience in *the strong will*. This last will finds the spring of self-legislating in itself, as the destiny of all other subordinate, even if autonomous, wills.

And indeed the thrust for qualification and relativization does appear from different directions. There is the relativization that asks that the other be taken genuinely into account, that heteronomy must not be placed in the bad position that, say, Kant puts it. This relativization opens out beyond autonomous freedom to a different kind of freedom and release of transcendence. This will come. But there also is the relativization that springs up *from within autonomy itself.* I mean that autonomy always risks the qualification that the upsurge of a strong will insists upon, as it insists absolutely on itself alone. *Within* the freedom of autonomy, the absolute willing of itself by the tyrannical will comes to arise. This tyranny is not the opposite of autonomy; it is the monster that has always slept in the cellar of will willing itself and that now crawls out triumphantly under the mask of self-legislation to proclaim itself finally as the absolute work.

Tyranny is immanent in the truth of autonomy that wills to absolutize its own self-legislation. The dream of reason does indeed bring forth monsters, but the monster was there from the beginning, biding its time, as it made mask after mask for itself to lull naive reason itself into sleep. Then in the witching hour, its hour comes round, it slouches from its hiding and casts its skin. What does it show itself to be? It shows itself as a god. It is less God than the evil genius that wills itself to be as one of the counterfeits of God. Such autonomy strikes one, so to say, as the ruse of Satan. It is nothingness become being. It is the spirit of negation become lord—the self-will that wills all others to be nothing, or as nothing that it may be all in all.

Fifth, nevertheless, there is a prefigurement of a *further form* of freedom. The triumph of the tyrannical will is *one possible outcome* of the equivocity of autonomy. If the equivocity is faced differently, we can see ahead of it to a further freedom— not self-legislating but released beyond self into the between, where community with the other is respectful of a relativized autonomy, but mindful of a more ultimate freedom that takes the other differently into account. We also will come to this, but I will put this prefigurement in terms of the following argument.

The question would be: What happens with self-legislation when there is more than one self, more than one center of self-legislation? Kant's categorical imperative is one effort to answer this, and as completely as possible in terms of self-legislation. This I argue is impossible if we consider the relation *between* two such beings of self-determination. This between is their community, but its possibility cannot be defined by *self*-legislation. *It is defined by an open intermediation*, a metaxological interplay that is always more than another self-determination. Take Kant's kingdom of ends as a name for ethical community: the moral subjects are autonomously self-determining, but what of the relation *between* self-legislating subjects? It cannot be just self-legislation again, cannot just be a more

inclusive self-mediation. There has to be a pluralization of mediations and deter-
minings and indeed legislatings that cannot be reduced to one form of self-mediation. What is the other freedom that is released into the between and seeks to
shape it beyond self-determination? It is a freeing beyond autonomy in which
transcendence is for the good of the other, and not just freedom for the self. As
we will see, it is the community of agapeic service beyond erotic sovereignty. This
is the true relativization of self-determining freedom, for it transforms its "freedom to" into a different transcending, beyond self-mediation. The relativization
is *to be in relation to the other* in terms of the agapeic vocation of the ethical.

To conclude: "Freedom to" as autonomous is a *dialectical freedom*, in a number of respects. At its best, it reveals the power of human selfhood to become
itself through a determination of itself that is not locked within itself but adven-
tures towards what is other. It expresses the exigence of self-transcendence in the
process of self-becoming itself: no self-becoming without self-transcendence.
Relation to the other is necessary if the genuine self-relation is to be or become
itself. There is a transformation of "freedom from" into a relativity to the other
that serves the "freedom to" of a self-becoming in transcending activity. Then the
relation to the other is not just a threat to my uncurbed freedom but becomes a
condition of my being enabled to be free at all. The idiocy of freedom, otherwise
potentially monstrous, is disciplined by the relation to others. This discipline
transmutes this idiocy from a merely idiosyncratic self-insistence into a self-
expression that communicates outside of itself with a characteristic singularity.
Opposition also contains the seeds of its own reversal into a more ultimate concord: the opposition of freedom with its limits, with the material conditions of its
emplacement, with the other free beings that sometimes threaten, subject, violate, even hate it—all can serve something more than opposition.

Nevertheless, the relation to the other remains double, open to serving two
purposes: first, the self as its purpose, and the one for whom the other is to serve;
second, the other as its own purpose, not as for the self simply but as standing
before the self with its own integral "freedom to." This second possibility comes
out more fully in another form of "freedom to" or "freedom towards." My main
point now is that even this double purpose leaves an equivocal possibility in the
first form above. This form itself is double: First, the other can serve the self,
hence it can be subordinated to the mediation of the self with itself—and this
subordination can take the form of a minor exploitation to a massive domination;
then dialectical self-mediation, as autonomy, subjects the other to its own becoming subject. Second, the other can serve the self in offering the gift in which the
self is *given or offered back* to itself—this offering back is not subject to a logic of
domination and submission (as in the first option), yet it is a dialectical happening in which the self-becoming is empowered to be itself.

In the nature of the case, where dialectical freedom serves the mediation of
self-determining autonomy, there is necessarily the temptation to silence this sec-

ond possibility. For if the offering is clearly acknowledged, it must imply the relativization of any claim to absolute autonomy; by contrast, the other possibilities are just what serve this latter absolutization. In a word, from whichever extreme we look at the dialectic, there is an equivocity never completely eradicated. This is because the self, being defined or defining itself, is by its nature equivocal.

This is reflected in a previous point: that along one pathway autonomy leads to tyranny. What is tyranny but the most powerful will willing itself in relation to the other? This means that autonomy, as this tyranny, is exactly *heteronomy*. The logic of the one willing itself is that there but be *one absolute* autonomous self-determination. Short of that, there will always be others to relativize the absolute autonomy. This logic of autonomy must become totalitarian, hence must produce the most tyrannical heteronomy, relative to all others except the all-devouring one. Some of this we have seen in modernity. Heteronomy of the most repressive type grows out of a culture that absolutizes the autonomy claimed to be the very opposite of the *heteros*.

If to absolutize autonomy produces its opposite heteronomy,[12] it seems that there is no defeat of heteronomy, only a corrupt form of it. Perhaps, in the first place, there should never have been a project to defeat heteronomy absolutely. For then freedom ends in being reconquered by a tyranny indistinguishable from the servitude said to be overcome. Indistinguishable, even though the tyranny becomes ever more dissimulating, since it now calls itself by one of the names of liberty. Satan has put on God's semblance. What better way to do the work of evil than in the name of the good?

The dialectical nature of freedom is revealed in the self-subverting nature of autonomy. The equivocity at the heart of autonomy comes out and shows how it becomes the corruption of freedom, in the name of freedom. "Freedom" produces "tyranny." Opposites generate each other, and show themselves to be identical at a certain point in their self-becoming. Thus this "freedom to" is dialectical in its structure with respect to self-mediation in the other; it is dialectical as self-subverting, and showing the limits of self-mediation in the other. We will need to recur to the "*dia*," the double, and move to more metaxological forms of freedom. Before this, however, we must turn to erotic sovereignty, which claims to take the measure of these equivocities, in terms of a *higher* selving of "freedom to."

---

12. In a way, Sartre gives rise to Levinas. Why? Because an unexpurgated equivocal logic of dominion and servitude infects their thinking from different extremes. Hegel, I think, was more subtle already in his discussion of the master/slave dialectic, which we now see turning up in the most unexpected of places—in the places that claim to be philosophies of freedom beyond mastery and slavery!

CHAPTER TEN

FIFTH ETHICAL SELVING:
EROTIC SOVEREIGNTY

Freedom and Erotic Sovereignty

The most affirmative upshot of the self-mediation of "freedom to" I call erotic sovereignty. Sovereignty is connected to autonomy, as to power (we speak of sovereign power as brooking no subordination to another power). It is bound up with social relations between people(s), or the people's power and its representation to itself and outsiders. Sovereignty is bound to the self-mediation of power through its representative expressions. These latter aspects are more appropriately addressed in terms of the *intermediation* of the good, since self-representation of power as sovereign cannot be accomplished without reference to relativity to others, and so is beyond any notion of self-mediation, however total (see Chapter 15).

Why speak of *erotic* sovereignty? Because the form of freedom here does not have its origins univocally in power but in a mixture of power (to be) and precariousness (of the "to be"). Finite beings mix the exigence to be and lack. The elemental self-insistence of a being is inseparable from its lack of its full self. It insists on itself in the face of its own lack and to overcome its threat.[1] The becoming of desire shows the urge to be free, and to be free as self-affirming, in such a wise that the lack internal to finitude is met and mastered. This is to will the overcoming of fear of one's death. This cannot be accomplished at one fell swoop; for lack returns, ontological lack, and dread of death, no matter how secretly hidden. *Fear and I were born twins*, said Hobbes. But the birth of the human also is a temporal *rebirth*, as newly becoming itself in the unfolding of its free power, and with each rebirth the rebirth of new fear, and the new need to overcome fear.

By erotic, I mean more than sexual eros, though this is important. At issue is our ontological exigence to be, in despite of our own possible nothingness and the concretion of this doubleness in our desire, hence also in all of our becomings

---

1. Thus Plato suggests (in the *Symposium*) the double parentage of eros in *penia* (poverty, lack) and *poros* (resource).

as forms of self-transcending. (As oriented to pleasure in being and to fecund generation, sexual eros expresses this powerfully in incarnate form.) The lack drives us out of ourselves, but out of ourselves in order to become and secure ourselves, selves otherwise paralyzed by the dread of our nothingness. Eros is the exigence of the power of the "to be" as self-insistent, but as thrust beyond itself, out of its own lack, towards what is other, as needful to mediate the fulfillment of its own need of full being. To be itself and to be itself fully, it must be other than itself as now needy. It must other itself and hence be self-transcending, as both beyond itself and in necessary relation to the other. Without the thrust of self-transcendence, it will be nothing; without the needful other, it will be nothing but inconsolable need.

Eros then refers us again to our inordinate restlessness as desire without determinate limit, restlessness in a finite being signed with infinity. There is a quality of absoluteness about it, even as its disquietude searches for what is absolute. Its will to be is singularized in this finite self, yet it exceeds all finite determinates. We are the paradox of this double nature: the mixing of power and precariousness, grandeur and wretchedness, serene beauty and fermenting chaos, elevation and abasement. Eros seeks sovereignty over this doubleness. Selving struggles with its own amorphousness, its twilight nature, the equivocal chaos out of which it would create. To know the turn of twilight into dawn, it must go into the night. What does it mean to "come to itself" (again that phrase)? It is not any simple selfishness. Sovereignty is pursued in view of a *purpose greater than the particular self*. Recall the fanaticism of purpose mentioned before: it takes over the whole self, seems to be greater than one. So with sovereignty, the search is to overcome the shabby condition of one's present limits. There is something "more" in self, expressed in the passion of its eros and its restless search for something more than itself, something above itself, something above by which it comes to what is more in itself, what indeed may be above itself (thus the higher self, as in the *Übermensch* of Nietzsche).

Erotic sovereignty can be connected to *the hero*. Let "hero" be metaphorical of the restless sweep of human self-transcendence in its search for the "more," in its will to live the "more" in its own self-becoming. Self-becoming is a self-overcoming; it releases the original power to be sleeping in the potency of "freedom to." This, in the overcoming of limits, cannot be merely indefiniteness, for then one would have the futility of self-becoming without any purpose. This means that purpose here cannot be any merely finite aim. The hero is the self of infinite purpose. He or she may not be able to say this; it may remain a longing, or a calling, or the solicitation of something more that only progressively can become more determinate. Self-becoming that is called to something more beyond the limit comes to itself in the discipline of the limit. The coming to itself is immediately converted into a self-becoming that knows it can never come to itself in an entirely determinate way.

And so we meet a creature of achievement and disquiet; a creature, we should say, better suited to conditions of war than of peace—war as spurring the creation of the new, not war as simply the destruction of the old. War is the restlessness that freedom wages against its own bondage, both to itself and determinate limits. The hero reaches up for more, climbs higher on himself, as his own pack mule, or reaches down into his abyss by himself as a ladder, or a shoot into himself where more lies buried than yet is brought up—climber, diver, prospector of danger and promise.

Erotic Sovereignty and the "More"

First, there is "more" within than we often acknowledge, and a more intensive dwelling with self shows that mostly we do not face the "more" because it is not always easy to integrate it into domestic life. It exceeds that determination; it is disruptive. To become sovereign, this well of eros must be given its upsurge, in one way or another. Often it is released in more usual ways—sexual love, work, or family life; or sometimes in an inordinate will to power that wants to be ruler of its own house, and indeed the houses of others; or sometimes there are other "sublimations" of this "more" in the works of culture, such as art or philosophy.

Second, the "more" within is not easily faced because its beauty blurs into darkness, and beauty seems to mask a pitchy kernel of enigma. What is the "more"? Is it the labyrinth of the heart? Suppose this is the place where the key to paradise is lost? If so, it also is a place of purgatory and houses its infernal chambers. The "more" is the chaos wherein base and noble make converse—or torment each other. To come to terms with it asks the courage to come before the monster. We are the monstrous. The one who would be sovereign must wrestle with the monster that comes to be born in, borne along on self-transcending itself. We can all come to communicate our bale. Struggle seeks the communication of "more" than bale.

We are Theseus. One enters the labyrinth, ostensibly a sacrifice to the minotaur, but covertly a warrior against it. One does not enter unaided, and those who do, do not emerge again. The aid of an other is necessary. Ariadne gives the promise of a return from darkness to new life. One still has to go in oneself and fight oneself. What does one fight? The minotaur. Who is this? The one who demands human sacrifice, indeed, the death of the most beautiful youths. One has to fight oneself and one's fear of death to be able to face the minotaur. This one knows: the young must struggle against death and the sacrifice of young ones, but it cannot be youth that *emerges* from this struggle. For youth dies when youth begins to struggle to save itself from death. The struggle against death, even when successful, is not successful, and the *metanoia* forced upon the victor means it is the victim of its victory. And there must be a *metanoia*, if the person is to emerge from the journey underground.

Theseus wins and comes out a hero, but he could never have become a hero alone. Coming out and coming to himself, he also has lost—lost the vital freshness of youth that glories in the good of the "to be" and of its own "to be." Mastery is a joy that embraces sorrow, even in its joy. Victory over death is its death as youth, and its first destiny to posthumous life. The sacrifice confronts a death that is postponed in its being surpassed. The sacrifice points beyond victory of self to another sacrifice that is a more ultimate victory, and the only saving from death. And still one must never forget the aid of the other.

The labyrinth is underground. It is a cave. It is the place of the masquerade, in the inwardness of idiocy. It is the place of bewitchment. Who is the minotaur? A legion of names, many contradictory: beast and beauty and devouring desire, and I myself the monster. There is an offering to savage power. There is a transcendence of savage power. There is power glorified. There is power transfigured. This is erotic sovereignty. There is the tie with nature, or the need to regain this tie. The erotic sovereign remains in tune with the elemental in the ethos. He or she joys in the pagan glory of the equivocal earth, pagan glory pulsing in self and the release of its freedom and free power to be.

Paganism is in love with the erotic sovereign. One thinks again of Anteus and the earth: his strength is from the earth, and he loses it if his feet lose touch with the earth. But the journey can be into the *heights* as much as into the underground, as Prometheus knew in stealing the fire of Zeus. Not surprisingly, modern philosophies of erotic sovereignty, whether political or existential, will laud Prometheus: he who challenged the perceived injustice of the gods, their coldness to the wretchedness of needy humans; who gives them the fire, allows them to work on nature, transform it into metallic bodies, bodies that will extend the body of flesh, bodies that may outlive the bodies of flesh and their death, metallic bodies that are weapons against the threat of the other; and fire, first that lets us cook, to make ploughs, and iron swords. There is equivocity in the turning away from the dominion of the divine, in a "freedom from" that becomes a "freedom to," freedom to become self, in work on nature, in defense against enmities, in contempt against the divine wrath—for all risk forgetting that the divine fire is still thieved, and there would be no freedom to become ourselves did we not have the aid of that fire.[2] The heroism of Prometheus in refusal or revolt is impossible without the divine against which the refusal is directed.[3]

---

2. Here theft is in relation to the jealousy of Zeus. What if the agapeic origin is not jealous? Fire is a gift, a gift that becomes a theft when the gift is denied to be so, or forgotten, or refused as gift. Thus expropriated, it is claimed as one's proper freedom, one's property rather than gift.

3. So with erotic sovereignty, which turns into revolt, as with, say, the French revolution, and other aftermaths of revolution—some more violent because more efficient, and more godless, and more violent because more intent on defacing any trace of the gift. Nor is the "valorization" of Prometheus confined to Marx alone, as many studies show.

Third, there is a coming to oneself after the ordeal of oneself, the ordeal that is oneself. Suppose one comes to know oneself and to accept oneself? This knowing is an intimate of the darkness in oneself. One wills oneself but wills oneself as more than what is within one's will. If there is a confidence in self as having taken the measure of the monster, there is a diffidence about claiming too much for oneself; one pays for overcoming with bruises that do not clear. One is buoyed on self by victory over self, but self is chastened knowing what self is, of what it is capable. It never leaves one—trepidation that the monster can revive, come back to itself, even as one comes back to oneself.

To come to self, become self by the ordeal of oneself, involves a dialectic of self and *one's own* other. There is oneself and oneself as "more"; and one comes back to oneself as "more," and hence as other: the same as what one always was, but other and different, for a new light converts the older features. The transformation is mediation between oneself as what one is and oneself as other. In going beyond self one becomes other, and yet comes to oneself in a context of otherness that threatens to rob one of self-identity. In the face of this crisis, a struggle commences that shows the self-mediating character of the dialectic: in becoming other to oneself, one is coming closer to self, though seeming to go away from self, and hence one is returning to what one is and was, always. The self is itself but must properly become itself; but it cannot do this until it enters the ordeal of self-opposition and emerges from it, recharged with the mission of being itself, not in the light of lacking itself, but in an achieved way, being full of itself.

Of course, one is tempted to forget the thread of Ariadne, the help of the other without which the ordeal of self-opposition might well become self-evisceration in the ordeal of oneself. There would be no return from the labyrinth without the help of the other, hence no coming to self. Since it is this coming to self that is stressed by erotic sovereignty, there is always the danger of *ingratitude*. (Why do I think of those healed lepers who never came to thank the other who spoke the word of healing?) Thanking the other deepens the trepidation into which one has come. It does not so much destroy confidence as guide one to a different consent, wherein one is more than consent to what is "more" about oneself. For the "more" within, as the otherness that is inward, is not exhaustive of the "more" or the other. Self-transcending will have to pilgrim further to come to these more truly.

Fourth, nevertheless, this "more" within can be freed into a kind of sovereignty that shines with an affirmation of being, for its radiance of self-affirmation is redoubled in its having fought the monster, and thereby faced its own fear of death. The erotic sovereign is not only involved in a fight to the death between masters and slaves, such as Hegel insightfully describes. This may well be so, in that the threat of the other human may be a major occasion in which the manifestation of the monster seems incarnate over against one, and in which the fear of death is called up, like a malign spirit always waiting its chance. No doubt

about it, many do enter into some erotic sovereignty in their contrast and contestation with the other that threatens the loss of freedom, thus threatening one's
being and its self-affirmation. Yet there is a deeper struggle. *This sovereign is
beyond the master.* The master is defined in a reciprocal dialectic with the slave;
and there is an autonomy and measure of sovereignty emergent from this; but
without denying the inescapability of relations to the other, whether sustaining
or hostile, there is more.

This is named by metaphors of the underground or the heights, or the monster, or the divine. Eros in its full sweep is not exhausted in relations with human
others, hospitable or hostile, nor with natural things, supportive or life threatening. Eros is more radical in going down into the deepest ontological roots where
the abyss of selfhood in its idiocy opens up, opens into a darkness that has no
limit, and no natural light that would illuminate the gloom that descends on the
waking mind upon entering this nothingness. This eros is more ultimate, in that
its energetic restlessness sweeps beyond even mastery over self, over others, over
the things of nature; it extends all the way to the divine. There is no way to understand this erotic ultimacy without recognizing that it concerns, at the end, *our
being there with the ultimate* that is from the origin in the idiocy of our beginning:
the divine even in the monstrous, at the beginning; the divine beyond the monstrous, even at the end, and even when the monstrous in us had set itself in hostile opposition to the divine. The true erotic sovereign struggles with the divine in
struggling with self, struggles with the divine in struggling with the monster.

If self-transcendence here surpasses itself towards itself, the self it comes
towards *sends it back* to its origin in the idiotic, and the overdetermination of
being out of whose merging enigma it had before emerged as being for itself. In
going beyond itself, it recurs to what is deepest in itself, in the inward otherness
as thus idiotic. But this is the place of intimacy between the origin and the freedom given as gift. One lives in the water in the well, water one has both drunk
and muddied. It is now being drunk again, and its mud now is the mud of self.
Drinking in the flowing of life, there is a going down into the mud of the idiotic.
One comes to the edge of nothingness within, for this is the emptiness that plays
around the earth, when the breath of the divine is not exhaled or drawn. It is in
the earth as humus; it is in the shock of nothingness that startles one into a
refreshed appreciation of the being-there of the creation, given out of nothing; it
is there in the gift of life that no finite reason can rationalize, or father; it is there
that there is the hint of the divine. It is in the earth, and the nothingness we are,
and the gift that makes us be at all and not be nothing, that the finding of the
divine can commence again.

This is not the end of it, since the finding at this point has too much of self,
as it has already come to be. The finding is not pure openness. It is full of willful
self-affirmation. These, our *realized* powers, are what make a struggle inevitable.
Much worse can come from the struggle of erotic sovereignty than from the

moderate liberty of an autonomy that refuses extremism. The extremes, however, are what are at stake here; for human self-surpassing is an energy of the extremes; and these extremes are the gift of being at all, the origin that gives the gift, the nothing out of which the gift comes to be, the good of the divine that solicits the full promise of the free creature. The struggle for erotic sovereignty is in the between as a site of strife and striving, but as the ultimate powers and nothing contend there, there too we must make ultimate and parlous choices. Erotic sovereignty is tempted to choose *itself*, often more ambiguously than not.

Going into the mud of the idiot, one is the slime again, the humus, source of our humanity, also of our earthiness, also of the excrement we make of the gift. In the humus, the breath of inspiring transcendence blows with a freshness that we have not felt since the day of youth when the wind blew off the limitless ocean and one marveled at the glory of things in excess of one's ken and power. Now the glory of this freshness feeds one's ken of power, hence the wind is a harbinger of bewitchment with one's own glory, as well as the glory of the gift of being and its giver. Why not be the sublime oneself? Why not be the strong and steadying earth, the fertile always new, ever-renewing ocean? Why not be the cleansing air, and the fire itself that comes to earth out of the swollen cloud? Why not, indeed, as Zarathustra might say. One says, even if one says nothing: I am the bolt of Zeus. It is I who stand here, I who stand here still.

Fifth, is there a fatal flaw risked by this erotic sovereignty? This. Just in its glory it risks losing self in its affirming of itself, as glory turns to self-glorification, turning the circle of eros into a "higher" autonomy that hiddenly is an autism of spirit, a solitude curved back into itself—freedom thankless, even though counting itself king of infinite possibility.

Consider the curvature. Erotic self-transcendence goes out of itself towards the other. It goes out needing the other to fulfill its lack, and finds its own desire to be more than lack, for how else could it surpass itself, were it not already an affirmative center of transcending being? It cannot be at one with itself without the other and what the other gives to it. It can be given back to itself by what the other gives, as the look of love in the other's eye makes it *love itself differently*: differently to the elemental self-insistence, not yet properly doubled between itself and the other. Erotic self-transcending more fully effects this doubling: it allows our opening to the other's gift, less in the mode of pure receptivity as in the vitalization of one's search for completion in and through the other. As one's openness is doubled in being able to allow the other, so one's self-insistence is qualified by recognition of the other's need; and yet the qualification may or may not take one beyond self, since it qualifies a self-insistence that remains with itself and at root still insists on its own "to be," as the center, as number one. Then this doubling between self and other turns the between into a medium in which the self mediates with itself in mediating with the other. The important thing then is the self-mediation, not the intermediation with the other, such as to carry one more completely out. What the other gives is taken as the means by which the self mediates with itself; it is a means to an end, and the end is the self. The giving is not received with the thanks that opens fully to what is given and sings its motiveless appreciation. It is received as a due, hence not as a gift: a necessity needed by me, not a gift given, means *I must take* in order to be myself. Thus the curve around from my openness to the gift to the taking of what I insist must be possessed by me, if I am to be self-possessed at all.

Thanking has given way to seizure. Erotic self-transcendence has become self-completing by its usurpation of the otherness of the other as other and its expropriation as the means by which I insist I will come to myself. Another form of the *will willing itself* here overtakes the possibility of a willingness that opens out beyond self-insistence to the glory of the other. Ingratitude in glorious self-love: the simple splendor of elemental thanks has been missed, and with it a kind of childlike freedom that is happy in the marvel of the gift of the other; instead a greedy grabbing of life.

True enough, there will be those grown old in their greed, those now contemptuous of the coarser forms of grabbing. They will coldly look on this vehemence of expropriation as vulgar and count themselves sovereigns beyond such vulgarity. The coldness of this superiority may not be so superior. The heat of greed shows life, and shows something unguarded to life's surprise possibilities, possibilities that may yet rock one back on one's heels, communicate the splendor of its mystery, and invoke one's unguarded thanks or praise. By contrast, the coldness of that sovereignty, with the fire of its greed gone out, may just be so guarded about itself and about such surprises that its superiority is closer to the condition of hell—there where the self coldly circles around itself in a hatred of the despair that it is, having become this hatred out of love, love turned back on itself. Its coldness to the vulgar greed and to itself is not its superiority, but its hatred, though it feels its hatred just as superiority. It has become the icy monster.

Once again, I stress that this is not the only possible outcome. Erotic self-transcending that comes to selve with a measure of sovereignty can retain its memory of the way the other has given one back to oneself. One would not be freed into the fullness of one's own powers without this person or that, my parents, this teacher, that teacher, none ever really knowing how much they have given; this childhood friend; this stranger whose unsolicited smile on a dark stretch of life made it possible for me to rise in the morning and continue; those whose gift is their simply being there, a mute reminder of the mystery of the gift, and a reminder of the violence of a self-insistence that has not been freed from itself into the splendor of the elemental good. One remembers, and then one's sovereign exercise of power is an act of thanksgiving. It is will to do the good. Because of the gift of the others, the help of the helpers, there is no heroism alone. Heroism may be singular, but the singular carries the good given by all the good others; and it is those goods that have given one back to oneself. Remembering this, there can be a peculiar modesty and humility in this sovereignty. This does not make it any the less powerful.

Those who identify power with its more evident exercises will be blind to the subtleties here. Those not purged of coarser self-insistences will not see any greatness in power that does not insist on itself. They lack finesse for the reticence of such power. There is a reticence of power that seems indistinguishable from powerlessness, but it is much more. This reticence is at the verge of what is in human power. The gift of the other is absolutely important, the waiting on the other, but it is not so much those human others who would insist on power in standard models of domination. One is standing before the demand for a kind of greatness of spirit. One's judge is not time; not even one's fellow humans; though time and others will judge one; it is with the divine that one is occupied; an occupation that may well break one and reveal a greatness in this shattering that even the glory of the world cannot contain. The first thing is being truthful to the solicitation of the highest; doing the best one can in light of standards of excellences not measured by the determinate goods of time; not insisting on success, or recognition, though one's vanity will rise up rebellious and insist on these things in a touchy way. There is something more. These other vanities will be counted as extravagances of breath.

We live, of course, in an extraordinary age that hates the extraordinary and rationalizes its hate in terms of its love of the ordinary. What is said seems odd. (Just over there a leering voice mocks: Oh, you are quite a greenhorn!) At odds, the erotic sovereign may decide that silence must be its mode of stealth. Indeed, it seems to create work for "the few" and not directly "the many"; in fact, "the many" are the beneficiaries, for their unsatisfied longing for perfection is buoyed up in the vision of exemplars dedicated to ascend to the heights. Some are as if they have died many times, just in living to the full, as if dead towards certain things that foster bewitchments and illusory powers that imprison in false freedoms. They are freed by time from time, freed by necessity from false freedom, released into struggle with and for the divine.

The many, not lacking gratitude, appreciate greatness more than the few who have turned against greatness, and who lack gratitude for greatness because lacking it themselves. They hate it because they are the eunuchs preaching to the fertile about the impossibility of conceiving works of higher excellence. They discourage venture because they have already been defeated, and they are resentful of the adventure of transcending that would try anew, where they now erect their "no trespass" sign. One is reminded of those who say metaphysics is impossible: eunuchs in a harem who construct a theory as to why fertile love is not possible, and should not be even tried, since, after all, we ourselves cannot do it. The licensed dog in the manger preaches against the freedom of open wilderness; barking out, the world is its bare manger.

Others will be attuned to the reticence of power as a quieter radiance that does not have to insist on itself. One need not raise one's voice. One reaches an

edge where this comes home to one. One's shout makes false the subtler truth of
freedom. This sovereignty here, come to itself, has nothing to prove in the mode
of self-insistence; it is quiet about its excellence, for it no longer matters, the
excellence itself is the thing. That is broadcast into the world, there to find its
recognition, if it will—that is not up to us. Coarse souls will not have the discernment to see beyond the quietness of this greatness. This may well be on the
verge of breaking through to another reality, or of beginning a different journey
that listens to a more radical call of the good.

Sixth, the subtle truth of freedom means that everything becomes more parlous the more one descends into the depth, or ascends up higher. The path down
into innerness is slippery with the slime of idiocy: the thrill of excremental transgression may give some the taste of a parodic divine specialness. The path up is
treacherous with the upsurge of exhilaration that ascribes to itself the power to
carry to the heights—our transcending takes itself for transcendence simpliciter.
Whether down or up, there is the archaic danger of pride: archaic not in reference
to time past, but as coeval with the elemental, and the elemental power of willing.
The divine gift of freedom takes itself as divine in its freedom. The natural temptation
more normally arises, of course, out of the contrast of the few and the many, the
sovereigns and those still subject. These are, what we might term, the equivocities
of the heights or extremes. The deeper or higher one goes, the more there is an
intensification of the equivocities of freedom. Here the stakes are not any ordinary
selfishness, but a spiritual pride. A more radical evil tempts, just in the glorious
achievement of erotic sovereignty. As freedom tastes itself more deeply, the more
is a deeper evil possible. With any higher, nobler freedom, the greater is the fall in
ignobility. The corruption of the best is the worst: *corruptio optimi pessimi.*

The Prodigal on the Throne

Shall we return to the prodigal son, *retell his tale,* now from the angle of
achieved sovereignty? If so, our focus now is not on slaves or hired hands but on
masters and more. See it this way. The prodigal son is still prodigal, though he
no longer spends the patrimony he was given but claims he is spending the
resource he has created for himself. He has thrown off the father, but he has
worked his way up from the slime, so he has reason to feel proud of the self-making he has effected. He is master of himself, not in debt to another and not cowed
by the conditions of life that subject many to external necessity. He is sovereign.
Suppose he is nagged by the suspicion that sovereignty ultimately derives its
power from a more ultimate transcendence that is not the transcending of human
self-mediating freedom? How deal with this suspicion?

If let speak, it might say something like this: ultimately all power is from the
divine, as is all freedom; to believe that power and freedom are purely self-mak-

ing is perhaps to fashion a god, but the god is oneself and one is engaged in self-idolatry. I am the counterfeit of God or the false double. As long as there is the trace of a God other than my own divinity, this admonishment sounds noise-lessly, forever making me uneasy with my supreme ease with myself. Now the supreme struggle for freedom can take place: supreme because it is the struggle for last supremecy, the struggle of freedom with itself, as it struggles with the God who has given the gift of freedom. The erotic sovereign must face the trial of spiritual pride.

Will this fall on deaf ears? Who are the deaf? *First*, those bewitched by the modern rhetoric of autonomy; they will squirm at something theologically florid in discussion of such wrestling and pride. *Second*, those grown indifferent (because of this autonomy) to the solicitation of God will yawn, for they have made themselves an emptiness without God, the easier to fill their life with bewitchments of their own magic making. Since everything of this is now called into question, it is sweeter to slip back into yawning intermittent mindfulness in which the strain of the extremes does not alarm one with the dread of one's spir-itual indigence. *Third*, will be those whose intellectual theory has educated them into a coarseness of religious discernment: they may even be among the cultural elite, with exquisite taste for the treasures of the artistic past and the nose of a fastidious connoisseur for the refinements of the present; but this refinement and fastidiousness will make them suitably weak when it comes to this struggle, for this is a brutal struggle, or rather an elemental struggle that requires nothing in the way of advanced degree in literary criticism or art history or aesthetic appre-ciation. The struggle is in the element of freedom rising up in the heights, but rising up with the same elemental self-insistence that has now been educated into the belief in its own absolute sovereignty. The rising up will have all of the incon-trovertible, even brutal, power of the elemental, though it will not express itself with any kind of coarse brutality; and yet just the refinement at stake here may have a brutality to it that no mask of cultural sophistication can hide from those who have the requisite spiritual discernment.

Fourth, there will be more domesticated sorts, the many who now and then have an inkling of the great struggle and who in their lives are gifted with the great struggle in the moments of passage in life: birth, marrying, begetting, and dying. They will suspect a drama more intensely fought in some rarer souls and will not always know clearly the outcome of the struggle; they will have intima-tions about the ultimates of the struggle and the chiaroscuro of the outcomes. But they will not dismiss the matter, or translate it into another idiom that makes it a literary fiction, or an interesting metaphor for a psychodrama that properly ought to be presented in prosaic and reductive terms. They have not been edu-cated into a cultural sophistication that habituates them to a self-incurred tute-lage, a self-incurred stupidity. For the heart is often more stirring in them, and they know in their own unprotected existence the blows of life, blows that do more than bruise, blows that wring from their secret souls an inconsolable cry of horror and revolt. The blows that crush them place them on the heights, just in that outcry. For the outcry is in the face of God. The sophisticated have learned to smother the outcry of the heart, and they have made themselves more inhuman in becoming more humane. Refined humanity refines itself to humaneness, which turns into godlessness, and in the process makes itself inhuman. Why this humanization that issues in the loss of the human? All because the splendor of the gift does not count for the marvel it is, and is usurped by a human construction of autonomy put in its place.

I suggested something noble in not denying the "more" slumbering within, in honestly engaging with it, though this is to risk freeing it. But there also may be something ignoble, as we now rationalize a release of savagery. One has itched to give the monster its chance to glut itself. And lo! one has an obliging philosophical theory to prophesy the stunted deformity to follow, if the monster is kept chained. When he barks, let him loose, let him roam; there will be relief in the release. Evil is being released, and not always to bring it back to its own good, but simply for its own sake—and all with the comfort of a theory that prognosticates worse evil (say, an unsatisfactory sex life) if one does not heed the barking.

Behold will to power dressed as honest, wholesome will to affirm life, or itself. It is a little mum about the negation entwined with the self-affirmation. I am blithe about others: I bestow my affirmation on them. If they are not up to it, what is that to me, I who am full of bestowing? What if the other stands in the way of my bestowing? My self-affirmation cannot escape its Janus side of negation. It incites itself to willing but as energized by negating. So negating risks swamping affirmation, while singing itself as self-affirming. The affirming is thus secret refusal that cannot be itself except as stamping itself on the other. But there is nothing bestowing about stamping. The excessive self dictates to the other, to the whole of being: it dictates itself to the whole. Let it become a god, but gods create in their own image. And if by bad luck this god arrives a little late on the scene where so much is already *not* made in his image, he has the regrettable task of having to *erase* the traces of these idols in the already given other. Never mind the violence, it all serves the good cause of divine work. For what else can a god do, when by some puzzling cosmic lag its creative work starts just a little too late? The god must redefine the gift of what is already given as nothing, or almost nothing, since it is really nothing till the god goes to work on it.

Of course, this redefinition of the gift as almost nothing or as nothing is the negation of everything that makes possible the exercise of derived freedom and creativity. So this project cuts the ground from under itself, just as it claims to be more radically completing its task to be itself, in its willing itself to be and its willing to be itself. Its will to be prior to everything is itself an expression of a derivation that, as derived, deforms its own nature, and all paradoxically in the name of absolutely being itself, absolutely fulfilling its own nature. It is full of impossible equivocation, but this does not deter it from pushing through into impossibility. For its freedom, not self-produced but originally given, is what makes it possible to will the impossible, and to will it as the only possibility that makes its own actuality to be its own. This is the fatal discord: to will to be one's own when the will itself arises from what is not one's own. What is not one's own must then be negated supposedly in order to be one's own; but if one succeeds in this negation, one must fail, for one can no longer be one's own, once the ground making this possible is negated. If this is an impossible equivocation, nevertheless it is lived and enacted in its futility, again and again.

And if this self-affirmation runs against the other, the other runs against one, also in a negative posture. The other also transcends, is the mixing of "yes" and "no" that exceeds itself in transcending towards itself. *There is more than one monster, and they meet.* Each is the flesh of excessive desire. So, like our dreams, the monsters walk abroad in the day. They walk down all the roads of daily decency. They do not howl for blood under the yellow moon. They go about the business of the everyday, in the gray light of daily commerce. They wear the masks of normalcy. (I mean not, so to say, Hitler meeting Stalin but the daily agents of the banalization of evil.) All honor to the temerity of those who name the monster, such as Thrasymachus, or Nietzsche, perhaps Hobbes. But do they remain in the equivocity of what they named, and of their own naming? Do they understand why the monster has to mask itself? It is the presentiment of shame before the truth of the good that reaches for the mask. They see it more as a new ploy whereby the monster seeks its own sly way. That is true, but there are masks beyond even this knowing sophistication. There is a shame beyond this shamelessness: a shame that is a modesty of vulnerability when the deepest "yes," beyond the "yes" to self, beyond all self-affirmation, is spoken to the self. In the eye of God, no masks.

So it will be announced—God must die, if I am to be absolute sovereign. (And what new horror there is in the way this announcement is now received as kitsch or passé.) Death reappears in the sovereign who seems to have conquered his or her own fear of death. This is the return of the nothingness of finitude: coming to nothing waits in quiet vigilance, waits too the destiny of the sovereign as also having to face its own coming to nothing. The truth is uttered by Job: Naked I came into the world, naked I will go out. The erotic sovereign knows this too, but alone is unable to utter the prayer of consent that follows on the lips of Job: Blessed be the Lord forever. God gives, God takes: the gift is lifted into being over nothingness; it is taken out of finite being. The sovereign is tempted to refuse this taking, and hence the coming to nothing that is the mortal pathos of the gift. Not blessed be the Lord, but I will be blessed, I will to bless myself. But self-blessing is a grotesque; it defeats the meaning of blessing and being blessed. When this refusal takes place, there is a loss of the heights by the sovereign; blessedness is forfeited in the act of insisting upon it; the insistence gave space to a will that counters the very freedom of blessedness, which again always implies the gift of blessing. In the resurgence of nothing and its refusal, blessing is turned into curse. This curse is the cursing of God.

The curse curses those who curse. The living of freedom cursing can let loose its apocalypse. When this curse is thoroughgoing and enacted in the whole, a reign of death follows. The curse of some modern revolutions bears witness to this. Some revolutionary happenings grew out of a refusal of derivation: the human was not a creature of the divine, but though a child of nature, capable of making self, and hence capable of being more and more self-derived through its own free original power: not creature but creative and self-creative. To speak of God's goodness can seem the greatest scandal to one who would be absolutely self-creative. No creature can be such, none can be absolutely self-determining, so none can have the sovereignty claimed by absolute autonomy; God must die that I be free. And though tired latecomers will yawn, this is more than romantic hyperbole. How many of the better intellects of the last two centuries have been bewitched by this rhetoric of absolute liberation, and still we hear reverberations of it and muffled afterlives. We are the gray inheritors of these muffles. We live in the age of Nietzsche, and it was Nietzsche who sought to uplift erotic sovereignty to the heights of an atheism that would take the measure of our murder of God. One cannot be tolerant of a rival god. There is an old argument, in Aquinas and others, that there can only be one absolute; were there two, one would limit the other and hence be the absolute, or if both were limited by the other, none would be the absolute. You might say that there is an *inescapable monotheism* written into any claim to be absolute sovereign. (Again the logic of number one.) The rival must be subordinated. God is the rival of my sovereign autonomy here rather than the giver and sustainer.

Call Nietzsche the prodigal sovereign, or in his own accepted name, the anti-Christ.[4] Nietzsche did not preach political revolution, yet his views have had long fermenting effects, some revolting. They make the human revolt, and in another sense, revolting. The serene face of released freedom is distorted in the phony jubilee of Dionysus, for any jubilee can only be fake or horrifying when the roots

---

4. On the matter of deciding the issue of spiritual superiority, see my "Caesar with the Soul of Christ: Nietzsche's Highest Impossibility." Nietzsche, a prodigal, without father, with attenuated relations to the other, except the "softer" feminine others of mother, sister, aunts (the injunction "Be hard": against this softness of pity), in which, as son, he found it hard to attain either erotic sovereignty or to see beyond it to a different freedom. Far from any father, he seemed to will to create himself ("If there were gods, how could I tolerate not being a god!"), though he too longs for a house of the other, and this he calls the temple of Dionysus, there to sing hymns to the universe, hymns that are different "songs of myself." Where is the father who enacts, beyond erotic sovereignty, the higher freedom of forgiveness that forgets itself and calls for the feast of thanksgiving on homecoming?

of religious jubilee in reverence have been lost, and all reverence means submission to the ultimate power, but this form of sovereign autonomy refuses all submission, hence all reverence. I know Nietzsche wanted a new reverence, but the effect of many of his words is to proliferate what he himself has honestly called the Ugliest Man—the modern atheist. This ugliness breeds death, and not only the death of God but the death of millions of humans through the ugly men who have dreamed the nightmare of the totalitarian state. They raised the art of Hobbes's Leviathan to a new level of homicidal efficiency. This is the mortal god, Hobbes's ominously precise phrase. The kingdom of this god is the realm of Moloch. The monster wants sacrifices again, not now the minotaur in the labyrinth, but a self-crowned hero Theseus who has set himself above God, and who now finds himself fated to a course of negation in which innocence must be turned into its opposite, before it is cannibalized. And all in the name of an autonomy that would absolutize itself, and this all in the name of the good of the human. This is indeed humanization, but it is the monster in the human that has grabbed the reins of the beasts of apocalypse and accelerated their gallop.

Revolt, terror, politics in the grand style, murder on a grand scale—all grow from the corrupted mustard seed of freedom. This was evident early on: can we forget, as we might want to, that the revolution of liberty, equality, fraternity produced better prisons, more inclusive war, and the efficient homogeneity at the guillotine? The king must be killed. Why? The divine right of kings must be destroyed, yes; but it is divine right that also is destroyed. I am not arguing for monarchy, for it too manifests all of the equivocities of erotic sovereignty concentrated in one figure, evident to all the world when this one is a tyrant. The tyrant is just the one who has rejected divine right, and taken on himself or herself the counterfeit divinity of absolute sovereignty. Death of the divine, whether enacted politically in a spectacle of execution or more hiddenly in the idiocy of being, creates a shudder of shock, as this awful transgression tempts the inner heart, touches freedom with the temptation of revolt, temptation once felt in its revolting truth, but then eagerly sought out as a true signpost that we are on the royal road to freedom. How many times since has the divine been executed in the soul of the singular human? We are on the road to nowhere, projecting ahead onto the empty way the freedom by which we bewitch ourselves.

Why road to nowhere? Because man has no end, it is said, and ends limit one. Why projecting? Because we create our future out of ourselves, it is said; we create ourselves by projecting ourselves ahead. But if there is no end ahead, and we have no end, before us actually is nothing more than death and nothingness and the emptiness that should be called by its proper name, namely, futility. Schopenhauer had seen far ahead on this road, and perhaps we might have learned something from his travels, but then along came a new magician by the name of Nietzsche, and he redefined emptiness, nothingness, futility as novel scope for freedom, creativity, and an unheard-of goal in the superman. His magic held many spellbound again with a song of themselves, and they fell back into the old enchantment of the erotic sovereign. We have not yet woken from this bewitchment. Its truth is still haunted by the despair that Schopenhauer had the greater honesty and superiority to name for what it was. Nietzsche's greatest lie was to rebaptize despair as Dionysian affirmation. When sovereignty claims to kill God, there can be no other outcome but despair, and despair is still despair, even when it dances around wearing the mask of Dionysus. Nietzsche did not awaken us; he has sent many, too many back into a metaphysical sleep, shaken only by feverish dreams of Dionysian sovereignty.

Is this a reprise of Hegel's brilliant insight about freedom and terror? Yes and no. All should know Hegel's claim that terror must emerge from the abstraction of freedom. Nevertheless, Hegel is only half right, because he is in thrall to a more sophisticated version of the same error. He will say that abstract freedom gives rise to terror, will perhaps indicate the empty negation of "freedom from," and rightly; but the affirmative "freedom to" will be the apotheosis of socially self-mediating autonomy, and the other will always be potentially ambiguous in his basic logic of dialectical social self-determination. This ambiguity can breed the sovereignty that wills to throw off God, as in the dragon's teeth of his children, such as Feuerbach and Marx, the latter a changeling who cannot be exculpated entirely from the systematic horrors enacted in the name of his systematic thoughts. Hegel's limitation for these, his children, is that the father was not radical enough, not revolutionary enough, not taking the knife of negativity enough to the religious absolute and properly freeing humans. I think Hegel did not adequately think through the equivocities of erotic sovereignty. His absolute is indeed an erotic sovereign. In the Hegelian erotic sovereign, the relations of self and other entail a dialectical appropriation of otherness within the self-mediating totality. In less subtle hands like Marx's, this dialectic breeds a revolutionary logic that is potentially murderous. Let us not mince words, since it is by their fruits that they will be known. Marxism produced a corruption of something that in potency is good.

The Erotic Sovereign and the Daimon

The higher autonomy of the erotic sovereign is tied to the dynamics of power, where a secret exigence to will to power has a kind of karma of its own, the unfolding of which tends to consume those who believe themselves sovereign exercisers of will to power. They do not think they ride the tiger, they think they are the tiger. There is a destiny to the illusion. It is self-consuming in devouring the tiger and its rider. The master can remain fettered by self-destroying equivocities.

What are these? They are flowers of the unexpurgated violence in the elemental self-insistence at the root of freedom as given. Freedom is given as for the self, and the self is for itself, expressing its own self-affirmation in insisting on itself and willing itself to be itself. At the origin there is an intertwining of origin as giver and self as given to itself, but after the origin the latter has qualified power to give itself to itself. This is where the equivocity of will to power has its root: willing to be oneself also entails the power to negate the other, even the ultimate original other who gives the gift. And the play between self and other ambiguously favors the self-affirmation that wills itself. It can take the cruder forms of wanting to dominate, even to enslave the other, as we normally associate with will to power. It can take "higher" forms in the supposedly creative will that wills itself. Even here, will to power is still a kind of self-glorification, no matter how exalted its particular formation, and so it makes secondary the giving other, and in the extreme it asserts its absolute power by holding over the other the power of life and death.

Self-affirming will to power easily deceives itself into thinking that it is the highest freedom when, in fact, it lives the law of the elemental self-insistence, which secretly worms its voracious way into all of the passageways of the heart, consuming all offered traces of the gift, and indeed glutting itself on its effacement of its debt and its involvement with the other that lets it be what it is. It takes its glut for self-fulfillment, but it is like the locusts eating up the fields, leaving nothing behind but waste. In this worming through the passageways of the heart, there is a harvest of waste, and the final desolation when sovereignty is revealed to itself as dry nothingness incarnate in an urn of dust. The monster is the tyrant, and the tyrant is not the bad king, or the leader who feeds the cult of personality. The tyrant is what one is, as willing all being to be for one, as willing the good as my good, as will willing itself as the absolute will, for which everything other serves. There is no service of the other in all of this, and no true release of self.

You object, it seems to be your passion to demonize erotic sovereignty. But no, erotic sovereignty, qualified by openness to transcendence as higher than itself, can show us the glory of the world. In the upbuilding of communities of justice, sovereigns who have come into a maturity of self-possessed freedom, are essential. They are essential to show us something of the realized promise of immanent excellence: such are heroes and exemplars—originals to imitate, paragons to emulate. They are essential to give us judges free of the tendency to say only what many will want to hear. They are not panderers to a public opinion that sometimes hardly knows what it thinks, not panderers who effect to revere but actually despise opinion (opinion seems to be their master, but their cunning is to remain masters while pretending respect for the others). Free humans are needed who have faced their own death and who will to live by standards of excellence that transcend the bewitchments of the day. Communities need such leaders, though they effect to despise any singular hero who rises above the many and will sometimes harbor long resentment. Not always, sometimes, and perhaps not often, since memory of wrong here is notoriously short lived. Success can purchase its own pardon, even when it has not earned it.

I do not demonize the erotic sovereign, but I do say there is the peril of the demonic in all of its ventures. The erotic at its full sweep, intensively and extensively, is demonic: it is a daimon, a power between mortals and divinities. This between is one *at the extremities* of the human, and here the challenge of nobility also faces a deeper danger of betrayal. The daimonic then becomes demonic in the infernal sense; it is the dark will for evil that takes over the excitation of the willing. This we witness too in an age that has moderated the human to a manageable medium, a tepid milk and watery middle. In our egalitarian and democratic and utilitarian age, the romance of this extreme is especially palpable to those whose energy of transcendence is more vital or vehement.[5] The force of their will to power will court the daimonic and risk the infernal, and this too on the scale of grand politics.

But the infernal is not coeval with, it is *second born* of divine possibility. Since we are in the between, we must struggle to stop the second born from becoming the cuckoo that clears the nest of every rival. One could endorse Pascal's point here: Atheism is an indication of spiritual vigor, but only up to a certain point. Or Dostoevski: There is an atheism that is just a little lower than faith, an atheism in a way superior to the faith of many mindless. I connect both points to the perils of the between at the height of transcending, or in the depths of the idiotic intimacy where the soul is alone with God. The vigor of these atheists carries them beyond those who are indifferent to the great strife of the human heart, but they have decided the strife in their own favor rather than in terms of a more radical exodus from themselves into the night of the divine and its holy terror. Behind it all, they fall for bewitchment with the magic of their own demonic powers.

I name the "daimonic" with express consciousness of its double possibility. I do not mean the diabolical. I mean being between and the double possibility that can turn either to the divine or the diabolical. Not to grant that one's autonomy can be as straw is to cut oneself off from a further release of freedom. When the erotic sovereign truly knows the perils of its own diabolical possibility, he or she may exclaim: I am worthy of hell; I am unworthy of heaven. Why worthy of hell? For hell has assumed flesh in the evil genius that whispers the temptation to be god in my intimate ear; and I listen rapt by the possibility, seduced by possibility, enchanted with self as the absolute possibility. Being rapt, I have already taken the first step towards hell, into myself as hell. We take that first step more often than we know or acknowledge. Making myself the most worthy, I make myself worthy of hell, that is, I make myself worthy of what I have made myself to be.

---

5. Have we not seen something of this romance of the demonic, since around the time of the deicidal politics (say, in de Sade, or Byron, or Baudelaire, or Nietzsche, or Bataille, or perhaps Foucault)? Of course, the Faustian suggests just that infernal freedom.

Beyond Erotic Sovereignty

We must speak of the dethronement, abdication, and transcendence of the erotic sovereign.

Dethronement: As already suggested, sovereignty is many faced, mostly connected to worldly, political power, though often bound to forms of spiritual mastery or dominion. Philosophy itself has been concerned with theoretical or spiritual sovereignty, as in the Stoic sage,[6] or even Socrates.[7] Mastery of thought is like the divine, and it seems to make us masters of being. In modernity, when

---

6. The sovereignty of the Stoic sage echoes Aristotle's God as thought thinking itself. *Megalopsuchia* is a social variation of sovereignty. Epictetus: what is within our power, what is not: the Stoic attracted to self-power and acquiescence. (Why do I think of Heideggerian "resoluteness" and authentic Dasein's recovery of itself from lostness in Das Man?) See Spinoza's *acquiescentia in se ipse* (*Ethics*, pt. 5): each entity is marked by the sovereign right to act according to its nature; all beings do, and there is no distinction between human beings and other things; all beings are units of self-affirming power; there is no distinction between reasonable and unreasonable. *Nature's right* forbids only those things no one can do or will do. The life of passion, violence by right of nature, is no different, no worse, than the life of reason. Natural right is limited only by power. The supreme law of nature is self-preservation: *lex summa naturae; ius summum*. All agreements rest upon utility. I say, there is a *more primordial affirmation of being to "self-preservation."* This affirmation "contracts" to self-preservation under *threat* from what is other to self. But do not simply blame the other: there is ontological frailty already there from the start in the union of lack and will to be. Moreover, that perceived threat is operative from the very onset of determination, the start of determinate being. This fixes the affirmation into self-affirmation. It is very hard then to get beyond this fixation, for the fixation makes us forget the "fluidity" of primordial affirmation. But the same "threat" from the other also can do the opposite—the other calls us beyond fixed determination into the primordial affirmation as *embracing both* the self and the other. This happens in love, for instance; not only the more normally recognized forms, but the more hidden; and in a way the primordial happening of affirmation, in diverse forms, is just love of being, love as ontological happening.

7. In *Philebus* (28a–c): the wise elevate their own god, perhaps really elevate themselves, in making *nous* king of heaven and earth. But with eros, in *Phaedrus*, notice Socrates's *shame* in giving the first speech: it debased divine eros into calculated gratification, will to power that camouflages itself as prudent love. The other time Socrates's face is covered is when he is about to die. Divine madness is related to sovereignty as erotic. In recent times, this matter often is named in terms of "genius." Some have grown embarrassed of that (let the poet be a good technician or "professional" writer), though the kitschy version of genius still goes the rounds—the divine is now caricatured into, say, a kind of priapic buffoonery. And yet despite it all, there is still the gift that none can command. The poet is right who speaks of wooing the muse: this is an erotic devotion that is not domination: wooing is "mastery" in submission to the more ultimate power.

freedom is understood as autonomy, theoretical sovereignty is related to the mastery of the equivocity of being by means of the new *mathesis* of nature; it takes practical form through the technologies that will make us masters and possessors of nature and especially (as Descartes suggests) give us the fruit of mastery over our bodies through medicine. Such autonomous sovereignty is erotic, though it may present itself as a servant of reason. It is really not servant but initiator of a *project* of reason. This project finds one ambiguous culmination in Kantian autonomy (see Chapter 4): rational, self-legislating sovereignty. This Kantian effort is an extreme rationalization of the eros for sovereignty, one that indeed hides its own eros, hides from its own eros, in the mask of pure practical reason. That absolute rational sovereignty cannot be sustained, as we see with its subsequent dethronement. True, Hegelian sovereignty tries to complete more radically this sovereignty. Its very success began to reveal the failure in it. Sovereignty has an ambiguous relation to the other, dualistic in Kant, dialectical in Hegel. Hegelian dialectic seems to deal with the ambiguity but restates it in another form. Hegelian sovereignty mounts the throne by its dialectic overcoming of otherness. The included other does not lie down quietly in the place assigned to it. The other rises up—be it the inward otherness of eros itself that refuses the claim of its complete rationalization; or the "included" other that sows seeds in the inclusive self that its inclusion is not after all completely inclusive.

We see the first uprising in the revolt of sovereign autonomy against its own rational form. *This is the widely acknowledged dethronement* in motion in post–Enlightenment thought. This dethronement of the sovereign rational ego is merely a shuffle in the palace powers. For the overthrow of the rational sovereign sees the ascent to the throne of a different erotic sovereign: the sovereign of more explicit eros, of will as prerational power, or will to power that actually brings us back to Hume in post–Kantian form: reason is and always must be the slave of the passions. If Nietzschean erotic sovereignty is the acme of this,[8] it leads to the so-

---

8. Nietzsche, *Genealogy*, 59, speaks about breeding man as the animal with the right to make promises: this is moral man, and as predictable; this is the price of a free will, a truly autonomous and "supramoral" individual: "'autonomous' and 'moral' are mutually exclusive." Nietzsche uses the rhetoric of autonomy in a "supramoral" sense—a higher "freedom from"—free from the restraints of morality, hence a higher "freedom to," freedom to be self autonomously—the apotheosis of the will willing itself, the self-glorification of the strongest will to power, beyond the everyday constancies of "morality," that is, beyond good and evil. Consider the *Borgias* as examples of erotic sovereigns: erotic in depraved form, sovereign in the glorification of their own power. Nietzsche loves the depraved contradiction of their ascendancy in Rome as the primary seat of Christianity. And this lush glory of the Renaissance, orgiastic and exuberant paganism seated on the throne of Christendom, all of this destroyed by Luther—so Nietzsche laments. See my "Caesar with the Soul of Christ." On the theme of Nietzsche as prodigal, see my "Dream Monologues of Autonomy."

called postmodern dethronement of the sovereign ego. This is all equivocal, since freedom still seems bewitched, half-bewitched with such sovereign autonomy, albeit rhapsodic rather than rational—more concretely erotic, you might say, for the night of the human soul is allowed to fall, and the infatuations of the dark are given asylum in the day. Postmodern thinking will perhaps deny a certain sovereignty, but one is tempted to think that it really is another form of erotic sovereignty, now in a frenzy of fragmentation or self-laceration, now in the orgy of a generalized *libido dominandi* that prefers to think of itself as a new libido, now bitter, now truculent, about the failure of its previous big ideas or grand narratives.[9]

This revolt of the inner otherness can take many forms. Consider, for instance, the aestheticism of much post–Kantian culture: it was between Enlightenment and Romanticism, a tension first resolved in terms of the Romantic dethronement of Enlightenment, then in terms of a post–Romantic dethronement of the Romantic. Genius was the aesthetic sovereign, and the duties of genius seemed to be accepted more and more. Shame over religion is coupled with the migration of religious transcendence into art—the religion of art. Then this paradox: everything was asked of art, now nothing is asked of it; made absolute, it mimicked absoluteness, and now nothing of it is absolute anymore.[10] Or the revolt can take a political form in the revolutionary movements of the nineteenth century: the most "creative," the most destructive. Two centuries after the strain was first struck, we find someone like Richard Rorty still singing the same tune, as if for the first time: strong poets and political revolutionaries. One marvels at such fetching faith.

The revolt of the inner otherness is not the same as the return to mindfulness of the other in whose debt one is. Think here of Kierkegaard in relation to Hegel: the God who is other and the God who is thought thinking itself. Or perhaps even Marx at his best: justice for those who are oppressed and defenseless. This recalls the best from the Biblical tradition. Nevertheless, the society beyond masters and slaves will be one grounded on a kind of communist erotic sovereignty: the humanly self-made social totality that through its own mobilization of power will create for itself and through itself the realization of social autonomy. There is no gift here, or ontological gratitude. The godlessness of this giftless world eventually sows the seed of its corruption of justice: its militant atheism, individual in the revolutionary, social in the new society, is its enactment of the struggle with the superior powers, a struggle that did turn its own demonic

---

9. True, some postmodern thought strikes us as the tease of foreplay ("not yet"), or the frustration of *coitus interruptus* ("stepping back," "disunion"), or the melancholy of post-coital dissatisfaction with a rush of pleasure over before it really happened ("always already over," "a past that was never present").

10. See "Art and the Impossible Burden of Transcendence."

potentiality into the diabolical. The matter was not only a lack of nuanced mindfulness about the temptations of erotic sovereignty but a clear-minded choice for a sovereignty that refused or willed to exclude the divine gift, for every gift makes one other than absolutely autonomous.

Abdication: It is only when our unease about the other as other has taken on conviction that we seriously think about the abdication of erotic sovereignty. Abdication does not here mean an abject giving up, though there is a giving up; does not mean a lifeless surrender, though there is a surrender; does not mean a submission to impotence, though there is a consent to powerlessness. Abdication has to do with the reticence of power, and the reserve of the power of freedom beyond autonomy. This is power that is, so to say, not of this world. Neither Marx, Nietzsche, or Freud understood this. Abdication is awakened by a dream of redeeming freedom. One wakes in the night overcome with mysterious grief: grief about nothing, not grief because one is disappointed, or has suffered wrong; strange grief out of fullness, grief betrothed to gratitude. Something is impenetrably mysterious about life, marvelously mysterious, and yet there is sadness that this is so completely beyond us. We come into the world naked, and will go out naked, and in between we make masks of power to protect and assert ourselves. It is all nothing—a scene acted on the stage, and a brief wind blows and it is blown away. Erotic sovereignty can be a mask of power that hides from itself its own despair, keeps from itself its futility, without the divine. In the night one does say, it is good, and one's sorrow is just one's love of its goodness. One is not disappointed—it is that something so good could be as elusive as a soft breath. The abdication springs from a gratitude, for one has sensed the sin in *that* striving and its futility. One is as elemental and vulnerable as a child, for whom the world in its otherness, the mystery of God, evoke unknowing reverence.

Transcendence: One might say that eudaimonia is related to erotic sovereignty, just in light of the daimon in eros, of eros as daimon. Noble sovereignty depends on the blessing of the good daimon. Erotic sovereignty can also be cursed, or itself given over to cursing, when its false absoluteness meets unavoidable resistance in the nature of things, and in the limit of the human. That there is blessing and curse here signals that erotic sovereignty must look beyond itself. Blessing and curse are not an affair entirely of sovereignty and are themselves signs of a further transcendence. They may or may not come at the limit of our self-transcending, but transcendence is not exhausted by human self-transcendence. The transcendence of the erotic sovereign stands at a limit where the sovereign may become willing to face the divine in a more ultimate communication.[11]

---

11. This transcendence might be illustrated by the three *temptations of Christ*. (I give a somewhat different discussion of these in "Caesar with the Soul of Christ," to a degree reflecting the different order of the second and the third temptation in Matthew 4, 1–11,

This willingness is already a mutation of will; for one cannot simply will what happens here. One can be willing but not will it and expect an answer to one's will. Willing here means patience, hospitality, waiting—waiting for what will come, if it will come, one cannot say, one cannot force it, one must consent to the space between that cannot be filled by what one wills. One's willing has to hollow out in itself, or allow to be hallowed, a zone of hospitality that invites the other to come, and come as it will, on its own terms. The person whose willing mutates into this transcending expectancy is waiting for God. This waiting in fear and trembling is at the verge of surpassing erotic sovereignty.

---

as below, and Luke 4, 1–13.) These are all the temptations of erotic sovereignty. Jesus must go into the desert, the waste, the noplace, to fast, to struggle, to overcome, to pray and be brought before the ultimate, as well as its dark counterfeit. The final struggle is at the extreme, and more dangerous than for "mere" self-mastery: this is spiritual temptation, connected to power and absolute sovereignty. *First temptation*: Turn the stones into bread. This is the temptation of the Grand Inquisitor: give the many bread and they will exchange it for freedom. This bread can be many things, not just the basic staff of life; it may be any necessity of life we need to preserve ourselves and prosper. Nevertheless, freedom is to be given up—not freedom as "freedom from" or "autonomy" but freedom of spirit to enter into search for, converse with, or struggle with God. Stones into bread: this also signifies power over the elemental necessities of life; mastery over the material conditions of life, power that frees one from submission to matter, such as might be dreamed of by the magician or the alchemist. *Second temptation*: Throw yourself down, and the angels will bear you up. Call this the temptation of spiritual power, pride that one commands the powers, the demons (daimons). This is the temptation spoken of above: the temptation of the spiritual elite; perhaps sometimes found in spiritualized gnostic claims, or in the revolutionary elite that know the Adamic alphabet of history, or the scientistic gnostics for whom knowledge is more than physical power but knowing transformative of the basic conditions of life in which they are the spiritual powers. *Third temptation*: If you bow down before me, I will make you master of the kingdoms of the world. Absolute, worldly dominion asks the price of submission to the evil power. Answer: the kingdom of God is not of this world. Its transcendence does not mean that it is not among us, for it is, just in the transcendence of the equivocities of erotic sovereignty. All temptations are rejected in favor of dedication to the life of a different transcendence: agapeic service. It is subsequent to the temptations and their overcoming that Jesus undertakes his public mission, beyond the equivocities of erotic sovereignty. What now is "being free"?

CHAPTER ELEVEN

SIXTH ETHICAL SELVING:
AGAPEIC SERVICE AND FRIENDSHIP

Agapeic Service and Servility

Erotic sovereignty seeks a freedom beyond autonomy, but it is still not released beyond its own self-mediation and the will that wills its own glory. How might it be given over, give itself over more fully to this freeing beyond autonomy? I think here in terms of agapeic willing: this shows the further promise of ethical selving. Service and suffering are crucial here. I come to suffering in the next chapter, but service makes us ask if there is a being for the other beyond autonomy? Is there an agapeic relatedness to the other that relativizes any claim to absoluteness by self-determining freedom? Does this extirpate self-determination or rather imply that it ceases to be the highest value? And what of the place of friendship in being for the other? What of the relation of erotic and agapeic self-transcending? In both of these surpassings, the human being, in being freed, is freed both to be itself and to be beyond itself; but the second orients us more fully towards being free beyond self-determination. This is freedom at the limit of its own freedom, as it wills the good beyond itself. "Beyond" means "preceding" as well as "exceeding," something "before" as well as "after," something "prior" to self-determination as well as more "ultimate." If now I seem to tilt, so to say, more "teleogically" than "archeologically," this does not imply that *arche* has nothing to do with agapeic freedom. The latter already constitutes the ontological promise of our being from the beginning, prior to the other formations of freedom. What we come to in the end here is already at work from the beginning, an incognito companion to all of freedom's forms in the middle.

Certain widespread presuppositions about mastery and service turn the latter into the merely servile, hence put it *below* autonomy. Often we think of service in terms of a certain relation of subordination. If I serve you, I am subordinated to you. You determine my activity, perhaps even my being. There is good reason for this. The word "service" has many associations, but it is related to the root "*servus*": this can mean being more than a servant; it can mean being a slave. To be in the service of another seems connected to being enslaved. This being so, quite clearly it seems that to be free, one must transcend service. Of course, there are forms less extreme than such servitude.[1] Yet something of the extreme form infiltrates our attitudes, especially when we are under the sway of a certain ideal of autonomy. For example, if I am a server at a meal or a mass, I do indeed help, but I am *adjunct* to the main event.[2] We find it hard to avoid a negative connotation. It also is interesting that *servus* has a certain feudal connotation, namely, to be in service to a lord, to be in fealty or bound by a duty or a bond with the lord. "Serf" is related to "*servus*," but also, of course, to "servile."

Evident here is the double face of service. As something positive, service calls for virtues such as trustworthiness, reliability, and fidelity. To serve entails a willingness to help, an availability to the other. One has a bounden duty; one is bound to the other; one's being is enacted in that service. The opposite connotation lurks here also: servility. Servility is a word of deprivation; we are not able to be ourselves through ourselves; an external imposition has laid its imperious hand on us. I am servile; I bow before the other; I am deprived of my glorious liberty and moral dignity. Instead of being answerable for myself, I answer to another. I am at the disposition of the other who is my master. Notice that this equivocity is itself doubly ambiguous, in that just to be there at the disposal of another also can take on a positive connotation that is beyond autonomy. I can say, "I am at your service," and I mean by that my willingness to be there for the aid of the other, beyond any external imposition, but just because I have been freed beyond myself into another relation of generosity for the other. "I am at your service" may mean, I am here for you, and not here because I have been compelled by force to be here, but because there is an availability beyond use.[3]

---

1. Think of "civic service," or being a civil servant or a public servant; or "seeing service" or "being in the services" (a phrase that interestingly seems to be less in use). *The Book of Common Prayer*, in the collect of morning prayer, speaks thus: "O God, whose service is perfect fredome."

2. Think of "being adjunct" in relation to education. In some universities today, humanities courses can sometimes be called "service courses." Implication: they are not the main point of pedagogy; they form a perimeter, or an ornament, but they do not excite the strong evaluation of "non-service" courses. This involves a kind of historical reversal. In the Middle Ages, the humanities were not service courses in this sense; they were the free arts, *artes liberales*, not *artes serviles*, those arts subordinated to pragmatic purpose and mechanical utility.

3. One thinks of the Third Commandment to keep holy the Sabbath day. This was sometimes expressed as the prohibition on "servile work." Beyond servility, the holy frees us into leisure, into *skolē*. We do not have to do anything for the day to be consecrated. Can you *command* this freedom? Yet this free day is a service beyond servility. One can force some forms of service, but not this.

In our culture, the image of a certain negative servility frequently associates service with an essentially instrumental relation. As serving, I am no longer an end in myself; I am a mere means, and a means not for myself but a means for you as the commanding other; you may be the end, but I am the means of your ends. What I am as servant is what I am as a tool of the other. As we know, Aristotle defined the slave as a "living tool." Yet many uncomfortable with Aristotle's complacent views often share a similar disdain for the servile servant who is nothing for himself or herself but only something by being the tool of another. This instrumentalization of service is again not entirely wrong, though it is incomplete, especially when it is defined exclusively in terms of a certain ideal of mastering autonomy.

This instrumental service also can be modulated in a variety of ways, as when, say, a business promises, "Service with a smile!" The smile too serves you, as a customer, not because it is the elemental language of a bodily generosity but because it is the means by which the other can be instrumentalized. "Have a nice day!" so says the server chirpily. But this "Have a nice day!" may have nothing to do with having a nice day and everything to do with keeping the customer happy, a keeping that itself has nothing to do with actually keeping the customer happy but much more with keeping in profit those who have invested in providing the service. It is not only the server who is instrumentalized by the served, the served also are instrumentalized and serve to keep the circuit of profitable consumption continuing. It seems to me that this kind of circuit departs both from the essential promise of service, as from that of a freedom beyond servility. This is related to what I call "serviceable disposibility" (I come back more fully to this in Chapter 13).

Our notion of self-determination also is often shaped in contrast to servility. No servant without a master, no master without his slave. Consider two of the most discussed views, namely, Hegel's (see *Phenomenology of Spirit*) and Nietzsche's (see *On the Genealogy of Morals*).

Hegel: There is a struggle between master and slave, but in truth, neither master nor slave can be defined in abstraction from the other; the master's independence is itself dependent on the servile work of the slave. Through his servile work, the slave actually manages to free himself from bondage to the material conditions of life, and so can initiate a rise above his condition of slavery. Mastery inverts into a kind of slavery; slavery harbors the seed of its own possible mastery. With Hegel, the dialectic of the two, in the end, is with the view to a more absolute form of self-determining being, beyond mastery and slavery. I do not think it is oriented to a service beyond self-determination in the sense I will mean.

Nietzsche: By a subterranean dialectic, the slaves reap their vengeance on the masters for being the superior beings they are. The superior are sovereigns; below them are the servile ones; but their being above as sovereigns means they breed the resentment of those below. The slave seeks his revenge and calls it freedom but it is the freedom of the slave that is glorified, and this "freedom" really just means the belittlement of the superior sovereigns. "Freedom" then takes the form of a leveling of all forms of superiority. For Nietzsche, our democratic age is this revenge. But in its secular, political form, our age is only the secular realization of the servility he claims is the meaning of the Christian life. For Nietzsche, there is a "higher" autonomy beyond this servility. Is there a service beyond this sovereign autonomy? Is there a freedom beyond it? If there is, and I think there is, Nietzsche did not, could not, see it.

What these two philosophers say shadows much of our view of service: self-determination is beyond servility. Who would be servile as lacking self-determination? The image of serving is of being supine or prostrate before a domineering other. The servant is like the worm that turns up when trodden on by the boot of the powerful; or like an obsequious dog that delights in approaching its master sideways or even backways.[4] We thus invite being crushed. This is not what we want. We want to be in control of our lives. We would be the decider of our destiny. This edifying wish sends out ripples in interesting directions. Why, for instance, do we despise the *imitator*? Because the imitator is a mere copy of another, subordinate to an external original. Imitation is servile. Or, as Emerson said in revealing hyperbole: Imitation is suicide! We would be an absolute original. This is an *interesting* original: affronted when its *inimitability* is not recognized, then, paradoxically, purring with self-congratulation on receiving the tribute of *multiple mimicry*. (Think of the philosophers of difference who all sound the same.) And service? If service is essentially defined in relation to an other, the pretension to being absolute originals makes no sense. We may not be mere imitations, but nevertheless what we are and do is inseparable from our being defined by the other. If imitation is suicide, so also must service be.

What if there is a service that is given for the other as other, a service wherein one comes to say, "What do I matter, I count almost for nothing?" But the will to be an absolute original cannot say, "I am nothing," hence cannot serve, cannot be of service. I think the Nietzschean sovereign cannot serve in that sense, for that service is a certain death to the self. And Nietzsche is quite right to see his hostility to Christianity on this issue. There is a service that cannot be included in his notion of sovereignty. The question is whether this service is always the base servility he claims it to be.

We need not think in terms of the rhapsodies of Nietzschean sovereignty. Self-determination also is the *earnest* autonomy pervasive in everyday modernity, to which *Te deums* are daily sung. If we are not self-determining, we may be at an immature stage of human development, say the necessary stage of childhood; but when we become ourselves truly, we break loose from the thrall of elders; becom-

---

4. Think of Hegel's tart rejoinder (some might say, cheap shot) to Schleiermacher's view of religion and the feeling of dependency: the dog would be your best Christian!

ing our own enlightened persons, we become anonymous Kantians. But if no one but we ourselves can make the determination of our being, what of the debt we have, not only to named others such as parents and teachers but to the nameless others who have silently aided one along the way—all of those others whose generous contributions allow one to stand up finally for oneself and claim the right to be self-determining? Is this debt just an unfortunate necessity of biology, or history that one would were not? Would one rather that one was self-determining from the start, hence in debt to none other than oneself?

This is absurd, of course. Some of the philosophies of self-creation, such as Nietzsche's and Sartre's, edify us with songs to self-creation sung against the darkness of the absurdity of being. Nor is the notion of *causa sui* too far away from the ideal of self-determination. God in modern philosophy is *causa sui*. Are we modern originals in the image of this God, or it in our image? Even those grown embarrassed by this talk, one suspects, are often more sullen that this hope of self-creation is not redeemed than released from its extravagance. If there is a nostalgia here, it is not for God but for ourselves as our own glowing god. "Being one's own creator" has become such a cliché that we barely blink upon hearing the phrase.[5] If one thinks that this is hyperbolic language, one probably respects an older language for which human self-creation was seen in its potential for deep distortion of finitude, perhaps even demonic self-glorification—*non serviam*.

We are first given to ourselves; we do not first give ourselves to ourselves. We may become *relatively* self-determining but always in relation to the numberless others in whose debt we are, whether we know it or not, whether we ever discharge this debt or not, and indeed this may be a debt that requires no discharge, precisely because what was given was given in the service of a generosity that did not calculate for itself alone. Does the will to draw a circle around self-determination risk rationalization of what at bottom amounts to ingratitude? One would rather not be in any debt to another. This is the autonomy that finds it hard to say thanks. And what about self-mastery? Does this make sense beyond a certain point? Is one servant on one level and master on another? What is one mastering when one masters oneself? Is it just one's base side, say one's body? But then just the so-called autonomy that is won is not at all free from the self that has been mastered. The autonomy of self-mastery is enslavement to oneself. Is there a freedom beyond self-mastery? What about the coherence of the notion of self-service? If one serves oneself, is one both servant and served? What serves, and what is served? Does not service always entail relation

---

5. See my "Creativity and the Dunamis," in *The Philosophy of Paul Weiss: The Library of Living Philosophers,* Lewis Hahn, ed. (La Salle, Ill.: Open Court Press, 1995), 543–557, for some remarks on "creativity." Also, on imitation and creation, see *PO,* Chapter 2.

to an other? Is serving oneself just serving oneself as an other?[6] Do not both notions, namely self-mastery and self-service, toy with the desire to close the circle around the self, closing it into itself in terms of an image of self as self-sufficient unto itself, and in this, closing the self off from a deeper sense of service and freedom?

Hegel, one must say, has a more complex view of freedom than one simply defined by the opposition of the master and the slave. I have spoken of this in terms of dialectical self-mediation through the other. Hegel recognizes that our freedom is defined in relation to another, and not purely through itself; but in relation to the other, I come to be related to myself; I interplay with the other, but the other is dialectically ingredient in my own being for self; the other serves the mediation of my own self to myself; if there were no others, I would not be able to be self-mediating, hence, self-determining. Thus my own self-determination comes to be inclusive of the other. Why not be satisfied with this? It is still the case that my relation to the other serves my self-determination, hence service is such that either the relation to the other is lacking in ultimacy, or ultimately the true form of service is self-service. In a real way, Hegel's view of the absolute is a kind of *absolute self-service*: the absolute is serving itself in its relation to the other, *the other that is the absolute itself serving itself* in the form of otherness, the other that hence serves the ultimate self-service of the ultimate. The absolute one is autonomously at home with itself in the end; the ultimate and absolute being is sovereign, self-determining being.

Such a self-serving absolute is not unrelated to a temptation to idolize autonomy. Self-determination passes into and through other-being as a means to itself as the true end. This need not be just "freedom from" external constraint or "freedom to" in an indefinite sense, but freedom to become the power of being we are already in promise. Why an idol then? Self-determination becomes an idol when the relation to the other serves primarily as a medium of self-mediation. What we absolutize thus cannot be thus absolutized. If the primary stress is on self-determination, the other will always be secondary, serving for the self. Perhaps one calculates for the other in the equation of one's own benefit or self-advancement. Or suppose one says, my self-determination must coexist with the other's self-determination. This can be said by Hobbes

---

6. Clearly, Paul Ricoeur's *oneself as another* (in *Oneself as Another*, trans. K. Blamey (Chicago: University of Chicago Press, 1992) does not go far enough. The notion of "inward otherness" and self-othering, as a kind of self-doubling is recurrent throughout Part III of this book; but this doubling of oneself as other is not the same otherness as the otherness that comes to one out of its own being: not oneself as another, but the other as for itself as other, and for one because thus other as other. The absolute service as *self-service* in the other that is oneself—is this not Hegel again?

or Mill or Kant or Hegel or Rawls. But if we take this seriously, this shows already that no self-determination can be absolutized: something other always ruptures all claims to self-sufficient self-determination.[7]

There is a deep fault line here. I put the point in terms of what I called the antinomy of autonomy and transcendence. Recall that the ideal of autonomy stresses our power to be self-determining, and perhaps not out of relation to the other; but even in relation to the other the primary stress is put on the *nomos* of the *auto*, not that of the *heteros*. By contrast, transcendence puts stress on a certain otherness; for the *trans* is a going beyond and a going across towards what is not now oneself, or a coming towards one of what is not oneself. If this otherness is irreducible to self-determining, this transcendence cannot coexist with an absolutized autonomy that is entirely for itself. If autonomy is primary, transcendence has to be subordinated; if transcendence is primary, autonomy cannot be absolute. The choice of modernity has been for the first option. Yet there is a service that puts transcendence towards the other before autonomy.

You might object that true self-determination is just our own fulfilled self-transcendence. The human being is an immanent transcending power. In self-transcendence, we have both autonomy and immanent transcendence. There is no need for an other transcendence at all. This looks like a solution, but only if we stay on the surface of self-transcendence. In truth, the more self-transcendence delves into its own immanent powers, the more it realizes how enigmatic that original power is, and the less it is wont to hold, without complex qualifications, to the ideal of self-determination. Explore the self as transcendence, and you will see that it does not only go beyond itself to what is other as outer but that it goes beyond itself into its own depths, depths bottomless, depths mysterious and murky and startling abysses. The infinite restlessness of our self-transcendence in its outward throw is the external side of an infinitely enigmatic abyss in inwardness itself. And when one enters that abyss, there is no simple autonomy at all: there is an inward otherness; and of the energies that erupt or emerge or surface, the "self" is no master but an expression or outpouring. Autonomy is not the sovereign it takes itself to be but itself the issue of an origin or a source, enigmatic just in its intimacy. Autonomy as self-transcendence opens into, or up to, transcendence beyond autonomy. Erotic sovereignty already knows this, but free selving needs to go further.

---

7. As we saw in Chapter 1, idolized autonomy is consistent with a devaluation of other-being, so that the idol human self must create the world anew in its own image. There is a project of will to power lurking here, and this too is part of the project of modernity, and it is no secret. All other-being will serve us. We seize this mastery and find that autonomy mutates into tyranny.

Freedom As Agapeic Transcending

Being free is bound up with the meaning of self-transcendence. To be free is to be free not only of false constraint on one's being but free of constraints in one's own being, namely distorting, corrupting limitations on the promise of one's being. To be more fully self-transcending is to be released from such constraints, both into fulfilling the promise of one's self and also towards the others with whom one has one's being in a community of togetherness. So seen, the freedom of self-transcending cannot be exhausted by autonomous self-determination. There is a self-transcending beyond autonomy, and this is released in a service for the other that cannot be determined in terms of our own self-determination.

Consider again the contrast of erotic and agapeic self-transcending (see *BB*, Chapters 10 and 11; *PU* Chapters 4 and 6). The expansive sweep of human self-surpassing shows us as erotic beings in search of fulfillment but aware of ourselves as lacking. Eros is a mode of transcending in which we are impelled beyond self in order to attain some wholeness of being beyond the initial lack. It carries self beyond itself from lack to wholeness, and does so in relation to an other who serves to overcome that immanent lack. I go towards the other out of lack, but in coming to the other, I come to some wholeness of self, and being whole I can claim some freedom of self-determining being. The surpassing of self towards the other comes back to the self, in the fulfillment it seeks in possessing the other. By contrast, agapeic self-transcending is a movement out of self and beyond self, not from lack but from a certain wholeness or fullness already realized. I do not seek the other as filling my lack, but I go towards the other because the other makes a call on me for its own sake. There is no inexorable circuit of self-return, though there may be something of self-return, but that is not the point of going towards the other: the other does not serve self-wholeness, but what I have as a whole is put in the service of the other who may be in need, in need not perhaps of things but of the gesture of solidarity that restores faith in being. Or the other may not be in need, yet there is a communication towards the other which is not for any return to self.

We humans are not simply lacking a completion that we must only seek by an outward thrust of self-transcending. This outward thrust arises from an original plenitude more elemental than the lack we also are. Agapeic self-transcendence arises from an overdetermined source of origination, not from a deficient condition or a merely indefinite possibility. Its power is the very definite power of generosity, an excess of original being that also is the expression of the primal freedom of the self. Rather than being our assertion of power over against the valueless absurd, real creativity reveals the generosity of being, the free power to give itself to what is other to itself. Agapeic self-transcending is a giving of being to the other, and for the other. There is no insistence on a return to self. The self goes forth from itself, like Abraham at the command of God, not knowing where the wandering or exile will end up, and not asking where, and not demanding a return to the first home in the end. It goes beyond itself in giving itself; and though there may be a return to the self, this is not the point of the first giving. The giving is not for the self; the giving is for the other; and though it may be the case that the other returns the generosity, that return is not asked or sought; if it never comes, the agapeic self would still give beyond itself.

The closure tempting the erotic sovereign is opened up, as is any temptation to idolize autonomy. Possession of the other, self-possession, is not the point. So also at the end there remains an excess never to be reduced to complete determination, or to a process of self-determination. The end is not unsurpassable completeness but renewal of self-transcending as a generous going towards other-being as other. This excess at the end is not failure. Erotic transcending might be tempted to see it as a failure of complete self-possession, but perhaps such an end sought was unwise in the first instance; unwise because eros did not understand its own lack as underpinned by a more affirmative participation in the plenitude of being. This participation remains open in the end, after all of our efforts at mastery fall short of their putative absoluteness. The "failure" is no failure from this other angle. The truth of things is that we are not the truth of things. The quest for mastery is always doomed when we invest self-determination with absoluteness. A different humility is needed before the call of the other, indeed the transcending enigma of being, in the beginning, in the middle, and in the end. If erotic transcending at best leads to a certain sovereignty, even beyond autonomy, agapeic transcending participates in a community of service, beyond self-mastery, and sovereignty, and for the other as other.

We come back to the equivocity in service. On the one hand, we find the servility that implies that the servant is deficient, lacking in what the master possesses; service is a mode of being for the other of the deficient self, for the servant has no being for self. On the other hand, we find an affirmative being for the other that is there available for the good of the other, there not out of defect of being but out of affirmative surplus. Between these two notions, the modern stress on autonomy as self-determination takes shapes. In the main, it takes shapes reactively to the servile sense of service. It sees itself as filling what service lacks, of fulfilling human self-transcendence by making it its own being for itself. But just by defining itself relative to the negative servility, it not only fails to see a service beyond autonomy, but in its own satisfaction with itself it risks a profound defection, just in its seeming success: its sovereign mastery becomes an amnesia of agapeic service beyond autonomy. Rather than complete self-transcending, it turns the self circle back around itself. The self-transcendence genuinely released for the other as other is denied it, or denied by it.

Understood in light of agapeic self-transcending, the meaning of service is consummate being for the other, indeed, consummate self-being. Such service beyond autonomy, beyond sovereignty, reveals a maturity beyond the opposition of being for the other and being for self. It is the free release of radical generosity that asks nothing for itself in return for its being there for the other as other. This is an almost impossible generosity for humans. We always find devious pathways of detouring back to ourselves. This generosity is a divine service. And yet to this release of freedom we are called.

This "being beyond" also reminds one of a connection between work, service, and being freed. Think of the children of Israel: slaves to the Egyptians, they work for them; then they are brought out of bondage. It is not just their work that brings them out of bondage, but their work has schooled their will in some constant decisiveness in inconstant circumstances: work hardens the will as it frees it, hardens it to resoluteness and decisiveness; work firms character, for the burden of travail makes the worker capable of enduring suffering, hence gives the worker both a deeper draught of bitterness and despair and a longer seeking for hope, more intensive and extensive. If it is through the intermediacy of Moses that God brings the Israelites out of bondage, nevertheless, Moses has known *both sides*: both the Egyptians and Israeli, both masters and slaves: he is himself both master and slave; he faces the masters and leads the slaves, and not because he channels their resentment, as Nietzsche would have it, but because he is charged with the mission of being beyond both, even as he has been both, and is capable of being beyond both just because he has been both master and slave. He is between, hence can be beyond in the double sense of *meta*. It is the origin that enables freedom from bondage, but the human can be either or both, and both and beyond both. Yet as we move beyond being both, the point is not to become again a master who has escaped slavery, or a slave who has become a master: it is a different "being with" the others, hence also a special attentiveness to those still in slavery. To be free is to be open to service for the slave, hence to be available for the occasion of their liberation. This service leads also to agapeic being for the other, including those who are not slaves.

Freedom and Friendship

The full meaning of freedom beyond erotic sovereignty can only be understood in the community of agapeic service (see Chapter 16). But what role has friendship in the becoming of freedom and the selving of the good? Is not *philia* an *intermediation* of the good? Is it not itself an intermediary—between our self-mediation through the other, and our being given over to the other in intermediation, between the selving of being good and intermediation with the good as other? I place friendship somewhere between erotic sovereignty and agapeic service. *Philia* mediates the latter in respect of the saying: greater love than this no man has than that he lays down his life for a friend (John, 15: 13). Such friendship shows a willingness to die, shows a love that is posthumous, beyond its own life. To serve, to suffer, to give, these may show a renunciation that is the patience of a supreme affirmation.

I put the point in terms of Aristotle's discussion of "friendship to self" (*philautia*) and to others.[8] As is well known, Aristotle differentiated three types of friendship: those based on pleasure, on utility, and on virtue or the good. These can be related to three kinds of freedom: friendship based on pleasure relates to a kind of aesthetic "freedom from"; friendship based on utility and virtue reflects two types of "freedom to" or "freedom towards." The first is more instrumental, the second more inherent. We move towards autonomy and sovereignty and then begin a step beyond. You might say that friends help mediate between power and its actualization. Previously, we saw this mediation with work, but friends work *for one another*.[9] In my working, I work for my friends, my friends work for me. They are at work in facilitating the realization of one's own *ergon*. They are not treated as "living tools," even though there is a tendency to this in the friendship of utility. The choice of what is *best for self* in friendship as *philautia* does not preclude *sacrifice* (*NE*, 9: 8). Nevertheless, the *philia* of utility is intertwined with an ethos of will to power, in that the other is useful to me as empowering me, as enabling me to use or fulfill my own powers, useful as a means to an end, not as an excellence to be celebrated for self (*NE*, 1156a10–12). We find the necessary instrumentalization of the relation of give and take that would be more take than give, if one could get away with it.

There also is giving and receiving in the third friendship, for I need the other to realize my own powers (*NE*, 1169bff.). Though Aristotle stresses *philautia*, this is based on virtue and the best: "Reason in each of its possessors chooses what is best for itself" (*NE*, 1169a18). We might say that this is the fulfillment of the elemental love of the good in the good of one's being. It is not the self-insistence that sets itself in opposition to the others. It affirms the good in itself, hence it is open to the good, in itself, in the other. This self-love is not at all to be extirpated. It is one side of the doubleness that has to be affirmed, and in the right form. This is the kind of self-love that is the fruit of the best erotic sovereignty. For the erotic sovereign is as much given to himself, as giving himself to himself. He is in the debt of the others and is grateful for them. When he does not forget this, it tempers the character of his self-love, which is first and foremost love of the good in self, love of excellence. The love of self is already under the judgment of excellence and can only esteem itself properly when it has lived up to the excellence that is the proper fulfillment of its being. This self-love is love of the best.

---

8. *Nichomachean Ethics*, 8–9, is of course the *locus classicus* for this discussion.

9. Ibid., 1169b10: "Friends are thought of as the greatest external goods."

Aristotle emphasizes the *mutuality* of friendship: there is a reciprocity. This tempers the tendency of erotic sovereignty to lay the emphasis on the return to self. The doubleness is kept, and in a balance and equilibrium. There is giving as well as receiving in this reciprocity, but not of an instrumental kind, such as we find in less ultimate forms of instrumentalizing freedom, wherein the other simply serves me. This mutuality is based on loving the other as that other is (*NE*, 1156a18–19), hence it presupposes the transcendence of self towards the other as that other is as other to me. Friendship is living well together (*NE*, 1170b11). Is there something similar to Kantian respect here? Is it the reciprocity of the Golden Rule? If there is a primacy of a noble self-love here, this self-love is disciplined by love of excellence. The noble man could not love himself if he did not love the excellent and in his life realize what is his proper excellence. Hence the respect between such friends is like the freedom enjoyed in the togetherness of erotic sovereigns who have come to themselves, not merely as insisting on themselves but as being exemplars of a proper excellence.[10]

We might say: eros returns the self to itself through the other; *philia* finds a mutual giving and receiving from self and other in a reciprocal exchange of the good; agape exceeds the self towards the other, sometimes when there is no return to self or even reciprocity with or from the other. These are three different releases of human willing.

Thus we must acknowledge a form of self-transcendence that is a relativity to the other different to erotic sovereignty, or agapeic service. This is friendship, in which there is granted a reciprocal interplay between self and other, an interplay where mutuality and a kind of symmetry between self and other is at work. There is a point to erotic sovereignty that is not entirely reciprocal, and a certain asymmetry in which the return to self is given a kind of privilege. Similarly, in agapeic service, there is a willingness beyond sovereignty that does not ask for or demand or always expect some reciprocation from the other served. There is an asymmetry in which the other served may be offered a more important place that the one who serves. With friendship (of Aristotle's third kind), there can be a kind of symmetry between erotic sovereigns in which they learn to serve each other, and serve in such a way that they themselves also are served.

Consider this: when noble, the erotic sovereign knows and grants that sovereignty is as much given through the other as self-achieved. I am given to myself, and I now am able to give myself to myself, because I was first given to myself out of the goodness of the other and in being recognized by the other as a being by myself and for myself. Often this gift of the other that turns us and returns us to ourselves is forgotten or ignored or rejected, because we are taken up with our being sovereign for ourselves. We do not have enough of the grati-

---

10. See Ricoeur's discussion in *Oneself As Another*, 181ff.

tude that grants that the other first granted us to ourselves. We are tempted to claim self-granting as always having been given to itself. But the noble sovereign does not lack gratitude and reverence and the willingness that is gracious in saying thanks. The fact that one does not have to insist on oneself makes it all the more possible to be gracious in granting what has been bestowed on one as a gift, and speaking the thanks, living it. It is in that superiority of sovereign freedom that integral humans can turn to each other in (third) friendship, and be together in a community in which there is no need for dualistic antithesis between being for self and being for the other. Erotic sovereigns may have learned to endure great solitude, but they take joy in the company of others who show some fullness of being that can give out of itself. Together they broadcast a space of freedom in which a noble community of *philia* is possible.

This community is indeed a great necessity, for it is one of the ways in which the erotic sovereign can be aided to take the way away from the excess of a hubris. The companionship of others who incarnate excellence mitigates the ferocity of self-assertion, not because one is cowed but because one can see from the outside the comic character of vanity, even as it rears its ugly head with the best. The other does indeed balance one in a relation of self and other, in such a way that the potential asymmetry of erotic sovereignty is given a kind of ballast in companionship. As one is recognized, one is no longer quite so insistent that one be recognized. One trusts in the other in a new way, hence one trusts in oneself, because one finds oneself being trusted by the other.

This kind of companionship in excellence is always open to the destabilizing effects of competition. There is no way to dispense with this entirely. Those who are erotic sovereigns do judge themselves against others, and strive for an excellence that is sometimes beyond them. One may be riven with a most peculiar envy at the sight of great excellence in the other, an envy that makes one ashamed of oneself. The excellence is excellent, but because it is in the other, one cannot quite stomach it, one would have it for oneself. Noble erotic sovereigns despise themselves, if they are overcome with that vain envy. Honesty means confession that they are overcome. There is superiority in not denying this inferiority.

Companionship with others in their excellence can temper this envy of highest competition, and make the demand of a higher justice in which one rejoices in talents even higher than one's own. This is sobering, indeed humbling. But there is a difference in being humbled by greatness and being humiliated (the one who feels humiliated is the one full of envy and a secret hostility to excellence, just because it is not his or her own). While sobering, it also is releasing, for one is not only being released to the other but also to the excellence of a good that is not of you or me but is beyond all of us, and that is excellent because it is excellent. To rejoice in the splendid excellence of the excellent is to be freed from the insistence that the excellent be *for me*. The excellent is not excellent for me, but it is for me to grant it as excellent for itself.

A balance between self-love and love of the other is struck in human friendship, but the balance is always shadowed by the equivocation that vacillates between these two. Friendship is a way of being together in the between, and just so the form of togetherness is full of ambiguities, hidden, hard-to-detect impurities, distorted selfishness, reticent openhandedness. Human beings can be masters of their souls and in that sense sovereign without any mark of social rank or distinction. Sovereignty has its universal promise. But, in fact, some seem to be born slavish, in that first character seems to lack the fullness of a proper reverence for itself, which it does not seem to make up for in life. Others are possessed of themselves as if from nature. The recognition of others confirms what is at work.

Of course, sovereignty is denied to most humans by the relations of subordinating power which, in one way or another, define all social orders. Often, those on top of the order of rank exude the confidence of sovereignty. There is evil in the order of the social; of this one is as much victim as is in collusion. This evil is not a fate. For sovereignty can come from the least places, since its first secret root is in the idiot self, and there in everyone the root self-insistence does its business. That said, certain orders of companionship are necessary to bring it to the fruit of erotic sovereignty. "Show me your friends, and I will tell you who you are." So mother admonishes her child, and was she right! Granting this provides no spur to self-congratulation but rather thankfulness and intimate cognizance of indebtedness. Companionship opens us up to an ethics of generosity and the transcendence of sovereignty as erotic.

If Nietzsche had found a proper friend, or a friend found him, might his fate have been different? Might he have seen through the emptiness of his songs to solitude and the despair at his own aloneness, though it seemed to offer the consolation of the heights? The muck of his relation to Lou Salome, he thought, was turned into a kind of gold, but the loss of hope for the human friend led to an increasing substitution of an empty projection into *futurity*, as the space where companions *will* be found. Hence the allergy to those nearest, the neighbor, and hyperbolic expectation that those furthest from the now can be truer companions. This is solitude making its own fantastic other, as in the end its own self-image—a kind of narcissism of futurity when the present self will be recognized by the true companion that cannot be found in the now. Instead of the father, God being the eternal one who recognizes, a future community of sovereigns, called *Übermenschen*, will constitute a companionship of creative friendship. Nietzsche's allergy to the nearest, his flight from those present into futurity, substitutes a futurely otherworld for a transcendent otherworld.

Is not Nietzsche's flight into that otherworld of projected companions similar to the "sin" he accuses religious "afterworldsmen" of committing? Except that hope in the goodness of God is a more worthwhile hope than this baseless hope for absoluteness in exceptional humans. This is Nietzsche's empty piety, bred out of the dynamics of erotic sovereignty seeking companionship in its solitary height. Were a true companion found, the friendship would temper, indeed resist, the self-glorification of will to power, and ask that it turn its transcendence in a more agapeic direction. As it was, it is hard to see Nietzsche consenting to this tempering. I believe he did not really want companions with genuine otherness but mirrors to give back the reflection of self-glorifying will to power—and this, despite some of the things he says that would seem to welcome the resistance, even the hostility of the other.[11] He seems to say, God give me enemies! Why does he want enemies? Not because he wants to prove himself greater than them, but because he can *prove himself greater by overcoming himself* in relation to them. Self-overcoming is self-glorification, again, even in willing the enmity of the other! It is a perversion of the command "Love your enemies." The promise of agapeic transcending is twisted around into another version of erotic sovereignty that really feels happy with itself, that still coils around itself as the superior power—power superior to the overcome other, *power superior to itself in being superior to the enemy.*

The word *companion* shows us something in friendship far more than the competition of excellent humans (though this is not excluded). There is a peace beyond *polemos* in the companion. The companion is not one's rival, not even the other who spurs one on to greater achievement or excellence. The companion is the one with whom one is at home, even if both are far from home, and indeed not at home with self, or with much more. The companion is the one with whom one shares a meal. *Cum panis*, with bread: the companion is the one with whom one breaks bread. The breaking of bread together is the release of a peace beyond *polemos* in a free togetherness. This breaking together breaks down the boundary of wholeness that the erotic sovereignty may seek to erect around his or her own superiority; breaks this down, and lets break through a commonality that is both elemental and exalted. Elemental: we sit down together, perhaps even on the ground, and consent in homage to the earth and its fruits. Exalted: generosity finds body in handing the other its daily bread, but lifts up the giver as well as the receiver, lifts up without false pride. Breaking bread together, the sharing of a meal, humble or lavish, welcomes into a feast whose embodiment of the good cannot be measured. Breaking bread: the feast of life, the agape of being which is too much, because one has been offered the sustenance of life by an other, and one also is willing to offer it on to another.

---

11. This throws some light on strange talk about *creating* the friend (in the section on the neighbor) in *Zarathustra*. Primally, one finds or is found by a friend; one "creates" a friend only in the sense that one *fosters* the promise of the *philia* of excellence; or perhaps the letting go that allows further for the agape of being, and the friend being given over to a providence that takes him or her away from one. I look in more detail at Nietzsche's attitudes to the neighbor and the friend in "Caesar with the Soul of Christ."

Freedom on the Frontier

We are reaching a frontier where freedom seems to be freed into a being beyond freedom. What can this mean? Freedom may find itself in the companionship of friends who bring us to the pride of achieving something of our promise in a community of excellence, but even so, we are beyond self-mediation and into the intermediation of the good. Our community with the other and both of our communities with the good give expression to our common esteem of the excellent. But we are not at the end of the process of ethical selving. There is still some ways to go, perhaps the whole of a life, in which we are turned inside out and made a being for the other.

The further selving of being good is not any simple "freedom from" or "freedom to." If there is here a "freedom from," it comes back to its debt to the other, not only the human others, but the gift of being itself, and the source of that being, the origin. In this coming back to oneself, the different "freedom from" is not so much from external interference but *from oneself as the inner limit* that constrains one to an excessively narrow love of oneself. One asks for release from the narrowness of self-love when one is no longer the barrier that constrains itself, no longer the wall of itself over which one is content to look. Freedom has taken wings from itself, but it finds itself lightened and on the wing beyond its own being. "Freedom from" is itself lightened by the agapeic transcending of the origin. It is from the origin, and from itself, out beyond itself, as itself, but not as itself so narrowly, and there out there with the others, as if it were not there, and certainly not there as insisting that this here now I is the center of the show. The show of being is the show, and it is spread out in the universal impermanence, and it is the between that is centered beyond itself in the origin.

If here there is a "freedom to," this is not just to be itself. It is another "freedom towards": there is a direction in its transcending, not only to itself in its own self-becoming; its self-becoming moves it towards what it is not, and not what it will become, but what it would love, as a good that is itself and for itself, and not at all a product of our self-becoming, and without which no self-becoming on our part would at all be possible. It is a freedom beyond self-determination, in which *proximately* we are released to being with others differently. They have as much call on the good as we; more, we often feel, since we have known the depth of our unworthiness—though this too is false, since we are to be loved with the same consent to the good as the other human. Companionship has taught us that. It is wrong to hate oneself if that means failure to consent to the good one is. Yet one must hate oneself, to the extent that the circle of a self-regarding autonomy closes its door on the other. The closure of the door is already hate. It is this hate that is hated, yet not to be consumed in negation, but to fall into the grace of release.

But *proximately* is not *most intimately*, and this is where "freedom to" points beyond all proximity into deepest idiocy, the inward intimacy, and otherness wherein the divine dwells. There is an intimacy deeper than any proximity, for what is here proximate cannot be objectified, or imagined, or named, or determined. It can only be desired and loved. Desire is freed into a dark night. One cannot say if the good that touches one is before one or behind one, above one or below one, inside or out. It seems everywhere and nowhere, hence this "freedom to" is a movement towards nothing and towards God. There is an excess and an indeterminacy about this freeing, which has difficulty giving any image of its releaser, and putting any name on the power that keeps it safe from evil.

I speak of a free willingness that is more than any determinate willing, more than any self-determining, for it does not will itself, or to be itself. It also is more than love of the proximate, the nearby, the neighbor. This willingness comes to know itself in the love of the neighbor, but it is still more than that love. There is the ultimate other the religious name God. This free willingness is not this or that will. It entails a return to the indeterminacy of the idiotic, but also a return from that return. For one is not dissolving in formless night but seeing the day itself enshrouded with the most extraordinary mystery. Everything is as it is, yet it is not as it is; or it is as it is, and it is not as it is; it is itself and also the showing of more. It is doubled into an icon of what itself is beyond showing in showing, and that resists idolization; a showing that entrances without bewitching, for one is falling into a love that holds one fast, yet lightens one. Nothing is as it seems to be, or it is as it seems to be; but in what seems, one sees something shown, not shown when the self-mediation of freedom was not released to the mystery of the gift.

I previously noted an *indeterminate willingness that consents*. This is the opposite of an indeterminate negativity that can only say "no," the rancor that does not primarily refuse this or that good but rather anything in its excellence, battening on any good to vent its spleen. By contrast, this willingness that consents is closer to a purer openness to the good such as it may be, always beyond what I can determine it to be. It is beyond what I determine myself to be also; for what I determine to be is infected with the false idolization of the I that I am. All autonomy and sovereignty is potentially idolatrous, and in some measure, actually idolatrous. This willingness is beyond one's self-determination, and hence a strange willingness, since in a real sense one cannot just will it to be. One cannot will this release through self-determining willing.

This release comes to one, it is given to one. One can await it, one can purify oneself in advance in hope. One can pray. One can struggle with one's demons, and the struggle is somehow the gift itself, as well as the preparation. One can will to enter the struggle, but the willing cannot make the gift be given. One can knock and knock on the door, but the knock does not open the door, for the door is opened from the other side, hence the opening comes to one, even though one has roused the night into noise that the gods themselves seem unable to ignore. The opening is a simple elemental gift that cannot be commanded. There is asked a willingness beyond will; a willingness that is a new will in us, but a will that cannot be described as self-willing or any kind of self-determining willing; it is a willingness beyond self-determining.

  Serving the friend is one step on the way to this new willingness, for this service is already a willingness beyond self-willing and beyond freedom as self-determining. It is attentiveness to the other, to its good; and not to its good because it too is my good; but to the other's good as the good as for the other. It is the genuine good that one wills for the other, and this transcends both the "for oneself" and "for the other."[12] Serving the stranger and the hostile other is a further step on the way. More often than not, we have to suffer to see this way.

---

12. One could desire a good for the other just to please the other, as a kind of indulgence or pandering. This would be a being for the other in which the good is made for the other, and the other is not desired as receiver of the good. Desire that does not pander wants the good. This may mean a difficult honesty with the other who may not always have reached the point of being released into the good, which is more than any good for you or me, though it is always there for you and me.

CHAPTER TWELVE

SEVENTH ETHICAL SELVING:
RELEASED FREEDOM AND THE PASSION OF BEING

Being Freed: Beyond (Standing on One's) Dignity

How relate an ethics of service and suffering? Can suffering be at the origin of a new willingness, breaking one open, asking one to understand the others who suffer (even tormented sovereigns)? Can the ethical and the religious finally be separated? What does suffering have to do with freedom? Are there sufferings that enslave? Surely, yes—sufferings can humiliate and mutilate. Sufferings that purify, bringing breakthrough? Why not? Can one be made more available? Does not sovereign Lear come to this exposure? But are we not also brought back to the intimacy of the idiotic? For is not all suffering elemental and idiotic? Is a new community possible then? At a certain extreme of suffering, are we not asked for unconditional trust in the good? What then say of freedom?

This: we must join the meaning of "freedom from" and "freedom towards." The "from" is from the origin as giver, but as freeing us, and into gratitude for the gift, even in suffering. This is not "freedom from" the other, which wants to be outside of community, but freedom given from the agapeic origin, and hence a "from" that founds elemental community. Here too "freedom towards" is beyond "freedom to" be oneself, since in certain sufferings there is an excess to self-transcending that is freed beyond itself and towards the good as other. This "freedom towards" has a vector that is ontologically intimate: both selfless and the deepest selving. One goes towards the good, sometimes sightlessly, in agapeic selving.

Put it thus: Suppose one touches a measure of erotic sovereignty; there can be a fulfilling but also a *new unrest*. Our infinite restlessness can only come to peace in a good itself infinite; we cannot be that good, though we have an infinite promise; and this our restlessness hearkens back to our first selving. It is impossible to rest with one's own fulfillment. Kant seemed deficient in awareness of this. When his moral man is conscious of his own virtue, he evinces "self-contentment"—not a sensuous satisfaction, but purely moral (see *Critique of Practical Reason*, 124). This is the self-contentment of the righteous: they have the satisfaction of having lived up to themselves. Is that it, then? I think not. There is a different sleeplessness, a new surpassing that suspects moral self-contentment to be so much straw. The intimation of a more ultimate good deprives one of the sleep of moral achievement. Kierkegaard liked to say: In the sight of God we are in the wrong. The Kantian paragon of dutiful virtue risks the pride of his own self-righteousness. I fall short of the moral law, but what distresses me? Am I not really more distressed by my falling short of *myself*? The righteous are conscious of their own worthiness. (Is this why one suspects Kant of a kind of "pharaseeism"?) The righteous do not cry out in sorrow: *Domine non sum dignus*. I affirm my achieved dignity: *Sum dignus*. After all, I have *earned* my dignity. I am content.

The question then: Is this self-contentment monstrous? Does my very moral dignity not cut me off from an ethics of agapeic service? Can my dignity stomach quite the stench of the unwashed that floats towards me from a distance? Think again of the dutiful son in the parable: the lost son comes home but still smells of the sty; he must be washed, before being granted cold entrance; and even then, the righteous son will demand that his brother *earn his forgiveness*. This moral self-contentment cannot just *give* forgiveness. Then I do not live the ethics of the gift and the gratitude and generosity that live in light of the gift. My dignified inability to grant forgiveness makes my moral uprightness immoral. My being in the right is my being in the wrong—perhaps even more than my straying brother. I am in the wrong, because I cannot recognize I am in the wrong. In my own eyes, I am in the right, and being thus in the right, I cannot see I am in the wrong. The wronging brother is more in the right, in confessing he is in the wrong. For he is open to forgiveness and willing to repent.[1]

The moral? Confession that one is in the wrong is higher than standing on one's dignity, standing on the dignity of one's essential righteousness. This confession is necessary for a deeper relation to the good, and for a more ultimate freedom as released. To make the leap to this new possibility, one has to be brought to nothing again, brought to the limits of self-righteousness, have one's moral integrity broken, pierced by a vision of its spiritual evil. Being good must come to know it is not the good, that it is evil; that its freedom also is bondage; that it owns nothing in clinging to the dignity of its self-contentment; that it must come to nothing and learn a new patience; that it must learn to forgive by granting that it is forgiven. It must learn to hate itself, and then learn not to hate itself, for it is already loved, even though it is hateful. And when it comes to be hateful in its own eyes, it must learn a new consent that cannot be described in terms of moral self-contentment. For it finally has no right to this. Its consent emerges with a new serenity that is on another plane to self-contentment. Only

---

1. See "Dream Monologues of Autonomy."

by knowing that it knows nothing will it learn to enter the nothing differently; know beyond the darkness of its own self-knowing that there is a communication of ultimate goodness, blown towards it from the bourn of enigma.

This further ethical venture cannot be entered on without exposure to suffering—suffering of spirit. Everything here seems an affront to the will to self-legislating autonomy. The ethical will must lie down again in itself, and see that it lies in the sty that is itself, and from the place of refuse come to itself as preparing for a different return to home. The divine is there in the muck, as in the cold and crystal stars, as in the moral imperative within. Our suffering being, our temporariness, our aging and dying bring us back to the earth, to the humus out of which our humanity is formed, and God is there in the humus, and this we come to know as His spirit is breathed in it, breathed in in the vital surge of growing life, breathed out as the spring tide ebbs, and the gift is taken back, perhaps given back.

I am not advocating something like the extirpation of will as in Schopenhauer's will-lessness. The new willingness can be called will-less, if by will we mean the will that wills itself; but in truth, it is a transformation of willing that is here at issue. Clearly also the point is not the ostensibly opposite view to Schopenhauer: Nietzsche's self-glorifying will. At best, this is the apotheosis of the erotic sovereign. In question here is a willing beyond the will willing itself. It may well be the case that the new willing cannot become itself without some kind of askesis: not the askesis that simply denies or negates; more the suffering that wears away, strips the masks of false selving; the suffering that mediates self in its most elemental love, as well as releases it to its being free beyond itself, suffering that returns willing to an intimacy with the good deeper than its intimacy with itself; embarking it on a voyage of love in which its harbor lies in the transcendent good beyond finite measure. Infinite depths, infinite restlessness: desire turned to the abyss of inwardness, desire turned to the height of transcendence.

Of course, there are many sufferings, but in one guise or another, all bring us to limiting others where our powers of self-determination cease to be king. We may retain the trappings or habits of king or insist that it is not so, like a tyrant or a child of tantrums. We can whip the sea, as Xerxes ordered sovereignly. The sea submits to the lash, but it also laughs. It continues its flow and ebb, beyond our shout to stay it and make it obey. Suffering may issue in a refusal, knotting us back into ourselves, or release a consent in which we are released. This consent regards "the good of the to be," "the good of it all," even in the ebbing away, or vanishing, of the timed "to be" of finite being. Can there be freed a "yes" to goodness in this undergoing? Is there an ethical comportment that comes out of this?

The limiting others we encounter can be correlated to different unfoldings of ethical selving. Correspondingly, we may focus on different sufferings relative to idiotic, aesthetic, erotic, and agapeic selving. Suffering is subtly different relative to each. Relative to the *idiotic*, we find the first suffering of being given to be; we find an intimacy and an indeterminate innerness of suffering that resist all complete determinate objectification. Relative to the *aesthetic*, we find suffering variously located in the body, often in such equivocal form that it cannot be univocally pinned down; bodily suffering expresses the encounter with outside otherness, though it affects the vulnerability of the more intimate innerness. Relative to the *erotic*, we suffer the spontaneous upsurge of self-surpassing desire, even though we shape our desire to be more self-determining. Our will to autonomy has a deeply uneasy relation to the suffering out of which it originates and which returns, as we reach out towards others beyond our self-determination. This is crucial with the *aging of the will*, as mirrored in the ebbing of aesthetic vitalities, and in the finessing of the idiotic innerness into a wiser acceptance. Erotic suffering has to do with being overcome, with letting the other love one, with longing and love for what is beyond one. There is always some frustration to autonomy and unrequited love that knows failure as inherent in the course of desire. And there can be refusals, some proper, some exacerbating the failure of love. Then there is the extreme suffering in the *agapeic*: given over to the other at the limit of sovereignty, one can say, "It is beyond me," and this is not abject failure but a surrender that opens into a different being for the other. This last is not a limit at the end but sends us back to the beginning: to the origin and to the idiotic, where the suffering of freedom as gift happens. The sending back is like *the passion* of all the closures on self in all the forms of selving. It is like a Golgotha of all closed self-insistences, and the coming back of the promises of selving in a resurrected freedom.

Idiotic Suffering: *Passio Essendi*

Suffering is of universal human concern, but there is an idiocy to it that makes its universality different to any objective generality. That we *are* suffering beings cannot be completely objectified, for it is most intimate to our being. This one necessity none will ever escape, though the fortunate may escape its more violent forms. Suffering reveals this doubleness: something we cannot escape, yet something we all want to escape, it being most natural to suffer, and most natural not to want to suffer. It shows a necessity of our being, a necessity we would were not necessary. It shows us as singulars up against necessity, and it shows us as the passion for freedom beyond necessity.

This idiocy of suffering concerns the fact that we do not first choose our being or freedom; both are first given to us; and being given, we begin to give ourselves to ourselves. Rapport with "all is gift" is perhaps most vital when we are young, or when overtaken by a joy that surprises us into fresh astonishment at being at all. Mostly it is submerged in the determinations of finite life that come to overlay the first gift. I say this is a suffering, for there is a *patience to being* at this elemental level, and a patience to the good of being. The nonobjective intimacy of this patience can be as much of the joy of being, as of the agony.

This intimacy also is beyond determinate subjectification: there are sufferings whose rhythms and currents in "subjectivity" we cannot univocally pin down. Innerness itself is floating and predeterminate, and we may be in suffering and not definitely know that we suffer, or what and why we suffer. This is a side of suffering turned away from definite cognition and determinate self-awareness. Often only the *crude* sufferings enter definite consciousness, whereas there are secret sufferings whose elusiveness stamps the tonality of one's entire being, yet they are almost completely hidden from self-consciousness. This is suffering going down into the root and primal self. It is there also that the fundamental resolution has to take seed and penetrate to the innermost. Extreme pains sometimes forcibly return us there, when the supporting comfort of determinate objectifications and subjectifications falls away. So much so, it is as if one were being returned to a nothing or a void, though it is not an absolute void, for there is an elemental agony in this void and that is what one is then.

This idiotic suffering has to do with our *being as pathological*. Our being is a *pathos* with *logos*. But the *logos* is not adequate to the *pathos*; it cannot give a univocal *ratio* of this *passio essendi*, as I will call it. We are not first *conatus essendi*, endeavor to be, but passion of being. Music, for instance, is powerfully in rapport with this *passio essendi*. Sometimes, too, the idiotic is revealed enigmatically to itself in dreams, when paradise and nightmare appear. It is at the level of this *passio essendi* that, for instance, we are subject to enigmatic *hypochondrias*. These, of course, are idiotic from the standpoint of determinate rational univocity, since we cannot assign a one-to-one cause for the suffering as "effect" (such an approach is simply misguided relative to the floating indeterminacy of idiotic selving). Such hypochondria might be the unreleased hugging of self to itself in fear and anxiety and an absence of real freedom; or it might be what Hamman called a "holy hypochondria."[2]

Finally, one cannot escape oneself at this level, even though many determinate selvings seek to offer escape. One suffers oneself and from oneself. One is riveted to self and is not free to be anything but oneself. One is one's own most intimate necessity. It is not easy to consent to oneself at this level. For being given thus, one also is given as free, thus can realize the promise of this necessity, or else shape self in forms that actually refuse this necessity. More difficult still, much of the shaping takes place unknowingly, through the shaping influence of others, before one wakes up to what one has become. And what one has become may not

2. Kierkegaard cites Hamman thus in *Either/Or*. "Hypochondria" is a contradiction to univocal logic: a sickness that is no sickness, yet is a sickness; and of the whole self, affecting body, mind, and spirit. See my remarks on Hegel's "hypochondria" in *BHD*, 132ff. Hegel sought to be released into the universal of his system and the Idea. I suppose that psychoanalysis is often concerned with varieties of hypochondria of the *passio essendi*.

be consonant with this deeper necessity. A new suffering then can come to be in this dissonance of *not being what one is*. Yet there is no escape in all the escapes, for in all the false trails to freedom they circle back around to this necessity. The elemental truth is that there is something radically unchosen about what one is, yet one can choose to accept, or not, this unchosen given. In this suffering of the unchosen, our choice can either institute a different suffering of self-discord, or a different freeing of self, flowing from consent to the given.

If the idiocy of suffering brings us back to the origin, this means it is bound up with *the sacred*. Because suffering is thus idiotic as well as universal, philosophy does not always deal with it well, since philosophy's universals often are such as to shun the idiotic. Hence it would be philosophically dishonest to avoid significant suggestions offered outside of philosophy, particularly in art and religion. Art and religion often are superior at naming the idiotic in its sacredness.

Today, our dominant models of knowing and being, whether instrumental or autonomous, are mainly intent on flight from this idiocy of suffering, or at least on pragmatically diminishing its sway. Nietzsche said: Dionysus versus the Crucified; and he is often seen as anti-religious; but here he suggests two ways of understanding suffering, *both religious ways*. Nietzsche may reject, so to say, suffering under the sign of the cross, yet he names a god, for the meaning of suffering is inseparable from the sacred. Much of life in modern Western society (even when it thinks it is Nietzschean) is in flight from such a view of suffering; we want to secularize suffering (get out from under the sign of any cross, as it were; or Dionysus). Instrumental and objectifying modes displace other appreciations of its place, and the value of life as suffering, even to the extreme. Suffering is redefined as a problem to be solved or as demanding adjustment or adaptation. And when it goes beyond that, the objectifying madness is continued, either in excessive technological interference, or in consigning the sufferer to idiocy in the worst sense: the refusal of meaning to it. The idiocy of suffering in a truer sense always brings us back to the *ontological intimacy* of the matter, beyond the limit of all objectifying and instrumental powers. There too the sacred is. Where? In the promise of holiness in suffering rightly lived.

Aesthetic Suffering

The sensuous and sensible body is perhaps the most evident place of suffering. It too raises the question of freedom. The *passio essendi* is concretely enfleshed. In aesthetic selving we are incarnated, yet in interplay with being as other. To suffer is to undergo; it is to be the recipient of something one does not produce entirely through will; so it is tied to the involuntary; it happens to us; hence its obvious connection with our bodily being. From the outset, the world's otherness makes its impact or impression on us in and through the body. This suffering in the aesthetic makes apparent our vital transcending to the given world as other. It also makes us vulnerable to shock and outrage from outside. We might say that the *passio essendi* and the *conatus essendi* are promiscuously wedded in the tensed singularity of the body. The aesthetic suffering is in waxing and waning, in the blossoming of bodily energies and their erosion as time wears them away, as we pass along time's way. The extremes meet here: say, the surging pleasures such as come in sexual excitation (we do not *do* these pleasures; we do certain things and we are pleasured); and the appalling agony of some fatal ailments (we do not *do* these; we are done in).

Philosophers often have sought to escape this suffering into knowing, rather than coming to know in the suffering. They use the ascetic strategy that minimizes our suffering of the aesthetic. To be effective, it has to impose a discipline—itself not void of suffering. Then the body is an aesthetic sickness, philosophy a dianoetic medicine whose healing pain will overcome the first suffering. In premodern epistemologies, we do find a stress on the knower as receptive to something other than self, say Platonic *noesis*. (We shall see that it is important to grant sufferings beyond the aesthetic.) This also is true of epistemologies emphasizing experience, which entails some essential acknowledgment of a givenness (however we interpret this). Being is other to knowledge, though related to it in knowing. How do we know? By spontaneous communication with other-being through the body. If so, the body's vulnerability enters knowing. Bodily knowing is an undergoing of something other than ourselves, a suffering. Of course, we also find the opposite emphasis: knowing as defined completely through the knower. While not absent in premodern philosophy, the attitude is more powerfully expressed in modernity. But at issue is our response to aesthetic suffering and its equivocity—the quest is for "freedom from" this. Many philosophers are implicated. Thus Platonic reminiscence entails some subordination of the senses. Even Aristotle's emphasis on the sensory basis of our knowing is counterparted by his fleshless God: thought thinking itself. Divine knowing is beyond the vulnerability of flesh, of any undergoing of otherness—thought completely at home with itself, knower and knower at one. What has this God got to do with suffering? Nothing. Hence the doctrine of divine impassability—God free from suffering, free beyond suffering. Hence the great enigma of how to think of the God shown in the biblical tradition. If God is involved with suffering, must we not conceive of God as other than thought thinking itself?

One might ask, do many philosophers avoid making suffering an explicit theme, because they desire the sovereignty of thought akin to this God? Are they driven by the eros of thought to be sovereigns of thought beyond eros? Even so, is not suffering still their companion, however much recessive? Philosophy is a therapy for suffering. The Stoics and Epicureans are only some among many examples that might be consulted. And where philosophy shows the will to be rationally self-determining, beyond all incarnate patience, it reveals itself as a project to overcome suffering. It then becomes one form in which the *conatus essendi* seeks to conquer the *passio essendi*, and to conquer the body as more elementally in rapport with that passion. But does not suffering mean we must now be different philosophers who must seek to think the other to thought thinking itself?

Erotic Suffering

With this we come more overtly to the relation of erotic sovereignty to suffering. This is the rub here: eros, at the source of our active self-surpassing, is something we suffer. It is the *passio essendi* as it becomes articulated in the sweep of our desire: this happens to us: we do not choose it (for example, "falling" in love). The *passio essendi*, emergent in and through the suffering of the idiotic and aesthetic, puts us off balance with a power that surpasses us, even as we find ourselves as self-surpassion. It lives us, but we live ourselves in being lived, and so we seek to live it. Thus the *passio essendi* more mindfully becomes *conatus essendi*, insofar as we seek for our own sovereignty in the happening of desire.

The doubleness here between *passio essendi* and *conatus essendi* can be tilted in favor of a claim to sovereignty beyond all passion, beyond all suffering of the power of being as other. I think that an ontologically rich sovereignty *remains in rapport* with the *passio essendi*, hence always knows that its *conatus essendi* emerges from a more basic gift of being given to self; thus it remains open to what is transcendent to its own sovereignty. In its passion, it knows it suffers the gift of "to be," more primal than its will to be, and will to be itself fully. Devoid of this fidelity to the *passio essendi*, the *conatus essendi* becomes univocalized into a will to mastery, in which erotic sovereignty seeks to surpass its own suffering of being in a will to power that, affirming itself, betrays the splendor of the gift of the "to be."

I note only a few aspects of this relative to the modern will to power. While ancient philosophical ways were not devoid of a *theoretical* will to master the world as other, in modernity the will to make *knowing the master of itself* is more pronounced. The modern quest is for the most complete autonomy of knowing. There is also a praxis to this. Beyond every patience in knowing, anything other is to be redefined in terms of knowing that is fully self-determining. Not incidentally, the beginnings of modern science are connected to alchemical desires, especially the possible medical benefits of the new knowing. Suffering is the shadow from which knowing flees. It also is the shadow it brings with it. What of the religious? It may ask us to have faith, and the meaning of suffering will be given. But faith itself is a kind of suffering, since one cannot will it into being. A more divine patience will redeem the mundane sufferings to which the flesh is heir. But if the answer to suffering is another suffering, this does not sit well with our impatient will to autonomy. Consequently, the new science will find it hard not to rival religion as a fundamental rejoinder to suffering. It will redefine suffering as a *problem*, which it will solve, most powerfully through the new technologies engendered by the superior controlled cognition of nature. Science is salvation. It seeks power over sickness, and age, and the last frontier of mystery, death itself.

Relentlessly the will to autonomy pushes suffering into the background, even though secretly suffering shadows its driving motive. As suffering beings, we will to overcome the suffering of being. How? By manipulating the life-threatening conditions of life itself. By meeting suffering with ontological aggression against the sources of suffering. But life-threatening conditions are themselves *conditions*. To destroy them completely would imply revolt against something inherent to our being at all. The will to overcome suffering through completely autonomous knowing diminishes human receptivity to otherness. In seeking to eliminate suffering, it risks dehumanizing us, dulling us to the promise of the gift in the *passio essendi*. Strangely then it is our hypersensitivity to suffering that ends up making us insensitive to suffering.

The objective does not suffer; the objective does not weep; only vulnerable flesh weeps.[3] Often knowledge is pursued to alleviate a kind of suffering rather than simply to know. What indeed is ignorance? The ignorance that is bliss does not know that it does not know. The truly ignorant know nothing and do not know they know nothing, hence no restlessness disturbs them. None of us is ignorant in that sense. As double and intermediate, our ignorance is not mere ignorance; a kind of lack, felt as such, we undergo it as a form of suffering.[4] Human ignorance, suffered as such, is overcome by the eros of perplexity.[5] The oppression *intensifies* when ignorance gives way to perplexity—a kind of intractable bafflement from which we seek alleviation. The knowing of other animals is geared to biological necessity, but our knowing ranges more universally, hence our sense of suffering has a range and an intensity nowhere else evident.

---

3. Science and technology dovetail with our desire for mastery, especially in relation to medicine. But notice the ballooning business that medicine has become, especially in the West. The suffering we seek to overcome becomes our rampant obsession. Would we rather be as if we were stones, or to have invulnerable or disposable bodies, or minds mindless of suffering, like a computer? The dream of invulnerability is not confined to the cybernetic thinkers. As Nietzsche, that supreme rhapsodist of will to power cried out against pity: "Be hard!" A cry taken monstrously to heart by the Nazis.

4. A man suffering from total amnesia: he was in ecstasy; then as memory returned, so did sorrow.

5. You are in a strange country where you lack the language, do not know what is going on, and do not have the means to communicate, much less gain some transparency on what is going on; you suffer a kind of oppression. Ignorance can be that kind of oppression.

We suffer not only in our physical frailty, but suffer from the fact that we know our vulnerability, and we know that we know. Our knowing enters intimately into our distinctive suffering, especially in relation to our death. We know our mortality in a way that is awake, compared to the sleeping presentiment some animals may have.

Thus the intensity of suffering and the range of powers of a being are proportionate. This is paradoxical: one would expect that the more powerful one is, the less one would suffer, or have to suffer. Yet the more extensive our powers, the more intensive the suffering possible. The possible range of our knowing cannot be definitely limited beforehand. This entails our potential openness to everything other; but it also means the intimate knowing of our radical vulnerability, just in our being able to be in relation to all else. Because our range of powers is greatest in creation, so also is our suffering. This too applies diversely to the potencies of the ethical.

This paradoxical doubleness of power/impotence is at the source of religion, art, and philosophy.[6] It also means an extremity of suffering at the height of the powers of erotic sovereignty and the potencies of the ethical called into play on the boundary between erotic sovereignty and agapeic service. Of course, this paradox may be *doubled falsely* due to the false selving that comes when we translate "being greatest in creation" into "being the greatest." Greatest simpliciter! The being greater than which none can be or be conceived! Does not the will to absolute autonomy now turn this into a new ontological argument but for *man as the absolute*? This idolatry is, in one sense, closest to the greatest truth, but the last step it takes turns a great truth into a great falsity.

Of course, there are more mundane responses to pervasive bafflement. We discipline our knowing in determinate directions, thereby diminishing the feeling of oppression. Life seems less to happen to us as that we live life in a definite direction we set. The oppression of suffering issues into pragmatic control of the conditions of life. It goes with the instrumentalization of life and the valuelessness of being. The end is to increase progressively our power over the conditions of life, mediated through a scientific understanding of those conditions. But at the bottom of our noble wish to lighten the burden of existence is the elemental reality of suffering. And, anyway, are these paths adequate to this elemental reality? Different religions deny this, whether Jewish, or Moslem, or Christian (the divine suffers—in suffering, the divine is revealed). The Buddha saw it: he was

---

6. Shelley put it thus (Jullian and Maddalo, i, 543): "Most wretched men/Are cradled into poetry by wrong:/ They learn in suffering what they teach in song." If range of ontological power is correlated to ability to suffer, then God must be most capable of being open to suffering. Radical love of the other is this suffering; from love it lets the evil refusal be, the evil that is the act of spiritual violence towards itself.

prince, king to be; then sudden witness of suffering that baffled; then later released beggar, with wise compassion.

Consider Pascal: one of the greatest mathematical minds, an eminent scientific one too; he underwent a conversion, and things could never be the same. When we turn to human beings, we need the *esprit de finesse*, not the *esprit de géométrie*. There is no geometry of suffering; there is no geometry of God, or our relation to God. There may be finesse. Finesse knows the wisdom of suffering. Becoming wiser means having suffered. There is no painless geometrical method to attain finesse. Geometry does not weep, does not laugh. The point applies to the cult of artificial intelligence: computers neither laugh nor cry; they store immense information and perform extraordinary feats of calculation, but they can never be wise, for they do not suffer. Who would gainsay empowering knowledge? Or the relative autonomy that allows us to do and answer for ourselves? The crux, however, lies with the absolutization of an effective univocalization of power, and the deficit of discernment concerning power's enlargement.[7] The issue is one of finesse, not geometry. And we live in a time of widespread geometry, but very little finesse. There are situations, constitutive of our condition, where we are brought to the limit of our power, and where the proper response is not the feverish rush to augment power once more. It is to consent.

This is true of aging and death. It is true of our own character, as is suggested above by idiotic suffering. Instead of flight from oneself in search of one's "true" self, one must accept oneself, who one is. (This is joy in the *passio essendi*.) We suffer from ourselves, but we should suffer from ourselves, and not spuriously seek ourselves. I am not saying we should not find ourselves or not be true to what we are, but there is a kind of seeking of oneself indistinguishable from a distraction from oneself. I ought to take a good look in the mirror. (I am going to die.) I need not go elsewhere to do that. I myself am the Everest I must climb. Horace: *Caelum non animum mutant qui trans mare currunt*: they change their sky, not their soul, those who run across the sea.

In consent to self there is more than consent to self. There is a freedom at the suffering of limit, but not one that defines and dominates life, that enhances power, that enlarges an autonomy. Wordsworth knew of this and spoke of a wise passiveness. There is a knowing that passes into us in the event of suffering itself: a happening that breaks us down, and that consented to from within may turn into the breakthrough of a wisdom we cannot get from anywhere else than from suffering itself.

---

7. Some sufferings are crippling of human powers. Lives are blighted, say, by a physical disability. Now we have resorts that free the person into a freer being for himself or herself. This freeing, properly understood, is sourced in a release of the agape of being. The good of the "to be" is made available again, resurrected. We can cooperate in this "giving again." But to see our being as such a cooperation is to be on the way of finesse.

Agapeic Suffering

I confine myself to three considerations: relative to our sense of evil; relative to passage beyond negation in suffering; relative to the allowance of an agapeic ethics.

First consideration: Often we think of evil in terms of a recoil from suffering, as we seek to maintain our integrity of being; what threatens us with harm or destruction we deem as evil. Here *conatus essendi* seems to counter *passio essendi*. Does this lie at the back of many ethical systems? It is not *all* that is involved. Yet it is something that surely makes us unsure, something that strains all self-centering, and in another sense, all being self-centered. I refer to a threat, not just to safety and perpetuation, but to life itself. This is the assault of death and nothingness. Everything in being affirms itself, despite nothingness and the threat of death. That there is death at all is hard to comprehend, as the testimony of earlier peoples shows. Something happens in life to life that negates life. This suffering is concretized in death, and this even though death eludes our efforts to fix it determinately. And perhaps all definitions of evil finally trace back to some such fatal destruction visited on being as good. Is this contradicted by the witness of those willing to die for a truth or a good? Yet they die into faith in a larger life because to live the current life would be to live a death.

In perhaps a less extreme metaphysical sense, the *passio essendi* shapes the sense of evil in ethical views such as Epicureanism, Stoicism, Kantianism, utilitarianism. They respond in different ways, but mainly they seek to overcome the *undergoing* in suffering and to be free beyond undergoing. In that respect, they are untrue to the deeper truth of this deeper suffering. Thus, Epicureanism is a therapy of desire to free us from suffering desire, from being its victim. Stoicism is similar: a retreat into the inner self would avoid the disturbance that contact with external things can bring. *Autarchia* or *ataraxia* seemingly offers a being-at-home-with-self, beyond the turmoil of disturbance, suffered from beyond our control. Kantianism sees our moral nature as being above the pathological, beyond desire as pathetic, or *esse* as *pathos*: we must be active and rationally self-determining, even to the point of dualizing our being. Utilitarianism is motivated by the secular wish to diminish suffering and quantitatively extend well-being, defined in terms of the satisfaction of desires—the greatest happiness principle is a democratized moralism driven by flight from suffering.

Second consideration: Why the untruth to the deeper truth of the deeper suffering? Because a truer "overcoming" *in* suffering is distorted by this claim to the overcoming *of* suffering. Flight from suffering can produce a flattening of the soul. The will to alleviate suffering may be moved by the best of moral intentions, but the result may be souls deficient in depth. (The "Prozac phenomenon": we can all now be happy campers!) The suffering that comes with life is treated as an aberration to be eliminated. There is a metaphysical truth in the recoil from suffering, but what if the stifling of the suffering is an untrue recoil from the *pas-*

sio essendi? Suppose the recoil is part of a process that shatters us and opens us to something beyond? Then the *passio essendi* asks for faith in goodness, not of one's making, asks nakedness to goodness beyond control or calculation.[8] This world is a vale of soul making, Keats suggested. There is no growing of souls without suffering. Take away suffering and we become either flat and soulless, or we become monsters—Strulbrugs who hate life, and who cannot die. Death can make us monsters, but without death, we would be more monstrous.

Third consideration: Can an *ethical* meaning be given to evil as suffered? Socrates, the so-called founder of morality, offers an extraordinary view: *better to suffer evil than inflict it.* Is this just the domestic suffering of a headache or a toothache, or a different suffering of evil? Our immediate response is negation: we greet evil, if not with evil, certainly with a kind of violence. There is a robust vigor that brings strength to bear on the rejection of evil; this is the natural recoil from the evil that threatens our being. But is there not more here? There is a reference to good beyond the more normal distinction of life and death. The goodness of this suffering suggests a good that transcends even the evil of death. Some deaths must be endured to pay witness to that good. Suffering evil brings us to the threshold of transcendence. Ethics brings us to the limit of the ethical, as determined by autonomy and erotic sovereignty. At this limit, a witness to something more is solicited.[9]

I would put the issue more extremely, beyond the temptation of any mundane complacency. There is a suffering of evil that is *more* than exposure to the threat of death. There is a different pathos when the monstrous face of evil, and our exposure to it, places an infinitely oppressive burden on us. We do not know how to respond. We try to hold fast. *Suffering evil*: darkness comes on us; a malignancy happens to us; we are at a loss, beyond the bond of fidelity with a mysterious transcendence. Think of the suffering of evil of Jesus in Gethsemane: agony of evil; nothing to be done; the struggle is within the deepest recesses of intimacy; the cup of bitterness must be drunk; holding fast and praying for comfort; and the angel came.

---

8. To move to a new stage of life, often one must be open to suffering. A child goes to school for the first time and has to endure the trauma of leaving the mother, and going among strangers; it can be heartrending to be as if bereft, but the child can be the better for having passed through the suffering. Are there not "therapies" for suffering that are evasions of suffering?

9. I take seriously Socrates's self-description as servant of the god. Such service is not a mere metaphor. It is witness to transcendence, on a verge between what we call life and death. It is a philosophical faith in a good beyond the good and evil of mortal life. In willingness to suffer evil, something of this is intimated. Is this the moralizing Socrates, the flat rationalizer of life? I cannot see it.

One remembers some survivors of the Shoah: witnesses of evil; and their afterlife is sometimes a suffering of evil that comes upon them unbidden; they cannot but be sufferers of evil; and their trust in life is tested to the utmost. They cannot simply live, cannot simply die. What help is there in Epicureanism and its undisturbed soul, or Stoicism and its inner sanctum, or Kantianism and its moral autonomy and self-contentment, or least of all utilitarianism? All are simply inadequate to the suffering of evil and its blasting of us.[10] A radical being at a loss brings us into the company of a darkness not itself passive. This darkness attacks us, invades us, seeks to assault our trust in the goodness of life. Brought into radical darkness, and the suffering of the darkness—what kind of knowing could this be, what life could come from this?

We are brought to Golgotha, the place of skulls. This place goes into the soul's most intimate recesses, for the struggle with evil is fought there, not just with arguments up here in the head; the Gethsemane and Golgotha are down there in that noplace of desolation. What knowing then under the sign of the cross? What living? I know these latter images are Christian and not Greek or Jewish, but the point is elementally human, and at the limit of the human: the suffering is *beyond human measure*, for were it possible, one would not choose it, but once being visited with it, one must taste its bitterness and what one is is tested by it. One comes to a crisis. In the suffering, is there more than the evil suffered? And one might well turn from this, resorting to responsive evil, and with the justification of fighting evil on its own terms. Or one might simply be shattered and be given over to despair. What is the "more" that beckons beyond despair? Transcending suffering is useless from a biological, a utilitarian, and even a Kantian moral point of view. We cannot completely rationalize its meaning, just as we cannot ourselves conquer death. Our ultimate helplessness is the shadow side of the fact that to be at all is an ultimate gift. We may ask for the releasing consent of an ultimate gratitude; we may show ourselves as ungracious in an ultimate sense. The fuller response to such suffering surpasses our autonomy and erotic sovereignty, as the religious surpasses the ethical.[11]

---

10. I may be wrong, but the suicide of Primo Levi makes one think of this "too muchness." Levi claimed to find meaning in his mission to be a storyteller of the evil of the Shoah, keeping alive the memory. Is this suffering of evil disproportionate to what can be "redeemed" by any human telling? Human memory is not enough. Did Levi come to despair on this point? In his own human terms, the storyteller cannot save, cannot redeem.

11. Religions give meaning to suffering, for often it is not suffering we find hardest to accept but meaningless suffering. In a religion such as Christianity, God is said to consent to suffering, to share in the condition of coming to nothing: not thought thinking itself, not sovereign master, or majestic power broker, or cosmic *autarkia*, but the agapeic servant who transforms the nothingness by consent to it, even in the most radical negation of death itself.

Suffering Nothing and the Good of It All

I try to say something more. In this suffering of evil, there is nothing definite one can exactly isolate, nothing definite, yet that oppresses one. One falls into a *being oppressed by the whole*. One has an indeterminate global feeling of things not being right, or of oneself as not being in tune with perhaps a deeper rightness in the nature of things; or perhaps one has a taste of horror that at bottom things may not be right at all. You cannot determinately pin down this oppression. Generally, we "encounter" something like this with all evil, and such suffering calls forth something related. At the limit of our power, it hints at our nothingness. Such suffering seems to bring a strange *knowing of nothing*. To know evil is to suffer from nothing.

Perhaps such suffering has more to do with wisdom than with knowledges in more determinate senses. A wisdom in a knowing of nothing—how fit this with any determinate scientific ideal? Science deals with determinate cognition of determinate processes, happenings, things. But there is no science of nothing, nor indeed of this suffering. Nor could one have a self-determining cognition, or any technology, to bring us to this knowing of nothing. It is life itself that tutors us in the knowing of this nothing. It brings us to this knowing of suffering, to attunement to frail nobility, to the mystery of the evanescent world, to the subtle vulnerabilities of the soul, to the terrifying shocks inflicted by cruelty and malice.

To come into this knowing of nothing, there is no formal discipline or subject matter. It is being religious that keeps it most in mind. I cannot get out of my mind these astonishing words: blessed are those who mourn. Today it might be: blessed are they who do not mourn but take control of their lives, who insist on being empowered; mourning is futile, and there is no comfort beyond; anyway, mourning avails nothing, is only the outcry of a powerless child crying for his or her mother or father; now that we have come of age, no mourning, no childish comfort from beyond, no ardor for God; we do not need it, we do well alone. I find it more interesting that Aquinas claims that this beatitude is especially relevant to those who are seekers of knowing. All increase in knowing brings increase in suffering; the seekers in knowing are being brought beyond their present knowing, and this is like a grieving process that must leave behind its present limit. It is like an elegy, or a leave taking, or an exile, or a kind of dying.

Can we here connect suffering and posthumous mind? For it is posthumous mind that allows us to see again the good of the "to be," to be resurrected to the ethos as sweetly, inexpressibly good in the good of being there. This reversion is a re-vision of affirmation. It is like the prodigal son coming home and being given the embrace of the father who makes no issue of forgiveness but offers again the feast. The prodigality of goodness is given in the feast, in festive life. The stray has spent his season in hell, and he has died perhaps many times, and now is come back to life: coming to nothing means coming back to being again as good.

Entering into death is the suffering that also the erotic sovereign faces. He or she is the hero who faces death, who seeks to surmount death, coming to self in this struggle. But there are *further* deaths. These are not a matter of overcoming one's fear of death to be oneself as master or sovereign. They concern death of the mastery of sovereignty in a new exodus of transcending. This is a suffering the erotic sovereign must undergo, though everything in its nature fights against it, for it does not want to be a suffering, patient being but active and overcoming. There are deaths beyond sovereign mastery of the fear of death, yet the sovereign's death and coming back to life presage these deaths and resurrections. Again, the doubleness of posthumous mind is important here: in the between with knowing of the beyond as well as the middle, of transcendence itself as well as rich immanent creation; brought to the neighborhood of the divine in one's death as sovereign, and forever looking on life differently, as newly seen in the inexpressible sweetness of its "to be."

The more there is a loss of religious, the more there is a forgetfulness of this suffering. You might say, so much the better. In fact, we would be much the worse, both in denying our patient being, and blocking receptivity to the radical healing our being craves absolutely. The issue is not the diminishment of the human by sneering at finitude. This charge of nihilism is a cliché, repeated too mindlessly since Nietzsche. No doubt, religions can vent rancor against our limits or denigrate our naked frailty. That is the human condition, namely, to flee itself, not to want to consent to finitude. I am concerned with a more elemental honesty about our suffering condition. This has to do with coming to a fundamental consent to the good of life, even in the undergoing of death, to which all must come. We may achieve much, may do extraordinary things, and yet we must face into the night when it seems that much, if not all, of what we do simply comes to nothing. (I think of Vermeer's painting "A Woman Weighing Pearls": behind her is a representation of the Last Judgment; before her are spread worldly goods, bits of gold, necklaces, and so on; and you might expect gold or pearls to be weighed in her scales or balance; but on closer looking, it seems to be that the balance is *empty*. *There is nothing there.* There is a different judgment beyond this empty weighing, or this weighing of emptiness. All this is shown with the aesthetic perfection of harmonious balance and beauty.)

This coming to nothing, in the wisdom of suffering, knows nothing. We come to ourselves as being broken, as breaking down. The question then: What is the point of it all? The good of it all? This is not only a question of the meaning of a life as whole in the face of death. The coming to nothing raises the question of the *good of life*, but with respect to a more open and indeterminate sense of the good—not the good of this or that, but *the good of it all*. The coming to nothing mocks this good and that good, all finite determinate goods, in fact. In exposure to the indeterminate nothing, the issue is raised of a good not exhausted by or defined as this good or that good: the good of it all. Can we somehow come into consent to the good of being at all? This is something both embracing and elemental—embracing as potentially extending to the whole, beyond our own erotic sovereignty; elemental as implicating each human as a singular self in the idiocy of his or her most intimate soul.

This more than determinate good puts us in mind of God. To be related to God sometimes seems like being related to nothing, since God is not this thing or that thing. If God is the good, God is not this good or that good but a different, excessive good. Suffering makes us question God, but it also makes us unable to evade perplexity about God. The hardened atheist, told of his cancer, demands, "Why me?" "Why me?" makes no sense outside of the spontaneous upsurge in the idiocy of the human heart of a profound perplexity before God and the palpable evil that now afflicts it. It is a rage against nothingness that is an involuntary prayer of anger.

We come to nothing, and still we struggle to say "yes": consent to life itself as good, and good as gift, and good thus because given out of goodness. The gift of life is given, we fall in love with it, we might even want it to be eternal, but it is finite, and we must die. Do we say "yes" in the spirit of gratitude, or turn back protectively into life as inexpressibly sweet, or turn against it in rage? It is because life is inexpressibly good that we do not want to cede gracefully our mortality. Suffering wears us down, erodes attachment to our own and limited goods, prepares us for another affirmation, a good asking consent more inexpressibly sweet than even the inexpressible sweetness of life. We are brought to the absolute pass of absolute "yes" or "no" to the good of it all.

Suppose we *are* brought into some ultimate consent. Is that it? Yes and no. Yes, in that a peace (simpler and more ultimate than sovereign power) is given to one. No, in that the consent and peace are paradoxically insistent, restless. Suffering points us to a knowing of the suffering of others, as well as our own. Changed by the knowing of our own nothingness, suffering can turn us towards those others who suffer. In this peace there is nothing quietistic but an appeal that we turn to those, or not turn away from those, who most suffer—the rejects, the refused, the defenseless, the downtrodden. In opening us to this appeal, the knowing of suffering can become an ethical wisdom that is compassionate. This is a knowing that asks to be enacted in a changed life. Compassion is a knowing of the other that is both beyond the *conatus essendi as mine*, and yet returns behind it to the origin, resurrecting a rapport with the *passio essendi* in which is given the ontological intimacy of the community of being as good.

And the Patience of Job?

Job was an upright man, good. Yet he was subject to what looks like a malicious ordeal. Why? Because Satan believed there was evil in every man. The challenge: take away everything from him, strip him, make it all come to nothing. The refrain rings out, and his wife goads him: curse God and die! Job does not curse. Being brought to nothing, his prayer is still gratitude for the gift: "Naked came I out of my mother's womb, and naked shall I return. The Lord gives and the Lord takes away. Blessed be the name of the Lord."

Satan is allowed to tempt a further turn, and to touch Job more intimately. Job is cursed and afflicted with illness, and his life becomes a burden to him. The day comes when he curses the day he was born. *This is a good man cursing the day*: "Let there be darkness. Let God's light fade."

This is a terrible cursing by a good man. The hair stands on end, the flesh shakes. The comforters try to persuade him of the good things of life. To no avail. There is nothing more terrifying than the curse of a good man. Nothing, except the voice from the whirlwind. It does not argue or persuade; it tells Job. And by a barrage of ultimate questions no human can answer. Who is man that he would curse life? Where were you when the foundation of the world was laid? Why were you born? Job has no answer. Silence. Consent. The incomprehensible gift of life.

This is the terror of the unholy: the enigma of the good man brought to nothing and cursing this good . . . the good gift becoming a terrible burden . . . the failure of even the highest consolations . . . being brought to an impasse in which the worst curse is uttered: do away, not with any light, but away with the light God gave . . . away with all that makes all good.

This is the terror of the holy: the majestic violence of the response; the good beyond good and evil; the nothingness of creation, even in its astonishing glory; the nothingness of the human being, even as it can hold glorious converse and contestation with God; the enigma of the ultimate good that allows curse to follow suffering lived but not comprehended.

This is the gift of the ultimate: life given again . . . out of nothing, beyond immeasurable suffering. For the suffering is, as the good is, beyond measure. The first children of Job: each an immeasurable good. The suffering of their death, also immeasurable. The gift of new children, also immeasurable. But is it all not so differently for Job now? He has been buried in death and been given life back. He is given a posthumous life.

The question then: If Job is a good man *before* immeasurable suffering, how do we describe him *after*? He is a good man, and so is the same, but he also is immeasurably different. The doing of the same good, being good in the same way, has become being good in an immeasurably different way. What is that difference?

PART IV

ETHICAL COMMUNITIES

CHAPTER THIRTEEN

THE FAMILIAL COMMUNITY OF THE INTIMATE: THE ETHICAL INTERMEDIATION OF THE IDIOT

Familial Intermediation and the Potencies of the Ethical

Communities in the between move from the idiotic, to the aesthetic, through more erotic forms, to touch on the agapeic. This movement is mirrored in this and the following chapters, as we move from the family, to the network of utility, to the communities of erotic sovereignty and agapeic service. In these diverse social formations of loves, trust is basic, as is the interplay of trust and distrust. There is the idiocy of agapeic trust at the origin, at end, and in the between. All of this is complicated because of the equivocal doubleness of the human being. We must come to some discernment of this complication.

We start with the ethical intermediation of the family, for this is most elemental. We are all born of a woman, and this first bond is intimately of the flesh itself. Birth shows a universality of the singular idiot: elemental idiocy, elemental universality. Yet the family has influences on all of the potencies of the ethical. An overview follows.

First, the family intermediates the good of the idiot self. It enters into the intimate, and one will never be entirely free from its influence. Second, it shapes the aesthetic: our bodies and their pleasure are mediated through the presence of our parents, the attractiveness of a mother's beauty, a father's smile. This is full of equivocity. Third, it orders the intimate and the aesthetic with its own sense of dianoetic norms: rules, formal and informal, come to one from the familial others; sometimes these are harsh, sometimes benign enough not even to be noticed. The family is an order that allows the intimacy of the psyche and the well-being of the flesh to flourish, to be pleased. It supplies the need of an ordered environment to set limits within which children come into their own: mere formlessness is as inimical to freedom as excessively rigid form. Fourth, family intermediates a transcendental sense of the unconditional: there are calls that we must answer, commands we must obey. In that familial others already embody something of the unconditional, in the trust and love they offer us, a fluctuating image of unconditional goodness can be called forth into mindfulness. Fifth, family inter-mediates eudaimonia: special reverence for the singularity of the child lays down a ground in early formation for integrity over a long life, and the integral func-tioning of human powers. Sixth, it intermediates the opening of transcending: the unrest in desire, lured on by an ideal not now fully realized, is offered hope that our being stretched out into infinity is not futile. Yes: seek the highest. Sev-enth, it intermediates the presentiment of the transcendent: familial togetherness can incarnate an image of the divine. A family without reverence is lacking—children are deprived of what is most deep and most high by not being told reli-gious stories: most intimate, most sublime is transcendence itself.

The Chicken and the Egg: First Familial Intermediation

Our ethical selving is massively indebted to what is given by familial others: a giving inseparable from our own giving, as well as our taking and grabbing. We might call our first family the "family out of which" we come, while we might call the second family (through marriage, or some other arrangement) "the family into which." We start with the first family, since when we come to the second we can be more mindful agents of the ethical intermediation, as well as more maturely capable of giving love as well as receiving it. In the first family we are immediately intermediated, though in such wise that the good passes into us, and we take no note of it, we so take it for granted. The intermediation is at work behind our back. For that reason, it is all the more influential. The communica-tions of the others pass without self-conscious barrier into the secret recesses of the idiot self, the intimacy of the heart.

We seem here to have the problem of the chicken and the egg. So do we focus on being children first, or on being in relationship with grown-ups? Since there are no children without grown-ups, must we not focus first on the second, since the child presupposes an intermediation that generates and grounds it? Our egg here is not the cosmic egg but *already a procreation from another* before it becomes itself a grown being for itself. If there is a circle here, this is perhaps to be expected with intermedi-ation, since there is no way to begin, as if we were not already intermediated. This means that we are already given to be ourselves, before we give ourselves to ourselves; grown by relations to the others, before we can grow up to be ourselves; already reared and grown in relativity, before being grown up and giving ourselves in relations.

We immediately grow in the light of the others, or sometimes the darkness, and we do not know determinately what is going on. The child could not grow to be itself were it not grown by others. The more it is thus grown in ethical inter-mediation, the more is its power to grow into itself, the more also its power to stand for itself, and stand alone, and to do for itself what before was done for it. Of course, "standing for self" may feed the illusion of complete autonomy; just as "being in need of the other" may prompt an infantilizing in which we resistlessly acquiesce. A delicate middle between these two is necessary. Initially we are the recipients of that intermediation rather than the agents, beneficiaries rather than benefactors. The process of growing up ethically turns the first into the second. But the second is grounded in the first, so that we may be beneficiaries who live thanks as benefactors. Reverence for what one was imparted inspires what one would now impart. *Ancestor worship* shows a religious form of this. Hence the first constancy addressing the human: honor thy father and mother. This is the first commandment after the primal commandments dealing with our relation to God: the absolute intermediation is followed by the neighboring absoluteness in finite creation of reverence for what one is given, out of which one gives.

But the familial ethos is equivocal, as the parental others show the child the double face of care and superiority: care, as offering security, even to the allowance of taking them for granted; superiority, as standing above us, sometimes invoking fear and trembling in our weakness, sometimes awe and adoration in a greater presence. The equivocity concretizes doubled possibility: as intermediated from the other, the child grows into its own self-mediation, but since the latter would be for itself and yet must come to itself through the other, *thanks and resentment are mixed up*. The child may be happy to be helped, yet may hate to be helped, since this shows it as helpless.[1] These words express the tensed mix: *being grown into being grown up*. Being grown shows our roots in another; being grown up seems to show us standing free on our own. If our roots are in another, standing free on our own is always relative. So we are caught between self-assertion and gratitude.

Since the family intermediation is rooted in a *fleshed bond*, its intimacy is the most powerful and subtle aesthetic togetherness: the bodies of spouses together, the flesh of children growing from that union, the children growing in the milieu of incarnate others, brothers, sisters, relatives. In some ways, it is a paradigm for being related[2] and having one's being from the other. Not surprisingly, we speak

---

1. *Helplessness*: the child is given over to the others; if the others are good, the helplessness is turned into enjoyment of the marvel of being; if the others lack goodness, the helplessness is compounded, and the goodness of being at all is turned into an unchosen misery. Mostly we are in between these extremes. The second helplessness fills the victim with despair or rage, as it may fill others who understand deeply the waste of life and its goodness. But helplessness is not necessarily a bad thing; it can be the other side of trust, out of which good is affirmed, one side of the inseparability of being good from the good of the other as helping, say, the old or the sick. They too may rage against this helplessness and may fall into despair. The aid of the other may help them fight, when this is the right thing, to consent when this is the way we must pass.

2. Hence its continuous use as an image of societies beyond family (for instance, by Aristotle). Consider political movements that speak of "fraternity," or religious communities as brotherhoods.

here of *our relatives*. The family is based on natural sexual differentiation and on the processes of generation by which we come to be and enter into an interme-diated network of relatives, themselves spread out over generations.[3] So too the familial bond is always more than a contract. To think in terms of contract is a dianoetic misunderstanding and superimposition on the aesthetic. The bond also is more than enlightened self-interest. It is more than a compact for mutual self-development. It is in excess of the determinate wills of its participants, since it also is intermediated in the web of anonymous relatives. Of course, there are fam-ilies who operate in terms of dianoetic calculation, for example, the arranged marriage calculated to seal a compact between powerful rival families. This is not the elemental level. There can be great dissonance between the two: for instance, "reason" in the form of calculative self-interest can be at war with the spontane-ity of love or passion, to be overcome by it, or to seek to stifle it.[4]

The exceeding is not only in the intimacy of the flesh and the heart. Mar-riage is called an *institution* because it is a public togetherness that exceeds the particular wills of its participants, and not only with respect to law, public respon-sibilities, and so forth. This also is with respect to its basis: the idiotic, the inti-mate—the singularity with intimate fleshed roots in elemental primal commu-nity. This is acknowledged by more modern "Romantic" notions but also in some religious traditions, where it is understood sacramentally, in relation to God as creator, and nature as the matrix of procreation. The family is not just a unit of biological procreation but the elemental metaphor for being together, in which the bonds of love exceed what people as their own can comprehend, in which the love can serve as a metaphor for the ultimate love of the absolute origin.

We are as nothing without the intermediation of relatives, yet also we are as a well of aloneness. This comes out in the loneliness that people feel in longing for an other to love and to love them. This frail loneliness is shaped in a longing inter-mediation. We grow anxious that the one for whom we long will not come. We are as nothing without the beloved, and are overcome by love's agonies. How inter-

---

3. This does not mean that a human being cannot be reared, and reared well, by grown-ups who are not the biological parents of the child. There are many ways of rearing and care—for instance, forms of fosterage. The important point is that the primary rearers meet the indeterminate trust in the child with love that is also unconditional and directed to the singularity as for itself. This is agapeic in being for the child as other, not erotic in being for the self-satisfaction of the carer (erotic does not mean sexual here).

4. Some of the best novels deal with this tension of the intimacies of the heart and the dianoetic exteriorities of social life. The first, as much as the second, is a form of interme-diated community. Think of Darcy in *Pride and Prejudice*: his *reason* knew Elizabeth was *socially beneath him*, but he cannot deny his passion and love; and initially he clearly does not feel at home with what goes counter to "reason," though love does win through.

twined we are with others, we come to know when we lose the beloved others. One has grown to be what one is with the other so that when we lose the other we lose ourselves. A person deprived of the beloved can come to die. Hearts are broken in many ways. But breaking a heart is always more than breaking a contract.

The bond here is often an incognito intermediation that is partially thwarted if we think of ourselves as entirely separate singulars. More basic than the separateness of "mine" and "thine" is the effective becoming of "ours." This "ours" also can free us from insisting on "ours," though it also can fortify itself into an "ours" that is a mutual egoism. Such an "ours" forgets the exigence of intermediation and circles around itself in an exclusive self-mediation. Think of couples so lost in themselves that their love is a failure to love; for no such exclusive circle can be true to love's self-transcending exigence.

Flesh to Flesh

The bond beyond contract is evident in "flesh to flesh." There is a transformation of sexual gratification that satisfies itself in the pleasure of the other; transformation into the giving of flesh as a gift. This too can be made also "for me." Sexual love is full of equivocity: it shows the body as the soul, communicative of what one is. Consider just these three possibilities.

First, sexual love might be a calculated exploitation of the other: the aesthetic being of the other is objectified into a means by which I gratify myself; the body of the other is instrumentalized; this is not animal simply in that the natural instinct of procreation is not the point. That humans are always more or less in heat indicates something distinctive. Heat is not seasonal; there is no rutting season; our desire exceeds the univocal drive of the animal. The equivocity of self-transcending emerges, for our desire has no fixed limit that completely determines the form of its manifestation. The indeterminacy in our being comes out in the equivocity of our desire, the lack of univocal limit, the excess of self-transcending. We require of the other its excitation of desire as pleasuring in the energy of its own self-excitation. In this requisition of the other, desire is born as instrumental. Just as only we can objectify the other, only we can be involved in seduction. Seduction involves always some self-relating exploitation of desire's equivocity, a dissimulation that is both self-relating and self-serving.

Yet there are sources deeper than our seductions. There are the secret enchantments of the glorious earth, its dark springs of invigoration, rising up in the body. Elemental energies are at work in bodies, ecstatic in immersion in the flesh as itself an elemental affirmation of being. We must say: the goodness of the flesh, of all that is fleshed. The sources of affirmation come from deep down; and *we are affirmed* by sources deep down that are not first within our control. This is the inward otherness of the flesh itself that escapes self-mediation at the start.

The body becomes self-mediating, but out of intermediated sources that themselves point to original power beyond determination, hence beyond complete
mediation, even intermediation. Behold the marvel of a beautiful body, seen
without instrumentalizing, as if one were still in Eden, the flesh itself gloriously
ecstatic and shameless. For innocence is shameless, though not as corruption is.[5]

Second, sexual love can be erotic in a deeper sense: not calculated objectification or secret dianoetic exploitation of the aesthetic, but releasing the energy of
self-transcending in the flesh. The passion for the other shows desire that is taken
over by its own exodus from itself towards the other; taken into an aesthetic
"being pleased" that erupts from depths of unknown intimacy and seeks in the
other similar depths. Desire is overwhelmed by the return of the indeterminate,
as when the skin is the surface of the between in us.[6] Sexual eros mingles lack and
plenitude; while driven towards the other, it is partly its own lack it is overcoming; hence the self-serving character of eros mingles with the gift of the body to
the other. One comes to oneself in the other, and that is the sweetness of love
consummated. So too the danger of a tyranny in eros: you are for me, mine; the
love is jealously demanding of the other, dictating to the other; not only eros
turannos in oneself, but oneself as a tyrant of the other. This is a peculiar danger
of dictatorial possessiveness, just in being given to the other; you are mine and
mine alone; I build a tower around you to protect my treasure. Jealousy shows
how deep is the desire to claim the other as one's own; it shows the intimate possessiveness: the root self-insistence absolutely holding the other as its own, intol-
erant, anxious that its own be threatened by an outside other.

Third, there can be an *erotic giving* that so becomes for the other as to border the agapeic: the body is available for the other, a gift of what one is in the

---

5. Even if sexual obsession is polymorphous—sadistic, masochistic, bestial, excremental,
recreational—the aura of the *secret indeterminate* is being sought in and through this and
that determinate sexual object. It is like a kind of *perverse adoration*, or a bewitchment in
bondage to the fascinating. Magic, religion, and sex twist around each other.

6. See above on the skin. Think also of the *kiss*: as devouring of the other, as a mouth that
wants to incorporate the other; or the kiss as an arousing caress that breathes a freer passage of passion back and forth between the flesh of lovers, a passing between that is the
erotic flesh itself. I kiss we kiss who kisses we are kissed we remember the apple we ate
just a while ago and shame flushes in a different thrilling way and the serpent extends its
temptation anew a secret place is sought in shyness and shame the mouth devours as much
as caresses, probes the rough tongue as much as feels its own throb, and the hurried tongue
says yes yes and the secret place offers itself as the moist serpent flares as secret place and
probing flesh thrust and flush and oh flow of a sudden glory and brief peace and the glowing fading glory it goes as the flood of intimacy ebbs slowly from the skin into the
retracted idiocy and brief slumber in fleshed accord and the world divides again to difference and desire again again and oh again.

openness of the most vulnerable body. To strip naked before the gaze of another is always to risk being objectified, to risk being an objectifier. Nakedness before the other is a potential offering that can be repulsed or shamelessly used. The offering offers a different loss of shame, in the giving of the body that is for the other. The meeting of bodies in the between is the meeting of surfaces that do not want to be surfaces but that would let surface in their aesthetic intimacy the show of what they are as loving. The offering seeks to bring this to the surface, a resurfacing of the deepest idiot intimacy.[7]

Sexual love as a giving of the flesh bears fruit in the mutual love of those espoused, and in the children that are the offspring of their union. We, today, under the dictation of self-fulfillment and self-determination, find the necessity of children hard to think deeply enough (to say nothing of espousal). Children risk being made another personal option, a preference. One is concerned with satisfaction of self, and having a child is another thing needed for satisfaction of self. We are fortunate that nature is powerful enough to seduce us with ruses, away from the poverty of this self-satisfaction. Having children, we find ourselves called upon to change ourselves and to be less concerned with self-satisfaction. This is as it should be. The self-satisfaction should be worn down by lack of sleep, by inconvenient squawking, by dirty diapers and pee in the bed. In the domestic mess, another kind of self is being born. Of course, we may resent the new demand because it does not fit our self-satisfaction. (After all, now is the time I *always* play tennis!) We may ourselves refuse to grow up, and want to remain children of our satisfaction. We do not let our children make *us* grow up. For we do no simply help children grow up. *Children ask that we grow up*, that we finally become grown up and become a more generous being for the other. This is agapeic service in the flesh itself.

Were Adam and Eve Married? On the Couple

This is an old theological worry, and whether we say yes or no, their story tells us much. An equivocal dialectic of eros is there in Arcadia. Is sexual eros awakened before or with the fall that brings us to know our nakedness? Is there

7. This is why pornography, as a public display of the most intimate, is grotesque. The intimate by its nature is not to be thus open to the public gaze—it must thereby be debased. The truth of the intimate is intimate. And it must be intimated to be communicated, not explicitly shown. Hence, silence, reserve, modesty, reticence are all absolutely necessary. The corruption of our "frank" society is tied to an idolatry of the objectified that, in claiming to make the intimate known, knows nothing of the intimate. Its will to exteriority is less a will to express the truth as the exploitation and corruption of what it claims to love.

sexual eros without the shadow of shame? And I do not mean *after* the shadow may be chased away. The fall, we may say, is somewhere between the intimacy of the idiot self and the intimacy of aesthetic presence before the other. And because all desire is in this between, sexual eros too is in the presentiment of shame, even though overcome by bliss. Being a couple, coupling, brings difference beyond any self-difference of the idiot selving. Shame is the shadow of equivocity haunting this promise of rapturous univocity.

But further, the doubleness of Adam and Eve turns against itself with the loss of the rapturous univocity; it turns into mutual recrimination in face of the superior other. I blame you for both of us waking up to nakedness as shameful; you blame me. The double as couple turns to mutual sullenness and suspicion. Blame itself becomes our bond, recrimination our new togetherness. For vulnerability means lack, and lack means my lack, and my lack needs the other to fill itself up. Thus the potential hatred of the other becomes the dialectical indirection that creates a different love, always ambiguous, ineradicably equivocal. This love of the couple is shadowed by suspicion and jealousy and quickly can veer into its opposite—hatred of the other for not loving me the way I require. This is the promiscuity of the opposites going with the step into evil, or into the vestibule of evil doing.

This dialectic takes place behind our back as the power of suspicion leads to its opposite condition of some "being together." Fear of the other, or trepidation of the other's betrayal, or abandonment, forged in the self-knowledge that at bottom one is selfish, creates a simulacrum of solidarity. This is a solidarity but not a released one, since it is secretly driven by the desire to dominate. Even this, our fallen condition, has the immanent standard of a free community, hence a mode of togetherness comes to be, despite the mutual antagonism of the couple. We are forced to be more than ourselves. The logic of cold war embodies this dialectic: hatred or suspicion finds its point of equilibrium in which the opposites somehow balance, and there is the appearance of a kind of peace. It is not true peace, merely the absence of overt war. It is war as peace, or peace as war. The opposites are more or less the same. Peace is latent war; cold war is the counterfeit of peace. (This is mad: mutually assured destruction.) Hobbes's logic shows insight into this dialectic. Overseeing power is needed to domesticate unbridled power. Forceful desire is needed to moderate the force of desire. Will to power is necessary to tame will to power.

Nevertheless, the doubleness of Adam and Eve is subserved by the call of an unchosen unity: the erotic and procreative urge makes the two one flesh. The sexual difference is need and more, need as vulnerability, and need as need to transcend self as set over against the other. The shadow of death falls over this, for death and procreation are mingled. One is one's bodily being: a man or a woman, and this radical singularity of incarnation one must accept. Sexual difference goes with the sense of bodily otherness, but this again is ambiguous, for shame and modesty are twins, and both are born in facing the other, and not merely in being over against, but in facing towards the other. Seeing and being seen, offering and being offered, bodily otherness and sexual difference become the basis of a reciprocal communication and interchange. Communication blossoms within this equivocal ethos of double possibility. The promise of reciprocal interplay shows an *affirmative* intermediation in the doubling of the couple. In the acceptance of bodily otherness, its very joy comes out partly from under the shadow of death and is given over to procreating new life. The couple become one flesh, and in time a child is born. Beyond the dialectic hidden in desire's equivocal doubleness, there is the promise of a metaxological community: eros exceeds even the *sunousia* of the couple, into the promise of agapeic service—living not for self or other, but for the other, beyond the couple.

This is the gift we find: exiled to mortality, an astonishing love of the mortal springs up. We love the child. I know my death, but knowing the death of the child fills me with far greater anguish, not because I see my own death in the death of the child, but because I love the child beyond definite measure. I am not loving myself in the child; I am loving the child as other. The shadow of death brings me around to a stuttered form of agapeic love of the other as other: the child loved beyond finite measure; I do not matter. In that regard, parents often can love their children more than the children love their parents.[8] Though, when children become parents, they are turned back by life and often come to realize what was given while they slept in the joy of growing up. They come to love the parent as an other. Then the opposites meet once more. Life asks us to care for the aged. We are not now returning a debt for love given. We are being asked to be new, in a love for the old. This love has no utilitarian function, it is beyond univocal measure. The aged and the dying burden us with their care, but the burden is the way they honor us with the opportunity of agapeic love. We may feebly answer the call, but how we love the powerless is a sign of the good, or its absence.[9]

What is this love of the mortal? It is a kind of posthumous love: beyond life and death, beyond the clinging to one's own life, as if one owned life; loving as if one had died and yet lived fuller beyond death, though we now actually are in the midst of the travail. This love of the mortal is a taste of the love of the good for the mortal: the agapeic God that loves the creature immeasurably, and for itself completely.[10]

---

8. Of course, there are the usurpations of sons beating fathers (see Aristophanes) and the usurpations of parents who will not gracefully yield time and place to children. King Lear paid for his lack of grace; his ungrateful daughters helped him to his season in hell.

9. Dostoevski said we might gauge the ethical quality of a society by looking at its prisons. The point applies also to how we treat the young and old, our agapeic care for the powerless, and those beyond usefulness.

10. The infinity of this love of the mortal does not entirely fit any of the conventional schemes we have: utilitarian, Kantian, Marxist, Platonic. It is consonant with Jewish, Christian, and Islamic views, insofar as the origin is agapeic. God is the love of the creature. It is

Being Reared: Second Familial Intermediation

The happening of familial intermediation is grounded on the promise of an *indeterminacy* of trust. Hear the child come into the world: it *screams!* But when we hear the scream, we are relieved, for this means that the child is healthy. The scream is not a howl of anguish but a first bawl of the lust of life. The scream is joy and gives us joy. The scream also is an indeterminate communication to the other in raw helplessness; helplessness that anticipates that the other will come to serve it, will come to its aid. The scream shows the good of the "to be," albeit also as full of ambiguity.

The basic bond is not proved by this or that act of trust. The trust is already given in the orientation of the child to the parent. The being of the child is *to be trusting*, in relation to the others that come towards it and define the between for it. Being trusting is more basic than being in distrust. The spontaneous activation of the expectation of good from the other indicates the intermediation of a community at work in the fleshed being of the child. It is a condition of our being at an elemental level. This is implied when later we see a child's trust violated by an abusive parent or some figure commanding social respect or authority who betrays his or her respect to exploit the child. Our outrage at this violation is the obverse side of our spontaneous acknowledgment that the being of the child is first trusting. Even a whining, colicky child proves the trust, even though it may try the patience of those who care for it.

The indeterminacy of trust fastens on determinate others, because those others are in intermediation with it: it does not just determine itself, but it is determined by the coming towards it of the gift of the other. The other helps anchor the trust. If there is no such anchor, the trust will find nothing in which to rest, hence it will mutate into varieties of anxiety and suspicion, sullenness and truculence, disquietude and restlessness. The intermediation of the good through the parent or the first other that cares for it is very important in intermediating the determinate shape of this indeterminate trust. The ardor of a nameless love, a love that does not know itself, transmutes into sorrow, thence into rejection and hostility, when some loving other does not give it the anchoring it absolutely needs.

This indeterminate trust is not a willing of this or that, a "yes" to this or that, but is prior to determinate willings.[11] It needs some determinate others to inter-

---

hard to give an account of this love of the mortal, outside of reference to God as the good. Is there not something extraordinary in the way the West seems to have jettisoned reverence for age? Will it change as the population ages? If those now aging never had reverence, they will find it hard to know it in their old age; they will hate age, and their children without piety will hate them: for both, their lives will be a burden.

11. It can be resurrected later in the excessive willingness of agapeic selving that goes beyond all will that wills itself, when the loving has passed into one, so that now one is to become the other that gives for those in need.

mediate with in order to become properly determinate itself. The other that intermediates with it cannot be any qualified other: it must be an other that holds towards it the promise of an unqualified willingness. The parent is the other who holds out this promise, the answer from the other to the indeterminacy in the intimate idiot self, and that answers, less with this or that answer, as with the willingness to be there in an unqualified way, the personal presence of a thereness on which one can count, without any determinate qualification. The family is the ethical milieu wherein the indeterminate trust in the child and the indeterminate acceptance of the parent come to meet. Out of this meeting, the child is given to be itself determinately. As so given through intermediation, it is enabled to begin the process of giving itself to itself, as self-determining, as self-mediating.[12]

Unconditional acceptance by parents is tied to the self-worth of children. A marriage issues from a betrothal, where trust and truth are intertwined; a family is a happening of elemental trust. Being true is being trustworthy: what will be reliable, and faithful, what will stand by you, and you by it. Because marriage is that trust, fidelity is of supreme importance. It is not a commitment that is half-hearted or conditional. This fidelity is not a provisional trust in which my self-mediation can override the intermediation when it feels it is not being served. There is the need for surrender and sacrifice. This is not easy to accept if one makes an idol of autonomy. Marriage is a good kind of heteronomy.[13] Divorce shows a breakdown or failure of the life of trust. Nor is it good when an attitude of calculated fidelity enters: calculative fidelity is no fidelity. Breakdowns may be unavoidable and unredeemable, yes, but social intermediation should not be indifferently supportive of a laissez-faire attitude. Against utilitarian thinking, there is the mystery of a fidelity that seems impossible in terms of calculative self-interest, and yet it grows and deepens from sources other than calculative self-interest. Fidelity is a sign of the good for children: it the intermediated embodiment of the trust that is not provisional.[14]

---

12. The upsurge of this indeterminate trust, as in need of the intermediating anchor of the other who loves it, also is deeply connected to our first conceptions of the divine as loving us: God as mother, as father; God as love.

13. Does Kant not show a gross way of thinking about sexual love in his *Lectures on Ethics*? He speaks from the "moral standpoint," yet there is something vile in the degradation of sexual love—as if the sexual organs were obscene machines that necessarily deprived us of our humanity and dignity. Is this moral superiority an ethical coarseness?

14. Some research now indicates the ill effects on children of divorced families: less able to trust others, they have been disappointed, perhaps crushed; their work at school may suffer; perhaps something is eating away at them, as if they ask, is the breakdown my fault? They seem to have a higher propensity for depression, even crime; have less stable adult relations, have more suicides, are less interested in general public matters, have

The elders are both the loving others and the beloved. The child's indeterminate trust regards the second, the parents unconditional care should enact the first. Ideally, the two meet in the middle. This meeting is an intermediation, but one in which there is an *asymmetry* between the parent and the child. It is obvious that parents are not always loving and beloved. They may be closed into their own self-mediation, so the child is not for itself first but is for the circling back of the parent to itself. To some extent, this must happen in all familial relations, because every human, young or old, is double: every human shows the self-mediation that comes to itself through the other and the intermediation that comes to the other through passage beyond the self. Parents are selfish just like children, because each lets dominate the circle that passes through the other back to the self as circling round itself. Family relations as intermediations disrupt that circle, hence are the elemental place of intimacy where love of the other is learned. The learning is aided by the child's indeterminate trust, but since this can be abused, the form determinate love takes also can become abusive in the image of the abusing parent. The inherited love knows not that it is not genuine love in this abuse.

I mean that the indeterminate trust reproduces the self of the child in the image of the parent, expected as loving but actually abusive. Since this is not known as such, the abuse is taken for love, and it is the corruption of love that gets reproduced in the mimetic behavior of the child. We live as we are first loved. If that love is loveless, we may never properly know what love is, as being for the other in a genuinely agapeic way. As the parent comes into the middle to meet the indeterminate trust, so the child's definite selfhood is crystallized determinately. Abuse crystallizes the indeterminate openness differently than does genuine love. The child here finds its receptivity victimized before it knows what is happening to it, for it is not determinately formed prior to the crystallization. What it is takes form from the other, and if that form is corrupt, so too it will be deformed in unfreedom. The opening as opening is formed as deformed, that is, as closed in its opening. From the start, such a child is pitched into the mystery of its own self-contradiction, of its inner woundedness and tornness, tornness due to the loveless love of the other, but crystallized in the indeterminate innerness of intimacy, thus in the idiocy that resists determinate approaches that might heal. In a way, there may be no *determinate* healing henceforth—it is rather only

---

more children out of marriage. Obviously such claims are controversial, and their meaning is not univocal. But there are children who have been put in second place relative to the personal self-satisfactions of the parents. They live as *seconds*, in some deep way, not always formulable, as *castoffs*. In some ways, the reticences and hypocrisies of marriages that stay together "for the sake of the children" *can* be better than the frank self-satisfactions of autonomous, freelance adults.

the openness of a new and renewing indeterminacy, a renewing love that might communicate opening and welcome to the wounded closure in the idiocy.

Around that wound determinate scar tissue has formed, and this tissue acts as a protection and a barrier; it even hides the wound from the knowing of the wounded. It cannot be healed by a determinate operation that would cut through the scar, for this would be a new wound and another scar. Rather, the suggestion of love must offer its welcome, and hope that the offer is registered on the other side of the determinations of selfhood. The offer does not know what is going on on the other side of the scar; though there is an eye of love that can see beyond barriers, normally protective and prohibitive. A good parent, a healer, has to have this extra eye.

There is no *technique* of healing at this level. Technique deals with determinate problems, but these wounds are not determinate problems; they are the indeterminate source of such problems, and hence the approach has to have *finesse* and discernment, not univocal mind, not geometry. Humans do not grow if they are not loved. There is indeterminacy in this too: the loving other must simply be there, so that the trust passes into taken for grantedness.[15] Need that is habitually met turns support into forgetfulness. The grounding is forgotten. There is, once again, the danger of the usurpation and end of proper thanks. Children are not asked for thanks, but thankfulness keeps proper reverence alive, without which humans are monsters.

Parental Bodies/Original Nostalgia

Family is the intimate intermediation of the desire of the child, and undoubtedly, the bodies of parents enter into that intermediation. Should we see this as a matter of childhood sexuality? Yes and no. Yes, insofar as every desire has a secret complicity with other desires, love of the parent with a vague sexual longing, perhaps, but this insofar as every form of desire is a formation of a more basic eros. Is the more basic eros simply sexual? This is to identify the determinate with the indeterminate, hence we risk wrongly characterizing the indeterminate opening in terms of one powerful form of desire it determinates. Of course, every determinate form always seeks beyond univocal limits, hence seeps

---

15. In this light, "quality time," so-called, lacks quality. The parent just has to be there; be there in order to be taken for granted. Generous granting is to allow oneself to be taken for granted. People too busy for their children cannot grant the space of this gift of being taken for granted. Real "quality time" comes from allowing the other to forget the fact that one is there. Love allows *this* forgetting. Advocacy of "quality time" is *another* forgetting, guilty about its neglect, but anxious to exonerate itself with a theory of child rearing.

into other formations, thus the indeterminate eros is alive in all desire, equivocally alive. This is true of love of the parent, the indeterminate trust as charged with determinations that more clearly belong to particular forms of desire.

The same point could be made for eating and drinking as for sexual desire. That our parents feed us and give us to drink is potentially surcharged with the indeterminate power of the original opening. Is Freud equivocal here, not always clear that a determination of desire mingles with the indeterminate desiring, taking on some of the overdetermined charge of the latter, being surcharged with the elemental power of the idiocy of being, and as surcharged liable to be identified with the indeterminate desiring? Of course, sexual desire itself is a powerful form of desire that returns us to the intimate idiocy, after the human being has assumed complex determinate forms of being; it shows the vehement resurfacing of the power of the indeterminate eros. Sexual eros is intimate with the original eros, so to say, which is not itself only erotic. There is a promiscuity of the indeterminate and the determinate, but for just that reason we must avoid taking the latter as the univocal clue to decipher the plurivocity of the former. One sometimes wonders if Freud is in the grip of a peculiar univocalization when he obsessively focuses on such things as the castration complex and penis envy, though what he says may be full of suggestive ambiguity. Do we risk misinterpreting the promiscuity of the indeterminate and determinate?

The body of the parent is not a sexual object first but the aesthetic presence of value. The parent's body as aesthetic personal presence is the other that intimately intermediates the idiot self of the child in its intimacy. The parental aesthetic presence is inseparable from the value of personal goodness expressed in the love of the child. The indeterminate opening is what is being given more definite form; sexual desire is a formation of that opening, but it does not exhaust it, and there are other formations that also are surcharged to a degree by the powerful indeterminacy of the more original eros/agape. The very powerfulness of sexual desire tempts us (or those in thrall to the Freudian bewitchment) to think that it truly reveals the truth of the original opening, but we have to be more discerning.[16]

Certainly, the bodies of loved others, mother and father, are charged for the child with value, surcharged with personal power that resonates in the idiotic reserves of the child's most intimate being. It would be surprising were there not such echoes that stir desirings in this resonation. It would be surprising if the

---

16. Consider Schopenhauer when he talks about the genitals as the metaphysical organs of the Will; they are expressions of the ultimate Will. This relation of organs and Will might help us better state the issue. Though I do not think the origin is Schopenhauer's Will, or sexual desiring, or even eros, the issue is whether such a way of speaking is adequate to *what comes to opening in us, in the idiot*. Does Freud risk mixing too much the "objectification" with the more primal source?

promiscuity of the indeterminate and determinate in the familial intermediation did not resonate with the sleeping sexual. It is another thing to say that the determination and the indeterminate opening are sexual. This is to confuse the promiscuity and to take a derived determination for the deriving indeterminate source, and it is the latter that is the deepest mystery.[17] The charge, surcharge of value of the bodies of the parents *must* be initially equivocal, since these bodies are the aesthetic shows of love, but love that from the other mingles self-love and love of the child as other. Necessarily, these bodies aesthetically incarnate both welcome and threat.

Again, not unexpectedly, the bodies of mother and father are plurivocal: they speak many things, allure and recoil, beauty and distance, goodness and forbidding. The equivocity is tied to desire as equivocal and the plurivocal nature of bodily presence.[18] The plurivocal presence of the parent's body also is tied to the awakening of the plurivocity of original desire in the child, a plurivocity that harbors its own frailty and insecurity, as much as trust and self-affirmation and love of life. This equivocity of the child's desire can double, redouble the potential equivocal presence of the body of the parent, lead to an image of the parent, as much due to the parent's aesthetic show as to the imagination of the child. This is another version of the doubleness of the *image* as mixing self-mediation and intermediation.

In ambiguous ways, the images of our parent's bodies shadow us in later life, and we fall in love with those images, or recoil from them, unbeknownst to ourselves, when later we fall in love with others. What has passed into the intimacy of the idiot self does not die there, vanish there; it adds dynamically to the inarticulate reservoir of our promise and power, to resurface or reshape itself in new form, when we are surprised by the intermediation of an other who crystallizes some longing, now long forgotten, or a memory of a love lost in time. (Sometimes this is like a wound being reopened, or an aching yearning. Something seemed aborted, but it did not die, only pined in secret.)

---

17. Freud: "We have to conclude that all the feelings of sympathy, friendship, trust, and so forth which we expend in life are genetically connected with sexuality and have developed out of purely sexual desires by an enfeeblement of their sexual aim, however pure or nonsensual they may appear in the forms they take on to our conscious self-perception. To begin with we know none but sexual objects; psychoanalysis shows us that those persons whom in real life we merely respect or are fond of may be sexual objects to us in our unconscious minds still." See "The Dynamics of Transference," 1912, *Collected Papers* (New York: Basic Books, 1959), Vol. 2, 319.

18. Desire is always marked by some plurivocity, even when it becomes definite, for there is the promiscuity of the indeterminate source and the definite formation; hence there can be overt desire, covert desire, and hints half-guessed about other vaguely suggested longings, all embodied there in this seeming univocal desire.

The image of the mother and father that passes into one in the familial intermediation *has to be double.* The mother or father intermediates the crystallization of one's intimate indeterminacy into the beginnings of determinate selfhood. This means taking on one's own identity, even as one arrives on the scene with the initial shock of difference. The doubleness is not only between child and parent, it is within the child. So there is a redoubled doubleness in the child, crystallized out of the sleeping intimacy of the predeterminate idiocy. Thus this double—intense longing, need of the mother, say, but also the stirrings of anxiety that one will be lost in the mother; a yearning to die again into nonseparateness, but also a trembling that one will be devoured by nondifference.

This might be called a nostalgia for the predeterminate rapport; for determinate difference and identity bring pain (*algia*); but this is pain for one's own (*nostos*). But one's own is the beloved other, not oneself simply; the mother or father, but one is the mother and the father too. So this nostalgia is not a narcissistic retreat to solipsistic ownness but sorrow for the immediate rapport that is an elemental intermediation, hence always a *predeterminate being with the other*. (Think how *consoling* the simple *touch* of another can be.)

An account of nostalgia as a regressive flight from difference is only true at a level that does not go to the deeper level where the predeterminate rapport with the other is working, a rapport stupid to describe as flight from difference. At this more primordial level, nostalgia shows a love of difference, the other, though it is a love that cannot truly name itself, since it is lost in the other, though at a more superficial level it seems to be consumed with itself and its own anxiety before difference. Such an account does not do full justice to the love of the other already ingrained in one's intimate being, a love whose elemental unnamed effectiveness resurfaces in the experience of "nostalgia." The deeper account shows: One's own is not one's own; or what is not one's own is one's own.

Our attitudes to *death* carry something of the doubleness, mentioned above in relation to the parents. Death too is related to nostalgia, as it is to the self-forgetting ecstasy of sexual abandonment—the little death. We seek, at one level relative to the destruction of difference, but at a deeper level, I think, relative to the more primordial rapport in which *one is excited to be*, through the intermediation of the other. This rapport is an unconscious love of being as good, shown to one in the loving other, whose love has namelessly passed into one, making one, rearing one.

It is interesting that nostalgia can befall one in times of idleness, or fallowness, or doing nothing, or in exile. Doing nothing—as if this lets open the space for something from of old to come to the surface again, forming itself into a ghost come to haunt, a presence taking body in the nothing, and gathering around a longing that did not know it existed till it appeared there, as if from nothing. It emerges with a kind of return to nothing, to the death of the grave. But it shows more than nothing, for something thought dead is resurrected in that grave of nothing. We come to know it was never dead. Rather, we are more like the dead, the living dead, who wander about unknowing of the borrowed life that infuses our self-important busyness. Doing nothing, the self-importance drops off, the ghost of the gone-by floats up again. And what if we are the living dead, in our life always carrying the dead with us? As if we were always tombs of others, but these dead are not dead? What if to be alive is to let them in on the life we lead, or to be let in on the life they too did lead, for they are not nothing but the ancestors without whom we are nothing?

Asymmetrical Relations and the Ambiguity of Authority

Since the elders are others who make a *determinate* between, the family is an order of relations. This order is an intermediation of openness and limit: openness to welcome the growing up of the child; limit to offer it the otherness that reflects its identity back to itself, so that the limit orders a determinate self-becoming. The order is double edged. For instance, openness can become so indefinite that its very amorphousness welcomes nothing—the child growing up does not encounter the resistance of otherness that lets it know that there is someone definite there. We have a simulacrum of openness that turns welcome into an indifference, and this is felt when the permissiveness of the parent is not a genuine permission. Contrariwise, limit can be so recalcitrant and constraining that it is felt as an order that returns the child back into itself, *before* it has had the proper opportunity to come out of itself. This repressive return of the child is not the return to self in which it comes to itself in a self-becoming.

Limit also is related to openness insofar as limit offers a shelter from the overwhelming otherness the child cannot yet deal with or assimilate. The shelter is a framing of a space of freedom, proportioned to the maturity of the younger person. Too much otherness and the excess will overwhelm and perhaps destroy; too little and the child will not be challenged to grow. Ideally, openness and limit, permission and direction, are done for the good of the young. Alas, the elders are equivocal too, and children still. They are caught in their own self-mediation, or limited versions of it, and they may want the children to reflect them back to themselves (e.g., parents who invest their own ambitions in their children). There is an asymmetry here that makes the young more recipient, thence sometimes more victims of the misplaced self-mediation of the old. Then the order of the family communicates the frustration of desire and of self-becoming. The children do not come into their own; the parents are alternatively insistent and disappointed with the children. These parents, as still childish themselves, do not form the milieu of a metaxological intermediation in which the agapeic good is honored.

Reconsider desire's doubling as *between* the singularization of self-mediation and the pluralism of intermediation. Reconsider the doubleness in self-transcending: transcending may serve the selving, or the selving may serve transcendence. This means that *always* there is selfishness along with trust, and this doubling applies to *both* the child and parents. In the child, the root self-insistence has a spontaneous power of self-affirmation; this is rude and must be shaped, which means encountering the recalcitrance of other independent centers of being. Hence the double again, namely *between struggle and cooperation* between children and parents. The root self-insistence also means that one must not forget the idiocy of the monstrous. Parents have to cajole the monstrous. They may be tempted to resort to violence to break the recalcitrance that will not open to the other.[19] Finally, however, the recalcitrance of the child's inner otherness cannot be so directly dominated without destructive consequences. This inner otherness must be persuaded to come into the openness of self-transcendence, willingly, freely. It is only love that guards this freedom without violence. This persuasion of love is the solicitation of the powers of agapeic self-transcendence in the child. Love shows hope that the monstrous in the idiotic will come to itself, come to love, in coming out into the openness of free intermediation with the other. In the end, this cannot be forced. Forcing it is a confession of betrayal, indeed, a confession that force cannot do what it seems to do.

This doubleness of struggle and cooperation is intermediated in the family, and this then is no innocent ethos. To heed only the self-insistent root in the child is wrong if we overlook the same root in the parents. To overlook this is to be complicit in certain subordinations, implicit in the asymmetry in the intermediation of the child and parents. This asymmetry is not the superiority of parents per se but their responsibility, hence their deeper defection when they do not serve the helpless ones, when serving them is the ethical obligation. Parents can be exemplars of love, they can be vilely self-obsessed. Their personal presence can be the aesthetic show of the life of goodness and being good;[20] it also can be the incarnation of evil. As there is an immediate mimesis of one, there also is of the other. Parents can be evil originals too. We are all imitations. Parents can have murderous thoughts towards their children—sometimes out of a sense of helplessness that the recalci-

---

19. Thus the deep ambiguity in some older traditions which speak of "breaking the will" of the child.

20. "Goodness appears to be both rare and hard to picture. It is perhaps most convincingly met with in simple people—inarticulate, unselfish mothers of large families—but these cases are also the least illuminating." I. Murdoch, *The Sovereignty of Good* (London: Routledge & Kegan Paul, 1970), 53. Murdoch is right in one point, but from a novelist, one might have expected a little more imagination as to what might be illuminating about generous mothers!

trant integrity of life of the child is resistant to any influence or shaping. To care for the child demands reserves of patience and a willingness to put with sleeplessness and discomfort, and sometimes this is too much. A child incessantly cries; a grown-up "snaps" and loses control. Do not say parents have not murderous thoughts—this is the monstrous emerging out of the intimacy of the idiotic.

The root self-insistence also means that the monstrous is waiting its entrance with the very young. The incessant cry of "mine," "mine," "mine" expresses in words the greed of expropriation in which the other is taken to be entirely for me. This is well before the elemental word "mine" is used at all. Murderous thoughts towards a brother or sister—we mildly call it sibling rivalry. Its truth is not mild. Family intermediation must find ways to divert the murderous thought from destruction. Evil also is intermediated through the other. Augustine speaks of a child marked by a kind of hatred of the brother at the breast. Many scoff at this as a despicable superimposition of sin on the sinless. Augustine is closer to the truth of the idiocy of the monstrous than all those liberal preachers who, with the best of intentions, offer effortless innocence. No peace is possible without vigilance to the dogs of war garrisoned in the restless soul. The idiocy of the monstrous is the "mine" that usurps the open play of good in the intermediation, with its own self-insistence: I am the good, and all that is of me . . . and that I will to be all mine. This "mine" is the primal egg of a universal usurpation. Family intermediation serves to enable the I to see that its "mine" is embraced in an "ours" in which it can be more truly its own, its own because it comes to own that nothing is absolutely its own.

The asymmetry in familial intermediation means that its differentiated order of relations is inseparable from the presence of *authority*. Authority now conjures ideas of authoritarianism, suggesting the aura of command that lacks final legitimacy. This has much to do with the bewitchment of autonomy that stupefies us into incapacity to see that heteronomy can be good. Authoritative others can have our good in sight and at heart, and we are subject to such others, in light not of power but of the good. Authority comes from the power of the good; it is a responsibility for and a service of the other. Authority is not in virtue of owning children, as with the Roman *paterfamilias* but in virtue of agapeic service. That is, the power to command is *given to one* in virtue of the ethical command and responsibility under which one is placed as parent. It is not because we are bigger[21] and more set in society, or more powerful. It is in virtue of the call of the

---

21. Undoubtedly so-called "transference" is related to the perception of a superior other and to bewitchment. It also relates to sovereignty (the "being above us") and thus to authority (see Chapter 15). Self-mediation occurs through intermediation with the other, hence in some sense "transference" is absolutely necessary, if we mean something of being mediated to oneself through the other, even though the other is an ambiguous bearer of plural possibility. Without the intermediation with the other, the self-mediation would be threatened with a collapse into formlessness.

bestowing of good. This is a form of agapeic service, and should be so, even when parents puff up with pride over their own brood. Parents are the receivers of power before they are the exercisers. Power is already given from other others, not self-produced. Parents and children are not "friends," as if there were no asymmetry.[22] The asymmetry is not absolute, but it is absolutely necessary when children cannot yet exercise command over themselves. Being in command of oneself is important relative to self-determining, eudaimonia, and transcending. One can command, because one has come into command of oneself, but this has been made possible first through bestowing others.

Authority is given to those whom one would expect are mature enough to exercise command over themselves, hence are in a position to exercise command over others not yet mature enough to do so. Authority and commanding are not dictatorial. The dictator is the one who, in being commanding, cannot command authority in virtue of justice. He commands in virtue of the power to enforce his will, against the will of others, not in cooperative intermediation with them (I return to this in Chapter 15). Tyranny is the *failure of authority* in this respect: being authorized by the good to command those who cannot yet command themselves. Parents lose their authority in sight of their children, because they do not understand or abdicate the ethical power of this asymmetry. They do their children a disservice—disservice in a literal sense: doing a disservice means not serving them well, in accordance with what is good for them. Their failure is the defect of not living the presence of superior virtue. Genuine authority has nothing to do with forcing power; it has to do with bestowed power and bestowing virtue (where *virtus* is power that does not violate).

Fear will enter into the authority of command. How could it be otherwise, given the double power of the image, the asymmetry in intermediation between child and parent, and the openness of the trust that has not yet confirmed itself, or had itself confirmed by the love of the other coming towards it? Indeed, one can never have that confirmation in an absolutely determinate form from another human being, since even if the love of the other is, in fact, unconditional, it has to come into the between as veiled in its show. It retains a reserve of hiddenness, even in its revealing of itself. Thus the indeterminate trust *must* coexist with frailty, trepidation, and dread, since the child is called forth in a mixed way by the coming towards it of the commanding other.

Fear can still serve the good, insofar as it brings the child to its senses, brings it to itself. Fear of the lord is said to be the beginning of wisdom: we come to know ourselves as ourselves over against the other; fear crystallizes us

---

22. A friendship can *come to be*, but this presupposes the child as coming into its own, to some degree. Thus the oddness of a view of the parent as a "buddy" or even a kind of "coach." (See Chapter 11 on friendship.)

out of the promiscuous immediacy of the given rapport, like a shower of cold water in a humid drowsiness. The fear can serve the command of the good, and be the helpmate of authority that is exercised for the good of the child, not the self-aggrandizement of the exerciser. (Are mothers often better intermediators of anxiety and love; fathers of fear and respect?) Since the adult is also selfish, fear can be a weapon of domination, and a way of maiming. But there is no way to rid the intermediation of fear. The good disposition of fear plays with the ambiguity of the intermediation for purposes of promoting the good, itself ambiguously promised in the familial fear. Fear is not roused for the sake of fear, though it can be.[23] It is hinted to sober the child and quiet them to receptivity of the gift of the good. There is here a *necessary pretense*: a noble lie; no sanction may be enacted, even intended; the suggestion alone should be effective. (A similar point applies to the discipline of fear in situations of sovereignty, political and otherwise.)

Boys will be Boys

The traditional family (which tradition?) is said to be breaking down. The results seem appalling: loss of respect, spilling on to violence on the streets; children are not loved; adults are grown to be loveless. Is there truth to the traditional view? I would formulate it somewhat like this.

Women are often closer to the idiotic and the aesthetic, while men are more distanced from sources and origins, from life as a gestation and a birth. They are given more to dianoetic rule: imposing themselves on things; more inclined to abstract transcendental sternness, to duty and the law; to autonomy and the illusions of autonomy. This is not to put women at the bottom of a hierarchy, since when we ethically move beyond the will to dianoetic and transcendental autonomy, happiness brings sovereignty back to its sources in receiving, while agapeic service shows the superiority of the higher freedom to be for the other, and this is more immediately at work in the idiot/intimate and in the aesthetic as celebrating the sensuous incarnation of good. These two brings us back to personal goods of a most nuanced and subtle sort: the first seem to be made last, but the last come to be first, at first and also in the last place.

---

23. There are malicious adults who like to terrorize children. To terrorize a child is to reduce it to an idiocy where it is retracted into an intimacy sheerly dissolving of its determinate selfhood. This is a nihilation in an active regard, making the child be nothing, to taste bitterly its own nothingness. Such vile cruelty does not serve the coming out of the soul, only its melting in its own terror. Even certain sarcasms (say, of a teacher) can serve this reduction of the child to nothing.

For the erotic sovereigns too must become as children again, else they will not enter the kingdom of the good, though they outlast this or that kingdom of the world. That too comes to nothing. None of this is to deny that all humans, regardless of sexual difference and familial order, are self-mediating, and hence self-determining, hence agents of relative autonomy in the metaxological community, and this extends beyond the family. Nor is it to deny that women are often deprived of the opportunity of externally directed self-transcendence. It is often redirected back into the intimacy. Dwelling more with this, women can be more prey to profundity, so to say; but you have to pay a price for profundity. Men are more superficial.[24]

Boys tend to be less in tune with the idiot, at least initially, in so far as we find a more aggressive extroversion of their being as aesthetic show. Their bodily energies seem more given to show themselves in transcendence towards exteriority, away from the intimacy of the idiot. Then they are often socially taught to repress, or not show, what is at play in the idiocy of the intimate. In their aggressive aesthetic show, their determination from the other needs to be offered a limit where the extroverted energies reaches a term that sends them back to themselves. Often this means an older male who will stand there as a limiting other who shows them themselves, as they bounce off the wall, so to say. Boys fight and wrestle among themselves, and would indeed fight and wrestle with the father, because this is the way of being determined back towards themselves out of the formless aggressive intermediation. I need to fight against the father as the wall that sets a limit in which I can come to myself. This struggle is itself a form of *cooperation in self-becoming*. In the fight with the father, the father should be good enough to embody forbearance.[25]

If there is not this restraining limit, young male energies go on indefinitely and they are not reflected back to themselves, and hence do not come to self-mediation out of the intermediation. The energy does not come to selving, and

---

24. See Jane Austen's *Persuasion*, Chapter 11, the conversation between Anne and Captain Harville (overheard by Captain Wentworth) regarding the difference of women's love and men's.

25. Thus, with many men we find the need for an opponent, perhaps a hostile other to crystallize one's identity, out of the perplexity of the indeterminate; to be oneself, one needs another to stand opposed to one. Thus, the fanatic: he needs an enemy to give form to the formless rage within himself that has not been properly crystallized; he needs an enemy to justify his own *will to death*, the will to death that is the formless energy become formless rage. Here the will to death is, in some ways, more basic that the need of an enemy. Death and the enemy are both *means of self-mediation*—at the *extreme*. The will to death makes one *be* something, just as the enemy does. This is to be found in politics (communists versus capitalists) and in religion, especially where the fanaticism of purpose (as "the cause") takes over the indeterminacy of eros. It is earthed, more or less harmlessly, in some competitive sports.

hence the desire of the boy sours on others, others now as limits to be despised, or no limits at all. Energy become rage into the void, and rage against others. The lack or impotence of the father or respected elder short circuits the return of the boy back to his own self-mediation out of the intermediation. The boy needs the fight or limiting constancy of the father, to fight with his own amorphous powers. He needs the intimate sympathy of the mother to remain in touch with his own idiotic intimacy, easily lost in the kind of self-return given out of the agonistic intermediation with the father, easily lost in the quasi-sovereignty that gains its mastery by saying "no" to deeper subtleties in the intimacy of the idiot. We cannot say "no" without paying for it at some point. The intimacy with the mother keeps the seed of another self-transcending alive, self-transcending beyond mastering sovereignty, beyond dominion and agon.

Thank Heaven for Little Girls

The girl, as aesthetic being, is more intimate with the idiot, not so given to aggressive extroversion that easily severs itself from the intimate sources. She too must be given to herself, but not in the agon that strikes against a determinate limit and then is bounced back to itself as itself. The coming to self is more entwined with the indeterminate, the sources of generation being more inwardized. (This is so even in the literal aesthetic sense that the organs of generation are turned into the innerness of the hidden and the intimate, while the male organs of generation are turned outward and cannot do the work of generation if they do not come out of themselves.) In that regard, the coming to self is less univocalized than the case of the male, more attuned to the nuance of the equivocal (hence the truth of female intuition).

The intermediation with the mother is fraught with ambiguity, just because women are generally superior in being in rapport with the indeterminate sources of generation, and the nuance of the equivocal. The girl needs the older female to confirm her out of the indeterminate. Otherwise she can be lost in too great an anxiety about the indefinite. Women live more dangerously with the indeterminate, in that their aesthetic being gives them to be incarnately mindful of what males will to reduce to the more externally determined. Since both the older and younger female live close to the intimate, their intermediation is fraught with subtler ambiguities than that of older and younger males, where the element of fight in the determinate open seems to simplify things—but also makes them more superficial, on the surface.[26] The female intermediation is not superficial,

---

26. *Armies*: armies are organized defense, but also organized death, offense against the other as threatening one's life. Women do not organize death, do not organize armies.

not on the surface thus, even though as attuned to the aesthetic, the woman is more mistress of surface. (The surety and anxiety of the female is different to the surety and anxiety of the male. Men want to prove themselves in agon with other males; women want . . . who knows what woman wants? Does a woman? Finally this has to do with the overdeterminate, not the indefinite as lacking.)

Women generally are capable of a more attentive mindfulness of the intimate and aesthetic: the senses, feeling, emotion, the more nameless rhythms of the bodies. Men are more like slobs, just because they parade themselves in more exteriorized, objectified form. They are more oblivious than women of the rhythms of innerness, and the body, and the very feel of being, just because of that aesthetic extroversion. Paradoxically, their extroverted objectifying bodies make them less mindful of the nuance of the body; while the more nuanced rapport with the intimate in the woman's body makes her often more mindful of the subtle powers of aesthetic show, on the outside. Rapport with sensuous innerness manifests itself in attention to the show of the beautiful outside. Inner rapport with the idiot and aesthetic shows itself in concern with the beauty of the body as aesthetic show. Thus the concern with adornment. Men too were once more attuned to this. The objectifying instrumental mentality of the modern West stripped them of their flamboyant adornment with such things as outlandish hats, plumes, and codpieces. This univocalizing development of the instrumentalizing mind dimmed down the power of aesthetic show, and more and more lost touch with the rapport with the intimate.

And the girl and her father? The father is an anchor that is not always quite drawn into the doubling over of ambiguity in the female intermediation, though he can be drawn into an intermediation in which a secret rivalry of mother and daughter is being enacted. The specialness of the mother-daughter bond may often be claimed, and it has to do with this redoubling of the intimate. The unspoken is rich with possibilities never determinately crystallized into this or that exercised option. There is a *crisscrossing* of ambiguities in the play of the determinate and the indeterminate. The father can be the anchor of determinate self-mediation that resists being engulfed by the crisscross of ambiguity of the female intermediation of mother and daughter. Of course, there can be a laughable vanity on the part of the male in his belief that he somehow escapes all that. More subtle intermediations may be going on just behind the back of his vain belief that he at least is not victim of the crisscross of ambiguity.

They make children, grow them intimately. Men redouble themselves with creations more likely to be counterfeit—false doubles of God. Men make mass death. This reflects inferior intimacy with the origin in the idiot and the aesthetic. Artists and saints can be less alienated; philosophers need not be, but they often do fancy themselves as hard men.

What I am saying does not signify the one and only univocal formation. There is not one absolutely univocal formation. There tend to be dominant formations. Yet, given that the indeterminate source is opening in all of the participants in the family crisscross, a multiplication of free formations of determinacy and indeterminacy is possible. There is a plurivocity possible here that per impossible could not be reduced to one univocal essence. Males are bitches, fathers are sons, sons sissies, daughters dolls and tomboys and bossy boots, and women we know wear the pants. Just the point of metaxological intermediation is the impossibility of reducing the pluralized intermediations to one, univocal essential form, and certainly not to any dominating self-mediation. The point is not the self-mediation of the family; it is the open happening of an intimately plurivocal intermediation.

Family Piety and Prodigal Release

The piety of the family mixes love and fear. There is a natural reverence here, tied to the bodied presence of the parents, and on both sides putting roots into the inarticulate depths of the intimacy of being. Thus the death of a parent can bring a profound shock. The anchor of a piety seems undone, and one is loose, but not loose. The natural reverence is inevitably tied to power, but it is more than power. It entails the transformation of power, not only by justice but more deeply by love. This love is not feeling merely. It is feeling and more, since it comes out of the silence of the flesh, even before feeling is aware of itself. When it comes to awareness, it is in the order of a certain dedication, indeed, a devotion.

Piety for parents means that as they will care for you, you will learn in time that you must care for them. Dedication and devotion are forms of service. They need not be servile, though they can be. Service is a loyalty and a trust, reliable over time. The service of a parent extends a trust over the time of a self-becoming, even when it seems to be turning out badly—as the father of the prodigal son must have felt in his sinking heart. The devotion is openness to forgiveness and reacceptance into the order of the family. Home says: we will stand by you. "Home is where they have to take you in." It is a basic ground on which one can count.

Dedication and devotion mean that each is involved in each. One older expression of this is the *honor* of the family: my disgrace is yours, for it is our disgrace, since what you are, I am. Similarly, the *good name* of a family can be tainted by the black sheep. Today we pay less attention than before, but this sometimes reflects the loss of intimacy, not necessarily deeper toleration. The older language was one expression of the interinvolvement in one of every other. Dedication is a "being for the other" as well as the other being for one. The "being for the other" can be asymmetrical in the parent and young child, but it can move towards more and more symmetrical relations when the intermediation of the one for the other effects a peculiar reversal, wherein the young and old turn around differently towards each other with age and time. The child is the parent, and the parent must be helped, nursed.[27]

This move towards more symmetrical intermediation becomes the basis of a move towards more symmetrical intermediations with others *outside* of the family. Love takes on different forms; an adolescent meets another, and the arousal of eros seeks that other in an intermediation different to that within the family relation of parent and child. The transformations of one's "being for the other" contains within itself a principle of transcendence that points beyond the family. The principle of transcendence in the family points to a transcendence of family—pointing beyond in a movement that carries the virtues, the powers disciplined by love, outside of the home. And so, not surprisingly, we find the powerful nature of the family metaphor (*metapherein*) with respect to other forms of being with the other that are intermediations of the good: the teacher/school are said to be *in loco parentis*; the economy is the *nomos* of the *oikos*, law of the household; government looks back to founding fathers, citizens fear "big brother," statesmen dream of the family of nations; revolutionaries and others dream of the brotherhood of man; and religious communities pray to God, the father, honor the fathers of faith, and ask to become the children of God.

Familial piety is enjoined in the Fourth Commandment: honor thy father and mother. This is the first commandment after God-bound commandments.[28] Father and mother are not honored for what they do, or their achievements, but because they are father and mother: those who intermediate the gift of life are co-givers; to them we owe proximately what we are. This reflects basic reverence towards the gift of life itself and what we become through love, education, and discipline. Parents are the link between our beginning and the origin. They are the most proximate beginning. One might distinguish proximate and intimate: intimacy involves ontological reference to the origin; proximity refers to the

---

27. See *PO*, Chapter 6, on what I call "reversed time" relative to fathers and sons, and what is thrown up over time in the generations.

28. Apropos Levinas: the first command of the face is not "Thou shalt not kill." This comes later, for already we are touched by love in the face of father and mother, as the proximate intermediators of the good and of God. The face is extremely important, as Levinas rightly reminds us—though it is not "the face" but the particular faces of father and mother—singular, unique to this family—that bear, less the general command, as the enactment of the good in the singular and possibly exemplary parent. This is where the seed of ethical upbringing begins to grow. If there is no mother and father, others will have to accept the place of the parent. Without parents (or others properly in *loco parentis*) in an ethical sense, as well as a biological sense, we do not become human, given into solidarity with the community that intermediates the good.

intermediators of the generosity of the origin. This is why God is called Father, because the proximate father can mediate the origin, as the most intimate transcendence as other to human self-transcendence. There is no reason why it could not be God the Mother, the proximate mother intermediating the intimate origin. We have lost layers of the familial piety of pre-modern times, and so, for better or worse, we have lost sight of the family as a sacral community, mostly for worse. Intimacy refers to the deepest ontological immanence as well as the highest metaphysical transcendence. Proximity refers us to the human neighbor, and first to the father and mother and the family.

The matter is not one of being carried beyond the family in a Hegelian way. There is an idiocy to the family that exceeds the process of public self-determination that begins with education, work, economy, political sovereignty, and so on. Because the bonds of love put their roots down into the ontological source of human being there, there too the memory of transcendence remains most alive: hence God as father, not as teacher, or chief executive officer; though we have spoken of him as sovereign; as agapeic servant. Family intermediates the superiority of love of the singular; it forms agapeic mindfulness, superior to the universal as the general.[29]

The monotheistic decalogue places the family command as the first in relation to human relations, but something profoundly originary about it is reflected elsewhere. Think of Socrates, accused of impiety, in his dialogue with the laws (*Crito*): there is an intertwining of different pieties—familial, local/place/civic, and religious. The laws grew him, reared him, like his parents; they were there before him, and his continued life in Athens was his pledge and piety. The laws already give us to ourselves before we come to ourselves; they are such that they educate, mediate the kinds of beings we are becoming. Notice the connection of civic to familial piety: Socrates's politics and jurisprudence are not "Oedipal"; he has no desire to kill the father.

Inevitably, and by contrast, one thinks of the filial impiety of the three *magi* of modern suspicion: Marx, Nietzsche, and Freud. Their therapy of enlightenment insinuates war on the fathers: be they the theological fathers of history and the bourgeois fathers of modern industry (Marx); the psychological rivals for

---

29. See Kierkegaard on the personal good of the singular human (cf. my "Being at a Loss" in *PU*, Chapter 2: on the "once," the irreplaceable). Kierkegaard denies mediation here: the absurd, the paradox that the individual is superior to the universal (see *Fear and Trembling*). But there is mediation: agapeic being is intermediation—it is love of the singular. For Kierkegaard, Abraham's silence is beyond mediation, but does it not have to do with the idiot, with an idiot wisdom, and the community in the idiot: radical intimacy of father and son, and Abraham and God? When the angel stays the sacrificing hand of Abraham, does not this restraint show the *release* from such sacrifice, and from the need to choose between God and love of the human singular?

erotic primacy, perhaps monsters in the way of the son's erotic sovereignty (Freud); or again, theological, religious, philosophical "higher" fathers of the history of culture (Nietzsche).[30] The three magicians do not bring gifts to the son of the most high father. They bewitch us to feel, as oppressive, the power of all fathers, divine and human. We must come into the son's legacy, on the son's terms. New prodigals must declare our glorious liberation from all fathers, human and divine. Does the glorious liberation bring glory or liberty? They wander off on coming into our generous portion; they think we come to themselves by resolving not to return to the father's house. Do they know, or want to know, the forgiving father? Do they rise out of the pigsty, to find everywhere another pigsty? And *in there*, is legion driven out into swine, or more deeply into ourselves?

And yet, the piety of the family does *make way* for our *being freed* by the family from the family. The piety of the family includes the agapeic service that allows, so to say, the fledgling to fly the nest: the grown child is released into its being for itself and the new beginning of its own self-becoming. This is the prodigality of its agapeic release. Being a child is a reposing in being, nestling, without yet the burden of responsibility for self. One is taken care of, cared for. One has the expectation that another will do for one. The dread of the night comes, and the touch or voice of another is shield enough to restore the trust. The porosity of one's being, as still indeterminate, is full of wonder. Agapeic astonishment gives way to perplexity often and before too long, and perhaps to harsh disappointment.[31] Nevertheless, the roots of faith are in the child. The credulity can be exploited, will be. Yet its openness to the other, prior to suspicion, is the ground of the greatness that resides in reverence.[32]

---

30. See my "Dream Monologues of Autonomy." In *Religion within the Limits of Reason Alone*, trans. and intro. by T. Greene and H. H. Hudson (New York: Harper & Row, 1960), 163ff., Kant shows his own ambiguity, not to say hostility, to paternal principles in relation to religious piety: "This name (*Pfaffentum*), signifying the authority of a spiritual father *(pappa)*, possesses a censorious meaning as well, only because of the attendant concept of a spiritual despotism, to be found in all forms of ecclesiasticism, however unpretentious and popular they may declare themselves to be."

31. See *BB*, Chapter 1 on agapeic astonishment: the metaxological rapport with, or wonder towards the goodness of being prior to determination into curiosity towards this or that—this is where the child can dwell. Perplexity comes to be in face of the same astonishing otherness, and with this, trouble and the sense of lack, and the assertion of one's own powers as overcoming the lack. But underneath it, and with it always, is the promise of the agapeic astonishment; and also the doubleness of openness to the other and self-becoming that wills its own will. Yes. Of course, I believe in Santa Claus.

32. Without reverence, we are base. Becoming as children again: this means regaining reverence beyond the responsible self-assertion claimed by autonomous self-determination.

What of the prodigal release and the fall of virgin eros into nature's blossoming round? The eros of adolescence: the infinite loneliness resurfaces with the self-becoming of the body. Puberty stirs up the idiot/aesthetic self. This stirring is not dianoetic or transcendental, but *transcending*, even oriented to transcendence as such. Desire's urgency is in search of something in excess of finite objects. The longing and ardor of adolescence may be vague and indefinite, but it recurs at a level of self-consciousness not present previously. Hence a new sense of shame and embarrassment, as well as a new self-assertiveness. There also is self-retreat in the face of more complex mindfulness of self and other. The loneliness seeks an other to assuage the indefinite longing: the other gives a shield against the formlessness and the infinite strangeness beyond self. I look into a distance that has no limit, but the appearance of the other against the empty vista shields me from the terror of nothing, the presentiment of futility in the unlimited expanse.

Because of the restlessness that keeps turning up, and the opening of transcending beyond this limit, with young love there is both intensity and shallowness in attachments. This is not to say that love at first sight cannot be real; there are early loves that stay the long course of a faithful life. The music of indefinite desire makes one swoon in the clinging embrace of another. But we cannot live in a swoon, thus come the comedies and tragedies of love. Young eros shows the freshness of humans in nature, hence aesthetic beauty serves the intermediation of a good beyond individual will. Falling in love is beyond will, yet has everything to do with indeterminate willingness. The ruses of nature produce the comedy of the body. We are being bewitched and are hardly aware of it, but we also are being intermediated in this comedy. The ironies of this intimate intermediation live on in a comedy of errors. There is a goodness in the bewitchment, despite its shadow, as in the seducer. For this is a masquerade, with always the hint of festivity and holiday. Marriage lies at the end of Shakespeare's comedies,[33] as death does at the end of the tragedies. We are fated to love, fated to fail. Prodigally released into our own self-becoming, we know gains and losses beyond individual control, beyond self-mediation. Seeking our own ends, we end up serving something beyond ourselves.

The paganism of the child and youth can be closer to the first goodness of Eden. We have sailed the sea, drawn in air not of the earth, been struck by light shimmering off the waves and reflected from the world as other, tasted a tang of brine that salts wounds of longing that find no final healing here—and all that was drawn in and savored, sensed in the wind among wild grasses above the sea, all this was inexpressibly sweet, as at Knockadoon.

33. There are mythic aspects here: the marriage of nature and human community: the feast celebrates the sacredness of love: the *hieros gamos*, and the marriage of earth and heaven.

CHAPTER FOURTEEN

THE NETWORK OF SERVICEABLE DISPOSABILITY:
THE INSTRUMENTAL INTERMEDIATION
OF THE AESTHETIC

Turned to the Commons

Intermediation, by its nature, tends to turn us away from the intimate, just so far as others call us out from self and enjoin our participation in the shared between. There are different ways of participation. If the family remains more in touch with the intimate, there are more objectifying participations that might be called *commons*. What is a commons? A commons constitutes a public space of intermediation, wherein a plurality of participants is together, either joining freely or being enjoined, whether through external compulsion, secret suggestion, exploitative use, or persuasive solicitation. The milieu of being, charged equivocally with value, and diversely stressed by the ethical potencies, is the primal ethos; a commons crystallizes a more particular formation of these potencies. A commons shapes its own derived ethos and is marked by its own purposes or common good, by its normalized ways of acting and its standards. Here, intermediation in the public space is more accentuated than the intimate. A more embracing sense of commons can be dominated or overlaid by more particular commons—which contracts the promise of the larger commons. Ethos, in the derived sense, is always a mix or mixing. Thus pure utility is an abstraction, expressing a human self-understanding, the strengths and deficiencies of which are reproduced in the character of the commons. The dominion in our time of this abstraction, which is socially real, merits notice.

Beyond aesthetic show, there comes to be a gap between the intimate/idiot and the space of the commons. The between can be "neutralized" into a particular public domain. So we always find a complex dialectic of trust and distrust in a commons. The others, to some degree, are always strangers. They do not know me as my family does. Their ambiguity as shown is more recalcitrant to my giving of trust. How are we to know if the other is hostile or hospitable? We cannot always be certain. We learn to be wary, on guard. A commons is both a togetherness serving shared purposes and the possibility of hostile otherness. Both are reflected in forms of inter-mediation not attuned to the intimate. The social between appears thus as more objectified and externally determined. Likewise, a more determinate self emerges, insecure and over against the others. This intermediation with the possibly hostile stranger shapes the social milieu in which I come to stand over against the other.

There are a number of resulting configurations of intermediation. There is the process of *education* (formal and informal) that a society offers to its mem-bers by which is effected the transition from the intimacy of family to a more public space of togetherness. This is schooling. What is a school? Education is intermediation: a bringing into the commons of knowing, as well as standard forms of doing. What is a teacher? One who is there for the good of the learner, knowing something the learner has yet to know; a being for the other that draws the other out into the between, the learner becoming self in the drawing out, and moving to the point where the learner can become a teacher and show the way to others. The teacher gives something of what has been given. We find a move from asymmetrical intermediation to more symmetrical, then to asymmetrical again. Always to think in terms of symmetrical intermediation may show a fail-ure of nerve: teacher and learner are not simply on a par. Here asymmetry must suggest less a superiority that looks down on the learner as the opposite—the teacher must be for the other, hence is called to something like an agapeic ser-vice. Moreover, the teaching passes back and forth under a norm that is possessed neither by one or the other. This service of truth is not the service of you or me. We participate in an intermediation in which we must be willing to be servants of a good superior to either of us. The teacher makes a way, a passageway in the between in which the learner can come into knowing. So too the teachers of the good; their teaching is a being good, hence the best learning is done from imita-tion of people already good. They show us the way as made incarnate in the ethos. There also is the process of social teaching that both formally and infor-mally educates one to deal with the possibly hostile other or stranger. This is con-solidated in the formation of ethical civility (see *PO*, Chapter 4).

Serviceable Disposability: On Work and Use

The commons I most want to consider now concerns the web of utility in the world of work. This web, delicate and entangling, is yet an interconnecting, driven by the exchange of instrumental goods and services. A dominion of use-values pervades the ethical milieu and infiltrates all of the levels of ethical inter-mediation. This dominion is unavoidable, but it is not finally sufficient, indeed, it is pernicious when totalized relative to the ethos. In certain respects, I am con-cerned with what in *Being and the Between* I call the community of equivocal desire. How does the web of utility give communal expression to the equivocity of human desire and its exploitation by a dianoetic rationality insofar as the latter tends towards a univocal instrumentalization of the ethos? This tending is itself an ambiguous contraction of human transcending. Its exploitation is proximately directed to the shifting ambiguities of the idiotic and the aesthetic. But it also produces, as we shall see, a mutation of the eudaimonic, transcendental, transcending, and transcendent potencies of the ethical.

The world of work shows the dialectic of trust and distrust in our participation in the social between. At one extreme, shadowed by death, we feel our hungry vulnerability to the elements: we work because we worry. At the other extreme, work expresses our power over ourselves and the elements: we work to take the measure of time and secure our tomorrow. This is reflected in two very basic views of work: as punitive for an original fall, reflecting our subjection to nature's necessities; and as the promise of our independence from these necessities, through our power to subjugate nature (see *PO*, Chapter 4). Mostly we work between these extremes: our subjection to necessity and becoming the subjects of our own doing. In the first, there is a service, but it is not agapeic: its relation to the other is mostly functional, and often servile. This is the functional service of utility. Nevertheless, this can prepare the second possibility, enabling a relative freeing, first into some sovereignty beyond utility and then into the fuller release of agapeic service beyond sovereignty. These latter intermediations will be discussed in subsequent chapters, but a dialectic in our doubleness leads to them. The community of equivocal desire points beyond to the communities of erotic sovereignty and agapeic service.

The human being is *homo faber. Verum et factum convertuntur*: Marx cites Vico, but with vastly different historicist implications (see *BHD*, Chapter 1). The stress on *homo faber* in modernity has a more totalizing tonality and an unprecedented emphasis on human powers. One of my purposes here is to take issue with this. Nor are we immune to something like the gyre of Vico, as below we will see in relation to what I call the karma of the equivocal. But what are some of the ethical ambiguities in the systematic organization of human life as laboring? Work, as we have variously seen, shows the dialectical power to mediate a sense of our free power. As such, it is releasing of the adventure of *enterprising* humans. The tight hearts of entrepreneurs will be warmed. They will swell in the humidity of the "blessings of work." But there are bewitchments here and distractions to enthrall. *Mercury*, the god of trade and tradesmen, also was the king of thieves.[1] Work is an intermediation, not just a self-mediation but an intermediation dominated by use-values, especially in our times. Working and using are

---

1. Latin *Mercurius* is related to *merx* ("goods for sale"), from which derive "commerce" and "merchant." *Mercari*, meaning "to trade," is the source of words such as "market" and "merchandise."

inseparable. But what is using? How does something become useful? And if the useless is what is beyond utility, is it thus no good? What form of intermediation constitutes use?

Using, like work, entails an intermediation that determines other-being, in its potentiality in the between, as an object or a resource we can appropriate, thereby turning the promise of its being for itself into its being for us. We make it desirable by changing its otherness into a form serviceable to our desire and will. To use is to respect otherness and not to respect it. Respect: otherness has to be first granted and appraised in its potentiality in order for its promise to be appropriated. Not respect: its very otherness as other is subverted by the dynamic of using, which alters its being for itself into its being for us. We seize its promise and realize it not for itself but for ourselves. If other being cannot be so seized, it seems useless. Thus use and *serviceability* go together. Some things are spontaneously useful: they serve one's desire without intervention. Other things do not serve like this. They must be dominated to be made serviceable. I must coax or force them into rapport with my desire and will. They are to be *made* useful; I must *make them* serviceable. Work makes them thus serviceable, that is, work makes them work, places their own being at work (their *ergon*, or *energeia*) at our disposal. Use works the promise of beings into what I call their *serviceable disposability*.

Interestingly, the language of serving crops up in all of its equivocity: the servile and serviceable, and service beyond use. Clearly some things must be forced into service and made useful; but this necessity is deceptive, since ruthless exploitation is the friend of forced service. The elemental necessity of making serviceable, taken to an extreme, produces tyranny over others and the earth. Beings become disposable. The *artes serviles*, so to say, produce the servility of other-being, as we assert the use of all other-being for us. I am not saying this tyranny is necessitated. This tyranny is the temptation of freedom. Thus to instrumentalize all being is to degrade the ethos to a milieu of resources ripe for our plucking. Were work exhausted by this, we could hardly evade ethical nihilism.[2]

The inherent dynamic of using must involve some loss of mindfulness of the more intimate sources of ethical intermediation, for this dynamic is *necessarily extroverted* onto objectified externality. This means not only the objectification of things as resources for us, it tends also towards the reduction of persons to objectified resources, consumers, or producers. Persons too become defined in their serviceable disposability. The between as ethos becomes a network of instrumentalized relations, made possible by the quasi-univocalization of things and per-

---

2. Husbandry of the earth, or its midwifery, is more metaxological. In Greek, "economics" contains reference to the order of the home or house (Aristotle). Economics still intermediates the intimate, but from a great anonymous distance. Yet the husbandry of the earth haunts even rapacious times. Ecological discernment intermediates a renewed ethics of husbanding.

sons in interplay. The between is open to the reign of an instrumentalized exteriority. And the gap of intimate and exterior does not mean that the intimate is not exploited. Rather, the exploitation must be always less than what the sources of freedom in the intimate require. There is a fall of intermediation into a kind of instrumentalized bondage: a "being together," in one sense, community, in another sense, not. This "being together" is always in danger of falling out of inherent relation, in relation itself. Under the dominion of serviceable disposability, this is impossible to avoid. How respond? Not in terms of any simplistic nostalgia or return to simple innocence or intimacy—our need is for fuller ethical intermediation. Yet, as this falls more into the anonymities of the univocally instrumental, "value" takes on characteristics of objectified determination, to the exclusion of the deeper sources.

We find, for instance, a kind of dianoetic exploitation of the aesthetic and the intimate (as in the economism of consumer capitalism). Also, the emergence of a claim to property comes with this objectification. The paradox here is that though property may be said to be private, it is necessarily from the start turned away from the private, in the sense of the intimate. Private property emerges in a *turn to the public* and is itself always determined in a public domain (by ownership laws, deeds, contracts, and the like; money too is always social—a reserved power of social intermediation). The public exteriority of private property determines a will to security, as property itself emerges from a will to secure oneself and one's own in the vagaries of externality. The dominion of serviceable disposability creates, ironically, a clinging to things. Without them, we fear we are nothing.

The fetishism of property is thus very basic. It is necessitated by an instrumental turn from the idiot/inner to the public as the appropriation of the thereness of other-being in the between. What was other turns into "mine," because I have taken it, taken it to myself. (When Locke says, in *Two Treatises*, Bk. II, Ch. V: "Every man has a property in his own person," he seems relatively innocent of these turnings.) Property is a self-mediation that in owning the other falls out of intimacy with the more primal intermediation. *Homo economicus, homo faber*, must be over against the other. Inevitably, to some degree, intermediation is overtaken by a will to self-mediation through the other, but this "takeover" can never be absolutely successful, since it is inherently *dependent on the other*. Not surprisingly, much economic intermediation tends to mask the exploitative nature of this dependency.

Consider the specialization and division of labor as showing an unfolding of the dynamic of using. Using is more effective if work is more efficiently apportioned. If the efficient exploitation of effective power is our *raison d'être*, this will seem self-evident, indeed, hailed as inevitable. What if this inevitability is dominated by an instrumental univocalization? The division serving the efficiency of human power proves divisive of human being. As it enables, it also disables. This is especially so if all functions are so narrowed as to meet a univocal measure of standard manipulability. The plurivocal promise of humans is contracted into a specific function. Their work is their whole, but this whole is lacking in whole-ness. This instrumental univocalization breaks down the flow of time into manipulable units; then time-managed functioning is geared to the quantified reconstruction of time, with the view to control, to pressure the worker into being more productive. The resulting growth in effective power also effectively hides the imposition of chains. The person is not whipped by a lash. The discipline of efficiency is enough to stress the worker to perform in terms of a predetermined, univocal grid of productive measure. The technique of efficient management shows the same univocalization. It will be called "rationalization," but the agents of "rationalization" do not themselves like to be "rationalized." How "rational" when others are "downsized," how outrageous, how "irrational," when I am!

The fall out of the more intimate sources of ethical intermediation means that the powers of the anonymous grow. Massification and homogenization are built into an unrestrained logic of use. The medievals distinguished between the *bonum honestum* and the *bonum utile*. Now, however, it seems literally that *the use-ful is not fully honest*. The dishonesty of use is its reduction of integral good, whether of self or other. An unqualified dynamic of use deprives beings of any value of their own. There is no inherent value; all value is "for self." The human self too has finally no inherent value. The self is then a means for other selves, or for itself. Each is alien to itself and the other.

Once again, as we make things as useful for us, we also are tempted to *make other human beings into the useful*. Their being too is their serviceable dis-posability. The temptation of use is dominion, subjection, and slavery. Of course, the using of other humans is different from the using of things, even though others are treated as things. Humans as other to us are centers of self-mediating power that are potentially free, free indeed to use others, to enslave others, if the occasion arises. The asymmetry in the use of things is not the same asymmetry in the use of other humans. Humans are not ethically dis-posable. The latter asymmetry of use coexists always with a potential symme-try, or the promise of it. But if we insist on the asymmetry of this use, it must be enforced in a redoubled way. It follows that the potential for ethical vio-lence in this intermediation of using another is more intensive and more extensive than first appears.

Many of the vices are connected to an unqualified dynamic of using. *Pride*: to make all others serve me, while I serve none; the others are serviceable, I am to be served, thus I am above the others in a relation of subordination, looking down on them. *Vanity*: the other is to be used always as my mirror, reflecting back my self-esteem, as I insist on appearing good in the eyes of others. *Envy*: the other has something I cannot use and call my own. Envy is the first curl of hatred, malice: I cannot subject the other, and my freedom comes to abhor that indomitable freedom in another. *Greed*, covetousness: the other has what I want; I want it only because I do not have it. I profit—at the expense of others. In fact,

I cannot profit at all without the other. My using is always in debt, a debt never acknowledged, a debt hated for giving the lie to my superiority.

One must say that there can be a *totalizing effect* in the dynamic of using, if under the dominion of serviceable disposability and not qualified by discernment of ethical worth beyond use. Then the *ethos as a whole* is reconfigured, and all of the potencies of the ethical are redeployed as resources of use. The ethos becomes exploited for purposes of our satisfaction as units of effective power, whether conceived of in terms of production, management, or consumption. True, we cannot survive or prosper without use and exploitation in some regard. The intermediation of the good *must include* the reconfiguration of the ethos, so that its being there as good offers itself or is remade into its being good for us. We also need an ethical therapy for *pleonexia*, the greed for "more," as Plato saw, to give measure to the equivocal limitlessness of our desire. The crucial matter is whether there are limits to this reconfiguration, limits inherent in the ethos and the given promise it offers us. Such limits would check any proclivity to extend limitlessly the range of this reconfiguration.

There are such limits, both inherent and called for, that demand *ethical qualification* of the dynamic of using. But first I must look more closely at the reconfiguration. The will to use the between objectifies it in our own image, makes beings within it serviceable and disposable, mirrors our more functional desires, produces an equivocal mixing of power and justice, and thus risks the subordination of justice to power. The web of use produces effects in all of the ethical potencies. What are these effects?

The Reconfigured Ethos under the Dominion of Serviceable Disposability

First consideration: What will we call the reconfiguration of the *idiotic*? Let us call it *the invasion of privacy*. At this level, our sense of *the proper* is fostered. This is tied to property and "mineness," but here as contracted into itself by the spirit of a utilizing univocity. Of course, a sense of what is proper to me is inextirpable, but a certain using univocalization can feed the spirit of a secret hatred. For the other as exploitable is always a possible enemy; so one must keep on guard; and if the other is for me, the law of social life is distrust; one must beware, be ready to fight. Each person as a unit of predatory power becomes also a cell of aloneness. Smile, but be sure to carry a big stick.

A particular formation of *private* and *public* goes with this. Perhaps this also reflects modernity's dominant ontology: "objectivity" out-there, neutral, universal, subject to univocalization, *mathesis*, calculation; "subjectivity" in here, emotive, merely personal, subject to incalculable variability, not rational in any hard way, though easily manipulable with the right tools. "Privacy" is the sphere of the second, "public" the sphere of the first. These two are dualized. The commons is effected by such a "publication" of social life. The "private" is allowed in its psychological idiosyncrasy, but the "public" is subject to rule, procedure, and rational debate.

Instance: the privatization of religion. Clearly, religious fervor can produce war and much madness. To inoculate ourselves against this, we relegate religion to a subjective preference. If everyone has freedom of religious belief, this is a private matter and should be kept out of public discourse—all in the interest of tolerance. Sometimes this remarkable tolerance shows remarkable intolerance. One is allowed religious freedom on the condition of its emasculation in public discourse.[3]

Private and public lives reshape themselves coherently with serviceable disposability within the web of utility. Each person is a private, autonomous unit of desire and effective power, entering relations as a means to satisfactions. Society is a public market, where buying and selling are the essential observances, enabling satisfactions. Each individual is a buyer and seller: of himself or herself as a resource or commodity; of others and things as resources and commodities. Of course, if there is no self-mediation without social intermediation, this dualism of "public" and "private" cannot be maintained. For each is always complicit with the other, and public space itself effects the idiocy of being.

Does not Nietzsche's remark about the anarchy of the instincts have some point? Is there something hollow here, a corruption of the intimate? No seed of genuine greatness can be sown in the small souls of the last men. We are lacking a sense of otherness that would make us cast our glance beyond. Our consuming society offers us the social cultivation of our narcissistic impulses. It makes a culture of self-realization into one of the self-absorption of "wounded children." It is a nursery of various operas of complaint, complete with soaring arias to our narcissism that, now sung, seem to promise finally to make us "comfortable." Even so, the will to "feel good" balloons into a monstrous system in which elemental emotional needs are subject to massive social technique. Such a society is

---

3. See Locke's *Two Treatises*. Of course, Locke's celebrated tolerance did not extend to atheists and Catholics. While not irreligious, the framers of the U.S. Constitution produced results that were ambiguous concerning the subordination of religion to political order. The American Founding Fathers rightly sought to avoid the religious wars of Europe. The polity facilitates liberty and the pursuit of happiness. Commerce and capitalism mediate new forms of civic religion. Tolerant liberals can get hot under their rational collars about the distinction of secular reasons (real reasons) and religious reasons (unreal reasons). Does reason discriminate between secular and religious reasons, if both are reasons? Yes, I do tolerate you, but your reasons must be reasons, the right kind. Still not satisfied? Very well, let religion be another interest group among others, say, a "lobbying group" for "values." Very well, religion might even come in useful when public order seems a little shaky. Something is rotten in the state of Denmark? Then call in the "values experts"! Let us have a values workshop! Why, then, do you look at me with pity?

just this side of hysteria. One suspects that some would keep us on the verge of hysteria; all the easier to stampede us in a desired direction, when that proves profitable. Meanwhile, we feel that we are "following our dream," being faithful to our "bliss." We are being led by the nose.

I do not say we are being secretly ripened for authoritarian dominances, but my memory is long enough to prevent worry from sleeping. What if things were to become too pinched for covetous powers? Will a big daddy put a bit of stick around, not use the whip because it will be enough just to show it, and we will all cry out for redemption? Come now, this is to have the shakes from a fevered imagination. And yet, odd propagandas for war do arise, directed at the most intimate, idiotic level, and we often find this out too late. Politicians and advertisers try to pitch their message here—"subliminally," they say. Hypnotize them, send them into a trance, as the Musak soothes their frayed nerves. It is better to be bewitched gently, with no offense to our comfort levels. Therapists, managers, and bureaucrats (with a bow to MacIntyre) put their diverse skills to work on the sources of our communal narcissisms, coaching us well in the safeties of adaptation. What is advertising now? The smokeless opium of the masses.[4]

The thesis is sometimes proposed that in modernity the nation-state was the most comprehensive social institution (see Hegel, among many others); but now, in "postmodernity," we are said to witness the decay of the authority of the nation-state, as it is superseded by the power of anonymous global corporations and transnational markets that exceed the regulation of even the most powerful state. What are the principles governing these corporations? In fact, they are not essentially different than those denominated under the notion of serviceable disposability, and which have had vigorous lives long before the advent of "post-modernity." The major ones would include, first, that the human being is a unit of power or resource; second, that desire is exploitative and even predatory, if the chance arrives; self-interest is the essential value; third, that rationality is self-interested calculation; fourth, that efficiency is perhaps the highest value; fifth, that the purpose of being together in society is product (GNP), and perhaps consuming;[5]

---

4. Against Marx: Religion is the hope of a freedom that is not sucked into this bewitchment. If there is a transcendent good, one cannot forget that everything in the network of serviceable disposability has a relativity and equivocity that is potentially corrupting.

5. See Rousseau, *The First and Second Discourses* (New York: St. Martin's Press, 1964): "Ancient politicians incessantly talked about morals and virtue, those of our time talk only of business and money. . . . They evaluate men like herds of cattle. According to them a man is worth no more to the State than the value of his domestic consumption" (First Discourse, 51). A person interviewed in Hong Kong (before the British left) said: "You in the West honor human rights; we in Hong Kong honor the economic boom!" The economic boom did not honor them; now a bust, they have their (lower) price, but what dignity?

sixth, that consuming may be for the *demos*, but there are the "captains of industry," as they used to be called—a professional elite of technicians, cybernets, managers, economists, social scientists, and the like. The "elite" constitutes a problem, even in a "positive" age, as Comte, among others, realized, but these seem to be like the Platonic guardians, but without Platonic wisdom.

Such views hardly get to the self-mediation of the good, for how conceive of erotic sovereignty, and agapeic service, if we are bewitched by the univocal exploitation of the equivocal? This is not even Hegel's civil society—for there grew the notion of *civil service*. There is no civil service of the global corporation. This is a self-moving quasi-machine, smiling everywhere with a thousand faces of advertising, yet for all that "presence," faceless and nowhere. Why moan that people retreat to the private, the idiotic, in face of this faceless quasi-machine? We have thought of that too. For this also is exploited by the quasi-machine: not right now to stir up war, but to make people anxious/comfortable in their cocoons, comfortable through the products they must anxiously purchase to feel comfortable. Their "privacy" serves the quasi-machine, even as they feel themselves free of it. For the power of this dominion of serviceable disposability is sustained by the exploitation of the equivocal: as in the use of ads, TV and so on, to produce desires in humans, in order next to reassure with the product that must then be bought. This is an omnivorous equivocity, except for the univocal calculators who have the "expertise" to manipulate the equivocity in others. We seem to be inside a global leviathan, devoured into its belly, as we ourselves devour there.

Why is the exploitation here often directed to the young? Because their idiocy is susceptible to suggestion, that is, to bewitchment. We pander to their plasticity, now in its idealism, now in its insecurity, now in its rebelliousness. Do we adults escape? We are earnestly counseled to listen to our feelings, but are we being slyly *weaned backwards*—into a new infantilism? Someone is always selling dreams, but the seller stays cold. Cool calculation is needed to sell hot desire, and sell through the simulacrum of hot desire. This dominion of serviceable disposability is quintessentially one of bewitchments. Children are made into changelings. But who are the witches? Among others, the ad men, and those who reckon before and after, and who can squeal "Wonderful!" at the drop of a hat. But the squeal too is cold.

Second consideration: How might we describe the reconfiguration of the *aesthetic*? Let us speak of *the exploitation of superfluous show*. For at the level of the aesthetic, we find less the show of the good and more obsession with externalities, with honors and being recognized, with appearances and the exploitation of appearances, sometimes to deceive, sometimes to sell. Riches seduce us to deference. One's position is the color of the ribbon one is permitted to wear. Dress is social intermediation. To be a celebrity becomes the highest apotheosis of the aesthetic, corrupting even those whose excellences are higher, such as artists who come to love the limelight of the chatter shows.

Just as the principle of thrift produces superfluities, the principle of use produces sheer uselessness. So too the network of utility makes us aesthetically obsessed with the body beautiful. We work on our bodies, with an earnestness devoid of the light touch of real aesthetic pleasure. We look into the mirror and mournfully see our ugly sister, the *body obese*. What is the society of the *body beautiful*? The thin twin of the obese society.

We also find the exploitation of sex here in such corruptions of intermediation as pornography (the "sex industry"—did you say *industry*?). This goes one step further than advertising's objectification of the body for its use in selling. It exploits the most intimate. In the process of seeking to show its hiddenness, it loses the intimacy of the intimate. Its objectifying use of the intimate debases the intimate, just in its showing of the intimate.

The calculative exploitation of the body and body parts as objects is not confined to their disposability for aesthetic pleasure; there also is trade in body parts for transplants; serviceable disposability makes one lung of a man from a poor country a resource to be consumed by another from a rich country, with the usual cohort of agents of disposability—the middlemen—in between.

Third consideration: How does it look in relation to the *dianoetic*? We worry that there is one law for the powerful, another law for the others. Have laws become merely tools for enforcing a peace? Laws are necessarily instruments of power, whose justified purpose is to stand as bulwarks against civil war. Sometimes, of course, they add to injustice. Laws are necessary but not always necessarily just. Rulers may need to bend evil towards the good. I think a major expression of the reconfiguration of the ethos is the change in natural law with Hobbes and other early moderns. This entails a continuation of the definition of beings and their good in terms of the efficiency of their being units of productive, predatory power. Law, at bottom, is then identical to the power one can command. This is not the same as pre-modern natural law, where there is a sense of the reasonable good and of justice more primal than the expression of power: the expression of power is to be judged in the light of this more primal good. Now natural right and the expression of power are coeval: a putative right, impotent with regard to its own self-empowerment, is not properly a right at all. If you say we have natural rights by virtue of our human nature, very well. But if our nature is what it is in virtue of being a unit of effective power, there is no right without its corresponding power to effect its claim. Law, then, is inseparable from power, but power here is taken to be the more basic name of the natural condition. Relative to effective power, justice will inevitably be reconfigured as an artificial construct, such as a contract. There are no laws "moral" or "political" in "nature." The justice of law becomes relative to the distribution of effective power(s) in the web of use, the worldly name for effective worldly power.

What then? In the web of using, the rules themselves are there for effective exploitation. They are the legal money of serviceable disposability. Money, as a currency of exchange value, will greatly ease the intermediation of exploitation. Marx has an insightful and cutting essay on the inverting power of money relative to nature: money will turn ugliness into beauty, age into youth, contempt into deference. It is the inverted world that follows from its lordship of the network of social intermediations. Money can buy one the justice of law. The best lawyers are sometimes paid the most by the most successful criminals. The inversion is the collusion of crime and justice in a venture that profits both. Even Marx himself has become a fashionable commodity: after the fall of communism, *The Communist Manifesto* is reissued, but now as a chic fashion statement, as an accessory to style.

Am I missing something? Am I missing something, when I see in all of this the social exploitation of the *equivocity* of use-dominated intermediation? When I wonder if the truth of the equivocity is the voracity of the powerful and rich who, from a distance, are predators on the weaker and the poor? Am I missing something, when social institutions will protect the gains of that voracity, while ostensibly giving the victims the protection of the law? When justice increases the oppression of the many; while the protests of the subjugated are treated as treasons by those who oppress? Justice must homogenize, yes, treat all as the same, reduce the many to the same, to almost nothings. The many too, if not serviceable, are disposable.

Fourth consideration: What shall we say of the *transcendental* potency? It becomes hard to avoid the suspicion that, let me be delicate, *the hand washes the hand*! There can be no unconditional claim in the reconfiguration if the norm of serviceable disposability reigns. We need contracts not only because we fear others will renege on their promise and exploit our trust, but because deep down we are made to think that everything has its price, and nothing its dignity. (Hobbes prided himself on his shocking superiority: the worth of a man is, as with all other things, his price. I sigh and say: Not back to Kant!; but come back Kant!) Everyone is for sale, if only the deal is right. Everything can be arranged; even as misarrangement loudly shouts out at us here. Fear not, protocols will protect us from the harshness of honesty. Euphemism will allow us indulgence in insincere sentiment. My left hand strokes the face of philanthropy, while my right hand is deep in my neighbor's pocket.

Is this the unapologetic reign of what, for Aristotle, is the least excellent, albeit necessary, form of friendship: the friendship of utility? We have something in common, but it is not ourselves, but how we can serve our mutual self-interests. We are serving ourselves in seeming to serve the other. Or rather, the point of the friendship is for the other to serve me; but I can contract his service only on condition of offering him service in exchange. To me he is as nothing, as is his friendship, without that *quid pro quo*. The hand washes the hand. These hands need frequent washing, as their greasy palms are frequently crossed. They lack something of the integrity to purge themselves without the sticky grip of another self-serving hand. The sticky grip does not wash, finally.

Studied silence about my duties and responsibilities will match strong words about my rights. Moral earnestness may mask my self-assertive will to success in the agon. But my right means—I am to be noted, I am to be taken care of; the devil take the others, until I am taken care of. "I have my rights" means "To hell with you." The other shouts back: "I have my rights," meaning "To hell with you too." We balance each other in our asserted lack, and a simulated peace intervenes. An ethics of agapeic generosity will have to filter into hearts, and people become less noisy about themselves, for the claim of the other to be heard. This is true also of hearing ourselves, as an integrity of dignity beyond price.

Fifth consideration: What of the reconfigured eudaimonism of the ethical? We are converted to *the religion of shopping*. Shall we call it a "preferential option for the rich"? What is happiness here? It is the happiness of having; and of having more and more. The rush for acquisition stirs up a storm dust of wanting, but when the dust comes to rest, what happiness is there in the desert of possessions? Hard to say. Is it that oasis on the horizon, or is it a mirage? Do we find it there, in the temple of convenience of the religion of shopping?

If advertising is the opium of the masses, shopping is its ritual ecstasy. What is a shop? A place where you can buy things, to be sure. What strange source then makes the shopping spellbinding? Surely gods are near. Who now thinks of the thrifty shopkeeper balancing his or her accounts, content with the frugal "blessings of work"? Now we hear of "a shopper's paradise." (My oh my, this is too much for me.) This heaven cannot wait. A bower of bliss where I eat and eat, sweets, without cease. Blessedness: buying without care, buying beyond care. Not just sweets, but everything and anything. Shops, shoppers, shopkeepers, suppliers, credit cards, consumers, shopping by mail, by internet, by phone . . . for what we do not need—truly a religious passion. This divine madness reaches a crescendo in Christmas shopping. A divine coming is announced—only seventy-five more shopping days until the glad day! To see those precious days slip by, what sorrow, what grief! What madness! Most human beings worry about their next meal. They get by from hand to mouth—when they get by at all.

Enough. The dominion of serviceable disposability midwives the nativity of this artificial man ("Artificial Man"—Hobbes's name for the political state): the product of his own work; driven by artificial desires; always busy, always anxious, fearful that he is not getting something important someone else is enjoying; lacking in repose, stressed from Monday to Friday, and alternatively lethargic and hyperactive over the weekend; the lassitude being no different from the excess of stress; the hyperactivity no different to the enervation; envious of the rich and famous; fearful of his children who despise him anyway; ingratiating to his bosses, cold to his subordinates, fawning in the company of celebrity; rushing, rushing, everywhere and nowhere; so much to do that the point of doing it gets lost along the way; friends are casual, for there is no time, and deeper intimacy is time consuming; it is easier to be entertained; so busy with the business of life that one is deprived of life; so demanding of its pleasure that nothing pleases one; and the acme of self-fulfillment a wretchedness so absorbed in itself it does not know its own misery; so lost in itself, it is lost to itself.

Sixth consideration: How does serviceable disposability reconfigure the meaning of *transcending*? Our self-surpassing becomes nothing but surpassing, and so a *surpassing of nothing to nothing*. Remember that the web of utility is produced out of the common energy of transcending, shaping itself and being shaped in instrumental intermediation. Infiltrating all of this shaping is the dream of becoming masters and possessors of nature. Realizing the dream depends on stripping down the givenness of the ethos, making it ready for exploitation, stripping down humans also into resource material or units of productive power. A reconfigured ethos of serviceable disposability then builds up more and more complex conglomerations of such units of power. At bottom, the project is very simple, but it grows into a grandiose monster. We end in artificial cities, creating monstrous humans that prey on each other as exotic beasts. We flee nature innocent, and end in a society red in tooth and claw, even when no blood is drawn.

Transcending is inseparable from the *ideal*, and the meaning of that is inseparable from sovereignty and service. I will come to these more fully. And here? Here we are jaundiced by a self-proclaimed realism that pooh-poohs ideals as empty fantasies, suitable for a preacher's edification but incredible in the realistic school of hard knocks. In that school, we are taught the bottom line, the cunning that knows the tissue of human hearts to be self-interest first and last, that nothing lasting is built from hope but only from profit and cash flow. Who will deny this reality? But to affirm this reality and deny the ideal is to contract the reality to less than what it really is. Human reality is plurivocal.[6] One of the strains runs, as here, to a more reductive univocity, yet threaded through the whole reality is the exigence of the ideal. For the transcendental potency of the ethical, and more dynamically, its transcending potency, reveal our restlessness for the best: having done good, one wants to do better, indeed, the best. One cannot define the best in terms of what counts for real in the school of hard knocks. The best serves a higher excellence than serviceable disposability. There is a higher commons. Our desire is love of excellences—qualitative consummations of essential human powers, and recognized in common. These are beyond any calculative instrumentalism. Excellences are sought in a movement of transcending; they are ends; and

---

6. How evident, even in exploitation! There is the exploitation of the more unstated self-surpassing, and not just sexual eros, as in pornography, but in politics, in power, in honor, in winning, and in dominance of others; markets have their own madness; James Stewart likened the "market" to an agon and playful war; this is to collapse erotic sovereignty into the web of serviceable disposability.

the means to them, our passage towards them, is not itself an instrumentality merely; the passage of transcending itself is suffused with the character of excellence, imbued with the excellence of the consummation sought. As their seeking is sometimes reckless, their attainment is beyond reckoning. The excellences ask discipline without the guarantee of a payoff. They solicit a love of the good beyond all instrumentalizing. As ideals they are useless, and yet they are most useful. They give honor and glory to a life, and the majesty of a freedom beyond utility. They reveal our ethical actuality as an incarnate ideal.

From the idiotic to the transcendent, a higher exigence is effective in every instrumentalization of serviceable disposability. Devoid of fulfilling excellences, the instrumentalization impoverishes the material it puts to use. Its use amounts to abuse. True use is not the abuse that sees nothing but use. True use sees beyond use. It is in love with the ideal, not with the reduced real. Its love is its participation in a higher commons. It is not easy to communicate this to prisoners of the reduced real. They claim the obvious is on their side. This is the obviousness to the worm of the earth on which it crawls. It is not the obviousness to the eagle of the sky that is the element of its flight. It is obviousness as perspective absolutized, not perspective expanded to do justice to the ethos.

Works of art, works of love, works of mercy point to the transcendence of the instrumental within the instrumental itself. This work can reach out to the whole realm of *culture* in which the human being is shaped as artistic, as religious, as philosophical. Works of art, of religion, of creative imagination, of speculative thought transform the work of serviceable disposability from within. Our commons is never an economy simply but always a mixing of many commons. Pure utility makes no sense, since by our cultivating nature the useful is adorned from the origin, lifting its possibility to higher forms of self-mediation and social intermediation. Art, religion, and philosophy are rupturing and transforming ways of being mindful in tension with the instrumental mindfulness of serviceable disposability. *Poiesis, mythos,* and *logos* transform *pragmata.*[7]

---

7. Ideology is bound up with the equivocities of ethical intermediation but is not always a manipulating superstructure of masked power. A system of "ideological" images can be so thoroughly appropriated, so proper, that it constitutes the second nature of the people. It is not a conspiracy to keep them subjugated; it is what they are, and what by their lives they consent to be. What they are may entail falling under the bewitchment of the dominant images; but the critics of ideology may be spellbound by a different bewitchment. How helpful is the idea of narrative identity? Telling our stories makes us what we are. Of course, this is true. But I cannot suppress the thought that narrative identity fits for certain professors as the glove fits the hand. The professor spends a lot of time reading books and thinks, audaciously, what if life is like a book or reading books? Ergo, I am not cut off from life in my study; I am life's true reader. Voila! There goes the difference of the professor and life. But life is not just stories, though it contains stories; there is more: suffer-

The bewitching power of the web of utility is such that the reverse now happens in the "culture industry." The artwork is assimilated to a commodity. We obliterate the distinction between the creation of artworks and the production of commodities. Art's power to release human self-transcending is redirected back from transcendence into the instrumental circuit of utilitarian exchange. The higher freedom is made servile to lower exploitation. Hence the position of *strangeness (bios xenikos,* Aristotle) of the genuine artist, or philosopher, or religious person relative to the network of instrumental values. (Alas, artists, philosophers, and religious people also fall under the spell of the bewitchment.) The totalizing of serviceable disposability devours forms of worth that are beyond instrumentalizing, and makes it increasingly difficult for other freedoms to stand against this devouring. The network multiplies images that become unanchored from any original. And this "postmodern" intermediation does not mediate humans back to themselves; it scatters them abroad into the network in an endless production of all absorbing images, which finally turn out to be images of *nothing.* We absolutize the means. Means to what? Perhaps first for themselves. But then, in the end, the means to nothing. Serviceable finally for nothing. The images are disposable, for we have already disposed of originals. The "original" of the "postmodern" network of images is its despair and flight from despair, and the despair that is its flight, and the future of the flight.

Seventh consideration: Does the reconfiguration twist the truth of *transcendence itself*? Suppose we answer: Give to Caesar the things that are Caesar's, and to God the things that are God's. A fine answer, indeed. Yet we can so give *that* answer that the religious is *denied* its proper truth. Where religion insists on persisting, the eye of use will quickly spy its expedience for social obedience. It will be made to serve as an ideal tool for those who oversee the web (consult Machiavelli, Hobbes, Spinoza, among many). Its value is less its own value as its value in the services of reigning powers. It too is serviceable and disposable. Its edifying stories shape the ethos as a commons of submission, overtly to the divine, de facto to those now in charge.[8]

---

ing, whose most radical intimacy has no story; horror that cannot be told; joys that would be besmirched were one to make them material for stories, as some writers besmirch their art, in the holy name of art.

8. One might see a certain univocalizing trend even in the modern claim of *sola scriptura*: ostensibly freeing biblical interpretation from heteronomous powers (alias, Rome), but effectively being hard to distinguish from a kind of Spinozistic enjoinment of the many's submission to the interpretation of the sovereign, as the one with power to subdue the anarchy of interpretations and the social turmoil it occasions. Spinoza's hermeneutics of interpreting scripture only through scripture is not unlike the *sola scriptura*, though the intent is the evaporation of all claims of a transcendent God, and the redefinition of the

We pay sincere respects to the spirit of enterprise, and in reverent moments of economic excelling we bend the knee at the shrine of man the worker, the businessman, the organizer, the master of the world. We remember the money-changers were once driven from the temple, but wink in the knowledge that the money-changers are an enterprising lot. They are back, will always come back, in droves, and see there is good money even in religion. How have the expelled returned, and there hardly seems a temple anymore from which they might be asked to leave again, or into which we might turn for sanctuary from the dominion of serviceable disposability. When there is no temple we know the ethos has been overlaid and groans under the burden.

Not only can reigning powers instrumentalize religion, religions can collude with such powers, deriving benefit for their own will to power. In some regard, this is true of all religions insofar as they are well established as communal intermediations. There can be the work of genuine intermediations in the complex interplays of politics and religion. The opening to the transcendent can transform the ideal of community and the reign of power. The ruler may bow before none human, but in sight of eternity, may tremble with terror. Power is made more chaste by such holy terror.

Conversely, the reigning powers can be partners in a social bewitchment in which the transcendent good is made an idol of the state or the people: our god, our good. There is no otherness to this god or the good, for it is our property. The dominion of serviceable disposability reaches out to transcendence, but in embracing God, it makes God its god. Its god serves the self-mediation of the instrumental commons, does not open transcending towards divine otherness, does not shock humans into the sacred sobriety that knows it is not the good.

Great violence follows from making God one's god, as we march off to war, bearing before us a mounted idol. One cannot always point this out without danger, for the spirit of a bewitchment has entered into the people, and that spirit will brook no opposition. All counsel otherwise is perceived to place one on the opposite side, the side of the enemy. Speak out, and you will be hacked to pieces.

---

sacred in terms of its socially useful function of soliciting "piety" or expedient submission. Does a univocalizing mind (one tilted to faith, the other to *ratio*) govern both, leading both to not dissimilar ends? (I think of Luther's docility before the reigning powers in relation to the uprising of the peasants.) Spinoza's view is dominated by a rationalistic version of the community of erotic sovereignty, and for a number of reasons, including his view of *conatus*, and a deficit in properly thinking agapeic community. Inevitably, politics and religion become skewed in a certain direction. Religion may seem socially "useful," but its withering away does not bring the sunrise of enlightenment but the shadow of ethical nihilism. And even then, at that extreme, we might hear once again appeals for "religion," and again too in terms of its socially useful function. The appeal, put in those terms, is part of the problem, and it shows itself not to understand the problem.

We give to Caesar the things that are Caesar's and to God the things that are God's. But now there is no god but Caesar, hence we righteously give all to Caesar, to god. Effectively, this is to be under tyranny, the rule of power identifying itself with justice, and where there is no justice but such as this exercise of power determines. This tyranny is the retraction of ethical intermediation into the dominant will of the reigning power, before whom all others bow in secular adoration. This Leviathan is a mortal god. In peculiar ways, I agree with Hobbes about this terrestrial god, but it is a monster. Hobbes asks us to bend the knee, but we must not adore. We are bewitched by a false double of God, but who will break the bewitchment?

Beyond Serviceable Disposability and the Karma of the Ethos

Where do we go from here? As we will see, there are ethical intermediations of sovereignty and service beyond utility that call for works beyond use—works of art, of love, indeed, works of mercy whose promise is smothered by the dominion of serviceable disposability. This promise needs redemption. Yet there are recalcitrances to the above reconfigurations. All of the potencies of the ethical limit the reconfiguration sought by an unqualified dynamics of using. There are limits, both inherent and solicited. The first limits were always surmised by mindful people, even if they could never be made univocally self-evident: respect for the possibilities of life as not subject to our utilization, indeed, presupposed for our use to be at all possible, whether in nature, in human nature, or in power neither human nor natural, yet ingredient in the karma of the ethos. What we have denied as inherent hits back at us when our reconfiguration of the ethos passes beyond a certain measure of responsibility.

The idiotic recalcitrance: Instrumental value is always subtended by a more basic sense of intrinsic value. Though often repressed or stifled, this cannot finally be denied. It often is exploited, thus distorted, and yet then it returns to surpass once again the instrumentalization, and in the instrumentalization itself. It is the intermediation at work from the beginning whose promise does not disappear, because it has not been acknowledged or respected.[9] In any commons, it

---

9. Rousseau tends to give a certain privilege to the idiotic and aesthetic potencies (calling them "nature") while divorcing them from the other ethical potencies (which then become subsequent sources of moral corruption). See his *Second Discourse*, 95–96: "I believe I perceive in it [the soul] two principles anterior to reason, of which one interests us ardently in our well-being and our self-preservation, and the other inspires in us a natural repugnance to see any sensitive being perish or suffer, principally our fellow men. It is from the conjunction and combination that our mind is able to make of these two principles, without the necessity of introducing that of sociability, that all the rules of natural right appear to

is impossible to sustain the instrumentalizing in an absolute way. In the intimacy of being, a more inherent community of being is at work from the origin. Thus, for instance, while pursuing the selfishness of instrumental self-mediation, people can unwittingly *serve*, serve the intermediation of the more basic community. How is this? Because the other, from the start, is *before* self-mediation: an incognito intermediation grounds self-mediation. Its continued noninstrumental work serves to draw together a pluralism of egotisms. As Socrates suggests in the *Republic*, among a band of thieves, honor and justice are necessary if they are to be effective thieves. A more primitive harmony of community must be presupposed. No complete denial of the *inter* is possible.

What of war? Auschwitz? Here we have a diabolic mimicry of an order of togetherness. Evil involves the turn back into the idiocy that strikes at the intermediation in the most intimate of intimacies: destruction of God in the soul. Evil is killing the egg of love in the nest, lest it grow. But love has already grown and allowed the turn back. Evil lives by the forbearance of the good.

The aesthetic recalcitrance: Our own bodies are not our own. We cannot use them as we will, not only because there are biological limits to be respected, but because our being as incarnate is given to itself to be, before it can claim itself as for itself. Our body is the limit to property in what is most considered the basis of property. It opens us to the presupposed aesthetic givenness of incarnation, as gift of the power to be.

The point might be explored in many directions, for instance, relative to the reserves of sexuality, or their brutal violation. If the bodies that are our own are not our own, the meaning of incarnate freedom cannot be seized in terms of autonomy. The pervasive exploitation of the sexualized body in consumer societies is exposed in its irreverence for the body it ostensibly celebrates. More often than not, we are titillated into aesthetic corruption.

Consider something that seems more innocuous—the forms of *politeness*. These concern the aesthetic show of the ethical. Politeness often has to do with a civil reserve that grows as much from diffidence towards to the other as respect.

---

me to flow: rules which reason is later forced to re-establish upon other foundations when, by its successive developments, it has succeeded in stifling nature. In this way one is not forced to make a man a philosopher before making him a man. . . . It seems, in effect, that if I am obliged to do no harm to my fellow man, it is less because he is a reasonable being than because he is a sensitive being." See his remarks on pity (*Second Discourse*, 130ff.: ". . . a pure movement of nature prior to all reflection. Such is the force of natural pity . . . ," 131). From it "alone flow all the social virtues . . ." 132. He returns us to something elemental in the ethos vis-à-vis the idiotic and aesthetic, but because he is so intent on freeing these from dianoetic, instrumental exploitation, he does not do justice to the other potencies, nor finally then to the immediate intermediations already at work in the idiotic and aesthetic. In seeking so to be free from one corruption, he risks a different corruption.

We are aware of the hiding ugliness of monstrous egotism. We gild the ugly and speak politely to each other, with icy reserve, yet without overt violence. The unruliness of the monster is kept in check by the reticence of politeness. It is a very weak check, as we know in situations of stress. When war breaks out, humans descend into such barbarism as to make them shameful in their shamelessness. There is a courtesy, an ethical civility, that should be described in more positive terms. Nevertheless, all politeness has its function in the masquerade: of showing and concealing what, were it shown, would be disruptive or destructive of the commons between the other and the self. True, politeness can be as much a form of egotistic self-regard as of care for the other. And yet the veneer is still an *acknowledgment of the other*, despite the darker passions that roil on. We may be perennially hypocritical when we are polite, but the hypocrisy is necessary for egotism to be effective, and to be effective, it must pay its tribute to the other. Egotism grows forms of life that show the deeper inescapability of the intermediation that grants the other as other.

Behold the green-eyed monster, *envy*! Envy is inseparable from egotism, for the other has what I admire, but I lack it, hence I hate the other for what she has, and I begin to hate what I love, just because the other has it and I lack it. *Sour grapes*: a sly assault on the good one desires because one is deprived of it. Envy is the love of a possession, soured to hatred of the other in possession. And yet this promiscuous passing of love into hate shows a *concealed self-transcending*. What I envy, I still secretly want, and envy can drive the surpassing of what one now is as lacking. See envy work in the web of serviceable disposability: what the others have, I too must have. Why if others did not have it, I might not want it at all. Because the others have it, so must I.

I cannot forbear another remark on advertising. Often advertising first creates the feeling of lack and anxiety; then it offers the product to still the anxiety; it arouses envy, but only in a mild form; a passionate envy is ungovernable; we need a constant mediocre envy, dribbling into an anxiety to have what one lacks, dribbling also into a low grade alarm at any excellence that rises above the rest. Everyone else is buying hula hoops! Am I missing something? Best not be left in the lurch. Once nudged into the initial movement, see how quickly the herd stampedes! How easily we are led by the nose by properly orchestrated envy![10] We pass from the discordant multiplicity of secret egotisms to their docile conformity. And obviously this is a community that does not go deep, but still it is a kind of community, an intermediation beyond egotism out of egotism.[11] Seen in

---

10. Think of *Tom Sawyer* in seducing the other boys to do his chore of painting; so utterly tedious as a chore, but oh so desirable, when the bewitchment of envy is cast.

11. A similar point holds true for diffidence and glory. Egotism is expressed in spite, backbiting, ill will, mean-mindedness, and the like but expressed always in relation to the other

this light, only a small difference separates propaganda and advertising. Advertising is the propaganda beamed to shore up faith in the religion of shopping. The military-industrial complex and the consuming society are too alike, with variations of sameness in their mechanisms of conformity and intermediation. There is a totalism in the consuming society, when all value is homogenized into the same form of serviceable disposability.

What of *the dianoetic recalcitrance*? Here I will just mark the inescapable law of the other, even when the rhetoric of predatory individualism fills the air. In the web of serviceable disposability, a negative form of intermediation must be at work: the other *must be acknowledged*, albeit as a means and a possible resource for me. The temptation to unbounded egotism is kept in check by the nature of that egotism, which must in fact take into account the other in order to make the other of use to itself. Thus the slave-master must care for his slaves, or he is undercutting the prudence needed for his own profiting from the other. Similarly, in capitalism, those who exploit others must in some measure allow the good of the others used, or else the exploited will be useless and hence of no profit to the exploiters. Even in the death camps there was a graded calculation in the use of the inmates: some were worked to death without any mitigation, if they were older and less healthy; others were treated with slightly more "care," for longer use. Even the vilest exploitation cannot do away with intermediated granting, hence it is tied to what it would exclude, were it possible. It is not possible.

The fear of the others that drives the will to ascendancy also keeps egotism in check. If I were not afraid of you as a possible threat, what malice might pour forth from me? We find ourselves watching each other for subtle signs that might reveal the monster in the other—the monster now muzzled, but perhaps to be unleashed, were the other to gain rule and be less in fear of what others might do. Fear gives body to a wisdom, but it is not the beginning of any wisdom—it is merely a way of keeping the lid on the monstrous in us, in the other. Fear of the monstrous makes us work together, for we fear that without that cooperation, and the friendship that shared utility brings, we will be more vulnerable to hostile forces. Cooperation is then protection against the always-present threat of hostility—springing as much from egotism's own surmise of its own monstrousness, as of the other's unbounded will to power. That is why every society has to make use of the instruments of fear to enforce at least the outward show of cooperative behavior. It is called deterrence in regard to certain crimes. The threat of violence is needed to keep the monstrous in check, for more often than not this is the only language the monster understands.

---

being dragged down, even as he or she must be acknowledged. There is no escape from the other, only a twisted relation. The other is twisted into conformity with my claim, the intermediation deformed into a self-mediation.

The communists were not wrong in holding that the absolutization of capitalist utility cannot provide the basis for human community. Can communism itself? It became a monster that kept the many monsters in check. As classically expressed, communism was infected by the same spirit of devalued being as is capitalism. Defined in the social formation of ethical nihilism, it was one more will to power presenting itself as the noble, saving power. Intentionally or not, humans were returned to the base in the noble. The ideal of communist solidarity stems from the recognition that work need not be dominated by the chain of instrumental exchanges. Nevertheless, totalitarian communism also was an absolutization of property: not of private property but of state property, in which the tyranny of a devouring instrumentalized relation subjected the more delicate seeds of social solidarity to a blasting and an uprooting. Insofar as intermediation is more basic than self-mediation, the ideal of social justice (intended by communism, whether adequately or not) cannot be sidestepped. Yet ethical intermediation itself is in solidarity with the promise of the singular, and hence the supportive basis of self-mediation. Capitalism willy-nilly lets a space for that support, not because it is its primary intention, but because without it the exploitation of the proper could not be effected at all. Capitalism is wed to something that implicitly harbors what cannot be fitted into its scheme.

In the exchange of services and goods, needs and desires are satisfied, thus disparate people, pursuing their own selfish interest, are bound together in a shared network. The invisible hand? Because the hand is *invisible*, we cannot be quite sure whose hand this is.[12] Hegel gives a fine account of how this system of needs finally turns out to serve the universal. Whether the universal is as Hegel describes it is another question. What is true, in any case, is that the intermediation at play is always equivocal between self-mediation and social intermediation, between self-serving and service to the community of the universal. This does not mean that the fuller community is exhausted by its determination in the web of utility. What the latter serves, it also distorts.

What of *the transcendental recalcitrance*? There are many conditions of the possibility of use (such as origin, ethos, and metaxological community), but it is enough here to point out a basic condition of the possibility of serviceable disposability. Serviceable disposability conceals the ontological/ethical conditions

---

12. The "invisible hand" of Adam Smith as the immanent theodicy of serviceable disposability? But even Smith has some sense of what is "before" use: sympathy and the social; still, "by nature," every man is "principally recommended to his own care"; political economy is founded on an area of morality specifically dealing with self-interest; justice is an "artificial virtue." One thinks of sympathy for Hume also: sympathy is pre-moral and still understood in terms of the modern view of nature: these impulses are subrational, connected to our animal inclinations and aversion and an ability of the imagination to put ourselves in the place of others (*Treatise*, Vol. II, Bk. III, Pt. I, Sec. I; Pt. II, Sec. I).

on which it is dependent, which both enable and limit it. I confine myself to the basic point: the notion of serviceability points to something deeper than useful disposability. It implies that things offer themselves, that there is something about them that is made *available* in a more basic way than use. Things and beings are given; they are gifts. And because they are gifts, they give themselves. In brief, *using is made possible by gift*.

An unqualified dynamic of using seeks to change gift into possession—to seize the given, to take it rather than to receive it; and taking it thus, not to receive it with gratitude, but to think itself free, as supposedly beholden to none but itself. Thus the generosity of being is denied in terms of its availability to our power. This loss of gift and gratitude distorts the meaning of offer, availability, serviceability, and disposability. This loss feeds a false form of freedom, a self-deluding autonomy. Nevertheless, the distortion is still dependent on the elemental gift, the ontological milieu as good, and mediately the good of the origin as the ultimate source of giving. Proper using is qualified by this more basic sense of the good of beings as gift. The serviceable disposability of unqualified using lacks the mindful acknowledgment of the living of this sense for things. Proper use is to use with ontological gratitude. This too is inseparable from the claims made above concerning respect for life, the intimacy of the agape of being, the aesthetic body, and the other.

We cannot but use. How use? That is the question. Proper use is not serviceable disposability but service available to the good that respects, while receiving, the gift of beings and things. Not: things serve us. But: we serve the good; hence as things service us, and serve our good, we too serve their good, to the best extent possible. This does not preclude appropriation, but it mitigates the violence of seizure. Perfect use is impossible for us. There is always some seizure. There is only moderation of this, not eradication. The moderation in use is itself gratitude for the gift that makes use primally possible.

What of *the eudaimonic recalcitrance*? The picture above of the artificial man tells us enough. The recalcitrance here is especially striking, since it is the search for happiness that generates wretchedness. The seeking flattens desire while seeming to flatter it. The hedonistic paradise is a place without peace. It is a cauldron of arousal and discharge and disappointment and the recharging again of tiring desire. The masquerade of desire excited proves more important than the worth of any goal sought. Desire comes to desire desire itself, inflating itself until satiation breeds boredom. To break desire's own lassitude, the pitch of provocation must be raised again, but outrage and shamelessness are the extreme outcomes.

This is daimonic without being eudaimonic. The sweetness of *hedone* itself becomes embittered. We are not blessed with any wholeness or integrity of being but cursed with loathing of the futility. We seek ourselves, but if we are lucky to find ourselves, or unlucky, our misfortune becomes plain, for we find ourselves as this loathing. This is the karma of the loss of gratitude for the gift of the good.

What of *transcending recalcitrance*? We here find the second kind of limit, solicited limit, discerned in an open process of becoming. Our power is notorious, both to exceed and disrespect measure. Previously this failing was called hubris, even though it is a close cousin of the noble faring that drives greatness. Hubris runs against limits in the ethos, limits initially not forced on us but learned in transcending itself. In self-surpassing, we come to discernment of measure. Hubris is a breach of this discernment, reckless disregard of what it teaches. Limit breaks in and teaches, through the shock of a shattering of over-reaching power. The measureless immoderation calls forth the nemesis. Nemesis is the karma of the limit that springs up on the other side of the breached limit. It reminds us bitterly of constancies in the course of things that cannot be disrespected with impunity.

The point could be put with more elegance, but here is the issue. The reconfiguration of the ethos under the dominion of serviceable disposability crowds out the slow patient thought, the discerning moderation born of long time and its wisdom. We become unballasted as we jettison this weight of wise finitude. We become giddy and take this giddiness for creative energy. This is commingled with secret presumption, as an excited flight to futurity rushes us along, skimming the surface of the ethos, and not skimming it lightly but voraciously, for this very surface is what is to be used, and used not to come to a stand, but to feed the flight, feed the light-headedness.

Since this unballasted energy of a time-devouring transcending is future intoxicated, it must remain indefinite. This utilization of the ethos exceeds this use, that use, is out beyond the slowing effect, the moderating effect of determination here and now. And for what? Perhaps for a basic security that should be easily reached, but it is not. For nothing in particular then? Perhaps for the excitement of the mastering feeling of reconfiguring the ethos? We set the stage and think that we are in charge of what is there before us; but then strangely, *it is as if no play happens*. Ballasting goods of tradition are thrown overboard; future goals orienting the excited flight are shrouded in suitable obscurity; they may not exist at all. It hardly matters if there are any such. Were there such, limit would reenter the picture. And there is nothing like limit to puncture the hysteria of self-excitation, self-creativity.

No limit in past, no limit in present and in future, means that the reconfigured ethos seems to stretch out indefinitely, whichever way we turn in the between. We fill up the between with the desire of our own self-satisfaction, with the powers we annex to make being for us, with the excited powers of our own immanent productivity that justify themselves with the picture of the between as being empty of value until we have filled its vacuum with value for us. A network of interlocking instrumentalities is made, in one sense saturated with value, in another sense, entirely indigent of value, and saturated just because of its indigence, and to hide from ourselves the threadbare lives we live in this glut of too much.

The longing for inherent value does not die, but this reconfiguration is such that it is hard to give genuine expression to the longing. Even to express the longing can present great obstacles, for the requisite words have been degraded into the language of serviceable disposability, thus embody the loss of the good longed for. Then longing for the lost is itself lost or at a loss. Those who manage to remain mindful of the other way will sound like someone speaking a foreign tongue: incomprehensible, fantastic, given to gibberish. Their stammering is the truer.

There is no easy way beyond, for people born into the reconfigured ethos will be grown in its image and likeness. Their presentiment of the other way will be overlaid with an idiom which, for all of its incessant talk, is deaf to the matter at issue. The talk silences us, dampens us down into a kind of moral autism in the network. This autism will take itself as the norm, but it is a norm baffled at limit, viewed in terms of a more deeply inherent norm. In another regard, this is not at all a silent autism; it is a chattering autism. But a chatter that is lost is really a silence of which the chatter has almost no comprehension. Since the source of the silencing and autism is in the reconfiguration of the ethos, we seem gripped by a fatality outside the power of any individual. And this despite the fact that the rhetoric of the reconfiguration talks incessantly about "being in control." No one is in control.

Thus is the bewitchment nurtured that all things are for our use, but each will be cast as the inmate of a cell of solitude, without the language to communicate with the sun that rises beyond the bars, or the sparrows and thrushes singing regardless in the forgotten hedgerows. Our socially useful freedom will be our spellbound chatter.

What of *the transcendent recalcitrance*? This arises when we come to ask, almost despairingly, how do we break out of this network, if it is like a net cast over us, hampering every movement of mindfulness? The more we struggle, the more we seem enmeshed. Must we succumb to a helpless fatalism? Fatality follows oblivion to the measure of limit; the net is thrown over an ethos of promise in which are buried, always, seedlings of hope, exceeding the totalized network of serviceable disposability. These spring up despite the inhospitality of the network.

The instrumental is subtended by deeper sources of value that are not exhausted, even when subjected to the dominion of serviceable disposability. The absolutization of the relative (here we have one form of it) must undergo the karma of its own hubris, and the reinstatement of measure between relative and absolute. The relative falls to the ground, undergoes its own downfall and decomposition. The ceaseless endeavor to shore up the serially absolutized finitude does not prevent the karmic hollowing that accompanies this fateful hubris. We live in the network and call this hubris our "can do." The karma is already ready, and it will exact the justice of measure in time. Discerning mindfulness will prophetically see the karma already ready.

The karma cannot be cut off from the idiot self, from what is at play in the intimacy of the agape of being that is prior to any instrumental objectification of the between. There is an indeterminate intimate intermediation with the good that works prior to the network, and that is never completely defaced by the network. It comes out again in elemental situations: when we confront suffering, we respond to the appeal of the other as of inherent worth, regardless of our habituation to utilitarian pricing. Our response has the character of an elemental agape, calling us to transcend ourselves in sympathy and compassion towards the other, especially those *in extremis*.

When the other seems fine, we have little bad conscience about instrumentalizing him or her. However, we can do this less complacently, when the other is in distress: it would be a double violation to use the other when the other is *in extremis*. The distress calls forth a response deeper than instrumentalizing. We may be suddenly turned around from a relation of using to a different concern. I have just used a person, say sexually, but the sudden distress in her eyes issues an appeal that strikes through the colder attitude of exploitation, and I experience remorse. I may hate the remorse, of course, but I also may be changed and vow there and then not to use the other. The appeal strikes through to an intimate depth prior to the instrumentalizing, which exceeds it and shames it for its reduction.[13] (God shadows the intermediation happening here. Our guilts reveal the

---

13. Schopenhauer (in *On the Basis of Morality*, 184) makes some remarks of relevance, I think, when discussing Rousseau's view of compassion and the origin of the *social virtues*. Compassion often, we might say, sneaks around the discursive intellect, by a kind of immediacy that needs no rational concepts: this is a prereflective rapport with the good of the other. Often it is more alive in those who lack a sophisticated education than in those whom sophistication has made cold to warmer human involvements. (The instrumentalizing intellect can be turned to evil—consider the very high percentage of Ph.D.s among members of the SS. Satan was brilliant, but cold.) Something opens up that falls outside of the mastery of instrumental intellect. Compassion, or an agapeic regard, works *prior* to instrumental rationalization (sometimes perhaps called "sympathy," "intuition," "moral sense"). It cuts through the hard crust of instrumental rationalization, preceding it and outliving it, as more in rapport with the more reserved sources of being good. It is capable of a deeper fidelity to these sources. It disrupts the instrumental network, giving hope for more, making us ashamed, spurring us to a more fundamental solidarity with fellow humans, indeed with all beings, especially those who are in suffering. It is the immediate intermediation that is reconfigured and distorted by the instrumental intermediation; the agape of the good is still offered in the dominion of serviceable disposability. Schopenhauer tries to explain this compassion in terms of the monism of the thing in itself and the pluralism of the individualism as phenomenal (see Supplement in *Basis*). In my view, the agapeic origin grounds the pluralism of creation in a different way, grounds love of the singular, as singular—the point is not a noumenal unity behind the singular. I do not understand the one and the many in terms of the noumenal and phenomenal. The agapeic

seed of sorrow at the gift abused and our defection from the good of the origin. The seed can become a thorn in the heart; the defection can be turned to penitential resolve.)

An insuperable limit to the dynamic of using is evident insofar as the network of instrumental relations circles around itself meaninglessly. The network is dedicated to a kind of freedom, but it is a vacuous freedom when it always concerns a means, and none can state what the essential ends are. Indeed, the network can mask the absence of essential ends, because these might disrupt the endless circling of use and exchange. They would bring us to a pause, ask us to contemplate *the point of it all*. What good was to be attained after all? We seem to have unlimited resources, but absolute indigence follows if their squandering, finally, is pointless. The need of a more sovereign intermediation and agapeic service is felt.[14] These latter intermediations seek paths on which the dominion of serviceable disposability can be redeemed from emptiness. They seek to give ethical point to the will to power in the network of utilities. There are illusions in all of that, but they are necessary illusions, and so they must be understood.

---

origin grounds the real pluralism of creation, in an ontological goodness that gives the finite other its being for itself. Creation is already agapeic as a love of the singular. There is no need to reduce the singular to the monism of an underlying ground. Differences are good, not mere phenomena. They are the basis of a metaxological community that itself shows the intermediated promise of agapeic service. Nietzsche sees a kind of giving over, but on this point, Schopenhauer is more phenomenologically rich than Nietzsche. In both cases, the metaphysics is not adequate. If Nietzsche rebelled against Schopenhauer, thinking to undercut all agapeic being for the other, he did not succeed, indeed, he proves to be still too captive to a defective dialectic of the one and many.

14. This is not entirely antithetical to the critique of instrumental reason in thinkers such as Adorno, Habermas, and others in what loosely might be called the "left-Hegelian" line. My concern is a rethinking of the ethos and its plurivocal ethical promise. And, of course, what we mean by "emancipation" depends on what we mean by freedom and community. This "left-Hegelian" line remains too tied to a dialectic of social self-determination—the freedom of agapeic release calls for a different kind of community; of this, monotheistic religious traditions have most often had the best sense. Short of some granting of agapeic community, we risk a joyless self-determination in which freedom becomes flat. The communities of the between are not understood, because the meaning of the between is not fully understood. See the thought-provoking work of James Marsh, who tries to bring Habermas together with thinkers more sympathetic to the religious, such as Kierkegaard and Lonergan, especially in *Critique, Action and Liberation* (Albany: State University of New York Press, 1995), and in *Process, Praxis, and Transcendence* (Albany: State University of New York Press, 1999) and also my review, *Tijdschrift voor Filosofie* 61: 4 (1999): 820–825.

CHAPTER FIFTEEN

THE COMMUNITY OF EROTIC SOVEREIGNTY:
THE INTERMEDIATION OF IMMANENT EXCELLENCE

Sovereign Intermediation

Intermediation in the web of serviceable disposability is dominated by the dianoetic exploitation of the aesthetic through an instrumental univocalism. This usefull intermediation cannot attain a fully ethical comportment vis-à-vis the good of the other, or indeed of the self, despite the surface pervasiveness of self-interest. Its necessity in relation to pragmatic affairs is governed by useful expedience rather than excellence beyond expedience. Its relativization of the good to use-values is dissembling, since a complete occlusion of inherent ends would precipitate an inexorable slide towards nihilism. The togetherness of the many may have many purposes, but it also would have no purpose. There would be no point to it as a whole, other than the infinite multiplication of finite satisfactions, none of which proves satisfactory in the end. And so a community lacks ultimate purpose if the business of serviceable disposability exhausts its creative energies. Its freedom refashions itself into a bondage to the products it consumes to slake its own emptiness. The omnivorous devouring of worldly resources does not, cannot, slake this emptiness. Something more is needed: a different gathering of creative power, another release of freedom transcending serviceable disposability, which would give it a purpose more ultimate than the expenditure of power on the useful.

This something "more" is first intermediated in the community of erotic sovereignty. By sovereignty, more is meant than an individualistic aristocratism, as in Nietzsche. At issue is a distinctive intermediation, hence an interplay of selves and others, thus something always communal, even when the flower of the intermediation is an extraordinary individual. If work is mostly bound to the web of utility, sovereignty is a kind of play of power, a freer power beyond utility.[1] Sovereignty is

---

1. Kant suggested that if Plato was play, Aristotle was work. Did Kant have enough discernment to see the sovereignty in Plato's play? As a valet of work, did he lack a certain sovereignty—for all of his talk of autonomy? For play is a kind of grace. In antiquity, sov-

not servile. It lives in a transcending to positions of "being above." "Being below" is not fully in accord with the full release of our power to be. To "be above" is to come into one's own. This freedom of "being above" is more than the network of utility can define, where everything is a means and nothing, in the end, a supreme end. To be sovereign is to approach the supreme and useless—beyond serviceable disposability. It is useless but as such more supremely useful: it gives use the self-justifying excellences the network of serviceable disposability lacks, and without which the whole seems finally pointless.[2]

This worth beyond serviceable disposability can take different forms. Examples: the worth of a work of art, beyond the instrumental work ruled by a schema of means: there is something sovereign about the great artist or work; or the great athlete: to play not just for professional success, but for glory—glory is a mark of sovereignty; or the philosopher whose mindfulness lives in, and through, and beyond the breakdown of limited categories and into a breakthrough of the other dimension of thinking. Sovereignty can be shown elementally in someone resolved about life's elemental enigma through suffering and self-knowing. These examples are beyond more usual sovereignties, which are tied to mastery of social power, as in leaders, kings, caesars, captains, or exemplary originals who gather an intermediation of power into a community of purpose beyond utilitarian goals.

If I connect serviceable disposability to the dianoetic exploitation of the equivocal, I connect erotic sovereignty to the dialectical intermediation of social power. It directs a many beyond mere equivocity towards some sense of itself as

---

ereignty is connected to the *agon*—whether relative to a cult of the heroic warrior or the artistic *agon* of tragedy, or the intellectual *agon* of dialectic. Nietzsche revives ancient agonistics but equivocates between the warrior as involved in the struggle for aristocratic honor, and as struggling for artistic creativity. Hence his praise of war and the need of an enemy (a need of which Carl Schmitt makes much). While the management of conflict and war is crucial to modern political theory, in Plato's *Republic*, warriors are not the highest humans, though the rulers do have something of the warrior in their transcendence of war. Consider Aristotle's *megalopsuchia*—aristocratic honor civilized within the polis in the *agon of outdoing liberality*, but not for the sake of the other: generosity to show self, the outstanding character of great soul. Nietzsche's "gift-giving virtue"(*der schenkenden Tugend*) has something of this: I honor myself in bestowing gifts. Neither is the same as agapeic generosity. Are Plato's rulers closer? Nietzsche is right to see the family resemblance of Platonism and Christianity but is deficient in his understanding of agapeic generosity, hence is unjust in his negative judgment.

2. The sovereign also can become a *coin*: a measure of value, even in the network of serviceable disposability. The other sense of the value of supreme power is more basic. The sovereign coin has its value because it has stamped on it the countenance of the sovereign: the power who stands surety or pledge for its genuine worth; it is not a counterfeit token. A counterfeit coin is the false double of power.

a whole. In some instances, this direction may even involve a community *staking its claim to destiny*. Is this end the end? No. Beyond servility and sovereignty is the community of agapeic service. This I connect to the metaxological intermediation of the good, beyond will to power. And this final community is not just at the end, but is our participation, most unminded, in the always already effective communication of the agape of the good.

The matter is complex and extensive, so I propose to order my remarks in terms of the different potencies of the ethical. I claim no incontrovertible univocalism to this ordering. Nevertheless, we can broadly correlate the idiotic with the enigmatic sources of sovereignty; the aesthetic with the charisma of power; the dianoetic with the legitimacy of leadership; the transcendental with the constitution and representation of a sovereign people; the eudaimonistic with the sovereign intermediation of a common good; transcending with the intermediation of a commons beyond sovereignty; the transcendent with sovereignty and the sacred.

The Idiocy of Sovereignty: Erotic Transcending, Social Sources

Sovereignty is connected to the problem of power in society in relation to the highest governing authority in a community or people. The sources of sovereignty have to do with the idiocy or *intimacy of communal being*. I mean that there is an indeterminacy of reserves of social power not to be identified with this power or that. There is a surplus source of power that often remains uncrystallized. Modern theories that speak either of a contract or a general will are already too determinate. The intimate overdeterminacy of the reserves of power needs to be connected to the openness of transcending power in the human. This transcending power has an erotic and agapeic side. It is with the former that sovereignty is most often aligned. So instead of Rousseau's general will, I would speak rather of *general eros*. The eros of a people is as much at work as the eros of the rulers. This eros inchoately circulates in a community and is not known more determinately until some exemplar or exemplars incarnate it. Sovereignty crystallizes itself in that incarnation. Will is a particular determination of eros, and the origin of sovereignty is not a determinate will such as that but a more indeterminate energizing of social being, at work before any explicit mindfulness or willing at all. That is why the "people" do not quite "know" what they desire, much less will, until the desire and will are incarnated in sovereign exemplars. People do not have first a definite, univocal will on the basis of which they decide. The situation is more indeterminate and fluid, hence also more perilous.

The sources are not in a contract, since this images the social expression of a people's power in terms of too determinate acts of calculated will. There is an unknowing social fidelity operative before calculative reason and its contracts.

General eros is not a general *will*, for will also is too determinate. Nor is it divine *will*, if we think of this as an absolutely determining source that determines univocally all that flows from it, marking it with a univocally predetermined plan (which those in power claim to know, represent, and execute). The source of power is more primordial than determinate will. Rather, humanly speaking, the source has to do with the intimate eros of transcending power to be that is more than every determinacy, and that, as rooted in the intimacy of being, is finally never separable from the agape of being. Nor is it separable from the *gift* of the power to be that comes from the overdeterminate origin. So also the source of power is more primordial than will to power, though the intimate indeterminacy incubates ambiguity from the outset, ambiguity that will allow the closer link of sovereignty to some forms of will to power. But let us walk before we run.

Further aspects of this view of sources will emerge as we proceed, but the view is not immediately evident from what seems implied by the word "sovereign." The word is derived from the French *souverein*, from vulgar Latin *superanus*, "someone who is above." We connect *super* with *huper*, above, with *über*. We connect it with "being supreme." What is supremacy? "Being above": being in the position of height, not being subservient. But how connect "being above" with sources in the *intimacy* of communal being? Sovereignty emerges in the flowering of the eros of human self-transcending. This, as seeking to "be above," points back to the deeper sources of power immanent in our being. The idiocy of being also is the place of the seed of divine promise. So eros reveals a double potency of power and lack. Power is expressed and developed in a process of self-transcending, which also is a process of self-becoming, oriented to a goal in which the lack is overcome and the human comes into its own fullness. We seek a wholeness in the consummation of power to be, which seeks to overcome lack by the developing of power, which proves itself relatively autonomous in this self-development, thus reflecting also the good of self-determining being. Erotic sovereignty stands for the achievement of a powerful wholeness wherein the human comes to govern itself. This achievement may presuppose immense struggle and suffering, and the discipline of a purpose over a lifetime, indeed, many lifetimes, since we stand on the shoulders of our ancestors.

To speak in individual terms here is misleading, since erotic sovereignty cannot be understood without relation to the other. Sovereignty is a social concept—a form of intermediation, even when it defines the autonomy of forms of life that are relatively self-mediating. Erotic sovereignty is a coming to be above, through an intermediation with the other, out of the overdeterminate intimacy of being, with its equivocal mix of power and lack. Out of our lack, and all the chaos hidden therein, we go towards the others, but the others give us back ourselves, and given back to ourselves, we come to ourselves as relatively self-determining. We are given to ourselves beyond lack out of this intermediation with the others. The intermediation serves a self-mediation. Were there no confirming others, we would not come back to ourselves. Power would throw itself further into extro-verted adventure, until it touches the other that in return touches it. The process passes towards and into and through the others. The return of power to itself as confirmed power is served by the process. We may well forget the others who have given us to ourselves and think our "being above" has been generated purely out of ourselves. This ingratitude of autonomy becomes mindless of the ethos of rel-ativity that is its own supporting medium. It is so supported by the social medium that it forgets the medium and takes its relative freedom to be absolute autonomy.

Since erotic sovereignty is entangled in the bonds of intermediation, and since these dialectically mirror a social self-mediating back to itself, the sovereign inevitably relates to these bonds equivocally. Given its freedom to be above, out of which it wins itself, it also is potentially resentful of *having being given anything*. It resists being in the debt of any other, for debt shows it not to be absolutely above but to be in an incontrovertible solidarity. It is tensed between its indebtedness and its being above; between its need of the others and its being fulfilled in itself; between its support by the social medium and the drive to be through itself. This fundamental ambiguity, as we shall see, runs through all of the configurations of sovereignty. There is no way to separate a sovereign individual from the social medium; nor separate a social sovereignty from its implication with what is other; nor separate claims to be above from deep indebtedness to the other and to unmastered intimacies of power; nor separate being supremely powerful from being powerless without what is given to one from the other.

The ambiguity is reflected, not surprisingly, in perhaps the two main tradi-tional views of sources of sovereignty. (These also reflect the different emphases of erotic sovereignty and agapeic service.) One view sees sovereignty as ultimately deriving its power from the divine: all power is from God, says Saint Paul, for instance. The other view derives it from the will of the subjects: popular sover-eignty. Of course, these two can be related in diverse ways. All power is a grant-ing of the origin. This has nothing to do with the advocation of totalitarian theocracy. Often the theory of divine sovereignty is viewed as an ideological superstructure hiding the absolutist will to power of the monarch or the ruling few. This is too simplistic. We speak as if we know what God is being invoked. We rarely do. Depending on our view of God, the derivation of sovereignty will appear quite differently. Overt politics hides covert theology.

Did the medieval theory of the two powers, temporal and spiritual, derive temporal power from God, only to sanction an absolutism of temporal power? This also would be too simple. This theory placed severe qualifications on tem-poral power, not just by subordination to the higher truths of spiritual powers but to the eternal law that was before natural law, that itself was before positive law as proclaimed and enacted by the worldly sovereign (Aquinas). The divine king was not God, and the difference between being delegated power and the ultimate source of power was ultimate. The sovereign was a representative; the sovereign was a servant. Political power was a service of God, in being a service of the good of the people. Transcendence as agapeic service infiltrates the transcendence of the erotic sovereignty and mitigates the indigenous temptation to *superbia*. Justice is sovereign, not power, and the highest power is the power of justice, as itself the expression of divine justice. Fear and trembling are the proper penances of this power.

In modernity, changes in the metaphysics of power go with changes in the notion of God. The sense of divine sovereignty shifts in accord with monarchical absolutism. We think of modernity as the time of "naturalization" and the liberation of humanity, and we think popular sovereignty is a modern creation. Is it so simple? For instance, Jesuits such as Suarez, Cardinal Bellarmin, and others did not think that God directly chose his representative but mediately through the consent of the people. And suppose divine power is not univocal relative to monarchy—suppose it were plurivocal, and the sovereignties it permits equally plurivocal? If modernity seeks a univocalization of power, its monotheism also is univocalized. Result: a war between human and divine power, insofar as each is claimed as the one and only source of power; a logic of univocity guarantees that one must subordinate, or subsume, or erase the other.

Modernity also witnesses the consolidation of power as *for itself* and the assertion of its priority to justice, considered as a transcendent norm. As God undergoes a change in our conception, we undergo changes in self-conception. The process of radical univocalization is reflected in the way the logic of self-mediation tends towards being absolutized, ostensibly in terms of the high value of freedom. It comes to the same: freedom as autonomous self-determination: the law of the same. Developed in a certain way, the logic of such autonomy turns into a royal road to tyranny, that is, to absolutism that is its own law, and above every law. It is this that we see in the drift towards absolutist monarchy. This has less to with a piety of the origin as other as with the self-glorification of the human sovereign. Hobbes is so far right about Leviathan: it is a mortal god.[3]

Modernity's reconfiguration of the ground of power tilts towards a stress on will to power as seeking autonomous self-determination. As God moves towards univocal, unilateral power to determine, human self-understanding moves towards conceiving itself as univocal will to power. The latter, just as univocal, eventually wills to dispense with divine origins. Inevitably, we have difficulty thinking of the divine as agapeic origin, which as other limits, qualifies, and obliges our use of

---

3. Popular sovereignty can produce its mortal gods, and not only the Marxist humanism that creates the earthy paradise of totalitarian society. Nor is democracy immune, especially when the relation to the other is retracted into self-determination, and prevalent cultural forces degrade the ethical value of agapeic service. The invocation on the dollar is deliciously equivocal: "In God we trust." What God?

power. This would take the wind out of the sails of our autonomous self-determination. We resent that. We see in divine power a tyrannical heteronomy. *Our* will to power creates the idol of divine tyranny. The shaping of power in modernity in terms of autonomous self-determination produces now a relative freedom, now a tyrant, whether divine or human (the god-men who make a waste of the earth in the name of making it a new paradise). This ambivalence between the divine and human is central to sovereignty, and will return.

The Aesthetics of Sovereignty: The Charisma of Power

The hidden sources of social power are shown through the sovereign or sovereigns. There is a communal aesthetics of sovereignty. The sources *show themselves*, albeit ambiguously, in the *charisma of power* that flares from the sovereign. This charisma can be concentrated in an individual, but it also can adhere to a group, as well as to the communal ceremonials that are the adornments of social majesty. Charisma is a loaded word, as is proper: it carries the suggestion of ultimate reference to the divine, but this is made indirect by being embodied in the figure of the sovereign. Hence, charisma is *equivocal between* the divine and the human. This between is mediated by the erotic sovereign who comes into the majesty of power in not being dissolved in the chaotic maelstrom of the equivocal. The intermediation of excellences in a society is impossible without certain singular selves called leaders, who take on the majesty and burden of sovereignty. But this is impossible to understand without social intermediation, even if a kind of self-mediating master emerges from the intermediation. In deepest truth, this singular self actually *serves the social intermediation*, even while seeming to be its ruler. Leaders manifest the charisma of power to the extent that the communal energies of erotic transcending find their figuration in their persons.

Won out of the equivocal, the figuration continues to be double edged. The ethical and political issue is one of rescuing social power from internal dissension and discord, say from the tendency towards the "dog-eat-dog" world of raw instrumentalities. The issue is a *higher commons* raised above this, with a social order affording a measure of peace and unity. This means the elevation of power above oppressive force and tyrannous use. The shaping or composition of the sources of power is a *raising up* and civilizing of human energy. It is its aesthetic education, so to say, but this is a social struggle with the equivocity of will to power in the form of vehement self-insistence. This double edge must be borne in mind in what follows.

A people needs a sovereign to express, confirm, and protect its sense of superior power, its "being above." The charisma of power does more than adorn or varnish the relations of utility; it guards a more basic sense of worth. Sovereignty is a way of confirming a higher freedom, though in the process it runs the risk of the tyrant, hence the loss of freedom.[4] A people need sovereigns because its indeterminate powers remain relatively diffused until crystallized in a definite figure or figures who embody and channel these fermenting and percolating powers. In Nietzsche's terms, a many remains a herd until it throws up a leader. Then it begins properly to become a people. This is why the leader can be adulated to the point of worship—without him, the people are almost as nothing, the people is not a people. He or they show the charisma of power in being the father or fathers of the nation. Indeed, often a group or community invests its sovereignty in someone like a father figure.[5] In some political contexts, the king is a kind of father of the people; in some religious communities, God, the father, is defined as sovereign. The leader is invested with the character of supreme, if not incontrovertible power. What seems lacking in the many seems present in a seamless wholeness in the sovereign.

Not surprisingly, the sovereigns are the ones who dare to stand out from the crowd, by an act of courage or transgression. Where the many fear to tread, the sovereigns go first.[6] The vehemence of their eros drives them to danger in order to find, not just what is there, but themselves. Risking dangerous otherness and coming to self, they show something of the realized promise of human being, and it is in this show of realized promise that the subordinate many find their own alleviation from the sense of their own lack. Eros as lack seeking fulfillment is shown a kind of fulfillment in the erotic sovereigns. They take on the image of wholeness, within which the lack of the many is brought, in a mediated way, to a kind of fulfillment. We identify with the leaders; they are the others of power in whom our own dream of power is mirrored back to us.

In the play with danger, there is a subterranean connection between *death* and the charisma of power. (Death too is inseparable from the danger of the

---

4. Rousseau, *Second Discourse*, 164: "It is the fundamental maxim of all political right, that peoples have given themselves chiefs to defend their freedom and not to enslave themselves. *If we have a prince*, said Pliny to Trajan, *it is so that he may preserve us from having a master.*"

5. See Aristotle, *Politics*, Bk. 1, on fathers, households, cities, and kings. Among many others, Locke connects fathers and sovereigns.

6. Freud asks us to think of this "standing out," this "standing above," in terms of a primal patricide that confers on the murderer the power of the father, and the "primal horde" bow to him. Certainly in some criminal communities, the willingness to commit outrages, to be fearless in evil, is taken as a mark of outstanding difference. A man is marked as different, perhaps even ambiguously superior, because he is known, or thought to have murdered; the power of life and death plays around his person, as a magical aura that might well bewitch. The erotic sovereigns seem *beyond shame*. Many are attracted to this, even ashamed people. Hitler and Stalin were beyond shame. So were Jesus and the Buddha; but they were differently "beyond good and evil"—as good, not evil.

sacred.) The network of utility is driven by power and the fear of death. For work is tied to worry about the future, which we seek to secure, hence it is implicated in an ontological distrust of the gift of being. The useful worker is haunted by the fear of nothingness and the sense that all things come to nothing. What use then is usefulness? The impetuous business of work keeps at bay this coming to nothing. It allays the ontological distrust. We hide from the nothingness which haunts us by keeping relentlessly busy. In its link to erotic transcending, sovereignty concerns the surpassing of this nothingness. Sovereigns face the nothing and seek to be above it; they seek to come to life, to a different "yes" to being beyond utility. They can come to a useless affirmation, the affirmation of life in the elemental good of its "to be."

So the erotic sovereign cannot be reduced to the *Hegelian master*, as defined in dialectical struggle with the slave, where there is a risk of death in the life-and-death struggle. There must be more than risk and more than struggle and more than the search for recognition. Erotic sovereigns may be caught in risk and struggle, even if they point beyond it. But if there is this pointing beyond, it means a different relation to death than risk and struggle. There is a different consent, and not just struggle, and this consent is not just resignation, which only means giving up the struggle. This consent is beyond resignation, since it is not beneath struggle but above it. It is given up without giving up. "Being given up" is a sign that self-transcending is carried by an energy of surpassing that is not self or simply of self. (Recall the equivocal space between the human and divine.) Nor is erotic sovereignty a matter of a mutual recognition in which a symmetrical mediation of the self and the other is granted. There is a relativity in asymmetry. Undoubtedly, the will to be recognized can infiltrate this, but it is not exhaustive of it. There is a transcending in the grip of sources of power that exceed even the ratification of the recognizing other, even though that recognition is necessary to constitute a sovereign social order. Hegel's dialectical way of thinking about the master is too tied to an affirmation of self that has to struggle for recognition with others, even if it finally comes to some peace *with itself* in relation to the other. Hegelian peace with self is not the deepest affirmation that is peace with the other to whom one is given up. Hegelian peace with itself is too self-mediating, even when intermediating, hence it does not do justice to the extremity of transcending that is *not* brought back to itself, even in erotic sovereignty itself.

What of the sovereignty of the *Stoic sage*? We are to live in terms of what is up to us, and so to conquer the fear of death. There is resignation in consenting to what is up to us, but ambiguities of unresolved resentment hide under the surface of this resignation. Despair and defeat are never far away. Stoic resignation is too close to a resentful consent, and out of resentful resolve there can burst a new agon, not to say revolt and usurpation. In its peace with self smolders hatred (albeit masked in milder, more sullen forms), unless it has let itself be transfigured into peace with the other. Stoic sovereignty shows the will for nobility in the desire to *master the monster*. The social sovereign seeks to master the monster. Sometimes, alas, *the master becomes the monster*. Beyond resignation, more is needed, and not revolt and usurpation, those defiant twins of sullen resignation.

The *inspiration of genius* throws some light on the recessive sources of power and the aesthetic charisma of its show. Inspiration is related to this other transcendence that makes transcending to be more than self-transcendence.[7] One might say that the difference of genius and talent is relevant to the distinction between the social sovereigns and those who are managers of the network of instrumentalities. Sovereignty asks some genius, not just talent. Talent is tied to the more controlled realm of *technē* and the calculative consideration of means. Genius is more than such *technē* and calculation. (Kant: genius those *favored* by nature, through whom nature gives the rule to art.) There is a being beyond rules, a being beyond the law. This is to be outlaw, and perhaps yet also a sovereign source of law. Sovereignty as majesty has more to do with the sublime than the beautiful. This relates to the *excess* of the sources of powers that are intermediated in the sovereign.

Erotic sovereigns court life, as if death itself were nothing; as if life itself were immortal, eternal—but court life as having taken the measure of its mortality, and of time. This is to be resurrected to the glorious now, dying now to the safety of finite and prudent calculation. A community outlives its own death through its erotic sovereigns. They become the heroes revered by later generations. Their stories, immortalized in myths, will give the community its "narrative identity" in time. Social sovereignty is mediated through the mythic stories of heroes whose exemplary lives and deaths intermediate to the community its sense of enduring value, its own enduring value (even unto being an empire of a thousand years . . .).[8] If to be sovereign is to "be beyond the fear of death," this "being beyond" cannot be simply so in a Hobbesian way. Death is not the master, for there is a community of being beyond death itself that breaks out in a *festivity of life beyond death*.[9]

---

7. Salieri had talent, hence was the successful court composer/musician. Mozart had genius, hence showed the glory of sovereignty, indeed, the majesty of the divine as the origin that favors some with singular creative power. Philosophers of genius show sovereignty in that sense.

8. Is our consuming society poor in such stories? To the extent it is, it is indigent in social sovereignty, despite the superior power of its greater efficiency. Its utilitarian superiority is its sovereign inferiority.

9. Think also how sovereignty is given its material existence in public buildings, monuments, memorials, and so on. These are the *posthumous stones* of sovereignty on which we find inscribed the petrified recollection of social power—and impotence. Festivity of life beyond death can take a more liturgical form in the community of agapeic service.

The network of use sought to produce this in utopian form in the communist state. But because this lacked the genuinely sacred, its will to sovereignty degenerated into diabolical tyranny, and the deadening of the human soul that makes the people into the living dead, as a zombie is: a macabre, parodic double of our being freed into posthumous mind and its song of being. Capitalism lacks sovereign festivity insofar as it is gripped by use-value. As seeking to absolutize serviceable disposability, as enmeshed in the net of instrumentalities, it is one of the least sovereign forms of society. Of course, there is no dearth of surrogate formations of sovereignty, such as the venture capitalist, the so-called elite of power and knowledge. The latter are the neutral universals, rooted finally in nothing but their own advantage. The venture capitalist may be inferior even to an inferior political leader of a parochial community, relative to sovereignty. He or she does not intermediate the community beyond use but turns it into a mass of shoppers. True, he or she tranquilizes the many against the fear of death—endless shopping sells us the illusion we are exempt from the fear of death. Such shopping, as we saw, is the opium of the people. The shopper's paradise replaces the sovereign affirmation of life in the good of its "to be."

The erotic sovereign is the genuine other for the many in which there is an intermediation that serves the self-mediation of the many: they come to themselves in the other. We see this too in religious communities in which God as sovereign mirrors back to humans their self-understanding of power. I stress that with the erotic sovereigns, the dominant consideration is *power to be as intermediating with itself in and through what is other*. Hence there is always the temptation of will to power to place the other in a subordinate position, as unilaterally as possible. We are so bewitched by power and dreams of power that our image of God mirrors that dream—the divine sovereign will be such unilateral power absolutized. So also will our image of the worldly leader. And what seems the proper response to this overweening power? Submission. Sometimes the follower will adhere with blind obedience, nor shrink from violence, and with joy, since it is the will of the sovereign that commands that this be done. Nor will guilt be felt. Why? Because the lack of the follower is anchored in the erotic sovereign, and no, not I live, but the erotic sovereign lives in me, and hence where is responsibility, if any, but in the erotic sovereign? Not only do I find myself by losing myself in the sovereign; I lose myself in finding myself in the sovereign. The sovereign seems to resolve for the many the burden of freedom and transcendence.

Thus the sovereigns must be commanding figures in many senses: commanding in giving commands; commanding in being beyond the doubt of self, the equivocalness of the ordinary vacillators; commanding in radiating an aura of bewitchment. All come from the glorification of power as figured in their charismatic persons. The subordinate many anchor themselves in a larger source of transcendence when they submit themselves to the sovereign. They may even welcome being shamed by the superior self, since just the shaming will show the superiority of that self. The superior self puts us in our place, and though we resent that, we also revere it.[10] Why do the many revere the sovereign and resent him? The same thing: his being above them. What before made them love him, in time will also make them hate him: his being above them. Love and hate are hard to disentangle, in the end.

The many create the sovereign. Did they not invest him with their dreams, his will to power would not swell to the monstrous proportions that are desired: he would be a mere swaggerer. Without the noughts of followers behind him, his oneness would not dilate into the multiplicity: the noughts behind him make him big, measureless in his majesty from behind.[11] Suppose one says that the many alienate their responsibility in the leader, transfer it there, leave it there; yet they are responsible; for did they not invest him with this surge that comes from numbers, he would be as nothing. Void of the charisma of power, the leader would be a boaster: an extravagance of breath. (That is often all he is, invested or not.) A mediocrity can take on the majesty of the sovereign, simply by having office thrust on him. What is office? The magic door to the power of social inter-mediation. In another sense, the erotic sovereign *ceases to be himself* when he becomes the intermediating leader of a group or community. He is his function, his office, which now is greater than what he is. He can no longer be himself simply, for it is his place in the dynamics of intermediation that defines how he is to be and how he must be. Instead of being autonomous, he is a servant of that dynamic. The best leaders somehow learn to combine sovereignty and this service, which they turn to the good. The many create a new identity for their sovereigns by investing them with hopes, fears, desires, and so on. But just as the many can lose themselves in the sovereign, the sovereign can lose himself in the many. The sovereign becomes the creation of the many's bewitchment; it is never only the sovereign bewitching the many. The social dynamic is both; it is bewitchment working from two directions. It is a double dialectic, a double

---

10. Note the social intermediation of *sadistic* leaders who call for their *masochistic* followers, and vice versa. Sovereignty is enforced by violence on the followers who, in one sense, welcome the violence, just because they are nothing without the superiority of the sovereign, and the sovereign nothing without the violence on the subject many. To be something, the many are subjected to violence. We find this in totalitarian regimes, and on a smaller scale, hence more visibly in, for instance, certain sects, cults, or gangs: the leader's approval and threat go hand in hand. "Why do you bang your head on the wall?" "Because it feels so good when I stop!" The situation is driven by a logic of degraded erotic lack: degrading will to power as the impetus of impotence.

11. When some ex-Presidents of the United States leave office, they become celebrity golfers; the aura of power, its sovereign magic, evaporates, though perhaps never entirely, as we find with relics of the first degree.

mediation, an intermediation. When the spell of this dialectic is broken or its charisma wears out, the result is sometimes death for the sovereign. He is the creation of the people, no self-creation, and when their power is withdrawn, he must vanish or die: as in those ancient tribes, when kings became scapegoats, since they no longer served the power and so they were put to death.

Only to emphasize the violent power of the sovereign is to make monoform this double edge. The deeper issue is one of *nobility or rank*. Nobility is a social worth beyond the useful. One might be the most useful agent, beavering away night and day, seeing opportunity, helping the workers work more efficiently, seeing news ways of exploitation, new inventions to lighten the daily burden of everydayness, but one might be lacking in nobility. Nobility is useless in the network of utility, but it has a use that transcends usefulness, for in nobility, a society celebrates ranking value that embodies something of self-justifying worth. Sovereignty seeks to be justified because of what it is, not because of what it has, nor of the useful services it can perform for the people. Nobility embodies transcending worth.

Traditionally identified, sovereignty was invested in a sacred caste or class, or with a ruling group, which traced its social ascendancy to a divine dispensation and felt no need to justify its being what it was. Modernity is the era in which nothing is justified. If so, no true sense can be made of the charisma of power. Usefulness steps in as the ersatz surrogate of justification. The fact is, nobility cannot justify itself in terms of a use, for its majesty comes from another dimension of power beyond. In the modern web of serviceable disposability, nobility suffers a refusal of this beyond when rank and status is reduced, say, to money. Money purchases reverence, or just the perception that one is monied may seem enough. Money then carries the charisma of power. I am revered when the aura of money surrounds me. Money, it will be thought, can buy one other statuses, including political power, nobility, and recognition. This is a cheapening of what is worthy beyond use. In pricing nobility, nobility is simply not prized.

The loss of the sacred is bound up with this as indeed is the desacralization of politics. And still we in secular democracies both crave and hate leaders, and again crave and hate for the same reason: their "being above." We crave, because we relish being shown an excellence beyond utility, a glory that is self-justifying; we hate, for secretly we envy those seeking to be above, serenely indifferent to the rush of homogenization and equalizing exchange. This network of serviceable disposability is our prison, but it also is comfortable, and when we look up, we are uneasily made aware of bars in the window. We long to be outside and above, yet we hate being tempted by the above, since here inside the cocoon of utility things are nice and cozy, and this cocoon becomes more cozy by the day with each new technological innovation. We love erotic sovereigns for being reminders of transcendence, but we hate them, for we hate the dangerous passage of transcendence beyond the comforts of utility. We hate the risk of useless excellence; it guarantees us no return on our investment, and above all, we must be prudent with our investments.

But the radiance of charisma is not the *possession* of those with power, and it is shown even in the absence of power. I mean the sign of a joy beyond sovereignty in someone who lives life simply as the gift of the divine, such as Francis of Assisi, embracing lady poverty and singing love hymns to possessionless freedom. The life of the saint is useless and indeed beyond sovereignty, yet a healthy commonsense society knows that its own life is merely banal if its domesticity and everydayness is not punctured by unpredictable visitors from beyond, visitors to be treated with the utmost reverence, lest it be a god or an angel that visits. Of course, care also is needed, since monsters too come to visit—looking like angels.

The Dianoetics of Sovereignty: On Leadership and Legitimacy

The dianoetics of sovereignty have to do with the issue of *legitimacy*, insofar as the dianoetic potency bears on the general rule of law. Just laws are requisite for the social intermediation of power in the often contentious, sometimes very dangerous, ambiguity of the communal milieu. The dianoetics of sovereignty thus concern the legitimacy of the rule of law, through which the justice of the lawgiver gives guidance in the equivocal ethos. The charisma of power is not only a matter of enforcement. Claims to sovereignty sometimes may have their inception in a brutal seizure of power, but to continue, the brutality must be transformed, hence hidden. The aesthetics of power intermediate a reformation from seizure to acceptance. The dianoetics of sovereignty may so discipline the outlaw that he or she becomes an enforcer of the law. The usurper becomes a charmer.

Is the charm all a Machiavellian pretense? The charisma of power means commanding and being able to count on obedience, but why does a many obey? A many seems to have power quantitatively in superiority, yet there is a docility or willing subjection to others carrying commanding power. Whence that power? A basic social trust allows the expression of the secret sources of power and its circulation. Law gives determinate social form to that trust and the expectation of it. This cannot be abstracted from the way in which the power of the many is reflected back to the many, in and through the figure of the sovereign. This makes possible an open self-mediation of the obedient with themselves, when they submit to the command of the sovereign. They make the sovereign sovereign, as much as the sovereign makes them subjects. In the self-mediating circuit of this intermediation of power, each is in a certain way both commanding and commanded.

This circuit can break down, of course, and the many no longer find themselves in the sovereign. The intermediation of the many in community falters, that is, the many is denied domestic repose in a commons that is taken for granted. It is important that the social trust that invests the circulation of power between people and sovereign have a stability sufficient not always to be called into question. Trust entails a dimension of taking for granted. One can rely on what is granted. The granting is still at work, even when it is taken for granted. The trusting is still in act even when no notice is taken of it, and the authority of the law is granted. The real effectiveness of this granted trust is often only noted when there is a defect of trust, when it is betrayed, as in a miscarriage of justice, or a blatantly unjust law, or a political treachery, or surrender to the enemy.

In times of peace, that is, of effective trust, the question of authority and legitimacy hardly comes up for discussion. Its constancy, more or less formalized in the institutions of law, permits people to get on with their daily lives in a framework not noticed, just because it works well enough. By contrast, in times of disruption and war and the breakdown of law, the question of legitimacy becomes extreme, when the exercise of power leads to widespread destruction, when in seeking to express itself in irresistible force it undermines the legitimacy of taken-for-granted trust. War itself becomes the struggle of distrust for supreme power. The force of power seeks to enforce its own legitimacy, not by winning trust but by relentlessly carrying through the consequences of distrust. The justice of its legitimacy cannot help but be dubious, though none has the power to stand against it, or even permission to say that this is so: that the justice of the victor seems as threadbare as the justice of the vanquished. Such a victory is not the emergence of a new sovereignty but a return to zero, in which the sources of social power must again seek secretly to sow the mustard seeds of trust.

Think again of the analogy with genius: the genius is a creative originator who gives the rule to art but is not himself or herself a rule, and in that sense is beyond rule. As the genius is the one through whom nature gives the rule to art (Kant), the sovereign is the through whom the sources of power give the rule to society. Both are *intermediaries* between idiotic sources of power and their communal mediation, though each may claim an untrue being for self, and usurp the gift. The source of indeterminate power out of which rule creatively emerged is not itself a rule, or simply subject to rule. Subjection to rule comes *after* the genius of original giving is confirmed in the work, not before the work. The legitimation comes with the work itself in its becoming determinate. We cannot anticipate this justification in advance in a completely determinate way. This openness must always mean risk and peril. This is not to deny precedent, or preceding originals that give direction to present endeavors, as some of the French revolutionaries looked back to Republican Rome. But the same basic problem of justification also arises with respect to precedent.

This does not mean that the justice is simply the *product* of the work. There is a justice that is, so to say, the *anonymous companion* of the entire exercise of power that only properly emerges from its anonymity in process, and comes to have a name, say, in the law, at the end with the justified work. The secret anonymity of this justice does not mean it is nothing until that end. Rather, it is the most essential that keeps itself in reserve in the unfolding of tasks, until the vessel of its proper incarnation allows it to reveal its name. Law may be one vessel, but there are others. If the wrong vessel is being created, this justice may not be allowed to proclaim itself. The creator cooperates with the nameless god, friend of the friendless, until it stands revealed and the world is astonished at its glory, or appalled at its horror. We participate in preparing the proper vessel to announce the always-present work of the good. We are not justified; the good is justified; but its willingness to be anonymous, and not named, also shows that it is beyond demanded justification. It is for the sake of the good itself, let fools put whichever name they like on the exercise of power. Similarly with the work of sovereignty. Legitimacy of power and its sovereign exercise *come to be together*. This does not make them necessarily arbitrary. It all depends on the companion justice that gets a name in the exercise. And the point is not to assimilate the work of social justice to the work of art simply—there are great dangers in that assimilation. The point is the just rhythm of power unfolding.

What can we say of the sovereign as social lawgiver? Can we speak of the self-legislation of society? Or the subjection of the social intermediation to the rule of the sovereign as supremely self-mediating, so that the social intermediation becomes the subject in which his or her power is exercised or confirmed? Does not the intermediation of sovereign power always show a tendency to favor a logic of dialectical self-mediation, whether from the side of the ruler or ruled? If the sovereign is the source of law giving, is the sovereign subject to law, or beyond law? We have all of the old issues of legitimate or arbitrary power. Is legitimate power always established as legitimate after the exercise of power, not prior to its exercise? If so, is not all power self-legitimating, and if it is, is there no ultimate distinction between self-justifying power and arbitrary power?

In one respect, there seems no legitimation of power prior to its proper exercise: the justice of power establishes itself in its very unfolding. Is this to make its exercise arbitrary? Not necessarily. The exercise of power may be differently understood, depending on how we see the source of origination. If law is a determination of power, the determination is the issue of a source prior to determinate law, and in that sense indeterminate. How we understand that source affects the character of its coming to be exercised. If we treat it as a neutral or an indifferent force, justice is mere might. If we understand this indetermination as the erotic lack that must fulfill itself by its determinate exercise, justice will tend to be self-legislating. Alternatively, the lack may suggest that there is a source of good that we do not possess, hence justice cannot be self-legislating but requires relation to that other source. Or we might understand the indetermination as an overdetermined source that, in some sense, is already full in itself and that does not exercise itself to fulfill itself but to give the good for the other. This kind of overdetermined source issues in justice as agapeic origination.

If we connect the source of sovereignty to erotic self-expression, there is no necessity that such a self-expression be an arbitrary exercise of capricious power. There will be some difficulty in properly recognizing the place of the other, and less justice will be done to the community as metaxological intermediation. The claim will be made for an inclusive self-legislation, but this inclusion will be, in fact, a contraction. The extreme of this contraction would make legitimate power reflect the strongest self-assertion and self-insistence. But even if sovereignty contracts the power of self-mediation out of the intermediation, it still may be *relatively just* in taking the others into account and recognizing their due in the most inclusive sense possible.

Thus there can be powerful leaders whose own approximation of a dialectical wholeness makes them *just bestowers*, relative to the social intermediation of the many. These just rulers must be both powerful and just, and through them, power becomes the instrument of justice. But they are justified by their just exercise of power, not by a justice *cut off* from the exercise of power. The situation remains shrouded in ambiguity: such a sovereign seems to be an embodiment of justice for the others, and yet the drive to be that exemplar is wedded to a great love of glory in which the name of the ruler is raised to the heights. If you like, a kind of *superior selfishness* finds its peace with doing good for the other. The sense of the origin as lacking and needing the other for itself always puts the other in an equivocal position relative to the exercise of power. Is this exercise for the good of the other or for the self-glorification of the self? Mostly it is both, but justice is not for self-glorification, but simply for the good, whether of the other, or for the self, insofar as it too is in the community of the good.

The matter is clearer in the case of agapeic power. There is not merely a subsequent definition of the good and of justice as the achieved result of a self-completing social eros, initially lacking. The good does not simply come to be in the end as a result of the exercise of power; rather, it comes to be determinately, because the origin is already full of good, already a good that exceeds itself in its bestowing of good for the other. The power to be exercised is itself the power of good: here it makes no sense to abstract justice from power or power from justice. Agapeic power originates the work of goodness; and that work is not just a matter of doing determinate good things, or creating laws that are determinate regulations of a power that is amorally lawless. There is an overdetermined sense of good and the power of this good, *before* determinate laws or rules and the power consolidated in this or that definite formation of social life. The agapeic source is lawless in that sense, but not as less than law but as more.

Its power gives the good for the sake of the giving of the good. This is a self-justifying giving of the good, not for the sake of self-justification but for the good of the recipients of the good, that is, the others who are the beneficiaries of the gift. Here general eros points towards an indeterminate good willingness, beyond determinate will and beyond will to power. This more fundamental power of the good takes us beyond sovereignty, insofar as the latter is bound up with the erotic process of social self-mediation through the intermediating other. The ambiguities of power with sovereignty cannot be seen properly without seeing beyond sovereign power. In any case, we cannot consent to a simplistic dualism of power and justice, or think of power as dominating force, or of justice as some impotent ideal. To see what is more is to see the ambiguities of the sovereign intermediation of justice through the power of a society. And so we become guarded about the slide of power into tyranny, while realistically appreciating that the power of justice calls out for effective worldly embodiment to concretize justice's disturbing demand. The justice of powerful sovereigns is tempered by skepticism about themselves as the ultimate power, with a humility in their pride, indeed, a secret spirit of penitence, lest the ambiguities of their gift seduce them to the black bliss of power exercised without justice.

Transcendental Sovereignty: On Constitution and Representation

The transcendental potency relative to sovereignty concerns the constitution of a people, for this refers us to grounding principles that serve, so to say, as the historical a priori conditions of possibility.[12] This cannot be a complete self-constitution. Sovereignty is always a social intermediation that shapes the medium of communal power in which a people comes to itself, hence something *more* than self-mediation is at work. This means that this constitution can never close into a self-sufficient whole. Sovereignty is an intermediated communication of the power of people to itself, a communication at once deeply intimate, yet over and above, more than the intimacy of any particular self. It is at once deeply singular and essentially communal, idiotic and public at once. Its will to maximize the self-mediation of its own intimate sources of power already shows the exigence of excess which, in fact, points to the limit and the breach of power as self-mediating. The temptation to hubris is inevitable: seeking the maximum, measure is exceeded. Measure is more outrageously exceeded in some social intermediations than in others. Sometimes sovereignty will insist on itself, manifesting itself through outrage itself (in analogy with the agapeic servant, but reversed: profane parody of the *skandalon*).

---

12. Not all peoples have a written constitution. This is a relatively recent development and has the advantage of a seemingly more univocal statement of the explicit grounding principles of a people that become its historical a priori conditions of possibility. Nevertheless, the relentless interpretation and reinterpretation of written constitutions, such as the U.S. Constitution, indicate the illusion of a merely univocal claim. Peoples lacking written constitutions are not necessarily devoid of grounding principles of possibility; they may have an effective a priori rather than a written one.

The sources of sovereignty can be intermediated to a constituting focus in a plurality of ways: monarch, elected assembly, dictator, president. . . . The ways are not all equal, since not all intermediate and free the sources of power. The dictatorial way may as much block the happening of sovereignty as facilitate it, when to sustain itself it has to stifle massive sources of original power in the community. Democracy, in principle, seems to be a form in which sovereignty draws most widely on these sources of power. In practice, it may stifle extravagant sources of power; the tyranny of the mediocre may suppress, by an aborting silence, the more outrageous, or noble, manifestations of power beyond utility.[13] Other forms of intermediation may, in surprising ways, draw forth into creative expression strange and original sources of power. The people is not the ultimate source of sovereignty; the people is emergent with sovereignty. The community and its reserves of power are the sources of sovereignty that facilitates the transformation of the community into a people with a self-mediated sense of its own identity. The claim of the people to be sovereign is to be granted, only because this process *has occurred*; the self-mediation has been effected, and then is thought to be original, not the result of a process of intermediation. The claim of the people to be its own original sovereign mixes result and source. There is a communal being together more original than being a people; the latter is a crystallization into self-mediation, through the intermediation of the sovereign, of the former's reserves of power. This being together, and the mysterious ways in which powers are communicated in its intermediations, is the more original source of sovereignty.

What then of *representation*? But are we not again, with representation, beyond self-constitution and self-mediation? For the representative is a being for an other; the represented is a being empowered through an other. The representative is a one who stands for many, or is for many, or serves as self for the others or many. One is for the others; and in the one, the many are for themselves. The many become one in this one, hence their plurivocal community is communicated in and through the representative. Nevertheless, there has to be an *ongoing passage back and forth between* the one and the many for the process of representation to be a form of vital and legitimated sovereignty. Representation, then, is a dynamic intermediation in the between. Thus it is a double process: the *selfmediation* of the many in the one and the *intermediation of the many* to and with itself, in and through the one, or representative. Sovereign representatives are ones who stand for the others, stand in and become the passage ways through

---

13. See the incredulity of a utilitarian mentality towards manifestations of sovereignty—extraordinary, excessive spectacles, spectacular shows of power disproportionate to utilitarian aims. They offend the inverse snobbery of the utilitarian: middling life is superior. And then, as if in revolt against the atrophy of spectacle, we greet the kitschy excess of *celebrities*—the mediocre aping of majesty in an age of utility.

which a community knows its power, its eros, its mind, its will.[14] The constitution of a people that comes to be itself in and through representing others is not univocal but plurivocal. In fact, different forms of representation, corresponding to the fourfold sense of being, can be discerned. This fourfold plurivocity itself illuminates something of the classical topology of forms of governance through one, some, and many. Let me elaborate.

First, if the sources of power are intermediated through *one powerful figure*, we tend towards forms in which patriarchy, or monarchy, or dictatorship dominates. This can be the appropriate form, depending on the state of virtual powers in the community, its social self-mediation and self-understanding, how these flow into an understanding of the form of intermediation best serving the good of the ethical that is now possible in this particular configuration of the ethos. There is a *sovereign univocity* here: the univocal sense of being shapes a community's way of seeing itself as a people only as intermediated in the *sovereign one*. Obviously, too, this representation of sovereignty is promiscuously linked to the power of the sacred, understood in terms of God as the sovereign one or as the all-mighty father. The many are represented to themselves as children of the one of power, the father of all power. Sometimes they see themselves as mediated back to themselves as subordinated moments of an all-encompassing whole, which is their enactment of the intermediation of the people. Differences hardly count or are suppressed if their dissident waywardness emerges. I should add that this is *one form* of paternalism: it does not exhaust the meaning of the father, as the almighty power does not exhaust the meaning of God, just as there may be kings whose power is the propagation of justice rather than the imposition of an order in which the many are held in subjection to the bonds of a social totality.

Second, this sovereign univocity must eventually come under strain, for the differences of plurality must emerge beyond the majestic difference of the absolute one and the exception of the incontrovertible monarch. After all, the one serves a *social intermediation*, and hence is impossible apart from the plurality it mediates and sometimes suppresses. Its very success as sovereign intermediation means that the many themselves will in time be empowered, and the prodigious might of plurality must come to exert itself differently, in its differences. Indeed, it will represent itself in a variety of forms of *equivocal manyness*: a *few* or *some* will manage to insist upon their power and right to rule; the power of sovereignty will

---

14. Representation prefigures a being in the place of the other which is not a projective will to power only. The agapeic representative may be more than the represented and may show the represented the more that is its own promise, hence may open up a way of transcending. See *BHD*, Chapter 3, on the doubleness of representation and the preservation of the "beyond" against dialectical immanence. Levinas may speak of "substitution," yet I find the whole critique of "representational" thinking full of equivocity, and not only in Levinas.

be more widely distributed in a many. Moreover, there will be strains in this many, since the power of the many may only be partially intermediated; power seems to have lost its focus in the one and is more elusively distributed among the few. Often here the sovereign who emerges is the one who is attuned to the equivocal flows of power, just in this elusive distribution, and who turns that flow in his own direction. Think of the despot emerging from the internecine strife of a many, which initially grabbed for the reins of potential sovereignty with the breakdown of the power of a previous sovereign one. Think of Stalin as the cunning power of the sovereign in waiting who could read the equivocal signs of will to power in his party cohorts and direct the flow of power to himself, as its flows from the dying or deceased Lenin. And what matter if many eggs must be cracked to cook this omelette!

Another possibility is an equivocal many who live in an ambiguous equilibrium, determined by their love of money (plutocracy), or power (oligarchy), or honor (timocracy), and so on. This equivocal sovereignty of a few often mirrors the network of utility, in that instrumental values tend to be in dominance. These few often fail to represent any excellence except what serves their own satisfactions. They are all more *mediocre versions of the tyrant* who previously unashamedly served his own satisfaction. And there will always be fear and suspicion in this social intermediation of sovereignty. For, in addition to the comfort of utility, the only other form they know is the power of the sovereign one, and they wait in trepidation, or hope, for the reemergence of a new dominating one. Their own manyness is something to be intermediated through a leader, who may return them to something like the old firm orientation or tyranny, or lead them forward with promises of a land that will be home. Among them lurks one or more who would be lord. And there can be forms of democratic manyness as treacherous, as debasing as the worst in the rule of the few. The equivocal many hides itself basely in the rhetoric of the equality of all, which is a weapon by which exceptional excellence is torn down or dismantled. All can be equalized, that is, flattened in the web of serviceable disposability. The people as a many can be as monstrous as any cruel despot or gang of fanatical rulers. Sometimes the difference between a lynch mob and a court of law is only slowness of procedure, and the play of order. The lethal outcome is foreordained.

Third, a form corresponding to an *open dialectic* will make good on some of these deficiencies: the tendency of the first form to repress the power of the many, while representing it; the tendency of the second to shortchange the power of the many as it expresses the power of the few, all the while lacking the superior excellences of the one. We might correlate this third form with an *aristocratic* form of sovereignty. The best is what is important for the aristocrat. Put aside the image of the decadent aristocrat, the ignoble noble. Think simply of the aristocrat as one who lives in terms of the best, or the excellent. Aristocracy is an intermediation of the community in which sovereignty is invested in a few who exemplify all that seems best about human promise and power. It makes good on the exclusiveness of the sovereign one in more widely communicating the majesty of power itself; power won in the achievement of the excellence, and hence a justified mirror of a human wholeness wherein the many in the community can encounter the self-mediation of human powers at their highest. The excellence of the one is communicated through many and not through one; hence the hope of a more universal communication of ethical excellence is shown to the community; thus the community may be enabled more explicitly to become a people of ethical excellence.

Sometimes if a society is blessed with a few good humans of outstanding ethical excellence, and if they attain social positions where they are "on show" to the community, the community is welded into a people participating in the community of higher excellence, represented to itself in just that social show. The communication of higher excellence is shown and shared through these few good humans. The society is energized with a higher purpose, beyond the kitschy poverty of the money loving plutocracy, the mediocre honors of timocracy, and the hollow crassness of the oligarchic few who cling to power for its own sake.

Aristocratic sovereignty can correspond to an open dialectical self-mediation of the sources of power, as coming to social recognition in a few humans of superior wholeness—the erotic sovereigns who have struggled out of the difference-less one, and also out of the shifting and treacherous equivocity of manyness without unity. In themselves as whole, these sovereigns enact and represent a balance of one and many, sameness and otherness. They become ones who can mediate the sovereignty of the many through the richness of their wholeness that contains within itself manyness. Just because their integral wholeness includes rich manyness in itself, they can justly be said to stand sovereignly for the many, to *represent* the many not as mere interchangeable substitutes, but as embodying even the higher powers that are dormant or stifled or denied in the many. They are representative humans because they are representative of what is best in humanity. They are exemplars of human excellence, not just mere messenger boys from the many, or gofers for an ascendant mediocrity. If they have any "right" to rule, it is because they represent excellence, and ethical wisdom concerns the rule of the best.[15]

Such representing sovereigns communicate to the people the power of achieved wholeness through the unity of oneness and manyness manifest in their selves; but they cannot be understood as solitary heroes or humans who on their own come into the possession of higher excellence. Their excellence comes to be out of an extraordinary complex *social* intermediation that provides the ground of support for the crystallization of singularity. This achieved singularity, by being

---

15. Interestingly, Plato's aristocratic communism and Nietzsche's aristocratic individualism converge, relative to the best, even as they diverge on what is the best.

what it is as a self-mediating wholeness of personhood, already *shows back* to the supporting ground of the community the richness of the soil on which it grew and which secretly fertilized it. In that *showing back*, the anonymous greatness of the community can come to be named, can put a name on itself, and can celebrate itself in its celebrating of the singular it has helped to grow. The society enjoys its own *festivity with excellence* in the feast of excellence that its own outstanding singulars put on show. The festivity is a fulfilling enjoyment, not only of the singular but of the society itself: it enjoys its own superiority in the great achievements of its singular best, or best singulars.

There also are great dangers here,[16] connected to *subtler equivocities in oneness itself, in wholeness itself.* I mean that these aristocrats can be seized by a hubris that unleashes disequilibrium in the intermediation of sovereignty. They will be *full of themselves*, so full they will think of themselves as the social totality, hence be tempted to usurp as solely their own what is, in the deeper measure, the gift of the community. They will want to be kings, or tyrants; or a group of them will, or give themselves over to the temptations of baser forms of rule by the few. The bewitchment of excellence itself will turn their heads. The power bringing them to excellence and the excellence bringing them to power will be perverted. The excellence of power and the power of excellence, in building their palace, will court their own ruin. Instead of being free in power, they become unfree in perpetuating power. Power becomes their bondage, as what makes them great is haunted by miserable anxiety, and on the very heights. They will cease to represent the best of the many in their own oneness. The oneness will contract, even as its seems to expand its power more inclusively. Being for themselves, unknown to themselves, they will have cut themselves off from the secret sources of power.

Of course, some singulars may have stored enough of this sticky honey to last their lifetime. Or they may be so well attuned to the equivocal flow of these sources that miraculously they find their way back to them again, just when they seem about to founder. So they survive and outlive their immanent deposition. Since the wholeness balancing oneness and manyness is a dynamic achievement, it is always fragile, and more so since it draws up its energy from the secret reserves of power in a community. In its highest wholeness, its temptation is to

---

16. The danger of organic totality, for instance. There is danger in that the idiotic sources of sovereignty are in excess to complete self-mediation. The idiotic infinity of these overdetermined sources is beyond finite measure. Think of the abyss of the singular self; think of this infinite abyss pluralized, without any univocal limit. This idiotic infinity is intimated in the majesty of sovereignty. But the spectacle of the sovereign, its *spectacular* powers, is related to the *monstrous (monstrare* is an excessive showing). Thus sovereignty can be a spectacle of the monstrous, a spectacular monster—a public enlargement of the idiocy of the monstrous: evil made socially manifest, magnified to world-historical dimensions, as in and through Stalin or Hitler.

collapse the plural interplay of intermediation into the single play of self-mediation. On seeming to achieve its wholeness, the root that links it to the secret reserves is tempted to think of itself as for itself alone, as self-sufficient. It is not. Its deeper ethical truth is this: *It has come to be whole for its own sake in order to be for the sake of the others: its own highest good is its being good for the others.*

A similar point must be made relative to *the community that enjoys itself* in its own best. The nature of its self-enjoyment may mean that it closes itself off from what is other to itself. It may turn towards these others in the spirit of sharp condescension, or the hostility that names its own feeling of superiority. The community enjoys its superiority, its being above, in the superiority of its dialectical sovereigns. But "being above" here means *putting down* the others who are below—that neighboring nation a mass of barbarians or breeding vermin. The *people itself* is tempted to its own holistic hubris just in its highest excellences. Out of that holistic hubris, out of that excellence, the worst barbarisms of war and imperial exploitation can flower. Once again, *corruptio optimi pessimi.*

In this instance, while the few intermediate the many, the many must be *our own.* The many others who are *not our own* must be below us—the unclean, the unelected, the servile outsider now destined to amplify our sovereignty. The aggression of this aristocratic sovereignty can euphemize its ferocity in the rhetoric of excellence: it has a mission or manifest destiny to bring the same excellences to the unwashed others, and for their good. But the clear truth to these unwashed others will be despoliation, subjection, pillage of their specific difference. The mission of excellence will be another usurpation. (God will be on our side, ready even to help with a cleansing disaster, such as a famine.) The dialectical sovereign grows its own incubus of opposition to the unregenerate other who, to be whole, must be included in the self-expansion of the original whole. But now this more inclusive whole is indistinguishable from a devouring of the other, or if the other is already akin, a kind of *Anschluss.* Sovereign intermediation returns to destructive equivocity in new dualistic opposition and the omnivorous drive to annexing wholeness.

A fourth form of representation extends the intermediation of the sources of social power beyond the one and the few to all—at least that is true in principle. A full understanding of *metaxological community* entails that the other is not just a means of self-mediation but has its own value for itself. While the togetherness of the many occasions self-mediation, more fundamentally it is a matter of intermediation in which the metaxological between supports the being of self and other as their own and for themselves, and yet also as each a being for the other, and at the highest, a being for the other who generously transcends self in the mode of agapeic service. In principle, the intermediation of the social sources of power is inherently marked by the exigence ethically to distribute original power to all within the embrace of the community. Insofar as the principle is recognized and enacted, a different meaning comes to be of the people as embracing. The embrace is not a merely inclusive whole; it grants community beyond any logic of part and whole. Given the implicit commitment to an ethical transcendence to all, the embrace turns away from figuring the other as the mirror in which I am reflected back to myself. Rather, the relation between selves and others becomes an opening into a venture of the good that tests the promise of agapeic generosity. Self-transcendence is turned away from self towards the other, and yet not turned away in a mode of denial but in a mode of bestowal out of what richness or poverty the self has. It gives its share to the other who now needs it, or who now is the companion in a communal enjoyment of the goodness of being, the goodness of the good.

We here reach a point of passage beyond the intermediation of sovereignty, for the latter always deals with some precipitation of the self-mediation of a community to *itself* out of the overdetermination of intermediation at work in the togetherness of the many. We are pointed to the community of agapeic service. Sovereignty touches the hem of the metaxological universal. In a complexly ambiguous fashion, we find some correspondence to the promise of certain *democratic* forms of sovereignty. These *can* correlate with the metaxological: insofar as the meaning of the many opens towards a universal ideal of human community in which each is given to be as an end in self, hence absolute, but none is closed in self as the absolute, and so each is absolved into a more absolute being for others. The drive from wholeness to inclusiveness that we find in the movement from one to many is articulated as the ethical hope of a community not of abstract humanity but the concrete singular others with me, and with whom I am always.

Can the sources of social power be distributed among all? In practice, the human universal must be mediated through the particular. Does this mean to the many through the few? The notion of representation by its nature means that one or some are for the others. Being one and being for others exist in inherent tension: being one is tugged towards its own self-mediation; being for others demands a transcendence of that self-mediation. It follows that in the representation of the many by one/some, the self-mediation of the latter can usurp the intermediation of the former. The great challenge is in devising social institutions in which this usurpation is avoided, or at least held in check. Were it not, the will to power of the one/some takes over, all the while claiming the legitimacy of all for its unrighteous exercise.

There is no way that this tension can be avoided entirely, since it is rooted in the nature of human being and its social intermediation. *Positively*, this tension calls us to metaxological intermediation as a *task* that is never finished. In practice, however, we often find the splitting of the larger many into smaller pluralities, each with representatives who fight the case of their faction or sect against the others. This may be positive in curbing the will to absolute power through, say, a system of "checks and balances." It may be negative in institutionalizing social life as low-grade civil war. Then in the political field, we find something like a doppelgänger of the network of serviceable disposability in which the many use the others, and indeed the whole, for their own self-mediation. Social intermediation is then instrumentalized in terms of a plurality of power groups, each insisting that it is the one that the social intermediation should serve, hence narrowing the potential for ethical openness to the other as other. Not surprisingly, many forms of contemporary democracy are in deep collusion with the network of utility. We preach the principle of the equality of humans as an end in itself; in practice, this equality is the individual's opportunity of becoming a unit of productive or consuming power, a partaker of the social exploitation of serviceable disposability.

This latter equality implies a reductive homogenizing, entirely at odds with the *intensive equality* implied by the self-mediation and social intermediation of the ethical. Intensive equality points to the *measureless value of the human being*, as an end in itself, of infinite character. This truth of human equality can never be fully institutionalized in a network of utility since it transcends it entirely. So also, corresponding to intensive equality, there is a fraternity and freedom that must transcend mutual exploitation and individual autonomy. To the degree that "democratic capitalism" is a contraction of intensive equality and fraternity and freedom, its final truth does not differ from that of serviceable disposability, namely, a disguised will to power and a secret despair. We need to transcend to another ethical dimension to do justice to what is the real truth of democracy, which is tied to the social intermediation of the power of the good to all humans.

As I suggested above, some forms of democratic manyness can be as debasing as the worst in the rule of the few. The rhetoric of the equality of all can be used to mask a particular strategy of will to power. The call of equality becomes a means by which excellence is surreptitiously undermined. One of the conceits of those who preach democratic piety is that the sacrosanct people always knows its mind. Clearly this is dubious, especially if we grant "general eros" as at the more intimate source of social power. On that score, advertisers in "democratic capitalism" are better political philosophers than are many political philosophers. So are "public relations" people, or "spin doctors," or (not to euphemize) propagandists. They seek to insinuate their images closer to the subliminal formlessness of the general eros. Plato saw the danger when he suggested that democracy was the form most likely to produce tyranny. Why? In our terms: because the indeterminacy of mass eros is always plastic to the charms of the charismatic sovereign who, intimate with the aphrodisiac effect of power, seduces the many with dreams of its own erotic sovereignty. The charm having worked, the monster in the charmer steps out, steps out if the people's general eros is so fluid as not to keep in strong check its own monstrous possibilities.

I know Plato is often hated as supposedly a proto-fascist, or enemy of the "open society" (Popper). But clearly, if he has any enemy it is *tyranny*. His honesty does not blink the possible connection of tyranny and democracy. The desires of the many can be driven (again with the goad of propaganda, advertising) to a frenzy of equalization that makes every excellence the same, hence making every excellence nothing excellent. Likewise, openness to otherness breeds an indifference to otherness, which mutates into hostility to the other, when the other is genuinely other, and not a reliable mouther of the catch cries of the day. This frenzy of equalization flattens intensive equality. It discharges the energy of self-transcending into the horizontal meeting of self-interested satisfaction, now comfortably housed in the dominion of serviceable disposability. The many acts collectively, like an autocrat who grudges the transcendence of higher excellence—a prophetic reminder of the slough of mediocrity in which the community lies. There is a fickle bewitchment abroad as we eagerly await the novelty that will tickle our tired palates, or the inconstant excitement of the new that will dress again our anonymous despondency. Lacking the discernment of intensive equality, we are victims of the equivocity of equality, and especially so when the intermediation of social sovereignty is overspread by the hegemony of serviceable disposability.

There are social excellences beyond utility without which utility is a mean-spirited and threadbare efficiency, effective into the void. The best democracies produce the best, namely, an aristocracy of character and spirit, in principle open to all. This aristocracy is not a distinct social class, or an hereditary noble class, or a managerial elite that imperiously claims to know what is best for all. It is the flourishing of the best of human power in the best human beings, as intermediated and supported by the sources of social power. The best should be sovereign, not in the mode of self-mediating will to power, but in service of the community as a whole, and with special attunement to the justified cries of those who are powerless. The aristocrats of the ethical are to be sovereign, but sovereigns who hear the call of a strange reversal from will to power to a willingness to sacrifice enjoyment of power, its pleasures and majesties, in order to dare social and political actions that enable the social intermediation of the good to all.

Equality, fraternity, and freedom here are in the dimension of intensive infinity. So also the task itself is an infinite one, always begun and never completed. For completion would be the claim of total self-mediation, and what is important here is not primarily the self-mediation of power but the communication of the good between self and others: at once real or being realized, but also an ideal and a hope for which we strive. Emphasize the realizing only, we easily become complacent or smug: the good becomes only what is always here now. Emphasize the hope only, we lose contact with the current social intermediation: the good becomes only an always elsewhere other. The good is truly always here now *and* always elsewhere other. We have to accept this tension and live this doubleness, paradoxical though it may seem. On the blasted heath of time, we meet again the weird sisters, and must turn around, again and again, their wicked refrain: fair's not foul and foul's not fair; yet the hurly burly's never done, and the battle's always to be lost and won.

The Eudaimonics of Sovereignty:
The Intermediation of Common Good

Social representation by one or some for the sake of others points towards
the notion of the common good. Call this the eudaimonics of sovereignty. The
intermediation of social power looks to an as wide as possible distribution of the
benefits of that power. The ethical communication of the power to be concerns
the good of the community as a whole. Thus the justice of a community is in the
effective communication of the common good. Obviously this communication is
not any quantitative sense of the common. The common is not an aggregate of
atomistic individuals represented in their external commonality through the sovereign. There are no such individuals. There are singulars that in their being are
communally intermediated from the outset, and so again the issue is more the
communication of powers that well up from idiotic reserves of commonness.
These reserves are elusively prior to the determination of different groupings
within a community, or the crystallization of this or that individual insisting on
its own power.

This means, on the one hand, that the common good is not simply defined
as if through a poll of individual preferences. De facto we may often have to be
oriented that way, but few are univocally certain of what is good for them. Nor
do leaders, claiming the right to tell them, have this certainty. We share the dis-
concertments of muddling in a fog. The so-called common good is often the
apparition of a set of flattering bewitchments. On the other hand, one cannot
finally *dictate* to people what is the good. Astray in a mystery, we settle for the
obvious and bark at any insinuation we know not what we are about. Those who
intermediate the community's sense of itself may be simply enforcing their own
commitment to a particular bewitchment, and not so much bewitching as breeding covens of happy zombies.

Can the common good be reduced to the sum of instrumental goods? Not if
sovereignty, in its eudaimonics, involves more than mediating the play of
exploiters in the network of utility. Were that all, there would be no common
good that is common, except the separate goods of the separate exploiters, or perhaps the homogenizing power of serviceable disposability as the only value the
same for all. What of the basic necessities we need as vulnerable beings? Self-
preservation, security of property, and so on have their place. But we want protection and more—we now want comfort. Does our comfort forget the struggle
to secure these goods? For the struggle reminds us of the bleak Hobbesian world
of scarcity, and we are tempted to think that any feast of creation is secondary,
subtended by a bitter, infertile rock on which we eke out a grim living. Is this
place of hostility and hunger the secret source: cold, forsaken, full of pitfalls,
crushing us if we do not work against it? If so, it is no surprise that will to power
emerges from it. And is this too hidden in our desire for comfort? Nietzsche, the

younger one, will serenade war, not always remembering the older Hobbes, who fought a grimmer fight for peace—but on the terms of war. Both this war and peace are children of the will willing itself. But—here we come to the deeper point—this is already an offspring of something more basic: the commons that is the intermediation of the self-mediating center of existence to itself. The hostile is an offspring of the common; the common is not a product built up from a dominance of the hostile or a balance of hostilities, nor the precarious comfort built on that balance. More basic than comfort and preservation, than threat and will to power, prior to self-insistence and the will that wills itself, is the gift of the power to be as good, given out of an ontological generosity that is peace, not war. The eudaimonics of sovereignty as the common good seek to give integral social form to such a condition of peace more fundamental than war.

This is social peace as the community at home with itself in the ethos as good. This is not peace that comes from the stalemate or compromise of warring powers, nor the dominance of one power over rivals. Certainly the dangers of will to power reflect the connection between sovereignty and erotic will to be. But the community of erotic sovereignty is grounded on a peace that is more agapeic, since it is out of an already effective excess of harmony that power is effective for further good. This peace is not a stale stasis but the surplus dynamism of harmony, the many at home with each other and themselves. To be good is to be at home. To be at home is to be at peace. This is the energy of the good, festive and affirming of the joy of "to be." The common good is in this peace, though more often than not there will be a mixture, where the balance of competing powers, even hostile powers, contributes.

The eudaimonics of sovereignty can be appreciative of the depth of the common, and indeed of different depths of peace. That is *first* the community between the origin and creation. The goodness of creation is a communication that comes to the given world from its being a gift of the origin. Basic ecological respect of creation as other echoes the basic love of the origin for the good of "to be." *Second*, there is a common good in the nature of nature that is not man-made. There is something of the blessing of gift on this. Forget this, and we are fouling our own nest, though we move serially into a virgin nest, once having made a dump of that last one. *Third*, there is a common good between the origin and the human. Humans are distinctive in the intensiveness of their ethical promise and range: they can care for the creation, enter into a relation that shows some trace of agapeic generosity: not merely respect, but a kind of elemental love for things that are there. In that love we recoil from the unnecessary destruction of life, including that of things not-human. The ant we stamp on is a marvel of singular life. We are insects ourselves with our shells placed inside. *Fourth*, there is a common good between humans, insofar as each is a singular source of self-transcendence, and end in self of infinite value. The community between a plurality of such beings cannot be of univocal reduction, or equivocal dissemination, or dialectical inclusion, nor of autonomy, or holistic self-mediation. The commons is in the between, and the relation of integral singulars, each self-mediating and bringing to show its infinity, cannot be autonomous self-determination. There is a commons beyond inclusion, as there is a freedom beyond autonomy. The energizing of that commons, of that freedom in the between, is the common good, as if we are simply to enjoy the good of being in the between: as when I am with the other, and the others are with me, and "being with" in the between is an energizing of our highest energies, not to possess others or even oneself, not to plot domination or ingratiation, but simply to be there to enjoy a consummation of being with and together; as if the human community itself had become a festivity of goodness communicating itself towards all the others, as at a great banquet.

Thus the eudaimonics of sovereignty has much to do with festivity, in which a community takes joy in itself, simply in the good of being with the others. Singulars are freed from the solitude that locks them in a circle of lonely or self-satisfied or longing self-mediation. We are snatched up into a larger life that does not engulf us but releases joy. The common good as enjoyed in the festival contradicts the claims of autonomous individuality. If people are in thrall to autonomy, they may refuse in themselves the festive opening that calls them beyond themselves, that makes they shrug and laugh and say: what am I, I am as nothing; and yet here I am, here with the others, and some are ugly, some beautiful, but lo the ugly—is it the feast that turns my head?—seem strangely to glow with an aura of beauty, and dare one say it, a holiness, as if the halo of an unearthly goodness glimmered around them. Is this what the agape of the common good does?

How far this eudaimonics of sovereignty is from contract! The derivation of sovereignty from contract makes as little sense as the above abstraction of the individual. Sovereignty is before contract and exceeds contract; it is already happening before the order possibilizing contract is given. Contract theories work with abstractions from already effective intermediations. The individuals are already abstractions from an effective common good. To say the minimum, the individual could not grow into an effective unit of self-interested or predatory power, whether hostile to the other or self-affirming, if the social ground did not give the soil on which his or her self-mediating could come to itself, come into its own. Contract theory always starts much too late. How could the individuals in a so-called state of nature, or behind the veil of ignorance, or whatever, even recognize the possibility of such a thing called contract if they did not already have the benefit of social intermediation, hence know, in perhaps some indeterminate way, the meaning of community, or being in common. Contract presupposes significant social cultivation for it to be possible, hence it cannot be the ground of the common but must occur in a common space that is more primordial.

Aristotle and Hegel are more correct than Hobbes, Rousseau, Locke, and Rawls. Many contract theories seem to mirror (whether in crude ways or subtle) the metaphysical frame of the modern *mathesis* of nature: the abstraction of atomized individuals, as if these were prior to intermediation; relations as merely contingent connections or customary contiguities between entities with no inherent connection; individuals as units of power, driven to protect, preserve, and perpetuate their power; communities having their basis in aggregation, even let the aggregate take on forms that seem to mimic more holistic or inherent connectedness. What you have at the beginning is not even neutral thereness, certainly no community of origin and creation, hence the efforts of humans to construct communities are such that value has to be an ingredient added to the aggregate in terms of what is considered basic or primitive to the exposed unit of power, namely, self-preservation and the expansion of its buffer of power, its *Lebensraum*. The solitary individual animals, the aggregates, founded on fear, calculative of benefits, are abstractions from primal intermediations. And where then are the eudaimonics of sovereignty and its festivity? Replaced by a sovereign, the supreme enforcer, perhaps cowing the many into submission to superior might, or holding together into the artificial concord of serviceable disposability the contending powers that both hate and need each other. If this sovereign is another mortal god, it also is a god who loves nothing. For no inherent good flows from it, no breath of love, or warmth, or care: calculative power at the milder extreme, but at the other extreme, colder power, cruel and crushing when necessary, and the counterfeit connectedness of the rule of power without justice. The counterfeits of peace come to be out of submission to that power. Strange peace, the last refuge from the destruction of peace, a refuge itself the destruction of peace, namely, tyranny. If that were all, life would not be the flourishing marvel it is but the desolate land left behind by plundering warriors, when they make of our eden a foretaste of hell. This mortal god needs hell, and the fear of hell, to keep the many in submissive order—not as punishment for what they have done, but simply for what they are said to be: nasty, brutish, and carnivorous. A daimon is let loose here, but it is not eudaimonic.

In our mixed condition, without the intermediation of the eudaimonic sovereign, the common good does not become express. The eudaimonics of sovereignty show something of the common good by being the communication of what is good in the community. If power falls to those who show less than the good, the commons does not have the representation in which can be seen the promise of its own more noble good. Since sovereign and many are in an intermediation, we cannot blame the sovereign always, as if this were always an external imposition on the pure many. The despicable or malicious sovereign tells us something of the malice and spite of the many. Not always, but it can be so. Perhaps it must be so to some degree, since the intermediation of the sovereign is always in a matrix of mixture, in which will to power willing itself mingles with the willing of the good of others.

Transcending and Commons beyond Sovereignty

The common good, and the meaning of its communication, suggests that the intermediation of sovereignty has inherent limits. These limits are both constraining and releasing. They constrain us in our claims to absolute sovereignty; they release transcending further, transcending already working in eros, but now placed at the threshold of a different sense of absoluteness beyond sovereignty, and a commons that cannot be included in the community of erotic sovereignty.

Thus the necessity that one/some represent the many also is testament to a gap between the sovereign one/some and the many. This gap both calls for communication and entails the limit of the common in the very intermediation of the common good. There is no absolute representation of the community in the fullness of its sources of ethical power. Representation testifies to the necessary finitude of sovereignty and its intermediation of the community. We will always have *slippage* between the many and leaders, *always misunderstanding*, too often exploited by those in power, sometimes with disaster as the result. Deep divisions call for the healing word that communicates peace, but they are answered with incitement to war, serving the enhancement of those with power, or the resentments of those outside power. Such a cure continues to contaminate what it would seem to heal. It pays too well those who will not cede power to keep the wound infected.

In addition, the intermediation of power in erotic sovereignty is always tempted by a will to power lured to its own affirming of itself, and liable to turn the common good into its good, or if not able to do that, to undermine it to enable its own self-aggrandizement.[17] In all relations of power, the bewitchment of tyranny is never totally exorcised. It is inherent in the beings we are and the communities in which we are and wish to dominate. Not only a guardian angel but a guardian devil attends the sovereign, hovering over the common good like a bird of prey waiting to swoop and scatter those gathered at the meal of fragile justice, if it thinks its own share is slighted. In the scattering, it thinks to possess more power than in the peaceful discipline of fragile justice. Perhaps such predatory opportunism often more marks those who *would* become sovereigns. Those who *are* sovereigns can be disciplined by their situation, as servants under necessity in the discipline of justice. How does Hobbes hit the bull? By naming those would mend a bad game by a new shuffle. Who wants a new shuffle? Those now with an unsatisfactory hand. Their care is not the common but the power their

---

17. For instance, in democracy, when the "mediating institutions" of family, religion, civic associations, and so on are weakened, power is not always distributed to the people but becomes more centralized in the state; the state grows as the center, while other centers are weakened.

own hand gives them. It is better to bring hubbub to the common than to consent to the limits of one's hand.

Then again a limitation at a more ethical level concerns how here an erotic transcendence that wills to be whole tends to receive primary emphasis. By its nature, sovereignty invites us to conceive of the common good in terms of an inclusive whole. This is a limit relative to freedoms that are not to be included, and also more subtle forms of otherness that ask for different forms of community. If a privilege is given to freedom as self-determination, and if the sovereign is its representative, such autonomy is not fully compatible with the common good, nor with the intermediation of the social. It operates in terms of a self-mediation in the other, not an opening to the other that exceeds the bounds of self-determination. The common good demands an opening to the place of the other beyond autonomy. Absolutized autonomy is tyranny, be it grandiose or everyday. A healing humility also can come in the inevitable slippage between the one/some and the many. For this slippage gives birth to skepticism about all absolute sovereigns. It gives birth to patient willingness to work for the good of the common, just in the equivocity of the slippage. Our small idols mushroom into monstrous gods just in that space of slippage. Reacting to the perils of inhabiting the commons of the between, sovereign autonomy becomes impatient with the recalcitrance of the others, ceases to be representative of social freedom, and becomes social enslavement or enslaver.

The secret recesses of the sources of social power are more than any representation can show forth, thus there is an excess at work *beyond* sovereign intermediation. The slippage intimates this. Even the sublimity of the sovereign shows something of this; there is too much, more, something superior, something from above, coming to communication from what is below in the unformed community. No one knows what is going on in a society; no one has a clear idea of what is being intermediated out of the intimate sources of social power. No doubt, some have a better idea than others, but nothing human is on a par with the excess of indeterminate power that is at the reserved origin of the social intermediation. Even the tyrant who thinks he is its master is, in fact, its beneficiary, given permission by what is beyond to work his domination. He is not master but debtor to a power in excess of all human discharges. He is not a good steward of that power but a waster. That no one knows, that no one is master, is this cause for pessimism? Not necessarily. It is counsel for vigilance. And for reverence willing to place open love where impatient power reigns in blithe self-satisfaction. It is quietly to answer the call of agapeic service, as the living of the good in the mysterious between.

What is the excess? The excess is not the power of the people. It is the companionship of the incognito God. The excess communicates the power of transcendence as other to human social self-transcendence, a transcendence of which we can never be the sovereign representative. In fact, it should not be represented as sovereign power, since it is more than that. Being what we are, we almost immediately fall on our knees before the magic of such sovereign power, drawn to what seems divine about the rulers. There is some truth to that, in this regard. All idols are idols by virtue of the permitting power of the divine, agapeic power that is the ground and permitting source of idolatrous as well as reverent power.

And so this social intermediation needs to be surpassed, as freedom is released beyond autonomy into an agapeic relation to the other. As the erotic sovereign surpassed servility, so the erotic sovereign is surpassed by the agapeic servant. Self-determining wholeness is good, but not good enough to the intermediation of the many. The promise of the universal is contracted just in its concretion, curtailed in its representation, since it cannot be completely communicated to all without the slippage coming from embodiment in the sovereign one/some. The common good relativizes the sovereign intermediation of it, for there is a relativity that puts strains on the self-expression of will to power such as to transfigure self-love into a willingness beyond measure that is there for the good of the other. Then the intermediation of social power transcends the power of will to power, for the power of the good is not exhausted in the will to power that wills itself, even the most noble and majestic. That power finds its most subtle form, its most ultimate communication, in a willingness that is agapeic. It seeks its social intermediation beyond sovereignty in a *community of agapeic service*. The majesty of all sovereignty is already let be as itself by the ultimate excessive and reserved source of agapeic allowance.

Transcendence, Sovereignty, the Sacred

What this means is that sovereignty cannot finally be separated from the sacred. We come to the transcendent good as the first and last potency of the ethical intermediation. The energy of transcending is revealed in erotic sovereignty, but in this energy the metaxological relation to transcendence itself is present: sometimes overt, sometimes hidden, sometimes expressed in communal mimesis of the divine, sometimes mimicking the divine in idols. This ambiguous reference to transcendence as other can equally affect religious traditions and secular standpoints, since neither is immune from the bewitchments of the idol. The long tradition of treating God as the absolute sovereign has its own bewitchment, especially when humans are bewitched by the dream of absolute determining power. How is (divine) sovereignty described then? Unilateral power to command absolute obedience. Power dictates, does not open to response—it does not ask, it tells. Sometimes this implies that power is not ultimately answerable to any law, since law is what power would will to be law. Does this mean the lawlessness of the source of the law, the power beyond all accounting? Human communities that dream of or seek such power often dream of their God as unilateral absolute determining power.[18] What if the power of God is not to be imaged on this sovereignty, this imperial power to command without controversion? What if there is a power higher than such sovereignty—God as the agapeic servant who does not determine but frees? I take Jesus as suggesting this, in his life and death, in parables such as the prodigal son. The tension of the higher good and sovereignty can lead to a struggle between the "prince of the world" and God. The prince of the world is the erotic sovereign thinking itself the last absolute, and hence having to stand over against God in spiritual agon.[19]

God as univocal, unilateral sovereign seems to be coupled with the beginnings of centralized sovereign power in early modernity.[20] We find this too among some religious people (such as the Calvinists, Jansenists, and Pascal). The unilateral determining power of the absolute sovereign seems also to be interlinked with the absolute determining power of nature as godless mechanism. The bewitchment of univocal determination appears in the realms of both nature and grace. In the latter case, there is predestination. The results seem odious when we think that unbaptized babies are consigned by the decree of the divine sovereign to the eternal torments of hell. This absolute sovereign seems constrained by determinations that more agapeic humans find abominable. Divine and human power are intertwined, and the sovereignty of human power takes on a divine aura, hence much depends on how we conceive of the divine. Some conceptions are full of the violence of a kind of power that will absolutely

---

18. The notion of predestination suggests a variety of theological determinism tied to the notion of absolute sovereignty as imperial power: the sovereign destines some to salvation, some to eternal damnation, and it must be so, for sovereign power cannot be controverted by anything, not even by itself; its innerness remains inscrutable to us; hence the appalling image of the divine sovereign as destining innocence to hell, just because it wills it so.

19. This does not prevent the image of the sovereign, in the Gospels, and in the history of Christianity. The struggle between God and the prince of the world is not for divine sovereignty conceived of in the above terms—it is for the superiority of agapeic service, being for the other. See my "Caesar with the Soul of Christ."

20. Jean Bodin, a sixteenth-century French theorist of absolute sovereign power, is remembered as an author of the modern theory of sovereignty. In a period of turmoil, he believed that one institution must be elevated above all others to impose order. It was to be the absolute power (endowed with "absolute and perpetual power"). He thought monarchy was perhaps the best way to achieve this, though he noted that in England, Parliament seemed to have come to perform a similar function. In any case, there must be one power above the rest, otherwise final responsibility and decisiveness give way to a war of different powers. Burke: "Nothing turns out to be so oppressive and unjust as a feeble government."

determine, that will command, and there will be no "ifs and buts." Such power is lacking in the generosity of agapeic being for the other.[21]

The usurpation of power is not confined to monarchical sovereignty, and similar results of dualistic opposition can be found in doctrines proclaiming their secularity. Thus the political fanatic who, like the religious fanatic, has an all-or-nothing attitude: intransigent, lacking the heart of flesh, because he or she thinks all is determined as his or her logic univocally determines it to happen. Marxist fanatics: History is the absolute sovereign power. This is a more dialectical than univocal determination, but it amounts to a dialectical univocity in the end. Stalin is the sovereign: this sovereignty degenerates into the reign of mass death; and this god also fails.

What of the sacred and popular sovereignty? The acting sovereign is, in the end, nothing without the consent of the governed, and this is well accepted. But the circulation of power through the sovereign does not necessitate the effective mediation of power back to the people; for the means of intermediation can take to themselves what is to be distributed back to the others. Government grows and concentrates in itself more and more power; instead of being the means, it determines itself as a kind of end in itself. If popular sovereignty is not open to, and in some way pious towards, a more ultimate source of granting power, its circulation of power and the distribution of goods within this circulation tend to close in a self-serving circle. The service of the other, the call of justice towards the others who are not served by the circle of power, is curtailed. Without the work of agapeic service, the power of the people's eros, serving its own good, closes into itself as a mortal god. It will be a jealous god, it will have none other beside it. It will launch

---

21. One suspects Pascal sometimes of a univocal attitude of "all or nothing" in relation to God, hence a kind of disgust at the creation as a fallen world, and the body. Despite his plea for finesse and his strong emphasis on the order of charity, Pascal has not always finesse enough to think of agapeic power beyond sovereignty; he seems caught in oscillation between geometrical univocity and an equivocity finally like the dualistic opposition we find in a gnostic degradation of the goodness of creation. Compare Pascal to the image of the divine generosity we see in Rembrandt's prodigal son. Rembrandt has finesse. Pascal's finesse often extends primarily to the equivocations of the geometric mind, the self-distractions humans devise, as well as our frivolity and bondage to bewitchments. Is there enough of the heart of flesh in his heart, enough finesse of the heart of flesh? We risk a different, *religious heart of stone*: the sovereign determination of the predestining God is hard to distinguish from an iron necessity that cannot swerve from the logic of damnation that must follow, it seems, if all of us merit nothing but perdition for our being born in sin and to sin. Is this God perilously close to an idol—an idolized determining and determined power, mirrored in the work of univocal determination in the mechanism of natural process, and in the stony necessity of geometric proof?

itself into conquest, or find itself at war with the sovereign gods of other peoples, or descend into secular sectarianism. We come to the war of the idols.

For the ambiguity of the connection between the sacred and social sovereignty is concentrated in the communal rapture of festive being. As "erotic," it is still tied to "will affirming itself"—it is not always a fully freed "yes," beyond death. The festivity of a community is ambiguous: struggling between breakdown and breakthrough, it *glories in itself,* and the sacred becomes an idol. A fuller affirmation faces nothingness in the *universal impermanence* and seeks to say "yes": gratitude for the gift of the good of the "to be." This is extraordinarily difficult to enact socially. The consummation of the sovereignty of a community in festivity is the social analogue of the acme moment for the individual. *Being full*: this is between being full of oneself and full of the energy of the gift of the good of the "to be." True festivity is impossible without the sacred. The eros of sovereignty is ambiguous beyond self and other, between self-glorification and surrender to the sacred power. In the mixture, there is always the tendency to mistake self-glorification for the power of the sacred. Thus we must be open to the topsy-turvy world of the festival, humble enough to let the Lord of Misrule have his mocking day. The ruling lords must be laughed at; the king must have his correcting fool. Thus are the idols laughed into relief. The sovereign must be matched with the twin of derision: idiot wisdom to dissolve the false doubles of God (on festive being and idiot wisdom, see *PO*, Chapter 6). Otherwise, the sovereign becomes the tawdry mediocrity that is the efficient manager, or the diabolical power that is the tyrant. The idol is not set in relief, nor do we suffer the intimation of the holy, beyond the relief of the idol. Thus we generate then a different idiocy, such as the Great War. Nations of the West were mortal gods wanting to extend their power and rule the world. Grim feasts—they danced in the streets when war was declared. Erotic sovereignty loses the lassitude of tame times and exults to expand its self-affirming power. In fact, hell was declared, and none could stay the advance of death. The lesson was not learned with the peace that suspended war. The erotic sovereigns sought to carve up the world anew. They were incubating monsters and sowing dragons' teeth. We have not recovered from that trauma.

Sovereignty is inseparable from the bewitchment of idols. Social power casts its spell of self-mediation in the other: the sovereign as "other" is invested with social power's own self-fascinating infinity, the implicit infinite self-love of social will willing itself, rival to God in its general eros to be *causa sui*. Absolute monarchy shows this bewitchment of power, incarnating in the command of obedience that enforces its spell in punishments on the body of the subjects. Are we released from the spell with changes from sovereign monarch to sovereign people or nation? From one idolatry of power, yes, but there is now another bewitchment. The sovereign nation can more effctively enforce its spell, just because its power to command is more distributed in the demos. We praise the democratic distribution of power, but the demos also can be like a god that watches with eyes, not single eyes but anonymous eyes. Their namelessness makes us anxious and subject: not subject to the squinting windows of the proximate neighbor, but to the eyes of self-scrutiny that the modern state sets in motion through its media, propaganda, institutions.

What are some of the bewitchments here? The compassionate autocracy of the mass mind-set. The comforting idolatry of bourgeois utilitarianism in which calculative mind erects monuments to its own exploitative shrewdness. The clever despotism of now open, now secret, scientism. The adroit technicism that regulates the imagination, killing in the womb the show of sacred mystery. The charm of the liberal state that preaches tolerance, while practicing the subtle intolerance of shaming what is not now pious to it (such as the so-called traditional family, religion, etc). I preach openness to the other, and when the first other to be genuinely other opens its mouth to voice its genuine difference, I mount my high perch of self-righteous judgment and denounce the other for not being open to the other. (The cheek of this preaching!) The reassuring bewitchment of the economistic state: we will give you more efficient markets, but you will have no souls, nor will we, the experts, who know what is rationally best. We will sanctify free competition, and in this make the offering of lives that count for nothing beyond their calculated price in a profitable exploitation.

Did the communist version of social sovereignty help? Hardly. We are workers, and our dignity is in the self-mediation of work. But if I am a slacker, I will be treated with less than dignity. Free labor will quickly become forced labor. The sovereignty of the toiling masses will finds its consummate expression in the dictatorship of the proletariat, with its executive branch, the party, stuffed with executive officers, underlings, and underlings of underlings. The sovereignty of the people, the dictatorship of the proletarian, the tyranny of the party, the divinity of the leader—all built on the brotherhood of man, the new man who builds the gulag for the old men, the black sheep. The sovereignty of absolute power—all dignified with the equality of the *lumpenproletariat*. You demur and say the solace of capitalism is to hand? But so also is the downward slide to the cheapest vulgarity and the triumph of the *lumpenconsumer*. As much as monarchy and communism, liberal society has its tyrannies. One of its tyrannies is the self-serving image of itself as being free of all such tyrannies. This is the bewitchment of its own self-righteousness. This righteousness is a form of wickedness.

These forms of sovereignty all show the bewitchment of power that wants to circulate back to itself. We learn the language of the other to circumnavigate the mystery of genuine otherness. We want an infinity of mirrors, but we only want to see one face in all of those mirrors, and lo, mirabile dictu, we behold ourselves! Since some bewitchment is unavoidable, it seems best to make a virtue of necessity: let there be a plurality of idols to keep in check their diverse claims to absolute divinity.

The metaxological view demands a plurality of mediating centers of power to prevent the social intermediation of erotic sovereignty from the project of seeking to become the one absolute center that seeks to ingest all others, subjecting them to itself as mirrors of itself. This middle way respects the pluralism of centers of power, keeping alive in the *metaxu* the promise of power beyond sovereignty, the power of agapeic service that frees from bewitchment. For this service there is only one God, and the first commandment it hears is the prohibition against false gods, and the graven images that constitute the embodiments of historical bewitchments.

What cannot be absolutely incorporated into the power of the ascendant sovereign? At one extreme, there is the idiot self—the void, you might say sometimes, the indeterminate source of innerness that is never exhausted by any determination, though its determinate existence be in bondage to them. The idiot is not absolute solitude but is intermediated prior to determinate mediation: God is in the immanence of the soul. From that deepest intimacy the call of agapeic service comes again, shattering the determinations that hold us spellbound, returning us as to nothing, offering anew a recreation of our being, out of the plenitude that twines around our lack. There is the released religious "sovereignty" of the idiot, the sacred fool.

This idiot extreme points to the other religious extreme, namely, the community that tries to live in the between in light of its acknowledged metaxological relation to the divine: in light of the generous finitude of its being, given the goodness of the "to be," out of nothing and for nothing but the good of being. This is the religious community of agapeic service that enacts the intermediation of the good beyond erotic sovereignty, and in ethically likening itself to the generosity of the agapeic origin. If at the first extreme erotic sovereignty gives way to mystical consent, at the second extreme the festival of a community becomes a sacramental drama.

CHAPTER SIXTEEN

THE COMMUNITY OF AGAPEIC SERVICE:
THE INTERMEDIATION OF TRANSCENDENT GOOD

Consummate Community: The Commons of the Divine

As there is a community beyond use, intermediated by sovereignty, there is a community beyond sovereign power, and beyond politics. This is the apotheosis of the bond of trust inherent in all forms of communities; it is at the ultimate, at the extreme, in relation to origin and end. It intermediates trust in good in an ultimate sense, and in relation to the extremes of life: birth and death, and the ordeal of suffering. In the face of our coming to nothing, it is trust in the good, by love of those who are as nothing, in facing their nothingness. It is community seeking to live in absolute service of the good. We might say: Christ is beyond the Grand Inquisitor, and Caesar.[1] Signs of ultimate community are not confined to one tradition. A prince, groomed to be a king, leaves the palace of his father. Beyond its cushion, he is shocked by suffering into a different mindfulness. He abandons the place of regal power, becomes a wandering beggar, homeless, seeking a way. The way enlightens, and he becomes Buddha.[2] If I say this community

---

1. See my "Caesar with the Soul of Christ." Think also of Francis of Assisi: there was much of erotic sovereignty in his young desire to be a glorious knight; off he went, though he did not get very far; and who knows what suffering there was in his time in prison. We do know that in time it was the call of agapeic service that he answered, as he chose a sacred poverty over his father's mercantile comfort.

2. Consider certain Indian practices—a person matures, has a family, is perhaps successful in business, and then at some point begins a different spiritual journey, perhaps beyond family and business. Perhaps also this person may go on a pilgrimage, even withdraw, though the point is less physical or psychical separation as the granting of a higher community, growing on these others, and unfolding the energy of self-transcending towards transcendence itself. In capitalist practice, one fears it will be money until the end, when despite all the wealth generated, one is unsure one can count on the solidarity that offers the freedom of the last pilgrimage. Some aged people fear the terrible degradation of

is beyond serviceable disposability and sovereignty, "beyond" does not mean dualistic opposition or hermetic separation, since we are always in the between and our reality is mixture. As serviceable disposability and sovereignty mix, this community also will find its shape in the midst of use and worldly powers. Its truth will not be captured by either of these. Of course, these can captivate it by degrading influences, bringing it into line with their determination of good. Alternatively, they can be transformed in light of this higher commons, so that use and worldly power are converted from the baser purposes perennially tempting them.

Since the middle as ethos offers many possibilities of freedom, we cannot determine in advance whether degrading or conversion will occur. Whichever occurs, it is not simply determined by individuals; communal movements shape the middle as ethos. There may be heroic individuals who set in motion such social transformations that lead to conversions within community. (There also are leaders who can corrupt a community.) As there are sovereigns who intermediate to a community a show of higher excellence, and so enable the community itself to be a people of excellence, so there are ethical heroes who show a way of transcendence to many others, inspiring them to try or seek likewise. They reform and transform the life of community in light of the transcendent good. They should be called heroes only with reservation, lest they be assimilated to the sovereigns whose goal is the intermediation of worldly power. They are more ethical servant than hero, or if hero, hero in the service of the transcendent good.

Both the sovereign and the ethical servant are moved by the self-surpassing energy of transcendence. Both ambiguously move on the border between human transcending as reaching for the ultimate and the good as transcendent. If in the sovereign there is an ambiguous mixing of the power of self-transcending and transcendence itself, in the ethical servant there is more of transcendence itself than of self-transcending. In the middle between transcending and the transcendent, the sovereign tilts to the former, the ethical servant to the latter. In the middle ethos, as always, there is no complete eradication of ambiguity. A sovereign may be a secret servant of the transcendent good, though appearing as lord of will to power; an ethical servant may be a double creature, whose great devo-

---

being stripped of human solidarity, of being appended to machines, anxious about who cares, who cares for them, tested by despair, if the social support is not offered. The final commons is in a different dimension. Of course, clever captains of the "care industry" will see at this extreme even the *usefulness* of religion, as they will see the usefulness of "values," but they will be shut out from the inner truth of that which they would now exploit. Even if religious practice reduces blood pressure and crime on the streets, this its usefulness is not its inner truth: these are fruits that, even as fruits ("outputs"), are qualitatively beyond instrumental quantification, though it may be said that they have been quantified, as in studies of religion and healing.

tion to the transcendent good is incompletely freed from human-all-too-human self-insistence. Even Jesus prayed, let not my will but thine be done.

This struggle with the doubleness of transcending and the transcendent good is intermediated in this community. It is not always struggle, for sometimes self-transcending is freed effortlessly from self-insistence and the energy of agapeic generosity is gently released towards being as other, the otherness of creation as good, of the neighbor as good, a release itself made possible by the release of agapeic generosity visiting us in the between. The communication is graced, becoming in turn a community that bestows good on others still estranged. A communal way of life may be formed wherein is intermediated this struggle and this release.

Consummate community might be called religious *kononia* or the commons of the divine. I grant that there are many religions, the study of which is voluminous beyond measure. Modern Westerners may put the secular before the sacred, but we are the anomaly, relative to humanity in history, of old, as well as much of contemporary humankind. For much of that history, and humankind, the fixed separation of sacred and secular lacked an ultimate basis. All power ultimately is from, or comes from, the divine. We saw this in the aura of sacredness glimmering around the sovereign. Western modernity has wanted to separate sovereignty from this aura, figured forth in the body of the king. Rightfully, it refused the abuse of power arrogating to itself the claim to be absolute. Yet the sacred does not evaporate. Let it be *vox populi, vox dei*; or the leader who fosters a cult of personality; or in less baleful form, the glimmer of tinsel divinity glinting on statesmen as political celebrities. Forms of sovereignty, as we saw, equivocally mix up with divine power. Their highest excellences are not simple human products but flower from an incognito divine accompaniment. That very mixture lets sovereignty set itself up as God's representative on earth.

The divine also is incognito in the network of serviceable disposability. If we look with eyes cleansed of the slur of instrumentalism, we see the frenzy of seeking, the cunning calculation, the glut of commodities, the dissimulating kitsch by which propaganda and advertising incite the network into spasms of getting and spending. At the center of this network of bewitchments, we see a brood of devouring idols. Not a neutral context without gods, in which units of power optimize their secular satisfactions; gods yes, but idols binding their subjects in invisible straps of craving and anxiety. We dethrone the divine, destroy idols of the tribe, breathe free of God, but our debunking sprouts its own new idols, all the more enslaving, since now we think of ourselves as being free of all idols, and this is the subtlest idolatry. The first step to the divine commons is confession we are never free of idolatry.

The divine is mixed in with the family. The family can be the commons of the most intimate human piety. If the seed of piety is not sown there, it will be

hard to recover reverence in other public commons.[3] Political piety is more ultimate than the piety expressed in the religion of shopping. Without something
more intimate before it, such as the family, or more inherent higher than it, such
as the sovereign, this religion is enjoyment without joy and impious pillage. Religious community intermediates humans to the ultimate power, albeit imaged or
represented in the available terms that the human community has, terms that are
never the best and often are mixed in with much that is idolatrous, or potentially
so. Religious community binds together (*re-ligare*—Augustine) the human and
the divine, and out of this it transforms the bonds holding humans together. The
sources of social power undergo a transformation that carries human power to
the edge of its humanness. We understand power as given all along, a gift from
motiveless generosity, motiveless goodness beyond the goodness of the gift, rousing in community the vision of humans living together an ethics of generosity in
the finite image of the ultimate generosity.

   Use and sovereignty may offer enabling matrices that support the open space
for this higher freedom.[4] They also may not do so, and if not, the space for the higher

---

3. "The family that prays together stays together." Scoff if you must, but is there more wisdom in such saws than in tomes of sociological analysis of the breakdown of the family?

4. Many philosophers such as Plato, Aristotle, Augustine, Aquinas, and Hegel point to a
life higher than politics. Politics is necessary, but not necessarily noble. With *Plato*, the
guardians are not just erotic sovereigns: they are servants of justice who have been vouch-
safed a glimpse of the good itself; servants of the harmony of the whole, in light of a good
passing beyond the human whole of political life; servants with no possessive claim on the
good; servants under an ethical exigence to return to the cave, serving the good of their
fellows; servants with a compassion (*eleos*) for our solidarity in darkness, not tyrants who
dictate their own desire to the other. Can one here separate the transcendent good from
politics and the call for politic's ennobling by just doing? For *Aristotle*, ethics is part of politics, but there is a higher life, reserved for the *theoroi*, though the relation between this
higher life and life in the polis may not be entirely clear. The Aristotelian metaphysician
seems more detached than the Platonic. This perhaps mirrors his sense of the divine: Aristotle's god as thought thinking itself is perhaps similar to the higher life that the philosopher now and then tastes—separate, aloof, occupied with its own higher joy in itself.
Plato's Good, as imaged in the Sun, is transcendently other but is not thus for itself: it
gives being and growing and intelligibility to all it lightens; it broadcasts its light beyond
itself—as transcendent, it is self-transcending, communicative goodness itself. Thus the
joy of the Demiurge in *Timaeus* in the created cosmos: he delights in its beauty and goodness; his bringing it to be is a celebration. Is the Platonic philosopher similarly a celebra-
tor, a player of divine games, as the *Laws* have it? *Hegel* often is seen as a philosopher of
the sovereign who is the worldly embodiment of the absolute, yet there is something
beyond the "earthly god" of the state. This last belongs to objective spirit, not absolute.
There is a different community of humanity and the divine in absolute spirit where art,
religion, and philosophy reveal both a higher freedom and communion with the ultimate.

may be closed down on a wide scale and the community corrupted on these lower levels as well. Even when these other intermediations work against the higher communion, they cannot stifle our transcendence towards the transcendent good. It will break out in stray individuals or groups, or else assume a disguised, even tortured, form where it is most publicly repressed. This is not "merely" private as opposed to public. It is the most intimate on one side, but this is inseparable from the call of a most intensive and extensive communion: vocation is called to convocation. The call for transformation is felt in prophetic social movements; or in the creation of institutions which enact a social mimesis of the ultimate good; or in utopian or apocalyptic movements, one looking forward in expectancy to the social concretion of ultimate communion, the other having a presentiment that the present order is passing away, and will go under in an ultimate judgment showing up its ambiguous fidelity to the ultimate commons; or in eschatological fervors alive with faith that some forms of present communion anticipate, hence realize, the ultimate commons, whose proper fullness in the consummate end is not simply of time itself.

The ultimate good is, in one regard, beyond politics, and in another regard, is not, since a community that recognizes the call on it by this beyond also shows a different immanent definition of itself, as already socially enacting the self-understanding that points beyond human community. It immanently creates, it must do so, the social space hospitable to welcome the communication of this beyond, this transcendence.

Is this all merely a transcending into an empty "beyond"? We are tempted to think so, if bewitched by use and erotic sovereignty as ultimate. Religious transcending breaks the bewitchment. But this "beyond" also is "before," say, in our participation in familial piety that engages our innerness as persons. We are less likely to empty the "beyond" if we are formed into thinking beyond self in love of the familial other, and shown agapeic service. "Before" serviceable disposability and sovereignty, in the idiocy of the family, the divine has the freedom to let its seed grow quietly in the heart raised in love, and raised up to love.

Likewise, any dualism between the "beyond" and creation seems not to the point. This "beyond" has everything to do with us, as transcending in the joys and

---

Hegel vitiates this point with his logic of dialectical self-mediation, since this compromises just the truth of the transcendent good, giving an emphasis to its necessary immanence that distorts the agapeic character of the ultimate communion into an erotic being at home in the whole. And yet, as he says, the state is no work of art; it exists in the realm of caprice and contingency; it lack the fullness of the ultimate communion with the ultimate. Hegel's failure here is in not properly laying out the implications of this communion to show how it undercuts all of the forms of idolatry that invest ultimacy in other forms of community, especially the state; how, indeed, the absolutization of immanence must be relativized, relativized as seen for its potential to idolatry, relativized as seen in light of the more ultimate relativity, namely, the agapeic commons of the human and divine.

sufferings and offerings of immanence. This transcending is mindful of the excess of the divine to any appropriation by finite being. The between as the milieu of divine communication is not the divine. Community means involvement and also freedom, hence immanence and transcendence. Thus "beyond" implies no dualistic opposition or hermetic separation. This commons is a *metaxu*: its *meta* is both a "beyond" and an "in the midst"; outside and inside; at home and not at home, both sides espoused. It is the intermediary in and through which transcending is energized. Were the religious commons merely outside, an opposition would result towards creation and other forms of human community. Setting itself over and against the other forms, it might be their implacable judge instead of being released towards their good as other, and the thankless task of their transformation. Were it simply inside, religious community would be degraded to an ideological buttress of the powers that be, not in their just exercise of power but also in their rapine.

Mere outside: and then we have something like religious critique—a religious hermeneutics of suspicion that debunks any good that is in the finite other as created immanence. This is not to serve the divine that gives the world as good and remains in solidarity with its good. The transcendent good is not the spirit of resentment projected by vengeful humans into the heavens to be used as a weapon to destroy what in the world is good and worthy to be praised and sung. Nietzsche says so, and no doubt, with some formations of the religious, it is so. The very qualified correctness of this view blinds us to the fuller truth. Interestingly, some of Nietzsche's children, the atheistic hermeneuts of suspicion, display an analogous righteousness—but applied to religion—not now the religious wail but the atheist whine. If such atheists were alive and bewitched in a theological age, they would be the thunderers against the world. They still thunder, but now against the other world. They cannot appeal to God to justify their righteousness. They appeal to the earnestness of their moral intentions or their purity of ideological correctness. They appeal to themselves as god.

Mere inside: and then the old story of the priest serving as the valet of the king; throne and altar stroke each other's certainty that they two are most close to the divine sources of power, for, after all, they *are* the powerful. This insider degrades the "beyond" to an immanent domestication. The Jesuits: convert the king, and the sheepish many fall into one's lap. Too comfortable closeness to the king makes the servant of the greater glory of God cozier with the greater glory of the king, and of himself and his company, in the company of the glorious king. AMDG. But who is the god? The king, the priest. The revolutionary atheist repeats the old story, in the name of his godless god. For he is king and priest and god in one.

The *meta* of religious intermediation is double: both inside and outside. Inside, for that is where we are in the between. Outside, for we have a presentiment of transcendent good, not to be identified with any finite good. The agapeic good is intimated through them as their giving source which, as other, is not other in the mode of transcendental opposition, but is the supporting source giving the otherness of creation to be as other, and good as for itself and in its own otherness. Outside: we see the goodness of creation, its worthiness to be praised and appreciated. Inside: a fundamental gratitude is resurrected, expressing itself in an ethics of generosity towards the frailty of beings in the between, human and non-human. The outside makes us uncomfortable with our idols, the inside shows us the appeal of love, the comfort of community given to us by others, which we also may give to others. The two great commandments arise in relation to this doubleness.

How better articulate some sense of this most elusive community? As before, it is helpful to think in terms of the different potencies of the ethical, even though this community also takes us beyond the ethical.

Hidden Showing and Community: On the Idiot Potency

In the commons of the divine, we come closest to the primal sources of goodness in the ethos. There is hiddenness as well as overtness to this community. Its participants are involved in a drama in the most idiotic intimacy, of which there often is no clear overt show, or only the most subtle. The struggle with oneself and the divine is a perilous adventure and trial. It often has no name, or an as-yet unknown name beyond the well-established names of past struggles. We are full of a reserve, since the truth is deeply reserved. We cannot say for sure. Even more, silence is often best, since something mysterious is enacted here. This might lead to the rejection: there is here no community at all. Like moths, we fly to the brightest light, but for us the most immediately bright light often is the most crudely forceful one. We set our course by this and navigate by rocks of darkness.

The hiddenness constitutive of this community means that participation cannot be completely shown in the securer publicities of objectified togetherness. Discernment is needed for the seeking in secret and the discipline of a public way of life. As we saw with sovereignty, there can be a slippage between overt show and what is at play in the intimacy of being. Intimacy means communion, and communion is given sensuous show, but without the eyes to see or the ears to hear, it is a dumb show, a mime meaning nothing. Slippage is always threatened between the community as intimate and any public institutions claiming to be its embodiment. The universality of the intimate, its being turned to the One (*universum*), cannot be absolutely embodied in the body of a public community that witnesses to the community between the human and divine. Nevertheless, this embodiment is needed. It offers the social framework of a public way of life that shapes the seeking and release of the intimate communion. The intimate truth of this community also is shown in the communication of the elemental drama of

God being with humans. But as we move from the intimacy of love to its public ceremonies, a different language must be spoken, and so we must take care.
The objectifying power of public language risks misproportioning the language
of the intimate. Sometimes one speaks out loud when one should murmur.
Other times one should not whisper by the wall but pronounce fearlessly and
without prevarication. Then again, this public expression can so solidify in a tradition that it comes to stifle the first language of love. Those who live out of the
secret source may even be scourged by the officials who have become custodians
of the public language. The institution then becomes the police guard rather
than the steward of the community, and even less the servant. The public is
caught up again in its intoxication with its own sovereignty, its will to power
bolstered by its faith in its own divine election to power. The we get inquisitions
for the truth; laws that imprison rather than free; and void of love, the whole
thing brass and tinkling cymbal.

Equally, of course, the intimate can become idiotic in a bad way, if it rebel-
liously refuses to face the community of others, and simply insists on the specialness of its secret communion or pact with the divine. (I am God's pet.) The
first is the communal tyranny of power claiming divine sanction; the second is
the individual tyranny that claims itself as the elect one, hence liable to no law,
subject to no authority, proclaimed in the name of the father, but actually asserted
in my name. I speak for God means I am God. The idiotic needs the ordeal and
test and anchoring of the public community, needs the sustenance of some tradition, needs the humility to confess publicly that all may be chosen, not just I. It
is all very well to say that it is an inward drama or covenant, but the good gives
beyond itself, and hence it must flow beyond the intimate into the public, into
the family and the community, or into the network, or politics, or public religious
communities, where it gives again to the others, out of the gift it has been given,
either from the divine or the tradition or the preceding community that helped
it to where it is now, on the way.

The public show must respect the hidden drama; the hidden drama must
acknowledge and overflow into public show. The good is communicative, all the
way down and all the way out, and the communication of the good is its nature,
everywhere and always. Nor should communication be confined to more normally recognized forms. It can be the most unpredictable rupture and shocking
crash, or a humming quietness so delicate it vanishes away into an aphony.

Doubled Face and Divine: On the Aesthetic Potency

Concerning the aesthetic potency, we find that there are equivocities concerning the highest. I will focus first on our usurping the agape of the good and
then on the bewitchments of transcendence.

On usurping the agape of the good: The showing of this commons in its social body is an adventure of a religious people, so there are pitfalls here. Over these, anomalous secularity also advances. We want to snatch the sun. It shines on good and evil, monsters and beauties, and we say: we are in communion with the divine, and behold, we are favored, behold, we are representative, and lo, those there with strange tongues and affronting gods, they must be chastised, and we rightly wield the rod, not because we have might on our side (we do), but we have God. The community that is potentially open to the otherness of all others, even the rejected and repulsed, turns back into itself, bearing the god it has communed with, as its talisman of superiority. The metaxological intermediation that should take it outside of itself in an agapeic surpassing *turns back*, and just because of its communion with God, into itself, and it sets itself up as the whole that can absolutely mediate with itself, for it has God within it. Its communion has been turned back into its own social self-mediation, and the adoration of its own counterfeit double of God. The very truth of communion with the divine lends itself to the absolutizing of the community that has tasted the communion. Why not? God is with it, is at work within it, has been taken into its immanence, and now as a commons with God, and with God as within it, it rightly presents itself as the absolute community, hence all other claims to community have to be relativized, or subordinated, or perhaps even destroyed, if their ways conflict with the way of the absolute community.

This is related to the problem of the *sect*: religious communities may promise the universal, or point beyond to it, and claim to embody the divine communion. They may indeed do so, but they are always, as human, a particular community, concretely differentiated from other communities. The sect is caught in a between: between its own specialness and universality; between the communal particularity that can turn back to itself and exalt itself above the others, and the promise that opens it to others and denies it the hubris of placing itself above the others. And, of course, by its claim to absolute community, in a way it is right to think of itself as above others, if it is a representative of the highest. But what if the highest is not itself so exclusive? If it shines on all with agapeic generosity, it belongs to no one. There is no chosen people, because all are chosen. All are loved with agapeic regard. God has no favorites, because God has only favorites.

The religious commons is not the tinsel sect that shores up its own resentment through the reversal of high and low, letting it make a lord of its own inferiority as the higher form of spiritual superiority. If it is the higher community, as higher, it is not the sovereign, or sovereign community. The meaning of "higher" is overturned relative to will to power. Highest power is not will to power at all, but the willingness to love the other that has been called to agapeic service. What it means to be higher is not to insist on power to subordinate. Inevitability, again, there is hiddenness and reserve. We cling to the public majesty of the sovereign, and this too in the sphere of the higher community, and then the sinuous subtleties of sly will to power insinuate themselves into the communal transcending towards the transcendent. It bends its agape back into a self-regarding whole, a self-mediating totality that short-circuits the unreserved opening to the other in metaxological intermediation (see *PO*, Chapter 3, on the closed self-mediation of the sect).

This turn back of the religious community into an exclusive self-mediating whole leads to the conflict of wholes, conflicts of communities each claiming to be absolute, but in a mode of self-assertive will to power which, though it carries the banner of God, must end in war with other communities, and must sow seeds that spring up as godlessness. These seeds only reap their own, since they are the seeds of godly godlessness. The war of religious groups, each insisting it is absolute community, seems to reveal that religion is a violent madness, not the highest inspiring communion. The thoughtful may turn away in silence; the impatient turn against in contempt; the proud turn towards themselves as proudly godless; the godless proceed to make new gods of themselves and their communities; and then godless communities claiming to be the absolute community will bring the gyre around again to war; but now the war lacks the restraining shames of the first godly wars.

Here we see again how the changed orientation to power in early modernity is plurivocally refracted through our conceptions of human community, as well as of nature and of the divine. These diminish reverence for the agape of being; and even the God who surveys and sanctions the process as a whole is a majestic unsurpassable will to power, whose unsurpassable unsurpassing will is recalcitrant to all reason. Such absolute power is too uncomfortably close to tyranny. If God is not responsible for this change of orientation, who or what is? The power of an understanding of the between that has lost deeper communion with the agape of being, so that nature becomes a valueless matrix of effective power, humans become units of predatory power, and communities become circulations and concentrations of that power, represented in sovereigns that claim more and more absolute power, mirroring a God that over time seems to show more and more of its masked face as that of the absolute tyrant. The *turn back*, mentioned above, which takes centuries to effect, has now turned back into the human, finding in itself the nothingness of its will to power. Except sporadically, the turn back has not dipped deeply enough into this nothingness to rediscover the agape of being and to *turn again*, now to God as agapeic origin, and turn again out of this turn towards the renewal of creation as good, of the human as the promise of agapeic self-transcendence, and of highest commons as the community of service that lives for the good, of the other, as much as for the self.

On the bewitchments of transcendence: Coming to highest community, we are more exposed than ever to bilking forms of bewitchment. Bewitchment is the accompaniment of all developments of being ethical. Essential is the turn back to the self, steeped in the equivocity of the ethos, which does not know that it is enthralled with itself when it seems to be enthralled with an other. To be in thrall is to be unfree, for freedom means being released beyond the confines of a self-limiting self-insistence that is not good, namely, not in communion with being as other, and indeed with itself. Being released is being set free into communicative being, where what is communicated is what one is as good, as well as what in other-being is good. Hence being free is always simply to be good in a community. By contrast, bewitchment is a dynamic whereby the energy of being circulates and seems to find its goal in the other, but there is a hollowness to the supposed other, to the form of relation thereto, and to the self ostensibly now taken up into communion with the other.

The bondage of bewitchment in religious community, where the stakes are most high, is indistinguishable from idolatry. Idolatry is the dissimulating version of absolute community. It is devotion to false gods, offering itself as the true commons with the ultimate. Put that way, the point is reinforced that religious community cannot be confined to "religion." For idolatry is pervasive in all forms and aspects of human life, in all societies and individuals. Being ethical is the communion with the good that struggles always with the false doubles of God. To be in this communion is simply to be religious. The element of hiddenness of bewitchment and communion sometimes conceals their presence in the most unlikely places. Religious community is dedicated to the release from bewitchments, those that are the counterfeit doubles of absolute community. There is no such thing as solitary bewitchment: bewitchment is a social intermediation, since it is a form of interplay between self and other, especially attuned to the potencies of the idiotic and the aesthetic, though not only these. It is a distortion of the freedom of that interplay, mostly when a form of self-mediation dominates the openness to the other, though it can be that the self also is a victim of the other who imposes its dominating self-mediation. The distortion is formed by the play of determinacy and indeterminacy, the latter relative to the infinite openness of desire, the former relative to the search for a determinate good to love. In absolute community, there is some sense that the good is not just a determinate good; it is the overdetermined, transcendent good. The play of our infinite desire is oriented to community, in which our desire finds home. Yet this overdetermined good is mysterious and cannot be determinately univocalized. Since we are ineluctably oriented to determinate goods, and since our full orientation has an exigent, infinite sweep, determinate goods necessarily become invested with something of that infinity. Here begins the witchery of finite goods.

This is not only us projecting infinity on the finite. These finite others are themselves gifts of the good, and as such, they participate in the infinity of the overdetermined good. We fall in love with their genuine good, mingling our own infinite desire with the trace of the infinite good in the other. What is *good* about the interplay is itself bewitching, because the other is there as good, my love is good, and the infinite good is reserved. The latter keeps itself in the background, one might say, so as to ground the community of creation as free for itself. This very freedom opens the space of bewitchment, which is the *equivocal twin* of the genuine love of the divine, which is the consummate commons. *In the bewitchment itself is the reserve of the transcendent good*—as giving, without insisting on itself, the very excess of freedom and free desire, the excess of good singularized in the self and in the other, hence giving the space for absolute love between them. Just the latter allows both the highest nobility between creatures but also the most subtle loss of nobility; for this absolute love, if it makes itself the absolute, ceases to be absolute and becomes an idol.

One of the great works of religious community is to help shape the spiritual discernment that is alert to the formation of such idols, all the more difficult to face and exorcise, since our most intensive love is invested in them, invested in what in itself is good, but invested to displace this goodness from the good. Idolatry is the most natural thing in the world—like religious community itself. Mostly the two are inextricably twined around each other. And there are many idols—beauty, self, nation, class, sex, wealth, science, religion—as many idols as genuinely good things in the world; for idols name our unfree relation, our autistic communion with the absolute good, in and through the bewitchment of all finite goods, and these not at all as evil, but as actually good.

The finesse demanded by this spiritual discernment must see into the heart of love itself, the labyrinthine ways of its mystery, the hiddenness of its secret obsessions, the unexpected tendernesses behind the hard masks, the strange hatreds hovering on the other side of its smiles—an impossible task. And so we find ourselves appealing for help. We cannot comprehend the human heart, and the heart itself comprehends this about itself. Religious community is itself the appeal to the good for that help to be good. We cannot do it on our own, as we cannot free ourselves from bewitchment on our own. To ask to be free from the idols is to ask for the spiritual strength of a divine service.

The Agapeic Universal: On the Dianoetic Potency

In relation to the dianoetic potency, I make three points: first concerning ethical piety and universal community; second concerning the great commandments; and third concerning the idols of the universal.

On ethical piety and universal community: Life is so full of heterogeneity that any idea of universal community is problematic. Yet the between itself is a network of complexly intermediated communications between the plurality of beings (themselves metaxologically intermediated), so the truth of the ontological situation is, in fact, a community of communities. The between as ethos is this community of communities. This has ethical relevance relative to non-human others as well as human others. Relative to the first, it means that if we are to respect that community, we need a new piety of the earth. Relative to the second, we need a new piety of the human. The signs of the times point in their direction. The metaxological between points towards an ethical service that takes up its place of solidarity towards the earth and humanity, out of this piety towards creation as good.

How think of such an implicitly universal piety? Is it self-justifying? In one way, yes: we love the earth for itself, we love and serve other humans for their good, and just because it is good to do this. In another way, no: I mean that since the between is a between, it shows in itself the vector of transcendence towards the divine ground as its other, an other not in dualistic opposition to it, but in solidarity. One must ask: What is the ground on which we are willing to enter in agapeic service with the earth and fellow humans? If this service, as a kind of piety of the between, lives in light of the good of the other, that goodness is not from us. And while it is in the others, it is not simply from them either; it too is given to them. The goodness of the between is in it, but not from it, in the sense of being a production from itself as originally not so valued. The sources of the good of the between are not of the between, even though that good is in it. Of what then is this good? From whence that goodness? Does not this piety of the between suggest homage and secret joy in an ultimate source of the giving of the good of the "to be"? We name that source in many ways, "God" being one of the names, and in many ways, the best. I call that source the agapeic origin. The absolute origin of the good of the between is not itself the between and the good beings that come to be in it; the good of the between is given out of the ultimate origin.

The ground of goodness is a troubling perplexity. It is more than a perplexity. There is astonishment that what is given to be is given as good. To be is to be good; this is communicated in agapeic astonishment. Its source troubles our perplexed thinking. We often lose mindfulness of this astonishing goodness of the "to be." It is sometimes shockingly brought back to us in encounters with death, in ways connected to posthumous mind. Out of this can come a renewed piety of the between, of non-human and human others. What gives the goodness of being? What originates it? It is not self-grounding by the between itself. For the between as double is not absolutely self-originating. It too is involved in an intermediation with what is other to it. This is the source beyond it. This other is the origin. The ground of the goodness of the between is the origin that gives the between. This original ground must itself be good to give the goodness of the between. This good is above the good—the superlative good, it is *huperagathos* (see *BB*, 538ff.). Religious community lives the good life in the between in relation to this good beyond the good and evil of the finite middle. Hence there are different senses of the universal here.

The piety of creation, including non-human others and humans, has a universal dimension. We would never sense that universal if we simply affirmed diversity: to affirm diversity truly is to find oneself in community with the universal. The universal is the community of the between. The universal is to be understood metaxologically. Nor would we understand that were we simply to insist on unity over against diversity. What community as metaxological means here is that the nominalistic/individualistic particularism is not enough; nor is the universalism of which singulars are mere particular examples; nor is the holism that thinks of the universal as a whole that incorporates differences and singulars and others as parts of itself. Against the first: because community is from the origin at work in the singular, and the singular is idiotically deep beyond the measure of nominalism. Against the second: since a logic of dualistic opposition vitiates it and renders the universal too close to a transcendent emptiness and the particular to a flattened, emptied singular. Against the third: for such holistic inclusiveness is modeled on an incorporating self-mediation, hence the openness of intermediation is not adequately stated. We need a universalism as mindful of the richness of singularity as of the manifold togethernesses; a non-totalizing universalism, not closed to otherness; a non-reductive universalism not emptying of singularity. This is an agapeic universalism.

This agapeic universal opens to the good of creation, both of human and non-human others.[5] It could not be fully sustained in terms of these human and non-human others alone, for there is a transcending demanded disproportionate to any finite being, or even the aggregate of finite beings, or even their community. It calls out for a deeper universalism that seeks its solidarity with the ground of worldly universal togetherness. This further universalism is to be found only in relation to the divine origin as agapeic. Only that goodness of the origin can ground the requisite universalism, singularity, selfness, and otherness (see *PU*, 235ff.; also *BB*, 526ff.). In the between is the promise of community, because there is an original universal that gives and grounds that community. The good of the community within the between is sustained by its relation to this original universal. The work of the ethical universal within the between is grounded on the religious commons between the human and the divine, a community not founded on the between but in the relation of the between and its ultimate source. The religious community in relation to God would live in light of this universal good, which is not closed to any other, not reductive of any singular.

---

5. The Buddhist ethics of compassion often has been more sensitive to the non-human other than religious ethics in the West, which can reflect more the self-insistence of our will. Schopenhauer saw this, though his compassion is a knowing that the other suffering is the *same* as oneself: properly speaking here, one is not loving the other as *other*. Francis of Assisi lived an ethics of agapeic compassion, extending to non-human others. Is Buddhist compassion agapeic? Perhaps not quite, since this last asks love of the singular as singular, and as other.

On the two great commands:[6] The ethical urgency of this agapeic universal is reflected in the two great commands. What is the commandment of the law? Love God, and your neighbor as yourself. First love God. The point of "first" is not a temporal priority. In our living, we know ourselves as loving many finite goods and humans, before the restless desire grows on us that there is more to be loved. First, "love God" takes the form of a command, but the command is already immanent in us: it reveals the ontological truth of human being. The exigence is effective from our origin. It constitutes our being as being, not just what we become as constituted in time. A primal love is in our being, is our being. We are the concretions of this love. It loves in us before we know it loves. Out of its love we live, and out of it all our desire, knowing, and love come to be. Only because it is already, does the longing for more manifest itself in our being. We are in search of the ultimate good because it is with us, but with us such as to bewilder us, especially when we let our love fall under the bewitchment of the good of finite things, for then we occlude the more in our love of the thing before us. As we recur to the deeper restlessness, we pass from bewitchment to bewitchment, yet the passage enacts the love of God, even though we are in the thrall of idols.

Religious community frees the ontological work of this love into a knowing of itself and its enactment in ethical service that is being freed from bondage to bewitchment. The command comes as a command because it speaks the imperative exigence of the already at work community of that love that provides the supporting ground of all coming to be of self, all transcending that seeks human wholeness, all self-transcending towards the other, all awakened love that turns towards the source of love that till now moved it onwards incognito. The command is like a shock to deep metaphysical amnesia. It shocks the memory of God into wakefulness in us. We are so bewitched in the amnesia that it seems a trauma to our being. For how can one love God? We do not know what God is; and did we know, it would be too much for us. How love what is unknown, what seems nothing, or too much? Is love of this the way of life? I love this or that. God is not this or that. How love what cannot be given the face of this or that good? Love in a darkness? Love what one cannot possess? Love of what brings one along a path of emptiness and emptying? Love of what in the dark light of mystery fills desire with a delectable sweetness, issuing in song hardly of human making or of nature?

How love God? By joy. And in the joy to thank the origin out of which the feast of life is given, and our privilege to enjoy this thing, that thing, the places

---

6. "Thou shalt love the Lord, thy God, with all thy heart, and with all thy soul, and with all thy mind. This is the first and great command. And the second is like unto it. Thou shalt love thy neighbor as thyself" (Matthew: 22, 37–39). Interestingly, Jesus here is being tempted by a *clever lawyer*.

offering a home, the faces of people one loves. By silence. And in the silence, trepidation and expectation, and beyond the dry boredom that is sin the silent communication that comes from prayer. By song and dance. And in the movement of praise or lamentation joy breaks forth, or shy consolation is given. By suffering. And in the agony, to be brought to breaking point, to be broken, and in the erosion or the shattering to say "yes" still, and still to pray for power to say this "yes." By consent to death. And in the consent, to live (would that one could) the good beyond fear of death, and to affirm the good of the temporary, the boon of being at all, though one's time goes by, is by, and one faces the test of return to nothing.

How love God? After being driven to more and more by erotic self-transcendence, only by agapeic going beyond. One goes out into the dark unknowing of divine otherness, and one does not face a mirror in which one's face is reflected; one faces into an emptiness or fullness; it is the movement of transcending that demands nothing from this mysterious transcendence, that comes to seek nothing for itself in this ordeal of nothing, and that yet in the darkness expects all, not for itself, but in its trust that God is all in all, though now in its sojourn in twilight, it can only hazard its "yes" against the darkness.

How love God? By enacting in life the truth of the agape of being, and this most concretely in service of the neighbor. This is the second great command. Like the first, it is a primal ontological promise and exigence of our being, before it is an explicit, and sometimes shocking, imperative. We see it in the spontaneity of sympathy for the suffering of others, called forth without thought towards the broken face of a sobbing child. There are other broken faces. The heart goes out to the others; the heart is what we are in the core of the intimate idiot; the heart is what we are; transcending towards the other, out of a reserve of love of being, it cannot consent to the deprivation of joy in the agony of the other. Our being is a going towards the other, an unconscious love that is about the other. It is our being to be thus interested in the other. Agapeic interest is *interesse*, being between.

The command, as an explicit call, refers us to *ourselves* also. This is important: love of the other, the neighbor, is not hatred of the self; there is no room for hatred, not of the self, not of the other. Pascal is right and wrong: the self is hateful, as perverting the urge of self-transcending; but the self is not hateful, it is to be loved, and myself as much as any other self. Suppose I say I must hate self and love the other; then I must also love myself as I love the other, and hence not hate self. The point is the love of the good: good of the being of self, or of other. Love of the good in the command to love the other transcends any dualistic opposition of self and other (see *PO*, 187–192, on the two loves). The transcending testifies to a community beyond the disjunction of self and other. This is not exclusive of one or the other and points to the more embracing love, the love of God that already simply is the agapeic love of the good of the finite, hence a love of the self and other, not one against the other or to the exclusion of any. Love of neighbor as self is to be a love first; and while it focuses on one or the other, or both together, if it is not love of the good it does not respect the imperative, hence as not deriving from love, does not find its true home that is the love of God. Love is the name for the community of the good. The word is easily debased, but it is elemental and needs no justification beyond itself. The ultimate community, as a love, is divine commons, hence love of God—not our love of God, God's love for the creature.

On the idols of the universal: The primal love points to a universalism and solicits its social enactment in freedom from idolatry. The idols of the universal are the counterfeit doubles of God. Insofar as it generated totalitarian communism, Marxism proved to be an idol of the universal. Its desire for community is not wrong, nor is its cry for a universal solidarity. But if only God can ground the community of the agapeic universal, other communities, in advancing that claim for themselves, must set themselves in the place of God. The violence of the prosecution of religious communities by totalitarian communism is no mere accident. It enacts the logic of the position. As a thoroughgoing humanism, Marxism is an idolism of the universal: there can be no false gods, and no God other than it. The decades-long campaign, now more ferocious, now less virulent, to uproot God from hearts and minds enacts the project to produce the false double of God, and the counterfeit of the consummate commons.

A certain dialectical logic of perfection leads to this idolatry of the universal. The immanent dialectical necessity of time is said to produce the perfection of time. The communist society—it will come. The godless god reigning in history is a pitiless determining power, a dialectical determinist who mirrors another god, the God who predestines some to heaven and most to hell. It will be so, whether we will it so or not. Such dialectical science cannot do justice to the singular, and its freedom, just as predestinarian doctrines cannot account for freedom and its participation in the open good of providence. The dialectical logic of perfection—anticipated with certainty as emerging from history's dialectical self-certainty, the lawlike forms of which we claim to know—offers a perfect justification for enacting the destruction of the "has been" and the "now." There will be perfection *then*, but on the basis of the nihilation of what now is, said to be the imperfect that hinders us from the promised land. Erase it, leave not a stone standing, or an image in stone, or a tender thought in the hearts of men that send up desolate supplications to the God beyond this god.[7]

Human communities, especially when their power is extensive and overreaches imperially in the world, are tempted by this religious perversion: the emperor is no steward or servant but is the divine: Caesar is god. Centrally

---

7. See the discussion of this dialectical logic of perfection justifying complicity and the enactment of monstrous evil—all for the sake of the good—in *BHD*, Chapter 4.

organized communities, again when their power extends to imperium, tend
more to this idolatry of the universal than communities that cannot, or do not,
or wish not to control centrally the prodigal pluralism of a community. Hence
capitalistic formations have more of an inoculation against this form of political idolatry. This does not mean there are no idols here, but these are perhaps
more the idols of the network of serviceable disposability than those of sovereignty. The failure of the Marxist idol to do justice to the singular does not
imply we worship that other idol, the individual of capitalism—the unit of productive and consumptive power. The true singular has all of the idiocy of the
infinite image of the infinite, the absolute original. The community of the universal is not a circle above and around us that encloses the many in a self-mediating one. It is already at work in the idiocy of intimate being, even as it is
enacted in the public space of the between.

Should we call this universalism a catholic or ecumenical community—
catholic as *kath' holou*, ecumenical as extending the communication of the good
to the *oikoumene*, the inhabited earth, the whole world? If so, the notion of "the
whole" needs subtle qualification. If such a community communicates to the
whole, that whole cannot be one dialectical totality. It must be an "open whole,"
or a pluralism of "open wholes," because its participants open into infinitude,
and into reverence that exceeds every closure into totality. We must exorcise
from the language of wholeness such overtones of closed totality. Moreover, the
agapeic intermediation of the divine and human suggests that the singularity of
the latter is loved as good for itself. As thus singularized, we are never out of
community unless we freely refuse what is offered. The drama of this community, while radically intimate, is also worldly: a being with others, and a going
towards them, out of the transformation of absolute community within the intimacy of the idiotic. The love that is in communication with the singular, and
that is also universal, is an agapeic love. Communion with the ultimate is not
only a happening of agape, it is the overflow of it, not only into our hearts, but
out into the world as other.

To find the worldly forms of this community is extraordinarily hard. It is
never finally fixed—how could it be, given the surprise of every new overflow of
the agape? No one worldly community is catholic. Religious communities share
the same tension between universal and particular that we saw with sovereign
representation: one/some represent many. A definite community claims universality, but it can never be univocally identical to the agapeic universal. This chastens the hubris of each and every community, even those calling themselves universal. The excess of the origin guards the difference of the human and the
divine, even in their intimate commons. Love is not the forgetting of difference;
it is the communication of the good in differences and across differences. The
difference of the singularly loved other is supported, even as its hardening into
hostility is worn away.

The idolatry of the universal is ineradicable. We humans will baptize ourselves as the universal and forget the commons of the agapeic universal as between the human and divine. This idolatry we cannot overcome alone. To think one can overcome it and attain to the universal by oneself is just the idolatry again. Idolatry is just to claim to attain to the absolute by oneself, outside of communion with the ultimate. The communion is given to one, not produced by one. To proceed as if we could proceed by ourselves alone is, once more, to carry the idol with us—ourselves alone as the counterfeit doubles of God. The false baptism redoubles itself in false communion.

Monotheism of the Good: On the Transcendental Potency

What of the transcendental potency? Does the agapeic universalism suggest a monotheism of the good as its ultimate condition of possibility? What would this be? There is one absolute good; other goods are idols if they usurp the place of the ultimate. Some now see monotheism as being disrespectful of plurality, hence implicitly totalitarian in superimposing the one true view on the plurality. Universalism also can be thus tainted, namely, as camouflaging collusion between worldly imperialism and religion. While such collusion has undoubtedly happened, surely it is not the whole truth. The community of solidarity with all under the divine has been expressed in a service not imperial. Simply as a service, it has begun to free itself from the sovereignty of the imperial. This is not to deny often a too-strong reliance on that sovereignty to make smooth the way into strange territories. Can we rethink monotheism in terms of a universal free of the imperialism of power (indeed, disrespect, going to the extreme of genocide)? Monotheism is not Western property. There is no possession in this matter. No one possesses God. True monotheism knows that to speak of one's God, as if there were any owning, is already to fall under the sway of the idol.

The God of the between as the open whole of creation belongs to no finite thing or human, though this God gives being to all, and the good of that being. There is a transcendence to this God that stands against the idol, since this transcendence keeps an essential difference open, even granting an intimate solidarity between the God and finite creation. The most intimate form of that solidarity is in human freedom: the finite human is given to be for itself, and to define itself for itself, to be responsible for the shaping of its own self-becoming and the community of humans, wherein singulars find their home on the earth. That solidarity is inseparable from freedom means that the universalism of this God cannot be such as to enclose the otherness of plurality within a totality where, in the end, plurality is nothing for itself. Agapeic universalism frees plurality into its own freedom. From this angle, any imperialism of monotheism corrupts the ethical meaning of the universal. Transcendent good is not of the East or West, the

North or South. It haunts the decadent places of power in hope of return to the good, as the deprived places of poverty where hunger, sorrow, and desperate hope keep company. It is everywhere and nowhere, and yet again is not in the world as a finite being but as the origin that gives the promise of being good, ceaselessly even when immediately the good given is turned aside into evil.

What I am saying is hard to make intelligible without a fuller exploration of the God of the between.[8] Without God, there is no sense in talking about religious community as being more ultimate than sovereignty and the network; no point in talking about idols and bewitchment; no point in talking about the freedom that is beyond autonomy; no point in talking about self-transcendence in search of transcendence itself. Relevant to current concerns, I focus on three points: the ground of the good; the agapeic character of good; and the solicitation of the good.

On the ground of the good: This issue concerns the goodness of good itself. We have seen many ways of being good, yet none is absolute, short of the transcendent good. What grounds the good? It is not nature simply: there is goodness to nature, yet this is disproportionate to the good as we come to know it, both in human life and in our response to all being. That response indeed also is expressed in our question of the ground, which also is the question of nihilism. Does it all come to nothing in the end? This is a *hyperbolic question*. If it does not all come to nothing, then there is nothing in nature on a par with the good that has come to be in the process of nature itself. We are pointed to something more. Nor can nature ground the universalism of the ethical, such as we discover to haunt human communities.

Is the ground human freedom? It seems not. Our freedom is *already* in communion with the good and is given to be as a good from a source other than itself. Freedom is a good, grounded in a good other than itself, since its own good is not itself the product of freedom. The ground of freedom is what makes freedom possible, but freedom first has to be as a possibility before it can make itself possible; there is a prior source that makes possible its own derived power to make itself possible. If the human is a source of good, there is a more primordial source of good not human. This is not nature, not only for the reasons indicated above, but because even the human good is in excess, disproportionate to the good of nature. Since humans are endowed with the promise of freedom, this other source must be adequate to the pluralism of singulars without determinate number that constitutes the many humans that have come and passed away, and will yet come and pass away in lines of succeeding generations beyond all human ken. The ground of the good must be proportionate to, indeed, in excess of, this.

---

8. As I said, *God and the Between*, a work in progress, will be the third volume of the trilogy, along with the current work and *Being and the Between*.

The prospect staggers the mind, beggars the imagination. We either say there is no ground, there is nothing; and the between is the ultimately void space where humans come and go, brief flares of inexplicable life that inexplicably bind themselves to a sense of the good, as if it were absolute, and yet the flare is snuffed out, and the singular proven to be a nothing in the cosmic void. Or we say there is a ground, but it must be proportionate to the sense of the good we experience in the between. *If so, this ground must be disproportionate just to be proportionate.*

The astonishing thing about our being in the between is precisely the transcendence of the solicitation of the good we come to know, its demand on human finitude that exceeds finitude. This is an infinite demand made on a finite creature that knows the call of the superior in the experience of its own inferiority, the call of the perfect in its own imperfection, the call of a more ultimate success even in the necessity it cannot escape of having to fail ethically. Even more, how make sense of the springing up of a mysterious love of the absolute good in the urgency of its own desire as infinitely restless, the peace beyond understanding that slowly comes to companion the human, as it is slowly released from its own self-enclosure into a service that is agapeic? How make sense of the startling surmise that the freedom of agapeic self-transcendence, when it is given, is the sweetest gift of creation, hinting to us something about the ground itself?

We might grant an infinite restlessness oriented beyond itself to absolute good and still say that the good is but a universal principle that remains undetermined in its being. Can we leave it undetermined? I think it is not undetermined but overdetermined, and we must risk thought about the nature of its excess. To call it an impersonal principle has its rights, just as we might speak of the ultimate as transpersonal, to avoid the reduction of that excess, that transcendence, just to the dimensions of human personal transcending. Transpersonal cannot be merely subpersonal, however. It is a source of good that itself as source must be good, and since the concretion of good we most know as such a source is personal, we may speak of the good in some sense as personal.

This is the truth of the traditional identification of the good with God. God cannot be an abstract universal, nor a principle at odds with the singularities of creation, especially the personal singularities, where we find the emergence of a concretion of value that is for itself and inherently valuable in an infinite sense. Let us say that we must be as much Augustinian as Platonic in this matter. It is in relation to the living God that communication as intermediation is possibilized; that giving as originating is possible; that originating as letting the good of the creation come into its own is actuated; that creation is possibilized as the freeing of the freedom of the other, especially of the human, into its own responsibility to itself and to creation, and finally then to God. A ground less than the living God does not ground the exorbitant good that comes to manifestation in the between, does not do justice to what is communicated to being ethical in the between, and does not itself enable communication between itself and that very between.

On agapeic good: Can we say that the good is itself agapeic? To be agapeic is to be as a communicative source of being. Suppose this is what God is. God is communicative in relation to the between as the finite given creation. Does this mean that God in self is nothing; and if so, what of the claim of the transcendent good? My reply is that agapeic being is communicative out of excessive, overdetermined powers of giving; there is an intimacy, an idiocy, to these reserves of power in themselves; no one, nothing, can dream of this otherness of the divine good "dwelling in inaccessible light"; or we can only dream.

The view consonant with the metaxological approach suggests the following doubleness. The divine good is both self-mediating in self and intermediating with creation as other to itself. Its own mediating, communication with itself is a community that is just its absoluteness in itself and for itself; this is in a hiddenness relative to everything other. But if that communion with itself is its love of itself, is this not the majestic narcissism of a self-glorying divinity? No. Why not? Because if to be is to be good, to be absolutely is to be absolutely good; and to be thus is just to be the absolute love of being; it is the love that is the absolute, and this is not "love disporting with itself" in Hegel's ambiguous phrase. Agapeic transcendence is the being of transcendent good, but this transcendence constitutes its giving of the good, its relation to the world, the second side of the intermediation with the world. This giving is the happening of the promise of the consummate commons. If the ground of the good is itself good, we name it in terms of agapeic transcendence, to make sense of the giving of good to the creation as other, of the letting free of that creation as other, as well as of the freedom of the human to enter freely into communion with the divine. The ultimate giving remains mysterious to us, and we are not on a par with it.

It would be entirely facile to think we can just will by some deliberate freedom to come into that community. We are invited, and the manner of invitation respects the freedom to refuse, as to accept. The invitation may be offered in the most anonymous acts of dull dailyness. Let the offer be accepted and it is as if the dullness lifts and the anonymous receives its singular name from love. The open invitation is there, and the banquet was spread before one, and one grumbled sullenly about dull daily bread. To pray for our daily bread is to ask for life's necessities. It also is to pray to be transformed by the invitation to the good, the welcome that lays one open to the feast, already there before one. We are guests on the earth; we always were.

On the solicitation of the good: Communication with the divine is not a narcissistic spirituality that cultivates its soul as a certain aesthete cultivates his or her taste for the beautiful. The cultus of this cultivation is devotion, yes, but it also is ethical service. Ethical service is solicited in the divine service that is the consummate commons. God service is not a stage prop that helps to dramatize an essentially moral worldview, the dispensable metaphorics of an earnest, indispensable morality. Quite the opposite: ethical service arises from God service, though it is often incognito; ethical service is enacted God service. God service itself is liturgical, in the sense that liturgy is a public service for the people, a feast in service. Moralities are ethical services that, so to say, suffer from amnesia about their liturgical origin. Without God service, ethical service becomes a moral ritual of duty without joy, like a festive drama that has lost the festivity.

The agapeic good frees us into our own being for ourselves, and we may refuse or consent to the agape. As free, we may ourselves become sources of agapeic transcending. The agapeic good solicits agapeic service in us. This is enacted in divine service which seeks to love God. It is enacted in ethical service in which the human other is to be loved for itself. It is to be enacted in the stewardship of the earth that will not mar its fair face. Creation is a gift of the good asking for ethical service that loves its goodness. It is not the face of the human other that brings us to God. We are already with God, whether we know it or not. The face of the human other shocks us out of lived amnesia, and the shock shames us into memory of the forgotten. It is the shock of God that shakes us into seeing the face of the other as a reminder of the ethical service. This ethical service is the memorial of the divine service that is simply our being as creatures. The shock comes in the gift of otherness, given out of a good of which first we have no comprehension, and we mostly live our lives without a clue. God is first and always first, as the agapeic origin.

And, of course, one cannot separate the divine and the ethical service. Divine service is agapeic communication in relation to God; ethical service is agapeic communication in relation to creation and human others. There is not one without the other, though there may be an ethical service that does not comprehend its ground in divine service, as there may be a love of God so caught up in this love that its *singular form* of ethical service is just to show to others the fruit of that love which is *holiness*. That singular service is the life of the saint, for the *sanctus* is the sanctified one, the one blessed.

Divine service turns to the fructifying ground, the inspiring ground, the ground of a confidence that the good is at work even when our efforts reach their limit, that the work of goodness transcends into a mysterious dimension not human or the creation of the human which, were it withdrawn, would cause the between to fall in a flash to infertile ash. Our service of creation and human others could hardly dream of the heroism of agapeic love of the other if it were not sustained, kept afloat above despair, by a faith that the deepest reserves of the power of being were themselves good. Maybe this is too much for us, too much beyond us. It would certainly appear comic and freakish and ridiculously absurd if we were to claim its power for ourselves. We are not masters of the agape but its beneficiaries. Our participation in the agape is a human possibility, because the ethical service of the human is itself made possible by a community beyond humanity, the community of humanity and the beyond, as the transcendent good that is the agapeic source. So we might say that the ethos of the metaxological between is the secret commons of creation and God. This is said relative to where we began this exploration, in the overdeterminacy of the ethos.

The Communication of Blessing: On the Eudaimonic Potency

The eudaimonic potency refers us to the fullest human flourishing of ethical power, but this is referred beyond itself to the daimon, the intermediary between the human and the divine. Intermediation here is religious community as the communication of blessing. How does the communication of blessing show itself? In the double, redoubled service of agapeic community: the God service in which human service, neighbor service, comes to be. Religious service comes to be ethical service. Beyond sovereign power, this is living the life of gratitude and the ethics of a generosity that gives what good it has and is. There is a kind of abdication of sovereign power, insofar as such power is entangled in the subjection of others, and as calling forth fear and trembling in order that its will be done. The agapeic community does not say "my will be done," but "thy will be done." This is first with regard to the absolute willing of the good, which is the agapeic willingness proper only to the divine. I mean a willing not limited by this or that finite will, a willingness transcendent to finite will, yet as agapeic directed to the singularity, hence willing this and that good also, so not a merely formless willingness. It is imaged in the servant whose good willingness extends beyond this or that act of willing, yet is turned to the singularities whose good is willed in this or that act. This transcendent willingness that yet expresses itself in love of the singulars reflects the double service, as beyond and yet in the midst.

This willingness is a release of freedom beyond the will to power. Sovereignty can sometimes be a bestowing on the other, but it is rarely unmixed with its own self-glorification, even when it bestows itself on the other. This willingness is now freed from the need of self-glorification. It may seem not even to exist, so freed is it from this need. It does what it does and is happy to be anonymous, as long as the good is done. It will go where no glory is and show its solidarity with the inglorious. The neighbor is not only the other whose hand washes the hand; the neighbor is the one who suffers without the solidarity of the word of comfort; or the lonely who suffer because they are as nothing and see no smile to warm the deadened heart; or the destitute whose begging hand holds out an appeal, and to our discomfort or shame; or the unjustly accused unable to make their own case, stunned by circumstances into impotence; or the grieving who cannot shake off their sorrow, yet crave a word of consolation, even a feigned word. Lessen their suffering.

The well endowed are not always sovereign enough to bestow some of their excess on others. Those rich in power often are concerned either with augmenting or protecting what they have; and they will find a way of keeping those with nothing in a situation of being nothing; or dole out crumbs when the social situation is threatened with disturbance, when the disturbance cannot be crushed. This can be all the worse in a society where sovereign power has turned back and become enmeshed in the net of serviceable disposability, for then we are putting down paving stones of usefulness on the way to hell. The others who have nothing are as nothing. What do they contribute to the network of utility? Nothing. Not assets, they are liabilities; and, say it, perhaps chronic liabilities that ought not to be. Those who have nothing will be hated for draining the resources from those who already have too much. The nothings will be blamed. Those with power will speak the high-minded language of responsibility and autonomy (we take responsibility for ourselves; the nothings drain the public purse; why cannot they do as we do?). The meaning of it all? We hate you. We hate you for not being like us, for not being powerful, for making us insecure and even ashamed. You are not a resource, you produce nothing, you have no value. Your usefulness is zero, your worth zero, and as zero you deserve to be treated as nothing, and in the extreme, noughted. No longer serviceable, just disposable.

Beyond this nihilating hatred of those who have nothing, the agapeic community sees in the nothings the trace of infinite worth. Their being as gift is already this worth, even if in our eyes it counts for nothing. Ethical service is enacted in image of the divine agape that gives for nothing, including the singular being of the finite self. It too was nothing and would be nothing if its being were not given to be by the origin. That it is at all is ultimately a gift of the supergenerosity of the origin. Being as nothing brings us to an extreme where ethical service may image something of this giving. To treat the nothings with the love that affirms the good of their being is to image the generosity of the origin. This generosity is both before and points beyond the instrumentality of the network and the dominion of the sovereign. The ethical community that lives out of the love of the origin also is prior and beyond. In remembering its origin, it sees its life as dedicated to the end of loving, even those who are as nothing, even those who are now nothing, either in death or in birth still awaited.

This is an extreme task of love: in the face of nothing to affirm the good of life; to know that one will come to nothing and to live beyond this fear of one's own nothingness, putting it in place relative to the great good of the gift, even though the gift is for a time, and we must part with it (but ask, is there eternal life for those who do not want it? Perhaps God grants us our will); not to see the nothings as nothing but as gifts of the origin, and to treat them as if they were there for us as the absolute; to be related and not to relativize them into means; not to have an end in view for oneself, hence to be wrenched out of oneself, out of the circle of self-mediation that circles back to itself; to become an agapeic self that is as nothing but a passage towards the other as good, and the good of the other. All of this is to be beyond death, not as dead but as living in community with the divine, and so to be free from clinging to one's life, as if this could be possessed. In trying to possess it, we confine it. We do not possess our lives as gift, they are to be broadcast abroad, abandoned into opening. This is to be servant of the good that is not yours or mine or anyone's, since it belongs to no one, yet all are implicated in it, and in community with each other in their community with it.

The words expressing the ethical service of this community beyond sovereign dominion have an extreme character. We seem to deal in *impossible* ideals. I think of the beatitudes (Matthew, 5:3–10) as expressions of this service. They are not ideals, though people speak of evangelical ideals. They name blessing. They give word of the actuality of the commons of the divine, already equivocally effective in human communities. They are "ideals" in that there issues a call on us from out this actuality, a call to live up to what is at work in the promise of community. They are not ideals that utility or sovereign power can pooh-pooh as unreal fantasies. They are at work in the network and sovereignty, but they belong to a different dimension: the extremities of the divine and of the nothing. The beatitudes concern blessings, name ways of blessedness, name the religious and ethical service that goes with being blessed and blessing. The blessing is the gift of being as good; being blessed is to come into communion with the origin of the blessing.

The beatitudes take us into the service of the holy, for they live life as holy. They are very strange sayings from the standpoint of serviceable disposability and sovereignty. We may have so often heard them, we discount them, we are so immersed in the other forms of community. They are rupturing words from another dimension that ferment the now, leaven its powers. They speak words that are releasing of the holy, releasing of us for the holy. Least of all, are they secret modes of resentment and vengeance by those who have nothing against those who have everything (Nietzsche). This last view cannot comprehend a community of service beyond sovereign power that is not a servile community but is released into a freedom beyond self-mastery, sustained by the love that comes in its divine service. As there is an autonomy beyond servility, there is a service beyond autonomy and servility, and this service is the releasing of freedom beyond autonomy and subjection, beyond the instrumental domination and subjection of serviceable disposability, beyond the self-affirming dominion of erotic sovereignty. This service is release into community in which we live from the good of the absolute other, and towards the good of ourselves and finite others as others, and again through them live towards the good of the absolute other.

Extremities of Agony and Thanks: On the Transcending Potency

What of the transcending potency of the ethical? Say this: thanks and agony touch. Who is not touched by despair? Who has not felt ebbing the faith that life is good? Or has not skirted the desert's edge, perhaps entered it, perhaps never clearly to come out again, and not to find any oasis within it? We suffer loss of the good of the "to be"—the play of life a meaningless mime, gesticulating with the signs of life but miming mockery. And then the hardening of the heart, first felt with trepidation, then with resistance, but waning and growing fainter, settling into a resignation, prelude to petrification into contempt. Is this hardness not time's tale: bright hope, young energies, crushed by time, exhausted in lovelessness? It was life that bewitched us, and now it is the ashen morning of disillusion. We grow old and wake to find ourselves prisoners of the loveless heart.

There is worse. In the gray of disillusion, a cold hatred can congeal. We taste this hatred when what we love seems not to live up to the love. Glowing ardor reverses itself into glowering cruelty. How does the between seem then? The place of lies, not the promise of the good. But promises that lie are not promises but swindles. Do I paint phantoms? If I do, it is the lineaments of a phantom haunting the loveless heart I draw. I see visages that have known time, but the lines on these faces mask the quietness of horror. We are wonderfully busy, but our animation hides horror. We relax, and the emptiness shows in the subsidence of the mask. One may have no clue that this is going on. The glee of one's smile speaks one thing, but the hollowness empties out love silently. Some know it, and endure it silently, or seek to be relieved in pleasure or in work and its touted "blessings." Some turn their dying into a reiterated demand on life that it be as it should, namely, be as I will it. The everydayness that is despair, the resignation, the revolt, here return to roots in the loveless heart.

What heals the loveless heart? It seems unable to heal itself. An other then? What other? There is lovelessness so hardened that the other has to be divine, if there is to be healing. We can descend into absolute despair; we cannot ascend out of it. We need the aid of another. The heart coagulates, it cannot uncongeal itself. The healing comes with the absolute community. The heart is pierced by a blade of ice, but the thaw blows from a direction that is directionless, from a source not named as source, from a power beyond power, so uninsistent it seems powerless. It releases the flow of our finite self-transcending that has one source in lack (for it is a wounded transcending), but a more rooted seed in more than lack, in agapeic going beyond. We do not produce this release. Religious community is the place we come to thanks of its gift.

How is the healing shown? The answer is elemental. Double service: God service, religious service; neighbor service, ethical service. Service is the word for the enactment of this love. The word love too quickly withers into sentimentality, or into cynicism under the leer of those grown old with jaded enlightenment. This is loss. Only love lives the agape of being.

The double of the agape: daybreak and coming into the light, darkening and dusk and passing away into the night; both in the end as gift. The day comes. We

give thanks. For what? The day's simple gift. The night comes. Its quiet brings
affliction in recesses of the soul. The day comes again. There is storm, we are buffeted and slide. This day is night. Not love but the urge to rage; grief whose measure seems nowhere, and still the prayer whose defiance would be softened into
yes. The night comes on. We came with nothing, we go with nothing, and into
nothing. We ask to be blessed and to bless.

I said before that religious community is the apotheosis of the bond of trust
inherent in all forms of community. It is the absolute form of trust: trust in the
goodness of the divine, and in the extremes to which the good brings us: coming
to nothing, facing nothing, facing those who are as nothing, and ourselves as
nothing; and yet good. This trust is enacted in works. What kind of works? Perhaps all kinds. Yet there is work not defined by the spirit of utility; nor in service
to the sovereign, or the establishment, or fatherland, motherland; this is service
of the good of the other, which does not seek self-justification, that is even
beyond proportional justice. This reckless goodness is close to what used to be
called works of mercy. These works are communications of trust that seek to free
the other. They enact freedom without a why. Beyond morality in a more usual
sense, they are not dictated by duty. The freeing is not dictated by anything but
is shown in a pure movement of giving. Mercy is a giving of good beyond good
and evil. The divine good is beyond good and evil in that moralized sense. The
commons of the divine calls us out into a space of acceptance by goodness beyond
good and evil.

The apotheosis of trust in transcending also calls on the agapeic latencies
of memory and hope and in that regard has to do with the transfiguring of
time. Time itself is a mysterious interim. The agapeic latency of memory keeps
alive a mindfulness that extends to the nameless participants in the past. With
them we have unspoken solidarities, beyond present determination, for their
past gift has entered into the present good that we enjoy (there are, of course,
the sins of the fathers, inherited evils). We quickly forget this and barely
remember our debt to those proximately present, and even then grudgingly.
Others beyond number recede into namelessness. The agapeic latency of memory is thanks. What kind of thanks? Try as we might, we cannot finally remember the names of those deprived of their name by the disposing powers of the
network or sovereignty. Yet we can remember that we have forgotten, and cannot but forget. The love of memory is, in a way, hopeless. There is a beyond
here. We may shrug and say "so what." Worse, we may instrumentalize our pre-
decessors a second time for use in our current play of will to power. Alternatively, we can live with this beyond of time with a thanks that does not always
know whom it thanks, yet it knows it is under the need to give thanks. There
is a thanks in excess of singulars who can be thanked, and the excess spills over
into a life whose seedbed is thanks. One gives thanks to and for a giver one
cannot name always, yet an indeterminate thanks is asked by the goodness of

what is come to us. Such thanks is like a religious trust that wakes to itself as entrusted with the gift of coming to be, entrusted by a giver it does not determinately know.

And the future? Others will come, and the gift will be passed on. How will we pass it on? As we have lived it. If we live it mean-spiritedly, we do not now contribute to a community of generosity, or make the matrix of present possibility richer with future promise. We do not give beyond ourselves. What then is the agapeic latency of hope? We are given to ourselves, we give beyond ourselves, but it is the others we love, when we live in hope for their good. This is not exclusive of living in hope for our own good. It is the good we live in hope for. Hope passes towards what passes beyond us. We do not always determinately know what it is for which we hope. There is an excessive hoping in excess of definite hopes. We pass in a kind of indeterminate love, just as we remember. We will not see the faces of those who come after us. Yet we are called to love what we will never see.

This is not easy. To see and behold gives us the belief that we are on a par with what we see. When we hope, we are not on a par; we are exceeded by the "object" of our hope, and yet we are drawn on. The indeterminacy is not necessarily an objection. It may sometimes be a vague indefiniteness. It also can be fed by an overdetermined willingness to dare to hope for the ultimate good. Hope also is a form of faith, and each is a form of love that does not know determinately, or in a way it can determine for itself, the face of what it loves. That face comes to show in the shifting interplay of the between. It communicates itself and withdraws, is revealing and hidden at once. We have to live the tension of this double condition, of being between: seeking our love whose name we know not, and being sought by love we cannot name ourselves.

Faith and hope are forms of love of the consummate community, for they are given over to the other, given a taste of the absolute trust that is the truth of all community. Trust says: I affirm that you are good: you are good; my trust lives the affirmation of your good; absolute trust lives the absolute affirmation of your good. Only God is capable of this trust. Only the absolute agape is the power of trust—trust that extends to letting the finite being fall into distrust and refusal. It trusts that out of refusal good may come and a turn back to community. To live the agape of being is *to be trust*. What of the evils we inherit? Beyond our justice, we must forgive. And the evils we perpetuate? Beyond our injustice, we must ask forgiveness.

Hyperbolic Gifts: On Transcendent Good

Relative to transcendent good, there is the offer of hyperbolic gifts. What are hyperbolic gifts? Hyperbolic gifts are revelations of goodness given at the extremes. What are these transcendent gifts of the agapeic community? The healing word; festivity and rebirth; confirmation and consolation; ministration in the idiocy of the agape of God. These are, so to say, the sacraments of this consummate community.

Communication of the healing word: The word communicated breaks bewitchment, as a name is called and a man wakes from hypnosis. The proper word is spoken, and the spell of the idol no longer has the power to enchant. Bewitchments keep us in the security of a world tailored to our finitude investing itself with infinitude. Worship breaks that confinement, the infinite breaks through into the finite. Every bewitchment is shadowed by the sharp slap, or caress, that wakens us to life. We flee the slap or blow or touch, and we build new mutations of the reversal of finite and infinite. They are futile. The infinite will come over or through or under our best protections, reveal itself there at the void center of the bewitchment. A word or name is spoken, and we snap out of a trance.

Frequently, of course, awakening is more long drawn out. We snap a little, only to fall in love with a new bewitchment, flitting from bewitchment to bewitchment with such fleetness it seems that nothing other is between. There are cracks between, but we leap over them, like children playing a game on a sidewalk. We are infinitely variable in our ways of thus clinging to the finite. Our infinite suppleness is not turned to the infinite and release beyond bewitchment. We become alert to the gaps, and in a moment of lucidity suspect we have been astray. In those moments of truth, we may ask to be shown the way of truth. This way shown soon is overgrown with wild weeds, and we take the tares on the way for the way, and say there is no way, for we cannot now see it there.

Communication of holiday: Genuine feast days, days of festive being, are hyperbolic gifts of the agapeic good. The consummate community is one of celebration, of our solidarity with the ultimate power, despite evil, in our own good in its many forms, in our struggle to be released from evils into which we fall, celebration of the sweet gift of life, as well as the peace we seek facing the terrors of death. Rebirth to the good of the elemental things is now celebrated. Birth itself is a mystery at the origin; not just the neutral fact of a coming, or the seemingly indifferent occurrence of a valueless biological event but the mystery of the singular life given for no general universal reason, for no special reason we humans can determine, yet mysteriously arriving into this world of the between, not thrown, not condemned, though its beyondness to general reason may make it seem so. This is my life, your life, and not known by us at the start but intimated to those at the delivery. The gift of the origin is repeated in the baptism that names the community with the origin, that names for us a mindfulness that would be faithful to the first solidarity, and this throughout a life as a whole. At the beginning, being born, and the promise of being reborn again and again: that is keeping alive the good of the gift. One must always be born again posthumously—I mean now in this life, waking up again to the astonishing good of the "to be," like a child looking for the first time, enjoying for the first time. We do not will ourselves into birth, just as we cannot will ourselves into this posthumous rebirth. It is a giving of which we are the gift, though then we ourselves are to be givers.

Agapeic communication confirmed: Life puts its seal on this willingness to live the gift. It is not just a once affair, and once done, done. It is once and again, and again and again, for every once is the moment of communication. Every moment is the absolute community. We name this when we utter our willingness to be confirmed into this way of life. Life is always the same, yet always other, and open to the hyberbolic gift of the origin. Something of this might be seen in the transformation of family life. Marriage becomes a life of trust open to life as a whole, a dedication of fidelity more than the moment of romantic infatuation. One comes to know, in coming to know the other, how much one does not know, not in the sense of definite secrets held in reserve, but in the sense of the ultimate reserve of the other, reserve even to himself or herself. Growing in love is growing in knowing but also an entrance into unknowing. The mystery of another grows on those who are faithful, and whose togetherness does not petrify into being merely alongside. Being with the other even in silence, so that one takes on the rhythms of the other, and the other of one; there are two fleshes, and there is one flesh. The sign of the union is in the children who grow in reverence for the divine and in piety to other humans. Elders are renewed in the new life of the youngers, not merely given a "new lease on life" but released into a new life in which the good of the other comes to press back the overbearing reigning of self-concern. Family life too is a consecrated life.

Communication of consolation: The communication of consolation can be a hyberbolic gift. When we sneer at consolation, we reveal ourselves. We need no consolation, we say, and expose how much we are in need. Who is needless here? The brave face of hard self-sufficiency? The tough hiding from himself or herself the vulnerable invulnerability? Not being absolved to be consoled, not being able to console: both go together. Consoling has nothing to do with mawkish sentimentality. A sentimental person does not console, but indulges his or her own feeling, or self in the show of consoling. The sentimental person really wants to be consoled, while being impotent to console. Some people are gifted with this great and mysterious power to console: to speak the word of peace and see an unspeakable peace descend; to speak the word in the suffering of a person, or in an unbearable bereavement, or in an internal torment whose sources lie beyond even its victims' ken. The consoling word finds a wound and binds it up in finding it, begins to heal it simply by knowing it, by sharing the grief with the other, simply by being the one with the other in torment. The word of peace says, I am with you, I will be with you. The "with," extended into the ordeal or agony, mysteriously consoles.

Suppose one is in torment about an evil one has done, or has become. It is one's prison of guilt and hatred. The agapeic community speaks the word of reconciliation, the word that absolves, that speaks forgiveness and for forgiveness. The point of forgiveness is not just penitence but rejoicing in beginning again. Forgiveness is the highest festivity of life in the face of evil. This festivity is the penance for evil. Those who cling to themselves cannot enjoy this festivity, for they must consent to the release.

The word of consolation is most needed in distress and suffering. Our power is withdrawn, and we are tempted with revolt for being reduced to helplessness. In the helplessness, the word of consolation shows the way to a consent to the gift of suffering and death. Because of death, we often turn into monsters. But without suffering and death, we would undoubtedly be as monsters. Death saves us from becoming monstrous. Sometimes it does so by cowing us into submission; sometimes by a jolt of reminder that all is gift; sometime by making us quiet enough to hear the voice of the "It is good." We have been too busy devouring life, and devouring ourselves and others to notice. Then we are laid low, and it is the blessing of life itself that we come round to the solicitation of praise and thanks. This coming round also can make us monstrous. We hate the course of things for laying us low. Our refusal is an unstated imprecation on the origin. Blessing and curse are dark twins.

The agapeic community is there with readiness to communicate the word of consolation and to anoint the extremely ailing. Suffering and death too are consecrated. Death is our companion, the most terrible. And perhaps in the terror of the angel of death, the angel guarding our life will come to minister. A song of praise is raised, even when we are hosts to the coming of sister death, as Francis of Assisi, adding to his Canticle, at the last, sang with love.

Communication of the idiocy of God's agape: Some individuals are specially singled out by their unique vocation in these works of love. And yet we are all under orders, all called. How finally celebrate the commons of the divine? In prayer and liturgy. In deeds that enact justice and mercy. In study that is earnest about the ultimate perplexities, in keeping faith with the gift of astonishment. In silence and in solitude, and in the mystical intimacy of an unknowing companionship of the divine. In nameless acts of daily generosity in which one thinks, however inadequately, about the good of the other, being freed by generosity from worry about oneself and the anxieties piling up around. In singing, and in the energy welling up from places of mystery in the soul. In moments of sad satiation when one looks in love on clouds, and sea, and earth, and all of its fair gift, and loves its thereness beyond words, and knows the touch of its source in the gift. In sitting next to the sick, however awkwardly. In watching with the dying, however unbearable be the strain of being outside the mystery, and of attending the vigil of another world that it is not yet one's turn to enter.

INDEX

Abel, 295–296
Abraham, 411n
Abyss, 24, 45, 111, 465n
action, 254ff.; and agency, 233ff.
Adam, 312n, 392
adolescence, and freedom, 280–81; puberty and eros, 185, 413
adornment, 185–186, 189, 408
Adorno, T., 179, 441n
advertising, 230, 423, 424, 427, 434, 435, 468
aesthetic, 11, 12, 23, 52, 57–59, 64, 68, 71, 84, 88, 91, 92, 96, 97, 98, 100, 102, 103, 105, 119, 129, 151, 177–191, 204, 206–207, 215, 219, 391, 392, 424; as ethical potency, 11, 56–59, 87–91, 177–191, 419, 424–425, 433, 443, 445, 449–456, 490–494; and suffering, 370–372; and skin, 224–235; body of parent as a show of value, 385, 397, 398; bodies, boys, girls, and the family, 405–409
affirmation, ontological 5, 389
agape, agapeic, 13, 132, 159–62, 163, 164–5, 169, 171, 177, 178, 180, 182, 184, 191, 199–203, 207–9, 215, 217, 218, 219, 220, 290, 305, 314, 320, 365, 388n, 459, 462n, 471, 478, 492, 496n, 505–506, 509–510, 514; and servility, 347–348; and transcending, 354ff.; and friendship, 356ff.; and suffering, 376ff.; and good, 401, 402, 405, 440n, 472, 490–491, 478n, 504–506; and family piety, 411, 412;

and astonishment, 412; and service, chapters 11 and 16, *passim*, 403, 405, 424, 441, 441n, 447, 452n, 466–467, 475–476, 477n, 481, 483n, 491, 503; and public space, 416; and work, 417, 418; and allowance, 476; and communication, 472, 487n, 512–514; and generosity 426; and origin, 440n, 441n, 481, 492, 495, 505; and power, 459, 476, 478n, 510–511; and self-transcendence, chapters 10 and 11, *passim*, 209ff., 498, 503, 507; and universalism, 494–496, 500–501
agon/agony, 327ff., 333ff., 444n, 477, 513; and thanks, 508–509. *See also* struggle, suffering
ambiguity, 7, 11, 26, 27, 35, 51, 53, 58, 65, 85, 99, 104, 115; and aesthetic 97
amnesia, 29, 105; metaphysical 19
ananke, 192, 293, 297
ancestor worship, 387
angels, 8, 456
anorexia, 83–83
answerability, chapter 7, *passim*; 245ff.
antifoundationalism, 3, 81–82
Aquinas, St. Thomas, 75, 104, 193n, 379, 447, 486n; *Treatise on Happiness*, 90n
Arcadia, 391
Ariadne, 327
ardor, 242–244
Aristophanes, 393n; and *The Clouds*, 84
Aristotle, Aristotelian, 6, 18, 24, 26, 62, 65, 67, 69, 96, 105, 108, 120, 120n, 121n, 130, 163, 169, 206, 206n, 235n,